Fires Within

Fires Within

Political Violence and Revolutionary Change

Peter C. Sederberg
The University of South Carolina

HarperCollins*CollegePublishers*

Acquisitions Editor: Maria Hartwell
Project Editor: Susan Goldfarb
Cover Design: John Callahan
Production: Hilda Koparanian
Compositor: University Graphics, Inc.
Printer and Binder: R. R. Donnelley & Sons Company
Cover Printer: The Lehigh Press, Inc.

Fires Within: Political Violence and Revolutionary Change

Library of Congress Cataloging-in-Publication Data

Sederberg, Peter C., 1943–
      Fires within : political violence and revolutionary change / Peter
   C. Sederberg.
      p.   cm.
   Includes bibliographical references (p.   ) and index.
   ISBN 0-673-46873-9
   1. Revolutions.   2. Violence.   I. Title.
   JC491.S383   1994   93-7744
   321.0991—dc20   CIP

93 94 95 96 9 8 7 6 5 4 3 2 1

To the victims

Contents

Figures and Tables

Preface

Revolutions often begin in hope, proceed with cruelty, and end in disappointment. Yet however they begin and end, they stand as "peak experiences" in the political communities that endure them. As such they attract the attention of historians, social scientists, and political journalists. The vast literature on revolution generated by these people over the past two centuries offers not too few but too many explanations of these dramatic events. This book aims to provide a review and perspective on much of what we know, or think we know, about revolution. If it succeeds in doing so, then it will serve as a place to begin, not to end, investigation of this puzzling phenomenon.

The many explanations of the revolutionary puzzle fall into two related but still distinct areas of emphasis. One set of theories addresses the issue of why people resort to violence to pursue their political objectives. The other set attempts to identify the social conditions that produce a revolutionary crisis in society. Not all political violence, however, has revolutionary intent—sometimes quite the reverse. In addition, not all revolutionary crises involve the same degree of violence. In this book we draw on both types of theories to illuminate the connections between political violence and revolutionary change. This focus means that other important forms of political violence—in particular, interethnic civil wars—receive only secondary attention. We are primarily interested in struggles to control and transform the existing political community, not to break it up. This latter problem deserves a book of its own.

Broadly speaking, scholarship on political violence and revolution adopts one of three approaches, the first theoretical, the second historical, and the third a combination. The first type of scholarship offers a general theory of political violence or revolution illustrated with data and examples derived from a variety of sources. Critics sometimes condemn these theoretical offerings as "ahistorical."

The second approach offers detailed historical analysis of particular events of political violence or revolution. Unsurprisingly, critics castigate these studies as "atheoretical." The third approach attempts a happy compromise through comparative history. These works take a number of apparently similar historical events and attempt to account for their similarities and differences. In this way they try to provide a more general perspective than single case histories while making more modest explanatory claims than general theory. These limited, or middle-level, explanations still usually represent a single perspective on the phenomena under study.

In much of the literature on revolution, areas of interest to the revolutionaries themselves often receive only secondary attention. These include issues of leaders and followers, ideology and organization, and strategy and tactics. Historical case studies, of course, usually characterize these issues, but only for the case under investigation. More general theories tend to subordinate such concerns to the development of some larger theoretical perspective. There exists, however, a substantial literature on these issues, some of it written by revolutionary participants themselves, that needs recognition and synthesis.

Current texts on the problem of revolution reflect these divisions to some extent. One group essentially provides numerous case studies, but only limited perspective on more general issues of theory and practice. The other group provides some broader perspective on issues of theory and practice, illustrated with relatively context-free examples. Neither approach seems wholly satisfactory. This book attempts something considerably more ambitious.

First, we believe that students must understand the conceptual problems underlying the study of political violence and revolutionary change and should be given some criteria for evaluating the different, and often contending, theories that attempt to explain these interrelated problems. We provide this foundation for understanding in Part One, "Concepts."

Second, students must be introduced to the various theories in a fashion that highlights each theory's perspectives on the problem, indicates when different approaches actually ask different questions, and compares and evaluates these approaches. We provide such a comparative evaluation in Part Two, "Theory."

Third, students need a systematic overview of the problems of revolutionary practice, particularly relations between leaders and followers, ideology and organization, and strategy and tactics. We provide such a perspective in Part Three, "Practice."

Finally, students do not benefit significantly from context-free illustrations. They often lack the historical background to understand and evaluate the significance of such examples. Historical case studies, in contrast, usually lack any theoretical context. We provide both historical and theoretical context in Part Four, "Cases and Conclusions." We chose two cases—Vietnam and Iran—to illustrate the analyses contained in the first three parts. The case studies, then, explicitly incorporate the explanatory concerns of the book. We hope they will serve as examples to the students as to how they might proceed to shape their own inquiry into other instances of revolution.

As with most books, many people have made contributions to the final product. First, I would like to thank the University of South Carolina for its material support for this project, especially with respect to the sabbatical leave granted me for the spring semester of 1991. Numerous colleagues, both at USC and elsewhere, have critiqued part or all of the manuscript. I wish to recognize in this regard Shahrough Akhavi, Betty Glad, Paul Kattenburg, William Kreml, Jennifer Ring, and Daniel Sabia, all of whom were kind enough to read portions of the manuscript and save me from some egregious errors of fact and reasoning. I particularly wish to thank Mark Lichbach of the University of Colorado and my wife and colleague, Janice Love, who read and offered useful suggestions for the manuscript over the past year.

Also deserving of my gratitude are those at HarperCollins who encouraged this project from its earliest stages. In particular, I thank Maria Hartwell, the acquisitions editor, and my production editor, Susan Goldfarb, who pushed this project through to a successful conclusion. I would also like to thank the following reviewers for their helpful suggestions and general enthusiasm: Vincent Ferraro, Mount Holyoke College; Roy Licklider, Rutgers University; Curtis G. Reithel, University of Wisconsin–La Crosse; and David E. Schmitt, Northeastern University.

Finally, I wish to thank the hundreds of students, both graduate and undergraduate, who have taken my courses in this area over the years. Little did they know that they were being presented with a work in progress, but their demands for clarity certainly challenged me. I hope this book goes some way toward meeting this challenge. In particular, I wish to acknowledge the contributions made by students in my seminar "Revolution and Politics," offered in the spring of 1992. These students provided some of the background research for the two case studies included in this volume and are acknowledged in the appropriate chapters. Three other students, Ken Hicks, Kristy von Karowsky, and Susanne Fisher, contributed to a third case study that, because of length considerations, I did not develop. They too deserve my thanks.

Given all this wise advice, I wish I could assert that the book is now without flaws. Unfortunately, I sometimes stubbornly followed my prior path, despite the advice of others. Consequently, any errors of fact or analysis must be my responsibility alone.

PETER C. SEDERBERG

Introduction

Political violence and revolutionary change capture the imagination and provoke the fears of ordinary citizens, governments, and political commentators alike. In this introduction we briefly describe the dramatic events of recent upheavals in Vietnam and Iran. Although each resulted in an apparent revolution, they differ from one another in both character and process. We confront, then, the puzzles of why they occurred at all and why they followed the paths they did. The remainder of the book addresses these issues. After the brief review of revolutionary events in these two countries, we outline the basic structure of the book.

THE DRAMA OF POLITICAL VIOLENCE AND REVOLUTION

The media bathe us with images of violence. Nightly newscasts lay down a statistical barrage of the latest death tolls from terrorist attacks, civil conflicts, local wars, urban riots, and drug violence. The print media follow with grinding analyses of the significance of these reports from the front lines. Today's horror pushes yesterday's catastrophe from prime time and the front page. Seeking escape from the "reality" of the news, we might flee to a movie multiplex to view, more often than not, portrayals of grisly death.

In the arena of everyday life, crime statistics apparently demonstrate that people increasingly select violent means to pursue their private purposes. Outraged with someone's driving? Shoot at him. Disappointed with your mate? Kill her. Frustrated with your children? Beat them. Envious of your neighbors? Rob them. Protective of your "turf"? Slaughter your rivals.

In the arena of high politics, contenders for power often yield to the temptation of violence. Disaffected dissidents plant bombs and plot assassinations while frightened political establishments counter with concentration camps and death squads. Bitter divisions between races, religions, or ethnic groups fuel bloody cycles of civil violence. The rivalries between states engender clashes on the killing fields of modern war. And looming over hundreds of local conflicts and regional wars are the two global conflagrations of this century with their megadeaths. Nineteenth-century "social Darwinists" characterized nature as being "red in tooth and claw," but little in nature approximates the death inflicted by humans on members of their own species.

Those who resort to violence to achieve their political objectives see it, perhaps, as the ultimate testament to their seriousness of purpose. Circumstances have reached such an impasse that only strategies that place their adversaries and themselves in deadly peril seem appropriate. Unsurprisingly, such political

1

extremity attracts considerable scholarly, as well as popular, attention. From the time of Plato and Aristotle, philosophers and scholars have searched for the origins of civil violence in general and revolutionary political action in particular. Our purpose in this book is not to supplant 2500 years of effort with something purporting to be the definitive and comprehensive theory but rather to explore some of the fundamental issues of internal political violence.

Internal violence, that is, violence occurring within an established political community, cannot be absolutely distinguished from forms of external violence, most commonly war between nation-states. Internal wars attract the interest and often the participation of other countries and may even be instigated or encouraged by these powers. Our recognition of an external dimension to these struggles, though, should not obscure the essential difference between conflicts among competing sovereign political communities and the violent struggle within a single political community for dominance.

REVOLUTION IN TWO COUNTRIES

The diversity of the revoutionary experience, however, does not permit facile treatments of even the revolutions of the last fifty years, much less those over the past two centuries. Consider, for example, what lessons we might learn from the revolutions in Vietnam and Iran. Each of these revolutions appears to confound the conventional wisdom that prevailed a few years before their emergence.

Vietnam

A festive spirit prevailed in Hanoi on September 2, 1945. On this day tens of thousands of Vietnamese would get their first chance to see Ho Chi Minh, the shadowy leader of the Viet Minh. This Communist-led nationalist front fought against two occupying colonial powers, France and Japan, cooperating with the Allies during World War II. Ho Chi Minh had reason to be optimistic. After the surrender of Japan, his political and military forces were the most powerful native organization in Vietnam. Regardless of his Communist affiliation, he stood within a thousand-year tradition of Vietnamese resistance against foreign domination. The anticolonial rhetoric of the Roosevelt administration, along with wartime support from the United States, encouraged his belief that the American superpower would support Vietnamese independence. In his speech that day, he even echoed the Declaration of Independence in an effort to appeal to the somewhat moribund American revolutionary tradition.

His hopes were dashed. The triumphant declaration of Vietnamese independence turned out not to culminate a nationalist sweep to power but to presage a thirty-year struggle against Western states and their Vietnamese collaborators. During World War II, the Vichy French regime cooperated with Nazi Germany and its Japanese ally. Japan, in turn, allowed the French colonial authorities to maintain their presence in Indochina (consisting of Vietnam, Laos, and Cambodia). In March 1945, with the impending Allied victory in Europe, the Japanese attacked the French forces in Vietnam and quickly seized direct control over the whole country. Their subsequent defeat created the power vacuum which the Viet Minh hoped to fill.

Instead of welcoming an independent Vietnam to the family of nations, the Allies occupied Vietnam on their own, the British in the south and the Nationalist Chinese in the north. The British rearmed the French troops in Saigon, and these, with the assistance of 25,000 more French troops arriving in October, reasserted control over the cities of southern Vietnam (known as Cochin China). The Nationalist Chinese, for their part, withdrew from northern Vietnam in 1946, allowing the French to return there as well. Tensions between the French and the native nationalists grew until hostilities broke out in November 1946.

Independence plucked from their grasp, the Viet Minh now faced the well-armed forces of a European state, along with its local supporters, backed by the might of the American superpower. Few in 1946 expected several thousand lightly armed guerrillas to resist successfully the reimposition of French colonial rule. Yet resist they did, turning the French war in Vietnam from an embarrassing stalemate into a major defeat. For nearly eight years the guerrillas fought the French, growing steadily in strength. Communist victory in the Chinese Revolution in 1949 provided safe sanctuaries, ideological encouragement, and material support. Finally, in March 1954, Viet Minh regulars, armed with artillery, lay siege to the French fortress at Dienbienphu. On May 7 the surviving French troops surrendered. This defeat eliminated any remaining French interest in continuing the fight.

Again, however, the Viet Minh's victory was compromised. At the Geneva Conference, convened to resolve the conflict, the Soviet Union and China pressured the Vietnamese to accept the *temporary* partition of their country at the seventeenth parallel. This temporary arrangement soon took on the appearance of a permanent division. The South Vietnamese regime, led by Ngo Dinh Diem, a fervent anti-Communist with nationalist credentials, reneged on the agreement to hold a referendum on national unification. Diem, backed by the increasingly alarmed Americans, who feared Communist insurrections toppling dominoes all over Southeast Asia, judged that Ho Chi Minh and his northern-based regime would emerge as the victor in such an election. Instead of holding the election, Diem consolidated his power, first destroying non-Communist competitors and then turning to the elimination of the remaining Viet Minh political organization in the South.

Faced with a fading hope for peaceful unification along with the probable destruction of its southern political apparatus, the northern regime somewhat reluctantly renewed armed struggle in the South in 1959. Once again, they faced a foe that appeared well armed and strongly entrenched in the urban areas of the South. More importantly, the Diem regime received strong backing from the United States, first in terms of military and economic aid and then through increasing numbers of American military advisors. Countering these forces were an incipient revolutionary political organization and several thousand guerrillas.

From these unpropitious beginnings, the Communist revolutionaries organized a new united front in the South under their leadership, the National Liberation Front (NLF). Though initially relatively weak, the NLF received growing
support from their compatriots in the North. Southern communists who had
moved North after the 1954 Geneva agreement infiltrated back south; increasing
amounts of aid filtered down a network of trails; and ultimately southern NLF
guerrillas were joined by North Vietnamese regular troops, especially after the
massive American escalation began in 1965.

Thousands of American military advisors were insufficient to stem the steady
increase of NLF military success. Increasingly disgusted with the corrupt, incompetent, and autocratic rule of Diem, the United States backed a military coup
against him in 1963. This coup, while eliminating Diem, only worsened political
instability in the regime. By 1964 the NLF forces began to organize into military
divisions and to transform themselves from a guerrilla insurgency to a force capable of defeating the South Vietnamese army in conventional battles. In that year
nearly 100,000 South Vietnamese soldiers deserted. The American president,
Lyndon Johnson, and his military advisors concluded that either American troops
would have to engage the NLF directly or the Saigon regime would fall. At the
beginning of 1965, the communist-led nationalist forces were on the verge of winning their second revolutionary insurgency.

Even massive American intervention, however, failed to defeat this insurgency; it only postponed its victory. By 1968 the United States had over 500,000
troops in South Vietnam and over 200,000 elsewhere in Asia supporting the war
effort. Neither American troops fighting in the South nor massive air bombard-
ment of the North subdued the Vietnamese. The North Vietnamese regime threw
more of its regular forces into the struggle to counter the growing American presence. Though these forces were unable to directly defeat the Americans, eventually the United States, for both military and domestic political reasons, tired of the
stalemate and was unwilling to sustain the effort required to maintain the status
quo, much less defeat the revolutionaries.

In 1968 Richard Nixon was elected president partly because of his pledge to
end the war with "honor." The actual plan involved "Vietnamizing" the war by
gradually withdrawing American ground forces. Ultimately, after extended negotiations in Paris among all the parties, the United States agreed to withdraw completely, and the South Vietnamese regime agreed to form a coalition government
with the NLF and then negotiate a possible reunification with the North. Despite
a supposed cease-fire, all sides continued to maneuver for military advantage.
Finally, the North Vietnamese began a limited offensive below the seventeenth
parallel in 1975. Somewhat unexpectedly, the South Vietnamese army's retreat
turned into a rout, culminating in the collapse of the South Vietnamese regime
and the surrender of Saigon on April 30, 1975, almost thirty years after that heady
day in September when Ho Chi Minh announced Vietnamese independence to an
indifferent, even hostile, world. Unfortunately, Ho did not live to see the victory
to which he dedicated his life, having died in 1969.

Superficially, we might classify the Vietnamese Revolution as a peasant-based
guerrilla insurgency, where the revolutionaries fought their way to power from the

countryside, ultimately seizing control of the cities. However, as even this brief survey suggests, the Vietnamese revolutionaries had not one, but four victories: 1945, 1954, 1964–1965, and 1975. In each of the three earlier instances, the fruits of their victory eluded them, because they were either snatched or compromised away. They ultimately contended not only with a heavily armed domestic competitor, but also with two major Western powers. Few scholars in 1945 would have predicted perseverance, much less victory, against these apparently long odds. Tragically, the prize they ultimately seized in 1975 had been devastated by decades of internal conflict.

While the causes and, perhaps, the persistence of resistance might seem obvious—after all, history repeatedly demonstrates the potency of nationalist aspirations against odious external rule—the outcome remains puzzling. To paraphrase an often asked question: "Why did their (the Communist) Vietnamese fight so much better than our Vietnamese?" One tempting, if simplistic, answer is that "our" Vietnamese were fighting for us, whereas "their" Vietnamese were fighting for themselves. Behind this simple answer, though, lie the complex contributions made by leadership, ideology, and organization to the final outcome. The effort to understand any revolution must look to these factors.

Iran

Revolutions, at least since the French upheaval of 1789, are supposedly secular affairs. Propelled by passion, revolutionaries paradoxically claim they possess the theory for constructing an earthly paradise of independence, freedom, equality, and fraternity. Reason and science light the way to this new social order. Whether they invoke the ideas of bourgeois liberalism or radical Marxism, the revolutions of the past two hundred years have tended to express anticlerical Western sentiments of social engineering.

Except in Iran. In Iran, a government with the mightiest military forces in the Middle East, based on an economy bloated with the profits of soaring oil prices and led by the very model of a modernizing monarch who enjoyed the firm backing of the United States, was toppled by an aged and exiled holy man invoking a doctrine of Islamic revival. This remarkable outcome indicates a need to look for weakness behind the facade of state strength and strength behind the appearance of weakness.

The royal pedigree of the Shah-in-Shah (King of Kings) lacked roots. Despite pretensions of restoring the glory of the ancient Persian kings, Muhammad Reza Shah's dynasty was of more recent and somewhat sordid origins. His father, Colonel Reza Khan founded the Pahlavi dynasty in 1925 after seizing power in what was essentially a coup d'état. Owing to Allied suspicion of the Shah's loyal ties, he was forced to abdicate in 1941 in favor of his son and was then shipped off to South Africa. The young Muhammad demonstrated little of his father's ruthless drive and talent, but nevertheless he was thrust onto the Peacock Throne, beholden to the external powers who had placed him there.

The new Shah had to contend with the increasing power of the national parliament. Secular nationalists, appealing to the popular resentments against the way foreign powers continuously interfered in Iran's economy and politics, gained control of the parliament in the early 1950s. A National Front government forced through measures nationalizing British oil interests and imposing their candidate for premier, Mohammad Mosaddeq, on the Shah.

British and American interests became increasingly disturbed over the course of Mossadeq's economic policy, and they played on their governments' alarm over the growing influence of left-wing, especially Communist, forces in Iran. The initial attempt in August 1953 to remove Mosaddeq from office by force backfired, and the Shah was the one forced to flee Iran. Ultimately, forces loyal to the Shah, allied with conservative religious leaders and merchants fearful of the left-wing secularism of the anti-Shah forces, were able to prevail over those supporting the National Front government. Once again, foreign powers helped to maintain the monarchy, contributing to the erosion of its legitimacy.

The Shah returned, rewarded his friends and supporters in the army and the upper classes, and with the support of the CIA set up a powerful secret police (the Organization of National Security and Intelligence, known by the acronym SAVAK, from the Persian). So strengthened, the Shah proceeded over the next two decades to alienate almost every base, or potential base, of support for his regime, while retaining the enmity of leftists and nationalists.

Land reform programs, intended to institute a kind of White (that is, conservative) Revolution in the countryside and create a class of supportive independent peasant landholders, had the effect of generating millions of migrants to the cities in the 1960s and early 1970s. Efforts to redistribute the holdings of the Islamic clergy, though progressive in appearance, began to alienate the extensive religious organization. Other efforts to modernize and industrialize the country helped create new middle and working classes resentful of the Shah's autocratic rule. Programs to improve literacy increased the numbers of professionals who expected a voice in the government and resented the corruption of the Shah's cronies. The effort to create a single-party state under the direct control of the Shah further frustrated other political sectors who longed for greater voice in government and increasingly viewed the Shah as illegitimate. Extravagant spending of oil revenues on lavish displays and military equipment fueled both inflation and growing economic inequality. The influence of particularly the United States continued to reinforce resentment over foreign interference in Iranian affairs.

By the mid-1970s few supporters of the Pahlavi dynasty remained. Muslim clerics and their devout followers condemned the Shah's corruption, authoritarianism, and secularism. The merchants of the bazaar feared the economic competition arising from the Shah's development policies. Large numbers of peasants remained landless despite the land reform program of the 1960s. The urban poor, mostly recent migrants to the city, found their precarious economic position eroded by inflation, while the favored few flaunted their riches. Urban professionals believed they deserved greater voice in the government. Finally, left-wing students and intellectuals, along with the Communists, continued unabated in their hostility to the Shah and his corrupt cronies. Both secular and Islamic radicals organized guerrilla movements that began to launch attacks against the regime.

This multifaceted, multimotivated opposition began to jell around one figure, the Ayatollah Khomeini. Khomeini's resistance credentials were impeccable. As early as 1963, Khomeini emerged as a focal point of opposition to the Shah's policies. He condemned the Shah's White Revolution for both its anti-Islamic elements and the autocratic way the Shah imposed it. For his pains, Khomeini was arrested, released in the face of protests, rearrested, and finally exiled in 1964. From abroad he continued to attack the Shah and rally his supporters. As the most revered cleric in Iran, his opinions, smuggled in as taped sermons, found a ready avenue of expression through the thousands of mosques in Iran. Even secular groups, suspicious of the Ayatollah's fundamentalism, began to rally around this symbol of opposition.

As the opposition swelled, the regime launched an ill-considered personal attack on Khomeini's character in January 1978. Thousands protested in the holy city of Qom, and the regime's forces killed hundreds in attempting to suppress the disturbances. This act of repression, however, only triggered a cycle of protests that spread to other cities, including massive demonstrations in Tehran, and culminated in a general strike in December. By wisely avoiding direct attacks on the military, the protestors' tactics began to erode the morale and reliability of the armed forces, the last pillar of internal support for the regime. Even the Shah's external patron, the United States, began to waver in its support owing to the accumulating evidence of the incompetence, corruption, and brutality of his government. Faced with massive protests by all of his many enemies and doubtful of the loyalty of the military, the Shah fled Iran for a second, and final, time in January 1979. Millions of people greeted Khomeini on his triumphant return from exile on February 1, 1979.

The Iranian Revolution, however, did not end on his return. The collapse of the Shah's regime left a power vacuum in the center of Iran's political system. The disparate forces that contributed to the Shah's downfall were united mainly in opposition to his rule. Not only were secular and religious groups suspicious of each other's intentions, but each side was characterized by internal division between more moderate and extreme elements. In the subsequent struggle for power, the clerics supporting Khomeini proved far more adept at engendering mass support (again through the mosques) and coercive clout (in the organization of the Islamic Revolutionary Guard, a volunteer force that eventually grew to 200,000 men). Perhaps most importantly, no other faction had a leader of Khomeini's moral stature. Finally, after a bitter struggle that left thousands dead and thousands more in prison, the Khomeini-led Islamic revivalists triumphed.

The irony of the Iranian Revolution consists in the combination of its classic form and its "reactionary" content. The course of resistance, rebellion, collapse, and power consolidation echoes the so-called great revolutions of the West, especially those in France and Russia. But the victors and their ideology in Iran seem the opposite of the secular leaders and ideologies of these other revolutions. How, then, should we understand the process of the Iranian Revolution? Does the radically different character of the outcome suggest different origins as well? How well, if at all, do the theories developed to understand the causes and courses of other revolutions apply to this peculiar instance?

THE PLAN OF THE BOOK

This book concentrates on internal political violence, especially that used to bring about or to resist sweeping changes in the patterns of rule in a community. The first part, "Concepts," places the problem of political violence in a wider conceptual and political context. The notions of violence as a means and revolution as an end of political struggle receive special attention. Finally, criteria for evaluating contending explanations for political violence and revolution are critically assessed.

The second part, "Theory," reviews some of the major explanations for violence and revolution, beginning with an investigation of the influence of metaphor on our social thought and then continuing with an assessment of some popular explanations of internal upheaval. Social scientists, sometimes incorporating elements of these popular "theories," develop more systematic explanations. Some of these focus on the individual's motivation, either as a deprived or a rational actor. Other explanations concentrate on more inclusive levels of social organization, including theories of social and cultural disequilibrium or structural contradiction.

The third part, "Practice," looks at the problems of revolutionary ends and violent means more from the participants' point of view. Successive chapters explore issues surrounding the relations between followers and leaders, ideology and organization, and strategy and tactics.

In the fourth part, "Cases and Conclusions," the wealth of analytical material developed in the previous chapters are drawn upon to illuminate the dynamics of political violence and revolutionary change in two relatively recent cases. The examples selected for closer study are Vietnam and Iran. In the concluding chapter we turn to the tragic consequences often associated with the choice of political violence. We weigh the problems of justifying revolutionary ends and violent means. In particular, we focus on the outcomes, insofar as it is possible to know them, of the revolutions in our two cases.

The substance of the book, then, is conceptual and analytical rather than descriptive and historical. The case studies, though, provide some historical basis to test the value and limits of the various approaches to understanding the complex phenomena of internal political violence and revolutionary change.

PART
ONE

CONCEPTS

1

Normal Politics

Political violence is unusual in most political communities, and so the problem of violence as an instrument of political conflict is best understood in relation to political order. The essential goal of revolutionary political violence is not simply to destroy but to transform the status quo. To understand political violence, then, we should consider its apparent antithesis, political order. First we attempt to characterize order in psychological and structural terms, and then we explore how it arises and is sustained in our communities. Ordered social interactions, while necessary for survival, are not always benign. Consequently, we identify some of the common causes of tension and protest and assess the available strategies for managing social tension.

POLITICS AND ORDER

Violent discord, for all its drama, is the exception, not the rule, in most human communities. Even in nations convulsed by violence, orderly relations remain the common experience of most people most of the time. Violent disorder occurs against a background of social order. The real problem, as Erving Goffman suggests, is not why people resort to violence to achieve their objectives, but why they use violence so infrequently.[1]

To understand violent upheaval, then, we should first explore its apparent antithesis, social order. The relation between order and violence depends on how we understand each concept. So first we attempt to define order in psychological and structural terms, and then we examine how orderly interactions arise within reasonably stable political communities.

Social order, however necessary for the survival of a community, is not always benign in its impact. Indeed, the established bases for order often generate the tensions that contribute to protest and conflict, and efforts to maintain rigid social arrangements often contribute to disorder and violence. We illuminate this complex interconnection between order and disorder by identifying some of the common sources of tension and protest within an established political community and then assessing the major strategies available for managing such tension. After introducing these aspects of the problem of order, we turn in the next chapter to issues associated with the concepts of violence and revolution.

The Meaning of Order in Social Relations

Political commentators sometimes elevate "order" to the status of a first principle or fundamental value in political relations. When confronted with violent rebellion, government authorities commonly assert that "order must be restored" before discussing any grievances. On a more philosophical plane, some might argue that freedom to act without restraint becomes merely destructive license.[2] Psychologically, anxiety or fear may drive some people to sacrifice all other values so that they may secure order. The seventeenth-century philosopher Thomas Hobbes, for instance, argues that people submit to a ruler precisely to escape from the fear of bodily harm and violent death that pervades the essentially chaotic "state of nature."[3]

Despite such attention, the character of "order" in our social relations often remains poorly specified. Do we mean complete agreement, where each lives in happy harmony with all? Such harmony was the ideal of various utopian thinkers throughout the centuries.[4] Though we may dream of heaven on earth, antiutopian skeptics suggest that efforts to achieve this harmony will more likely produce at least boredom and, at worst, forms of earthly hell.[5]

Do we mean the absence of overt conflict? The absence of conflict may result from fear and suppression rather than shared values and temperate compromise. Suppressed conflict could well contribute to a more serious breakdown later.[6] Consequently, vital social arrangements provide for the *regulated* expression of conflict, thereby contributing to, rather than undermining, the maintenance of order. Conflict and disorder are *not* synonymous; we express conflict in orderly or disorderly ways, and even disorderly conflicts need not involve violence.

In our lives, order means predictability. *Unanticipated* events disorient us, whether the vicious attack of a midnight mugger or the pleasant shock of a surprise birthday party. From our individual psychological perspectives, then, order exists when we are able to develop stable and accurate expectations about each other's behavior. The violation of these expectations produces the experience of disorder, and even pleasant surprises generate anxiety as we struggle to adjust to the new situation.

Order so defined does not preclude the existence of conflict from orderly interpersonal relations, as long as that conflict develops along expected lines. Complete harmony of purpose and perspective supports stable and accurate expectations, but so might a regularized system of coercion. Habit provides a major contribution to the maintenance of order in that we learn to rely on the essentially automatic responses of each other in certain common situations.

The prevalence of order in our lives, like many other social psychological conditions, is a matter of degree rather than a simple dichotomy of presence or absence, order or disorder. In addition, we may more easily accept minor disruptions in some areas of our lives than in others, and some people may possess greater tolerance for ambiguity than others. Consequently, the same degree of unpredictability may produce varying levels of disorientation under different circumstances or in different people.

We cannot uncritically value all forms of orderly life. After all, peasants in Bangladesh may awaken each day to the same condition of wretched deprivation. The predictability of their lives provides no cause for celebration. Conversely, disorientation and disorder do not deserve automatic condemnation, despite the stress caused. Creativity involves devising something new and therefore disorienting. Revisionary works of art, for instance, are often first greeted with disbelief, dismay, and incomprehension before being embraced as embodying new insights into the human condition. Indeed, sometimes people rebel against the utter predictability of their lives. One commentator on John Milton's great poem *Paradise Lost* suggests that Lucifer, after eons of worshiping the Divine Being, grew bored and concluded, "Really, there must be *something* else to do."[7] This represents the first case of "revolution for the hell of it."[8]

We tend to underestimate the orderliness of our lives. I often ask my students to gauge the orderliness of their daily interactions, with zero representing perfect chaos and 100 standing for perfect predictability. Commonly, their replies range from 50 to 90 percent predictable. They apparently live lives of astounding disruption! Then I inquire whether, when they rose that morning, the light came on when they flipped the switch. Did the shower work as expected? Did they follow the same morning routine? As they drove to school, of the hundreds of drivers they passed, how many behaved in unanticipated ways, racing through red lights, randomly crossing the center line and smashing head on into them? When they arrived in class, did they take their accustomed seats, even though I do not have a seating chart? The point appears trivial, perhaps, but it illustrates the extent to which we take for granted the predictability of our lives.

For the students who remain unconvinced of the detailed predictability of their daily existence, I suggest the following experiment: that when they enter an elevator carrying several other people, rather than engaging in their "natural" (that is, habitual) elevator behavior of standing equidistant from all strangers and facing the front, they move close to someone, face the back, and start talking to themselves. They should then note how the other passengers respond.

The predictability of our taken-for-granted world does not mean that we exaggerate the significance of disorder. For our survival, and even more for our comfort, we depend on complex interdependent interactions. We rely upon a high degree of continuous predictability, and even an instant of surprise could threaten our survival. Of the hundreds of drivers we pass during the day, only one has to deviate for just a second to produce devastating results. The anxiety generated by the unexpected may seem exaggerated when compared to the relative infrequency of such surprises, but not when we consider possible consequences of the unanticipated.

From another perspective, these complex interactions constitute the *structures* of order in our everyday world. When particular patterns of stable interaction continue through time, we label them "customs," "institutions," "organizations," or even "societies," perhaps endowing them with misleading concreteness. References to "Congress," or the "Hizbullah," or the "Soviet Union," represent a shorthand way of alluding to complex sustained activity. Without hundreds, or even millions, of people behaving in mutually expected ways over extended periods of time, our institutions and organizations would not exist. Deterioration in these complexes of mutuality leads to the civil discord plaguing so many states around the world. Recent events in the former Soviet territories demonstrate how apparently permanent structures can essentially evaporate.

Even though the structures of order in the everyday world exist only through the sustained outpouring of our mutually expected interactions, we often lack control over them. The products of this outpouring, whether physical (like tools and other cultural artifacts) or behavioral (like language or institutions), attain a reality that confronts us as "external" and independent of ourselves. This apparently external reality turns back upon us and shapes our subsequent activity.[9] In this dialectical fashion we form and are formed by the structures of social order.

The Politics of Order—Two Views[10]

Justice "means nothing but what is to the interest of the stronger party."[11] These words, attributed by Plato to the Greek Sophist Thrasymachus, introduce one of the earliest statements of the *coercion theory of order*.[12] Bluntly, the strong do what they will and the weak do what they must, and the stronger party characterizes the result as "just," "good," and "right." Marx echoes Thrasymachus' analysis when he argues that the dominant economic class uses the power of the state to enforce its interests and then engages in ideological mystification to justify its exploitation.

In the coercion theory of order, mutually expected interactions between the strong and the weak arise directly through coercion or indirectly through manipulation. The strong and the weak in a coercive order possess a fundamental conflict of interest, though through deception and even self-deception neither side may fully realize it. The strong, who benefit from the prevailing order, have an interest in maintaining the status quo. The weak, who suffer under this order, possess a vested interest in change. Potential conflict and breakdown, therefore, lie at the heart of every coercive social interaction and do not represent unnatural intrusions into an otherwise placid relationship. These circumstances place pressure for change on nearly every social connection.

In sharp contrast, the *consensus theory of order* stresses stability and agreement on values. Plato, in rebutting Thrasymachus, develops a theory of a just society in which philosophers capable of recognizing the nature of the Good direct the policy of the state, a class of guardians protects the polity from internal and external enemies, and an artisan/agricultural class cheerfully provides for the economic needs of the community. Each of the three classes contributes to the well-being of the community by attending to its proper role, a task for which its members are, at least in part, naturally suited. The acceptance of one's natural and proper position in society underlies Plato's conception of justice.

Order, from this perspective, results from a consensus over mutually recognized and accepted norms and expectations, valued by all parties in a relationship. Everyone contributes to the stability of the existing social arrangements, and change, if it occurs, will most likely be for the worse. Conflict represents some type of breakdown in the established state of affairs, at least in a "well-ordered" community. In recent decades, social theorists who declare "the end of ideology" or "the end of history" in the advanced capitalist welfare democracies represent variations on consensus theory. They believe that these communities have essentially settled all the "big conflicts" over the distribution of wealth, power, and value and that only discussions of appropriate means to achieve consensually agreed-upon ends remain.[13]

Table 1.1   THE BASES OF ORDER IN SOME
             CONTEMPORARY POLITICAL
             SYSTEMS, 1970–1980[a]

Consensually ordered	Coercively ordered
• Austria	• Afghanistan
• Denmark	• Chad
• Finland	• China
• Japan	• Ethiopia
• Switzerland	• Yugoslavia
• Luxembourg	• Guatemala
• New Zealand	• Kampuchea (Cambodia)
• Norway	• Lebanon
• Sweden	• South Africa

[a] This listing is based upon an interpretation and extension of the data presented in Charles Lewis Taylor and David A. Jodice, *World Handbook of Political and Social Indicators,* Volume 2: *Political Protest and Government Change* (New Haven, Conn.: Yale University Press, 1983), especially pp. 106–175. This listing is intended to be illustrative, not definitive. Moreover, although these countries represent the empirical extremes, they do not embody theoretical extremes. Even the most well-integrated countries still experience acts of social violence and political discord; even the most divided communities exhibit a degree of consensus, at least among subcommunities. Moreover, the vast majority of contemporary political systems are probably distributed between these two empirical extremes.

Most political theories, whether academic or popular, do not embrace either view of the politics of order in an unqualified fashion, but many positions tend toward one or the other of the two theories. Conservatives usually adopt a consensus view of social order, seeing lapses in the consensus as signs of breakdown and revolution as a pathological condition afflicting the body politic. Radicals, in contrast, emphasize the pathologies of the status quo and embrace challenges to the existing order, including revolution, as comprehensible and even necessary responses. Empirically, a survey of contemporary political systems might find them essentially either coercively or consensually based, although none belongs at either theoretical extreme (see Table 1.1).

The Sources of Order in Social Relations

Predictable behavior must be under some form of control. The weaker the control, the wider the range of behavior exhibited. More effective control narrows the range of possible behavior and facilitates the task of prediction. Morse Peckham metaphorically characterizes this simple relation as the "delta effect."[14] Rocky strata narrowly channel a river, but when it enters the soft, marshy flatlands near the sea, the river spreads into a wide delta. Even here, though, the river's course encounters some resistance; if it did not, the delta would be indefinitely large. Analogously, the complete absence of controls on human behavior would result in pure randomness, a condition seldom approximated. The central issue, then, involves not the presence or absence of control, so much as the degree of control exercised over a particular area of interaction.

We often associate control with the workings of some malevolent power forcing people to behave in certain predictable ways. Such a view represents a coercion theory of order. Certainly, overt coercion and manipulation channel some behavior, but effective controls need not entail either one. *Anything* that narrows the range of possible response to a situation acts as a control, from biological tendencies to concrete threats. To understand the range and complexity of possible forms of control, we review some of the ways "inherent" needs, cultural directives, and external inducements progressively narrow the range of responses in a myriad of interactions. This channeling makes it easier for all the participants to form stable and accurate expectations about each other's behavior.

Similar Needs   Before anything else, we are physical and biological creatures. This restatement of the obvious reminds us that this taken-for-granted reality also shapes our behavior. We may flee from danger, but we will not, unless technologically assisted, literally fly from it. Our physical and biological properties and capabilities constrict the possible range of our behavioral responses. Such limits begin to lay the foundation for order as predictable interaction.

At the most fundamental level, sociobiologists argue that human beings are genetically predisposed to behave in certain ways to guarantee the replication of their genetic material in subsequent generations. As Edward O. Wilson asserts, "No species, ourselves included, possesses a purpose beyond the imperative created by its genetic history."[15] From this general notion, sociobiologists develop specific hypotheses relating a variety of behavioral tendencies to principles of genetic advantage and evolution, from forms of aggression and patterns of sexual reproduction and child rearing to the emergence of religion. Some evidence also indicates that genetic makeup influences the development of certain fundamental personality characteristics, such as the tendency toward extroversion or introversion.[16]

A somewhat less controversial proposition than the genetic determination of individual and social behavior is a related argument that biophysical properties limit our activities. At the individual level, a person's physical capabilities and biochemical makeup shape his or her behavior. At a more macrolevel, human societies lie embedded in the biosphere and ignore the ecological effects of their activities at their peril.[17] Socioeconomic activities that violate the fundamental requirements for continued life (for example, by generating excessive pollutants) will eventually encounter severe environmental reactions.

Common needs may also shape human behavior in somewhat predictable ways. Abraham Maslow suggests that in addition to the obvious physical needs for food, water, shelter, and some level of reproduction, human beings share certain psychological needs, including the need to belong, the need to love, the need for self-esteem, and the need for personal growth.[18] Erich Fromm posits a more elaborate set of "existential needs," including ones for a frame of orientation and devotion, rootedness, unity, effectiveness, excitation, and character structure.[19] Of course, sociobiologists might argue that these psychological or existential tendencies, if they exist, yield some genetic advantage.

Just as individual humans must fulfill certain needs, some sociologists argue that whole societies must provide for certain "functional prerequisites" to survive. Various inventories of what social systems "need" vary from author to author. Talcott Parsons, perhaps the best known of the functionalists, argues that all social systems from the family to the national community must fulfill four prerequisites: adaptation (to the external environment), goal attainment, integration (of the disparate parts of the system), and pattern maintenance (of the roles and structures that make up the system).[20]

Similarly oriented political scientists contend that all political systems perform certain functions, though they do so in different ways and through different structures. Gabriel Almond and G. Bingham Powell, for instance, identify these functions as interest articulation, interest aggregation, rule formation, rule adjudication, rule enforcement, communication, and system maintenance and adaptation.[21] If such functions must be undertaken by all social or political systems, then we presumably have a basis for rendering intelligible those structures and activities that might initially appear alien and surprising. Human behavior, then, at both the individual and societal levels cannot be completely random, for it must be channeled in certain directions to sustain life, whether that of the organism or of the social system.

All of these approaches remain controversial, whether they define the factors channeling the behavior of individuals or larger units of social interaction. While the constraints of basic biological necessity and some significant influence of genetic heredity appear undeniable, disagreement develops over just how far "nature" restricts the possible range of behavior. Categorizations of psychological and existential needs, though plausible, often appear tainted by the cultural biases of their authors. Both Maslow and Fromm, for example, seem to reflect the high premium placed on individualism in Western culture.

Hypothesized functional prerequisites of social and political systems suffer from similar problems of vagueness and potential bias. Nevertheless, whatever their precise parameters, shared characteristics of humans as biological, psychological, and social beings begin to lay the foundation for orderly social interaction. Activity that initially appears bizarre and disorienting might become more comprehensible when recognized as fulfilling a common need. In the first place, then, human behavior becomes predictable because it is *human*.

Cultural Directives   Whatever the conditions laid down by nature for our survival, they do not dictate a detailed, singular "way of life." Consequently, biology alone cannot simply define predictable interactions. Biology might determine the activities of the so-called social insects, like ants and bees, in this fashion, but humans learn to be predictable, albeit within broad natural limits. The difference between instinctual and learned behavior is crucial. As one anthropologist remarked, if ants are social animals, then human beings are not.[22] Our sociability depends to a great degree on how effectively our culture has been transmitted to us.

Simply defined, culture consists of directions for performance.[23] Cultural directives, whether stated in laws, embedded in customs, or incarnated in artifacts, serve to guide our behavior in a multitude of different settings. We share a culture to the extent that we respond to the same set of cultural directives in mutually expected and compatible ways. We learn such "appropriate" responses, essentially, by being repeatedly told how to behave in particular circumstances.

A complete catalogue of the cultural directives channeling behavior in a particular society would be an exhausting, if not impossible, undertaking, but we may consider a few illustrations. Take, for instance, student behavior within the typical college classroom. By and large the students sit reasonably quietly, attentively listening to the instructor, and when asked to participate, will do so in a fairly predictable and orderly fashion (that is, raising their hands to be recognized in turn, rather than engaging in shouting matches). These nineteen-year-olds have successfully learned, for better or worse, the first lesson of institutionalized education in this country: "Sit still and shut up!" And they started learning it the minute they stepped through the doors of their first institution of formal education, if not before. Those who fail to learn sufficient self-control are largely purged from the system.

Appropriate classroom decorum represents just one example of the broad class of cultural directives devoted to controlling impulsive behavior, a major source of disrupted expectations. An enormous variety of human interaction, from the way we eat our meals or drive a car to the techniques we master to fulfill the precise tasks required by our complex economic relations, requires that we suppress our impulses. If we followed the "natural" inclinations we exhibit as infants, for example, we would all eat like pigs. As we learn progressively more refined etiquette, the task of eating a meal grows increasingly (some might say dysfunctionally) complicated.

Six hundred years ago, knights were admonished not to spit across the table, but to either side of their chairs; only later was the refinement of spitting into a napkin introduced. The repression of impulse in the area of manners coincided with the progressive regulation of impulsive behavior across a wide range of human activity. The emergence and growth of the complex patterns of interaction comprising modern society demanded such regulation.[24] In a sense, the maintenance of order in modern society begins with our parents repeatedly demanding that we use our forks and close our mouths when we chew.

Of course, the fact that our parents repeatedly tell us anything requires another vast area of shared understanding essential to predictable interaction—common language. Human beings appear genetically "wired" to learn language (another illustration of how nature lays the foundation of order in our societies), but cultural redundancies determine which language a person learns. From the day of their birth, infants are continuously instructed in their native tongue. By the time children begin their formal education, they have already mastered the basic structure of their language. The relation between the genetic predisposition to learn a language and the cultural origins and structure of a particular tongue illustrates how nature and nurture combine in channeling our behavior.

Successfully ingrained cultural directives often grow into habits, creating a near permanent basis for predictable interaction. Mastering the rules of the road illustrates the habituation of cultural directives. This task involves an area of complex, interdependent interaction where mutual survival depends on highly predictable behavior. Consequently, our society develops a significant array of precise directives for this particular performance, ultimately codifying many of these into law. Initially, when we learned these rules and norms of conduct, we were unsure and awkward. After extensive practice, though, much of this culturally structured behavior developed into automatic, or nearly automatic, habits of performance.

These illustrations focus on how specific cultural directives channel individual behavior. From at least the time of the ancient Greeks, social thinkers also sought to discern the general cultural themes organizing the myriad detail of social life. They hoped to identify certain "macrocultures" that somehow unify the diverse particulars of individual social interaction. Scholars developed simple dichotomies—traditional versus modern, organic versus mechanistic, or individualistic versus collectivist—to represent broad cultural tendencies.[25] These polarities presumably constituted the alternative ways societies organized to fulfill the functional requisites of survival.

A more recent argument posits that five (and only five) basic ways of life are viable: hierarchy, egalitarianism, fatalism, individualism, and autonomy.[26] Each way of life subsumes particular patterns of social relations and the values and beliefs that support them. Different ways of life generally coexist in the same society, the same organization within society, or even compartmentalized within the same individual, depending on the particular situation.

The specific content of cultural directives may vary, but they will nonetheless reflect one of these broad cultural patterns. Thus, students in the lecture hall, workers on an assembly line, and officials in a bureaucracy all represent variations on a hierarchically organized way of life. In contrast, graduate students in a seminar or members of a board of directors reflect more egalitarian norms of interaction in relating to their immediate colleagues. Once we identify the way of life embodied in an unfamiliar pattern of social relations, we take a significant step toward rendering the pattern intelligible and predictable.

External Inducements   Within any social relation we may fail to learn the "appropriate" directives for smooth interaction, or learning the rules, we may choose to violate them (the reasons for failure and violation are explored below). At this point, the third source of order in social relations comes to the fore—external inducements involving threats of punishment for "misbehavior" and promises of reward for conformity. The efficacy of such inducements depends on the perceived severity of the punishment or the value of the reward, the likelihood of the specified consequences occurring, and the attractiveness of the alternative, directive-violating behavior. Effective threats and promises must be at least periodically fulfilled to channel behavior over time. If disobedience never brings punishment or obedience a reward, conformity will probably decline, and disorder will spread.

Again, the highly interdependent arena of driving offers an apt illustration. Socially appropriate operation of an automobile demands mastery of a complex set of rules.[27] To demonstrate this mastery, we must pass a written test, serve a period of "apprenticeship" under the direction of a (presumably) skilled driver, and then prove our ability and conformity in a road test. If we do all this, the state rewards us with a driver's license. A one-time demonstration of mastery, though, fails to provide an adequate guarantee of order on the roads. Consequently, our society codifies many of the directives of driving into law and invests considerable resources in the continuous policing of this activity. Assuming apprehension, violations of the law carry penalties of varying severity.

Legally enforced cultural directives constitute a minority of the norms regulating our interactions. Customary directives, even if not codified into law, still carry the threat of punishment or promise of reward. All of us continuously manipulate the resources at our disposal to channel the behavior of those with whom we interact. Even in the absence of concrete threats and promises, the collective validation of competence and "worth" provides a major means of social control. We never definitively establish our personal sense of worth; consequently, our need for validation is an "insatiable maw" devouring all signs of worth bestowed upon us.[28] This insatiable need helps to impose a continuous source of control on behavior. Even when directives seem ambiguous, we anxiously search for the response that others will deem appropriate.

Just as our fulfillment of others' expectations of appropriate behavior leads to their validation of our worth, violations of these expectations contribute to our shame and prompt others to shun us. (Shaming and shunning represent two underrecognized instruments of social control.) The desire for social validation suggests why, even in the absence of concrete sanctions, we try to live up to each other's expectations. Through the mutual desire for mutual validation, we sustain orderly relations.

Order, then, depends on predictable interaction. Mutually predictable behavior must be under some form of control, whether external or internalized. More effective controls produce more predictable behavior. Controls on the range of behavior take root in the biological and psychological character of the human animal; they take shape through the continuous repetition of cultural directives; finally, they take force from the promise of reward and the threat of punishment. Yet in spite of this impressive apparatus of behavioral control, unpredictability continuously intrudes on our efforts to ensure smooth interaction. And sometimes it should, for though order has its uses, it also has its limits.

The Limits of Order

We require order for survival. Unanticipated interruptions threaten our complex and interdependent forms of social interaction. Yet, however necessary, order does not guarantee survival. Rigid adherence to increasingly inappropriate patterns of behavior jeopardizes survival as surely as the randomization of behavior. Consider, for a moment, two extreme types of insanity, the wildly inappropriate behavior of certain types of schizophrenia and the equally inappropriate autistic withdrawal and rigidity. Schizophrenics, driven by the directives of their own personal demons, exhibit unpredictable and threatening behavior to those around them. On the other hand, the inflexible behavior of the severely autistic (for example, the character Raymond in the movie *Rain Man*) threatens the victim's own survival.

We confront, then, a "stability/innovation" dilemma, both personally and in our social organizations. On one hand, all forms of change, whether deliberate innovation or the simple behavioral drift resulting from weak controls, upset the predictability of any ongoing relation. On the other, rigidity, defined as resistance to necessary change, also eventually undermines an interaction. The dilemma sharpens further because we can never definitively know before (or even after) the fact whether a particular innovation will improve matters or make them worse. Conservative critics, for example, often argue that revolutionary innovation commonly serves only to replace a tolerable, if imperfect, regime with a postrevolutionary abomination, and usually at a catastrophic cost in disrupted social flow.

A variation on this dilemma contrasts "adapted" with "adaptability." From an ecological perspective, a social form "occupies" a certain environmental "niche," composed of other, potentially competing, social forms and the natural setting. A particular social form may fit more or less well into a particular niche. Highly *adapted* forms support smooth, predictable interaction, but they may well lack the resources to adjust to new challenges arising from their environment; that is, they lack *adaptability*.

In contrast, adaptable social forms may not fit well into an existing niche, because they exhibit patterns of deviation that allow them to adjust to environmental change. Where environmental demands remain constant, adapted social forms maintain the stability needed for survival, and innovation often makes matters worse. When environmental demands shift significantly, adaptable social forms (that is, those capable of innovation) transform and survive, while the previously well-adapted patterns of behavior may exhibit pathological rigidity. The disorder of transformation, under changing conditions, constitutes the necessary price of survival. Thus, for radicals, fruitful disruption necessarily accompanies the birth of a new and better order.

Apart from the stability/innovation dilemma, order has its costs. Even smoothly functioning social systems produce winners and losers. The controls of custom and law may function to ensure patterns of predictable interaction sufficiently well adapted to the demands of the environment. The interactions established and enforced, however, support a particular distribution of power and value. As Anatole France rather cynically observed, "The law, in its majestic equality, forbids the rich as well as the poor to sleep under bridges, to beg in the streets, and to steal bread." Those who defend the value of "law and order" deserve to be asked, "Whose law? What order?"

STABILITY AND CHANGE

Sources of Tension and Themes of Protest in Social Relations

Any social order, no matter how smoothly it functions, engenders certain inevitable tensions that lead to common themes of protest. The severity of these tensions, to be sure, varies from society to society and over time, but when they intensify sufficiently, isolated cries of discontent can combine into a chorus of rebellion.

The Repression of Impulse   Predictable interaction arises from the controls imposed on the potential range of behavior. Much of this control channels otherwise impulsive behavior into more manageable directions. In this fundamental sense, all societies repress their members. Sigmund Freud places the repression of certain impulses, such as a boy's sexual attraction to his mother, at the center of his theory of psychology. Civilization, to paraphrase the title of one of his books, generates discontent.[29] We need not embrace Freudian theory, however, to recognize that any society, to sustain orderly relations, must place considerable restraints on its members' impulsive behavior. From the incest taboo to the speed limit, cultural directives prohibit us from doing just as we please.

The repression of impulse, though, inevitably contributes to resentment. The policing of behavior imposed by the structures of social control provokes forms of protest ranging from evasion to open rebellion. In some sense, the wider political community continually replicates adolescent resistance against parental rules. We stretch the limits; we violate boundaries; we attempt to evade control; and, at the extreme, we attempt to overthrow the authority that imposes these restraints on our lives.

When revolution weakens the dominant structures of social control, a period of celebration commonly follows, entailing "the transgression of prohibitions, collective excitement and the proliferation of the imagination."[30] As the chorus in Peter Weiss's play *Marat/Sade* puts it, "And what's the point of a revolution without general copulation?"[31] For the celebrants, the brief period of release usually precedes a "morning after" hangover and the imposition of an often sterner regimentation, again accompanied by the inevitable resentment.

Recognition of the inherent repressiveness of society no more condemns all forms of social order than the acknowledgment that we require order for survival means that all forms of control deserve equal praise. We could declare our independence of society and become hermits (submitting, still, to the necessities of survival), but if we choose to exist in collective interdependence, we must submit to some restraints. The particulars of this restraint—and what constitutes a good order—require additional deliberation.

The Distribution of Power   Another fundamental source of tension inherent to any social order involves issues of *power distribution*. Power, defined as the capacity to shape mutual interaction, derives in part from the control of certain resources.[32] These valued sources of power include the following:

- **Economic resources** (the inputs and outputs of the processes of economic production);
- **Political resources,** specifically authority (the right to speak for a community and announce community policy) and legitimacy (perceptions of the worthiness or rightness of established social and political relations);
- **Status resources** (essentially the degree to which a person is esteemed so that others will follow his or her directives);
- **Information resources** (control of the information needed for the effective and efficient use of the other resources);
- **Coercion resources** (the capacity to inflict harm); and
- **Organization resources** (the capacity to orchestrate common action).

All of these resources may be more or less unequally distributed. Economic resources clearly demonstrate this point, but similar distributive concerns arise with respect to the other resources as well. Certainly every complex political system distributes authority unequally. In a democracy, for instance, each citizen controls a small piece of authority—the vote—but bureaucratic officials and elected officeholders possess far greater authority to shape the course of community affairs.

Similarly, the perceived legitimacy of particular political arrangements fluctuates. The bases of esteem may vary from group to group and over time, bestowing status unequally. Some people have privileged access to vital information giving them an edge in the competition for social control. The police and the armed forces of a regime usually hold the preponderance of coercion resources, though in a revolution these resources grow more widely dispersed. Finally, the size and quality of different organizations vary considerably.

Whatever the distribution of power, complaints develop. Clearly, unequal distribution pits the "have-nots" against the "haves," whose privileges the deprived envy. Alternatively, protests also arise from equal distributions, because some will undoubtedly believe that their talents and contributions are not appropriately rewarded. In any case, power tends to be unequally distributed in most social arrangements from the family to the state; consequently, inequality, rather than equality, becomes the target of protest. Only universal acceptance of the prevailing allocation as a fair reflection of relative worth would relieve the tensions arising from the distribution of power resources.

Cultural Inconsistency   Inconsistency develops whenever contradictory directives appear to apply to the same situation. Examples abound from the trivial to the profound. Consider, for instance, the confusion surrounding certain commonsense maxims:

"Look before you leap," but "he who hesitates is lost."
"A stitch in time saves nine," but "haste makes waste."

"Absence makes the heart grow fonder," but "out of sight, out of mind."
"Many hands make for light work," but "too many cooks spoil the broth."

Inconsistent directives, though, are no joke, for they engender considerable conflict. Contending centers of power often advocate competing directives in their efforts to structure behavior to suit their preferences. The tobacco companies, for example, communicate messages of virility and health through the images in their ads, while in the same frame, the surgeon general warns of the terrible health consequences that afflict those who smoke. Public policy reflects this contradiction, as well, in that the government both supports programs to discourage smoking and provides tobacco farmers crop subsidies.

At its worst the competition between cultural directives, each striving to order social relations, deteriorates into a conflict between largely incompatible ideological positions. In the United States the controversy over abortion illustrates how intense the competition between competing cultural directives can become, as the contenders pit ultimate principles of "the right to life" and "freedom of choice" against one another. The definition of this debate leaves limited opportunity to define directives satisfactory to all concerned.

Broad and somewhat contradictory ways of life coexist and often contend within the same society.[33] During the Cultural Revolution in China during the 1960s and 1970s, two comprehensive "ways of life" struggled for dominance, one representing the egalitarian ideals of "revolution" and the other the hierarchical demands of "order."[34] This broad conflict incorporated numerous subsidiary inconsistencies, including revolutionary purity versus technical expertise ("red versus expert"), political movement versus bureaucracy, and agitation versus technical education. The forces of hierarchically directed modernization emerged victorious by the 1980s, but tensions between modernization and revolutionary ideals still exist. In addition, the triumphant bureaucrats rejected Western-style democracy, embracing only technical modernization. Over the past decade, however, democratic, individualist cultural values have emerged to bedevil the aging bureaucratic elite that rules China.

Cultural Inadequacy   The presence of contradictory directives suggests that no single directive is fully appropriate for all occasions. Sometimes we should look before we leap, but at other times hesitation leads to loss. Moreover, the problem involves more than determining which of the competing directives provides adequate guidance for a particular situation, a task that might prove challenging enough. Sometimes *none* of the available directives provides adequate guidance. As in Sophocles' *Antigone* and other tragic dramas, the competing demands of different moral communities to which we belong may place us in situations where *any* decision we make "outrages the gods."

The inadequacy, at least to some degree, of all cultural directives stems from the inherent instability of categorical statements. Like other categories, cultural directives, even the most specific, abstract to some extent from the situation that they purport to address, creating the continuous possibility that they may be undermined by a surprising occurrence for which they failed to account.[35] The greater the gap between the hypothetical world of cultural directives and the world actually encountered, the more inadequate the directives become. The more inadequate the directive, the more likely the "world" will slap back, contributing to demands for revision. Of course, a dominant cultural order may choose to ignore evidence for a needed change, but often only the imposition of coercion will sustain increasingly inadequate directives. This "solution" to the problem of inadequacy will usually generate further discontent and only postpone the reckoning.

The dramatic collapse of centrally planned economies in 1989–1990 graphically illustrates how, beyond some point, even coercion cannot sustain inadequate directives. Yet the crisis of state economic control fails to demonstrate the adequacy of market economies. The United States, for example, bears the consequences of following inappropriate directives justified in the name of the free market in its savings and loan banking crisis. Moreover, environmentalists warn that the materialist directives underlying the production, consumption, and pollution patterns of the industrialized world threaten the survival of the species on this planet.

Cultural "Incompetence"   Imagine a happy place unvexed by inconsistent and inadequate directives; a place where, indeed, a consensus exists over the appropriate distribution of resources; a place, finally, where all acquiesce in the necessary restraints on their impulsive behavior. Tension, protest, and conflict can still arise owing to incompetence. Most simply, as Peckham trenchantly observes, "Nobody ever gets anything right."[36] This does not mean that everyone gets everything completely wrong, only that we do not always follow the directions as expected.

In part, *apparent* incompetence arises from the presence of inconsistent directives leading us to respond in ways others might not expect. Alternatively, inadequate directives may prompt us to innovate a new response. In addition to these two potential sources of disorder, we simply may not understand the directive in the expected fashion. "Appropriate" performance entails, at least in principle, two acts of interpretation. First, we must understand the situation as one to which a particular directive applies. Second, we must understand the directive as calling for a particular behavior. We may therefore mistake the situation, the directive, or both. Our incompetence will provoke those with whom we interact, who may demand that we be disciplined or reeducated in some fashion.

In all fairness, however, individual shortcomings are not the only source of cultural incompetence. Some situations and some directives are simply ambiguous and generate considerable anxiety for those unfortunates who must try to interpret how to respond. We encounter ambiguity most frequently when first entering an unfamiliar context, such as visiting a foreign culture. The unfamiliarity disorients us while, at the same time, our inappropriate behavior disorients and probably offends the natives.

         ☣   ☣   ☣

Tensions arise in all established social orders, though certainly not to the same extent. Resentment festers because of the inevitable repression of impulse, leading to evasion and rebellion. Protests erupt around the distribution of power, demanding redress of grievances about perceptions of unjustified privilege or unearned reward. Conflicts emerge as proponents of contradictory values attempt to structure social relations according to their preferences. A cascade of contrary evidence may undermine the asserted adequacy of a dominant way of life. Most bluntly, when people die because of the side effects of human activities, many will conclude that something is amiss. Finally, even in the absence of protests over power distribution and the definition of authoritative values, tensions still arise when we bear the consequences of each other's incompetence in interpreting both situations and guiding directives.

Managing Social Tensions

On the whole we interact with each other in a predictable fashion. Our predictability, however, does not emerge automatically from common genetic heritage, though an initial structure for order may well have its foundation in our biological constitution. Rather, our culture composes the details of our interactions, and we learn the tune through repetition, as well as through the blandishments of reward or the threat of punishment. Our behavior according to these cultural directives reproduces the culture through time. Nonetheless, all social arrangements reflect certain inherent tensions and echo with familiar cries of protest. Continued stability, then, depends on successful implementation of various strategies for managing these inevitable tensions.

Strategies of tension management often involve deliberate intervention by the regime in a community, although sometimes management emerges from tacit responses or unintended consequences of regime inaction. No strategy, or combination of strategies, is cost-free; each requires the investment of scarce resources, entails certain risks, and encounters barriers to its effectiveness.

Strategy 1: Conservative Change   The most superficially appealing strategy for managing tension initiates conservative change. This strategy aims to reduce the intensity of certain grievances through real, if modest, reform, while preserving intact the basic structure of power and value in a social order. The success of conservative reforms depends on the presence of certain conditions. First, the level of discontent must be modest. Second, programs to ameliorate discontent must generate less significant discontent than they cure. Third, the regime (essentially, the government and the social sectors that support it) must control the resources needed to undertake the reforms, repress those who remain alienated (see below), and control those who now protest the new dispensation established by successful reform.

The strategy of conservative change aims to buy off the moderately discontented, thereby isolating the radicals. The regime then attempts to control these radicals through other means. This strategy assumes that the prevailing tensions produce predominantly moderate protest. Intense alienation confronts a reforming regime with an uncomfortable dilemma. Modest reform may only further inflame the passions of the discontented, who take regime concessions as a sign of weakness; but the character of the changes they demand would transform the basic order rather than conserve it. Most regimes, not surprisingly, resist transforming themselves out of power.

Moreover, reform cannot reduce all forms of social tension. Reform most easily addresses tensions arising over the distribution of power resources, *if* improved productivity can increase resource supply. Under these conditions, competition for resources becomes *positive sum*, in that an expanding resource "pie" provides the opportunity to improve everyone's position. When, for example, an economy experiences a period of growth, the material well-being of everyone may improve, even though relative positions remain unchanged.

Sometimes, unfortunately, the resource pie fails to expand or, by its nature, cannot be expanded.[37] When the economy stagnates, conflicts over distribution often intensify, because improving the position of one person means another will endure an actual loss, not just a smaller gain, as in the positive-sum situation. In addition, some tensions arise over value conflicts that are neither divisible nor resolved through improved productivity. If a regime embraces one side of the abortion controversy, for example, it necessarily alienates the other. The attempt to stake out a middle position often alienates both extremes. Under such conditions, programs of modest reform may create more tension and protest than they cure.

Finally, even if reform in principle reduces some social tensions, the regime may lack sufficient resources to (1) redistribute to the discontented and (2) maintain the support of most elements of the existing establishment who benefit from the status quo, while (3) controlling those who remain or become discontented. Radicals, who consider the reforms inadequate, as well as newly alienated establishment factions, who believe the regime's concessions go too far, often attack a reforming regime. Confronted with these costs, a regime may well seek other alternatives of tension management.

Strategy 2: Deception and Deflection   Conservative change produces a modest improvement in the lot of the discontented in the hopes that this will suffice to reduce levels of social tension. A second, more manipulative strategy aims to convince (some might say delude) people into thinking that their condition is improving without making any substantive changes in the basic structure of power and value. Failing to assuage the discontented in this way, the regime may attempt to deflect popular discontent onto targets other than the regime itself and the order it supports.

The first manipulative goal involves a form of "symbolic politics," where one sector of the population receives the substantive benefits of policy, while another wins a symbolic, rhetorical victory.[38] Symbolic politics, when successful, convinces the discontented that they possess greater capabilities than they really do or that they have won victories on values that they have actually lost. In this way the regime finesses distributive conflicts as well as manages some problems of inconsistency.

Citizens easily recognize manipulative symbolic politics when it consists of blatant propaganda containing exaggerated distortions of reality, such as that often produced in wartime. More subtle—and effective—manipulation involves the rhetorical invocation of deeply held myths of a community. Insofar as Americans, for example, believe the myth of equal opportunity, they tend to accept the prevailing distribution of power and wealth as the justifiable result of differential effort. (Cynics might argue that myth allows us to rationalize the deprivations of others but see our own disadvantages as the product of some kind of unfair practice.) Additionally, to the extent that they accept the myth of democracy, Americans may well believe in their political efficacy without ever acting on this belief.[39] These types of symbolic persuasion enhance the stability of an established distribution of power and value, without the costs of reform.

If a regime fails to inflate its citizens' value position symbolically, it might attempt to deflect the consequences of tension away from itself. A regime accomplishes a diversion of discontent through various "scapegoating" techniques, blaming an "enemy"—internal or external—for the people's sufferings. An external enemy can prove useful in uniting a community and justifying sacrifices. An internal enemy helps explain away deficiencies in the dominant order. Stalin, for example, used the real fear of "capitalist encirclement" to justify the costly mobilization of the Soviet population during the 1930s. Hitler and the Nazis blamed both the German loss of World War I and postwar economic difficulties on the Jews (and leftists of various types), thus deflecting many Germans away from questioning the real failures of the system.

Strategies of deflection and deception, though, entail certain costs and risks. First, propaganda and other rhetorical appeals cannot be so divorced from reality that people readily see the discrepancies. They will find it difficult to swallow claims of glorious victories if enemy bombs continually rain down on their heads.

Manipulation of existing legitimacy myths may prove more effective, because these myths emerge gradually from the collective experience of a political community. The nature of their origins, however, means the regime cannot simply will them into existence. Moreover, these myths create certain expectations about regime performance that the regime may fail to fulfill. After all, the conditions defining the legitimacy of a regime also establish when it loses that legitimacy. Equality of opportunity, for example, justifies the existing distribution of power only as long as people believe that the system provides for equal life chances. As citizens increasingly experience what they see as unfair discrimination, the principle of equality of opportunity becomes a rationale for protest against the regime. This gap between expectations created by legitimizing myths and actual performance thereby develops into a form of cultural inconsistency.

The strategy of scapegoating must strike a delicate balance. An external enemy must be real enough to convince people a threat exists, but not so real that the regime's attacks provoke it into counteraction. When the Argentine military junta invaded the British-ruled Falkland Islands in 1982, they were attempting to divert increasing domestic discontent. Although initially successful (since the Malvinas Islands, as the Argentines call them, have long been a source of friction between the two countries), the junta certainly did not plan on their ultimate defeat by the British. This humiliation contributed to the downfall of military rule.

Internal scapegoating necessarily divides a community, a potentially dangerous consequence. The scapegoat must *appear* powerful enough to cause the problems blamed upon it, but not so powerful as to respond effectively against the attacks against it. Hitler found a perfect candidate in the Jews. People of Jewish background, through their drive and ability, disproportionately occupied positions in many of the high-status professions in Germany, as well as in world finance. The Jewish background of many left-wing figures also helped Hitler to draw his fateful portrait of conspiracy. Of course, if the Jewish population had possessed power to the extent Hitler claimed, they would never have allowed him to rule.

Finally, the fundamental shortcoming of these strategies lies in their failure to address the underlying causes of social tension. The distribution of power remains unchanged. Value inconsistencies and inadequacies remain unresolved. Ultimately, any regime relying too heavily on deception and deflection risks that eventually its people will reject symbolic rewards and excuses and demand concrete changes.

Strategy 3: Rituals of Rebellion   All social orders repress impulse, and the tensions arising from these social constraints produce evasion and possible rebellion. Stable social arrangements, therefore, provide for certain "safety valves" or "rituals of rebellion" allowing people to release their tension in ways that do not directly challenge the basic structure of power and authority.[40]

The rituals for releasing pent-up tension range from the "Saturday night drunk" to festivals like Mardi Gras, New Year's Eve, or sports victory celebrations. All these festivals relax conventional social controls for a time. The use of drugs such as alcohol and cocaine also represents a ritual of rebellion, in that those who might otherwise directly attack the regime dissipate their discontent. Drunks and dopeheads do not make revolutions. Without the existence of such safety valves, reactions to the repression of impulse could escalate into a direct challenge to the established order.

Nevertheless, though all stable communities must provide for such avenues of tension release, the costs and risks are high. Periodic festivals of celebration can rapidly become destructive, as the frequent reports of riots, and even fatalities, associated with sporting events attest. Widespread use of various narcotics may well deflate rebellious impulses, but it also jeopardizes the level of social performance required in complex societies.

Alcohol and drug abuse contribute to both health and productivity problems in the United States. Policies of eradication, such as those tried against alcohol consumption during Prohibition, generally prove futile. Nonetheless, the regime devotes considerable energy and resources to push substance abuse out of areas of complex interdependence (such as the operation of any form of transportation— cars, trains, planes, or supertankers). Cynics might doubt, however, whether the government really wants to implement serious programs to eliminate substance abuse among the underclass, as opposed to the middle class.

Ritualistic rebellions, then, always risk causing intolerable social disruption, even if they do not directly challenge the prevailing distribution of power and value. In addition, though providing a form of tension release, they fail to reduce the fundamental causes of social discontent. Eventually people may refuse to be bought off, manipulated, or drugged into passivity. At this point a regime can resort to a fourth strategy to defend the established order.

Strategy 4: Repression Even a reformist regime may encounter some dissidents who refuse to be placated by what they see as superficial alterations in a totally unacceptable status quo, distracted by symbolic victories or scapegoats, or deflated by rituals of rebellion. The regime may simply have to repress these challengers. Indeed, repression may be necessary to gain enough time for long-term reforms to work. As a regime grows less willing to reform, and if the effectiveness of other strategies declines, the regime will rely increasingly on strategies of repression when faced with widespread discontent.

Repression involves both short- and long-term objectives. In the short run, it strives to control protest by increasing the costs attached to any significant attack against the established order. Over the longer run, a strategy of repression contributes to passivity and acceptance. We might expect repression initially to anger people further, but sustained and effective repression may eventually lead rebels to despair. Protest, whether for reform or revolution, fundamentally expresses a sense of hope. People without hope generally do not revolt, though they may occasionally rebel.

As with the other strategies, repression suffers from certain practical limitations. The more extensively a regime relies on it, the greater the cost of the apparatus of coercion. Moreover, coercive organizations—the army and police—can threaten the survival of the regime. Over the past three decades, many leaders in the Third World countries have found to their dismay that using the army to suppress internal dissent has often encouraged the military to seize power for themselves.

Repression, even if consistently applied, fails to resolve underlying sources of discontent and can add to them. At best, it buys time for the regime while suppressing the irrevocably alienated. Inconsistently applied or insufficiently backed by the required coercive resources, a strategy of repression may only reinforce the strength of the protest.

Strategy 5: Compartmentalization Finally, a regime may deliberately decide to compartmentalize and ignore a problem. Every regime, constrained by scarce resources—symbolic as well as material—must decide which problems, protests, and demands to ignore, at least for the time being. In addition to problems of resource scarcity, the regime may face certain value conflicts that can neither be resolved nor manipulated out of existence. A regime will most likely seek to aid those sectors central to its survival and suppress those whose tensions it cannot cure but whose protests may prove disruptive to the social order.[41] On the other hand, the regime could safely ignore the needs of weak and isolated sectors and spend only minimal energy repressing whatever protests emerge. Compartmentalization has often victimized racial minorities, the poor and homeless, and immigrant groups, until they demonstrated sufficient disruptive power to attract more overt attention, if only of a repressive sort.

The strategy of compartmentalization and neglect runs certain obvious risks.

First, a particular sector must be weak enough to be easily ignored. A mistaken assessment in this regard could lead to unfortunate consequences. Second, neglect certainly solves nothing and may even intensify tension and protest.

No established order relies on just one of these strategies to manage inevitable tensions. Rather, policy, whether deliberate or tacit, consists of some ever-shifting mix. Success, never guaranteed, depends in part on the resources and skills of the regime and on the severity of the protest confronted.

Tension Management—The South African Case[42]

Perhaps no country exhibits more diverse and severe tensions, accompanied by increasingly desperate attempts by the regime to manage protest, than South Africa. The racially polarized distribution of power and wealth provokes intensifying demands for change. Economic growth depends upon an expanded involvement of an increasingly well-educated Black labor force, undermining the racial ideology and social myth of separate development. The increasing social and economic tensions reveal the incoherence and inadequacy of the entire cultural apparatus of Apartheid. And all the while, the simple realities of nonwhite population growth continue to worsen the contradictions in the system of white domination.

The fact that a system of such egregious exploitation and incoherence could endure for so many decades stands, though, as an inglorious tribute to the efficacy of the various strategies of tension management. Repression has been the most obvious instrument of social control, ranging from the welter of regulations covering residency, work permits, social behavior, and political organization to the overwhelming imposition of police and military coercion whenever protests from the nonwhite community grew too challenging.

The white regime, however, has not relied only on the use of direct repression. The authorities also assiduously pursued policies designed to divide the nonwhite population and deflect them into fighting among themselves. The artificial system of "racial classification" that categorized the population into broad categories of "Asian," "Coloured," and "Black" represents only the crudest illustration of this tactic of divide-and-rule. The policy of providing separate "homelands" for the different ethnic groups in the native African population further subdivided the oppressed. Finally, the regime has apparently provoked factional violence among Black groups over the years.

The perpetuation of an ideology of racial distinction supported the institutionalization of separate development. Religious doctrines, especially in the Dutch Reformed Church, entwined with the official myths of white superiority. The regime tolerated high rates of crime and drunkenness in the wretched urban townships not only as outlets for the tensions resulting from exploitation but also as evidence of the incapacity of Blacks for self-rule. All of these strategies combined to sustain the system in some form for decades, but they have not proven sufficient to eliminate swelling Black discontent or to resolve the glaring contradictions of Apartheid.

Consequently, continuing protest combined with external pressure forced the regime to attempt ever more significant reforms to buy off discontent while preserving essential white privileges. Over the past ten years, constitutional changes gave Asians and Coloureds a limited voice in the national government; educational and economic opportunities for nonwhites were grudgingly and inadequately expanded; the worst features of petty discrimination decreased substantially, at least in the major urban areas; and Black labor unions were legally tolerated. Nevertheless the regime continued to deny the majority any real voice in the national government.

Finally, by 1990, the white regime had decided to risk far more substantial reforms: it officially abandoned the homeland policy of separate development; it integrated all public facilities; it legalized the African National Congress (ANC) and released its leader, Nelson Mandela, after twenty-five years in prison; and, most significantly, the government entered into negotiations intended to develop a new constitutional system to provide Blacks with some meaningful political representation.

The ANC and other Black political groups demand majority rule and a redistribution of the wealth that they helped create through their labor. The divisions within the Black community, which the regime helped foster over the years, plague their attempt at political transformation. Meanwhile, the government faces an increasingly stiff and violent challenge from conservative segments of the white population who feel that their privileges, and perhaps their lives, are threatened by the prospect of further reform. In any case the regime seems unable to satisfy the demands of its majority population without "revolutionizing" itself out of power, a result which, if effected, would likely provoke many whites into even more violent reaction. Under conditions of such severe deterioration, the limited strategies of tension management may progressively fail, and the country may well slide into chaos.

CONCLUSION: DISORDER AND THE PROBLEM OF VIOLENCE

Order may be the dominant experience in social life, but the potential for discord pervades the very sinews that bind us together in predictable interaction. The sources of predictability generate tensions that lead to protest and even rebellion. At times these pressures result in outbreaks of individual deviance that violate established norms; on other occasions themes of protest combine into demands for systematic reform or revolution. In this case hopes for a new order justify the disruption of the old. Violent expressions of discontent may accompany either form of disorder.

The connection between discontent, disorder, and violence is, however, conceptually and empirically complex. Discontent need not produce disorder, depending both on the intensity of social tensions and the efficacy of regime strategies for managing emergent protest. Violence need not accompany disorder. Perhaps violence could become such a predictable pattern of social interaction that it establishes its own perverse order, although, at the level of the individual, the experience of violence is commonly disorienting.

Whether "orderly violence" posits a contradiction of terms, violent discord usually indicates the ineffective management of social tension. Neither disorder nor violence, however, is inherently perverse or pathological, for each may result from the pathologies structured into an established pattern of social relations. To sort these issues out, we must first clarify what we mean by the ambiguous concepts of violence and revolution.

NOTES

1. Erving Goffman, *Relations in Public* (New York: Harper Colophon, 1971), p. 288.
2. See, for example, the discussion of the meaning of freedom in Frithjof Bergmann, *On Being Free* (Notre Dame, Ind.: University of Notre Dame Press, 1977).
3. Thomas Hobbes, *Leviathan*, any edition, especially Chapters 13–18.
4. See, for example, any edition of Plato, *The Republic;* Thomas More, *Utopia;* Edward Bellamy, *Looking Backward;* and B. F. Skinner, *Walden Two.*
5. See, for example, any edition of Eugene Zamiatin, *We*, and Aldous Huxley, *Brave New World.*
6. The classic work discussing the vital role played by conflict in social relations is Lewis Coser, *The Functions of Social Conflict* (New York: The Free Press, 1956).
7. Morse Peckham, "Rebellion and Deviance," in Morse Peckham, *Romanticism and Behavior* (Columbia: University of South Carolina Press, 1976), p. 70.
8. Free [Abbie Hoffman], *Revolution for the Hell of It* (New York: Pocket Books, 1970).
9. Cf. Peter L. Berger, *The Sacred Canopy: Elements of a Theory of Religion* (Garden City, N.Y.: Doubleday, 1967), pp. 3–4.
10. This section is based on Peter C. Sederberg, *The Politics of Meaning: Power and Explanation in the Construction of Social Reality* (Tucson: University of Arizona Press, 1984), pp. 56–60.
11. Plato, *The Republic*, trans. by Francis M. Cornford (New York: Oxford University Press, 1945), p. 18.
12. Cf. Ralph Dahrendorf, *Class and Class Conflict in Industrial Democracy* (Stanford, Calif.: Stanford University Press, 1959), pp. 161–162.
13. Daniel Bell, *The End of Ideology* (New York: The Free Press, 1960); see also Francis Fukuyama, "The End of History?" *The National Interest*, 16 (Summer 1989): 3–18.
14. Morse Peckham, *Explanation and Power: The Control of Human Behavior* (New York: Seabury Press, 1979), pp. 164–165.
15. Edward O. Wilson, *On Human Nature* (Cambridge, Mass.: Harvard University Press, 1978), p. 2.
16. Hans J. Eysenk and Michael W. Eysenck, *Personality and Individual Differences: A Natural Science Approach* (New York: Plenum Press, 1985); see also William P. Kreml, *The Anti-Authoritarian Personality* (London: Pergamon, 1977).
17. Lynton K. Caldwell, "Biocracy: The Irrepressible Influence of Biology on Politics," in Elliott White and Joseph Losco, eds., *Biology and Bureaucracy: Public Administration from the Perspective of Evolutionary, Genetic and Neurobiological Theory* (Lanham, Md.: University Press of America, 1986), pp. 3–42.
18. Abraham Maslow, "A Theory of Human Motivation," *Psychological Review*, 50 (1943): 370–396.

19. Erich Fromm, *The Anatomy of Human Destructiveness* (New York: Holt, Rinehart and Winston, 1973), pp. 230–252. For a collection of recent investigations of the impact of human needs on social organization see Roger A. Coate and Jerel Rosati, eds., *The Power of Human Needs in World Society* (Boulder, Colo.: Lynne Rienner Publishers, 1988).

20. For a relatively late restatement of his position see Talcott Parsons, "Some Problems of General Theory in Sociology," in John C. McKinney and Edward A. Tiryakian, eds., *Theoretical Sociology: Perspectives and Developments* (Englewood Cliffs, N.J.: Prentice Hall, 1970), pp. 26–68.

21. Gabriel A. Almond and G. Bingham Powell, *Comparative Politics: System, Process, Policy* (Boston: Little, Brown, 1978).

22. Noted in Morse Peckham, *Explanation and Power,* p. 242.

23. Morse Peckham, "The Arts and the Centers of Power," reprinted in Peckham, *Romanticism and Behavior,* p. 335.

24. See Norbert Elias, *The Civilizing Process: The History of Manners,* trans. by Edmund Jephcott (New York: Urizen Books, 1978).

25. For a critique of some of these categorical schemes see Michael Thompson, Richard Ellis, and Aaron Wildavsky, *Culture Theory* (Boulder, Colo.: Westview Press, 1990), Part Two.

26. Ibid., pp. 1–15. *Hierarchical* relations are characterized by strong group boundaries and strong, externally imposed prescriptions for behavior; *egalitarian* relations have strong group boundaries but minimal prescriptions; *fatalistic* relations reflect weak group ties but strong prescriptions; *individualistic* relations entail neither significant group identity nor social prescriptions; finally, the *autonomous* individual is one who withdraws from social interaction of any form as much as possible (e.g., a hermit).

27. The absence of group ties combined with detailed prescriptions for behavior identifies this area of social interaction as embodying a fatalistic way of life. Traffic police attempt to control those who convert their driving into an individualist pattern (that is, not bound by externally imposed rules). A few people deliberately refuse to buy cars, remaining relatively independent of the whole pattern of relations in this arena.

28. Peckham, *Explanation and Power,* pp. 199–200.

29. Sigmund Freud, *Civilization and Its Discontents* (New York: W. W. Norton, 1962).

30. Jean Baechler, *Revolution,* trans. by Joan Vickers (New York: Harper & Row, 1975), p. 105.

31. Peter Weiss, *The Persecution and Assassination of Jean-Paul Marat as Performed by the Inmates of the Asylum of Charenton Under the Direction of the Marquis de Sade,* trans. by Geoffrey Skelton (New York: Pocket Books, 1966).

32. For a comprehensive development of a resource exchange model of political power see Warren F. Ilchman and Norman Thomas Uphoff, *The Political Economy of Change* (Berkeley: University of California Press, 1969). I have developed a more elaborate discussion of power resources in Peter C. Sederberg, *Interpreting Politics* (San Francisco: Chandler and Sharp, 1977), pp. 34–45.

33. Thompson, Ellis, and Wildavsky, especially Chapter 5.

34. See Lucian W. Pye, *The Mandarin and the Cadre: China's Political Cultures* (Ann Arbor: University of Michigan Press, 1988).

35. See the discussion of the inadequacy of categories in Peckham, *Explanation and Power,* pp. 96–99; see also Thompson, Ellis, and Wildavsky, Chapter 4.

36. Personal conversation.

37. This distinction between those resources that can be expanded and those that cannot reflects that made between "material" and "positional" resources in Fred Hirsch,

The Social Limits to Growth (Cambridge, Mass.: Harvard University Press, 1976), p. 27.

38.   Murray Edelman, *The Symbolic Uses of Politics* (Urbana: University of Illinois Press, 1967), Chapter 2.

39.   Some evidence exists that this at least used to be the case. See Gabriel A. Almond and Sidney Verba, *The Civic Culture: Political Attitudes and Democracy in Five Nations* (Boston: Little, Brown, 1963), especially Chapter 6. By the time the "civic culture" was revisited fifteen year later, attitudes of greater cynicism were found. See Gabriel A. Almond and Sidney Verba, eds., *The Civic Culture Revisited* (Boston: Little, Brown, 1980).

40.   "Rituals of rebellion" is an anthropological term. See N. L. Nieburg, *Culture Storm: Politics and the Ritual Order* (New York: St. Martin's, 1973), especially Chapter 7.

41.   Cf. Ilchman and Uphoff, pp. 42–47.

42.   For background on resistance movements in South Africa see Stephen M. Davis, *Apartheid's Rebels: Inside South Africa's Hidden War* (New Haven, Conn.: Yale University Press, 1987); for background on the regime's efforts to manage discontent see Stanely B. Greenberg, *Legitimizing the Illegitimate: State, Markets, and Resistance in South Africa* (Berkeley: University of California Press, 1987); for data on the patterns of social and economic deprivation see Francis Wilson and Mamphela Ramphele, *Uprooting Poverty: The South African Challenge* (New York: W. W. Norton, 1989).

2

Defining Politics, Violence, and Revolution

All social concepts suffer to some degree from ambiguity and multiple meanings. The concepts of violence and revolution exhibit these difficulties perhaps more than others owing to the emotions evoked by the phenomena they attempt to characterize. This chapter undertakes the necessary task of conceptual clarification. We first evaluate commonsense, behavioral, and structural notions of violence, and then we review forms of internal political violence. Since multiple definitions of revolution abound, we also sample and critically assess some of these.

POLITICS AND DEFINITION[1]

We usually associate politics in the contemporary world with government, especially national government. This commonsense association between government and politics, though, is too restrictive. We participate in many overlapping communities, at least intermittently, ranging from our families, religious groups, places of employment, and peer groups to a variety of national and international associations. In each of these communities, and through these communities, we can participate in politics.

We need, then, a concept of politics broad enough to encompass the richness of our political experience: *Politics consists of all deliberate efforts to control mutual interaction.* The mutual interactions of individuals and groups generate communities from the family to the nation-state. In order for these interactions to be "mutual," our responses to one another must be understandable and predictable. If we respond to each other in incomprehensible and unpredictable ways, our sense of mutuality, or community, breaks down.

We must immediately add three important clarifications. First, *efforts* to control need not imply success at control. Many times we set out to have an impact on some community in which we participate. We might, to select a conventional example, campaign for a particular party or policy. Repeated defeats, however, may eventually discourage us and redirect our energy to forums where we expect greater success. We could turn from the macropolitics of the national community to the micropolitics of our family or business. Alternatively, frustration with the conventional channels of political influence may incite us to disrupt or destroy what we cannot direct.

Second, attempts to control interaction entail more than the cynical imposition of the will of the powerful on their weaker subordinates. We may seek control through domination and manipulation. But political interactions also develop among relative equals. Even where inequalities exist, efforts at control may be mutual, involve bargaining and compromise, and lead to consequences that all participants view as beneficial.

Finally, those seeking control may pursue a variety of objectives. We tend to associate control with the goal of *maintaining* some established pattern of social relations. Politics, from this view, would be fundamentally conservative in nature. We also attempt, however, to *modify* our patterns of social interaction or *create* entirely new ones. These latter goals could require the destruction of established social structures.

Our broad conception of politics characterizes all deliberate efforts to control interaction, even that between two people, as essentially political in nature. Most useful perspectives on politics yield similar implications, despite efforts to restrict the conception to activities conventionally associated with government operations. More restrictive definitions, such as those distinguishing between "public" and "private" arenas or focusing on "whole" communities, commonly concede that "quasi-political" activities occur in other spheres, such as the family or corporation. Whether definitions of politics stress cooperation or coercion, imposed power or implied consent, they all focus on the attempt to control mutual interaction.

Despite its breadth, our definition does not equate politics with all human behavior. First, not all behavior is deliberate. Deliberate behavior consists of that taken in response to self-given directions. Deliberation excludes behavior resulting from either instinct or habit. We cannot be aware of when we behave in an unconscious, automatic fashion, but if we reflect back on our daily lives, we can recognize how much of our behavior is not deliberate. Indeed, such automatic responses make a major contribution to our mutual predictability and thereby help to sustain orderly interactions.

Habit, though not specifically political, has conservative political implications. Consequently, those aiming to transform established communities often feel driven to disrupt habitual interactions. Revolutionaries are keenly sensitive to the conservative nature of established habits. During periods of revolutionary turmoil, questions of ideological purity penetrate into realms of behavior previously considered nonpolitical, private, or even "natural."

Our definition of political action, moreover, does not include all deliberate behavior, rather, only that specifically aimed at creating, maintaining, or altering interactions. A hermit in contemplation or people carrying out some technical task may deliberate but with no intention of affecting a pattern of social interaction. Similarly, deliberation over how to interact smoothly within an established pattern is also nonpolitical, although such action may have conservative political implications. Drivers merging onto a busy freeway, for example, may calculate their moves quite carefully. Their goal of smooth interaction supports mutuality, but they usually make no effort to control others. A highway patrol officer, in contrast, deliberately intervenes to maintain certain behavior, by force if necessary, and so engages in politics.

The political universe, though significant, is not all-encompassing. Not all behavior is deliberate, and not all deliberate behavior aims at controlling interaction in some way. The political universe, in addition, continually expands and contracts. Revolutionary politics, to transform structures and habits of behavior, tends to expand the political realm, while a highly tradition-bound community may have a quite limited political sphere. A completely habitualized social order would have no politics at all, although such a community represents only a hypothetical extreme.

Our concept rejects identifying politics solely with the "public" arena or characterizing "private" life as nonpolitical. The definition of the boundary between public and private spheres itself constitutes a political decision often subject to considerable dispute. We might understand "privacy" as a kind of sovereignty. When we assert a "right" to privacy, we essentially demand self-rule in a particular arena, as opposed to being subject to the jurisdiction of some more inclusive community. Within this "sovereign" arena, political life may still go on, though free of external regulation.

Those who assert that parents have the right to raise their children as they see fit, without the interference of the state, make a claim to sovereignty similar to the claim of those who argue that the World Court has no jurisdiction over the activities and policies of the United States government. Politics, as we define it, would continue within the "sovereign" family just as it clearly does within the United States. In the former case, however, laws and regulations of wider communities considerably circumscribe sovereignty, or privacy. Parents cannot treat their children just as they please. Governments, though, still abuse their own citizens with little fear of external interference, though challenges are arising to this form of sovereignty, too.

The domain of politics also extends to debates over the meaning of the concepts we use in political discourse. Often we treat our terms of analysis as self-evident and commonly understood. This naive presumption, however, ignores the sordid and bloody history of human disputes over meaning, disputes that lay, for instance, at the core of the religious wars of the sixteenth and seventeenth centuries and are echoed in both the secular and sacred ideological conflicts of our time.

The process of definition does not entail the discovery of some transcendent ideal; rather, it reflects particular historical eras, intellectual professions, and even partisan positions.[2] The definition of terms, like other human actions, involves the interests of those doing the defining. The definition of the terms of a debate helps set the agenda for the community, whether this community is the nation-state or the community of inquirers in a particular academic discipline. Successful definition, therefore, involves the exercise of a kind of power.

Does this mean that all definitions, then, are equal? Equally arbitrary? Equally valid? Not at all. We need no more agree that all definitions are equivalent than concede that all human interests are equally tolerable or that all forms of the exercise of power are equally desirable. We must recognize the potential for arbitrary and repressive definitions, just as we acknowledge the existence of repressive relations.

Definitions offered in apparent sincerity often reflect political agendas, assume distinctions that are not universally self-evident, and represent distributions of power and privilege of a particular time and place. To remain unselfconscious about the concepts we use to make sense of the world means that the definition of those concepts (and the interests they support) will use us.

We should treat definitions not as received truths but as tools. The value of these conceptual tools ought to be determined in the same way as that of other tools: *in use*; rather than in terms of their presumed approximation to a transcendent ideal.[3] Definitions should serve the interest of making sense out of our experience. Nevertheless, we must remember that effective explanation, too, involves an exercise of power, but one that liberates rather than oppresses, if we strive to sustain a dialogue, not to shut it down.

THE POLITICS OF DEFINING COERCION AND VIOLENCE[4]

All commentators seem to "know" what they are talking about when they discuss "violence," but they are often not talking about the same thing. When I ask my students to define or characterize an act of violence, they come up with some common traits, but also some common disagreements and common omissions.

All agree that violence involves "hurt," "harm," "damage," or "death." Disagreements develop over the degree or amount of harm done before an action becomes violent. Loss of life, they concur, is certainly serious enough, as are other forms of major bodily harm, but usually disputes arise over the issue of property damage. Most students accept that accidents should not count as acts of violence, but they usually fail to specify the boundaries of "accidental death."

Further disagreements develop over the conceptual distinction, if any, between the police shooting a criminal suspect and the criminal shooting the police. Some want to say that if the authorities engage in the action, it cannot be violence. Others see no difference and want to characterize all intentional harm as violence. In these disputes violence often carries a pejorative connotation. Few students want to defend acts labeled as violent. If they identify with the action, they want to label it differently. Everyday understandings of the meaning of violence, then, stake out some common ground but generally fail to agree on the exact boundaries.

Scholars reflect similar disagreements in their own work. Consider two contrasting definitions of coercion, one excessively broad and the other too narrow. Samuel Dubois Cook says, "To coerce is to compel or restrain the human will by an outside agent."[5] He then elaborates:

> Coercion may be physical or nonphysical (psychological, spiritual, intellectual, aesthetic), violent or nonviolent, public (official) or private, individual or collective, overt or covert, legitimate or illegitimate, positive (rewards or promises of benefits) or negative (punishment or threat of deprivation), formal or informal, etc.[6]

The breadth of Cook's definition contrasts sharply with the narrow focus of Christian Bay, who limits coercion to acts involving "physical violence" or sanctions severe enough to deter an individual from a strongly desired course of action.[7] Bay thinks coercion is the "supreme political evil."[8] Given the breadth of his definition, if Cook had concluded the same thing, he would be condemning the vast preponderance of human political behavior. Consequently, he argues that coercion is "ethically neutral."[9]

Although each definition offers some insight, neither one seems satisfactory. Bay recognizes the essentially negative character of coercion—it involves harm—but he carries this notion to an extreme conclusion, thereby obscuring the full range and role of coercion in our political lives. Cook plausibly argues that we cannot separate the evaluation of coercion in politics from the character it takes and the ends for which people use it. He defines coercion so broadly, however, as to make it indistinguishable from the general notion of power, a none-too-precise concept in the first place.

We avoid both these extremes by defining coercion as *intentional harm*. The degree of harm may vary, and we may use coercion, or its threat, to pursue a variety of purposes, as we may with other forms of power. The distinctive characteristic of coercion, though, remains intentional harm.

Coercion permeates political life, from mild gestures of parental discipline to devastating military campaigns. Well-ordered political communities establish and enforce limits on the use of coercion in social relations. Rather than using "coercion," "force," and "violence" interchangeably, we consider the latter two terms as labels for two types of coercion. We label as "violence" those acts of coercion that *violate* the limits governing the use of coercion within a particular community, while identifying coercion within these accepted limits as "force." The notion of acceptable coercion or force implies that the benefits to the established order are seen as outweighing the harm done, as when the police use coercion to apprehend a lawbreaker.

The use of this term splitting to make some critical distinctions yields a simple progressive differentiation (Figure 2.1). Each of the distinctions, however, reflects the political process within a particular community. Outbreaks of violence do not signify the breakdown of politics; indeed, politics determines the forms of coercion considered to be violent. Even the definitions of "harm" and "intention" result from a continually dynamic and often conflictual political process. Yet conflict and dynamism need not imply chaos; in fact, they seldom do. The manner in which different communities establish, challenge, and change these distinctions, though, reveals much about the role of coercion in various social settings.

Harm

The nature of harm might appear self-evident, but it is not. We might recall the old philosophical conundrum concerning whether a tree falling unheard in the forest makes a sound. The answer, of course, depends on whether we define sound physically as a type of wave transmitted through a medium or "socially" in terms of a receiver who can interpret its meaning. Analogously, we might define

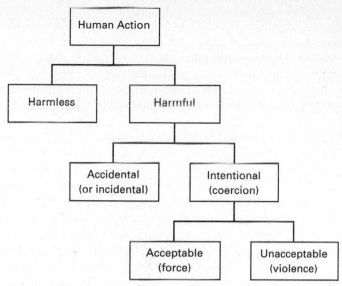

Figure 2.1 Defining coercion.

harm materially in terms of an alteration of a physical state (like changing an animate into an inanimate object or otherwise rearranging molecular states), or socially as the loss or limitation of some entitlement. In both cases, the social meaning presumes the physical but goes beyond it. Only the latter definition possesses political significance.

Political communities establish and maintain entitlements, but ambiguities and disputes often surround both the process and the result. In situations involving unclear entitlements, debates arise over whether "harm" in any socially significant sense has occurred. Some entitlements, like that to life, seem well established, while others, like that to various forms of property, are more nebulous.

Even the "right to life," however, is not absolute, unambiguous, or universally accorded. The abortion controversy aptly illustrates this point. Some argue that the fetus cannot be harmed by abortion because it possesses no independent title to life. Others consider the fetus's right to life absolute and believe that deliberately ending that life is murder. Intermediate positions also exist. Some people believe that the fetus possesses a limited entitlement to life and that abortion therefore harms it. Nevertheless, they might accept some abortions under strictly defined circumstances, such as to save the mother's life or if the impregnation resulted from incest or rape. Such intervention involves a type of "justifiable homicide." Therefore, depending on our political position, people might view the same act—abortion—not as harm at all, but simply a medical procedure; as an act of unacceptable coercion or violence; or as an act of acceptable coercion, or force, at least under some politically established conditions.

Harm, even in terms of deprivation of something so fundamental as life, lacks political reality until so recognized by a community constituted to define such entitlements. Animals who die for human purposes suffer no harm in a social sense, except to the extent that a community has bestowed certain entitlements on them. Those who empathize with the fate of animals butchered for food or used in medical experiments probably think not at all about the millions of microbes slaughtered when they take antibiotics. Microbes, unfortunately for them, are rather remote from our consciousness, unlike the "higher" life forms, like puppies and chimps, that share more closely in our humanity. "Man" is the measure of all things, for all entitlements within political communities derive *from* those communities.

Concepts of harm to life and limb have at least one foot, so to speak, in a biological reality independent of culture. Notions of harm to liberty and property appear completely culturally dependent. Generally, liberty implies some idea of space: most basically, a literal space within which to move; more figuratively, a "space" to express a range of opinions or engage in a variety of life-styles.[10] Positively, liberty suggests the possession of resources necessary to make use of the available "space." In any case, all communities restrict space to some extent. Both liberties and the resources needed to realize them are scarce. Harm to a person's liberty, therefore, involves the imposition of restrictions beyond those conventionally established. The definition of the "appropriate" limits on liberty, and thus where harm begins, often is itself disputed.

Similarly, the concept of property is culturally dependent. Whether harm occurs to property depends on who "owns" the property and the limits on this title. The range of this particular debate extends from Proudhon's dictum that private property is theft to Robert Nozick's claim that public taxes are theft.[11] Socialist communities tend to look more unkindly on acts that damage community property than those that affect the limited area of private property rights. Capitalist societies tend to reverse the emphasis.

The concept of harm, then, emerges somewhat unsteadily from the ongoing efforts of human beings to establish some consensus on entitlements within (and among) their communities. The definition of entitlements determines the extent and nature of the harm. Relatively stable communities establish widely shared agreements on these issues, but even so, the dominant position will seldom go completely unchallenged.

Intention

Coercion entails intentional harm; that is, the perpetrators must direct themselves to harm the victims. This condition adds the next layer of ambiguity to the concept of violence, for intentions are commonly covert and difficult to assess. Moreover, the coherence and consideration informing self-directives also vary. Nevertheless, the social significance of a harmful act depends upon the "degree of directiveness" underlying it. Acts identical in effect (for example, the victims die), differ greatly, depending on intention.

We might distinguish among four levels of intentionality, reflecting judgments commonly made in criminal proceedings. *Accidental harm* occurs when the consequence appears essentially unforeseeable, random, and unavoidable. The victim, though harmed according to established community standards, has not been coerced. *Incidental harm* occurs when those involved recognize harm as a possible outcome of an action taken for other reasons. The risk of death that accompanies all forms of major surgery provides an obvious example. Under normal conditions, if the patient dies, we would not consider this event to be an act of coercion.

Sometimes, though, the perpetrator could avoid the harmful consequences, even if they were not specifically intended. For example, if the surgeon had not been intoxicated, the patient might have lived. Such *negligent harm* introduces a degree of culpability, because the surgeon could foresee and avoid the harmful effects of drinking and cutting. Nonetheless, it seems dubious to consider negligent harm as coercion. Only *directly intended harm*, then, fits our definition of coercion. Even so restricted, though, some ambiguity remains, for the perpetrator may function under some form of "diminished capacity." Consequently, "crimes of passion" do not possess the same political significance as coolly premeditated acts of destruction.

Another's intent, especially in the complexity indicated above, is impossible to know directly. Nevertheless we cannot avoid assessing intention in our interpretations of the social world. This paradoxical plight injects an additional element of instability into social relations generally and into the interpretation of coercive acts in particular.

We need not conclude, however, that the assessment of intent consists of arbitrary guesswork. Rather, we may carefully develop a motivational construct based on what we know of the person and the context within which the act occurred.[12] Such analysis narrows the range of probable intention, even if it cannot establish definitive truth. Reasoning of this sort proceeds overtly in a court of law and somewhat consciously whenever we attempt to understand each other's motives. Yet, no matter how carefully we construct our interpretation, a gap will always remain between interpreted and actual intent.

Another problem associated with this approach to coercion concerns the biases of "methodological individualism."[13] By focusing on individual intent, our concept of coercion misses those social arrangements whose consequences are harmful, even though the individuals who embody the arrangements in their behavior do not specifically intend harm. Rather, they simply do their assigned tasks within an orderly system of mutual expectation. Richard Rubenstein, for example, notes the wide participation in the bureaucratic system that organized the genocide of the Jews in Nazi Germany:

> The destruction process required the cooperation of every sector of German society. The bureaucrats drew up the definitions and decrees; the churches gave evidence of Aryan descent; the postal authorities carried the messages of definition, expropriation, denaturalization, and deportation; business corporations dismissed their Jewish employees and took over "Aryanized" properties; the railroads carried the victims to their place of execution, a place made available to the Gestapo and the SS by the Wehrmacht.[14]

In most cases, however, those directing such social organizations are aware of and do intend the harmful consequences. This leaves open the question of the extent to which the contributing "cogs" of a bureaucratic machine are held culpa ble for the consequences of their collective actions. In those cases where all the participants, perhaps including even the victims, remain ignorant of the harmful effects of their social arrangements, the situation involves exploitation or oppression, as opposed to explicit coercion. From this perspective, then, we might speak of "structural exploitation" but not "structural coercion."

For the purposes of our study, coercion means intentional harm. This restriction, though, is pragmatic, and we must remain sensitive to the possible biases of our approach. Revolutionaries, for example, often point to how apologists for the status quo condemn the overt violence of the dissidents while ignoring the far greater harm done by the institutional arrangements of the established order.

Acceptability

Intentionally harmful acts range from the trivial to the devastatingly destructive, and whether we like it or not, people often resort to the threat or use of coercion in their political relations. All political communities, from the family to the "new world order," confront the problem of limiting the extent of coercion in their politics. The contemporary nation-state, in particular, attempts to define the "acceptable" uses of coercion within all the subsidiary communities that it comprises. The state does not so much claim a monopoly on the "legitimate" *use* of coercion, as Max Weber would have it, as claim the ultimate *responsibility* for establishing the boundaries defining the acceptable forms of coercion used by its representatives and members.[15] This distinction between acceptable "force" and unacceptable "violence" also emerges out of a continuous political process.

In a relatively stable community, the prevailing definition of acceptable coercion, whether set through custom or law, generally favors the status quo. The community as a whole will tend to tolerate coercion seen as basically defending established values and the existing distribution of power. Alternatively, coercive acts that increasingly threaten the established values and power will more likely violate the limits on coercion. This does not necessarily mean that "anything goes" as long as it is defensive, or that all "redistributive" coercive acts will be branded as violence. The definition of force favors the status quo, but the extent of the bias varies. A more "open" society may strictly regulate "establishment" coercion (for example, by limiting police powers) while tolerating certain forms of redistributive coercion (for example, industrial strikes). Figure 2.2 illustrates these alternatives, with panel (*b*) representing a more "open" society.

Our distinction between force and violence, then, rests on an empirical assessment of the dominant standards in a particular community. If no standards prevail, then the distinction collapses. This definition of violence does *not* imply a normative conclusion. We may, for instance, believe that the use of force by a tyranny is evil, while the use of violence by those resisting this tyranny is justifiable.

Though we may, in principle, empirically determine the range of acceptable coercion within a particular community, the boundary often lacks the clarity suggested by Figure 2.2. Inevitably, disputes arise over the acceptability of certain coercive acts, and in the modern state, courts exist to adjudicate such disputes.

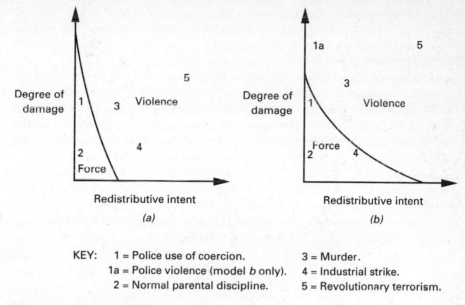

KEY: 1 = Police use of coercion.   3 = Murder.
       1a = Police violence (model *b* only).   4 = Industrial strike.
       2 = Normal parental discipline.   5 = Revolutionary terrorism.

Figure 2.2 The political definition of force and violence.

Moreover, boundaries based on conventionally established criteria change over time and often differ from community to community. In the United States, for example, the government has placed increasingly stringent restrictions on the use of coercion within the family.

When Is Violence "Political"?

Our actions take on political significance whenever we attempt to shape mutual interaction, yet the significance of different acts varies considerably. A father uses abusive coercion to assert control over his family, and a regime resorts to terror to repress all vestiges of opposition in a country. Muggers use violence to redistribute wealth from their victims to themselves, and a revolutionary movement expropriates the property of wealthy landowners in the territory it controls and redistributes it to poor peasants. A teenage gang murders those who wear rival "colors," while the death squads of a political party assassinate their opponents. In everyday discussion the latter example of violence in each of the contrasting pairs commonly carries the label "political," while the other instance does not. Why?

No answer can avoid ambiguity, because the "political" label, in these cases, depends on somebody's judgment of the significance of the act for wider, more inclusive communities. Judgments of significance, though, are themselves subjects of contention. Regimes often attempt to deny wider significance to acts of violence directed against them, labeling such attacks as the work of "common criminals" or "terrorists." The perpetrators of these actions, in contrast, might exaggerate the significance of their acts and describe themselves as "revolutionaries." Prison sometimes radicalizes common thieves who come to see their acts of theft as blows struck against the oppressive capitalist regime. The regime, unpersuaded by such ideological claims, resists reclassifying the convicts as political prisoners.

Despite the obvious scope for disputation, we may evaluate the political significance of coercive acts both logically and empirically. Differences might arise, but we can make general comparisons of the relative significance of coercive acts within their social contexts. The suicide of an aging individual suffering from a fatal disease approaches zero political significance. The self-immolation of a high-caste Hindu college student protesting the Indian government's policy of reserving some government positions for so-called "untouchables," possesses some political significance, but perhaps not as much as the suicide truck bomber that destroyed the American marine barracks in Beruit in 1982. A well-organized revolutionary insurgency waging war against the incumbent regime of a country represents politically significant violence of the highest degree.

🔥   🔥   🔥

Coercion, force, and violence take on meaning only within political communities. To coerce means to harm intentionally, but harm can occur only with the loss of an entitlement, and entitlements exist only within communities. Harm is a matter of degree, but the assessment of degrees of harm depends on community standards. Intention, too, is a matter of degree and can only be indirectly assessed. The distinction between force and violence depends on the existence of prevailing standards in a community, but these fluctuate over time and differ among communities. The political significance of acts of force or violence depends on their relevance to, or impact on, more inclusive communities.

We might wonder, given this complexity, how any common ground can be maintained. We need to remind ourselves, again, of the fundamental rage for order that we possess. We pour most of our political energies into determining, communicating, and embodying mutually agreed-upon standards of behavior, including those defining the nature of coercion and its acceptable use in political relations.

As analysts we build our understanding on the foundation of order existing in social relations. The importance of a particular event for our hypotheses and theories of political violence depends on our initial decisions about whether it was harmful, intentional, acceptable or unacceptable, and significant within an established community. With this in mind, we can undertake a preliminary classification of different forms of violence.

FORMS OF VIOLENCE—A PRELIMINARY INVENTORY

Coercion provides an instrument of control in our political communities whose contribution to orderly relations depends on its successful regulation. Acts of coercion that violate established limits disrupt the existing order, but not all forms of violence do so to the same extent. For the purposes of analysis, however, we certainly do not want to dissect anew each instance of violence encountered. Consequently, we need to develop at least a preliminary inventory of basic forms of violence to assist us in systematically comparing the particular violent events we observe.

Classification schemes, like definitions, are tools used to organize complex and diverse observations.[16] Useful classification yields, at a minimum, some bases for comparison and identifies puzzles in need of explanation. One common method of classification develops a typology constructed from two or more empirically grounded dimensions to produce "mutually exclusive and jointly exhaustive" types.[17] Exclusive and exhaustive means that each case of the phenomena being classified fits one category of the typology and *only* one.

Our ambitions here are more modest. We develop an inventory of different forms of violence, specifying a number of empirical characteristics of each (see Table 2.1). We cannot claim that our inventory is exhaustive as an empirical classification, for we may encounter some event that fails to fit clearly into one category or another. Mutual exclusivity is also compromised, for some forms of violence partly overlap on several dimensions with other categories. Moreover, certain kinds of violence may, in their various manifestations, reflect the full range of a particular empirical characteristic. Finally, most of our empirical variables use relatively primitive *nominal* (simple identification of differences in kind) or *ordinal* (differences in degree expressed in terms of "more or less" rather than stated in terms of precise intervals) scales of measurement.

Despite these shortcomings, this scheme provides a preliminary enumeration and a tentative organization of common forms of domestic violence. The empirical characteristics identified aid in distinguishing among the different forms of violence, indicate the significance of a particular form for the community so afflicted, and suggest some important empirical puzzles.

Empirical Variables

We compare forms of violence on the basis of six empirical variables. These, to be sure, do not exhaust the conceivable characteristics that could prove of interest. They emphasize, however, several areas of significant contrast, as well as illustrate the diversity of the phenomena grouped loosely under the broad concept of "violence."

1. *Location*   Different types of violence occur in varying social contexts. More detailed analysis of the context of violence might use variables of social class, group identity, or organizational form. We begin, though, with the simple recognition that some forms of violence develop in *rural* settings while others occur in *urban* locations. A few types, however, may be all-pervasive in terms of their locale. The urban/rural distinction is a simple nominal indicator.

2. *Political Significance*   All actions intended to affect mutual interaction are basically political in nature, but their significance for a wider political community varies. We estimate relative political significance on an ordinal

Table 2.1 FORMS OF DOMESTIC VIOLENCE

		VARIABLE					
TYPE	Location	Political Significance	Direction of Change	Mass Participation	Elite Participation	Destructiveness
1. Violent crime	Urban and rural	Low	0	Low/medium	Low	Low
2. Social banditry	Rural	Low/medium	~0	Low/medium	Low	Low/medium
3. Gangsterism	Urban	Low/medium	~0	Low/medium	Low	Low/medium
4. Peasant risings	Rural	Medium	-1 to 0	High	Low	Medium/high
5. Urban riots	Urban	Medium	-1 to 0	High	Low	Medium/high
6. Guerrilla raids	Rural	Low/medium	-1 to +1	Low/medium	Low	Low/medium
7. Revolutionary warfare	Rural	High	-1 to +1	High	Low/medium	High
8. Urban revolution	Urban	High	+1	High	Low/medium	Medium/high
9. Assassination	Urban and rural	Medium	-1 to +1	None	Low	Low/medium
10. Vigilante violence	Urban and rural	Low/medium	-1 to 0	Low/medium	Low/medium	Low/medium
11. Coup d'état	Urban	High	-1 to +1	None to low	Medium/high	Medium
12. Regime terror	Urban and rural	High	0 to +1	Low	Medium/high	High

scale that includes the benchmarks of *low*, *medium*, and *high* levels of significance. Some acts of violence have little significance beyond those immediately affected, and these events would be of limited interest. Such a scale, obviously, does not indicate the precise interval between acts judged to be of different significance. The assessment of significance depends on how a particular type of violence affects the national political community.

3. **Direction of Change**   We also estimate whether an act of violence attempts to preserve or change the prevailing distribution of power in the national political community. Simply defined, *reactionary violence* (−1) aims to restore a previously established order; *preservative violence* (0) aims to defend the existing distribution of power and value; and *revolutionary violence* (+1) aspires to create a new political and social dispensation.

4. **Mass Participation**   In most cases, relatively few people directly participate in acts of violence, even ones of considerable significance. Nevertheless, the range of participation among the "masses" varies considerably. We could attempt a census of those participating directly in the violence to produce clear, precise, numerical measures. In practice, however, few are willing or able to undertake such hazardous research, and in any case it might yield a false sense of precision. For our preliminary purposes, we use a limited ordinal estimate of mass participation ranging from *none* through *low*, *medium*, and *high*. So-called high levels of mass participation, though, still involve only a minority of the available population. Nonetheless the participation of only a few percent represents considerable numbers of people.

5. **Elite Participation**   Elements of the elite in a community may also engage in acts of violence. Most of the time, of course, the coercive processes that we characterize as "force" reflect elite preferences. Under severe conditions of social strain, however, "acceptable" coercion may not provide an adequate defense of elite position. Consequently, members of the elite begin to instigate and participate in acts of establishment violence. In addition, some members of the more privileged sectors of a society may empathize and affiliate with the disaffected and attack, rather than defend, the established order.

This variable, of course, presumes we can distinguish just who qualifies as a member of the "elite." Analysts commonly use indicators of class, status, and wealth, either alone or in some combination. Educational achievement provides another useful measure, with the elite representing the most highly educated segments of the population. In some communities, this might be anyone with a high school education; in others, it might mean higher education or even professional degrees. However "elite" is defined, some kinds of violence attract greater elite participation than others, often in leadership roles. Again, rather than striving for dubious precision, we simply estimate elite participation as ranging from *none*, through *low* and *medium*, to *high* levels.

6. **Destructivene**   All acts of coercion entail harm, but the degree of harm varies. We might equate the dimension of destructiveness with body

counts and monetary estimates of damage inflicted, lending it a false precision. We should resist, however, drawing too close an equivalence between
physical and political damage. Some acts of violence tear more grievously at
the social fabric than others, although the physical consequences appear
identical. The assassination of a president damages a political community
far more than the murder of an ordinary citizen, even though the body
counts are equal. This qualitative dimension again supports use of an ordinal scale of *low, medium,* and *high* levels of destructiveness.

Forms of Violence—Some Comparisons

Human beings engage in many distinct forms of violence. In Table 2.1 we take
some conventional categories and compare them according to the six empirical
characteristics just discussed. Though these comparisons are illustrative and tentative, not definitive, they serve to highlight some significant differences we need
to take into account in understanding various types of violence.

   1. Violent Crime   Even reasonably well ordered communities experience
violence, especially in the form of common crime.[18] Though crime is not confined
to any particular setting, its frequency appears to increase in urban areas. Most
common crime has direct political significance only for those immediately affected. Pervasive crime, however, may assume indirect political significance for the
regime charged with protecting the citizens' safety and well-being.

   Although many individual crimes involve some redistribution of wealth and
power, they seldom constitute a significant challenge the basic distribution of
power and value in a society. In a stable community the vast majority of the people, even among relatively deprived sectors, remain law-abiding. However, under
deteriorating social conditions, like those afflicting some American inner cities,
criminal acts spread widely among certain groups. Even so, participation remains
essentially atomized, rather than organized. Elite participation in violent crimes,
as opposed to so-called white-collar crime, is low.

   Except under extreme conditions, the level of destructiveness attributable to
common criminal violence is relatively low. Even in the United States, with perhaps the highest murder rates in the industrial world, the number of people killed
on our highways dwarfs the total killed in violent crime. Admittedly, the victims of
crime seldom accumulate in large bunches, diluting the social-psychological
impact. Were they all slaughtered at the same time and place, Americans would
more likely see the death toll as a national calamity.

   2, 3. Social Banditry and Gangsterism   Sometimes criminals coalesce
into significant organizations.[19] In rural settings we label organized crime as
"social banditry," and we use "gangsterism" for its urban counterpart. Specifically,
a gang, whether in a rural or urban setting, maintains a hierarchical organization
and persists through time. Whether the gang organization survives a generational
change in leadership provides one crucial test of its organization.

   Cohesive identities increase the political significance of urban and rural gangs. Their organizational resources may even directly challenge those of the regime, at least in local settings. Sometimes criminal organizations, like the drug cartels in Colombia or the rural banditry periodically afflicting China throughout its long history, undermine the authority of the national regime. Nevertheless, no gangs possess systematic programs of political change, and though they may contribute to the deterioration of order, they seldom guide its transformation.

As with more "individualized" forms of criminal activity, popular participation in organized crime remains generally low in stable communities but probably increases under conditions of social decay. Direct elite participation also remains low. Some members of the elite, though, may indirectly participate through political corruption, when organized crime attempts to influence political institutions through threats and bribes. The organization of criminal gangs also enhances their destructive capabilities, as the "narcoterrorism" in Colombia shows.

4, 5. Peasant Risings and Urban Riots   Historically, two forms of violence entail rather broad mass participation and often widespread damage, at least in the locales where they occur.[20] Peasant risings or rebellions and urban riots generally mobilize the more deprived, though not necessarily the most wretched, sectors of the population in relatively spontaneous outbursts of rage. Their targets range from rival communal or racial groups to representatives of the more privileged sectors.

The potential for disruption lends mass risings a degree of political significance; however, these demonstrations of anger and resentment usually lack any coherent program of transformation, even when expressing anger with the status quo. Some rebellions and riots develop in response to the perceived erosion of traditional rights, in which case they take on a reactionary character. Nineteenth-century Luddite riots against certain forms of industrialization in Great Britain, as well as some peasant rebellions, appear to fit this mold. The low level of elite participation, along with a related lack of organization, limits the political significance of such risings in either urban or rural settings.

6. Guerrilla Raids   Guerrilla bands engage in a form of rural-based violence that demonstrates a greater degree of political coherence and direction than social banditry.[21] Like participants in social banditry, guerrillas possess organizational continuity, but they also advocate a reasonably well developed political agenda. Analysts often associate guerrilla violence with revolutionary objectives, but as both the guerrillas in Afghanistan and the Contras in Nicaragua demonstrate, preservative or even reactionary sentiments motivate some guerrilla organizations. The presence of a reasonably coherent political agenda, whatever its ideology, lends political significance to even relatively small guerrilla organizations.

Generally, both mass and elite participation in guerrilla activities start off at relatively low levels. As the political movement engaging in guerrilla tactics expands its base of support, however, it mobilizes larger numbers of the populace. Eventually guerrilla organizations may grow powerful enough to stand and fight conventional battles with their adversaries. At this point their activities approach full-scale revolutionary warfare. Even before reaching this stage, the organization and tactics of guerrilla violence increase its destructive impact on a political community.

7, 8. Revolutionary Warfare and Urban Revolution Two dramatic, if infrequent, forms of violence present major challenges to the existing regime.[22] In each case a political movement representing a plausible alternative to the regime directs a campaign of violence against it. In a revolutionary war the movement mobilizes a sufficient segment of the rural masses to threaten the urban-based regime's control of the countryside. In an urban revolution the urban masses, often including elements of the middle classes, rise up and attempt to seize the centers of the regime's power.[23] The Chinese and Vietnamese revolutions involved rural-based revolutionary warfare, while urban risings largely propelled the Iranian revolution. Sometimes both forms of violence work in combination to bring down the regime, as in the Sandinista-led revolution against the Somoza regime in Nicaragua.

Since only highly developed, widely supported movements can mount such challenges, the political significance and mass participation tend to be fairly high. Moreover, it often happens that many members of the elite, especially disgruntled intellectuals and professionals, play key leadership roles in these movements. Organization and mass mobilization, finally, contribute to relatively high levels of violence, except in the case of an urban rising encountering such weakness at the center that the movement gains power rather quickly.

9. Assassination Assassination is a highly politicized violent tactic used for the full range of political purposes, from reaction through revolution.[24] Assassins often use considerable discrimination, killing only the intended target (an obvious exception occurs when the assassin uses an indiscriminate weapon, like a bomb, as the instrument of death). The notion of mass participation in an assassination appears almost logically contradictory, unless we consider rampaging mobs as a type of "collective assassin." Members of the elite, however, may conspire to engage in assassination, although elite participation is not necessary.

In quantitative terms, the destructiveness of an assassination appears relatively low, especially in comparison with the more indiscriminate forms of violence. Depending on the importance of the victim, though, the impact of some assassinations reverberates throughout a political community. In addition political contenders can wage assassination campaigns against their rivals, in which case the body count also rises.

10. Vigilante Violence Not all forms of violence, in the sense we have defined it, come from dissident sources. Even though the boundaries delineating "acceptable" coercion favor the status quo, regimes and their supporters periodically violate the limits on coercion formally established in their communities. Vigilante acts violate the limits on the use of coercion in the community but with the intention of defending this community from some form of subversion.[25] Often, such violence is sporadic and relatively spontaneous, though organized vigilante movements, under the direction of local elites, occasionally develop. Criminal elements, minority communities, and social or political "deviants" often feel the brunt of vigilante wrath.

Vigilante violence occurs in both urban and rural settings. Its political significance varies according to its extent and organization. Vigilante violence can involve essentially overzealous reactions to threats to the established order. Sometimes, however, it takes on a more reactionary coloration in response to a changing political order. Mass participation varies from low to medium, and more organized cases of vigilante violence involve members of the elite, as well. The police can exceed the limits on their authority to use physical coercion, and acts of police violence also seem essentially vigilante in character. Destructiveness depends on the pervasiveness and systematic character of the violence, and the extent to which the regime condones or at least tolerates it.

In addition to the private groups and the police, the armed forces may violate the limits on their coercive authority. Under conditions of internal turmoil or war, the struggle to maintain the existing order usually exceeds the capabilities of the regular police, and the threatened regime will mobilize the military. These circumstances increase the likelihood for abuse of military power. Military violence resembles vigilante violence in its aim, the defense of stability, though its potential destructiveness rises owing to the considerable coercive resources at the disposal of modern military organizations.

11. Coup d'Etat Sometimes a faction within the military strikes against the regime itself in a coup d'état.[26] Such a blow falls in the urban centers of a country because the conspirators hope to seize power quickly, not to wage a prolonged war from the countryside. Since the coup plotters seek control of the state, the political significance of this form of violence is quite high. The motivations of those instigating the attack on the regime, however, can range from reactionary to revolutionary. Mass participation depends upon the extent of military mobilization and regime resistance, but many coups involve relatively few military units. Top elements of the officer corps commonly lurk behind most such conspiracies, though at times disgusted middle-ranking officers attack their superiors in the military whom they see as part of the discredited regime. Since the plotters conspire to destroy the incumbent regime, the potential level of destructiveness rises, though actual bloodshed depends on the resistance encountered.

12. Regime Terror Sometimes a regime facing significant challenges will conclude that the authorized instruments of coercion lack sufficient "bite," and it will engage in a reign of terror.[27] A fully realized program of regime terror covers the entire population, mobilizes most of the coercive institutions of the regime, involves considerable elite direction, and entails widespread destruction. The political significance of a reign of terror is generally high, but a regime may use the violence for either conservative or revolutionary purposes (the latter case being a so-called "revolution from above"). Stalinist terror in the 1930s provides a dramatic case of regime terrorism used for both purposes.[28]

         ✿   ✿   ✿

Violence takes many forms in our domestic political relations, and these forms vary in significant ways. A comprehensive theory of violence, if feasible, would have to account for these differences in location, political significance, direction, participation, and destructiveness. We pursue a more limited interest in understanding those patterns of violence associated specifically with revolution, either as a means to promote or to resist such transformations. But what, then, is a revolution?

REVOLUTION

Contending Definitions

A not-quite-dead metaphor lies buried beneath the academic prose on the subject of revolution.[29] The word suggests a turning, perhaps physically embodied in an image of a wheel whose half-rotation reverses the positions of top and bottom. This notion of reversal captures the essence of some concepts of revolution, but other ideas reflect the original metaphor more weakly, echoing only the feeling of dynamism and change. In this more remote sense, publicists apply the label to any change they wish to emphasize from the Industrial Revolution to "a revolution in washday detergents." Apart from a weak commitment to the core metaphor, the meanings associated with the concept of revolution appear rather various. Consider the following sampler:

1. Political revolution, then, may be defined as a sudden and violent overthrow of an established political order.—*Carl Friedrich*[30]

2. [R]evolution is a sharp, sudden change in the social location of political power, expressing itself in the radical transformation of the process of government, of the official foundations of sovereignty or legitimacy, and of the conception of the social order. Such transformations could not normally occur without violence, but if they did, they would still, though bloodless, be revolutions.—*Eugene Kamenka*[31]

3. [Revolutions are] forcible interventions, either to replace governments, or to change the processes of government.—*Peter Calvert*[32]

4. A revolution is a fundamental change of social structure brought about in a short period of time.—*Johan Galtung*[33]

5. [R]evolution could be defined as that process by which a radical alteration of a particular society occurs over a given time span.—*A. S. Cohen*[34]

6. A revolution is a sweeping, fundamental change in political organization, social structure, economic property control and the predominant myth of a social order, thus indicating a major break in the continuity of development.—*Sigmund Neumann*[35]

7. [A revolution is] a breakdown, momentary or prolonged, of the state's monopoly of power, usually accompanied by a lessening of the habit of obedience.—*Peter H. Amann*[36]

8. The real revolution is the change in social attitudes and values basic to the traditional institutional order.—*Dale Yoder*[37]

9. Political revolution refers to abrupt, illegal mass violence aimed at the overthrow of the political regime as a step toward over-all social change.—*Mostafa Rejai*[38]

10. A revolution begins when a government previously under the control of a single sovereign polity becomes the object of effective, competing, mutually exclusive claims on the part of two or more separate polities. A revolution ends when a single polity . . . regains control over the government.—*Charles Tilly*[39]

11. A revolution is an acute, prolonged crisis in one or more of the traditional systems of stratification (class, status, or power) of a political community, which involves a purposive, elite directed attempt to abolish or to reconstruct one or more said systems by means of an intensification of political power and recourse to violence.—*Mark Hagopian*[40]

12. These two dimensions of structural transformation and class breakthrough from below effectively define and circumscribe revolution as "great revolution."—*Barry Schutz and Robert Slater*[41]

13. A revolution is a rapid, fundamental, and violent domestic change in the dominant values and myths of a society, in its political institutions, social structure, leadership, and government activity and politics.—*Samuel Huntington.*[42]

A casual reviewer of our sampler might conclude that the list is highly repetitious. Certainly, some of the definitions appear quite close, for example, Neumann (no. 6) and Huntington (no. 13). Despite overlap, however, these scholars do not generally describe revolution in the same way, and even where similarities exist, the distinctive characteristics of a revolution remain ambiguous.

Characteristics of a Revolution

Broadly, four elements together make up the concept of revolution: outcome, process, duration, and direction.

Outcome   The most common element associated with revolution focuses on what constitutes a revolutionary *outcome*. Revolutions cause change. But how much change makes a revolution? Amann (no. 7) seems to suggest that even a "momentary" breakdown in the "state's monopoly of power" suffices for a revolution. Other definitions stress that revolutions significantly alter or replace the structure of the regime or political order (nos. 1, 2, 3, 10). Rejai (no. 9) believes that the political change should be the first step toward more comprehensive alterations. The remaining definitions characterize revolutionary outcomes in more sweeping terms involving the transformation of social and economic structure as well as the political regime (nos. 4, 5, 6, 8, 11, 12, 13).

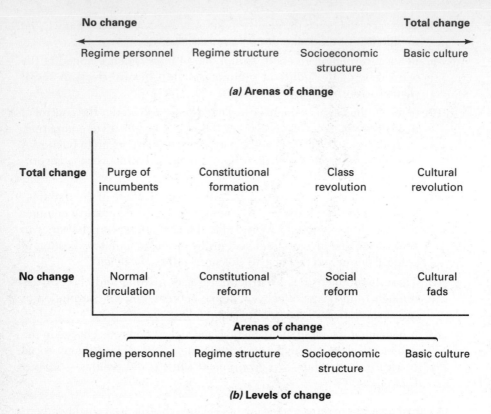

Figure 2.3 Defining revolutionary outcomes: (a) arenas of change; (b) levels of change.

Change, of course, is a concept of degree ranging between the theoretical extremes of no change through total transformation (Figure 2.3). We might think of change progressively involving more encompassing arenas of community life: first, simply the personnel in the regime, then the institutional structure of the regime, then the underlying socioeconomic structures, and finally, the basic culture (Figure 2.3, a).

This continuum considerably oversimplifies the problem of representing the degree of change, because each arena could change more or less significantly (Figure 2.3, b). Thus, turnover in regime personnel could proceed through normal circulation, say elections, or through major purges of top personnel. Alterations in regime structure could result from a gradual process of amendment or the dramatic formation of a new constitutional order. The socioeconomic structure may evolve incrementally through social reforms or change rapidly through the reconstruction of class revolution. Finally, cultural dispositions may alter superficially through the ebb and flow of fads and opinion or undergo fundamental reconstitution through cultural revolution.

Which outcomes, then, represent revolutionary change? No lower-scale alteration in personnel, structure, or culture is really revolutionary. A shake-up of the class structure or basic cultural values, in contrast, clearly satisfies the expectation of significant change. Commentators usually label outcomes of this sort as "great revolutions." Constitution formation and purges of personnel remain subjects of ambiguity and debate. Since purges simply change the faces but not the essential structure of power and value, they do not constitute revolutionary outcomes. Significant transformations of the constitutional order, however, represent "political" or "regime" revolutions.

We can find approximate historical examples of each type of significant change. Stalin's purges of the top party, governmental, and military leadership in the Soviet Union in the late 1930s, while bloody and unsettling, merely allowed for the promotion of subordinate and more docile members of each of these bureaucracies. The American Revolution, culminating in the Constitution (1789), created a significantly new structure of political relations for the newly independent nation-state. It did not, however, radically alter socioeconomic relations or cultural values. Indeed, some analysts argue that the new Constitution was designed to protect economic privilege and dominant values.[43] The 1917 Russian Revolution, powered by disgruntled masses of workers and peasants and ultimately captured by the Bolsheviks, resulted in a significantly restructured social and economic order. Finally, the Khmer Rouge in Cambodia probably attempted the most sweeping change of any twentieth-century revolution. Once they seized power in 1975, they forcibly evacuated the cities and eliminated thousands of "reactionaries," that is, those tainted by Westernization.[44]

Process   A second trait frequently associated with revolution involves the presumably violent nature of the revolutionary process. Mao Tse-tung observes: "A revolution is not the same as inviting people to dinner, or writing an essay, or painting a picture. . . . A revolution is an insurrection, an act of violence by which one class overthrows another."[45] Six of the definitions appear to agree with Mao about the distinctive and necessary role of violence in the revolutionary process (nos. 1, 2, 3, 9, 11, and 13). Eugene Kamenka (no. 2), though, observes that radical revolutionary change "could not *normally* occur without violence," but indicates that the outcome, not the process of change, makes for revolution (my emphasis). The remaining scholars, however, appear even less inclined to identify violence as a necessary trait of a revolution.

The logical and empirical association between revolutionary outcomes and violent political processes appears convincing. Logically, the drive for significant change in political, social, and economic structures must inevitably challenge vested interests. These interests will not surrender without resistance, particularly since they have the power of the state at their disposal. To overcome this resistance and consequent state repression, the revolutionary forces must bring to bear offsetting instruments of overwhelming power. This power will most likely involve violent blows against those defending the status quo. Empirically, the historical events most commonly identified as revolutions—for example, those in America, France, Russia, Mexico, China, Cuba, and Vietnam—entailed violent processes.

And yet . . . we might overvalue violence as a necessary component of the revolutionary process. Gene Sharp argues that all forms of power depend fundamen-

tally on the consent of the ruled. If the ruled withdraw their consent, then the efficacy of any instrument of power, including coercion, fades.[46] We exaggerate the
efficacy of violence, despite its bloody costs and many failures, while at the same
time ignoring the power of nonviolent (though not necessarily noncoercive)
action. Nonviolent alternatives demand serious analysis and consideration (see
Chapter 9). Suffice it here to recognize that many of the regimes swept away in
1989–1990 collapsed in the face of nonviolent resistance. In Poland, Czechoslova-
kia, East Germany, Nepal, and Bangladesh the people simply refused any longer
to obey or be coerced by their governments, while the regimes found their normal
organizations of social control to be unreliable.

In addition to conceding the possibility that nonviolent strategies might produce revolutionary outcomes, we also must recognize the diverse patterns of violence associated with revolutionary change. Coups, urban risings, guerrilla insurgencies, and even campaigns of regime terror all play a role in different revolutions. The intensity of violence varies considerably, but the reasons behind this
variation will elude us if we simply assume by definition that revolutions are violent in some undifferentiated fashion. We should treat the occurrence and extent
of violence in revolutionary transformation as a problem for investigation, not as
an unproblematic element of definition.

Duration   Almost every society undergoes dramatic changes if we wait long
enough. The United States possesses one of the oldest regimes in the world, measured by the longevity of its uninterrupted constitutional order. Despite over 200
years of political continuity, the society and culture of the country have changed
dramatically over the past two centuries. Yet, we normally think of our revolution
as ending in 1790.

We might try to resolve this conundrum by recognizing the dramatic alteration in social and cultural relations but argue that these changes were not
wrought through violent means. We have already seen, however, that revolutionary violence varies in both form and significance, limiting its value as a definitional characteristic. In any case, we often ignore the extent to which violence has
accompanied the vast changes in the United States, from vigilantism, frontier violence, and the near extermination of Native American peoples to the Civil War
and urban labor violence.[47]

Another way out of this ambiguity asserts that the revolutionary changes
unfold suddenly or over a short time span (see nos. 1, 2, 4, 13). Not all of our scholars agree, however, that short duration is a necessary definitional attribute. Many
make no mention of the time span for the transformation, while Amann (no. 7)
suggests that a revolutionary "breakdown" *could* be prolonged, and for Hagopian
(no. 11), revolution *is* a "prolonged crisis." In addition, how long is a "short" time?
A year? A decade? Surely, if a revolution extends over a generation, the notion of
"sudden" loses some of its meaning.

Moreover, the determination of a change as "sudden" or "prolonged" presumes we know when to begin and when to end our count.[48] When, for example,
did the American Revolution begin? In 1765, with the introduction of the Stamp
Act? In 1770, with the Boston Massacre? In 1775, with the Battles of Lexington

and Concord? Or in 1776, with the Declaration of Independence? And when did it end? In 1781, with the defeat of Cornwallis at Yorktown? In 1787, with the Constitutional Convention? Or later still, after the Constitution's ratification? The French Revolution presents similar problems. Most people mark its beginning with the convening of the Estates General in May 1789 or with the storming of the Bastille in July. But when did it end? In 1794, with the end of the Reign of Terror and the execution of Robespierre? In 1799, with the accession to power of Napoleon Bonaparte? In 1804, when Napoleon crowned himself emperor? Or in 1815, when he was finally exiled to St. Helena? The exact span of transformation becomes even more murky if we search for long-term underlying causes and effects.

Of course, we might focus on the actual struggle for power by the revolutionaries and forget its roots and consequences. The American Revolution, then, lasted six years (1775 to 1781) and the French, three (1789 to 1792), if we mark its end when the Convention finally abolished the monarchy in September of 1792. Even accepting this rather arbitrary definition of beginning and end, we still have the problem of what to do with the major Asian revolutions of this century. In China the communists fought from 1927 to 1949 before finally occupying the capital. In Vietnam the struggle for power continued for at least thirty years. Neither period seems aptly described as sudden.

Nonetheless we find it difficult to shake the association between the ideas of revolution and rapid, significant change. One possible explanation for this might be our intuitive recognition of the *objectives* of revolutionaries. They *intend* to bring about sweeping changes over the shortest period possible. They prefer to seize power swiftly. Who wouldn't? Whether they *accomplish* their goals depends on, among other things, the resistance they encounter. Strong resistance contributes to prolonged struggle. Overwhelming resistance results in the defeat of the revolutionary movement. Duration, like the issue of violence, seems more an empirical problem rather than a definitional attribute.

Direction   Wendell Phillips, the nineteenth-century American abolitionist, reputedly observed, "Revolutions are not made; they come."[49] His perspective minimizes the role of intention and direction in the process of revolutionary change. Rather, social forces far beyond the control of puny human agents catalyze the transformation. In contrast, some analysts directly or implicitly suggest that revolutions involve deliberate campaigns of radical social change. Hagopian (no. 11), for example, characterizes revolutions as "elite directed," and other definitions (nos. 3, 9, 10) imply a degree of deliberate guidance in the process of revolution.

The view that revolutions are directed helps to distinguish these special events from other major social alterations resulting from the aggregation of individual decisions not specifically intended to cause any systemic transformation. The "Industrial Revolution," for example, transformed European and American society, but not according to a deliberately imposed blueprint. Rather, millions of people over the decades, pushed and pulled by a myriad of forces and opportunities, undertook (and had imposed upon them) countless decisions that accumulat-

Table 2.2 CRISIS, BREAKDOWN, AND REVOLUTION: AN INVENTORY OF ATTRIBUTES (1 = ATTRIBUTE PRESENT; 0 = ATTRIBUTE ABSENT)

ATTRIBUTE

TYPE	Widespread elite/popular alienation from state	Elite revolts against state	Popular revolts against state or elites	Widespread violence or civil war	Change in political institutions	Change in status system of traditional elites	Change in economic organization	Change in legitimizing symbols and beliefs
Stability	0	0	0	0	0	0	0	0
Successful repression	1	0	0	0	0	0	0	0
Normal coup d'état	1	1	0	0	0	0	0	0
Conservative political reform	1	0	0	0	1	0	0	0
Dynastic civil war	0	1	0	1	0	0	0	0
Secessionist civil war	1	1	0	1	1	0	0	1
Political revolution	1	1	1	1	1	0	0	1
"Great" revolution	1	1	1	1	1	1	1	1

Source: Based on Jack A. Goldstone, *Revolution and Rebellion in the Early Modern World* (Berkeley: University of California Press, 1991), pp. 10–11. Copyright © 1991 The Regents of the University of California.

ed into massive social change. Wendell Phillips' aphorism aptly captures the nature of this change: It came.

The outcome of events more usefully described as revolutions, however, cannot be separated from those leaders, ideas, and organizations directing their course along certain paths. Admittedly, social discontents powered the American, Russian, Chinese, and Vietnamese revolutions. Historical contingencies and the concrete demands of seizing and securing power generally compromised prerevolutionary utopian ideals. Finally, the more successful movements adapted preconceived strategies to fit the opportunities of the moment. Nevertheless, individual leaders and consciously directed movements took advantage of the available possibilities to remake their communities.

The role played by deliberate agents in steering the course of structural change helps to distinguish *revolutions* from the more inclusive category of *revolutionary outcomes*. Not all revolutionary outcomes are the product of revolutions. Yet no revolution is fully the consequence of deliberate direction, so again we find that a possible definitional attribute, on closer inspection, reveals a more ambiguous concept of degree. Revolutionary events *more or less* result from direction of an adapting, responsive sort, rather than a preordained plan.

🔥   🔥   🔥

Jack Goldstone suggests a way of combining elements of three of our four characteristics to compare different forms of internal strife.[50] Table 2.2, "Crisis, Breakdown, and Revolution," adopts his binary system (1 or 0) to indicate the presence or absence of eight characteristics: widespread alienation from the state, elite revolts, popular revolts, widespread violence, and four levels of change—political institutions, status systems, economic systems, and culture. Thus, we define "stability" by placing zeros on all attributes; successful repression prevents widespread alienation from being manifested in any elite or mass action, and so on. "Great" revolution represents the extreme opposite of stability, with the presence of all eight attributes.

CONCLUSION: TOWARD UNDERSTANDING POLITICAL VIOLENCE AND REVOLUTION

What, then, is a revolution? If we could be satisfied with adding another abstraction to the sampler of definitions, we might say:

A revolution is a significant change deliberately wrought over a relatively short time through a strategy involving considerable coercion.

Such a definition, though, leaves unanswered what constitutes a significant change, the extent of the outcome explained as the product of deliberate direction, the brevity of "relatively short," and the exact role and forms taken by the strategy of coercion. It serves less as an answer than as an initial source of questions to guide research.

Significant change produces a *revolutionary outcome*. A political program of coercion deliberately designed to bring about this change is a *revolutionary strategy*. Those attempting to implement this strategy are *revolutionaries*. History provides cases of revolutionary outcome without a revolutionary strategy or revolutionaries; instances of revolutionary strategy without revolutionary outcomes (that is, failed revolutions); and revolutionaries so weak and isolated that they cannot initiate the strategy, much less accomplish the outcome. When the actors implement the strategy culminating in the outcome, we can say that we have witnessed a revolution.

The combination occurs relatively infrequently. Only rarely do *revolutionary conditions* arise that generate the revolutionaries, support the strategy, and produce the outcome. Theories of revolution attempt to explain when and why revolutionary conditions develop in a particular community that propel people to resort to extreme means to instigate dramatic change. Before we can explore some of these explanations, we first need to clarify the criteria we could use to evaluate such "theories."

NOTES

1.   This section is largely based on Peter C. Sederberg, *Terrorist Myths: Illusion, Rhetoric, and Reality* (Englewood Cliffs, N.J.: Prentice Hall, 1989), pp. 6–8, 3–5.
2.   Richard Rorty, "Philosophy in America Today," in R. Rorty, *The Consequences of Pragmatism* (Minneapolis: University of Minnesota Press, 1982), p. 222.
3.   This notion of definition approximates the "pragmatic-contextual" approach elaborated by Raziel Abelson in "Definition," in *The Encyclopedia of Philosophy*, Vol. 2 (New York: Macmillan, 1967), pp. 314–324.
4.   This section follows closely that in Sederberg, pp. 12–19.
5.   Samuel DuBois Cook, "Coercion and Social Change," in R. J. Pennock and J. W. Chapman, eds., *Coercion* (Chicago: Aldine, Atherton, 1972), p. 115.
6.   Ibid., p. 116.
7.   Christian Bay, *The Structure of Freedom* (Stanford, Calif.: Stanford University Press, 1958), p. 93.
8.   Ibid., p. 92.
9.   Cook, p. 126.
10.   This interesting notion is developed by Michael A. Weinstein, "Coercion, Space, and the Modes of Human Domination", in Pennock and Chapman, eds., pp. 63–80.
11.   The dictum of Proudhon is from *Qu'est-ce que la Propriété?* (1840), Chapter 1. Robert Nozick outlines his position in *Anarchy, State, and Utopia* (New York: Basic Books, 1974), pp. 169–172.
12.   For more extensive discussion of this interpretive approach see the essays in Paul Rabinow and William M. Sullivan, eds., *Interpretive Social Science* (Berkeley: University of California Press, 1979).
13.   For a good study of the limits of methodological individualism see Alan Garfinkel, *Forms of Explanation: Rethinking Questions in Social Theory* (New Haven, Conn.: Yale University Press, 1981).
14.   Richard L. Rubenstein, *The Cunning of History* (New York: Harper Colophon, 1978), pp. 4–5.

15. Max Weber, *Economy and Society,* G. Roth and C. Wittich, eds. (Berkeley: University of California Press, 1978), p. 56.

16. For a detailed discussion of this approach to classification see Alberto Marradi, "On Classification," in Anton Bebler and Jim Seroka, eds., *Contemporary Political Systems: Classifications and Typologies* (Boulder, Colo.: Lynne Rienner Publishers, 1990), pp. 11–43.

17. Ibid., p. 26.

18. For an analysis of trends in violent crime over the past 150 years see Ted Robert Gurr, *Rogues, Rebels and Reformers* (Beverly Hills, Calif.: Sage Publications, 1976).

19. Eric Hobsbawn, *Primitive Rebels: Studies in Archaic Forms of Social Movements in the 19th and 20th Centuries,* Third Edition (New York: W. W. Norton, 1965).

20. For a historical overview of patterns of urban and rural rioting see Charles Tilly, "Collective Violence in European Perspective," in Ted Robert Gurr, ed., *Violence in America,* Vol. 2: *Protest, Rebellion, Reform* (Newbury Park, Calif.: Sage Publications, 1989), pp. 62–100.

21. For a massive history of the role of guerrilla warfare over the past two millennia see Robert B. Asprey, *War in the Shadows: The Guerrilla in History,* two volumes (New York: Doubleday, 1975).

22. The literature on these two forms of political violence is vast. Two works that attempt to assess the respective contributions of urban- and rural-based revolutionary movements in shaping the outcomes of several "great" revolutions are Barrington Moore, Jr., *Social Origins of Dictatorship and Democracy: Lord and Peasant in the Making of the Modern World* (Boston: Beacon Press, 1966) and Theda Skocpol, *States and Social Revolutions: A Comparative Analysis of France, Russia and China* (New York: Cambridge University Press, 1979).

23. These two forms of violence are associated with what Huntington terms "Eastern" and "Western" forms of revolution, respectively. See Samuel P. Huntington, *Political Order in Changing Societies* (New Haven, Conn.: Yale University Press, 1968).

24. For a collection of theoretical articles on the problem of assassination see William J. Crotty, ed., *Assassinations and the Political Order* (New York: Harper and Row, 1971); for a history of the role of political assassination see Franklin L. Ford, *Political Murder: From Tyrannicide to Terrorism* (Cambridge, Mass.: Harvard University Press, 1985).

25. H. Jon Rosenbaum and Peter C. Sederberg, "Vigilantism: An Analysis of Establishment Violence, in Rosenbaum and Sederberg, eds., *Vigilante Politics* (Philadelphia: University of Pennsylvania Press, 1976), p. 4. See the other essays in this collection for a broad discussion of this form of violence.

26. For a collection of articles analyzing this form of political violence see Amos Perlmutter and Valerie Plave Bennett, eds., *The Political Influence of the Military: A Comparative Reader* (New Haven, Conn.: Yale University Press, 1980).

27. For a historical interpretation of this form of violence see E. V. Walter, *Terror and Resistance: A Study of Political Violence* (New York: Oxford University Press, 1969).

28. On Stalin's regime terror see Robert Conquest, *The Great Terror* (New York: Oxford University Press, 1990); see also Robert C. Tucker, *Stalin in Power: The Revolution from Above, 1928–1941* (New York: W. W. Norton, 1990).

29. For an intellectual history of the metaphor that is actually far more complex than we indicate here, see Melvin J. Lasky, *Utopia and Revolution* (Chicago: University of Chicago Press, 1976).

30. Carl J. Friedrich, "An Introductory Note on Revolution," in C. J. Friedrich, ed., *Revolution,* Nomos 8 (New York: Atherton, 1967), pp. 3–9.

31. Eugene Kamenka, "The Concept of a Political Revolution," in ibid., pp. 122–138.

32. Peter A. R. Calvert, "Revolution: The Politics of Violence," *Political Studies*, 15 (1967): 1.

33. Johan Galtung, *A Structural Theory of Revolutions* (Rotterdam: Rotterdam University Press, 1974), p. 9.

34. A. S. Cohen, *Theories of Revolution: An Introduction* (London: Thomas Nelson, 1975), p. 31.

35. Sigmund Neumann, "The International Civil War," *World Politics*, 1 (April 1949): 333–334.

36. Peter H. Amann, "Revolution: A Redefinition," *Political Science Quarterly*, 77 (1962): 36–53.

37. Dale Yoder, "Current Definitions of Revolution," *The American Journal of Sociology*, 32 (1926): 441.

38. Mostafa Rejai, *The Strategy of Political Revolution* (New York: Doubleday, 1973), p. 9.

39. Charles Tilly, "Does Modernization Breed Revolution?" *Comparative Politics*, 5 (1973): 425–447.

40. Mark N. Hagopian, *The Phenomenon of Revolution* (New York: Dodd, Mead, 1974), p. 4.

41. Barry M. Schutz and Robert O. Slater, "A Framework for Analysis," in Schutz and Slater, eds., *Revolution and Political Change in the Third World* (Boulder, Colo.: Lynne Rienner, 1990), p. 6.

42. Huntington, p. 264.

43. See, for example, Thomas R. Dye and L. Harmon Ziegler, "The Founding Fathers: The Nation's First Elite," Chapter 2 of *The Irony of Democracy: An Uncommon Introduction to American Politics* (Monterey, Calif.: Brooks/Cole, any edition).

44. See the essays in David A. Ablin and Marlowe Wood, eds., *The Cambodian Agony* (Armonk, N.Y.: M. E. Sharpe, 1987).

45. Mao Tse-Tung, *Selected Works of Mao Tse Tung*, Vol. 1 (Peking, 1965), p. 28.

46. Gene Sharp, *The Politics of Nonviolent Action* (Boston: Porter Sargent, 1973), Chapter 1.

47. See the essays in Ted Robert Gurr, ed., *Violence in America*, Vol. 2: *Protest, Rebellion, Reform*. See also Richard Maxwell Brown, *Strain of Violence: Historical Studies of American Violence and Vigilantism* (New York: Oxford University Press, 1975).

48. For chronologies of several revolutions see Thomas H. Greene, *Comparative Revolutionary Movements: Search for Theory and Justice*, Second or Third Edition (Englewood Cliffs, N.J.: Prentice Hall, 1984, 1990), Chapter 3.

49. Quoted in Theda Skocpol, *States and Social Revolutions*, p. 17.

50. Jack A. Goldstone, *Revolution and Rebellion in the Early Modern World* (Berkeley: University of California Press, 1991), pp. 10–11.

3

Evaluating Explanations for Political Violence and Revolution

In the absence of a clear theoretical consensus, many purported explanations for political violence and revolution contend with each other. We must develop some bases on which to compare the relative value of these contenders. In this chapter we describe some basic criteria for evaluating explanations. In addition, we preview some of the common problems afflicting "theories" of violence and revolution.

CONFRONTING CONTENDING EXPLANATIONS

Revolution is the exception and stability the rule in our political communities. Perhaps because of its exceptional nature, the drama of revolutionary conflict rivets the attention of political analysts. Three primary issues challenge our understanding: the origin of the revolutionary impulse, the choice of violent means, and the factors affecting the outcome. Though clearly related, these three problems generate somewhat different research agendas. A particular explanation often addresses puzzles arising from one or the other of the three agendas. As "consumers" of the research product, we must determine how, or if, these inquiries fit together to provide us with a more complete understanding of political violence and revolutionary change.

Within a single problem area we encounter contending explanations that we must evaluate, compare, and, if possible, combine. Unfortunately, multiple explanations often resist simple combination for several reasons. First, explanations for the same action may contradict one another. Second, explanations may address different "levels of analysis"; for example, some focus on the individual actor while others concentrate on groups, while still others deal with large social aggregates. Finally, and most troubling, different explanations may construe the nature of social knowledge and the conduct of inquiry differently.

Confronted by such multiplicity, we need some criteria to assess the various explanations competing for our attention so that we may establish their relative merits and limitations, as well as their possible compatibility. No set of criteria, however, will enable us to sort out all the various explanations and fit them neatly together in a completely satisfying theory of revolutionary violence. The puzzle, unfortunately, is not so neat.

We might consider the familiar story of the five blind men exploring different parts of the elephant. One feels the trunk and thinks the elephant is much like a snake; another touches the tail and concludes the creature resembles a rope; a third grasps an ear and deduces the elephant is like a large fan; the fourth embraces a leg and avows, to the contrary, that the animal is built like a tree; while the fifth runs his hand on the side of the beast and asserts that the animal takes after a wall.

We, of course, "know" what an elephant looks like and can afford to be amused by their blind gropings for understanding. We recognize that each blind man possesses only limited knowledge and falsely concludes that his partial vision approximates the whole truth. Our privileged vantage point enables us to recognize what is of value in each observation, how each is incomplete, and how to combine the partial visions into a single, true depiction of the elephant.

Imagine, though, that we are among the blind observers. None of us knows what it is to be an elephant, but we can move our hands around the animal and gather ever more information through these "experiments." We assume, after all, that a real elephant exists out there. As we gather the data, our idea of the appearance of an elephant becomes more accurate and complete. Moreover, as each of us follows along in the tracks of the others, we can replicate and refine their observations, leading to greater confidence in the validity of our shared image of an elephant.

This version, though, still assumes a more privileged view than the one depicted in the original story. There, the blind characters seem confined to their respective restricted experiences. They can only communicate the *results* of their experiences. They do not report brute sensory data. Rather, their reports have been organized by some preexisting conceptual scheme. The one who felt the elephant's trunk and reported a snake, for example, could not have done so without possessing the idea of a snake. They use different "theoretical" categories to understand their incomplete data, and they do not even recognize that they feel different parts of the beast. Even if they did, they could not facilely combine their reports into a more accurate representation of an elephant. Such a combination would produce the image of a monster. Given their limited experience and different theories, the blind observers are, in a sense, explaining different realities in incompatible ways. Finally, a critic might argue that were they to produce an accurate physical description, their understanding of the animal would remain incomplete until they provided an adequate representation of the world from the elephant's point of view.

Our retelling of this tale suggests three possible responses to the explanatory pluralism that confounds our efforts to understand violence and revolution:[1]

1. Single-Vision Objectivism   We could aspire to the privileged position of the narrator (or reader) of the elephant fable, what Donna Harraway calls the "god trick" of seeing everything from nowhere.[2] Dismissing the blind bumbling of unprivileged observers, we could strive to develop a unified theory of violence and revolution (or, for that matter, all social behavior) capable of subsuming anything of value in the contending explanations.

2. Naive Perspectivism   Lacking an "all-knowing eye," we might attempt to sort out and combine the partial visions on the problem. We assume these partial explanations share a common approach to understanding a directly accessible world, and we can, therefore, hope to assemble the partial perspectives into a more complete picture. "More complete" does not necessarily mean *entirely* complete; but if we believe that we will eventually synthesize all the parts into a comprehensive theory, then our partial visions will add up to a single vision. Alternatively, though we accept that we may never discover a unified theory of behavior, nonetheless we still believe our knowledge of the problem will continuously improve. In both single-vision objectivism and naive perspectivism, progress is possible. Indeed, in the former we may achieve essentially perfect understanding.

3. Radical Perspectivism   If we accept that different assumptions concerning the nature of the world and how we gain knowledge about it result in our "constructing" different worlds, then progress becomes much more problematic. We cannot synthesize explanations reflecting different worldviews into a more "complete" picture. Progress in our understanding, if possible at all, develops only within a particular perspective. What's more, since we lack any privileged vantage point, we have no real basis for choosing among contending worldviews.

Though pursuit of a single-vision theory seems unpromising, indeed presumptuous, we need not conclude that we must endure the cacophony of innumerable competing visions with no way of judging relative worth. The basic ways or "methods" of constructing social explanations are not indefinitely various. Each method establishes criteria for sorting out the merits of different explanations developed according to their methodological prescriptions. Although the methods embody different assumptions about the nature of the social world and the proper conduct of inquiry into it, some overlap exists. While insufficient to provide a foundation for a grand synthesis, this overlap presents opportunities for "dialogue" among different worldviews.[3]

In the remainder of this chapter we first briefly describe the three main methods for constructing social explanations. Then we discuss some major criteria for evaluating contending explanations, indicating which appear specific to a particular method and which seem more generally applicable. Finally, we identify some common problems afflicting efforts to explain violence and revolution.

CONSTRUCTING SOCIAL EXPLANATIONS

Whenever social analysts set out to discuss problems of "methodology," the eyes of the audience begin to glaze over, and more results-oriented colleagues criticize such meditations as unproductive navel gazing. Even worse, proponents of different positions often talk past one another, creating concurrent monologues rather than a true dialogue. Three methods predominate in the construction of explanations for political violence and revolution: logical empiricism, interpretive analysis, and critical theory. We do not pretend to resolve all methodological disputes nor to satisfy philosophers of social inquiry. Rather, we hope to introduce these major approaches and provide sufficient grounds for evaluating contending explanations.

Logical Empiricism

Mainstream American social science incorporates the methods of logical empiricism, and both its proponents and its critics characterize this approach as being the most "scientific." Central to logical empiricism, as Richard Bernstein argues,

> is the conviction that the aim of the social sciences is the same as that of the natural sciences. Collecting and refining data, discovering correlations, and formulating testable empirical generalizations, hypotheses, and models, all have important roles to play, but they are not sufficient to establish the social sciences as mature sciences. There must also be the growth of testable and well-confirmed theories which explain phenomena by showing how they can be derived in nontrivial ways from our theoretical assumptions. At the heart of scientific explanation must be discovery of and appeal to laws or nomological statements.[4]

We easily recognize works committed to this methodology by the distinctive emphasis on how the current project fits into and improves on past research, the explicit statement of hypotheses derived from some accepted theory, a conscientious concern for empirical, especially quantifiable, indicators, and the effort to identify areas for future research. This method assumes the existence of a real world that we can progressively understand through the cumulation of systematic observation guided by prior conclusions (theory). Social scientists, of course, revise these theories, if necessary, to take into account new evidence.

Logical empiricism views "facts" or "data" as real and independent of any particular observer, partial perspectives as potentially reconcilable, and therefore progress in our knowledge of the social world as possible, even inevitable. Moreover, this method implies a rather deterministic understanding of human behavior. Just as deterministic causal laws explain phenomena in the natural world, analogous laws will ultimately explain human behavior.

This approach imposes some rather demanding standards on explanations developed according to its strictures, making it possible, at least in principle, to sort out relative worth. Logical empiricists must place their research in the appropriate theoretical context. Their derivation of hypotheses and development of conclusions must conform with established standards of logic. Finally, the process of hypothesis testing must proceed with keen attention to rules of measurement and evidence. Ideally, other observers should replicate such tests. Other members of the community of inquiry carefully scrutinize conclusions inconsistent with existing theory, and they will tend to reject hypotheses weakly supported by logic and/or evidence. Finally, they will view irreproducible results with skepticism.

Logical empiricism appears essentially incompatible with radical perspectivism. In the past forty years, however, some philosophers of science have developed a more subtle and complex view of the scientific enterprise.[5] They argue that theories are verbal structures underdetermined by the "facts." Consequently, an "ugly fact"— an empirical observation that appears to contradict an accepted theory—will not necessarily lead scientists to abandon an elegant theory. Rather, only another, presumably more robust, theory can replace the first theory. Empirical observations in any case are not "pure"; rather, our theoretical orientation shapes our observations.

Those embracing this account of empirical investigation argue that though we may evaluate work done *within* a particular theoretical perspective, we have no way of definitively choosing between incompatible theoretical perspectives. Rather, our choice between them resembles a "conversion," more than a product of the reasoned consideration of indubitable "facts."[6] Conversions, though, more likely occur when a "challenger" theory addresses problems previously ignored by the established perspective. Consequently, progress in scientific understanding is more problematic than it initially appeared. We do not simply steadily accumulate more knowledge of the elephant. Instead, we periodically "revolutionize" our understanding of "elephant" and pursue an entirely different line of inquiry.

Interpretive Approaches

Some scholars reject logical empiricism, especially in its more objectivist versions, as an inappropriate method for studying the social world.[7] Social interaction, they argue, differs qualitatively from events in the physical world of the natural sciences, and we must recognize and account for these differences.[8]

First, the natural world possesses no innate meaning or value; it merely exists to be dealt with in some way. We impose our meanings and values upon it. In contrast, thinking, purposive creatures conduct social activities. Human beings give themselves covert directions (motives or intentions) and assign meaning to their own and others' behavior. For these reasons, we cannot equate social events with those in the inanimate or unself-conscious worlds. In some sense, the social world *does* possess innate meaning—the meaning that the participants assign to their own behavior.

Second, we cannot understand the meaning participants attach to their behavior in isolation. Rather, self-understandings take shape within a context of shared meanings.[9] Critics of logical empiricist methods argue that empirical analysis fails to account for intersubjective meanings. Intersubjectivity cannot be facilely reduced to the "brute data" of individual behavior but must be seen within a setting of mutually expected interaction. Empirical methodology, by concentrating on the observable behavior of individuals, without regard for its subjective content, obscures both the meaning of the behavior for the actors themselves and the mutuality that shapes these meanings.

Third, ongoing social action is *prospective* in character, in that the participants look forward to some *to-be-completed* act. Logical empirical investigation, in the critics' view, adopts a *retrospective* stance based upon the observation of *already completed* events. Only when we step out of the continuous flow of daily life and look back upon discrete actions we consider already completed do we adopt a retrospective position in our everyday lives. The prospective stance adopted by the participants in the ongoing process of life contributes to a sense of indeterminacy and free will, in that whatever we plan to do, we feel we could choose to do otherwise. The retrospective stance, in contrast, contributes to a sense of determinacy and causation, because we have completed the behavior and cannot alter it.

Interpretive social analysis, responding to these differences, seeks to "explain" observed behavior by rendering it intelligible through showing how a particular action reflects a wider context of shared meanings.[10] The anthropologist Clifford Geertz describes the process of interpretive analysis as involving a continuous "tacking between the most local of local detail and the most global of global structure in such a way as to bring them into simultaneous view." He continues, "Hopping back and forth between the whole conceived through its parts that actualize it and the parts conceived through the whole that motivates them, we seek to turn them, by a sort of intellectual perpetual motion, into explications of one another."[11]

The interpretive approach draws an analogy between the interpretation of social acts and that of literary texts. This association contrasts with logical empiricism's emphasis on the explanation of empirical regularities by subsuming them under lawlike generalizations.[12] However, we need not consider contending interpretations of the same action to be of equal worth. Although we cannot definitively resolve interpretive conflicts, we can judge the adequacy of an interpretation on the basis of the currently accepted understanding of the context in which the action occurs.

Most interpretive approaches embrace a kind of perspectivism, placing them in clear conflict with objectivist modes of analysis. Interpretation usually presumes that human action becomes intelligible only by explicating individual motivation within its cultural context. Consequently, cultural variation would seem to foreclose the possibility of a universally relevant interpretation of motivation. While perspectivism certainly characterizes several prominent forms of interpretive analysis—for example, biography, narrative history, and political anthropology— at least one form of interpretation, rational choice theory, sometimes displays more objectivist tendencies.

In somewhat oversimplified terms, one major application of rational choice theory attempts to predict individual choice on the basis of deductions derived from relatively few initial assumptions. For example, the actors are assumed to be utility maximizers who possess a clear hierarchy of preferences and near perfect knowledge about the outcomes of alternative actions.[13] Although some practitioners might resist characterizing their approach as interpretive, rational choice theory attempts to render behavior intelligible by positing certain motives behind individual choice in a particular context. Indeed, one commentator refers to rational choice theory as "formalized folk psychology."[14] In any case some proponents tend to universalize the postulates of rationality to all choice situations regardless of context. By doing so they seem to verge on a single-vision theory of human action, at least with respect to the process of choosing means to achieve one's ends.[15] The origin of a person's value hierarchy, however, remains a question that can be understood only in context.

Despite the qualitatively different ways of characterizing social reality, we should take care not to exaggerate the conflict between interpretive and logical empirical approaches. As we indicated, recent perspectives on logical empiricism reject some of the objectivist tendencies of earlier years. They recognize certain "interpretive" aspects in empirical explanation, even in the natural sciences. "Facts" (empirical observations) underdetermine theories, and theories partly structure observation. In addition most empirical accounts of social and political action implicitly or explicitly include some representation of the motivation and self-understandings of the actors. Alternatively, in developing and communicating our interpretations of human interaction, we do not simply engage in a "touchy-feely" empathy with our subjects. Rather, we must draw upon systematic observation and argumentation, particularly when depicting the context of the actions we interpret. These concerns suggest a possible overlap with empirical methodologies.

Critical Theory

A third major approach to social analysis castigates both logical empiricism and interpretive approaches for their failure to recognize the connection between knowledge claims and powerful interests in the wider political community.[16] Empirical analysis, from the critical perspective, reduces social actors to mere objects, rather than conscious participants in their own life-dramas, and pursues an often unrecognized interest in control. Critical theorists charge that logical empiricism is unabashedly manipulative and often serves, perhaps unwittingly, the agenda of the existing centers of power in society.

Interpretive analysts at least treat social actors as conscious participants in their own lives, but by representing the self-understandings of the actors, they tend to accept uncritically the particular cultural context. This acceptance, however, obscures the extent to which concentrations of power in the social setting distort the consciousness of the participants. The effort to render social action intelligible by representing false consciousness produces rather dubious knowledge claims.

Critical approaches attempt to illuminate the ways in which power distorts social understanding. But critical theorists do not stop at uncovering the delusions of both actors and observers. In addition, they aim to emancipate social actors from their false consciousness and thereby empower them. To complete this task, critical approaches must explain the nature and origins of the distorted meanings or false consciousness; how this false consciousness causes a social crisis; how to enlighten the victims of false consciousness; and, finally, how the newly enlightened can transform their societies.[17]

Critical approaches, then, aim not simply to understand the world, but also to act in it (a contrast often called theory and praxis). Though critical theory represents a minority position in contemporary American social science, it holds special significance in the study of revolutionary change. Scholars who simply *study* revolution often adopt empirical or interpretive approaches, but those who attempt *to instigate and direct* revolutionary action usually possess a fairly well articulated critical theory. Marxism, in particular, develops a critical analysis of the ways in which the capitalist order maintains itself through ideological mystification and stresses the need for the proletariat to be liberated from the resulting false consciousness.

Critical approaches, like the empirical and interpretive, may take either single-vision objectivist or perspectivist forms. Any critique posits some standard of enlightenment for evaluating ordinary self-understandings. An objectivist critique asserts an absolute standard, justified by invoking itself, resulting in a vicious circle. Perspectivist critiques subject themselves to critique, and that critique, too, can be critiqued, and so on in an indefinite critical regress.[18] Both of these alternatives cause problems for critical analysis. The former lends an air of false certainty to the process of criticism (unless, of course, the critical standard is, indeed, infallible), while the latter seems to guarantee permanent instability in our knowledge claims.

Despite the distinctive emphasis on the problem of distortion and the need for enlightenment, critical approaches partly overlap with the other two. Regardless of their commitment to action, critical theorists must still attend to systematic observation and argumentation, or else their critiques will prove unconvincing, and the actions they advocate could well prove disastrous. Moreover, since they wish to illuminate how the self-understandings of social actors are distorted in some way, they must first adequately represent these self-understandings.

🔥　🔥　🔥

When we study the problems of political violence and revolution, we confront multiple explanations that often contradict one another or speak to different pieces of the puzzle(s). Even worse, they sometimes reflect different assumptions about the proper way to develop social explanations in the first place. Only three major methods of inquiry, however, dominate social analysis, and, though they differ in significant ways, they do not seem totally incompatible. The criteria for evaluating the relative worth of explanations developed within any particular approach, therefore, may have some relevance to the other approaches as well. We now turn to these criteria

CRITERIA FOR EVALUATING SOCIAL EXPLANATIONS

Comprehensiveness

Many times a particular explanation addresses only part of a larger puzzle. This limitation by no means invalidates the offered solution, as long as we recognize its incomplete nature. We may find it possible to fit these partial explanations together, if they reflect compatible perspectives on the problem. On the other hand, we need to recognize that some explanations may be not only incomplete but also incompatible, particularly if they reflect different methodological assumptions.

Substantively, we face two related, though not identical, research problems. First, why do people (or groups) resort to violent means (that is, unacceptable coercion) to accomplish their political objectives? Second, what causes revolution? Political violence need not be revolutionary and not all revolutions involve the same degree of political violence (see Chapter 2). We can break both these research problems into a number of interconnected questions.

The problem of political violence, for example, might consist of at least four subsidiary issues:

1. What causes discontent? Presumably, satisfied members of a stable social order do not contemplate engaging in acts of violence. (Rational choice theorists challenge this assumption; see Chapter 5.) Empirical analysis might strive to identify the measurable correlates of rising discontent in an effort to form a causal theory. Interpretive and critical approaches will explicitly represent the motives and understandings of the participants. Critique also emphasizes that, because of false consciousness, the actors may be unable to recognize the true nature and origins of their feelings of frustration.

2. What politicizes this discontent? People may internalize their discontent or direct it outward toward more inclusive political communities. If they blame themselves or only their immediate relations for their frustrations, then their discontent will not directly possess wider political significance. We want to know, therefore, how the discontented come to hold the government and/or broader political forces responsible in some way for their plight. Again, empirical approaches attempt to identify measurable correlates of political mobilization, while interpretive and critical methods concentrate on representing the self-understandings of the participants. Critical theorists also explain how the actors overcame their false consciousness and discovered the "true" origins of their discontent in the structure of political oppression.

3. What inclines the discontented to violent expression? Discontent, whether politicized or internalized, need not result in violent tendencies. People may tend toward nondestructive expression, or they may sublimate frustration in one area of their lives into energetic activity elsewhere. Empirical approaches attempt to find the causes of destructive tendencies either at the individual or collective level. Again, both the interpretive and critical approaches try to represent the self-understandings of those prone to violence. Critical theories perhaps will argue that the existing proscriptions against violence serve the established order.

4. Finally, what affects the actual levels of political violence? Even significant political discontent among people inclined to express their anger violently need not result in the occurrence of widespread violence. In this final issue area we must identify the circumstances that encourage or discourage the expression of a disposition to political violence. Violent outcomes may depend on the degree of desperation or may result from a pragmatic assessment of possibilities or, bluntly, on either passion or reason. Again, we expect that logical empirical explanations will focus on concrete indicators associated with increasing levels of violence, whereas the other two approaches will emphasize the reflections of the actors. Critical theorists

may also posit theories of education and transformative action that reveal to the discontented the true basis and extent of their power and how they might use it.

While explanations for political violence often concentrate on the level of individual behavior (or action), theories of revolution commonly focus on collective levels of social organization. Here, again, several interrelated puzzles arise:

1. How does a revolutionary crisis emerge? Proposed explanations, whether logical/empirical, interpretive, or critical, usually concentrate on broadly construed socioeconomic forces and/or the interactions among somewhat abstract collectivities like "classes," "status groups," or "primordial groups" (ethnic, cultural, racial, or religious identities). Empirical theories might focus upon social and economic trends that contribute to increased polarization in society. Interpretive and critical approaches will assign collective motivations to abstractions such as class or status groups. In addition, critical theories will purport to reveal how various sectors misconstrue the nature of prevailing social forces.

2. What weakens the state (or establishment, if a theory sees the state as a mere instrument of some external group)? Economic or cultural polarization does not automatically produce a revolution. Usually something must undermine the effectiveness of the state and other instruments of social control. Thus, a revolution develops out of a crisis of domination as much as an upwelling of discontent. While empirical theories may focus on the factors that undermine the structures of domination, the other two approaches personify the abstraction of "the state," endowing it with motives and meaning. Critical theories, in particular, focus on "contradictions" that weaken the state or establishment.

3. What factors affect the relative success of the strategy and tactics of revolutionary transformation? The consideration given this final issue depends in large part on the extent to which analysts believe qualities of leadership, ideology, and organization at least partly explain revolutionary outcomes. If a theory proposes that social and political forces beyond the intervention and control of human beings determine the origins and course of revolution, then this final question is moot. If human volition and direction affect outcome, on the other hand, then issues of strategy and tactics assume greater importance in the revolutionary puzzle. Theorists may still stress structural factors, in that a revolutionary crisis must develop and the institutions of social control must weaken, but the character and success of the revolutionary strategy and tactics influence the specific shape of revolutionary outcomes.

Our identification of the various puzzles constituting the general problems of political violence and revolutionary change does not mean we should dismiss all partial explanations while searching for comprehensive theories. Rather, we should try to recognize the focus of partial explanations in order to recognize the limits of the contribution they make to our understanding. In addition, we should be suspicious of any effort to combine partial explanations in a simplistic fashion. Rather, we must be sensitive to both differences in approach, as well as merit.

Coherence

A good explanation must be logically coherent. This criterion may seem to reflect a bias toward *logical* empiricism, but we must not underestimate its broader relevance. Explanatory coherence involves more than the systems of formal logic developed by logicians and mathematicians.

Broadly speaking, "logic" includes any set of rules for linking statements to one another. In some sense the basic grammatical structure of a language is a kind of logic. A serious violation of the basic rules of grammar may make our statements incomprehensible to others.[19] Further, we expect explanations to be at least internally consistent and to avoid spurious conclusions. We dismiss those explanations, regardless of approach, that are self-contradictory or commit other commonly recognized logical fallacies.

On the other hand, we must also fault arguments that exhibit a false coherence. Social explanations, for example, often include forms of circular reasoning (where the conclusions are preordained by the initial assumptions) and spurious or accidental correlations (for example, the *post hoc ergo propter hoc* fallacy that involves causally linking essentially accidental sequences of events).

The formal rules governing either statistical inference or the deductive logic of rational choice theory provide detailed bases for evaluating explanations constructed within these approaches. Arguments developed according to precise rules of argumentation, however, are not necessarily superior for that reason alone. Explanations composed of weakly linked components remain unpersuasive even if we use precise rules of statistical inference to establish these relations.

The criterion of coherence provides a basis for evaluating explanations developed through any of the three approaches, at least by eliminating those containing internally contradictory assertions. It encourages skepticism about explanations depending on relatively weak associations, whether expressed in statistical terms, formal logic, or ordinary language. It also alerts us to cases of false coherence and circular reasoning. Nevertheless, this criterion alone offers little help when we must choose among equally coherent explanations.

Empirical Support

Coherent explanations may lack empirical support. Critics, for example, sometimes fault the empirical validity of rational choice theory despite its logical elegance.[20] Empirical validity seems to provide an obvious way to assess explanations, but the obvious in the social sciences often proves elusive. First, we face the fundamental problem of what, exactly, constitutes empirical support. The current view in the philosophy of science argues that theoretical perspectives shape observation, and that "facts," therefore, are not incontrovertible nuggets of unmediated reality. At the very least, a defining theoretical perspective determines issues of relevance, guides inquiry along certain paths, and influences the interpretation of observations.

Moreover, if a particular theory informs observation, we must also remember that the broader methodological orientation, in turn, shapes theory. Issues of empirical support often reflect the logical empirical approach. Interpretive theorists, however, question the significance of empirical data unless rendered intelligible through some representation of the self-understanding of the actors. Critical theorists, in turn, often condemn empirical analysis as, at best, reflecting of the will to control or, at worst, deluded.

Such disputes detract from the ability of empirical validity to provide the definitive basis for evaluating explanations, but they do not negate this standard altogether. Indeed, the criterion of empirical support raises at least four important subsidiary considerations:

1. Clear Conceptualization   We previously invested considerable effort in evaluating some common concepts of political violence and revolution. All inquiry requires conceptual clarity, if for no other reason than to communicate the boundaries of the problem under investigation. Sometimes explanations conflict simply because they conceptualize the problem differently.

Empirical clarity also requires that the concepts we develop be *operationalized,* that is, put "in a form that permits some kind of measurement."[21] Empirically rigorous explanations contain concepts precisely and reliably measured by empirically valid indicators. Poorly operationalized concepts necessarily detract from the explanatory hypotheses that relate them. Many explanations for social violence, unfortunately, suffer from ambiguous operationalization (see below).

2. Specification of All Relevant Factors   A good, empirically grounded explanation specifies all the relevant factors (and no unnecessary ones) in an explanatory relationship. Simplistic explanations fail to specify all the relevant factors; excessively complex ones multiply these factors unnecessarily. The challenge, of course, arises in determining the appropriate balance and avoiding either extreme.

Theory, as we stressed, informs observation, particularly by determining relevance. We undermine the validity of an explanation by identifying a presumably relevant factor it fails to incorporate or by pointing to irrelevant factors it includes. Unfortunately, many of these debates over relevance reflect different theories, and therefore we cannot resolve such disputes through an appeal to one or the other of the theories in contention.

3. Specification of Relations Among Factors   In more systematic empirical social science, the specification of explanatory relations involves the development of hypotheses stating the relationship between independent and dependent variables (the empirical concepts used in an explanation). Changes in the independent variable(s) presumably affect the dependent variable(s) in some predicted fashion.

Appropriate specification of empirical relationships presumes that we have identified and clearly conceptualized all the relevant factors. We may find that the relationships, even though clearly specified, are not especially strong (see above, the discussion of coherence), and weak associations limit the persuasiveness of any explanatory hypothesis.

4. Falsifiability[22]   Sound empirical arguments provide concrete indication of what would constitute evidence *against* their propositions. An unfalsifiable explanation has little empirical value, for all conceivable outcomes, even mutually contradictory ones, are considered confirming evidence. Such an explanation explains nothing, because it explains away everything. The fact that an explanation is falsifiable in principle does not mean investigators will in practice succeed in falsifying it. If an explanation resists falsification, investigators gain increasing confidence in its empirical robustness.

These four requirements taken together help us achieve two fundamental objectives of empirical inquiry: transmissibility and replicability. Any explanatory enterprise that aims to produce commonly accepted knowledge, whether interpretive, critical, or empirical in approach, shares the former objective. Private understanding, no matter how profound, makes no direct contribution to a community of inquiry. Considerations of empirical validity, though not the only way to establish mutual understanding, remain the most commonly accepted way of transmitting knowledge claims. Consequently, interpretive and critical approaches often incorporate, implicitly or explicitly, some concern for the empirical validity of their arguments.

The goal of replicability, in contrast, seems more important to those adopting a logical empirical approach. Replication refers to "the ability to repeat a study as a way of checking its validity."[23] The clarity, specificity, and falsifiability of the original study assist the attempt at replication, though they may prove insufficient. Other observers cannot exactly replicate certain forms of interpretive and critical analysis. For example, investigators can check anthropological research based on participant observation (see below) against other ethnographic studies and through subsequent observation, but the nature of the method prevents true replication. The conditions of the first observation cannot be duplicated.

Adequacy

Interpretive and critical theorists, though not denying the importance of coherence and empirical support, emphasize that qualitative differences between the social and the physical worlds must affect the conduct of inquiry. For interpretive analysis, social explanation must render observed human behavior intelligible. Essentially, good interpretive explanations adequately reflect the self-understandings of the participants in the social action.[24] This concern for *adequacy* encompasses some consideration for explanatory coherence and empirical validity. Explanations that fail to give an accurate account of observed patterns in social activity are unlikely to reflect the actors' motives and meanings adequately.

The most obvious means to check the adequacy of an explanation is to ask the actors themselves. This option, though, lacks reliability and often feasibility. People provide unreliable accounts of their own motivation, either because they deliberately lie or they lack a full appreciation of their true motives. In addition, we frequently wish to understand actors remote from us in terms of time and space, but we have no way of directly questioning them. Under these conditions we assess adequacy by making a construct of the historical context of the act to gain additional guidance for deciding whether a particular explanation adequately represents motive and meaning.[25] If the hypothesized understanding does not make sense within this historical context, then we have grounds for questioning its adequacy. The development of the historical construct, incidentally, again raises issues of coherence and empirical support. In this case, however, these concerns support the objective of evaluating an explanation's representation of the self-understandings of the social actors.

Any evaluation of adequacy, then, requires an interpretive step beyond that of judgments of empirical validity and logical coherence. In addition to determining, as best we can, the validity of the observations and the quality of the argument, interpretive adequacy requires that we check the representation of the meanings actors themselves assign to their activities and the cultural context within which they act. Consequently, in addition to logical fallacies and empirical discrepancies, an alternative representation of the actors' self-understandings and context can undermine an explanation for social action.

Authenticity

A particular explanation may adequately represent the self-understanding of the actors, but critical theorists point out that these understandings are often distorted. Basing social explanations upon a self-deluded sense of motive and meaning hardly provides a reliable foundation for understanding social reality, nor would uncritically representing a context distorted by concentrations of power.

The criterion of *authenticity* goes beyond concern for logically coherent, empirically valid, and interpretively adequate explanations. In addition, it recognizes how the observed action often reflects powerful forces of which the actors are both unaware and perhaps even resistant to acknowledging. For example, a psychoanalytic explanation uses theories of repression and displacement to characterize how patients distort or deny the real motives underlying their neurotic behavior. Similarly, Marxist critical theory applies its presumed insight into the fundamental links between the forces and relations of production to illuminate how dominant ideologies mask the actual character of economic exploitation. Both psychoanalytic and Marxist theories attempt to provide more authentic explanations for political violence and revolution (see below, Chapters 4, 5, and 6).

Once we accept a particular critical approach, the criterion of authenticity carries us beyond explanations that simply represent the actors' self-understandings to ones that critically contrast these representations with a construct of undistorted social activity. Unfortunately, it appears easier to accept the possibility of delusion than to agree on a standard for identifying and correcting such delusions. Indeed, any "authentic" critical standard may itself be distorted in either formulation or application and should be critiqued, and so on. Critical attacks on the authenticity of certain social explanations often enjoy greater success in unmasking distortions than in establishing a more authentic alternative.

Generalizability

Logical empirical analysis seeks to subsume many particular cases under an encompassing explanation; moreover, it seeks to unify a variety of explanatory hypotheses into an integrated theory. True science, from this perspective, entails much more than the accumulation of empirical data. Rather, scientific explanation must relate this data in a logically satisfying manner. Ideally we should seek to explain all instances of political violence or revolution by a single theory, universal in form and unlimited in scope. In reality few, if any, social theories achieve this level of generalizability.[26]

Generalizability is not identical to comprehensiveness. We might, for example, put forth a general theory on the origins of discontent that does not address the other elements of the puzzle of political violence. Alternatively we might develop a detailed study of how all the elements of the puzzle fit together in a particular case of political violence, while making no claim that our investigation has any general relevance. Of course, an ideal theory would be both comprehensive and general.

The lack of a commonly accepted unified theory of political violence or revolution does not invalidate this criterion. Even though we may never achieve a universal theory, we can still compare competing explanations according to the exact domain to which the explanations purportedly apply.[27]

The issue of general domain, though, reflects the methodological biases of logical empiricism and might seem irrelevant from the perspective of interpretive approaches. Certainly, interpretive analysts reject more general theories that are unintelligible "from the native's point of view," and they often focus on richly textured case studies. These tendencies, however, should not obscure a certain concern with a type of generality. The generalizations of interpretive theory perhaps remain more explicitly tied to the self-understandings of the social actors; nevertheless, some interpretive approaches demonstrate an interest in generalizability. For instance, rational choice theory, which we consider a formalized interpretive approach, claims general applicability to a wide variety of choice situations.

Logical empiricists recognize that interpretive case studies can provide the building blocks for more general explanations. This view partly overlaps with the interpretive notion of "tacking" between the particulars of a given situation and more general structures of shared understanding (see above). Indeed, some scholars argue that empirical social theories explicitly or implicitly represent the self-understandings of social actors and are more interpretive than often recognized.[28] Empirical generalizations, interpretive theorists argue, have validity only to the extent they adequately represent widely shared self-understandings.

Critical approaches as well incorporate some concern for generalizability, especially with respect to the standard of critique. Concentrations of power may distort understanding in many different ways, but enlightenment lies along a common path. Contemporary Marxists, in particular, sometimes promise a general theory to explicate the many different forms of ideological distortion and delusion in the world (see the discussion in Chapter 6).

The criterion of generalizability, dare we say it, has some general applicability for the evaluation of contending social explanations, but only if applied cautiously. We may never attain universal theory, and we must specify the domain of the limited generalizations we do possess. Unfortunately, explanations addressing different contexts may not be strictly comparable according to this criterion. Moreover, a "good" case study is superior to a "bad" generalization. The former may have limited relevance, but the latter is simply misleading.

♨   ♨   ♨

We need not accept some vulgar equality among all theories of political violence or revolution and give each theory the same weight and consideration as all others. Rather, we possess a variety of criteria for judging the relative merits of contending explanations. Indeed, since different criteria reflect the biases of alternative approaches, it might seem we have too many. The "playing field" each establishes is not level. Empirical criteria, for example, favor explanations formulated according to the principles of logical empiricism and appear slanted against more interpretive approaches. The criterion of adequacy reverses this bias. We might conclude, therefore, that though we may be able to judge the relative merit of explanations produced within a particular approach, we cannot make any valid comparisons between approaches. This limited ability to draw definitive conclusions as to relative merit ensures a certain irreducible perspectivism in our study of violence and revolution.

The three major approaches to the study of the social world—logical empiricism, interpretation, and critical theory—are not, however, completely incompatible. We noted several areas of overlap. Empirical explanations cannot ignore their interpretive elements, nor can interpretive and critical theories escape assessment in terms of the logic of their arguments and the evidence they muster. While this sharing cannot resolve all the disputes arising from different ways of construing and studying the social world, the degree of sharing provides a basis for a dialogue among explanations that reflect different approaches.

Moreover, two of the criteria—comprehensiveness and generalizability—seem equally applicable to all explanations, regardless of methodology. They judge not the quality of an explanation but its domain. Comprehensiveness reminds us that a particular explanation, whatever its quality, may address only part of the puzzle. Partial explanations are not inherently flawed; science generally proceeds on multiple fronts, with many researchers working on different elements of a puzzle. Frequently, however, a partial theory lays claim to an unwarranted comprehensiveness.

Generalizability recognizes that social explanations are seldom, if ever, equally applicable to all times and places. We might develop a persuasive explanation for a particular case, but it may have limited relevance elsewhere. Such limitations, when acknowledged, provide no grounds for rejection. Sometimes, however, researchers claim a false universality for their explanations, and we need to uncover these pretensions.

EXPLAINING VIOLENCE AND REVOLUTION: SOME PROBLEMS

We frequently encounter problems in the study of political violence and revolution, some common to most social research but others intensified by the peculiar hazards of the subject matter. In most cases we can neither wholly eliminate nor completely ignore these problems. By recognizing their presence, though, we minimize the extent to which they compromise our conclusions.

Identification/Dehumanization

Social researchers generally prize the virtue of *objectivity*. What objectivity demands of the researcher, however, remains subject to debate. Sometimes objectivity seems to imply that we must aspire to a godlike vision transcending all limited perspectives. More modestly, objectivity requires that explanatory contributions provide a sufficient basis for others to judge the possible impact of the researchers' interests on their conclusions. While private and social interests conceivably affect all systematic research in the physical as well as the social sciences, their influence seems particularly paradoxical in the study of social relations, especially extreme ones of violence and revolution.

On one hand, the psychological impact of violent political struggle challenges our detachment and tempts us to identify with one side or the other. Although we might offer a reasonable defense for our sympathies (for example, the choice of siding with the oppressed rather than the oppressor), that rationale will not fully compensate for the biases likely to creep into our analysis. Moreover, identification often results from a powerful emotional reaction rather than a reasoned philosophical analysis.

On the other hand, we might purchase apparent detachment at the cost of dehumanization. Often we encounter social analysis that copes with the potential problem of emotional identification by abstracting human beings out of the equation altogether. As Walter Kaufmann notes with respect to philosophy, social analysis often "helps one endure the sufferings of others by distracting one's attention from them."[29] The ordered abstractions of social inquiry fail to comprehend the extremities of "life at the limits."

Logical empirical approaches appear more likely to abstract and dehumanize their subject matter. In contrast, interpretive studies, given their objective of rendering the social world from the participants' point of view, seem more susceptible to distortions arising from overidentification. Emotional bias, however, may underlie even scientific abstractions, and simplistic stereotypes (a common form of dehumanizing abstraction) may twist interpretive efforts. Navigating between overidentification and dehumanizing abstraction will likely prove difficult for any student of violence and revolution, regardless of methodological preference.

Political Agendas

Emotional identification with the subject matter encourages the deliberate imposition of a political agenda on the conduct of inquiry. Even researchers in the physical and biological sciences sometimes subordinate their investigations to the purposes of a political ideology. Analyses of social problems central to powerful political interests, however, seem far more susceptible to political influence.[30] Outbreaks of political violence and demands for radical social change directly evoke the researchers' most fundamental political biases, whether for or against the established order in a community.

The epigram "One man's terrorist is another's freedom fighter" implies that our fundamental categories of political analysis often reflect our position on the political spectrum. Whether we consider an act "criminal" or "revolutionary" is, from this point of view, simply a matter of ideological preference. Consequently contending theories generally suffer from political, as well as methodological, incompatibilities.

James B. Rule refers to these emotional and political biases as the *rhetorical* elements of a theory.[31] Though we must recognize the possible influence of such elements, he argues that we can separate them from the *falsifiable* components. He rejects the conclusion that methodological or ideological factors necessarily render different theories incompatible. Rather, we must recognize and isolate rhetorical biases in any explanation while weighing the concepts and evidence that at least partly transcend the emotional and political identifications of a particular researcher.

Emotional and political identifications constitute some fundamental aspects of the way we, as human beings, know the world. Our feelings and values undeniably shape our understanding, and any effort to deny their influence probably contributes to a deluded tendency toward overabstraction. But if we wish to participate in a community of inquiry, especially one devoted to such volatile topics as political violence and revolution, we need to distinguish between purely personal insight and those knowledge claims that transcend our personal perspective and make a transmissible contribution to shared understanding. In part we rely on logical argumentation and empirical evidence to support such contributions. Unfortunately, in addition to the philosophical argument that our theoretical perspective influences observation, certain problems of research also impair our study.

Research Problems

Revolutions are relatively rare historical events, and even acts of political violence occur infrequently in most communities. From an empirical standpoint, however, we would like to have numerous instances of the phenomenon being investigated to develop more reliable explanations. When forced to rely on only a few cases, especially ones widely separated in both space and time, we find it more difficult to isolate common factors from those peculiar to a particular event. Of course, only a fool would wish for widespread political upheaval simply to provide a more fully developed data base. Interpretive studies, in any case, tend to emphasize the particular, arguing that an event becomes intelligible only when understood in its context. This type of analysis, then, is less confounded by limited instances than those seeking to develop a general theory of revolution.

Both interpretive and empirical approaches, however, encounter some serious obstacles to the conduct of direct research. A community wracked by political violence and revolution presents an environment hostile to both the participant observation favored by some interpretivists and the systematic surveys or other forms of direct data collection often used by empirical social scientists. With a few exceptions, social analysts do not relish putting their lives at risk to undertake their research. And even those who do will likely find that the information they require is unavailable in a community rent by extreme conflict.

Specific problems of measurement further complicate research. Many of the most interesting phenomena—like levels of frustration or alienation—are difficult or impossible to measure directly, forcing us to use indirect indicators. We might, for example, attempt to measure possible changes in individual frustration through shifts in aggregate economic indices like unemployment levels. Critics commonly attack the relationship between indirect indicators and the phenomenon they purport to represent. Efforts to measure states of mind or preferences directly, however, often raise questions about researcher or respondent bias (consider, for instance, all the problems that opinion pollsters encounter in relatively placid political communities). Finally, even phenomena amenable in principle to direct and reliable measurement may prove difficult to assess in a hostile research environment.

Unfalsifiable Explanations

Lastly, the complexity of the problems studied contributes to the formulation of unfalsifiable explanations. In many areas of social investigation, analysts commonly protect their propositions with the caveat *ceteris paribus* (other things being equal). When many factors conceivably affect outcome, the failure of a specific relation to hold as predicted seldom falsifies an argument. Rather, the investigator usually points to changes in some other factor that affected the predicted outcome. The limited ability to perform experiments in the social sciences that control for the effects of extraneous factors reinforces this problem.

Moreover, social science explanations generally state their relations in probabilistic or tendency terms; for example, "Increasing unemployment *tends* to increase political discontent." An occasion where increased unemployment has no measurable impact on levels of discontent cannot falsify such a tendency statement; it may simply be "the exception that proves the rule." Repeated failures to demonstrate any association between unemployment and discontent casts increasing doubt on the proposition, but even a number of failures would not, literally, falsify it. Such apparent discrepancies could result from a statistical fluke in the sample studied and might be corrected by including further cases.

CONCLUSION: MANAGING EXPLANATORY PLURALISM

We do not lack explanations for political violence and revolution; indeed, we may have too many. Perhaps if we agreed on one best way of studying the social world, we might hope to combine these different explanatory efforts into a complete and satisfying theory (a hope reflecting naive perspectivism). The lack of consensus on how best to approach the social world, however, frustrates this hope. The three major methods of social investigation differ in their objectives. Logical empiricism aims to identify empirical regularities, ultimately subsuming them under lawlike statements. Interpretation attempts to represent the observed social activities from the point of view of the participants. Critique strives to unmask patterns of domination and delusion in the social world.

Yet though they differ with respect to their fundamental explanatory objectives, some overlap exists. Empirical social analysis contains more interpretive elements than often recognized by its practitioners. Interpretive and critical investigators cannot ignore issues of empirical support and logical argumentation, and critical theories must first represent the self-understandings of the actors before demonstrating their delusion.

Partial sharing makes it possible to translate the concerns of one approach into terms partly compatible with the others. Such translations, though not definitive, serve as somewhat satisfying accounts of mutual intelligibility and relative worth.[32] Richard Bernstein argues that "plurality does not mean that we are limited to being separate individuals with irreducible subjective interests. Rather it means that we seek to discover some common ground to reconcile differences through debate, conversation, and dialogue."[33]

We have identified part of this common ground, and in the coming chapters we use this foundation to judge the contributions of different perspectives on political violence and revolution. In this way we seek not the final word but rather to participate in the ongoing conversation about the drama of political discord.

NOTES

1. For a good introduction to the different perspectives on social theory see Richard J. Bernstein, *The Restructuring of Social and Political Theory* (Philadelphia: University of Pennsylvania Press, 1978); for an introduction to the problem of "progress" in political inquiry see Terence Ball, "Is There Progress in Political Inquiry?" in Terence Ball, ed., *Idioms of Inquiry: Critique and Renewal in Political Science* (Albany: State University of New York Press, 1987), pp. 13–44.
2. Donna Harraway, "Situated Knowledges: The Science Question in Feminism and the Privilege of Partial Perspective," *Feminist Studies,* 14 (Fall 1988): 582.
3. For an extended discussion of these kinds of possibilities see Richard Bernstein, *Beyond Objectivism and Relativism* (Philadelphia: University of Pennsylvania Press, 1983).
4. Bernstein, *The Restructuring of Social and Political Theory,* p. 43.

5. The initiation of this change is commonly associated with Thomas Kuhn, *The Structure of Scientific Revolutions*, Second Edition (Chicago: University of Chicago Press, 1970) and reached its most radical statement, perhaps, in Paul Feyerabend, *Against Method: Outline of an Anarchist Theory of Knowledge* (London: NLB, 1975). However, anticipations include Michael Polanyi, *Personal Knowledge: Towards a Post-Critical Knowledge* (Chicago: University of Chicago Press, 1958) and some of the ideas of Ludwig Boltzmann in the nineteenth century.

6. The controversial idea of conversion is Kuhn's, p. 158.

7. See Bernstein, *The Restructuring of Social and Political Theory*, Part Three, pp. 117–169.

8. This discussion of differences is largely similar to that in Peter C. Sederberg, *The Politics of Meaning: Power and Explanation in the Social Construction of Reality* (Tucson: University of Arizona Press, 1984), pp. 28–29.

9. Charles Taylor, "Interpretation and the Sciences of Man," in Paul Rabinow and William M. Sullivan, eds., *Interpretive Social Science: A Second Look* (Berkeley: University of California Press, 1987), pp. 62–64. This collection of essays provides a good introduction to many of the issues in interpretive social analysis.

10. Alexander Rosenberg, *Philosophy of Social Science* (Boulder, Colo.: Westview Press, 1988), pp. 82–86.

11. Clifford Geertz, "From the Native's Point of View'. On the Nature of Anthropological Understanding," in Michael Gibbons, ed., *Interpreting Politics* (New York: New York University Press, 1987), pp. 145–146.

12. Terence Ball, "Deadly Hermeneutics; Or *Sinn* and the Social Scientist," in Ball, ed., pp. 95–112.

13. For a good introduction to this complex area see Jon Elster, "Introduction," in Jon Elster, ed., *Rational Choice* (New York: New York University Press, 1986), pp. 1–33.

14. Rosenberg, p. 65.

15. Elster suggests that rational choice theory may be viewed as normative (indicating how people *should* make decisions, not necessarily how they actually make them), descriptive (of certain observed patterns of decision making), or explanatory (that is, empirically valid explanations of behavior). Elster argues that rational choice theory faces some real problems as an explanatory theory from a logical empirical perspective (as, we might add, do all interpretive explanations). See Elster, pp. 1–3, 12–22. For an additional critique of rational choice as a causal theory see Terry Moe, "On the Scientific Status of Rational Models," *American Journal of Political Science*, 23 (February 1979): 215–243.

16. A good introduction to critical theory is Brian Fay, *Critical Social Science* (Ithaca, N.Y.: Cornell University Press, 1987). See also Bernstein, *The Restructuring of Social and Political Theory*, pp. 173–236.

17. Cf. Fay, pp. 31–32.

18. William E. Connolly, *Appearance and Reality in Politics* (New York: Cambridge University Press, 1981), pp. 34–35.

19. The basic grammatical structure, however, needs to be distinguished from rules for standard speech which deal less with issues of intelligibility than with "correct" speech. Failure to follow the former leads to incomprehension ("Have of riot the caused don't any what idea we"); failure to follow the latter leads to the judgment that the speaker is merely uneducated ("We doesn't have no idea what caused the riot"). See Joseph M. Williams, *Style: Toward Clarity and Grace* (Chicago: University of Chicago Press, 1990), pp. 176–177.

20. See, for example, Richard Ned Lebow and Janice Stern, "Rational Deterrence Theory: I Think, Therefore I Deter," *World Politics* (January 1989): 208–224. For a general critique of rational choice theory as unscientific, see Moe, cited above.

21. Kenneth R. Hoover, *The Elements of Social Scientific Thinking*, Third Edition (New York: St. Martin's, 1984), p. 55. This book provides a good basic introduction to some of the characteristics of empirical social analysis.

22. James B. Rule systematically applies this criterion in his *Theories of Civil Violence* (Berkeley: University of California Press, 1988).

23. Hoover, p. 37.

24. Alfred Schutz, "Common-Sense and Scientific Interpretation of Human Action," in Maurice Natanson, ed., *Philosophy of the Social Sciences* (New York: Random House, 1963), p. 342.

25. See Morse Peckham, "The Intentional? Fallacy?" in Morse Peckham, *The Triumph of Romanticism* (Columbia: University of South Carolina Press, 1970), p. 441. Social theorists are often tempted to use history to *exemplify* their pet theories without questioning whether the historical context supports such a construction of events. Adequate *interpretation,* in contrast, takes care to ensure that the historical constructs reflect the self-understandings of the actors, not merely those of the theorist.

26. James B. Rule, *Theories of Civil Violence*, pp. 227–230.

27. Ibid., pp. 230–238.

28. Ball, "Deadly Hermeneutics," *passim.* See also Peter C. Sederberg, "Subjectivity and Typification: A Note on Method in the Social Sciences," *Philosophy of the Social Sciences,* 2 (June 1972): 167–176.

29. Walter Kaufmann, *Life at the Limits* (New York: Readers Digest Press, 1978), p. 78.

30. For a discussion of the impact of Marxist-Leninist ideology on the course of natural science in the Soviet Union see Anatol Rapoport, *Origins of Violence: Approaches to the Study of Conflict* (New York: Paragon House, 1989), pp. 145–151.

31. Rule, pp. 280–281.

32. For an elaboration of the notion of "translating" different worldviews see Paul A. Roth, *Meaning and Method in the Social Sciences: A Case for Methodological Pluralism* (Ithaca, N.Y.: Cornell University Press, 1987), pp. 226–245.

33. Bernstein, *Beyond Objectivism and Relativism,* p. 223.

PART TWO

THEORY

4

Metaphors and Partial Visions: The Beginnings of Explanation

We generally try to understand the unfamiliar in terms of something more familiar. Such efforts often reflect the influence of metaphor on our thinking. By uncovering the influence of metaphor in theories of political violence and revolution, we better understand their character and possible limits. From there we critically review some popular commonsense explanations for violence or revolution. Finally, we attempt to classify these explanations with respect to the level of analysis they adopt, as well as whether they reflect essentially deterministic or voluntaristic depictions of social processes.

MAKING SENSE OUT OF THE "SENSELESS"

A massacre of elderly worshippers in a synagogue; a cheerful playground turned into a killing field by a man wielding an automatic rifle; poison gas dropped on a Kurdish village; unarmed priests executed by soldiers—just a few sorry instances of internal violence in recent years. When confronted by such horrors, we often recoil with fear and incomprehension and initially label the acts as "senseless." But do we really think they are inexplicable?

Some confusion arises from the different shades of meaning we give to the notion "senseless."[1] "Radical senselessness" characterizes an occurrence that lacks any apparent rhyme or reason. Perhaps a tornado that skips through a town killing some while leaving others unscathed approximates an event whose effects approach pure chance. The victims have no distinguishing characteristics other than being at the wrong place at the wrong time. When we look at the "whirlwinds" of violence that afflicted Lebanon, El Salvador, Somalia, or Sri Lanka in recent years, we might consider them senseless in this manner.

Despite such powerful images, we know that human beings commit such acts; therefore, the acts differ from the random forces of nature. A second meaning of senselessness acknowledges violence as a human activity, but considers it the product of a demented personality. We can understand (make sense of) such events but only in terms of some theory of pathological behavior. "Senseless," here, means insane.

A third variation on the meaning of senseless does not question the clinical sanity of the perpetrators; rather, they lack moral sense. Perhaps more honestly, either we do not comprehend or we disagree with their moral agenda. Many Americans, for example, find the religious beliefs of Iranian Shi'ite fundamentalists to be incomprehensible. Or, we might condemn the actions of a revolutionary movement or a repressive regime as senseless brutality, because we disagree with their ends.

Finally, we might be making a means/ends judgment when we condemn an act as "senseless." In this case senseless actions prove destructive of the perpetrators' *own* goals. Miscalculation or stupidity presumably underlies the choice of "senseless" means. Sometimes such an argument serves as a cover for the previous meaning; that is, we think the ends are morally repugnant, but we base our criticism on whether the choice of means "makes sense."

Regardless of our initial emotional reactions to outbreaks of violence and rebellion, then, we seldom find them completely *without sense.* Indeed, we demonstrate a strong compulsion to explain such interruptions in the flow of orderly existence. If we identify with the victims of violence, then we seek to explain such acts to protect ourselves from their reoccurrence. If we identify with the perpetrators, we seek to understand how we can further encourage the conflagration. Finally, as detached observers of the human condition, we strive to render these extraordinary events explicable or intelligible in terms of available explanations of human interaction.

The explanations we use as either participants or observers focus on one or more of four different levels of analysis: *individual,* the level of individual psychology; *group,* the level of social psychology; *culture,* the level of mutually recognized directives; and *structure,* the level of enduring patterns of social and economic arrangement. These levels of analysis interconnect in various ways, and some theories attempt to translate explanations at one level into the terms of another or to integrate the various levels into a more complex synthesis. Explanations, beyond proceeding at different levels of social analysis, reflect voluntaristic or deterministic biases. *Voluntaristic* explanations emphasize the role of human intention and choice in rendering social action intelligible. *Deterministic* explanations understand outcomes more as the product of forces beyond individual control, forces that perhaps determine outcome.

When we first encounter the exceptional, we generally try to understand it in terms of something more familiar. Metaphors often influence our thinking at this stage, even with respect to systematic social analysis. By detecting the influence of metaphor in theories of political violence and revolution, we reveal something of the character and possible limits of these explanations, as well as the level(s) of social analysis at which they operate. We then proceed to a critical review of some popular, though incomplete, explanations for violence or revolution. In the conclusion, we classify these partial theories with respect to their level of analysis, as well as whether they embody deterministic or voluntaristic depictions of the social process.

THE USE AND ABUSE OF METAPHOR[2]

Metaphors pepper our political discourse. With respect to style, the use of metaphor suggests a certain poetic impulse. Poetry is often richly metaphorical, and metaphorical images, devised for vividness and impact, may enliven otherwise drab social scientific prose. The use of metaphor, however, entails something more than the triumph of style over substance. "The essence of metaphor is understanding and experiencing one kind of thing in terms of another."[3] When the problems we confront are complex and obscure, we try to represent them in more familiar terms, by treating them as though they were something else. Political metaphors not only invigorate our writing, they also structure the ways in which we think about and respond to unfamiliar or difficult problems.

In drawing metaphorical comparisons, we must remain alert to the ways our linguistic tools can end up using us, rather than the reverse. Any metaphor highlights certain aspects of the problem so characterized and draws our attention away from those elements that the metaphor fails to represent. Like any limited perspective, metaphor provides only a partial way of seeing. As long as we recognize when we are speaking metaphorically, we remain sensitive to the limits on our way of seeing. Unfortunately, sometimes we mistake the metaphorical mask for the face of reality, and instead of developing a worldview we create a world.[4]

Once we identify the metaphor(s) lying at the heart of a particular explanation or theory, we uncover a useful way of delineating its perspective. Consider, for example, describing the drug problem in terms of "war." Despite its conflictual aspects, the problem of drug abuse in the United States is not, actually, a war. Rather, the war metaphor serves to characterize a complex phenomenon in familiar terms.

Insofar as we buy into the war metaphor, we then emphasize certain ways of thinking about and dealing with the drug problem. In short, "We act according to the way we conceive of things."[5] The war metaphor suggests seriousness of purpose and demands the mobilization of all our energies. Beyond this obvious political utility, certain aspects of the drug problem seem particularly warlike, such as the violence afflicting some of our urban areas.

Yet the drug problem is not a literal war, and the simplistic application of solutions appropriate to warfare will not resolve it. Consequently our political debates have produced a minor metaphor—the drug "epidemic"—to represent some elements ignored by the war metaphor. A comparison of what each metaphor entails illustrates the contrasting ways we think about the drug problem and how we should deal with it.

The war and epidemic metaphors overlap in at least one significant area that suggests why we also apply the war metaphor to various efforts to control disease, like the "war" on AIDS. Specifically, both suggest an external enemy that "invades" and traumatizes an otherwise healthy body, whether literal or figurative. Beyond this significant similarity, the metaphors diverge in important ways.

War suggests borders, front lines, and battle zones that we must defend or pacify. The threat resides in an overt enemy who occupies the other side of the battle lines. Epidemic, in contrast, implies a threat that suffuses the entire community, an adversary that we cannot easily track or isolate.

War mandates a military solution that inflicts casualties, takes prisoners, and incarcerates or even executes them as a form of punishment to deter future "aggression." Unsurprisingly, then, the "war" on drugs involves strengthened police forces, more prisons, the death penalty for drug "kingpins," and even the use of military force against the drug producers in other countries. As in the case of real war, the demands of the war on drugs also justify the expansion of government intrusiveness and power. Instead of loyalty oaths, we have random drug tests.

An epidemic, however, requires a curative/rehabilitative program, not a military one. The people who fall prey to an epidemic are victims who should be treated as patients and hospitalized, not imprisoned. Programs to stop the spread of an epidemic must emphasize prevention, not punishment. Policies reflecting the drug epidemic metaphor, consequently, stress drug rehabilitation programs and educational campaigns to slow and reverse the spread of drug abuse.

The war metaphor dominates both the political rhetoric and the allocation of resources, but curative/preventive programs receive at least a share of the available resources. We might believe that these contending metaphors together provide an appropriate and complementary characterization of the problem, though perhaps the emphasis should shift in one direction or the other.

A third metaphor, however, suggests that the drug problem may indicate something more profoundly wrong with our society than implied by either of the other two metaphors. This metaphor, largely missing from our political discourse, sees the drug problem as a "symptom." Unlike the other metaphors that view drugs as essentially an external threat to an otherwise smoothly functioning community, the symptom metaphor suggests that widespread drug abuse signifies a profoundly dysfunctional society. Drug use, from this perspective, reflects the normless, aimless existence of our privileged sectors and the hopeless condition of an expanding socioeconomic underclass.

Antidrug wars and public health programs, then, treat only the symptom, and other social pathologies will likely offset whatever success they achieve. For example, successful interdiction of the drug flow into the country may simply drive up the price of illegal drugs and, consequently, the crime rate.

Metaphors are not simply true or false. As the drug case illustrates, each of the metaphors provides a plausible, if incomplete, orientation to a difficult problem. A metaphor, to use a metaphor, illuminates part of an unfamiliar terrain. It may highlight significant aspects, but it may conceal others of even greater importance. Nor can we facilely combine multiple metaphors into a more complete depiction (naive perspectivism). Like the more formal explanations they influence, metaphorical constructions are often at least partly incompatible with one another. Thus, the three metaphors for the drug problem diverge in significant ways both in how they construe the problem and the policy responses they imply.

Metaphor, then, often initiates the process of explanation. Indeed, sometimes a powerful metaphorical image will terminate the process of explanation as well. Invoking the metaphor will suffice to close any further exploration of the issue. If we can identify the metaphors embedded in various theories of political violence and revolution, we will begin to ascertain the conceptual biases underlying these theories. The common metaphors for political violence and revolution include those of geological, hydraulic, organic, and explanatory origin. We start our analysis, however, with a metaphor rhetorically inflated to the status of a "theory," the domino theory.

The Domino Theory

One charm of the domino theory lies in the frank admission of its metaphorical status. Certainly no one believes that countries are rectangular chips with dots on them. Nonetheless, ever since the end of World War II American policymakers have invoked this "theory" to interpret the process of revolutionary change and to prescribe the appropriate response. This metaphorical construct particularly influenced American policy in Southeast Asia in the 1950s and 1960s and in Central America in the 1980s.[6]

The domino metaphor highlights a number of propositions about the revolutionary process:

- Regimes are stable unless acted upon by an external force (like a domino balanced on its edge).
- If one regime falls, then those in contiguous countries will fall or at least be destabilized (a falling domino will knock down the one next to it).
- Even if a revolution starts in a country geographically and politically remote, its fall will initiate a sequence of events that will ultimately affect an area central to our interests (like a row of dominoes falling in a chain reaction).
- The revolutionary sequence is best countered at the beginning rather than the end of this process (if the chain reaction never starts, the dominoes never fall).

The domino theory adopts a perspective influenced by classic Newtonian laws of motion. Essentially, an object at rest will remain at rest and an object in motion will remain in motion unless acted upon by some external force. Regimes "topple" and countries "fall" to Communist control because of externally sponsored subversion. When one country falls, the forces of subversion easily cross over the border to bring down its neighbor. The only way to stop this sequence would be through the intervention of another external force to check the fall by "propping up" the regime in danger of being toppled.

Proponents of this theory, however, sometimes seem to violate the principles of classical mechanics when they argue for some kind of "action at a distance": that is, a regime falling in one part of the world somehow causes a revolution in another region. This apparent violation of the domino metaphor, however, probably represents the combination of domino theory metaphor with the organic metaphor of contagion (see below).

Critics attack the metaphorical entailments of the domino theory on conceptual, empirical, and pragmatic grounds. Conceptually, the mechanistic roots of the domino metaphor misrepresent the nature of social phenomena. These critics decry what they view as the pernicious tendency to draw on metaphorical associations with the natural sciences incapable of representing the intelligible character of social interaction. This criticism reflects the interpretive position on the proper character of social explanation.

Specifically, such critics argue that the domino theory ignores internal conditions and treats the rebellious population as a passive "dependent variable," slavishly responding to the external forces imposed upon them. The domino theory denies the possibility that a revolution arises from the discontent and aspirations of at least portions of the populace acting in a relatively autonomous fashion. Finally, the theory tends to ignore significant differences among countries, because, after all, dominoes are essentially alike.

Because of these conceptual inadequacies, the theory cannot accurately predict where revolutions will occur nor explain these discrepancies. The most conspicuous empirical failure of the theory occurred in Southeast Asia, where American policymakers confidently predicted that unless the "aggression" of North Vietnam against its neighbor to the south was checked, all the countries in Southeast Asia would fall to Communism.

Superficially, the evidence for this argument seemed persuasive. After the first successful Communist takeover in Russia, the Soviet Union then aided the revolution in its neighbor China. Both the Soviets and the Chinese Communists aided the revolution in Vietnam. After Vietnam was partitioned in 1954, the North Vietnamese regime, with continuing Chinese and Soviet support, instigated a renewed revolution in South Vietnam, Laos, and Cambodia. Given this "evidence," who could doubt that if this "proxy" aggression succeeded in these last three countries, then Thailand, Malaysia, and Burma would follow, and Communist subversion would ultimately threaten even the archipelago countries of Indonesia and the Philippines?

Skeptics challenged this reconstruction of events on a number of empirical grounds. First, while not denying some contribution made by external aid and comfort, they argue we can understand the successful revolutions in China and Vietnam only in the context of their internal conditions and struggle. More dramatically, the predictions of regimes toppling throughout Southeast Asia proved wildly inaccurate. After the success of the revolutions in Vietnam and Cambodia in 1975, the victorious "dominoes" fell on each other rather than their non-Communist neighbors. The Soviet Union engaged in a propaganda war and a border conflict with China, and China attacked Vietnam after Vietnam invaded its erstwhile revolutionary ally Cambodia.

Finally, critics argue that the falling domino metaphor contributes to disastrous policy. Since toppling dominoes are best stopped at the beginning of the process, the theory encourages intervention in areas of remote concern. Failure to intervene early means that subversion will inevitably threaten core interests. In addition, since the theory emphasizes external factors, it obscures the internal origins of rebellion. Because it obscures the internal origins of revolution, the theory encourages alliances with regimes that have already lost the support of many of their people.

Despite the obvious problems with the domino metaphor as applied to events in Southeast Asia, it still influenced policy in Central America during the 1980s. In part, analysts clung to the metaphor because it captures, though imperfectly, some essential aspects of most revolutions. They do not occur in an international vacuum. They take shape in a global context that provides encouraging (and discouraging) examples, constructive (and damaging) advice, and sometimes critical material aid and even active intervention. On the other hand, counterrevolutionary forces also might receive critical support from foreign sympathizers. More systematic theories offer plausible suggestions as to how a domino effect might be produced. (See the discussions of the justifications for violence and the "bandwagon effect" in Chapter 5.)

More cynically, we might suspect that the metaphor captured the minds of so many U.S. policymakers for four decades after World War II because it fit their ideological preferences and political interests. They found it convenient and simple to view revolutions as a form of disguised aggression instigated by our primary adversary, rather than to understand them as complex processes reflecting unique local conditions. Response to the former would be unambiguous—we must stand up to aggression and defend friendly regimes. Response to the latter would necessarily involve complex and subtle policies, possibly beyond our capabilities.

The domino theory, then, illustrates some of the more pernicious effects of metaphor on the explanatory enterprise. We must not conclude, however, that more successful analyses of the problems of political violence and revolution avoid metaphor altogether. The metaphorical influences, rather, are often more deeply hidden rather than explicitly announced, as with the domino theory. We now turn to several of these more subtle metaphorical influences to determine the character of their portraits of revolution and political violence.

Geological Metaphors

In addition to classical mechanics, social analysis draws on other physical sciences for metaphors of revolution. Powerfully destructive geological forces, for example, often provide dramatic images for the depiction of revolution:

- The *tensions* produced by these social contradictions *accumulated* until they had to be released. (The forces causing a revolution build up along social fault lines.)
- The revolutionary *upheaval* in France began in 1789. (Revolutions are earthquakes.)
- The mob *erupted* in fury. (Mass violence is volcanic.)
- The regime quickly *collapsed*. (Institutions are structures that collapse in a revolutionary earthquake.)
- "Revolutions are not made; they *come*." (Revolutions, like earthquakes, cannot be predicted, promoted, or prevented.)[7]

These few examples illustrate the rhetorical influence of geological metaphors. More importantly, these images shape how we understand the nature and causes of political violence and the character of revolutionary change. The metaphor captures the power of revolutionary events and how difficult they are to control. The capacity of revolutions to bring about the collapse of apparently impregnable regimes suggests some equivalence to the natural forces in the earth that destroy our strongest buildings. Flexible, responsive regimes adjust to these forces, whereas rigid ones crumble, much as "earthquake-proof" buildings flex to absorb the shock of the upheaval. Such associations also suggest that we understand the causes of revolution only imperfectly. Although we know where the *potential* for revolutionary upheaval exists, we cannot predict or control their exact occurrence.

Even though geological metaphors for revolution draw on the physical sciences, they differ in one significant way from the "physics" of the domino theory. Analyses rooted in images of earthquakes and volcanoes focus on the *internal* causes of revolution. This contrasts with the metaphor of dominoes toppling because of the action of an external force. In addition, geological metaphors usually conceptualize revolution in collective terms as the product of clashing social forces rather than as a simple aggregate of individual frustrations and aspirations. Consequently, this type of metaphor usually shapes structural theories of revolution, even though they may not explicitly draw on geological imagery.

Geological metaphors conceal, as well as reveal, aspects of revolution. Obviously, an approach emphasizing internal factors may underestimate the significance of external variables on revolutionary outcomes. Geological metaphors, then, risk reversing the bias of the domino theory. More seriously, the equation of social and political phenomena with physical forces renders them virtually meaningless, lacking in purpose or point. Like earthquakes and volcanic eruptions, we may eventually explain revolutions by subsuming them under deterministic lawlike statements, but this metaphorical perspective will never render them intelligible. Rather, they resemble the vast and impersonal forces of the physical universe. And like other physical phenomena, they possess no moral component; no one is responsible. We cannot judge revolutions, only deal with them as we would other natural calamities.

So despite the power of geological metaphors to represent some significant aspects of the revolutionary experience, they, too, conceal some essential elements of the revolutionary process. Other metaphors, partly in response to such deficiencies, epitomize political violence and revolution differently.

Hydraulic Metaphors

In addition to classical physics and geology, some images of political violence and revolution reflect a third natural science field, that of hydraulics or fluid mechanics:

- *Frustrations increased* among the peasants to the breaking point. (Anger builds up in people like pressure in a boiler.)
- The increasingly frustrated peasants *exploded* into violence. (Eventually pressure leads to an explosion.)
- Repression only *increased* their anger. (Compression of a fluid or a gas increases the pressure.)
- The "Saturday night drunk" provides a *safety valve* for the workers' frustrations. (Frustrations can be released like steam from a boiler.)

Analysts draw on these metaphors to explain both individual and collective violence and thereby highlight a perspective on social discord obscured by geological metaphors for revolution. Like geological metaphors, hydraulic images emphasize internal over external factors in explaining outbursts of social violence. Unlike them, however, the participants become somewhat more the subjects of their own drama, rather than the depersonalized objects through which forces of history work. Through the idea that pressure "builds up" in an individual, hydraulic metaphors attempt to represent individual states of being.

Hydraulic metaphors address some of the deficiencies of theories shaped by geological images, but they possess their own characteristic blind spots. We might question, first, whether hydraulic metaphors represent individual consciousness in an adequate fashion. Like other metaphors rooted in the physical sciences, hydraulic images carry a kind of deterministic bias, even when focused at the individual level. In psychological terms the metaphor supports a simple stimulus/response (S-R) equation: Increasing frustration (stimulus) leads to violent outbursts (response). But this ignores individuals as thinking, purposive beings. Could not the response to increasing frustration be mediated in various ways by the actor (a psychological model of stimulus/organism/response, or S-O-R), rather than leading automatically to violence?

Second, whereas geological metaphors tend to highlight structural factors while obscuring the role of individuals, hydraulic metaphors risk reversing the bias by obscuring the structural context within which individual behavior develops. When we focus on the individual level of explanation, we tend to accept the context as a given. In a revolution, however, the significant question is not "why did these people rebel rather than those?" (explained in hydraulic terms of the rebels experiencing greater "pressure"), but rather "why did anyone rebel?" (explained in structural terms of the patterns of exploitation that lead to frustration or the weakening of controls that repress the expression of discontent).[8] Metaphors tend to direct investigation along some lines of inquiry rather than others.

Organic Metaphors

Geological and hydraulic metaphors, along with the mechanistic impulses of the domino theory, draw upon the inanimate world and the physical sciences for explanatory images. We might expect, however, that metaphors drawn from the biological realm would better capture the vital nature of social life. Political commentators from at least the time of the ancient Greeks have developed organic metaphors to evoke the essential nature of social and political relations.

The image of the "body politic," in particular, provides numerous entailments for theories of revolution:[9]

- To understand an *outbreak* of violence we must diagnose the *symptoms* of discontent. (Violence is a disease that affects a healthy political community and exhibits certain characteristics.)
- The *ideas* of the revolutionary agitators *infected* the people's minds. (Revolutions are infections spread by carriers who transmit the germs of discontent.)
- The reign of terror *consumed* the political community. (The revolution is a fever that intensifies and then eventually burns itself out.)

- Terrorism spreads *malignantly* throughout the world and must be *cut out*. (Violence is a cancer demanding radical surgery for a cure.)
- The revolutionary *movement* must *cleanse* the country of the reactionary forces that threaten the goals of the revolution. (The old order is diseased; revolution is the cure; and violence is the medicine that effects the cure.)

The images of disease, infection, and fever vividly capture a sense of how revolution spreads and, once started, of its prognosis and possible cure. In addition, we can work out the metaphorical entailments at either the structural or the individual level, depending on whether we conceive of the whole political community as the diseased organism or focus on how individuals become "infected." Moreover, contagion metaphors evoke how revolutionary ideas and successes spread both across geographic space and through time. This contrasts with the domino theory, which must violate the physical principles of its metaphorical origins to incorporate the "demonstration effect" of a "domino" falling in one part of the world somehow causing another some distance away to topple. Finally, though organic metaphors do not fully escape the deterministic tendencies that compromise metaphors originating in the physical sciences, they capture some notion of human agency through such images like ideas as "germs" deliberately spread by revolutionary "carriers."

Organic metaphors for political processes and relations often exhibit a certain conservative bias. They usually characterize the "natural" state of the body politic as one of healthy equilibrium, with each part making a contribution to the well-being of the whole. Various "pathologies" can upset this happy condition, as when the "infected" lower orders attempt to usurp the proper position of those best suited to rule. Such pathologies originate from outside the body politic, absolving the existing order of any responsibility. The counteractions implied by metaphors of disease and cancer, consequently, recognize little justice in the claims of the revolutionaries and often rationalize brutally severe "cures" to halt the progress of the infection or malignancy.

Revolutionaries, however, reverse this common conservative bias by simply claiming they seek to purge a body politic plagued by a corrupt regime. Through this twist the established order becomes the disease and revolution the cure. This reversal transforms revolution into a "natural" and defensive response to internal conditions, rather than the consequence of insidious, external infection.

Organic metaphors even suggest a third alternative, somewhat detached from the claims of either regime or revolutionaries. We might attach some role to external "infection" in terms of ideas or support but see these as contributing to revolution only when corruption and misrule have weakened the "body politic." This kind of adaptability to different levels of analysis and political agendas partly explains the continued vitality of organic metaphors in political thought.

Metaphors rooted in the physical world and the natural sciences play an important role in the history of social thought. Yet they all suffer from a key limitation. They cannot directly capture the self-consciousness of the social universe. Explanatory/linguistic metaphors, in contrast, explicitly reflect this self-consciousness.

Explanatory/Linguistic Metaphors

Interpretive approaches to social analysis decry the influence of the natural sciences, whether reflected in the influence of physical metaphors on social theory or in the slavish imitation of what some social scientists might take to be *the* scientific method (see Chapter 3). Interpretivists reject explanations of human action that subordinate it to deterministic natural laws. Rather, they strive to understand human action as governed by humanly devised rules that, when uncovered, render it intelligible.

We can exaggerate the differences between scientific (or logical empirical) and interpretive approaches. The natural sciences also possess interpretive components. Indeed, Colin Turbayne argues that the mechanistic determinism of classical physics itself reflects a metaphor—the universe as a machine. He suggests an alternative metaphor to explain the regularities we observe in the physical world. The organization of the universe resembles a universal language, and the regularities we find resemble not causal laws but the rules of grammar. "The former connote production of existence, necessity, and universality; the latter regularities that have exceptions."[10] Consequently, from the "linguistic" perspective, we learn about the physical universe much as we learn a natural language. Moreover, our understanding of language, at least in terms of use, generally surpasses our mastery of machines, providing linguistic metaphors an edge in translating the unfamiliar into more familiar terms.

Explanatory/linguistic metaphors should be even more applicable to puzzling aspects of the linguistically structured social world. Revolution, for example, could represent the clash between two explanations, one embodied by the established order and the other by the revolutionary movement. Revolutions occur because the dominant explanation within a community undergoes a crisis, at first experienced by only a few isolated individuals but eventually spreading throughout the community.[11] A successful revolutionary movement, then, constitutes a more convincing social explanation.

Jon Gunnemann provides a detailed elaboration of the explanatory/linguistic metaphor for revolution.[12] He argues that revolutionary polarization develops when a significant portion of the population challenges the prevailing "theodicy" of their community. His secularized use of the concept of theodicy involves "not justifying God but justifying evil and legitimating social inequities."[13] Following Thomas O'Dea, Gunnemann observes that human beings inevitably confront four forms of social evil in their communities: scarcity, uncertainty, powerlessness, and human perversity.[14] While a social theodicy does not concern all matters of social interaction, it affects areas central to the distribution of power and wealth. Any transformation of the prevailing theodicy would, therefore, constitute a revolutionary change.

Drawing explicitly on Thomas Kuhn's thesis about the nature of "paradigm shifts" in the natural sciences (see Chapter 3), Gunnemann argues that a revolutionary situation develops as more members of the community experience "anomalous evils," that is, evils that the prevailing theodicy cannot explain or justify. Anomalous evils alone, though, cannot produce revolutionary polarization.

Rather, presumptive revolutionaries must offer a new solution to the problem of experienced evil, and the affected population must accept it as providing a more plausible justification of the inevitable patterns of domination and subordination. Once such a challenge to the prevailing theodicy develops, disputes between the two theodicies over the justification of evil defy compromise.[15]

Kuhn, then, uses the metaphor of "revolution" to characterize fundamental shifts in perspective that occur periodically in the natural sciences. Gunnemann borrows Kuhn's characterization of scientific explanatory crises developing from the experience of progressively more serious empirical anomalies to represent metaphorically the fundamental moral process of political revolution. Both see the clashing explanatory perspectives, whether empirical or moral, as fundamentally incompatible.

Complex social processes, like revolution, seem aptly captured by explanatory metaphors. Most importantly, such metaphors avoid the deterministic implications of those drawn from the physical sciences. They render the experience of revolutionary crisis in terms that reflect the purposive character of human action. In the place of implacable forces, they emphasize the role of ideas and, by extension, those who create them. Rather than impersonal structures or atomized individuals, explanatory/linguistic metaphors place shared meaning, or culture, at the center of social theory. Indeed, these metaphors so closely portray the intelligible aspects of social interaction that we might think they are not metaphorical portraits at all, but actual mirrors of social reality.

Yet we should be cautious about mistaking the mask for the face here, as with other metaphors. Highlighting the role of ideas and explanation in revolution obscures the contribution of material relations that produce the explanatory crisis in the first place. We need not embrace Marxist materialism to recognize that experienced "reality" is sufficiently plastic to support alternative explanations. Those explanations backed by concentrations of power can partly create their own reality. Moreover, while rejecting the determinism of other metaphorical representations of revolution, we must not exaggerate the role of human volition and reason in constructing revolutionary outcomes.

🔥   🔥   🔥

Metaphors often lie at the heart of social theories, shaping their characteristic perspectives on the world. Sometimes an approach explicitly announces its core metaphor, as with the domino theory; at other times nuances of theoretical language subtly reveal the metaphorical influences. Even a compelling metaphorical portrait will both reveal and conceal. Uncovering the metaphorical spin of a theory provides us with clues to how it construes the social world.

POPULAR EXPLANATIONS FOR VIOLENCE AND REVOLUTION

For millennia philosophers and scholars have puzzled over the human paradox. How could a creature so close to angels behave worse than beasts? How could the same species that produced the music of Mozart and Beethoven also build death camps? Popular answers, often woven around metaphorical associations, retain a grip on our imaginations. Often these explanations contain plausible insights inflated into theories that distort our understanding. Nevertheless, since more sophisticated and complex theories often incorporate elements of these popularizations, they deserve critical review.

The Killer Ape Thesis

Human beings, like most other animal species, possess some capacity for aggressive behavior. From such an apparently innocuous observation, some explain the stubborn persistence of war and other forms of *intra*species violence (as opposed to *inter*species attacks, like that of a predator on its prey). In its baldest form the thesis states that human beings directly descend from a species of "killer apes," *Australopithecus africanus*. Consequently, "man is a predator with an instinct to kill and a genetic cultural affinity for the weapon."[16] Not only do human beings possess a genetically rooted urge to kill, but also heredity compels them to make ever more powerful instruments of destruction. In vivid images Robert Ardrey advances this viewpoint:

> Peoples may perish, nations dwindle, empires fall; one civilization may surrender its memories to another civilization's sands. But mankind as a whole, with an instinct as true as a meadow-lark's song, has never in a single instance allowed local failure to impede the progress of the weapon, its most significant cultural endowment.[17]

Though once adaptive, the killer instinct, when amplified by modern weapons, increasingly threatens human survival. To control this instinct, political communities devise severe restrictions on the expression of destructive aggression or attempt to channel aggression in ways that do not threaten orderly social relations. Obviously, these cultural defenses provide some protection, for we do not endure a universal and continuous bloodbath. Yet, just as obviously, cultural barriers and safety valves secure only limited protection from our destructive tendencies. The defenses are repeatedly breached, and we tear at each other both individually and collectively.

A veneer of scientific respectability covers the killer ape thesis. It seems consistent with both evolutionary theory and contemporary analyses of animal behavior, and gains indirect support from the very intractability of interpersonal violence in human societies. The thesis leads to rather pessimistic conclusions about the future of our species, now that our instincts have driven us to develop weapons of mass destruction. But before we despair completely, perhaps we should inspect the argument more closely in terms of its comprehensiveness, coherence, and empirical support.

The language of the killer instinct theory suggests that its roots lie partly in a hydraulic metaphor. Specifically, human beings possess a built-in compulsion that periodically bursts forth in destructive aggression.[18] This metaphorical association alerts us to the origins of the deterministic bias that violence is a biological inevitability. Many things supposedly excite destructive aggression in the human species, including the desire for sex, a quest for dominance, the need to protect territory, and so on. The thesis itself, however, directly addresses only one element of the problem of violence—the inclination toward violent expression. The answer it provides points to our destructive instincts. Therefore, even if coherent and empirically valid, it remains an incomplete explanation for the occurrence of political violence. But what should we think of its coherence and empirical validity?

Vivid language, for example, may disguise weak logic. The argument underlying the compelling images of an innate human blood lust sometimes resembles free association among words rather than coherent reasoning. Anatol Rapoport provides one example of this "freewheeling speculation by word association":

1. Killing in war is a by-product of "fighting for one's country."

2. Country means territory.

3. Many instances of territoriality are found among animals.

4. Therefore the origins of war can be traced to a deep-seated instinct for aggression in human beings.[19]

Fromm points out that the reasoning when it's not simply associative tends to be circular: "Man *is* aggressive because he *was* aggressive; and he *was* aggressive because he *is* aggressive."[20]

In addition to rather loose reasoning from archaeological and animal studies, the killer ape thesis suffers from some severe empirical problems. Human beings clearly possess a capacity for aggressive, even destructive, behavior, but saying so fails to establish the origins of this capacity or its equal presence in all people. A lack of conceptual clarity from the start impedes any determination of empirical validity. The capacity for aggression is not the same as aggression itself, and aggression, of whatever origin, is not equivalent to destructive aggression or a killer instinct. Aggression simply involves pouring our energies into our world to achieve some effect; it may or may not involve destruction.

Human beings possess other biologically conditioned responses in addition to a capacity for aggression. Fromm, for example, agrees that human beings possess an innate capacity to fight against threats to their vital interests. This capacity, however, closely resembles, especially in terms of physiological response, a similar capacity to flee from such threats. Indeed, rather than protecting us from our natural proclivity to fight, he suggests, some institutions are designed to keep us from following our natural instinct to flee from danger.[21] Military training, for example, disciplines soldiers until they become dependable fighters by curbing their instinct to flee. Cultural variables, in addition, mediate and amplify what we take to be threats to vital interests.

Even if we accept that human beings possess a capacity for destructive aggression, we explain relatively little about widespread political violence. If destructive instincts alone were the sole determining factor, or even the most important, in explaining violence, then we should find considerable uniformity in the patterns of violent acts, both across time and cross-culturally. We do not find this uniformity. In 1990, for example, the murder rate in the United States (murders per 100,000 people) was nine times greater than in Great Britain and eleven times greater than the rate in Japan.[22] Significant differences also exist over time, and evidence suggests similar variation exists among prehistoric peoples as well.[23] Perhaps most of the killer apes migrated to America over the centuries, but we suspect that factors other than presumed genetic proclivities play a more important role in explaining varied rates of violence.

Finally, the killer ape thesis suffers some rather serious shortcomings in terms of adequacy and authenticity. While some murderers may see themselves as "mad animals," most people committing acts of political violence probably possess some other self-image. The depiction of contending armies or conflicting sides in a revolution as bands of well-armed killer apes does little to render their actions intelligible. Of course, the reasons we give for our actions may simply rationalize our primitive blood lust. The killer ape thesis then emerges as a type of critical theory, stripping away the delusions with which we surround our beastly being. In this form, though, the killer ape thesis deflects attention away from the distortions arising from social and economic concentrations of power, against which we can, in principle, direct political action. Rather, biology bears the blame for our fix, a profoundly pessimistic and conservative conclusion.

The Cherry Pie Thesis

Violence, observed 1960s Black power advocate H. "Rap" Brown, "is as American as cherry pie."[24] He was responding to critics who condemned the increasing violence among American protesters in both the civil rights and the antiwar movements. Brown rejected the myth that the American political process allowed for peaceful change and that the resort to violence was therefore un-American. He emphasized, in contrast, the violent character of American political history and culture.

Violence secured American independence. Violence, as in the war with Mexico, expanded American territory. Violence preserved the union. Violence against the Native American peoples pacified the frontier. Violence against workers preserved industrial peace. Violence against Blacks and immigrant groups upheld the American status structure. Violence afflicts American interpersonal relations. Images of violence saturate popular culture.[25] Indeed, Brown may have underestimated the role of violence: It may be as American as *apple* pie.

The "cherry pie thesis" proposes a cultural explanation for different rates of violence in political communities. Some cultures sanction violence or, more accurately, destructive aggression as an appropriate or useful response to certain situations. This thesis conflicts with the killer ape hypothesis. Simply put, human beings are not *born* to kill; they *learn* to kill. The killer ape thesis falters in explaining different rates of violence across time or culture, but the cherry pie thesis predicts such differences based on cultural variation. The thesis can adopt either a deterministic or voluntaristic thrust, depending on whether it embraces the deterministic stimulus/response (S-R) model of learning or the more voluntaristic conception that the "organism" actively mediates between the stimulus and the selection of response (S-O-R).

The cherry pie thesis, like its opposite, lacks comprehensiveness and suffers from some problems of coherence. As an explanation for political violence, it addresses only the issue of the choice of violent means. The origins and politicization of discontent and the conditions that encourage people to move from violent dispositions to violent action remain unspecified. Logically, the thesis exhibits a certain tendency toward circularity. Violent acts typically serve as evidence for the existence of the violent culture that presumably produces them. Causal relations, if proposed, are probabilistic at best.

While plausible, the cherry pie thesis fails to garner unambiguous empirical support. The concept of a "culture of violence" lacks empirical validity to the extent that it treats the culture of a community as coherent and homogeneous. But if all "cultures" are complex and contradictory, then the culture of violence thesis faces the formidable task of sorting out the relative influence of contending cultural directives.

Though the cherry pie thesis may help explain different cross-cultural rates of violence, it fails to explain individual differences within the same cultural area. For this we must either turn to explanations that recognize the complex impact of contradictory cultural influences or incorporate the effects of differences in discontent, mobilization, and opportunity on the expression of destructive aggression. Indeed, we might hypothesize that people equally exposed to the same cultural directives encouraging violence might have different innate destructive proclivities (a modified killer ape thesis).

Despite these logical and empirical problems, the cherry pie thesis seems more adequate than the killer ape thesis. Rather than grounding the explanation of human violence in our bestial nature, the cherry pie thesis stresses the importance of what sets us apart from the other animals—our culture. The most significant aspects of human violence, from this perspective, are those that distinguish it from aggression in the animal kingdom. Our instincts do not drive us to violence; we choose violence because of our learning. Most of those engaged in more deliberate acts of political violence would probably appreciate this representation of their actions rather than being depicted as killer apes.

Critical theorists might embrace the cherry pie thesis because it reveals the hypocrisy of the established order and uncovers the role destructive aggression plays in maintaining the status quo. The political bias of the cherry pie thesis, then, reverses that of the killer ape thesis. The latter attracts conservatives, who embrace existing social restraints as the best, if fragile, hope to contain the human proclivity for destruction. The former, in contrast, stresses that the origins of human violence lie not in our genes but in our institutions. If the killer ape thesis encourages fatalism, the cherry pie thesis holds out at least the possibility of transformation.

The Insanity Thesis

Confronted by the brutality and horror of violence, we might conclude that only crazy people could perpetrate such atrocities. Violent acts require the suspension of normal standards of behavior and sever healthy ties of identification with our fellow human beings. As one late-nineteenth-century theorist put it: "Criminals, madmen, the offspring of madmen, alcoholics, the slime of society, deprived of all moral sense—these compose the greater part of the revolutionaries."[26]

The insanity thesis need not crudely assert that all those engaging in acts of violence are uniformly crazy; rather, it might posit a variety of more subtle variations such as the following:

- The leaders who instigate massive violence are psychopaths. Plausible examples include Hitler, Stalin, and Pol Pot.
- Movements and organizations that legitimize the expression of destructive impulses disproportionately attract people with psychopathic tendencies (see Chapter 7 for a further discussion of these two points).
- To prompt people to commit acts of violence, destructive organizations must make them at least temporarily "crazy" through such deliberate processes as the destruction of the autonomous moral identity of the perpetrator and the dehumanization of the victims.
- Wars, riots, and rebellions sweep people up into "crazy social processes," where they behave in an atypical, irrational fashion.[27]

The insanity thesis stands somewhat opposed to both the killer ape and cherry pie theses. The killer ape thesis asserts that human beings are naturally and normally destructive. The insanity thesis suggests the opposite—only abnormal human beings engage in violence. On the other hand, the cherry pie thesis rejects attributing violence to insanity, even though concurring that people are not naturally destructive. Rather, human beings learn how to behave in their social relations, and if their culture teaches that violence is appropriate and useful, they will learn this lesson. Though we might describe the culture of violence as "pathological," we cannot characterize the people who grow up within it as insane.

The insanity thesis, though undoubtedly identifying a potentially important characteristic of some participants in violent political processes, suffers from problems similar to those of the other popular theories. As an explanation for political violence, it clearly lacks comprehensiveness, addressing only the issue of why people *are disposed* to violence. The thesis gives little attention to the conditions that provoke insane outbursts of violence or to the factors that affect the extent of the violence.

The thesis, moreover, lacks empirical support. First, the concept of insanity slips and slides into various meanings. Are the perpetrators initially insane? Does the collective process that sweeps them up make them mad? Or do mad leaders simply mislead them? The key empirical issue concerns not whether psychopaths commit acts of violence, but whether all those who commit acts of violence are psychopaths, or at least temporarily insane. Any evidence of political violence as rational, end-directed, cost-efficient action falsifies the thesis. Instances of psychotic blood lust, at the individual or the collective level, undoubtedly occur during violent political struggles. The empirical puzzle requires that we sort out the relative contribution of psychosis while we avoid mistaking a partial explanation for the whole story.

The partial vision of the insanity thesis gravely compromises its adequacy. Perhaps a few people see themselves as "mad animals" in the grip of passions beyond their control. Most of the participants in systematic campaigns of political violence, however, are no more likely to describe themselves in this fashion than as killer apes. From a critical psychoanalytic perspective, however, we might see their denial as a form of delusion we expect from the psychotic. Failure of self-recognition, from this critical view, provides no basis to reject the authenticity of the thesis.

We can, however, subject the presumably critical character of the insanity thesis to critique. The attribution of acts of political violence to individual or collective madness has profoundly conservative implications. Psychoanalytic theory, though superficially critical in nature because of its claimed revelation of the hidden wellsprings of human behavior, often reflects a therapeutic bias toward encouraging "maladjusted" individuals to adapt to the existing social order. Similarly, theories that emphasize the presumed individual or collective madness of revolutionaries deny the rebels any legitimate interests or needs and conveniently excuse the established order from any responsibility for the people's anger.[28]

How then might we circumscribe the plausible domain of the insanity thesis? Perhaps insanity, or at least irrationality, plays a role in explaining the violence of socially isolated individuals or relatively spontaneous outbursts of collective destructive behavior. In contrast, organized and sustained violent activity directed toward concrete objectives undercuts the credibility of the insanity thesis and suggests that we inquire about the "sanity" of the existing social order.

The Misery Thesis

A popular explanation that blames the established order for widespread violence and revolutionary discord attributes such actions to misery and oppression. If the people seem mad, then who drove them to their madness? How can we dismiss the actions of those who finally lift a hand against their tormentors, even if they have little hope for success? Indeed, since tyranny provides no avenues for peaceful change, violence may well represent the only available recourse for those who reject their continued exploitation.

Contented citizens are unlikely to engage in political violence or advocate the revolutionary transformation of their communities. Historical accounts of revolutionary movements look to the prerevolutionary situation to identify the conditions that drove people to adopt such extreme means. Journalistic descriptions of contemporary political struggles commonly provide some depiction of the desperate economic and political conditions of the people recruited into revolutionary movements. Even the famous anthem of the working class, "The International," suggests the wretched rebel:

> Arise ye pris'ners of starvation
> Arise ye wretched of the earth
> For justice thunders condemnation
> A better world's in the birth
> No more tradition's chains shall bind us
> Arise ye slaves no more in thrall
> The earth shall rise on new foundations
> We have been naught we shall be all.

Geological metaphors underlie this thesis, as the imagery of "The International" makes explicit. The exploitation of the masses finally builds up enough force to to shake previously stable structures of domination and topple the old order. The sanity or rationality of the people living under such conditions is largely irrelevant; rather, the political tumult released by the "eruption" of the oppressed resembles the impersonal forces of nature more than the perversity of the psychopath.

As a theory of revolution, the misery thesis lacks comprehensiveness. Whatever its empirical credibility (see below), the thesis focuses on the origins of the revolutionary crisis. This emphasis ignores other important elements of the equation, especially those concerning the effectiveness of the instruments of social control and the factors affecting the success of the strategy and tactics of revolutionary challenge. The simple determinism of the formula obscures the contribution of calculation and choice to the course of a particular revolution. The misery thesis also risks falling into circular reasoning if the presence of revolutionary activity is used to demonstrate the existence of misery.

The danger of circular reasoning indicates that the thesis also suffers from some empirical shortcomings. First, we must demonstrate the existence of misery. Conditions of absolute deprivation may not directly indicate the *experience* of misery. Some people accept or, like monks who take a vow of poverty, even embrace their deprivations. Second, even if the experience of misery grows in direct proportion to increases in deprivation, growing misery alone does not seem directly linked to political violence and revolution. Deprivation may become so extreme that the wretched lack even the basic physical energy to rebel, whatever their desires. The truly miserable often do not rebel; they simply endure. Conversely, relatively privileged sectors often propel revolutionary movements. Moreover, the miserable might calculate that the risks of resistance outweigh any possible benefits. A more empirically persuasive theory must explain these differences.

The misery thesis crudely represents the motives and understanding shared by the participants in a revolution. While revolutionary movements undoubtedly contain many deprived people, this thesis provides a flattened depiction of the diversity and individuality of the participants. The image of the oppressed masses rising up to smash the established order deals in stereotypes rather than intelligibly representing the complex motives of these "masses." From a critical perspective, the misery thesis does not serve as an apology for the status quo, as do some of the previously discussed partial explanations. Yet because of its roots in geological metaphors, its consequent determinism, and its flattened portrayal of the revolutionary participants, the thesis contributes to a kind of fatalism. Revolution will come once conditions worsen sufficiently, but revolutionaries can do little to hasten the process or direct its course.

The Conspiracy Thesis

The misery thesis evokes images of inexorable pressures of exploitation increasing until they lead to a social earthquake. In dramatic contrast the conspiracy thesis blames a small group of plotters who deliberately instigate rebellion. To some extent this thesis contains a contagion metaphor, in that the conspirators "infect" an otherwise healthy and happy body politic with the bacillus of discontent. While a revolutionary earthquake represents a kind of "natural" process in that misery and oppression create tensions that eventually burst forth, conspiratorial infection "unnaturally" corrupts a stable political community.

During the civil rights struggles of the 1960s in the United States, city leaders around the country commonly blamed "outside agitators" for creating discontent among their minority population. The germ of truth in this accusation was that civil rights organizers often entered communities to develop voter registration drives or to help organize campaigns for social justice. Similarly, regimes around the world often blame the rebellions they face on the machinations of foreign enemies and their agents. Cuba's hand, for example, supposedly guided revolutionary puppets in Central America and elsewhere. Che Guevara's effort to spread the Cuban Revolution to Bolivia in 1967 lent some credence to such accusations. Importantly, however, Che failed miserably, dying in the attempt (see Chapter 9).

In perhaps the ultimate example of conspiratorial infection, the Germans sent Lenin back to Russia in a sealed railway car, in the hope that he would cause further internal discord for their wartime adversary. Lenin fulfilled their hope by using his tightly organized revolutionary party to seize control of the fluid political situation that followed upon the overthrow of the Czarist regime in early 1917. We cannot discount his role in any explanation of the outcome of the Russian Revolution.[29]

Some evidence, then, supports various versions of the conspiracy thesis, but only as a partial explanation of political violence or revolutionary change. Where applicable, conspiracy mainly addresses the issue of strategy and tactics of revolutionary transformation. Alternatively, in the area of general political turmoil, conspiracy may shape the direction of discontent, particularly whether it becomes politicized or violent. Conspiracy alone, however, seems less fruitful in explaining either the sources of discontent or the origins of the revolutionary crisis. A preexisting revolutionary crisis, for example, gave Lenin's tactical genius space to operate. In contrast, Che Guevara and his guerrilla band found themselves isolated in an environment in Bolivia that resisted their revolutionary intentions.

As a limited insight, conspiracy theory draws attention to the role of leadership, conspiratorial or otherwise, in political conflict. Deterministic theories, like the misery thesis, understate the role of leadership, while the conspiracy thesis exaggerates it. More balanced explanations, then, must delineate the possible contributions of leaders to the character and outcome of political conflict and then empirically establish the specific dimensions of their role in particular cases. The somewhat paranoid concept of "conspiracy" seems inadequate to the task of such specification (see Chapter 7 on the role of leadership).

As an interpretation, the conspiracy thesis at least puts "politics" back into political violence and revolution. If instinct or insanity causes political violence and if the structural strains generated by continuous exploitation produce revolution, then the notion of politics as the *deliberate* effort to shape social interaction slips into irrelevancy. These theories reduce human action to nearly automatic behavior (stimulus/response) or "physical" laws. Conspirators, in contrast, embody conscious purpose and cunning rationality, becoming actors in their own political dramas. Of course, though the conspirators possess autonomy, the masses they manipulate remain putty in their hands.

This biased and limited opinion of the consciousness of the people suggests that the conspiracy thesis lacks authenticity. Its apparent denial of the autonomy of most of the people engaged in political violence and revolution means that conspiracy theory makes only a modest improvement over the other explanations (killer ape, insanity, and misery theses) that reduce the masses to completely dependent variables. Ironically, some revolutionary leaders seem to consider the people incapable of recognizing their true interests, implying that they must be led, or even forced, to be free (see Chapter 8). Moreover, beleaguered regimes commonly embrace conspiracy theories as an explanation for their troubles, thus revealing another potential political bias in this approach. A thesis that blames turmoil and rebellion on agitators stirring up an otherwise satisfied population conveniently excuses the established order from any responsibility.

CONCLUSION: CLASSIFYING EXPLANATIONS FOR VIOLENCE AND REVOLUTION

Despite their flaws and limitations, these partial explanations make some contribution to our understanding of the problems of political violence and revolution. Though misleading if uncritically embraced, each provides an insight into the puzzles that confront us. Unfortunately, since they reflect different assumptions about the character of the social world and adopt different levels of analysis, we cannot facilely combine them into a comprehensive and true picture. In addition, some explanations address the origins of violence while others focus on the phenomenon of revolution.

We can, however, begin to sort out their respective contributions. We may classify these explanations with respect to the level of analysis adopted and whether they embody an essentially deterministic or voluntaristic understanding of social processes (see Table 4.1). Like any classification scheme, this one simplifies the complexity of its subject matter. The issue of determinism versus voluntarism in the social world, for example, obscures the varying degrees of restraint on human will and purpose. More sophisticated explanations attempt to indicate the relative balance between fate and will in directing the course of history. We somewhat arbitrarily divided the levels of analysis as well, and we make no attempt to resolve the debate about the primacy of any one level over the others

Despite such qualifications, Table 4.1 still provides some worthwhile comparisons of the essential thrust of the various partial explanations. The parenthetical comment under each level of analysis identifies its essential focus. In addition some explanations essentially address part of the puzzle of political violence (PV) while others focus on the puzzle of revolution (R). Most of the partial explanations we have covered possess a clear deterministic bias. The level of analysis adopted by these deterministic explanations is fairly clear, except with respect to the insan-

TABLE 4.1   CLASSIFYING EXPLANATIONS OF VIOLENCE AND REVOLUTION (I)
(R=REVOLUTION; PV=POLITICAL VIOLENCE)

LEVEL OF ANALYSIS (FOCUS)	DETERMINISTIC	VOLUNTARISTIC
Structure (stable patterns of social arrangement)	• Misery thesis (R)	
Culture (mutually accepted directives)	• Cherry pie thesis, S-R (PV)	• Cherry pie thesis, S-O-R (PV)
Group (social psychology)	• Insanity thesis, group (PV)	• Conspiracy thesis (R and PV)
Individual (psychology)	• Insanity thesis, individual (PV) • Killer ape thesis (PV)	

ity thesis. Here we have placed versions at both the individual and the group level depending on whether they emphasize individual or collective madness.

Conspiracy theory, which blames upheaval on the deliberate machinations of a small group of provocateurs, represents the only clearly voluntaristic explanation. We also place in the voluntaristic column a variant of the cherry pie thesis that emphasizes the mediating role played by the "organism" in selecting a response to various "stimuli." In this case human actors interpret cultural directives encouraging violence as opposed to responding in an automatic or uniform fashion. Two cells of the voluntaristic column remain temporarily unfilled, though we might reduce conspiracy theory to individual action.

We will return to this classification as we proceed to review more comprehensive explanations for political violence and revolution. In this way we will indicate some possible links among these partial visions and more ambitious explanatory undertakings.

NOTES

1. This discussion is based on that in Peter C. Sederberg, *Terrorist Myths: Illusion, Rhetoric, and Reality* (Englewood Cliffs, N.J.: Prentice Hall, 1989), pp. 74–76.
2. This discussion of metaphor is based on Peter C. Sederberg, *The Politics of Meaning: Power and Explanation in the Construction of Social Reality* (Tucson: University of Arizona Press, 1984), pp. 126–130.
3. George Lakoff and Mark Johnson, *Metaphors We Live By* (Chicago: University of Chicago Press, 1980), p. 5.
4. Colin Turbayne, *The Myth of Metaphor* (Columbia: University of South Carolina Press, 1970), p. 17.

5. Lakoff and Johnson, p. 5.

6. See Jerome Slater, "Dominos in Central America," *International Security*, 12 (Fall 1987): 105–134.

7. Wendell Phillips; see Chapter 2, note 49.

8. For a discussion of structural versus individualistic explanations see Alan Garfinkel, *Forms of Explanation: Rethinking the Questions in Social Theory* (New Haven, Conn.: Yale University Press, 1981), especially pp 151–155. He gives an example that might be clearer for students. Consider a class where only one student earns an "A." An individualistic question inquires why that student earned an "A," the answer being that he or she had the highest average. The structural question would be "why did exactly one person get an "A"? The answer in this case might be that the instructor decided beforehand to establish a curve where only one "A" would be given (pp. 41–45). The issue then becomes "why this distribution (that is, structure) rather than some other?"

9. One of the more systematic applications of the organic metaphor in a theory of revolution is the classic work by Crane Brinton, *The Anatomy of Revolution* (Englewood Cliffs, N.J.: Prentice-Hall, 1938, 1952; reprinted by Vintage Books).

10. Turbayne, p. 214.

11. For a discussion of the phenomenon of explanatory crisis and collapse at the individual level see Morse Peckham, "Romanticism and Behavior," in Morse Peckham, *Romanticism and Behavior* (Columbia: University of South Carolina Press, 1976), pp. 3 31. For a discussion of such crises from a broader cultural perspective see Michael Thompson, Richard Ellis, and Aaron Wildavsky, *Culture Theory* (Boulder, Colo.: Westview Press, 1990), pp. 69–81.

12. Jon P. Gunnemann, *The Moral Meaning of Revolution* (New Haven, Conn.: Yale University Press, 1979).

13. Ibid., p. 32.

14. Ibid., p. 30.

15. Ibid., p. 40.

16. Robert Ardrey, *African Genesis* (New York: Dell, 1961), p. 168. See also Ardrey, *The Territorial Imperative: A Personal Inquiry into the Animal Origins of Property and Nations* (New York: Atheneum, 1966). The more serious scientific proponent of this thesis is Konrad Lorenz, *On Aggression* (New York: Harcourt, Brace, Jovanovich, 1966).

17. Ibid., p. 324.

18. Erich Fromm, *The Anatomy of Human Destructiveness* (New York: Holt, Rinehart and Winston, 1973), pp. 17–18.

19. Anatol Rapoport, *The Origins of Violence: Approaches to the Study of Conflict* (New York: Paragon House, 1989), p. 24.

20. Fromm, pp. 18–19; emphasis in original.

21. Ibid., pp. 96–101.

22. Report of the U.S. Senate Judiciary Committee as reported in *The State* (Columbia, S.C., March 31, 1991), pp. 1ff.

23. Fromm, pp. 124–181.

24. Remark, c. 1966.

25. For a collection of essays substantiating the role of violence in the above areas of American life see Ted Robert Gurr, ed., *Violence in America*, Vol. 1: *The History of Crime* and Vol 2: *Protest, Rebellion, and Reform* (Newbury Park, Calif.: Sage Publications, 1989).

26. Scipio Sighele, quoted in James B. Rule, *Theories of Civil Violence* (Berkeley: University of California Press, 1988), p. 95.

27. The phrase is Karl Deutsch's. The idea that people can be swept into irrational behavior by a process of mass psychology is probably most clearly associated with the work of Gustave Le Bon around the turn of the twentieth century. See especially Gustave Le Bon, *The Crowd: A Study of the Popular Mind* (New York: Viking, 1960). This notion has received a more sophisticated treatment in subsequently developed theory of collective behavior. For a good assessment of this area see Rule, pp. 91–118.

28. Rule, p. 95.

29. See Edmund Wilson, *To the Finland Station: A Study in the Writing and Acting of History* (Garden City, N.Y.: Doubleday, 1953), pp. 456–474. See also Leonard Schapiro, *The Russian Revolutions of 1917: The Origins of Modern Communism* (New York: Basic Books, 1984).

5

Deprivation and Decision: Why People Rebel

Many theories attempting to explain the origins of political violence or radical political action begin at the individual level of analysis. They explain violent political movements on the basis of the motives and intentions of those who participate in them. We first evaluate relative deprivation theory, which attempts to identify what drives people to commit acts of violence, especially political violence. We then contrast deprivation theory with rational choice theory, which explores the puzzle of why rational individuals would join in radical collective action. Neither of these theories provides an exhaustive answer to its particular research question. Nevertheless, they illustrate the range of essentially psychological explanations for political violence, as well as the limits of such approaches in explaining revolutionary outcomes

MICROMOTIVES AND MACROEFFECTS

What *drives* people to political violence? What *attracts* them to radical movements? These two questions focus upon the psychology of desperate human behavior—the "push" and "pull" of political extremism. Theories addressing these questions usually begin at the individual level of analysis, rooting their explanations of violent political movements in the motives and intentions of those who comprise them. All such individualistic explanations must demonstrate how a multiplicity of individual motives and calculations combine to produce widespread social effects and collective action.

Each question evokes a different approach. When we ask what drives people to violence, we look for the compelling causes of individual and, by sometimes dubious extension, group violence. Our explanations tend toward logical empirical form and deterministic character. If we inquire what attracts people to extremist political movements, we focus more on people's intentions and purposes. Our explanations, therefore, tend toward interpretive form and voluntaristic character.

Several popular explanations concentrate on what drives people to violence. Broadly speaking, the killer ape thesis asserts that destructive behavior arises from our genetic heritage. The cherry pie thesis argues, to the contrary, that we learn violent responses from our culture. Finally, the insanity thesis, in contrast with both the others, asserts that psychological abnormalities compel our violent behavior. Only one popular explanation, the conspiracy thesis, really addresses the issue of what attracts people to extremist movements. In its view, clever and deceptive agitators provoke essentially satisfied people to engage in political violence.

None of these theories, despite some partial insights, offers a very satisfying explanation for individual or collective political violence. Social analysts, however, have developed two more sophisticated approaches over the past three decades. *Relative deprivation theory* purports to explain what drives people to commit acts of violence, especially political violence. *Rational choice theory* identifies the circumstances under which rational individuals would join in radical (often violent) collective action. Neither of these theories pretends to offer an exhaustive answer to its particular research question. People may engage in violence for reasons not in complete accord with relative deprivation theory. Similarly, people may join in radical collective action not because they are rational, in some narrow sense, but quite the reverse. Nevertheless, the two theories illustrate the range of essentially individually based explanations for political violence, as well as the limits of such approaches in explaining revolutionary outcomes.

RELATIVE DEPRIVATION AND POLITICAL VIOLENCE

Precursors and Problems

Plato and Aristotle both worried about the unsettling effects of inequality on the city-state. Throughout the subsequent centuries political philosophers often returned to the dolorous consequences of greed, inequality, envy, corruption, exploitation, and repression for the peace of the political community. Popular folk psychology also affirms that when pushed too far, repressed too long, or exploited too brazenly, people eventually rebel.

In the 1930s *frustration-aggression theory* formalized centuries of tradition and folk psychology. According to its formulators, "The occurrence of aggressive behavior always presupposes the existence of frustration and, contrariwise, the existence of frustration always leads to some form of aggression."[1] So baldly stated, the frustration-aggression hypothesis makes insupportable claims. Frustration need not directly produce aggression. Other responses, like sublimation and even resignation, may develop. Moreover, subsequent researchers distinguished between a *disposition* to aggression (that is, anger) produced by frustration and the actual occurrence of an aggressive act, which depends on other factors. Finally, aggressive responses need not involve violence or even destruction.[2]

However modified, a hydraulic metaphor clearly underlies the frustration-aggression hypothesis. Frustration builds up in a person until ultimately released through a burst of aggressive energy. Much remains *unspecified*, though, in this theory of political violence. What, for example, causes the frustration? What channels the anger produced into political directions? What directs the release of the anger in destructive forms? What affects whether violence will be widespread? Finally, how can analysts operationalize these individual psychological variables and demonstrate their relationship to collective political violence?

James C. Davies draws upon the psychological model of frustration-aggression to explain the emergence of widespread political violence. Specifically, he argues that "revolution is most likely to take place when a prolonged period of rising expectations and rising gratifications is followed by a short period of sharp reversal, during which the gap between expectations and gratifications quickly widens and becomes intolerable."[3] This sharp reversal of fortune produces feelings of *relative,* not absolute, deprivation. People may remain quite well-off, but the experience of improvement in the recent past leads them to expect continued progress for the indefinite future. Failure to meet these "rising expectations" leads to widespread frustration, laying the groundwork for rebellion.

Davies provides a vivid sketch of how generalized frustration contributes to eventual rebellion:

[The people's] state of mind, their mood, is one of high tension and rather generalized hostility, derived from the widening of the gap between what they want and what they get. They fear not just that things will no longer continue to get better but—even more crucially—that ground will be lost that they have already gained. The mood of rather generalized hostility, directed generally outward, begins to turn toward government. People so frustrated not only fight with other members of their families and their neighbors. They also jostle one another in crowds and increase their aggressiveness as pedestrians and bus passengers and drivers of cars. When events and news media and writers and speakers encourage the direction of hostility toward the government, the dispersed and mutual hostility becomes focussed on a common target. The hostility among individuals diminishes. The dissonant energy becomes a resonant, very powerful force that heads like a great tidal wave or forest fire toward the established government, which it may then engulf.[4]

Davies suggests, then, several stages in the emergence of collective violence and rebellion from the wellspring of individual anger. First, social, economic, or political reverses lead to widely shared frustration. Second, this frustration manifests itself in widespread increases in interpersonal aggression. Third, the people's anger focuses on the government, apparently because of the efforts of dissident leaders and their ideologies. Finally, interpersonal violence declines while that directed against the regime increases. Davies sees this pattern of progress followed by a sharp reversal in a number of historical instances of widespread political violence, including Dorr's rebellion in nineteenth-century Rhode Island, the American Civil War, the Russian Revolution of 1917, the accession to power of the Nazis in 1933, the Egyptian Revolution of 1952, and the protests of American Blacks in the 1960s.

About the same time Davies searched for specific historical instances of rebellion and revolution that fit his general theory, Ivo and Rosalind Feierabend undertook to apply a similar hypothesis to cross-national variations in domestic political instability. Specifically, they identified political instability as a form of aggressive behavior.

It should then result from situations of unrelieved, socially experienced frustration. Such situations may be typified as those in which levels of social expectations, aspirations, and needs are raised for many people for significant periods of time, and yet remain unmatched by equivalent levels of satisfactions. The notation:

$$\frac{\text{social want satisfaction}}{\text{social want formation}} = \text{systemic frustration}$$

indicates this relationship.[5]

Like Davies, the Feierabends specify a number of factors that intervene between systemic frustration and overt political instability. For example, constructive reform might buy off discontent, the regime might successfully repress or deflect potential dissent, or people may vent their anger in interpersonal rather than regime-targeted violence.[6] Nevertheless, they conclude that "in the relative absence of these qualifying conditions, aggressive behavior in the form of political instability is predicted to be the consequence of systemic frustration."[7]

Rather than identify a few historical instances that appear to fit their hypothesis, the Feierabends collected aggregate data on socioeconomic conditions, political repressiveness, and political instability in 84 countries between the years 1948 and 1962.[8] Their analysis of these data demonstrates some support for their basic hypothesis. They find that levels of socioeconomic frustration, as measured by aggregate indicators such as gross national product, caloric intake per capita, physicians and telephones per capita, relate positively with levels of political instability and turmoil. Significantly, they also find that highly coercive and relatively permissive states suffered from less civil strife than moderately repressive states. Highly coercive states successfully squelch all resistance, whereas permissive states allow for peaceful protest and evolutionary reform. The states in the midrange presumably fail to undertake either successful reform or repression.

Both of these early efforts suffer from common shortcomings.[9] Frustration-aggression theory is ultimately a hypothesis about individual states of mind and consequent behavior. Yet both Davies and the Feierabends characterize and measure frustration in terms of aggregate quantitative indicators of prosperity. Their approach obscures the problem of how individual frustrations add up to collective political violence. Rather, they assume, depending on the performance of the aggregate indicators, that politicized frustration is widespread throughout the community. Their studies, moreover, raise the question whether the aggregate indicators provide valid measures of the individual psychological states powerful enough to drive people to violence. Finally, neither approach successfully sorts out the relative contribution of intervening factors like leadership or the regime's coercive capability in determining the actual levels of political violence.

Despite these shortcomings, the underlying notions that frustrated people commit acts of violence and that some form of relative deprivation causes their frustration retain both intuitive appeal and some scientific credibility. Soon after these initial efforts an ambitious study incorporating these assumptions attempted a more comprehensive and systematic statement of the transformation of relative deprivation into widespread political violence.

Relative Deprivation and the Emergence of Violent Political Behavior

Why Men Rebel culminated decades of investigation into the psychological origins of violence and lay the groundwork for 20 years of subsequent research and debate. When published in 1970, Ted Robert Gurr's book received considerable acclaim: "outstanding as a piece of scholarly communication," "the most important book published on social violence in a good number of years," "the best effort to date" in the psychological analysis of political violence.[10] The book deserved such praise for its effort to specify the concept of relative deprivation and relate it in a systematic fashion to other variables that affect the transformation of frustration and anger into actual political violence.

Despite its complexity, the psychology of frustration-aggression remains at the heart of Gurr's explanatory model. "[T]he primary source of the human capacity for violence," he writes, "appears to be the frustration-aggression mechanism. Frustration does not necessarily lead to violence, and violence for some men may be motivated by expectations of gain. The anger induced by frustration, however, is a motivating force that disposes men to aggression, irrespective of its instrumentalities. If frustrations are sufficiently prolonged or sharply felt, aggression is quite likely."[11]

Frustration arises mainly from the experience of relative deprivation. Relative deprivation (or RD) develops from the "actors' perception of discrepancy between their value expectations and their value capabilities. Value expectations are the goods and conditions of life to which people think they are rightfully entitled. Value capabilities are the goods and conditions they think they are capable of getting and keeping."[12]

Several characteristics of this idea deserve emphasis. First, despite Gurr's tendency to speak in terms of collectivities, relative deprivation remains rooted in *individual* perceptions and self-assessments. Two different people in the same objective situation, therefore, may experience different feelings of RD. Second, since RD depends on self-assessment rather than objective conditions, absolutely deprived people may experience relatively low levels of RD *if* they fatalistically expect little from their lives. Alternatively, people who appear well-off may still experience intense RD if their expectations significantly exceed their capabilities.

Third, both expectations and capabilities represent an aggregate assessment on the part of individuals. We all possess many different values and aspirations. Gurr suggests a threefold classification: *welfare values*, including primarily economic well-being and self-fulfillment; *power values*, especially the ability to influence others (participation) while avoiding the unwanted intervention of others (security); and *interpersonal values*, such as status, communality (a sense of belonging), and ideational coherence (a sense that our lives have meaning).[13] Value capabilities also arise from multiple sources, and a capability that helps meet one value expectation may be irrelevant to another. Economic wealth, for example, may confer neither power nor status in some political communities. Consequently, people with the same assessment of their capabilities but with different value expectations experience different feelings of RD.

If we can compare aggregated value expectations with an assessment of aggregate capabilities, then feelings of RD emerge in three basic ways. First, in *decremental deprivation,* expectations remain constant, but capabilities decline over time.[14] In traditional societies, for example, stability depends on the avoidance of calamity. In ancient China the emperor could lose the right to rule (the Mandate of Heaven) if the people were afflicted by widespread disorder, floods, or famine. Expectations remained unchanged, but social and natural disasters eroded people's perceived capabilities. Similarly, political elites experience decremental deprivation when a movement of reform or revolution challenges their established power and privilege.

Second, a gap develops when capabilities remain constant, but expectations increase rapidly because people either acquire new values or expect to improve their position with respect to old ones. Gurr labels this pattern *aspirational deprivation,* and it sometimes carries the more popular label of the revolution of rising expectations.[15] In contrast with the rebellions that periodically break out in traditional societies, this form of deprivation underlies more contemporary notions of revolution. People experiencing aspirational deprivation do not simply want to return to the old ways of doing things; rather, they desire something new in their lives. Thus, new aspirations for liberty and equality inflamed minds in the French Revolution and its successors. Alternatively, simple exposure to the resource position of others contributes to feelings of RD as seen, for example, in the cliche of "keeping up with the Joneses."

Finally, expectations may increase at the same time that capabilities decline, producing *progressive deprivation.*[16] This type of RD subsumes Davies' hypothesis that political disturbances follow when a sharp reversal of fortune interrupts a long period of economic and social progress. Presumably, prior experience shapes expectations for the future. If people's lot in life has continually improved, they expect this improvement to continue, and thus any reversal doubly disappoints them.

Gurr, then, shares with his predecessors a basic psychological theory. Increasing RD leads to rising frustration that intensifies anger resulting in increased violence, including political violence, *other things being equal.* He attempts to identify just what these *other things* might be and how they affect his primary dependent variable, the *magnitude of political violence (MPV).* To do so, he develops a complex causal model that greatly complicates the psychological individualism of frustration-aggression theory.

Gurr's basic explanatory model (Figure 5.1) posits a direct and positive relationship among three primary variables. Increases in the *potential for collective violence (PCV)* contribute to increased *potential for political violence (PPV).* Increased *PPV* leads to growth in the *magnitude of political violence (MPV)* in a society. *PCV* refers to the "disposition among members of a collectivity to take violent action against others" and represents a special case of the aggressive disposition supposedly generated by the experience of frustration.[17] *PPV,* in turn, constitutes a particular form of *PCV,* in that the disposition to violence focuses on specifically political objects, such as regime personnel or institutions.[18] The grow-

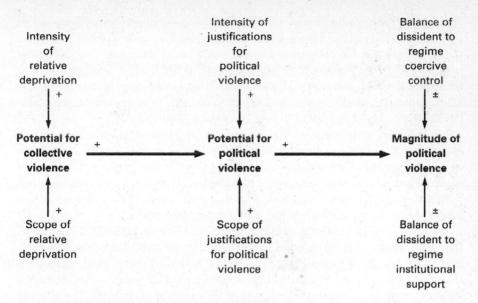

Figure 5.1 The primary and secondary determinants of the magnitude of political violence.

Source: Based on Ted Robert Gurr, *Why Men Rebel,* p. 320. Copyright © 1970 by Princeton University Press. Reproduced by permission of Princeton University Press.

ing disposition to engage in political violence leads to increased acts of political violence *assuming* nothing blocks the inclination to commit violence.

PCV, which powers the primary causal sequence, depends upon the intensity and scope of relative deprivation in a community. A number of general factors affect the intensity of RD:

> The greater the discrepancy we see between our expectations and capabilities, the greater our discontent. The greater the importance we attach to the values affected, and the fewer the other satisfactions we have to fall back upon, the greater is our discontent. If we have many alternative ways of trying to satisfy our expectations, we are likely to defer discontent over our failures; if we have few alternatives we are likely to feel the anger of desperation. A fifth determinant is time: if our anger is denied expression in the short run it intensifies before it subsides.[19]

The scope of RD refers to the degree to which feelings of relative deprivation extend throughout a particular community.

The factors affecting the intensity and scope of relative deprivation, however, add little to our understanding of how the anger presumably generated by these forms of frustration is transformed into a disposition to collective violence. We could relabel the primary variable, PCV, as the *level of collective anger* that then contributes to the *potential for collective violence.*

The unclear conceptualization of the primary independent variable carries over to the composition of the secondary factors affecting the intervening primary variable, *PPV*. According to the model, *PPV* increases directly with increases in *PCV*, but the intensity and scope of the justifications for political violence in a particular culture also affect it. Gurr identifies two broad classes of justification for political violence, normative and utilitarian. People "are likely to hold norms about the extent to which and the conditions under which violence generally, and political violence specifically, is proper. They are also likely to have expectations about the relative utility of violence as a means for value attainment."[20]

A political culture need not equally include both types of justification. People might accept political violence as morally justifiable but useless to attempt or morally unjustifiable but nonetheless effective. Gurr, however, argues that the two forms of justification tend to reinforce one another. If people believe that violence works, they will convince themselves of its rightfulness. If they believe in the moral justifications for violence, they often expect it to work.

Gurr also considers the interrelationships between the intensity and scope of the justifications. "The *intensity* of justifications for political violence is a function first of the *range of circumstances* to which actual or threatened violence is thought to be an appropriate response, and second of the *relative desirability* of violence, in normative and utilitarian terms, vis-à-vis other responses. The *scope* of justifications refers to the prevalence of supporting attitudes and beliefs among members of a collectivity."[21] He suggests that some of the same cultural factors tend to increase both intensity and scope of the justifications for violence.

When Gurr identifies these specific factors, however, it becomes clear that two distinct processes influence the potential for political violence.[22] The first process involves the factors and experiences encouraging or justifying the *violent expression* of anger. The second process, in contrast, concentrates on the factors and experiences that *politicize* this anger. For example, the factors associated with the disposition to violent expression of frustration include (1) extrapunitiveness of socialization, that is, the extent to which we learn it is proper to act aggressively toward others; (2) the density of aggressive symbols in the media; and (3) the historical magnitude of violence in a community. Other hypothesized factors, in contrast, focus on the politicization of the anger and include (1) the success of symbolic appeals (like ideology) in identifying political targets as the source of RD; (2) past regime effectiveness in relieving RD; and (3) differential regime response to RD. Some factors, though, might affect both the disposition to violence and politicization of anger, including (1) regime legitimacy (negatively related to *PPV*); (2) past success in relieving RD with political violence; and (3) other groups' success in relieving RD through recourse to violence. These dual contributors, however, should not obscure the two distinct puzzles in people's response to feelings of relative deprivation. Why are they disposed to express their anger politically? And why are they disposed to express their anger violently?

A more coherent presentation of the primary and secondary determinants of the magnitude of political violence, therefore, would relabel the primary independent variable as the *level of collective anger* and would thus turn the *potential for collective violence* into an intervening variable contributing to, but not the only determinant of, the *potential for political violence* (see Figure 5.2). Similarly, the secondary variables would analytically distinguish between those cultural factors

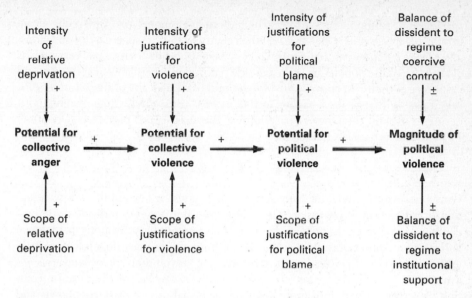

Figure 5.2 The primary and secondary determinants of the magnitude of political violence, revised.

Source: Based on Ted Robert Gurr, *Why Men Rebel*. Copyright © 1970 by Princeton University Press. Reproduced by permission of Princeton University Press.

that contribute to a disposition toward the violent expression of anger and those that encourage the deprived to blame political actors and institutions (rather than fate or themselves) for their failures.

In either version, the primary dependent variable remains the same—the *magnitude of political violence (MPV)* afflicting a particular community. When *PPV* increases, so will MPV, other things being equal.[23] In this final case, the "other things" that affect *MPV* refer to the balance of power between the regime and the dissidents. Gurr distinguishes between two basic sources of power, coercive control and institutional support. The two mutually reinforce one another, as an expansion or contraction in one area contributes to a similar movement in the other (see Chapter 9).

The relative balance of power between regime and dissidents affects the *MPV* in a curvilinear fashion (a relationship signified by "±" in Figures 5.1 and 5.2). This means, simply, that *MPV* will be greatest when the regime and the dissidents control approximately equal power resources. Equality produces the condition of "internal war." As the regime's power increases over that of the dissidents, the actual levels of violence decline. Ultimately, a sufficiently powerful regime represses even intensely frustrated people. Alternatively, if the dissidents' power position exceeds that of the regime, they overthrow the regime with more limited violence. If the relative power of the dissidents increases sufficiently, they could seize power in a bloodless coup d'état.

As with the other secondary variables, Gurr specifies a variety of more concrete factors that contribute to the power of the regime and the dissidents. With respect to institutional support these include such elements as (1) the scope of the effectively integrated population, (2) the quality of their respective organizations, and (3) the value stocks they control. Coercive support depends on factors such as (1) the size of the population that each side has under surveillance, (2) the size and resources of their respective armed forces, and (3) the loyalty of these forces. *PPV* might also influence these factors in that as *PPV* rises, the dissidents may find it easier to expand their power base among the disaffected populace. Declining *PPV*, in contrast, assists the regime.

❧   ❧   ❧

Gurr's behavioral model for "why people rebel" goes far beyond the simple equation of frustration = aggression. He draws upon not only the individualistic psychology of frustration-aggression theory, but also cultural justifications for violence and structural bases of relative power. By defining the primary dependent variable as the *magnitude of political violence* rather than "revolution," he expands the relevant domain of his theory far beyond the relatively few historical cases of revolution, however defined. Revolution becomes a special case of dissident activity and may include different patterns of political violence from terrorism to internal war.

His theory also covers forms of political violence that possess no revolutionary intent such as establishment violence, like vigilantism or regime terrorism, and military coups. It subsumes reactionary rebellions, ethnic violence, and secessionist civil war, as well as revolutionary civil war. Given these ambitions, *Why Men Rebel* has stimulated a generation of scholarship and criticism.

Evaluating the Theory That Covers Everything

Gurr formulates a theory that purports to account for the emergence of almost all forms of internal political violence by drawing on multiple levels of analysis. In part, the very grandeur of the effort contributes to the problems that emerge when we apply the criteria established in Chapter 3.[24]

Comprehensiveness *Why Men Rebel* provides a comprehensive reply to all the major explanatory puzzles of political violence, drawing upon and integrating several of the partial theories previously discussed. Relative deprivation improves upon the misery thesis as an explanation for the origins of discontent. Rather than rooting discontent in supposedly objective conditions, relative deprivation emphasizes the importance of how people evaluate these conditions in determining their level of frustration. By elaborating the culture of violence thesis, the model suggests how the frustration bred of relative deprivation is politicized and transformed into a disposition to commit political violence. Finally, through structural analysis of the respective power positions of the dissidents and the regime, the model defines the conditions that maximize the magnitude of political violence in a polity. The comprehensiveness and complexity of Gurr's argument gives it persuasive weight.

Comprehensiveness, however, comes with a price. By striving to address all the relevant issues, Gurr achieves comprehensiveness at the cost of simplicity. The partial explanations at least possess the virtue of clarity. Gurr's model, however, contains at least seven secondary variables (or more, if we separate normative and utilitarian justifications) and dozens of third-level variables hypothesized to affect the secondary ones, and even more suggested indicators of these third-level variables. Relations of such complexity inevitably raise issues of empirical validation and falsification. Complex explanations also beg the question of determining which part of the theory does the work. If it can be demonstrated, for example, that structural factors explain most of the variation in the *magnitude of political violence*, then the rest of the model becomes largely superfluous. Consequently, by striving for comprehensiveness, Gurr compounds problems of both coherence and empirical validity (see below).

Coherence   Precision of argument sometimes gives a false sense of coherence. Gurr carefully specifies the relations among his primary and secondary variables and the third-level factors that presumably affect them. Specificity, however, does not by itself produce coherence. Gurr's model, as we noted earlier, conflates explanations for how the frustration generated by relative deprivation is politicized and channeled toward violent expression. This confusion obscures the possibility forthe nonviolent expression of politicized frustration or the nonpolitical expression of violence-prone frustration.

A more fundamental problem of coherence arises from the different levels of analysis in the model. The frustration bred by relative deprivation supposedly drives the whole explanatory sequence. But frustration-aggression theory works essentially at the individual psychological level. The primary variables (*PCV*, *PPV*, and *MPV*), however, focus on the behavior of large groups. Barbara Salert observes, "There is no reason to suppose that individual behavior is in any way similar to group behavior or, saying it another way, that the behavior of people in large groups will follow the same laws as the behavior of isolated individuals."[25] Gurr's model tends to ignore the difficulty of moving from the individual to the group level of analysis by simply referring to group deprivation rather than convincingly accounting for its origins in diverse individual feelings of deprivation. People interacting in large groups may well develop expectations and capabilities distinct from those they possess as individuals.

Finally, Gurr states all the hypothesized linkages among the variables in tendency terms. He distinguishes among strong, moderate, and weak relations, but such distinctions fail to alter the essentially weak coherence of the model when taken as a whole. While a single relation established as "strong and direct" may give us considerable confidence, a series of similarly defined, interconnected relations that hypothetically combine to determine variation of the primary dependent variable is far less compelling. The many intervening variables that mediate between increases in feelings of relative deprivation and the consequent increases in political violence undermine the persuasiveness of this basic causal sequence.

Empirical Support[26] An explanation of political violence based on relative deprivation must demonstrate three critical empirical linkages:

> First, that the participants shared a single standard of justice, appropriateness, equity, minimal acceptability, or the like.
>
> Second, that the timing of the action ensued from the experience of the violation of this standard, as registered in evidence from the individual participants.
>
> Third, that the actual participants in the violent action were distinguished from nonparticipants in the same population by their sense of violation of the key standard.[27]

Why Men Rebel amasses an impressive array of evidence for its basic propositions, from the anecdotal to the systematic, from the testimony of other theorists to historical cases. However, fundamental conceptual ambiguities, indirect measures of presumed states of mind, and a failure to establish the specific contribution of relative deprivation to the choice of violent participation all limit the empirical support for the theory.

The concept of relative deprivation represents an improvement over the idea that absolute deprivation alone leads to violence, but it suffers from its own ambiguities. RD involves individual self-assessment of the extent to which value expectations exceed value capabilities. This definition raises questions about how people define their expectations and capabilities, whether these individual states of mind can be combined into a "collective" variable, and how we can measure states of mind in the first place.

Value expectations, as we noted earlier, presumably reflect people's beliefs about *rightful* entitlements. But expectations may also reflect what they *aspire* to gain, regardless of entitlement, or alternatively, what they see as the *best possible* position under the circumstances. Some may aspire to a position greater than the one to which they feel "rightfully entitled," though the human capacity for rationalization probably ties the two quite closely. Alternatively, others might lower their expectations to the best possible position under the circumstances, even if it falls short of their beliefs about entitlement.

The definition of expectations, then, affects the size of the gap between them and perceived capabilities. Not only must our measures of relative deprivation distinguish among the different types of expectation, but also we must determine which measure is appropriate in a particular case. Even if we draw such distinctions, we cannot facilely combine feelings of relative deprivation that arise from the violation of different standards of expectation.

Resolution of these issues, of course, presumes we can effectively measure and compare states of mind. Although sophisticated psychological techniques for measuring individual attitudes have been devised, *Why Men Rebel* depends largely on indirect, aggregate measures of presumed expectations and perceived capabilities. While indicators such as the economic improvement of reference groups, the exposure to new ways of life, or the effects of ideologies may all affect expectations, measures of such indicators do not directly assess states of mind. Similarly, economic downturns, inflation rates, and other indicators of economic and social distress seem plausibly connected to how people assess their capabilities, but again, they do not directly measure such assessments.[28]

In addition to the conceptual and measurement problems associated with the notion of relative deprivation, the complexity of the explanatory model challenges us to determine the relative contribution of such feelings to the outcome of political violence. It seems unlikely that all the secondary variables, for example, will prove equally significant in any particular case of political violence. Recent empirical studies, for example, suggest that factors such as perceptions of regime legitimacy, as well as calculations concerning the utility of violence, may account for far more of the variation in MPV than relative deprivation itself.[29] Such considerations, of course, correspond to normative and utilitarian justifications for violence and thus are incorporated in the overall model. Nevertheless, these findings diminish the direct significance of relative deprivation as an explanation for political violence.

The capacity to incorporate criticisms directed at one part of the model in another both gives the appearance of strength and constitutes a potential empirical weakness. The model appears to accommodate almost every conceivable influence on the emergence of political violence. This accommodation, however, not only raises the issue of the relative contribution of different variables discussed above, but also undermines our ability to falsify the argument as a whole. Every time we question a particular variable, another part of the model seems to accommodate the challenging evidence, thus "saving" the overall argument. Such complexity probably ensures that the model will endure, even as it undercuts its empirical clarity. Complexity also complicates judgments of the adequacy and authenticity of this approach.

Adequacy   *Why Men Rebel* represents one of the more fully realized examples of logical empirical political behavioralism. First impressions suggest an essentially deterministic understanding of the problem of political violence. Most, if not all, social theories, however, at least implicitly incorporate some representation of human intentionality, and this representation emerges not so much in the basic model outlined in Figure 5.1, but in the particular factors that contribute to variation in the secondary variables.

The adequacy of the deprivation model, therefore, depends in part upon what we choose to emphasize. Not only does the explanation for MPV proceed at the individual, group, cultural, and structural levels, but also each level incorporates both deterministic and voluntaristic elements. The basic psychological theory of frustration-aggression, in at least its simple stimulus/response form, certainly reflects a kind of psychological determinism rooted in a hydraulic metaphor of aggressive human behavior. Yet *relative* deprivation assumes that frustration arises when conscious actors contrast their expectations with their perceived capabilities.

Similarly, some of the variables that politicize anger or channel it toward violent expression, such as the historical or personal experience with violence or the "density" of violent symbols in the media, suggest a form of cultural determinism. In contrast, other normative and utilitarian considerations appear to involve deliberation over the costs and benefits of adopting a particular course of action.

Finally, the structural variables stressing the balance of power between regime and dissidents could mechanistically determine *MPV* (at a given level of *PPV*). In contrast, we might see regimes and dissidents, both as individuals and as groups, calculating the odds they face, weighing their alternatives, and selecting the best strategy for improving their power position and accomplishing their goals.

Authenticity   A curious political reception greeted the publication of *Why Men Rebel*. In 1970 the United States was experiencing considerable internal discord. The civil rights struggles of the previous decade had culminated in an ugly series of urban riots, and protests against American involvement in Vietnam had grown progressively larger and, at the fringes, more violent. Into this disturbed political environment came a book purporting to dissect in a dispassionate fashion the underlying determinants of political violence. Some condemned the work as a handbook for repression, whereas others denounced it as a cookbook for revolutionaries.[30] Faced with ideological critics from both political extremes, we might conclude that the book strikes an appropriate balance, relatively detached from the demands of any particular political agenda. Critics of its authenticity, however, warn against the illusion of detachment and suggest that the behavioral approach adopted by Gurr is particularly susceptible to manipulation by the political establishment.

An authentic social explanation must not only adequately represent the self-understandings of the actors but also uncover the ways in which these self-understandings may be distorted by the centers of power and interest in a particular society. Any social theory that reduces political action to a deterministic causal sequence at the very least denies the ability of human beings to be the actors in their own political dramas. Moreover, such an approach tends to reflect a strong orientation toward manipulation and control, a bias easily subordinated to the powerful in a community. A theory that purports to explain political violence in such a deterministic fashion represents a special failure in this regard, because it completely misses the potentially liberating effects of such rebellions, as the oppressed cast off the debilitating illusions that enslaved them.

By highlighting the deterministic elements of relative deprivation theory, we could easily caricature *Why Men Rebel* as a clear example of social scientism's dead hand. But such attacks neglect the subtle and multileveled argument made in the book. The complexity of the model, while complicating many issues of empirical support, allows the model as a whole to slip away from charges of inauthenticity just as it does concerning accusations of inadequacy. Some elements in the model, whether in the formation of value expectations, justifications for violence, or strategic interaction with the regime, can incorporate many of the concerns for authentic social explanation. For example, the critical goal of stripping away the false consciousness of potential dissidents appears similar to the success of symbolic appeals in identifying political targets as a source of relative deprivation. Though such maneuvers might not satisfy a committed critical theorist, they illustrate again how the intricacy of Gurr's argument frustrates simple rejection.

Generalizability   Finally, *Why Men Rebel* appears to claim a nearly universal applicability for both its general model delineating the determinants of *MPV* in a society and for the special significance of relative deprivation as the motivating force behind the recourse to violence. These two claims appear somewhat incompatible.

If, as Gurr suggests, frustration generated by relative deprivation is "the primary source of the human capacity for violence,"[31] then variations in RD should account for most of the variation in *MPV*. However, subsequent empirical studies, as we noted earlier, question whether variations in relative deprivation account for the occurrence of violent protest. Rule concludes that "successful social-psychological explanations of participation [in violence] will hold only within specific historical, cultural, and political contexts."[32] Of course, the remainder of Gurr's model incorporates such historical, cultural, and political variations. The limited generalizability of RD as an explanation for variations in political violence, then, fails to undermine the general applicability of the model as a whole. The very complexity and comprehensiveness of the model deny central significance to any one variable as the primary source of political violence.

The model, though, fails to specify the relations among its many variables in any precise fashion. The exact combination of these many potential variables carrying the explanatory burden probably varies from case to case. Once we identify the respective significance of all the possible factors—psychological, cultural, and structural—in a particular setting, we produce an explanation with a domain probably restricted to this single case. The model, if not specified in this way, retains general applicability not as a theory of political violence but as an inventory of potential factors, the levels of analysis at which they function, and some possible relations among them.

        🔥   🔥   🔥

Gurr's model of the determinants of political violence attracts so much criticism in part because of its ambitions, comprehensiveness, and clarity of presentation. Nonetheless, its many parts exist in uneasy relation with one another. In particular, we noted the difficulty in relating different levels of analysis and in reconciling the deterministic and voluntaristic elements. We chose to emphasize this work as the most significant example of a "push" theory of political extremism; essentially, relative deprivation produces frustration that *drives* people to violence. Not all the components of the model, though, embody this deterministic thrust. Some variables suggest that calculation plays a role in determining whether people choose to act on their presumably violent dispositions. The notion that some calculus "pulls" people into violent political action independent of their feelings of frustration suggests a more self-consciously interpretive approach to human action. Human action, from this point of view, becomes intelligible only insofar as we incorporate people's intentions, not merely their drives, into our explanations. The most systematic version of this approach in contemporary social theory is the rational actor model.

RATIONAL ACTORS AND THE CHOICE OF RADICAL POLITICAL ACTION

Why Get Involved?

Deprivation theory, in its various forms, suggests that the right combination of outrages eventually drives people to extreme action, other things, of course, being equal. Despite some problems, this causal sequence possesses a certain intuitive appeal and garners some empirical support. Certainly we can point to numerous instances where the perpetrators of violent acts seem to fit this model.

But what of more considered participation in a campaign of radical action directed at achieving some reasonably well articulated political objective? Does any explanation built on the assumptions of frustration-aggression theory convincingly explain why people engage in sustained radical political activity? Why should people participate in a revolutionary movement, whatever their level of alienation or deprivation? Indeed, why should people participate in political organizations resisting revolutionary movements, even if they identify with the status quo? Deprivation theory, with its suggestion that participants are driven by their passions, their instincts, or their individual and collective insanity, fails to deal seriously with such issues.

Suppose, to begin with, that we are angry with our government. The relative deprivation model suggests that as our anger increases, the likelihood that we will attack the regime with violence also rises. This simple "to be or not to be violent" oversimplifies the actual options available to us. We could respond in one of four nonconformist ways: through ritualism or withdrawal, through reformism or open rebellion.[33] *Ritualism* involves outward conformity with the expectations of the established order, even though the actor no longer believes in or identifies with it. *Withdrawal* involves cutting most, if not all, contact with the regime and the order it upholds. *Reform* involves activities, possibly at the margins of official tolerance but essentially nonviolent, aimed at modifying the established order in moderate fashion to alleviate some of the sources of frustration. *Rebellion* entails rejection of the establishment and commitment to the struggle to replace it with a radically restructured order. Only this last alternative involves extreme, though not necessarily violent, means.

We may compare these four alternatives on the basis of two different dimensions: *active versus passive* and *moderate versus extreme* response (see Figure 5.3). Deprivation theory, with its roots in a hydraulic metaphor, suggests that the more extreme the pressure the more extreme the response. But the extremely frustrated confront a choice between two extreme responses: rebellion and withdrawal (somewhat analogous to the point that fight and flight are closely related instinctual reactions to a threat). Similarly, the moderately frustrated actor must choose between two moderate responses, ritualism and reform. The opposite of rebellion for the frustrated is neither reform nor withdrawal, but ritualistic conformity. Why would we choose the more active responses, even if extremity of response varies directly with the degree of our frustration?

Those who look to psychological drives for an answer propose that other

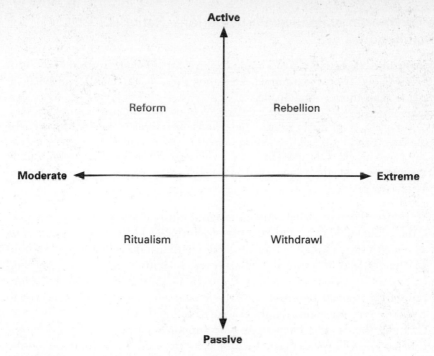

Figure 5.3 Alternative antiregime response.

aspects of personality, in addition to the level of frustration, affect whether we act directly against the source of our anger, through reform or rebellion, or manage our frustration in more passive ways, ritualism or withdrawal.[34] This approach preserves the essential explanatory thrust that people are pushed into violence by psychological forces largely beyond their control. Gurr, in his model, looks to cultural or historical factors rather than the individual level for an answer. Nevertheless, the basic tendency remains relatively deterministic. However, some of the factors he suggests that transform anger into a disposition to act violently seem to reflect a more deliberate choice.

The choice to become actively involved, whether through reform or rebellion, moves people into the public arena. Ritualism and withdrawal, in contrast, usually confine them to their private lives and individual pursuits (unless a person withdraws as part of a group, like those radicals in the 1960s who chose to go off and form a commune rather than engage in direct attacks against the establishment they despised). If we assume that the participants in collective action, whether reform or rebellion, are rational, then their calculation of the benefits of such action must have "pulled" them into the public arena. This conclusion stands in dramatic contrast with the argument that people's frustrations push them into desperate resistance. Unfortunately, the assumptions of rationality generate a serious paradox in the area of radical collective action.[35] To understand the origins and character of this paradox, we must first specify what we mean by a "rational actor."

The Oxymoron of Political Participation—Rational Revolutionaries

Rational choice theory starts with a relatively restricted characterization of rationality. Michael Taylor, for example, identifies three major features of what he terms the "thin" theory of rationality:

> (i) Rationality is relative to given attitudes and beliefs (which are each assumed to be consistent) and the agent's actions are *instrumental* in achieving or advancing the given aims in light of the given beliefs. (ii) The agent is assumed to be egoistic. (iii) In applications of thin theory, the range of incentives assumed to affect the agent is limited.[36]

To pursue the maximizing action, the agent must possess perfect information about the comparable costs and benefits of alternative choices. The second feature eliminates the possibility of an altruistic identification with a larger community that might lead to "rational" self-sacrifice. Incentives include only the end being sought, the resources the actors devote to the pursuit of the end, and a limited range of reasonably concrete "selective incentives" (incentives that accrue to the specific actors, depending on the course of action they choose).[37]

Consider the position of two potential supporters of a revolutionary movement: Maria and Che. Both desire the objective pursued by the movement—the New Revolutionary Order (NRO)—a public good. The NRO is a public good because it cannot be selectively allocated; that is, when the new order comes, all members of the society will equally enjoy its presumed benefits. In short, if anyone in a community receives a public good, everyone must receive it. (This requirement is commonly termed "nonexcludability.") Obviously, the NRO is not the only public good around. Any benefit provided to members of a community simply because they are members, regardless of their contribution, has the status of a public good. Examples include national defense or clean air laws. We also assume that the achievement of the NRO demands a mass movement where each individual's participation makes only a negligible contribution to the eventual outcome.

Maria and Che face quite a dilemma. Although they value the public good, their individual contributions make no noticeable difference on the probability of its achievement. In addition, they will share in the NRO regardless of whether or not they participate. On the other hand, their participation in a revolution involves some significant, selective costs. At the very least, they absorb considerable direct and opportunity costs (the other goals they sacrifice by devoting their limited resources to the movement). At the worst, they could get killed. As rational egoists, Maria and Che will sit out the revolution, even though they strongly value its promised *public* good. They will rationally choose to become *free riders* on other people's sacrifices.

If we assume that all the potential participants in the revolutionary movement make a similar calculation, then a tragic result follows. Everyone free rides and the revolutionary movement fails. Even more tragic, since we assumed that our actors possess perfect information, they *know* the universal decision to free ride will produce this result. Yet they still defect from the movement, if any one person's decision to participate is a one-time event, made without any interaction with other potential revolutionaries. It might seem that all would recognize that their "enlightened" self-interest dictates that they should elect to participate. But if Maria thinks that the others will choose to participate, the greater incentive she has to defect and free ride. Moreover, since everyone thinks the same way, if she elects to participate, she knows that the others will free ride at her expense, making her a sucker. This would produce the worst possible outcome for her: a failed revolution plus her payment of all the selective costs of participation.

Mark Lichbach refers to this situation as the "rebel's dilemma." Rational potential rebels will choose to free ride, but if they do, the potential revolution will never become an actual revolution, since no potential revolutionary would ever rationally choose to become an actual revolutionary.[38] Moreover, the passivity of the rational rebels is independent of both their feelings of relative deprivation and the value, however high, they place on the NRO. Even though frustrated and profoundly alienated, rational actors will still not rebel. They will select the more passive and private responses to alienation: ritualism or withdrawal.

Contrary to the expectations of rational choice theory, however, we can point to revolutions and attempted revolutions. Such evidence, however, does not appear to falsify the rational choice theory for several interrelated reasons. First, though some people join radical movements and engage in desperate resistance, their actions are the exception, not the rule. The powerful temptation to free ride goes a long way in explaining the relative infrequency of extremist movements and the generally unrepresentative status of their members, despite the plight of many people and the repressiveness of many regimes.

Second, when revolutionary movements gain adherents, perhaps the participants are not, for the most part, rational. They may not make the calculations required to weigh costs and benefits. They could ignore probable costs, exaggerate benefits, and join simply because they do not understand the consequences of their actions. Or participants may join out of pure altruism, willing to sacrifice for the group, regardless of their personal costs. Third, participants may join for a variety of selective payoffs in addition to the public good of the NRO. The right incentives can induce actors rational in the thin sense to participate in a revolutionary movement. The next section explores some of these possible solutions to the paradox of participation.

Why the Rational Rebel: Possible Solutions to the Paradox of Nonparticipation

The temptation to free ride subverts not only the revolutionary quest but also numerous other forms of collective action for public goods. Yet such collective action, from voluntary associations for political reform to revolutionary cells working for radical transformation, undoubtedly occurs. Rather than characterizing such activities as non- or irrational, rational action theorists suggest possible reasons why maximizing egoists might participate in collective action. Many of these hypothesized solutions apply to the rebel's dilemma.[39] We term a number of these proposals *first-order solutions,* because they address specific elements of the decision calculus of nonparticipation. We then survey a number of *second-order solutions*—those means through which potential dissidents try to generate the first-order solutions. Finally, we consider what happens if we alter the third assumption of "thin rationality" by including a "thicker" range of rational incentives.

First-Order Solutions[40]   Maria and Che desire the public good, the NRO, but their participation makes only a negligible contribution to its accomplishment. Yet if they participate, they absorb some selective direct and opportunity costs. Finally, regardless of their participation, they will share in the public good in the event of a rebel victory. Under these conditions, they rationally defect and choose to become free riders. If everyone faces the same calculus, then no one joins the revolution, guaranteeing its failure. We can suggest at least six first-order solutions to this quandary: (1) Increase the probability that their individual contribution makes a difference; (2) lower the selective costs of participation; (3) develop selective rewards for participation; (4) develop selective punishments for nonparticipation; (5) learn to cooperate; and (6) create a bandwagon effect.

1. Increase the Probability of Making a Difference.   The participation of the average "spear carrier" in a revolution makes no difference. The calculus of free riding changes, however, if a potential participant rationally believes that his or her participation significantly increases the probability of success. Consider the clearest case where Che's contribution guarantees success but his nonparticipation ensures failure for the revolutionary movement. If the value he attaches to the public good of the NRO exceeds the calculated costs of his participation, it would be rational for him to participate. If, however, the personal costs of participation exceed the benefits of the NRO, he still will not participate, even if his nonparticipation dooms the revolution. For example, if Che dies, then the value of the NRO may become somewhat moot to him (unless he seeks a narcissistic immortality through the revolution—see Chapter 7).

Che's decision becomes more difficult if he values his contribution more realistically; that is, his participation increases the *probability* of success, but does not guarantee it. Under these conditions Che must calculate a more ambiguous comparison of definite costs and possible benefits. Moreover, this solution begs the question as to who can rationally conclude that his or her participation makes a difference. Under conditions of perfect information only leaders of mass movements could rationally reach such a conclusion. So this solution still leaves us without any rational followers.

2. Lower the Costs of Participation   Unfortunately for advocates of radical action, potential participants can more easily calculate the personal costs of participation than the benefits of the NRO. Lower costs, then, would make it easier to mobilize rational individuals for action. This solution by itself, however, cannot motivate rational rebellion. Even if Maria estimates her costs at zero—an unlikely outcome—she will remain indifferent between participation and nonparticipation, since she still rationally believes (in contrast to Che) that her participation makes no difference to the achievement of the NRO. Lower costs do make a difference for Che, since his participation increases the probability of success. The lower his costs, the more likely that the increased probability of achieving the NRO with his participation will move him to action.

3. Develop Selective Rewards for Participation   Even with lower personal costs, Maria will still elect to free ride. However, if her participation is rewarded with some specific, concrete benefits of greater value than her personal costs, then she will participate. Such selective rewards can be immediate or long-term. With respect to the former, Maria could receive payment for participation. If she were unemployed and impoverished, for example, even the promise of food and shelter might suffice to induce her to join the movement. The possibility of plunder might also outweigh the potential costs of participation. In the longer term, a successful revolution promises not only the public good of the NRO, but also selective rewards of payoffs, position, and prestige allocated only to those who loyally supported the movement. Potential participants, however, will probably discount vague promises of future benefits more heavily than the immediate provision of concrete rewards. In addition, the lure of significant postrevolutionary selective incentives will be greatest for the leaders, rather than the followers, of a revolutionary movement.

4. Develop Selective Punishments for Nonparticipation   In the original calculation costs accrued only to participation in the movement. If nonparticipation entailed greater selective punishments than the expected costs associated with participation, then Maria and Che would reverse their decision to free ride. Dissident movements, then, try to establish a variety of selective punishments, as well as rewards, to maintain the integrity of revolutionary collective action. Like rewards, punishments may be immediate or promised over the longer term; that is, those who defect from the movement may escape immediate punishment, but they will not escape retribution in the NRO.

5. Learn to Cooperate   Maria and Che tragically recognize that if all potential revolutionaries act as rational egoists and decide to free ride, then the revolution will fail. Even knowing this, faced with a single decision point, they still choose to defect out of the fear of becoming suckers if they participate while everyone else defects. Another solution to the rebel's dilemma, then, develops if all potential revolutionaries learn to cooperate in pursuit of the public good of the NRO. If the value of the public good exceeds that of the costs of participation, cooperation can produce a more desirable outcome than mutual defection.

Potential revolutionaries may learn to cooperate if the "game" of deciding whether or not to participate is played repeatedly. Suppose Maria bases her decision to join on what Che does. If Che defects and free rides, Maria does the same, but if Che, for some reason, chooses to participate, then Maria also participates. Cooperation is thus rewarded and free riding punished. Perhaps if they play this game repeatedly, both will learn to cooperate. If enough potential revolutionaries learn to cooperate, they can avoid the tragic outcome of individual rationality producing the collective irrationality of failed revolution. The process of learning to cooperate in this manner is commonly described as the tit-for-tat strategy.

   6. Create a Bandwagon Effect.[41] Confronted with a powerful repressive regime, rational potential revolutionaries will keep their preferences hidden and choose the option of ritualistic conformity or, at the extreme, withdrawal. The fear of being played for a sucker deters any expression of dissent, no matter how attractive they find the public good of the new revolutionary order. Yet revolutionary entrepreneurs, assuming they can draw upon the solutions discussed above, may at some point start a bandwagon effect. The few who start resisting might succeed in altering the calculations of success and failure of a few more potential participants, improving the capacity of the revolutionary movement, thereby attracting some more participants, and so on. Increased numbers of participants also lower the probable costs of participation, as average followers may more realistically hope to escape regime retribution.

   At some point the process may begin to accelerate and affect not only the calculations of those who value the NRO but even previous supporters of the regime. Revolutionary movements typically attract a considerable number of opportunists to their ranks as they appear to approach victory. These opportunists attach little or no value to the public good of the NRO; rather, they see selective chances for advancement or fear being punished for standing aside from the triumphant revolutionary movement. Contrary to the expectations of relative deprivation theory, rational choice theory, then, suggests frustration is not even *necessary*, much less sufficient, for revolutionary participation. The rapid collapse of apparently strong regimes in China, Vietnam, and Iran suggests something like the bandwagon effect. On the other side, dissident organizations, since they lack complete information, may overestimate the likelihood of initiating a bandwagon through their tactics. Overoptimistic estimations of success contribute to revolutionary adventurism (see Chapter 9).

   The creation of coordinating organizations and the manipulation of concrete rewards and punishments to guarantee collective action characterize the operations of the regime. Those attempting to overthrow a regime must, therefore, become like a regime themselves—a counter-state. Once a counter-state exists, rational egoists may join in a revolutionary movement. But these solutions to the free rider problem simply push the question back a step. How does a revolutionary movement start and then acquire the capability to implement these solutions?

Second-Order Solutions   Revolutionary movements engage in risky political action, the costs of which would seem to discourage most potential revolutionaries from participation. First-order solutions to the free rider problem, unfortunately, beg the question of initiation. How does a movement start in such unpromising circumstances, and once started, how does it generate the capability to implement the first-order solutions? Rational choice theorists propose several significant "second-order" solutions to the problems of initiation and implementation: (1) generate revolutionary entrepreneurs, (2) mobilize patrons, (3) manipulate incomplete information, and (4) organize.

1. Generate Revolutionary Entrepreneurs.[42] Incipient revolutionary movements possess only limited capacity to manipulate selective incentives (either rewards or punishments) to overcome the free rider problem. Also, in the early stages of rebellion, those electing to participate are probably most vulnerable to regime counteraction, raising the personal costs of dissent. This leaves one major path of rational participation — for those who believe that their contribution significantly improves the chances of achieving the public good of the NRO. (For simplicity of argument we assume that such beliefs in personal efficacy are justified.) If participation in the movement is rational for these leaders, then entrepreneurial talent may be self-generating. Revolutionary entrepreneurs are probably risk takers; that is, they choose to risk much to gain much. Moreover, if they emerge, they facilitate other second-order solutions.

2. Mobilize Patrons.[43] Revolutionary movements in their early stages lack the resources to compete with the regime. Revolutionary entrepreneurs reduce this disparity by mobilizing patrons who provide the resources needed to improve the movement's ability to manipulate selective incentives. Entrepreneurs seek these patrons both inside and outside their political community. Internal patrons include elements of the domestic elites who defect from the regime. Revolutionary entrepreneurs often find external patrons among the foreign states that compete with the existing regime. Nonstate actors, like some of the extremist groups involved in transnational terrorism, may also provide limited support to the emerging revolutionary movement within a country. The support of such patrons ranges from ideological encouragement and strategic advice to the provision of concrete material and organizational resources.

The patronage solution, unfortunately, doesn't solve the free rider problem so much as push it back yet another step. Where do potential patrons come from? Why should they choose to support the movement rather than free riding on it? One possible answer points to how efficacious the potential patrons feel. They choose to support the revolutionary movement when they believe their participation makes a significant difference in at least discomforting their rivals and perhaps improving the chances for a NRO.

3. Manipulate Incomplete Information.[44] Rational choice theorists initially assume that actors possess complete information and accurately calculate the costs and benefits of their participation as well as the probability of their making a difference. While such a simplifying assumption clarifies the logic of their arguments, it lacks empirical credibility. People, including potential dissidents, possess imperfect information. Consequently, even though they may attempt a rational calculation of costs, benefits, and probabilities, they often make mistakes.

Revolutionary leaders commonly interpret the world for their followers, usually with the assistance of a reasonably well developed ideology (see Chapters 7 and 8). These interpretations both provide emotional support and guide political action. Since potential dissidents lack complete information, leaders can inflate the value of the public good, the chances of success, and the likely allocation of selective incentives, while understating the costs of revolutionary resistance. We need not assume that revolutionary leaders deliberately deceive their potential followers, though both dissidents and regimes, in the context of incomplete information, have an incentive to exaggerate their respective positions. Since leaders as well as followers lack complete information, they may delude themselves along with their audience. This solution, however, probably declines in efficacy over time, as reality eventually corrects inflated claims and expectations.

4. Organize.[45] Revolutionary entrepreneurs also attempt to overcome the free rider problem through organization. Potential revolutionaries might join an organization that promises to encourage cooperation and monitor defections. If the organization can reduce the likelihood of defection, then rational rebels might move toward their preferred option of cooperation. Moreover, an ongoing organization increases the ability of the revolutionary movement to allocate selective rewards and punishments. Successful revolutionary movements, especially those coming to power after a long period of revolutionary civil war, often seem in retrospect to have "outorganized" the regime.

An organization, once started, may be self-perpetuating. The problem comes in initiating it. Why should a rational actor invest the effort in starting an organization which itself is a public good? Why not free ride on the work of others until the organization offers attractive selective incentives? Of course, if everyone made such a calculation, the organization would never exist. Revolutionary entrepreneurs have an incentive to start an organization because they believe in their personal efficacy. Organizations mean little without followers, however, so the entrepreneur may try to create the revolutionary organization by building on the basis of preexisting social ties and community organizations that have already created some bonds of trust among potential followers and possess some resources for selective incentives.[46] This possibility, of course, begs the question of how these preexisting ties and organizations arose in the first place.

Our discussion of rational participation in revolutionary political action starts with a restricted, or "thin," depiction of rationality. A final set of solutions to the paradox of revolutionary participation argues that such a narrow definition guts the concept of rationality. If we broaden or "thicken" our idea of what it means to be rational, then the rebel's dilemma becomes far less severe.

"Thickening" Rational Incentives[47]

Critics of rational choice theory often reject the narrow concept of rationality, particularly with respect to the nature of rational incentives. Rather than simply being oriented to outcomes, rational people may attach value to the *process* of political participation, in this case revolution. Rather than simply being self-interested egoists, rational people may possess a strong sense of *other-regardingness*. Adopting these two assumptions about rationality reduces the free rider problem.

1. Process Incentives Thin rationality assumes that people engage in collective action entirely on the basis of some calculation concerning its consequences in terms of both a public good and selective rewards or punishments. They attach no inherent value to the means used to achieve these ends. Process incentives, in contrast, recognize that value also adheres to political involvement per se, independent of whether the participants accomplish the formal goals of political action.

Political philosophers from the time of the ancient Greeks have argued that political participation serves as a method of self-actualization. More recently Erich Fromm has suggested that human beings have an "existential need" to be a cause, to have an effect.[48] Moreover, people may gain entertainment value from political participation, ranging from adventure and excitement to the opportunity to express deep-seated compulsions. Revolutions, during some phase, often involve a relaxation of normal social controls which results in both celebration and innovation. Finally, people may even see the costs and sacrifices associated with participation as marks of value. Some people seek suffering and even martyrdom, contrary to what we normally assume about the value we attach to our own lives and pleasures. The personal joy a person receives from revolutionary action may outweigh the selective costs and thereby make participation in the movement rational.

2. Other-regarding Incentives   Some potential revolutionaries may join not from any egoistic interest but because of their identification with others or with the abstract goals of the struggle. In the first case feelings of altruism motivate people to pursue a public good from which they may stand to gain little or nothing as long they believe that the people with whom they identify gain. Those motivated by the abstract goals of the revolution, like fairness or justice, may see their participation as a way of demonstrating their attachment to a treasured norm.

Finally, other-regardingness may emerge as a form of group consciousness. Participation becomes an expression of solidarity with a larger group of which the individual feels a part, whether this be a class, kinship group, religious community, or, for that matter, a combat squad. In this case participants seek not merely their individual self-interest but the interests of the collective.

Incorporating a "thicker" concept of rational motivation multiplies the incentives for participation in a revolutionary movement. Potential revolutionaries choose to participate not simply on the basis of concrete individual incentives, which are often scarce, but because of appeals to their sense of self-actualization or identification with a wider good. Of course, such an approach begs the question of how such feelings and orientations emerge in the first place. In addition, the assumption that such values *could* serve as rational incentives does not empirically demonstrate that they *do* in fact serve such a role, at least with very many people.

          ◊   ◊   ◊

Rational revolutionary collective action develops if the calculus of potential rebels can be altered to counteract the temptation to free ride. The solutions proposed, alone or in combination, neither occur automatically nor guarantee success even when implemented. The regime, too, can manipulate the incentives motivating action, and it usually controls far more resources than the potential dissidents.

Consequently, in a head-to-head competition for the compliance of rational actors, even those attracted to the promise of an NRO, the regime should triumph. Revolutions happen infrequently, and those that succeed often face severely compromised regimes (see Chapter 9).

Rational choice theories of radical political action provide a major alternative to the deprived actor theories most fully exemplified by *Why Men Rebel*. Rather than trying to explain outbreaks of violence by isolating the frustrations that presumably drive people to desperate acts, the rational actor approach views individual participation in radical political activity as a product of a conscious calculation of costs and benefits. By recognizing the particular relevance of the free rider problem to the question of revolutionary participation, this approach offers an important explanation for the relative *infrequency* of such events. The major solutions to the free rider problem indicate potentially fruitful areas for research into those movements that have emerged and succeeded in achieving an NRO. Yet, despite its fruitfulness, this systematic approach to why and, more importantly, *when* people rebel encounters some significant challenges to its claimed explanatory status.

Critique of the Theory of the Rational Revolutionary

The theory of the rational revolutionary starts with a few simple assumptions about a value-maximizing egoist. On the basis of these assumptions the theory specifies the conditions under which such an individual would participate in radical collective action, possibly including violence. It concludes that most potential revolutionaries will forgo revolutionary action unless induced to participate by selective rewards and punishments. Incipient revolutionary movements find it difficult to assemble the resources required for such selective incentives; consequently, most potential revolutions remain unrealized. The theory, therefore, appears most successful at explaining why radical collective action *fails* to occur. Indeed, the rational choice approach may suggest some interesting research problems rather than actually explain revolutionary action.

Comprehensiveness   The rational choice approach to the problem of political violence and revolution directly addresses only one puzzle—the conditions under which potential dissidents would elect to express their dissent in radical collective action. Although it does not directly address the selection of specifically violent means, we could infer that rational revolutionaries choose collective violence only when they calculate that this instrument will produce the maximum net payoff. Rational choice theory cannot explain the origins of discontent or why potential revolutionaries hold their particular values, preferences, and beliefs. Nor does it explain the origins of a revolutionary crisis. These elements, rather, are simply assumed at the outset of the chain of reasoning that leads to predictions about the likely course of collective action.

Coherence   A high degree of logical coherence characterizes the rational choice approach to the problem of collective action. Predictions and implications follow deductively from the initial assumptions. The internal relations specified in a rational choice argument, then, take on a lawlike structure. Questions, however, arise concerning the empirical relevance of this internally elegant logic.

Empirical Support   All empirical theories make symplifying assumptions. Some critics, however, argue that the assumptions of rational choice theory lack empirical credibility.[49] Terry Moe, for example, observes that "rational models are problematical not because they contain theoretical terms, but because they are 'theories' about decision makers and decision-making contexts that do not exist."[50] The assumption of perfect and complete information defies the experience of all decision makers. The restriction of intentions to those reflecting only the narrow, egoistic self-interest of the participants represents an impoverished characterization of human psychology. The consequent limitation of incentives to only those fulfilling divisible, materialistic interests further constricts the empirical validity of the rational "model of man."[51]

Finally, the assumption that people respond only to narrow, divisible interests presumes that they can distinguish such interests from other potential motives. To lump together those who fight to defend only their own lives, those who fight to defend the lives of their close family, those who fight to defend the life of a stranger, and those who fight to defend an abstract idea as all reflecting "self-interest" is vacuous. On the other hand, "to try to partition these interests into either-or categories of self-interest versus altruism . . . distracts attention from a reality that has much more nuance."[52]

These limiting assumptions make it easier to explain inaction than the emergence of collective action, especially action of an obviously dramatic and costly sort like revolutionary movements. Even if widespread participation in such movements is the exception rather than the norm, we need to account for these exceptions. The available evidence fails to support the notion that mass participation in revolutionary action results simply from the manipulation of divisible, materialistic incentives.[53]

Rational action theory responds in several ways to the accusation of empirical implausibility. One response restricts the theory's applicability to certain clearly specified contexts where the restrictive assumptions appear more plausible (see below, the discussion of generalizability). But as Rule argues, this treads very close to "a claim that the theory can be expected to hold only in those conditions where it does in fact hold. If every collective action in which participants were not clearly motivated by selective incentives or some other form of divisible gratification to their narrow self-interests were relegated to the 'noneconomic' category, [the] theory would be circular."[54]

A second strategy of dealing with problems of empirical credibility broadens the characterization of rationality and adopts more realistic assumptions about the context of decision making. We used these tactics in trying to solve the dilemma of the rational rebel, for example, by assuming imperfect information or allowing for process and other-regarding incentives. While such moves suggest solutions to the problem of collective radical action, they do so at the expense of the elegance of the initial model and again threaten to turn it into a tautology.[55] Once having relaxed the original assumptions in this fashion, it seems that any manifestation of radical collective action could be deemed rational either because the actors were operating under conditions of imperfect information and/or they were responding to these "softer" incentives. In this case no conceivable outcome could falsify the theory.

A third response preserves the initial restrictive assumptions, regardless of their empirical implausibility, arguing that the value of rational choice as a scientific theory rests on its ability to predict aggregate social behavior.[56] As long as the predicted consequences come to pass, whether the actual decision-making process resembles the hypothesized one is irrelevant. This stress on predictive accuracy at the expense of explanatory credibility, however, reflects a distorted notion of science. As Alexander Rosenberg argues, predictive success is one means of certifying knowledge claims in science, not a substitute for them.[57] In any case, the unqualified theory of radical action predicts inaction, not action. To account for revolutionary activity, the theory either declares its inapplicability (conceding that the participants are not rational in the "thin" sense) or modifies its original assumptions (thereby treading close to circularity and nonfalsifiability).

Adequacy   Rational choice theory represents a formalized interpretive approach to the social world in that it renders individual and collective action intelligible by representing the states of mind of participants. This representation, or typification, incorporates assumptions about the values, beliefs, and intentions presumably held by the actors. Few of us would reject being characterized as "rational." Even the depiction of the self-serving, egoistic maximizer probably represents an adequate characterization of human actors in many situations, especially those appropriately defined in relatively narrow economic terms.

On the other hand, even though the rational rebel represents a formalized interpretive typification, something remains troubling about its adequacy. We already noted its impoverished depiction of the range of human intentionality, as well as its limited characterization of what counts as rational. The inability to account for the origin of beliefs and preferences—they are simply assumed— detaches political actors from their history and their current social context, both of which might explain the origins of beliefs and values. From one perspective, rational choice theory reflects a view of revolutionaries, potential and actual, as thinking, calculating, purposive creatures, striving to maximize the returns from their actions. From another point of view, the political actors are merely counting machines, programmed in a particular way by their preferences and production functions, whose actions result in a determined fashion from the assumed calculus of maximization. Of course, to point out that rational choice fails to account for preferences begs the question as to what theory of preferences we should use. (The approaches discussed in Chapter 6 attempt to address this issue.)

Authenticity   The restricted definition of rationality ultimately raises questions about the authenticity of the rational choice approach. The assumption that human beings act only in accord with materialistic self-interest may mistake a cultural peculiarity for a universal trait of human nature. The rational maximizer, from this critical view, is a creature, a creation, of the capitalist system.[58] The model might best describe behavior assumed to characterize the capitalist marketplace; indeed, this behavior essentially supports the existence of the capitalist system. To ensure the replication of the capitalist order, a critic might argue, the culture turns people into egoistic maximizers.

Rational choice theory, from a critical perspective, incorporates a model of human psychology that often serves the interests of the centers of power in contemporary Western society. The conclusion that revolutionary collective action is unlikely or impossible for such "rational actors" suits the capitalist establishment just fine. Rational choice theorists, by incorporating the egoistic capitalist consumer into their model, may unwittingly support the status quo. Such egoists cannot even imagine, much less implement, radical alternatives to the existing order.

The proponents of the rational actor approach answer such criticisms by arguing that their use of the approach assumes selfishness but does not recommend it.[59] Rather, the restrictive assumptions in their model of motivation help to provide useful insights into the character of collective dissent. These assumptions guide empirical inquiry; they do not prescribe how we should live our lives.

Generalizability   The foregoing evaluation of the limits of the rational actor approach suggests its limited domain. By addressing only the decision to participate, this approach leaves many interesting questions unanswered. Moreover, the restrictive assumptions of the rational actor model appear more plausible in some decision contexts than others. Lichbach, for example, suggests that the rational actor theory of collective action (whether radical or not) works best

1. with unitary rather than collective actors (collective actors like "regime" or "party" raise problems of social choice within the actor);
2. in concrete situations with well-defined actors, actions, and outcomes (mitigating the information problem);
3. with actors with fixed goals and stable evaluations of outcome (ideological flux undermines the definition of a rational preference order);
4. when outcomes are determined from actions (uncertainty as to outcome undermines definition of rational choice);
5. when differences among choices are moderate (rational choice doesn't matter when differences in outcomes are small; if differences are too large, then intense preference can override rational action); and
6. in situations with high penalties for nonrational action (low penalties undermine the importance of being rational).[60]

With respect to understanding revolutionary collective action, Lichbach observes, these approaches "work best when least needed and most poorly in the most interesting situations."[61] The decision context of a military conspiracy underlying a coup d'état probably fits the theory better than that of the mass movements propelling the great revolutions.

Despite the questions we raised, the rational actor approach to understanding revolutionary collective action remains particularly valuable. To suggest that it lacks credibility as an empirical theory hardly distinguishes it from many of the alternative approaches available to us, including deprivation theory. It proves its value in at least three significant areas:[62]

First, we may use it as a "theorylike" instrument for forecasting certain behaviors. We have seen that the initial model predicts that little or no revolutionary collective action will occur. It suggests that deprivation alone, relative or absolute, will fail to push people to rebel; revolutionary action requires something more. This argument coincides with deficiencies noted in the deprivation model of *Why Men Rebel* by suggesting reasons for the nonoccurrence of rebellion.

Second, our identification of some of the possible solutions to the rebel's dilemma posed by this approach suggests numerous areas of inquiry into revolutionary organization, strategy, and tactics that might prove empirically fruitful, even though such modifications risk turning the rational actor approach into a tautology.

Third, though the rational actor approach may have faults as an explanatory theory, it proves useful as a set of normative principles, offering guidance as to the choice of means, not ends (which are assumed).[63] These principles provide a basis, albeit a limited one, for critiquing the actions of revolutionaries.

CONCLUSION: WHY PEOPLE REBEL

Why, then, do people rebel? First impressions suggest that relative deprivation and rational choice offer radically different answers to this question. Relative deprivation focuses on the frustration that ultimately drives people to violent acts. Rational choice, in contrast, portrays people as carefully calculating the costs and benefits of alternative actions and selecting the one that offers the greatest promise of reward. If radical political action promises the maximum personal payoff, then rational actors will select this path. In terms of our classification of explanations, both relative deprivation and rational choice focus upon the individual, but the former is essentially deterministic, while the latter is voluntaristic (see Table 5.1).

More fully developed explanatory models of both deprived and rational actors go far beyond the simple psychological equations of their initial assumptions. In *Why Men Rebel*, Gurr elaborates a multilevel explanation for the emergence of political violence that includes elements at both the cultural and structural levels. Similarly, various solutions to the rebel's dilemma suggest the possible significance of leadership, collective identities (emerging from cultural experience), and the role of organization (indicating the impact of structure on individual calculations). Table 5.1 illustrates the multilevel nature of these more complex spin-offs from both relative deprivation and rational choice approaches. Note that rational choice theory focuses on radical collective action, not violence per se. The fully developed model of *Why Men Rebel* even softens its deterministic thrust by suggesting some role for calculation on the part of the dissidents as they form their ideas about the justifications for violence and its likelihood for success.

Table 5.1   CLASSIFYING EXPLANATIONS OF VIOLENCE AND REVOLUTION (II)
(R=REVOLUTION; PV=POLITICAL VIOLENCE; RCA=RADICAL COLLECTIVE
ACTION)

LEVEL OF ANALYSIS (FOCUS)	DETERMINISTIC	VOLUNTARISTIC
Structure (stable patterns of social arrangement)	• *Regime/dissident balance of power (PV)* [a] • Misery thesis (R)	• *Organization effects (RCA)*
Culture (mutually accepted directives)	• *Justifications for PV (PV)* • Cherry pie thesis, S-R (PV)	• *Other-regardingness (RCA* • Cherry pie thesis, S-O-R (PV)
Group (social psychology)	• Insanity thesis, group (PV)	• *Revolutionary entrepreneurs (RCA)* • Conspiracy thesis (R and PV)
Individual (psychology)	• *Relative deprivation (PV)* • Insanity thesis, individual (PV) • Killer ape thesis (PV)	• *The rational revolutionary (RCA)*

[a] New material in italics.

These two individualistic approaches complement each other to some degree, while their more elaborate manifestations suggest a common deficiency. Deprived and rational actor approaches complement each other in at least two ways. First, each suggests possible solutions for the explanatory shortcomings of the other. Deprived actor explanations, with their roots in frustration-aggression theory, indicate why people might be driven to extreme action even though a rational calculus suggests that a passive response is the maximizing course of action. Alternatively, rational actor explanations offer reasons why even severe relative deprivation may not suffice to drive people to rebellion, as well as indicating the circumstances under which even relatively satisfied people might rebel (see the bandwagon effect).

A second way in which the two approaches complement each other involves the inability of rational choice theory to specify just how people acquire their goals or value hierarchies. Rather, the theory assumes goals and focuses upon choosing the maximizing means to achieve them. Relative deprivation theory, in contrast, focuses specifically on people's value expectations, explores their formation, investigates their different composition, and hypothesizes how they are frustrated. We identified several critical conceptual and empirical deficiencies in relative deprivation theory. Nevertheless, the difference in emphasis suggests that the two approaches work in combination in specific empirical contexts to provide a fuller depiction of radical motivation. Perhaps essentially nonrational deprived actors initiate a sequence that makes revolutionary participation rational for others

Finally, we noted that both the complex model of *Why Men Rebel* and a number of the possible solutions to the rebel's dilemma move away from the individual level of analysis to include other factors. While we may explain particular violent actions or the decision to join a radical political movement by focusing on the individual, the phenomenon of revolutionary transformation involves something more. The unit of analysis becomes a whole society, and something seems lost by the attempt to reduce societal transformation to the atomistic interactions among individuals. Rather than cobbling group, cultural, and structural elements onto an individualistic approach, we might simply begin with a macroperspective. Group, cultural, and structural theories may better explain the origins of cultural crisis, structural strain, and revolutionary transformation. We turn to some of these alternative approaches in the next chapter.

NOTES

1. John Dollard et al., *Frustration and Aggression* (New Haven, Conn.: Yale University Press, 1939), p. 1.
2. For a discussion of subsequent research see Ted Robert Gurr, *Why Men Rebel* (Princeton, N.J.: Princeton University Press, 1970), pp. 33–37. For more comprehensive critiques of the literature on aggression in general and the frustration-aggression hypothesis in particular, see Knud S. Larson, *Aggression: Myths and Models* (Chicago: Nelson-Hall, 1976) and K. E. Moyer, *Violence and Aggression* (New York: Paragon House, 1987).
3. James Chowning Davies, "The J-Curve of Rising and Declining Satisfactions as a Cause of Revolution and Rebellion," in Hugh Davis Graham and Ted Robert Gurr, eds., *Violence in America: Historical and Comparative Perspectives,* Revised Edition (Beverly Hills, Calif.: Sage Publications, 1979), p. 415. Davies' "J curve" thesis originally appeared in 1962.
4. Ibid.
5. Ivo K. Feierabend and Rosalind L. Feierabend, "Systemic Conditions of Political Aggression: An Application of Frustration-Aggression Theory," in Ivo K. Feierabend et al., eds., *Anger, Violence, and Politics: Theories and Research* (Englewood Cliffs, N.J.: Prentice Hall, 1972), p. 137.
6. Ibid.
7. Ibid.
8. Ibid., pp. 137–181.
9. See James B. Rule, *Theories of Civil Violence* (Berkeley: University of California Press, 1988), pp. 208–210, for more extensive development of a methodological critique of both approaches.
10. These are the opinions of Chalmers Johnson, Lewis A. Coser, and James C. Davies, respectively, quoted on the back of the paperback edition of Gurr, *Why Men Rebel.*

11. Gurr, *Why Men Rebel*, pp. 36–37.
12. Ibid., p. 24.
13. Ibid., pp. 25–26.
14. Ibid., pp. 46–50.
15. Ibid., pp. 50–52.
16. Ibid., pp. 52–56.
17. Ibid., p. 29.
18. Ibid., p. 155.
19. Ibid., p. 59.
20. Ibid., p. 156.
21. Ibid., p. 157. Emphasis in the original.
22. For a complete discussion of all the secondary determinants of *PPV* see ibid., pp. 160–231.
23. Ibid., pp. 232–316.
24. For a good critique of Gurr's model see Barbara Salert, *Revolutions and Revolutionaries: Four Theories* (New York: Elsevier, 1976), pp. 50–74. See also Rule, pp. 200–223.
25. Salert, p. 64.
26. Gurr provides a systematic attempt to assess the empirical validity of a version of his model in Ted Robert Gurr and Mark Irving Lichbach, "Forecasting Internal Conflict: A Competitive Evaluation of Empirical Theories," *Comparative Political Studies*, 19 (April 1986): 3–38.
27. Rule, p. 223.
28. See ibid., pp. 207–212 for more extended discussion of these problems.
29. See especially Edward N. Muller, *Aggressive Political Participation* (Princeton, N.J.: Princeton University Press, 1979); see also Muller, "The Psychology of Political Protest and Violence," in Ted Robert Gurr, ed., *The Handbook of Political Conflict* (New York: The Free Press, 1980).
30. See, for example, Edward Hunter's review in the *Annals of the American Academy of Political and Social Science* (September 1970): 248, for a conservative reaction.
31. Gurr, p. 36.
32. Rule, p. 222.
33. This is based on David C. Schwartz, *Political Alienation and Political Behavior* (Chicago: Aldine Publishing Company, 1973), especially pp. 25–28. Schwartz bases his categories on the classic article by Robert K. Merton, "Social Structure and Anomie," reprinted in his *Social Theory and Social Structure* (Glencoe, Ill.: The Free Press, 1957).
34. See Schwartz for an elaboration of some hypothesized personality variables.
35. The problem of why rational actors would engage in any form of collective action is commonly associated with the classic work of Mancur Olson, Jr., *The Logic of Collective Action: Public Good and the Theory of Games*, Revised Edition (New York: Schocken Books, 1971).
36. Michael Taylor, "Rationality and Revolutionary Collective Action," in Michael Taylor, ed., *Rationality and Revolution.* (New York: Cambridge University Press, 1988), p. 66.
37. Ibid., p. 66.
38. Mark Irving Lichbach, *The Rebel's Dilemma: Collective Action and Collective Dissent* (forthcoming).
39. Lichbach provides an impressive and thorough summary and evaluation of two dozen possible solutions and their many variations in ibid.

40. The first four of these first-order solutions are discussed in Salert, pp. 33–41. Lichbach also discusses them in more systematic detail.
41. Lichbach. See also Timur Kuran, "Sparks and Prairie Fires: A Theory of Unanticipated Political Revolution," *Public Choice*, 61 (April 1989): 41–74.
42. Lichbach.
43. Ibid.
44. Ibid.
45. Ibid.
46. Ibid.
47. Ibid.; see also Taylor, pp. 885–890.
48. Erich Fromm, *The Anatomy of Human Destructiveness* (New York: Holt, Rinehart and Winston, 1973), pp. 235–237.
49. For a general critique of the scientific status of rational choice theory see Terry Moe, "On the Scientific Status of Rational Models," *American Journal of Political Science*, 23 (February 1979): 215–243.
50. Ibid., p. 226.
51. The phrase is Donald Moon's in his essay "The Logic of Political Inquiry: A Synthesis of Opposed Perspectives," in Fred I. Greenstein and Nelson W. Polsby, eds., *Handbook of Political Science*, Vol. 1 (Reading, Mass.: Addison-Wesley, 1975).
52. Rule, p. 39.
53. See Salert, pp. 43–47.
54. Rule, p. 37.
55. Taylor, p. 66.
56. For a development of this argument see Alexander Rosenberg, *Philosophy of Social Science* (Boulder, Colo.: Westview Press, 1988), pp. 75–77.
57. Ibid., p. 79.
58. See John E. Roemer, "Neoclassicism, Marxism, and Collective Action," *Journal of Economic Issues,* 12 (March): 147–161.
59. Lichbach, personal communication.
60. Mark Irving Lichbach, *The Cooperation Dilemma: Social Order and Collective Action* (forthcoming).
61. Ibid.
62. Based on Moe, pp. 236–238.
63. See also Jon Elster, "Introduction," in Jon Elster, ed., *Rational Choice* (New York: New York University Press, 1986), pp. 1–2.

6

Strain, Crisis, and Revolution: When Do the Masses Revolt?

In this chapter we review several explanations for revolution that begin at the macrolevel. We first inventory the presumed long-term causes and more immediate accelerators of a revolutionary crisis. We then examine ways in which these inventories are organized into theories of system disequilibrium to explain the origins of a revolutionary crisis. We next compare system disequilibrium theories to Marxist structural theories of revolution. These latter theories identify sources of structural contradiction and conflict that supposedly produce a revolutionary crisis. Finally, we investigate the argument that a revolutionary transformation will not occur unless the potentially revolutionary elements in a society have both the opportunity and the resources to act effectively. This opportunity/resource approach serves as a bridge between the concerns of the theorist attempting to explain revolution and the practitioner attempting to make revolution.

REVOLUTION AS A MACROPHENOMENON

Deprivation and rational choice theories address the puzzle of why people resort to extreme means, particularly violence, to achieve their political objectives. They are less successful at explaining why revolutions occur. Deprivation theory encounters difficulties in explaining not only collective action but also social transformation. Rational choice theory fails to account for the preferences lying behind the choice of radical action. Even combined, they provide better accounts of the origins of turmoil than explanations of the forces contributing to social transformation. Perhaps explanation of a macrophenomenon like revolution requires macrotheories, that is, theories that begin at some collective level of analysis—like group, culture, or social structure.

Analysts embracing methodological individualism (the stance reducing all social phenomena to the actions of individuals, and the one underlying both deprivation and rational choice theories) often criticize macrotheories for reifying conceptual entities such as "state" and "class" and making them causally prior to the individuals that constitute them. On the other hand, proponents of macrotheories argue that the idea "[t]hat these collective phenomena are themselves products of individual actions, aims, and aspirations in no way contradicts (let alone invali-

147

dates) the collectivist thesis that individual preferences are shaped by social processes."[1]

Microexplanations, like deprivation and rational choice theory, appear best suited to explain why *some* people rebelled rather than *others*. Macroexplanations, by attempting to account for the context within which individual action occurs, seem better at explaining why *anyone* rebelled and why the revolution *succeeded*. This added understanding, not surprisingly, comes accompanied by its own conceptual ambiguities and empirical shortcomings. In this chapter we review several approaches to revolution that *begin* at some macrolevel, whether group, culture, or structure.

The most simpleminded macroapproach attempts to identify the presumed long-term causes and immediate accelerators of a revolutionary crisis. Other, more systematic macrotheories concentrate on various forms of system disequilibrium that, if sufficiently severe, presumably lead to revolutionary readjustment. Marxism and its varied progeny stress sources of structural contradiction and conflict that combine to produce a revolutionary crisis. Finally, the opportunity/resource approach argues that, whatever the degree of disequilibrium or contradiction, revolutionary transformation cannot take place unless the potentially revolutionary sectors in a society have the opportunity and resources to act.

This last approach suggests a possible way both to combine micro- and macrotheories of violent discord and revolutionary change and to represent some of the factors considered by revolutionary actors themselves. It serves, then, as a bridge between the social scientific "theories of revolution" and the more pragmatic "revolutionary theory" of the participants.[2]

SOURCES OF STRAIN AND REVOLUTIONARY TRANSFORMATION

One problem in succinctly defining "revolution," as we noted in Chapter 2, arises from its historical origins. Though the term *revolution* suggests a sharp, sudden change, to so characterize a social process presumes that we know when a revolution "begins" and obscures the underlying roots of the revolutionary crisis. The most simple macroapproach to the problem of revolution concentrates precisely on the historical trends underlying the emergent revolutionary crisis. These long-term trends, of course, commonly affect countries that do not experience revolution as well as those that do. Consequently, commentators also identify short-term accelerators or precipitators of a revolutionary crisis, producing this simple equation:

$$\text{Long-term causes} + \text{accelerators} = \text{revolution}$$

Long-Term Causes of a Revolutionary Crisis

In retrospect everything appears clearer. After the culmination of a revolutionary crisis, we then look back and attempt to identify the long-term factors contributing to the crisis. The more important factors apparently underlying revolutions over the last two hundred years include the following:[3]

The Influence of the Scientific Worldview   Many people take the scientific worldview for granted, even though they remain essentially ignorant about both the methods of scientific inquiry and the substance of scientific conclusions. Since the sixteenth century, however, the growing influence and prestige of scientific inquiry has contributed to three fundamental tendencies in Western culture: secularization, disenchantment of the world, and rationalization.[4] The process of *secularization* reduces the role of religion in everyday human activity. *Disenchantment* increasingly subjects the natural—and by extension the social—world to human calculation, intervention, and control. Finally, *rationalization* involves achieving clearly defined ends through the practical application of carefully designed means.

These three tendencies both corrode the basis of traditional authority and provide the intellectual foundation for a new social and political order. The shrinking influence of religion in people's lives reduces the significance of a major prop for traditional social and political hierarchies. If God no longer ordains the "powers that be," then people can question the legitimacy of their rulers. If fate and other unseen forces no longer govern human lives, then people can hope to rise up and take control of their own destiny. Finally, if people come to understand the natural and social forces affecting them, then they begin to judge policy by its effectiveness rather than how well it accords with tradition.

The growing influence of science contributes mightily to the idea of progress reinforcing both the liberal's call for reform and the revolutionary's demand for radical transformation. Without the belief in progress, political upheavals commonly involved merely the contentions among rival elites (like the dynastic civil wars that plagued England in the fourteenth and fifteenth centuries); atavistic rebellions among peasants to protect their traditional rights from the encroachments of a rapacious aristocracy; or the cyclical turning of the wheel of fate, exalting the lowly and diminishing the mighty . . . until the next turn of the wheel. Once tradition loses its sacred aura and people become masters of their lives, they then dream of a better world built on the wreckage of the discredited *ancien régime*.[5]

The dynamism released by this cultural revolution propelled the previously insignificant European states to the center of the world stage and spread their power throughout the non-Western world. European imperialism either destroyed or subordinated established civilizations in the Near and Far East, Africa, and South America. It seemed that non-Western powers like Japan could effectively resist subordination only by successful imitation. Ironically, anticolonial forces ultimately drew upon the same cultural forces that undermined traditional rule and justified revolution in the West to challenge the authority of the Western powers in their empires.

Technological Change   The disenchantment of the world and the rationalization of human activities have also contributed to the continuous technological revolution of the past few centuries. Today we see a close relation between science and technology, but until the nineteenth century, the two developed relatively independently of one another. Improved understanding of the basic physics and chemistry of the natural world did not immediately translate into new technologies. However, the same cultural forces that reinforced the shift of intellectual authority from schools of theology to academies of science have also encouraged pragmatic inventions to increase the effectiveness and efficiency of especially economic activities.

At least two major social effects arise from the increased pace of technological intervention, one material and the other intellectual.[6] Materially, technology not only vastly increases economic productivity, leading to a long-term trend of improving material prosperity (see below), but it also contributes to the transformation of the social structure. New classes (capitalist entrepreneurs and industrial workers) emerge and increase in power, while others (rural peasantry and aristocracy) find their material position weakened. Intellectually, success in material engineering reinforces the idea of social engineering. If human beings can remake their material world, why can they not transform and rationalize their social relations, as well?

The political consequences of technological change are complex. The enhanced position of new economic classes along with increased confidence in the human ability to re-create the world encouraged the spread of revolutionary ideas. On the other hand, political conflict arises when established classes resist the inroads of the new processes, powers, and ideas. Participants in political violence and even revolutionary movements are not always consistently progressive. Often they rebel against the modernizing forces that erode the traditional foundation of their security.[7]

Economic Development   Technological change contributes to economic development. Economic development means something more than the simple expansion of material wealth, although wealth generally increases with development. Development fundamentally entails increasing the *productivity* of those creating the wealth.[8] Improved technologies of production constitute the most obvious way of increasing productivity; however, the organization, attitudes, and aptitude of the producers also affect their productivity. Agricultural productivity, for example, increased not simply because of the application of new technologies, but also because of the accompanying changes in the organization of agricultural production and in the skills of the laboring force. Similarly, a synergistic combination of technology, skill, and organization propelled the movement from craft to industrial production.

The revolutionary implications of economic development reinforce some of the consequences of technological change. The changing tools and methods of production are unevenly distributed. Groups without access to these new tools and methods, or who fail to adapt, find themselves unable to compete. The wealth created through improved productivity, therefore, is not evenly distributed. New economic cleavages emerge, or old ones intensify. Ironically, economic development creates the expectation of continuous economic improvement, a bizarre idea in a traditional subsistence economy where peasants view cycles of relative prosperity and deprivation as largely governed by fate. The periodic economic downturns associated with capitalist economies, therefore, provide a new source of frustration (see below, the section on accelerators).[9]

The spread of the capitalist world economy to Africa, Asia, and Latin America often proved more disruptive than the experience in Europe and America. Here the colonial possessions of the European powers and the imperfectly independent states emerging from the breakup of these empires suffered the costs associated with the destruction of their traditional economies but received few of the benefits of increased economic productivity.[10] Rather, the major economic powers and the transnational corporations largely expropriated these benefits.

Demographic Trends   In addition to the rise of science, technological change, and a long-term improvement in economic productivity, world population has surged, contributing to a related trend of urbanization. Population growth and urbanization first affected the early industrializing states, but by the nineteenth century, they had spread to the remainder of the world. A hundred and fifty years later, population growth has largely leveled off in most advanced industrial countries, but many of the developing countries still experience something of a population explosion.

Population growth alone, as Thomas Greene argues, fails to explain the occurrence of revolution.[11] Population expansion, though, can put pressure on the productive capacity of an economy, thereby contributing to increased deprivation. Growth can also reinforce emerging economic and social cleavages.[12] Migration to the cities presumably provides a pool of rootless, alienated underemployed, readily mobilized by radical social movements. Alternatively, allowing for the outmigration of frustrated peoples may serve as a safety valve for potentially dangerous social pressure. The opportunity for millions of Europeans to migrate to the United States between 1850 and 1910 may have helped to prevent the social upheaval many predicted for the old world.

The Rise of the Centralized State   A dramatic increase in the power of the state usually accompanies, or even precedes, these social and economic processes. The emergence and growth of modern bureaucracy reflect the drive for rationalization released by the scientific revolution. At the same time, expansion of the economic base of the society provides vastly more resources available to the state. Even the growth in population contributes to state power in terms of the resources it extracts (for example, larger armies) and the responsibilities it assumes.

Hagopian argues that modern revolution cannot occur in a feudal society because power is too diffuse. (Internal wars in feudal states are dynastic struggles rather than "true" revolutions.) Nor will revolution challenge a fully developed modern state, because power is too concentrated. In between these two extremes lies the *patrimonial* state, where a centralizing monarch attempts to increase the domain of the central government's authority and the effectiveness of its extractive capability. A national administration, though not a modern bureaucracy, expands the government's writ throughout the country. This emerging central government supplies a source of grievance, an enemy against which to organize, and a power base to seize and use to transform society.[13]

The Spread of New Ideologies   Modern revolutions involve restructuring society and polity according to unorthodox norms and values. In contrast, premodern rebellion often aimed simply to reestablish traditional prerogatives. Perhaps the two most significant revolutionary ideas are those of democracy and nationalism.

The growing influence of democratic ideals challenges the traditional basis of legitimate rule. Democracy includes several different ideas, all subversive of established hierarchies of wealth, status, and power. At the most basic level, democracy presumes an essential equality among people. If people are by their nature equal, then the unequal distribution of privileges demands explicit justification. Calls for political, economic, and social equality often form the core of a revolutionary ideology.

In addition, if all people are inherently equal, then governments rightfully arise only from the freely agreed-to compacts among these citizens. This *contract* theory of political consent implies that government failure to fulfill the terms of the contract dissolves the citizens' obligation to obey. Such a contractual notion clearly influenced the justifying document of the American Revolution, the Declaration of Independence.

Finally, democracy in its most reductionist form demands that legitimate rule directly reflect the will of the people. If the voice of the people is the voice of God (*vox populi, vox Dei*), anything less than the people's voice has no moral standing. Revolutionary movements often draw on this simple notion when they claim to be the embodiment of the people's will.

The idea of "nation" combines powerfully with democratic ideals to produce potentially revolutionary demands for "self-determination." The creation of an identity that transcends traditional ties of kinship and village provides a basis to transform the social order of a country. The idea that the territory of the state should coincide with the cultural identity of a people formed a compelling rationale for the consolidation of regime power in some countries (Napoleonic France), fueled irredentist claims of others (Hitler's Germany), and encouraged the breakup of multinational empires in Europe (the Austro-Hungarian Empire after World War I and the Soviet Union in the 1990s) and of European colonial empires after World War II.

Primordial Cleavages   The first six long-term causes of revolution in the contemporary world directly or indirectly reflect the complex and controversial process called modernization. Initially Western scholars embraced two misleading conceptualizations about modernization. First, they rather arrogantly equated *modernization* with *Westernization*. They expected countries emerging from the breakup of the European colonial empires to recapitulate the economic, social, and political experiences of their previous rulers. Second, they conceived of "modernity" as simply and directly opposed to "tradition." Modern identities, values, and institutions would replace traditional ones as these societies modernized.

In contrast with these simplistic ideas, many revolutionary upheavals seem partly rooted in preexisting, primordial divisions reinforced, rather than erased, by the forces released by modernization, democratization, and nationalism. Often established cleavages channel the intensifying struggle for economic and political power. So-called traditional identities define the quest for political autonomy and economic justice. When the new divisions created or exacerbated by the processes of economic and social modernization reinforce, rather than crosscut, primordial identities, internal strain within the community mounts.

Primordial divisions contributing to the polarization that precedes a revolutionary crisis include those of race, culture (including language), and religion. The last of these stands in especially ironic contrast to the expected secularizing effects of the spread of the scientific worldview. At the same time that science demystifies much of creation, millions of people turn to fundamentalist religions as a source of both identity and guidance in a disrupted and uncertain world (see the discussion of the revolution in Iran, Chapter 11).

◈   ◈   ◈

Our inventory of the potential long-term causes of revolution fails to provide a systematic theory. Nevertheless, it makes two important contributions to our understanding. First, the inventory suggests that the events we identify as revolutions generally occur in societies that have already experienced considerable cultural, social, and economic change. In a sense, what we call a revolution represents an intensification of processes of fundamental transformation rather than a clear break with the past. For this reason we cannot easily establish the precise historical boundaries of a revolutionary event (a problem we noted in Chapter 2). Second, though not a theory, identification of the long-term causes of revolution directs our inquiry and may supply some of the components for more systematic explanations.

The long-term causes represent global trends, but revolution clearly is not a universally shared experience. The relatively infrequent occurrence of revolution might reflect the intensity with which different societies experience the dislocations produced by these trends. Alternatively, these long-term processes might constitute the necessary, but not sufficient, causes of a revolution, leading us to seek other factors that further increase the susceptibility of a particular society to revolutionary upheaval. Analysts commonly call these reinforcing factors the *accelerators* of a revolutionary crisis.

Accelerators of the Revolutionary Crisis[14]

If revolution results from an intensification of fundamental processes of change, we might then look for the factors contributing to such intensification. These accelerators strengthen the underlying strains or encourage their expression in revolutionary upheaval.

Economic Depression   We already identified economic development as one of the long-term causes of revolution. Economic downturns amplify the strains generated by the process of economic transformation. Even before an economic reversal, tensions arise over the creation of new classes, the uneven distribution of the fruits of development, and the obsolescence of previously established economic groups. A depression not only further weakens the position of the economically disenfranchised, but also it jeopardizes the recently acquired prosperity of the beneficiaries of development.

War   No sociopolitical process possesses greater potential for havoc than war. World War I precipitated the Russian Revolution. World War II preceded the culmination of the Chinese Revolution as well as years of national liberation struggles against the weakened European empires. While defeat in war seems particularly corrosive of regime security, the events after World War II indicate that being on the victorious side provides no guarantee of political stability. Though dutifully recognized as one of the five great allied victors in World War II, the Chinese Nationalist regime fell four years later.

Regardless of the ultimate outcome, war intensifies the existing strains within society in a variety of ways.[15] First, war demands the mobilization of a country's resources and inevitably increases the experience of hardship. Though citizens may willingly make sacrifices in the name of national defense, these burdens clearly entail some potential for engendering bitterness, especially if the postwar situation remains one of continued deprivation.

Second, the conduct of war may weaken regime capability. Even an ultimately successful campaign can raise questions about the competency and authority of the regime. In addition to the sacrifices demanded of the people, the war may cause significant economic damage. The losses in a war could also weaken the regime's repressive capability. Indeed, a war against a foreign invader may create or strengthen resistance forces independent of the regime.

Third, war creates new values and interest groups. Returning soldiers make up one potentially disruptive new group. Their wartime experiences may well generate both expectations for change and a sense of solidarity that could form the basis for political mobilization. Even the people back home may develop new values on the basis of both their expectations of some reward for sacrifices made and the regime's own wartime promises. Previously disenfranchised groups may no longer accept their subordination. Finally, the demoralizing effects of warfare may lead to a loss of values—a kind of normlessness that makes people available for mobilization by movements promising new sources of meaning and direction in their lives.

Government Financial Crisis   Fiscal collapse also intensifies the strains produced by the long-term causes of revolutionary crisis. Accelerators like war and depression usually contribute to a regime's financial crisis. Depression depletes previously reliable sources of revenue, while war creates exceptional demands for resource mobilization.

Even without a war or depression, the long-term sources of strain can generate a fiscal crisis. Regimes face a dilemma. On one hand, economic development, the expansion of governmental responsibilities, the demands of demographic change, and the emergence of new ideologies all place greater burdens on the state. On the other hand, the imposition of new taxes to enable the regime to fulfill its growing responsibilities may further alienate important sectors of regime support. The alternative of printing more money to cover the costs of governance leads to inflation, while the failure to extract the needed resources results in bankruptcy.

Ineptitude of the Ruling Class   Confronted with the long-term sources of structural strain and the immediate challenges of depression, war, or fiscal crisis, a government may worsen matters with its response. Previously tolerated inefficiencies and corruption become increasingly onerous in the context of a crisis. Repressive reactions to emerging demands may only further alienate the regime from its people. Moreover, the population will probably hold the political leadership responsible for any economic or military catastrophe.

The cultural changes wrought by long-term trends such as the spread of the scientific worldview, economic development, and the emergence of democratic and nationalist ideologies also serve to undermine the authority of the old elites. In this emerging world aristocratic birth no longer guarantees automatic deference, and people will demand new forms of competency and upward mobility for those who possess them. Failure of the ruling class to renew itself in the face of these challenges further contributes to the emergence of a revolutionary crisis.[16]

Division in the Ruling Class   In the context of increasing social strain reinforced by the emergence of one or more crises, elite unity may crack. The term "ruling class" imparts a false sense of coherence to a potentially divisive collection of interests. First, government authorities possess interests distinct from those of nongovernmental elites. In particular the government must extract sufficient resources to carry out its obligations. Though the poor may not possess the resources to resist governmental impositions, they also lack the resources to provide much support. When the government turns to those who possess most of the economic resources—the economic elites—it also risks alienating an important component of its political base. Therefore, failure to extract the needed resources leads to fiscal crisis, while the attempt to extract these resources often contributes to elite divisions.

Second, divisions develop among the nongovernmental elites themselves. Different sectors, for example, possess different economic interests, as in the commonly recognized conflict between urban and rural economic elites. Rural elites (and peasants) benefit from high prices for their agricultural commodities, but urban elites (and the urban masses) benefit from low prices, a standard producer/consumer conflict. Alternatively, urban-based industrialists typically desire high tariffs to protect their "infant industries," whereas rural elites producing for export often oppose such tariffs. In addition to potentially clashing economic interests, primordial lines of race, culture, or religion may divide nongovernmental elites.

Third, primordial, ideological, and even organizational cleavages may divide governmental elites. The government of a divided society confronts a serious dilemma. If a regime reflects the divisions in society, it may encourage partisanship within the government by those who identify more strongly with others sharing ideological or primordial characteristics than with the governmental institutions. A failure to represent one or more significant sectors of society to guarantee governmental homogeneity, however, simply results in the unrepresented sectors growing more alienated from the government. Moreover, the structural components of a government also possess different interests, especially concerning the division of public resources. The military, in particular, may defect from a regime that fails to support it to the degree desired. Nothing weakens a regime more than the defection of all or part of its military.[17]

Alienation of the Intellectuals　Intellectuals, despite their pretensions of autonomy, generally serve the established order as "clerks" and "apologists." In the former role, they provide the expertise needed to keep the government and other elite enterprises running smoothly. In the latter role, they provide the ideological justifications for the status quo. The defection of elements of the intelligentsia accelerates the revolutionary crisis, for now the revolutionary movement benefits from both their organizational and ideological expertise.[18]

The regime may alienate intellectuals in both their roles. As clerks they may grow dissatisfied with elite incompetence and feel that their knowledge and skill are underrecognized and inadequately rewarded. As apologists they may perceive how the regime fails to rule in accord with its own stated values. Some, moreover, may empathize with the victims of the established order and begin to articulate the point of view of the disenfranchised. Finally, and more cynically, the regime may lack the resources to satisfy the number of "intellectuals" in a society. If the educational institutions produce more graduates than the existing social order can readily employ in the manner to which the graduates aspire, then a "class" of unemployed intellectuals may form. This class can prove a significant irritant to regime stability.

Insufficient Reform　To paraphrase a well-worn maxim, good intentions often pave the road to revolution. A major strategy for managing social tension entails instituting "conservative" reforms to reduce discontent while preserving the essential structure of power and value (see Chapter 1). The success of this strategy, however, depends on the nature of the tensions and the resources of the regime. If modest reform cannot buy off existing discontent or if the regime lacks the resources to carry out the reforms while continuing to control those who remain (or become) discontented, then reform may simply accelerate the revolutionary crisis.

Somewhat tautologically, analysts observe that revolutionary upheavals occur not against highly repressive regimes, but against those regimes that loosen their controls on the community and even attempt some serious, if incremental, reforms. The probable explanation appears fairly obvious. Weakening controls provide "space" within which a revolutionary movement can organize and operate. Halfway measures of reform often encourage demands to finish the task or even generate new demands. Reform policies may alienate powerful interests in and out of government, contributing to divisions within the elite.

Permissive World Environment[19]   Revolutionary upheavals, especially in the contemporary world, seldom occur in splendid isolation. Internal political struggles attract the attention of foreign powers. These may elect to support one side or the other in the political struggle, shaping the outcome. If successful, a new revolutionary regime frequently encounters hostile neighbors intent on restoring the old order.

Consequently, both the success and the survival of the revolution depend on a relatively permissive world environment. Foreign supporters supply guidance and materials, while hostile powers support the old regime and may even intervene to reverse the outcome of a revolution. On the other hand, initial allies of the regime may abandon their former associates, contributing to revolutionary success.

Intervention in an internal power struggle, however, often carries a high price, deterring even foreign powers hostile to the revolution. Foreign intervention, for example, postponed the outcome of the Vietnamese Revolution but ultimately could not defeat it. Though the United States presumably possessed the power to occupy Vietnam indefinitely, it could not do so at an acceptable cost. Widespread Western suspicion of the Iranian Revolution was not sufficient to support overt Western intervention against the new Islamic order. Finally, the transformation of the Eastern European regimes in 1989 occurred in part because the Soviet Union was unwilling, and perhaps unable, to intervene militarily as it had in the past to prop up discredited communist regimes. A permissive world environment, then, encourages revolutionary transformation, while a hostile one can delay and even defeat it. The international political context, however, is seldom so clearly aligned.

🔥   🔥   🔥

This inventory of underlying causes and accelerators of social strain helps develop a macroperspective on the origins of revolution as opposed to merely rebellious or violent behavior. It fails, however, to provide a systematic macrotheory for revolution.

Critique

Retrospective inventories of the causes of structural strain and the accelerators of revolutionary crisis suggest some possible components of an explanation for revolution. They do not constitute an explanation by themselves. However plausible or exhaustive, such lists cannot escape their pretheoretical status. Our inventory of causes and accelerators identifies some possible origins of the revolutionary crisis and reasons for the weakening of state control, but this catalogue of travail lacks both logical and empirical coherence. Moreover, even on its own terms, the inventory largely ignores a third puzzle of significance, the factors that affect the relative success of revolutionary strategy and tactics.

A list, however exhaustive, is not a theory. It fails to specify relations among its parts or to determine their relative significance. While the catalogue of factors contributing to particular instances of revolutionary transformation may be suggestive, it risks both circularity and spurious correlation. Simply because events preceded a revolution, they cannot be considered causes of that revolution until systematically woven into an empirical argument. A theory would propose why and how these factors, rather than others, produce a revolutionary transformation.

Since the long-term causes of structural strain afflict societies where no revolution occurs and ones where rebellion develops and is defeated, as well as those that experience a revolutionary transformation, we must be able to explain these variations. The list of accelerators suggests hypotheses that could account for the differences, but an empirical theory must specify the relevance of and relations among the many possible factors. Neither the long-term causes nor the short-term accelerators are equally present in every historical instance of revolution. Such simple inventories do not constitute an empirical explanation of any sort—good or bad—and therefore questions of adequacy or authenticity do not apply.

Their pretheoretical status, however, does not mean such exercises are fruitless. Our inventory of possible long- and short-term causes of revolution provides an initial orientation to particular historical cases. Identification of similarities gives us greater confidence in formulating systematic empirical hypotheses. Recognition of differences raises interesting puzzles requiring explanation. In this way, though not an explanation, these inventories may supply the components for more ambitious macrotheories of revolutionary transformation.

THEORIES OF REVOLUTIONARY DISEQUILIBRIUM

The sources of structural strain and revolutionary crisis suggest that revolution represents the intensification of existing processes of change. More systematic explanations must specify the ways in which a social system becomes sufficiently perturbed to experience a revolution. Such "disequilibrium theories" propose that revolution occurs when something disrupts the internal balances of the macro-order. Revolution, if successful—and success is not guaranteed—reequilibrates the macro-order.

Revolution in the Disequilibrated System

In the consensus view of order (see Chapter 1), a properly functioning society consists of a well-integrated system of structures and roles based on shared values and common adherence to the norms of social interaction. Each part makes a contribution to the smooth functioning of the whole system. Conflict in general and revolution in particular represent degeneration from this ideal state of affairs. Consensus theory, then, exhibits a conservative bias.

Chalmers Johnson, writing within this tradition, tries to avoid this conservative slant on revolution. Rather, he argues that "true revolution is neither lunacy nor crime [the common conservative explanations for deviant behavior]. It is the acceptance of violence in order to cause the system to change when all else has failed, and the very idea of revolution is contingent upon this perception of societal failure."[20]

From a conservative point of view deviant behavior and even revolt arise from three primary sources: (1) breakdowns in socialization, so that some people fail to learn the appropriate role behavior; (2) role conflict, where the demands of a role in one subsystem conflict with those of a role in another (for example, the norm of family loyalty may conflict with the norm of bureaucratic impartiality for civil servants making decisions that affect their relatives); and (3) norm conflict arising from inconsistent or ambiguous norms within the system.[21] All of these represent some deterioration from the ideal internal operations of the social system.

Johnson argues that other challenges may throw the system into more serious disequilibrium. He asserts that a healthy social system maintains a *homeostatic equilibrium* with its environment. This rather intimidating concept, borrowed from physiology, simply refers to the capacity of the system to adjust automatically to potentially harmful challenges.[22] The balance struck, then, is dynamic within certain limits rather than completely static. Since he draws on an organic metaphor, we might as well use a literally organic example. Our bodies adjust to changes in temperature to maintain a homeostatic equilibrium. When hot, we sweat to cool our body temperature; when cold, we shiver to generate some heat. Notice, though, that such automatic adjustments take us only so far. At some point we will die of hyper- or hypothermia, unless we consciously intervene to correct for the environmental challenge.

Analogously, a social system may also encounter challenges that overtax the established mechanisms of adjustment. The system is thrown out of equilibrium, and the adjustments normally undertaken to *maintain* equilibrium cannot *re-create* it.[23] The potential for revolution, then, arises in a seriously *dysfunctional* social system. The people do not fail the social system; the system fails the people.

Johnson observes that "so long as a society's values and the realities with which it must deal in order to exist are in harmony with each other, the society is immune from revolution."[24] Consequently, dramatic changes in values or in environmental challenges throw a system into disequilibrium. Our inventory of the long-term causes of revolution identifies precisely these kinds of changes. Modification in values arising from the spread of scientific, democratic, or nationalistic ideas undermines traditional bases of legitimacy. Alternatively, technological change, economic development, and demographic trends define some of the "realities" confronting the social system, particularly in the area which Johnson considers of greatest importance, the division of labor.

Disequilibrium, obviously, represents yet another slippery concept of degree. As the pressures of growing disequilibrium mount, the regime experiences a *power deflation;* that is, obedience to authority can no longer be taken for granted.[25] A disequilibrated social system, however, need not succumb to an inevitable revolution. Returning to the human analogy, just as we can innovate a response to protect ourselves from the dangers of extreme temperature variations, the political regime of a disequilibrated social system can undertake reforms to forestall a revolutionary challenge (see the discussion of "conservative change" in Chapter 1). The occurrence and quality of conservative change directly influence the likelihood of whether revolutionary change will ever occur.[26] A regime, however, may lack the wit, the will, or the resources to undertake "quality" reforms. Moreover, regime-initiated reform presumably can go only so far in restoring a profoundly disequilibrated system.

Even if conservative change fails to reequilibrate values and demands, a regime may forestall revolution by successfully coercing the required social interaction. Consequently Johnson argues that the final condition for revolution will be some "ingredient" weakening the regime's relative coercive position vis-à-vis the revolutionaries. He suggests three: (1) a decline in the unity and discipline of the regime's coercive forces, (2) an ideological belief on the part of the revolutionaries that they can overcome the armed might of the state, and (3) revolutionary military operations that erode the regime's aura of invincibility as well as the effectiveness of its armed forces.[27]

Figure 6.1 presents Johnson's overall argument in schematic form. Changes in social values and organization upset the social system, contributing to power deflation. Power deflation increases the ratio of dissident to regime coercive power, which increases the likelihood of a successful revolutionary insurrection.

Certain secondary variables affect this simple sequence. For example, the social system can, within limits, adjust essentially automatically to changes in values and organization, and this capacity compensates, to some extent, for disequilibrium. On the other hand, the system may fail to carry out its normal functions of socialization and role and norm reconciliation, thereby worsening the problem of disequilibrium. Disequilibrium contributes to power deflation, but a regime may respond through a deliberate strategy of conservative change. Failure to do so

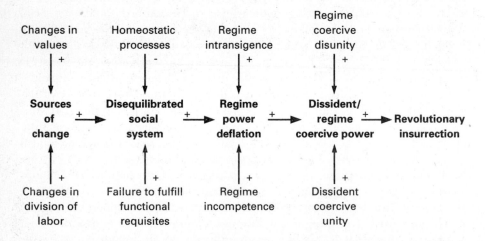

Figure 6.1 Disequilibrium model of revolution.

Source: Based on Chalmers Johnson, *Revolutionary Change*, p. 106.

through intransigence or incompetence contributes to further deflation and improves the power position of the dissidents. Regime coercive disunity and dissident coercive unity (as embodied in their ideology, organization, and strategy) also improve the relative power position of the dissidents, increasing the probability of a successful revolutionary insurrection.

Johnson's argument provides a more systematic "macroportrait" of the causes of revolutionary transformation than do simple inventories of presumed sources of a revolutionary crisis. Though drawing on consensus-oriented systems theory, he manages to avoid some of the conservative implications of this approach. A revolution occurs only in conjunction with a series of system failures: first, in the homeostatic processes of system adjustment, then in the adaptive capacity of the regime, and finally in the coercive unity of the regime. Nonetheless, even though the model specifies some important hypothetical relations, "Virtually all the components of the system are 'black boxes': we do not know how they operate."[28] Other disequilibrium theories, however, add some more detail to the content of these boxes.

Revolution as a Crisis of Modernization

Most of the long-term causes of a revolutionary crisis reflect socioeconomic processes commonly associated with modernization. Samuel P. Huntington asserts that the phenomenon of revolution "is the ultimate expression of the modernizing outlook, the belief that it is within the power of man to control and to change his environment and that he has not only the ability but the right to do so."[29] True revolution, in Huntington's view, cannot occur in either highly traditional societies or highly modern ones. Rather, revolution is possible only in transitional societies where demands unleashed by the processes of social and economic modernization significantly exceed the capabilities of the existing institutions to respond effectively.

> The political essence of a revolution is the rapid expansion of political consciousness and the rapid mobilization of new groups into politics at a speed which makes it impossible for existing political institutions to assimilate them. Revolution is the extreme case of the explosion of political participation. Without this explosion there is no revolution.[30]

Huntington's argument, then, provides some content for several of the "black boxes" left underspecified in Johnson's model. Changes in values and structure (division of labor) result from the spread of economic and social modernization to previously stable traditional societies. Modernization creates new classes (the bourgeoisie, the proletariat) and disrupts old ones (the peasants and traditional elites). New ideas spread among the population. Disequilibrium emerges in the form of increased demands for political participation by both new and previously passive sectors of society. Power deflation results from the failure of the political system to incorporate the emerging demands for participation. Huntington characterizes this deflation as "political decay."[31]

Revolution represents the ultimate crisis of political development. Unless the existing political organizations of a community can manage the social forces released by the modernization process, they will be destabilized at best, and swept away at the extreme. The emergence of a revolutionary crisis depends, then, on the strength of the existing political organizations. Huntington suggests two primary criteria for measuring this strength: *scope of support* and *level of institutionalization.*[32] "Scope" refers essentially to the extent to which the political organizations incorporate the population. Traditional political institutions generally possess limited scope, but this matters little if the mass of the population remains quiescent. But when previously passive sectors, or new ones created by the processes of modernization, demand to participate in the politics of the community, the existing political organizations face a crisis of support.

The level of institutionalization of a political organization depends on its adaptability, complexity, autonomy, and coherence.[33]

1. *Adaptability*   A strong organization must adjust to changing circumstances and confront new challenges. The severity of such challenges varies, and even relatively adaptable organizations may falter in the face of a dramatic increase in demands. Huntington suggests three possible indicators of an organization's adaptability: its chronological age (older organizations almost certainly have faced and survived at least some challenges); generational age (more adaptable organizations have successfully dealt with the problem of succession, replacing one set of leaders with another); and functional adaptability (the capacity to take on new tasks).[34]

2. *Complexity*   Complexity essentially refers to the degree of differentiation or division of labor in an organization. A complex organization is usually large, but not all large organizations are complex. Differentiation includes both the hierarchical structure of authority and the numbers of distinct functions performed by the organization.

3. *Autonomy*   A strong political organization must be relatively independent of other social groupings. Obviously, autonomy does not mean complete autarky. Every political organization needs to manage the demands placed upon it by other sectors in society and extract resources from these sectors. Autonomous organizations, though, express their own interests and establish their own procedures rather than mirroring the interests of or subordinating their procedures to another social grouping. Marxists assert, for example, that the state lacks autonomy because it merely serves as the instrument of the dominant economic class.

4. *Coherence*   The extent to which the parts of an organization function in a smooth, well-integrated fashion also affects its quality. Disunity indicates a low level of institutionalization. Autonomy and coherence reinforce one another. A divided organization invites interference from other social forces, whereas a unified one may be able to protect itself from unwanted intrusions and influence. On the other hand, as complexity increases, so also do problems of maintaining coherence.

Huntington postulates two broad patterns of revolutionary transformation which depend on the scope of support and level of institutionalization of established political organizations. In the "Western" pattern (so called because it approximates the experience in the French and Russian revolutions), the old regime's strength is so eroded that it collapses at the center. In the "Eastern" pattern (reflecting the experience in the Chinese and Vietnamese revolutions), the established regime maintains some level of support and institutionalization, and the emerging revolutionary forces must consolidate their own position and fight their way to power.[35] This difference affects subsequent characteristics of the revolutionary struggle.[36]

In the Western pattern significant political mobilization follows the collapse of the old regime, as emergent groups contend to occupy the centers of power. In the Eastern pattern the revolutionary movement must mobilize support, often under arduous conditions, to overthrow the old regime. Consequently, Huntington notes, Western-style revolutions often have clear dates marking their beginning (when the old regime collapses), while Eastern-style revolutions have clear dates marking their end (when the revolutionary forces finally occupy the capital), although, as we noted in Chapter 2, such clarity may be more apparent than real.

In the Western pattern moderate reformers and radical revolutionaries struggle for power, in contrast with the Eastern pattern, in which the revolutionaries contend mainly with the regime. In the Western model the group seizing control of the center must generally fight to consolidate their power over the countryside, as opposed to the Eastern pattern, in which the revolutionaries fight their way to the center from remote areas of the countryside. Finally, the use of terror intensifies in the final stage of a Western revolution, as the newly established regime solidifies its hold on power. In contrast, terrorism is the primary tactic in the early stages of an Eastern-style revolution, when the movement lacks the power to mount more significant attacks against the regime (see Chapter 9).

Neither path of revolutionary insurrection guarantees success to its participants. The collapse of the old regime in a Western-style revolution creates a power vacuum, but other elites, rather than the revolutionary radicals, may quickly fill it, preventing any significant restructuring of wider social relations. Alternatively, political decay may open space for radical groups to *initiate* a struggle for power against the established regime, but the regime may recover, perhaps with foreign assistance, and crush the rebellion.

Huntington also notes that a successful revolution commonly requires the participation of more than one sector.[37] Usually a coalition develops among revolutionary intellectuals, some elements of the urban middle classes and proletariat, and the peasantry. Such coalitions do not automatically emerge; indeed, coalitions must often bridge significant differences. Moreover, the same phase of the modernization process may affect the potentially revolutionary sectors differently. For example, as modernization proceeds, the urban labor force and the emerging middle classes may become more economically secure, while the situation in the countryside deteriorates.

A revolution, finally, cannot reequilibrate the system unless it creates new political organizations capable of managing modernization. Huntington argues that "the measure of how revolutionary a revolution is is the rapidity and scope of the expansion of political participation. The measure of how successful a revolution is is the authority and stability of the institutions to which it gives birth."[38] Ultimately the new regime must manage the very forces that fostered its emergence and success. Confronted with this challenge, many revolutions succeed in seizing power only to "die" in the aftermath (see Chapter 12).

❀ ❀ ❀

Huntington's analysis adds considerable detail to the disequilibrium model of revolutionary change, as well as offering some specific hypotheses on the course of the revolutionary process. Modernization causes disequilibrium by creating new social forces and relations while disrupting old ones. Disequilibrium takes the concrete form of increased demands for participation. The demands for participation create a revolutionary situation when they overwhelm the existing political organizations, whose strength depends on their scope of support and degree of institutionalization. The nature of the *ancien régime* determines the outcome of this process of political decay. Depending on its scope of support and institutionalization, the regime may either collapse in the early stages of demand mobilization (Western pattern) or resist the revolutionary demands (Eastern pattern).

Huntington's argument, then, develops some further interconnections, making the disequilibrium model more "theorylike," and it suggests ways to develop some empirical indicators of a revolutionary disequilibrium. Finally, although oversimplified, the two alternative patterns of revolutionary change recognize and attempt to account for obvious differences among various "great revolutions" of the last two centuries.

All this comes at a certain cost. As we noted, Huntington recognizes that his argument shrinks revolution to a "historically limited phenomenon."[39] True revolutions occur only at a particular stage of social development, though his theory does not preclude the occurrence of other forms of social and political violence. Neither highly traditional nor highly modern societies experience overwhelming demands for participation. The former place few demands on the political structure, and the latter's political organizations are too strong to be overwhelmed.

Nothing in principle is wrong with defining a limited domain for key concepts. Indeed, we might reasonably argue that the search for universal laws in the social sciences is not only misplaced, but misleading (see Chapter 3). The trick, of course, lies in circumscribing the appropriate domain. Does a "true" revolutionary disequilibrium arise only when the participatory demands generated by modernization overwhelm the capability of existing political organizations? Is this the only form of revolutionary disequilibrium? On the other hand, does the experience of modernization necessarily produce an escalation of participatory demands? Might the modernization process prompt responses other than an explosion in participation?

Cultural Disequilibrium and the Revolutionary Crisis

Johnson argues that a revolutionary disequilibrium develops in a social system when shared values diverge sufficiently from actual experiences. This contention is unhelpfully vague. Huntington, by focusing on the modernization crisis, may well define a revolutionary disequilibrium too narrowly. A recent thesis, however, offers interesting possibilities for developing a middle position.

Michael Thompson, Richard Ellis, and Aaron Wildavsky contend that identifiable patterns of shared values and beliefs (culture) and the interpersonal actions (social relations) they direct are not infinitely various. Indeed, they maintain that culture and social relations combine into five fundamental ways of life: hierarchy, egalitarianism, fatalism, individualism, and autonomy (see Chapter 1).[40] They construct these five types by combining two fundamental dimensions of social interaction, group and grid. "*Group* refers to the extent to which an individual is incorporated into bounded units," and "[g]*rid* denotes the degree to which an individual's life is circumscribed by externally imposed prescriptions."[41] These two dimensions join in alternative pairs to produce the five pure types of social life:[42]

- *Hierarchy* combines strong group identification with binding external regulations on the individual's behavior.
- *Egalitarianism* also stresses strong group identification but imposes minimal external prescriptions on behavior.
- *Fatalism* involves strong external regulation but with little group identification.
- *Individualism* defines a way of life entailing few externally imposed prescriptions and little group identification.
- *Autonomy* involves withdrawing from social interaction altogether.

Of these ways of life, three are socially active (hierarchy, egalitarianism, and individualism), one is socially passive (fatalism), and the last (autonomy) is simply asocial. Autonomy, as the asocial form of life, has no direct relevance for the emergence of social disequilibrium. Those drawing on autonomous ways of life, however, may provide a source of social innovation (see Chapter 7).

Each of the four socially engaged ways of life offers guidance to its adherents about the nature of the world and how they should act in it.[43] For individualists the world is essentially *benign*. Success depends on the skill, ambition, and hard work of the individual. Hierarchists believe the world is *perverse/tolerant*. Humans can prosper within limits, but the controlling organizations of the community must carefully regulate human activities to ensure that these limits are not violated. Egalitarians, in contrast, predict that the world is *ephemeral*, and the slightest excess of the individualist or hierarchist may cause a cascading catastrophe. Finally, fatalists see a *capricious* world where little can be done to control their fate, which may bring them unpredictable rewards or punishments.

The four social forms of life, then, imply four radically different socioenvironmental equilibria, each of which could be upset by encountering a world more consistent with one of the other three perspectives (see Table 6.1). Take, for example, the individualist way of life, which predicts a world that rewards human efforts and intervention. If those guiding their lives according to this expectation encounter a world where rewards are allocated capriciously or one where their activities lead only to disaster, they will begin to question the basis of their values and the social relations these values ordain. Reestablishing an equilibrium implies moving to the way of life more consistent with the experienced world.

Table 6.1   SOURCES OF DISEQUILIBRIUM IN ALTERNATIVE WAYS OF LIFE

FORM OF LIFE	ACTUAL WORLD			
	Capricious	Ephemeral	Benign	Perverse/Tolerant
Fatalist	*** [a]	No good luck	Efforts consistently rewarded	Efforts consistently rewarded within limits
Egalitarian	Caution does not work	***	Others' efforts prosper	Others prosper within limits
Individualist	Skill and work not associated with reward	Total collapse	***	Partial collapse due to violation of limits
Hierarchical	Unpredictability	Total collapse	Others prosper without guidance	***

[a] Asterisks indicate an equilibrium between a way of life and the actual world encountered.

Source: Reprinted from Michael Thompson, Richard Ellis, and Aaron Wildavsky, *Culture Theory*, 1990, p. 71, by permission of Westview Press, Boulder, Colorado.

Though this analysis suggests a number of paths leading to cultural crisis and political decay, not all of them possess revolutionary potential. Insofar as the idea of revolution implies a belief in the ability to control destiny, the unrelenting experience of a capricious world seems unlikely to lead to a revolution, but rather to *resignation*, on the part of those committed to other perspectives. On the other hand, the encounter with a world where the violation of limits leads to catastrophe (confirming the expectations of the hierarchist) leads those committed to the other three ways of life toward *reactionary politics*. Under these circumstances people subordinate themselves to a hierarchical order in the expectation that this will guarantee them prosperity or at least survival. Ironically, the unfulfilled expectations of revolutionaries often lead to the assertion of hierarchical control over the community (and possibly to the generation of a good number of fatalists as well).[44]

The disequilibria produced by unexpected encounters with a benign or ephemeral world, in contrast, offer greater potential for a revolutionary response, as we normally understand the concept. The perception that people thrive through their own efforts undermines the expectations of the hierarchical form of life, where only guided intervention should prosper. This disequilibrium supports the classic *liberal-bourgeois revolution* against both traditional monarchies in the eighteenth and nineteenth centuries and, perhaps, against the rigid and corrupt bureaucratic states in Eastern Europe and elsewhere in the late twentieth century.[45] The growing perception that the world rewards active intervention also transforms those previously committed to egalitarian and even fatalist ways of life. Certain elements of the modernization process contribute to this form of revolutionary disequilibrium. Both the promise of science and the performance of technology demonstrate the efficacy of intervention in the material realm, while the values of democracy and secularism promise rewards to those who take control of their fate in this world.

The experience of an ephemeral world may produce an *egalitarian* revolutionary disequilibrium. If the hierarchical order proves incompetent and the individualist way of life simply disguises the exploitation of the many by the fortunate few, then those committed to the egalitarian form of life can inveigh against the excesses of the others. The socialist revolutions of the twentieth century, especially those in China and Cambodia, rejected both traditional hierarchical order and the liberal form of life dominant in the West. In the view of radical egalitarians these cultures clearly failed. The trick for the egalitarian revolutionary movement, however, is to prevent the experienced failures of the hierarchical and individualist ways of life from being seen as evidence for the world's capriciousness, reinforcing fatalistic resignation rather than egalitarian millenarianism.

Disequilibrium and political decay, then, emerge in four basic ways, but only two of these are potentially revolutionary. The experience of a capricious world contributes to a spiral of decay without correction, and the experience of a perverse/tolerant world leads to political reaction and the imposition or reimposition of hierarchical order. On the other hand, the experience of a benign or an ephemeral world raises a potentially revolutionary challenge to the perspectives surprised by such occurrence. Interestingly, this cultural analysis echoes the alternative behavioral responses to the experience of alienation (see Chapter 5): ritualism (fatalism), reformism (individualism), revolutionism (egalitarianism or individualism), withdrawal (egalitarianism, if done collectively; autonomy, if done individually), and conformity (hierarchicalism).[46]

Modernization, as Huntington's disequilibrium theory argues, has indeed generated both benign and ephemeral world experiences. Modernization's successes have led to bourgeois-liberal revolutions in Europe, while its excesses have led to egalitarian revolutionary movements in the Third World. However, we need not conclude that *only* modernization generates the experience of a benign or an ephemeral world and, therefore, potentially revolutionary disequilibria. Rather, Huntington's argument develops an important special case of a general theory of cultural disequilibrium, albeit one of central importance for understanding the revolutions of the past two centuries. Nor need we conclude that modernization produces *only* the experience of a benign or an ephemeral world. For the victims of modernization the world may appear capricious, while for the hierarchists it may seem a tiger needing strict state control.

This culture theory provides an intriguing compromise between the vague disequilibrium theory of Johnson and the excessively restrictive focus on modernization proposed by Huntington. Unfortunately, as the authors themselves quickly point out, the world is stranger than their simple scheme might suggest. Although they posit only four forms of social life (or five, counting the asocial form, autonomy), they recognize that all are present to some extent in every society. In short, every real-world society possesses a pluralist culture; none is a pure type. The mix, of course, differs over time and across space, and we should be able to determine empirically which type dominates in a particular era or place.

Since we experience a complex, contradictory world, the dominant culture at a particular time may be an uneasy alliance between two of the activist perspectives. (We might consider the fatalists to be silent partners in any dominant coalition between two of the others.)[47] The authors consider a grand coalition among all three active ways of life a near impossibility and even dual coalitions necessarily exhibit considerable strain because of the contradictions between different worldviews.[48] Moreover, even an individual may possess all five perspectives, following the dictates of whichever one seems appropriate for the particular context (world) encountered.[49] In this case a disequilibrating surprise would be specific to a particular context. Cultural and psychological pluralism makes it less likely that a homogeneous revolutionary disequilibrium could arise in society and reinforces the common observation that a successful revolutionary movement must always forge a coalition among apparently disparate groups and individuals.

Revolution and Demographic/Structural Disequilibrium

The theory of cultural disequilibrium acknowledges that the world we experience sometimes diverges radically from what we expect. Since what we expect from the world influences how we structure social relations, significant divergence often produces a structural crisis. Revolutionary transformations can arise from these structural crises. Although culture theory specifies alternative ways in which structural crises could develop, it lacks empirical specificity. A recent work investigating revolutions and other state disturbances in the early modern era, however, adds substantial historical detail to this general disequilibrium argument and serves as a bridge to theories of structural contradiction.

Jack Goldstone, in *Revolution and Rebellion in the Early Modern World*, develops a demographic/structural model to explain the social disturbances that occurred across the Eurasian continent in the early modern era (roughly 1500 to 1850).[50] Goldstone notes a number of important puzzles bedeviling historical interpretations of revolution during this period.[51] First, contrary to Marxist theory (see below), revolutionary disturbances did not coincide with the intensification of capitalist modes of production. Second, contrary to those advocating linear theories of history, the disturbances occurred in cycles. The first cycle culminated about 1650, followed by 100 years of relative domestic tranquillity. In the 1770s, however, the crisis intensified again, inaugurating another century of disturbances. Third, contrary to those historians who explain particular state crises by reference to idiosyncratic factors like bad luck or ruler incompetence, the cyclical crisis affected a number of states about the same time. Such historical coincidence suggests that some common processes play a role, even though factors unique to a particular situation shape outcomes. Fourth, contrary to those who see revolution in the early modern period as a uniquely European phenomenon, Goldstone argues that similar disturbances afflicted both the Ottoman Empire and China at approximately the same time, culminating in significant structural change. In the West, however, these changes were often rationalized in terms of ideologies of secular redemption. In the East, in contrast, the changes were understood as restorations of a traditional equilibrium.

Goldstone draws upon geological imagery to epitomize his basic theory of revolution.[52] A profound disturbance causes some state structures to tremble and fall. Others, however, do not collapse. As with an earthquake, we might explain such variation in two ways. First, different structures might experience different pressures. Second, different structures might possess different capabilities to resist the same pressure. More concretely, Goldstone sets out to explain the origins of the disequilibrating pressure and both its cyclical rise and fall over the historical period, as well as variations among countries at the same time. He also attempts to estimate the effects of the pressure on existing state and social structures.

Population growth both initiates the crisis and generates its cyclical nature. Declining mortality rates, unaccompanied by an equivalent decline in fertility, underlay a rise in population between 1500 and 1650. Mortality rates increased again after 1650, slowing population growth for a time, until it began to rise again around the middle of the eighteenth century. During the period of slower growth most states across Eurasia experienced relative domestic stability, especially in comparison with the disturbances that preceded and followed this period of internal tranquillity.

Population growth alone did not produce the cycle of crises. Rather "growth, in the context of relatively inflexible economic and social structures, led to changes in prices, shifts in resources, and increasing social demands with which the agrarian-bureaucratic states could not specifically cope."[53] Population pressures generate a revolutionary disequilibrium only when they overwhelm the existing social structures and create multiple conflicts at different levels in society. Goldstone attempts to capture this multileveled crisis through a political stress indicator *(psi)* composed of state fiscal distress, elite conflict, and mass mobilization potential.[54] He summarizes these three interrelated trends as follows:

(1) Pressures increased on state finances as inflation eroded state income and population growth raised real expenses. States attempted to maintain themselves by raising revenues in a variety of ways, but such attempts alienated elites, peasants, and urban consumers, while failing to prevent increasing debt and eventual bankruptcy. (2) Intra-elite conflicts became more prevalent as larger families and inflation made it more difficult for some families to maintain their status, while expanding population and rising prices lifted some families, creating new aspirants to elite positions. With the state's fiscal weakness limiting its ability to provide for all who sought elite positions, considerable turnover and displacement occurred throughout the elite hierarchy, giving rise to factionalization as different elite groups sought to defend or improve their position. When central authority collapsed, most often as a result of bankruptcy, elite divisions came to the fore in struggles for power. (3) Popular unrest grew, as competition for land, urban migration, flooded labor markets, declining real wages, and increased youthfulness raised the mass mobilization potential of the populace. Unrest occurred in urban and rural areas and took various forms of food riots, attacks on land-

lords and state agents, and land and grain seizures, depending on the autonomy of popular groups and the resources of elites. A heightened mobilization potential made it easy for contending elites to marshal popular action in their conflicts, although in many cases popular actions, having their own motivation and momentum, proved easier to encourage than to control.[55]

Goldstone sees little role for ideology and mobilizing organizations during the period leading up to the state crisis and breakdown. Basic material and social forces dominate this period.[56] Once the state breaks down, however, ideology grows increasingly important in determining the course of the political struggle and the character of the reconstructed social order. The failure of the existing order to manage the multiple tensions emerging out of the material crisis caused by population growth discredits any value system associated with the status quo. Consequently, both disaffected elites and alienated popular groups turn to heterodox religious and secular creeds in search of a new value foundation.[57]

This summary, while providing little of the rich empirical detail with which Goldstone supports his argument, highlights some important differences with other disequilibrium theories. Unlike the others, Goldstone's theory gives only a secondary role to changes in values or social organization as disequilibrating factors. It stresses, in contrast, the impact of an ecological variable, population growth. Power deflation results from multifaceted, multileveled crises arising from population pressures and manifested in fiscal collapse, elite conflict, and widespread popular discontent. The course of the political struggle, and whether it produces a revolution, depends on the subsequent organization of these contending social forces around particular ideologies and political organizations.

The theory, with its combination of demographic, structural, and ideological elements, defies simple classification as deterministic or voluntaristic. The demographic source of disequilibrium appears relatively deterministic. The afflicted regimes neither anticipated nor understood the causes and the potential effects of increasing population. Nor was the decline in population growth rates after 1650 the result of deliberate policy. The structural component—inflexible social and economic organizations—also seems relatively deterministic, in that these structures resisted rapid adaptation to the new and poorly understood challenges. Nevertheless, even inflexible social structures result from the continuous outpouring of human action and thus differ from the "impersonal" whims of nature. Finally, the struggle to comprehend and respond to the crisis by searching among alternative ideological and social forms reflects a still greater degree of deliberation and choice.

Goldstone, therefore, is not a crude demographic determinist. The source of disequilibrium lies in demographic changes, but whether a fully developed state crisis ensues depends on the preexisting capability of political and social institutions. Finally, the consequence of the crisis—whether successful reform, revolution, or restoration—depends on the combination of political adaptability and the availability of ideological alternatives in the culture.

The demographic disequilibrium hypothesis distinguishes Goldstone's theory from those of both Huntington and Marx. Revolutions in this period represented neither crises of modernization nor capitalist economic classes sweeping away feudal fetters on their productivity (see the discussion of Marxist theory below). In conformity with Marxism, however, the crises arose out of a change in material relations, though not the way Marx expected. Like Huntington, Goldstone empha- sizes the inflexibility of existing institutional forms in managing emerging demands, but he more fully develops the multidimensional character of the struc- tural crisis. Moreover, these unmanageable demands develop out of demographic effects relatively independent of the modernization process. Indeed, Goldstone argues that capitalist modernization ultimately stabilized the European countries by dramatically increasing their material productivity and enabling them to escape "the cycles of overpopulation and food riots and of land shortage and state break- down that pervaded early modern history."[58]

Finally, the ecological crisis produced by unanticipated population growth in a relatively inflexible structural context supplies the disjuncture between an estab- lished form of life and the actual world experienced. In particular the multiple demographic effects undermined the legitimacy and competence of the essential- ly hierarchical structures of early modern monarchies. The availability in the cul- ture of other plausible cultural forms shaped the subsequent character of state reconstruction.

The two major elements of Goldstone's argument population growth as the source of disequilibrium and the multifaceted nature of instability—are logically independent.[59] His theory leaves open the possibility that other ecological vari- ables could supply the "earthquake" that shakes existing institutions. Population growth may instigate major disequilibria in the future, especially in the rapidly growing areas of Asia and Africa. On the other hand, environmental crises could generate equivalent challenges for the industrialized countries. In either case the intensity of the crisis would depend on the levels of fiscal insolvency, elite conflict, and mass discontent resulting from the ecological challenge. Unlike Huntington, Goldstone views the potential for state crises and revolution as arising not simply in a particular historical era but whenever an ecological disequilibrium over- whelms the adaptive capability of existing social structures.

Critique of Disequilibrium Theories

Disequilibrium theories represent an advance over simple inventories of the pre- sumed causes of revolution. They attempt to specify why and under what circum- stances the stresses and strains of social change lead to a revolutionary crisis. Though Johnson's original formulation of system disequilibrium seems vague, other statements add both conceptual clarity and empirical detail to his general formulation. The identification of four basic social forms of life and how contrary experiences undermine them, along with Huntington's thesis on the disequilibrat- ing effects of modernization, supplies more specific propositions on how disequi- libria might develop. In addition, Huntington's effort to estimate the strength of political organizations elaborates the concept of power deflation. His discussion of the Eastern and Western patterns of revolutionary transformation identifies alternative strategies of revolution as well as reasons why revolution might fail. Finally, Goldstone's recent interpretation of early modern revolutions provides an alternative explanation of disequilibrium by exploring the multifaceted crisis produced by structural inflexibility in the face of ecological challenge. Despite these contributions, however, certain problems remain.

Comprehensiveness A comprehensive theory of revolution must successfully address at least three basic issues: the origins of the revolutionary crisis, what weakens the state, and the factors affecting the relative success of revolutionary strategy and tactics. Taken together, the four approaches cover all these issues, at least to some extent. The notion that disequilibrium may arise from a culture crisis in general, or the impact of modernization or population growth in particular, proposes some intriguing macroperspectives on the inception of a revolutionary crisis. Huntington's argument on the connection between institutionalization and stability furnishes hypotheses as to the circumstances under which an established regime might "reequilibrate" the system. It also underlines the task facing the revolutionary movement in reconstructing the disrupted social order. Goldstone's stress indicator suggests a more precise way to determine the extent of the structural crisis. The major deficiency with respect to comprehensiveness emerges when we consider the factors affecting the relative success of the revolutionary movement. The two broad patterns of revolutionary transformation—Eastern and Western— provide an overall orientation to this issue but little basis for comparative evaluation. Similarly, Goldstone's suggestions about the potential role played by ideology in guiding the course of state reconstruction also lack specificity.

Coherence A theory, as we have noted, may display either too much or too little coherence. Indeed, a theory could manifest both problems at the same time. Too little coherence arises from self-contradiction—which disequilibrium theory appears to avoid—and weak or unspecified links among its component parts— which disequilibrium theory, like many social theories, manifests. Clearly, disequilibrium theory exhibits greater coherence than a simple list of causes, but the hypothesized links among the various components remain problematic. At best, the presumed "causal" relations are essentially tendency statements (see Figure 6.1), weakening the overall argument relating a disequilibrium crisis of some sort to a revolutionary outcome.

On the other hand, a proposed explanation reflects false coherence if it makes spurious connections or propounds an essentially circular argument. Whether the hypothesized relations represent valid causal links or merely accidental associations are essentially empirical questions (see below). Equilibrium theories, though, must struggle against a strong proclivity to circular argumentation.[60] Specifically, evidence of a prerevolutionary disequilibrium often becomes the revolution it produces. The logic of the argument, however, requires empirical validation of disequilibrium independent of the presence or absence of the predicted consequence, revolution. Goldstone, in particular, successfully avoids the pitfall of circular argumentation. By breaking down the social crisis into three components of fiscal distress, elite competition, and mass mobilization potential, he measures disequilibrium independently of the dependent variable of revolutionary upheaval.

Empirical Support Disequilibrium theorists, partly because of the logical problems indicated above, often offer anecdotal rather than systematic evidence for their argument. In addition, the central concepts, even when refined, generally exist at a high level of abstraction. Most of the variables—independent, intervening, and dependent—demand further specification of critical limits.[61] According to the proposition of homeostatic equilibrium, all social systems require continuous adjustment. When, however, does the "level" of disequilibrium become sufficiently severe to constitute a revolutionary crisis? When does political deflation or decay constitute a political crisis of authority or institutionalization? What, indeed, represents a revolution, rather than some other form of political turmoil?

The failure to specify critical limits or thresholds—a common shortcoming in social theory—combined with previously noted tendencies toward circular argumentation raises problems for falsification. If we do not know the important thresholds, we cannot determine if a specific instance of nonrevolution represents a falsifying counterexample or simply an instance where the critical limits of one or more key variables were not exceeded. Thompson and his coauthors note that if culture and social relations existed independently of one another, then this independence would undermine their theory.[62] Unfortunately, this suggestion too assumes some critical threshold effect, for they assert that all societies possess plural cultures. Such plurality helps explain the origins of both disequilibrium and transformation. Consequently, they must specify *whether* and *when* value pluralism demonstrates the relative independence of values and social organization.

Even Goldstone's demographic/structural approach, despite the specificity of its indicators of disequilibrium, encounters threshold effects. The disequilibrating impact of population growth depends on the resilience of the state's social structure. A state crisis develops only when several critical structural thresholds are breached. Each of the three major components of the crisis—fiscal insolvency, elite disunity, and popular mobilization potential—in turn include several subcrises. Elite disunity, for example, includes both intraelite conflict along various dimensions and alienation and defection of at least some elites from the state. Mass mobilization potential includes not only the immiseration of the masses as indicated by increased landlessness and the rising price of bread, but also related demographic shifts like migration to urban areas and expansion of the percentage of the population under thirty. While such complexity captures the character of a state crisis, it also provides many opportunites to "save the hypothesis." When identical population growth rates produce a crisis in one country but not another (as occurred between 1500 and 1650 with respect to Austria and northern Germany), the argument that multiple crises must combine to produce such crises provides opportunities to explain, or explain away, the discrepancy.[63]

Adequacy Macrotheories, because of their nature, tend to be relatively remote from the self-perceived realm of individual action; action that, after all, presumably embodies the "system" and makes it real. This reverses a problem encountered with microtheories of individual behavior where even adequate and empirically plausible accounts of the individual choice of political violence or other forms of extreme political action have difficulty explaining the occurrence of a society-wide revolutionary transformation. Macrotheories of system crisis and transformation, in contrast, often fail to represent the social world in terms that reflect the self-perceptions of individual actors.

In more refined statements of disequilibrium theory, however, the specifications considered draw closer to a more familiar social reality. Indeed, as we discuss the four ways of social life, we slip easily from considering patterns of social relations and the values that support them to viewing human actors as essentially one type of person or another—an egalitarian, an individualist, or whatever. The hypothesis that people possess "plural selves" carries the process of individual typification even further. This possible reduction down to the microlevel makes it easier to consider questions of interpretive adequacy, in that we can in principle ascertain whether people see themselves in the hypothesized manner.

Such reduction, though, generates something of a level-of-analysis problem. Are we dealing with a theory of personality and personal "disequilibrium," a theory of culture and cultural disequilibrium, or both? If both, then when and how does the former combine to produce a revolutionary crisis in the wider arena? Or is the process reversed: Does a culture crisis produce personal disequilibrium? If so, how?

A final problem with the adequacy of most, though not all, macrotheories involves their common deterministic implications. The focus on broad social forces and value changes obscures the significance of individual motives and purpose. Rather, these macroforces sweep people into social processes beyond their understanding and control. Later stages of the argument, such as those dealing with regime efforts to respond to power deflation, the revolutionary movement's strategy to negate the coercive power of its rivals, or the search for alternative ideological orientations, better represent individual purpose and choice. Nevertheless, usually some implication of ecological, social, or cultural determinism remains at the core of most disequilibrium theories.

Authenticity   Disequilibrium theory often stands accused of an inherent conservative bias. We easily slip into considering equilibrium as "good" and the forces that upset it as "bad." Such a tendency probably reflects the strong human need for order (see Chapter 1) as much as an inherent conceptual bias, but we might minimize it. As Johnson argues, we could understand disequilibrium as arising from the failure of the existing system to make necessary adjustments rather than as the evil influence of subversive forces or human perversity. Nevertheless, the reestablishment of order (equilibrium) remains the highest good, regardless of how disequilibrium arises.

Huntington's argument may contain a more subtle bias. If revolution is a problem of transitional societies, as he argues, then advanced industrial nations with their strongly institutionalized political regimes will never face a revolutionary crisis. His position directly opposes the classical Marxist prediction that the world revolution will begin in the most advanced societies (see below). Just because Huntington's conclusion might serve the interests of the capitalist establishment does not prove it is incorrect. However, if we have reason to doubt the validity of his restricted characterization of revolutionary potential, then the coincidence between the interests of powerful sectors and the conclusions of a social theory raises some questions about that theory's authenticity.

Alternatively, Goldstone provides a new critical twist on contemporary historical understanding. His theory to some extent challenges our confidence in the progressive character of history in general and revolution in particular. He argues that social and political institutions crumble not because they fail to manage the social forces of modernization but because they encounter an ecological crisis that overwhelms them. Though contemporary social institutions of welfare capitalism and liberal democracy appear more resilient than the autocratic states of the seventeenth and eighteenth centuries, their ability to survive a severe environmental or demographic disaster seems by no means assured.

Generalizability   Huntington restricts the domain of the concept of and explanation for revolution to a particular historical period. Goldstone also applies his demographic structural analysis to a specific historical period (roughly 1500 to 1850). However, he argues that a multidimensional structural crisis could arise in any historical era. Other disequilibrium theories also claim wider applicability for the idea of revolutionary crisis. Johnson's broad approach purchases its generalizability at the cost of vagueness. On the other hand, cultural disequilibrium theory, by specifying a limited number of basic ways of life, attempts to capture social variation more accurately while not entirely sacrificing some general perspective on the maze of idiographic detail. Unfortunately, once we recognize that all real societies reflect cultural mixes of one combination or another, we admit so much variety in the way disequilibrium might develop as to undercut any pretensions to general theory.

ϐ   ϐ   ϐ

Disequilibrium theories improve upon inventories of the long-term and immediate causes of revolution in at least two ways. First, they attempt to provide more concrete reasons why and how particular social and cultural changes combine to generate a revolutionary crisis. Second, they provide at least a crude sense of the stages of a revolution: disequilibrium, political crisis (power deflation or political decay), coercive struggle (recall that Huntington specifies two broad types, Western and Eastern), and reestablishment of a new equilibrium. Though they suffer from conceptual and empirical shortcomings, at least they offer a more systematic perspective on the problem of revolutionary transformation. The next macroapproach also attempts to impart a systematic understanding of revolutionary transformation. However, rather than viewing equilibrium as the normal state of affairs upset by some essentially exogenous material or value change, it stresses inherent structural contradictions and conflict.

STRUCTURAL CONTRADICTIONS AND THE REVOLUTIONARY CRISIS

Structural theories of revolutionary transformation, particularly those within a somewhat loosely characterized "Marxist" tradition, share several characteristics distinguishing them from disequilibrium theories. First, these approaches stress that stable patterns of social interaction— social *structures*—are the key variables in social explanation. This contrasts with both microlevel theories that focus on individual psychology and those macrolevel explanations that emphasize shared values.[64] Second, interests, especially material interests, define the bases of different structures. These material interests in some sense "construct" the values and norms that justify them. Third, material interests commonly conflict, generating the constant potential for overt discord. Most structural theories, then, see conflict as inherent in the structure of social relations, not as the product of periodic disequilibrium.

The Marxist "school" represents the most influential structural theory of revolution. First, we outline the major components of the basic Marxist explanation for revolutionary transformation. As a theory of revolution, however, classical Marxism explains the origins of a revolutionary crisis better than why it culminates in a revolutionary outcome. Second, we therefore review two major additions to the tradition, the Leninist stress on the role of the revolutionary vanguard and a more recent resurgence of interest in the state as a relatively autonomous player in the process of structural transformation.

The Structure of Revolutionary Transformation

Karl Marx, in contrast to the other analysts we discuss, was a revolutionary theorist in addition to being a theorist of revolution. As he expressed it, his purpose was not merely to interpret the world but to change it.[65] His life work produced not just a theory of but a program for revolution.[66] He never lived to see the revolution he prophesied and for which he toiled. Cynics might add we never *will* see his predicted outcome either, regardless of the pseudo-Marxist revolutions made in his name, because of the fundamental flaws of his theory. Consequently, any action based upon this flawed theory must be misguided.

Since Marx developed his thought over four decades and never produced a completely definitive statement, we find it difficult to represent his complex and sometimes contradictory argument, much less incorporate 150 years of its development by others.[67] Perhaps Marx furnishes his most succinct statement in *A Contribution to the Critique of Political Economy* (1857–1858):

> In the social production which men carry on they enter into definite relations that are indispensable and independent of their will; these relations of production correspond to a definite stage of development of their material powers of production. The sum total of these relations of production constitutes the economic structure of society— the real foundation, on which rise legal and political superstructures and to which correspond definite forms of consciousness. The mode of production in material life determines the general character of the social, political and spiritual processes of life. It is not the consciousness of men that determines their existence, but, on the contrary, their social existence that determines their consciousness. At a certain stage of their development, the material forces of production in society come in conflict with the existing relations of production, or—what is but a legal expression for the same thing—with the property relations within which they had been at work before. From

forms of development of the forces of production these relations turn into fetters. Then comes the period of social revolution. With the change of the economic foundation the entire immense superstructure is more or less rapidly transformed. In considering such transformations, the distinction should always be made between the material transformation of the economic conditions of production which can be determined with the precision of natural science, and the legal, political, religious, aesthetic or philosophic—in short the ideological forms in which men become conscious of this conflict and fight it out. Just as our opinion of an individual is not based on what he thinks of himself, so can we not judge of such a period of transformation by its own consciousness; on the contrary, this consciousness must rather be explained from the contradictions of material life, from the existing conflict between the social forces of production and the relations of production. No social order ever disappears before all the productive forces, for which there is room in it, have been developed; and new higher relations of production never appear before the material conditions of their existence have matured in the womb of the old society. Therefore, mankind always takes up only such problems as it can solve; since looking at the matter closely, we will always find that the problem itself arises only when the material conditions necessary for its solution already exist or are at least in the process of formation.[68]

This general outline suggests why many consider Marx to be an economic determinist, even though he expressed regret at the overly schematic way others applied his more subtle, dialectical analysis of history.[69] Despite such protestations the Marxist theory of revolution begins with a fundamentally materialist argument, however much it might be modified to account for historical diversity.

A revolutionary crisis develops out of an intensifying contradiction between the *forces of production* (FOP) and the *relations of production* (ROP) dominating a particular era. The forces of production comprise anything that is or can be used to create something of material value. They include technology, natural resources, and, most importantly, the organization and skills of labor.[70] Neither tools nor resources, Marx argues, have any value until combined with labor.

Relations of production—legally expressed in property relations—depend on who controls the use and product of the productive forces.[71] The relations of production determine the dominant or ruling class and the primary laboring class, as well as various peripheral classes. In the case of the capitalist era these classes are, respectively, the capitalist bourgeoisie, the proletariat, and the increasingly marginalized traditional middle classes and the progressively proletarianized peasantry. The sociopolitical "superstructure," including the state, dominant culture values and institutions, and ideology, reflects and defends the interests of the ruling economic class.

Marx assumes that the forces of production evolve continuously, improving the productive potential of human beings. Labor's skills and organization develop, technology advances, and the use of natural resources improves. Relations of production, which initially in any era further these progressive trends, increasingly hinder the full realization of human productive potential. Marx assumes the irreversible evolution of productive forces. At some point, then, the strain between these evolving forces and the increasingly obsolete relations culminates in a revolutionary transformation. A new class seizes control of the forces of production and brings into existence new productive relations. As productive relations change, so must everything in the superstructure; consequently, economic revolution involves political, ideological, and cultural transformations as well.

This fundamental contradiction finds expression in class conflict. Now the besieged ruling class will not slip quietly from the world stage; quite the contrary. After all, it controls the considerable power assets of the superstructure, including ideology, law, and, ultimately, instruments of coercion. Yet fundamental economic power inexorably slips to the challenger class, and ultimately it will sweep aside the old order. Since the old ruling class will likely defend itself through state coercion, the challenger class will probably have to resort to violence to overcome ruling-class resistance.

Though Marx gives passing attention to other epochal transformations (for example, from slave economies to feudalism and from feudalism to capitalism), as a revolutionary theorist he concentrates on his own era. He argues that the drive of capitalists to maximize their profits contributes to the emerging revolutionary crisis in a number of ways:

- The increasing concentration of economic power destroys the traditional artisan classes, drives the peasants from their land and into the cities, gathers the workers into ever-larger industrial sites, and even forces the weaker elements of the bourgeoisie into the proletariat.
- As the working class expands, it grows more alienated. Specialization in the workplace and the competition for jobs alienate workers from one another. Even though their labor is the primary component of the productive process, workers exercise no control over the forces of production. Marx refers to this condition as "wage slavery." Finally, since the capitalists expropriate any "surplus value" (value beyond what the workers need for bare subsistence), workers are alienated from the product of their labor.
- The structural cycle of alternating economic "boom and bust," essentially caused by capitalist overproduction in the pursuit of profits, periodically augments both the size and misery of the proletariat.
- The social interactions of the workers in their workplace gradually contribute to the growth of proletarian class consciousness. The workers, *objectively* constituted as a class by their position in the economic structure, begin to recognize *subjectively* their collective identity, common interests, and true enemy (the capitalist class).
- Increasing class consciousness provides the basis for organizing a revolutionary movement that, given the improving position of the proletariat in the objective forces of production, enables it to seize power. This organization expands in concert with the development of a collective identity, starting first with the organization in the workplace, and then proceeding to the industry, related industries, the national economy, and finally the workers of all nations.

Capitalism creates a world system, and the revolution to replace it will also be global in scope. Nevertheless, according to classical Marxism, the proletariat in the most advanced countries will lead the world revolution. By the time the revolution occurs, the proletariat will comprise most of the human race. Once the victorious workers eliminate the vestiges of the capitalist class, the new relations of produc-

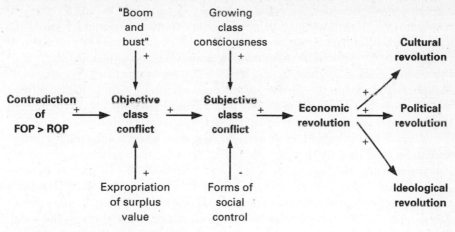

Figure 6.2 Basic Marxist model of revolution.

tion will consist of only one class—a working class now no longer alienated from the control of the productive forces. In this single class or "classless" society, the state, no longer needed for class oppression, will "wither away." Relations of production will no longer fetter the evolution of the forces of production, and human productive potential will blossom.

At the risk of obscuring the nuances and complexities of Marx's analysis of nineteenth-century capitalism, Figure 6.2 presents the basic Marxist model in a form somewhat comparable with the deprivation and disequilibrium models of revolution (see Figures 5.1, 5.2, and 6.1). The primary contradiction between the forces and relations of production increases "objective" class conflict. The depredations of the economic cycle and the inherent tendency of the ruling class to exploit the laboring class (or classes) reinforce this conflict. Increased objective class conflict contributes to the growth of subjective class conflict. The objective classes, defined by their position in the relations of production, become increasingly aware of themselves as a class and of their conflict with each other. Growing class consciousness and organization reinforce the growth of subjective class conflict, but the forms of social control (economic, cultural, and coercive) serve to suppress it (thus, the "−" sign in this relation). The intensification of subjective class conflict eventually culminates in a revolution in the economic relations of production. Since the relations of production determine the character of the superstructure, this economic revolution necessarily transforms culture, politics, and ideology.

Revising the Tradition: Party, State, and International System

Accepting for the moment Marx's contentions that material contradictions "can be determined with the precision of natural science" and that these contradictions lead to an emerging revolutionary crisis, does the theory explain, or simply assume, a revolutionary outcome? We could read Marx as arguing that evolving material conditions will inevitably lead to revolutionary transformation, and individual action can neither hasten nor defer this inevitability. In the case of the capitalist world system, the proletariat will ultimately throw off its economic shackles, establish new relations of production, and create a new superstructure. This argument, though, contributes to the passivity of the oppressed by asserting that underlying social forces will usher in the new age. It also assumes that the crisis produced by the material contradictions automatically leads to radical transformation.

V. I. Lenin, perhaps Marx's most significant heir as both a theorist of revolution and a revolutionary theorist, addresses precisely these problems of passivity and inevitability. He finds both conclusions insupportable.[72] Contrary to some other Marxists of his time, Lenin argues that left to its own devices the proletariat would never fulfill its revolutionary destiny. Yes, the contradictions would produce a crisis, and, yes, worker consciousness and organization would emerge. But a reality defined by the existing economic relations between workers and their employers would confine both consciousness and organization. So constrained, the workers could develop only a "trade union mentality." They would organize to improve their material condition within the existing relations of production, rather than to transform these relations.[73]

Lenin's critique of revolutionary inevitability anticipates the problem of the "rebel's dilemma" from the perspective of rational choice theory (see Chapter 5). Workers will defect from their collective interest in revolutionary transformation to pursue divisible material rewards within the capitalist system. We should also note that Lenin accurately predicted the course of worker activity in the advanced industrial nations of the West, at least thus far.

Lenin asserts that the workers can develop a revolutionary class consciousness only from outside the economic struggle with their employers.[74] He advocates, therefore, the creation of "an organization of revolutionists capable of maintaining the energy, the stability, and continuity of the political struggle."[75] Lenin's emphasis on the significance of an organization of professional revolutionaries serves to bridge theory and practice (see Chapter 8) and has proved influential in revolutions around the world. He also adds a significant, and voluntarist, component to the relatively deterministic Marxist model.

Lenin accepts that a vanguard cannot materialize a revolution out of a social vacuum. Fundamental contradictions must produce the conditions for objective class conflict. In the absence of the guidance of a professional revolutionary vanguard, however, only a reformist consciousness will emerge from objective class conflict. Again, notice that professional leadership represents a possible solution to the rebel's dilemma. The members of the vanguard can rationally believe their participation makes a difference. Once organized, the vanguard presumably implements some of the other solutions to the problem of free riding.

The revolutionary vanguard, then, serves to energize and organize the revolutionary class and maintain its discipline. This proposition rounds out the depiction of one side of the revolutionary equation. The other side, the position of the ruling class, still remains essentially determined by the underlying changes in the forces of production that eventually undermine the position of the ruling class in the economic structure. When the ruling class falls from structural grace, their other sources of power (for example, the state, the ruling ideology, and the other elements of the superstructure) presumably evaporate as well.

A second major revision to the basic Marxist model, however, challenges the simple economic determinism of this chain of reasoning. The essential issue involves the degree to which elements of the superstructure—especially the state, but also culture—are somewhat independent of the material interests of the ruling class. If parts of the superstructure are "semiautonomous," then they can possibly defect, weakening the instruments of social control maintaining the established relations of production. Marx certainly believed that intellectuals like himself could "reason" themselves free of their class origins. Indeed, these liberated elements of the intelligentsia, rather than producing the "mystifications" that legitimize the position of the ruling class, become important participants in the revolutionary vanguard and contribute to the raising of proletarian class consciousness.

Recently, some structural theorists have concentrated on the semiautonomous position of the state.[76] If the state as a political structure possesses interests other than simply defending the dominant class, then two possibilities emerge. The state could defect from the dominant class or the dominant class could defect from the state. Either defection weakens the defense of the established relations of production, opening up opportunities for the revolutionary movement.

The most significant, though not the sole, "semiautonomous interest" of the state involves its role in international competition. A state must be militarily and economically powerful to compete effectively in the international arena. Military strength requires extracting the resources needed to support the military organizations. Simply put, if the dominant class expropriates all surplus value from the workers and peasants, then the only source for the state to do *its* expropriating is from the dominant class.

Military power, moreover, ultimately depends on the underlying strength of a country's economy.[77] Consequently, military rivalry necessarily leads to comparative assessments of economic strength. A state may conclude that effective international competition requires certain domestic economic reforms, reforms that intrude on the entrenched interests of elements of the dominant class. For example, programs to protect new industries or carry out land reform to make the agrarian sector more productive often intrude on the interests of the landed gentry.

In both of these interrelated cases the interests of the dominant class and state diverge. The conflict engendered necessarily weakens the foundation of the status quo. If severe enough, elements of the dominant class may actually attack the state structure (or vice versa), weakening the major defender of its own class interests. The revolutionary movement can now seize the opening provided. This clash between elements of the establishment, if sufficiently severe, leads to the kind of collapse at the center that initiates the Western pattern of revolution. If less severe, it perhaps weakens state control sufficiently to enable a revolutionary movement to begin at the periphery, initiating an Eastern pattern of revolution.

These amendments represent only a few of the numerous variations added to the basic Marxist model over the past century. Even so, they soften the deterministic inevitability of the simple sequence portrayed in Figure 6.2. While underlying economic forces may indeed produce objective class conflict creating the potential for a revolutionary class movement, they will not suffice to propel this class to its full revolutionary consciousness. The fulfillment of revolutionary class potential requires the leadership of a professional revolutionary vanguard organization. Moreover, revolutionary class conflict alone may not sufficiently weaken the grip of the ruling class. Something must erode the power of the state that defends ruling class interests. Only with the added contributions of a revolutionary vanguard combined with a crisis of state domination will objective class conflict produce the conditions for a revolutionary transformation (see Figure 6.3).

Other major issues in the Marxist tradition include just who makes up the primary revolutionary class, whether the revolutionary transformation must be violent, what role tactics play in the transformation, and, of course, what explains the failure of the world revolutionary transformation (see below and Chapters 8 and 9). Despite this legacy of contention over basic issues, the Marxist theory of revo-

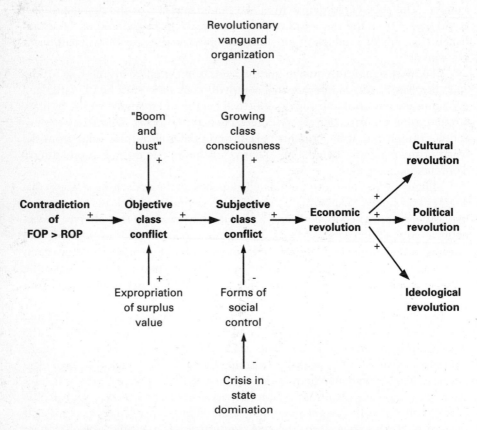

Figure 6.3 Modified Marxist model of revolution.

lution, broadly defined, remains the most influential structural approach to the problem of revolutionary transformation, influencing both analysts and revolutionary actors. Owing to its significance in both theoretical debates and practical politics, it also generates a major critical response.

Critique of Marxist Structuralism

Perhaps no social theory has received such thorough criticism as Marxism in its various incarnations. Certainly, Marx failed to fulfill his aspiration of developing a theory of social transformation deserving the same status as Newton's laws of physics. The influence of the natural scientific ideal, moreover, probably accounts for some of the determinism found in Marxist analysis. Indeed, the structural approach in general devalues the role of the individual human actor in accounting for large-scale social processes and thus seems inherently open to a deterministic bias. All this reflects the influence of metaphors drawn from classical mechanics.

The failure of Marxist theory to provide the apparent certitude of classical mechanics, however, cannot justify a quick dismissal of all its claims. After all, no other social theory provides such certitude. While we may fault Marxism for reaching beyond its grasp, we still need to consider the value of what it managed to grasp.

Comprehensiveness   Marxist theory addresses the issue of revolutionary transformation, not simply the problem of political turmoil and violence. As a comprehensive theory of revolution, however, classical Marxism fails on several counts. The basic argument of structural contradiction and economic crisis, as we saw, provides an account of the emergence of a revolutionary crisis but fails to explain what leads from crisis to transformation. In partial response to this short-coming, later Marxist theorists attempted to identify what galvanizes the potential revolutionary class to fulfill its historic mission (the vanguardist party) and what weakens the ruling class sufficiently to allow for effective revolutionary action (the crisis of the semiautonomous state). Even so, how revolutionary actors solve issues of strategy and tactics remains largely unaddressed.

Coherence   The logic of the Marxist theory of revolution contains three problems: tendencies toward circular argument, a related false certitude about some presumed linkages, and, ironically, a response to predictive failure that eviscerates the ability to predict the future of revolutionary activity.

The major problem of circularity arises with the proposed link between class conflict and revolutionary transformation.[78] According to the theory intensified class conflict characterizes periods of revolutionary transformation. Indeed, intensified class struggle constitutes the revolutionary crisis. This hypothesized connection tempts us to take a revolutionary transformation as a sufficient demonstration of extreme class conflict. Such reasoning, though, is circular. We need to demonstrate the existence and intensity of class conflict independently of the presence (or absence) of revolutionary turmoil. As in previous cases, solutions to the temptation of circular argumentation raise an empirical challenge (see below, "Empirical Support").

In addition to potentially circular argument, classical Marxist theory of revolution contains deterministic connections that both minimize the significance of individual action and posit the inevitability of eventual revolutionary transformation. The former aspect raises questions about whether Marxist theory adequately accounts for the motives and activities of the revolutionaries (see below, "Adequacy"). On the other hand, historical experience tends to undercut any sense of inevitability.

The heirs to Marxist theory add in elements of volition (the vanguard party) and nondeterminism (semiautonomous elements of the superstructure, like state and culture). While these changes soften an insupportable determinism and accommodate the desire of revolutionaries to have some control over their own fate, they do so at the cost of weakening the causal connections within the basic model.

Empirical Support   Problems with respect to comprehensiveness and coherence contribute to a crisis of empirical support for Marxist theory. The basic components of the abstract model, such as the forces and relations of production and the concept of class, all require clear empirical specification to convert the model into an empirically grounded theory. Unfortunately, encounters with the empirical complexity of actual historical cases of revolution demonstrate the weaknesses of these central concepts.

The concepts of class and class consciousness, for example, are central to the theory. These concepts define the nature of the relations of production and determine the intensity of class conflict, the presumed wellspring of revolutionary transformation. For these concepts to carry their explanatory load, we must be able to specify a number of aspects.[79] First, empirical theory requires that we define class boundaries. Second, the consciousness of the class members must reflect this definition; that is, people must recognize their membership in a particular class. Third, class differences, so perceived, must generate the basic conflicts in society.

Encounters with the real world frustrate these objectives in a number of ways. First, the actual patterns of economic relations in a society often reveal considerable complexity. Marxist analysts (and, for that matter, the revolutionary actors) commonly recognize multiple divisions existing in supposedly clear-cut classes. For example, working-class divisions might include a trade union "aristocracy" with little revolutionary interest, unorganized workers, both blue- and white-collar, and an anomic aggregation of the unemployed and underemployed with little perspective on their social plight (sometimes referred to as the "lumpenproletariat"). The peasantry may include rich, middle, poor, and landless elements. These divisions raise not simply questions of adequate classification; they also represent significant differences in social position and, therefore, revolutionary potential.

Second, whatever boundaries the analyst concocts, Marxist empirical theory requires that these relate, ultimately, to the self-definition of its presumed members. These members must recognize their class interests and act upon them. If a revolutionary class divides into multiple subelements of differing revolutionary potential, then any consciousness reflecting these divisions might fail to produce a common revolutionary consciousness.

Third, even a cursory review of various civil conflicts around the world reveals that cleavages other than class—for example, race, linguistic, and religious identities—seem far more significant sources of violent discord and even revolution than presumed economic class divisions. To dismiss this empirical reality as a product of false consciousness begs the question as to the adequacy of the concepts of class and class conflict in explaining actual, as opposed to hypothetical, conflict.

Mark Hagopian summarizes the empirical difficulties of a theory of revolution based on the concept of class conflict:

> (1) The term "class" is often misapplied to cases where the system of stratification is something else; (2) segments of the same class are often found on both sides of the revolutionary barricades; (3) the role and nature of "outside" (that is, from a different class, like the intelligentsia) leadership calls into question not only the "spontaneity," but also the very nature of ostensibly class-based revolutionary movements.[80]

Another area of empirical difficulty arises from the failure to specify all the critical empirical factors. For example, since class conflict presumably exists in all social settings but only periodically intensifies to crisis proportions, critical thresholds must be defined. Moreover, given the theory's historical character, some critics find the failure to specify time factors especially ironic. "Thus, we never know," Salert observes, "how long particular processes are supposed to take. If some predicted effect fails to materialize, then, it is never clear whether this means the theory is inadequate or simply that insufficient time has elapsed."[81]

Finally, the most potent empirical criticism of the Marxist theory of revolution emphasizes its apparent falsification on many points of prediction. The original theory predicted that the world revolution against capitalism would start in the most advanced capitalist countries. It did not. Moreover, although late nineteenth-century Marxists recognized some revolutionary potential in Russia, the theory claimed that the socialist revolution could not begin in such relatively backward countries. It did. Once begun, the revolution was to spread throughout the world capitalist system. It has not. The proletariat supposedly plays the key role in revolutionary transformation. It has not. Even in Russia, and much more so in China and Vietnam, the peasants made a critical contribution to the success of the revolution. Once established in power, socialism was to yield rapidly to communism, resulting in the withering away of the state. The state thrived in the Soviet Union, China, and the rest of the socialist world. Finally, history's progress is irreversible; a higher stage—socialism—cannot yield to its precursor. But socialism apparently yielded in Eastern Europe and the Soviet Union and is under pressure elsewhere in the socialist world.

Unsurprisingly, this record of failure leads to some serious efforts to "save the hypothesis." The most obvious ploy, as Salert notes, is to lengthen the time span needed for the transformation. Other conceptual escapes include Lenin's theory of imperialism and its successors that not only posit that exploitation of the "peripheral" territories in Asia, Africa, and the Middle East eases revolutionary pressure within the imperialist countries, but also suggests why the revolution might start in the exploited periphery, rather than the advanced core.[82] The tendency among Marxist theorists over the past century to assert that the capitalist system has entered its final crisis, however, eventually grows unconvincing.

One of the more interesting efforts to save the theory from apparent falsification argues that the revolutionary disturbances of the twentieth century, regardless of their ideological rhetoric, are not socialist, but late-capitalist, revolutions.[83] Edward Malecki points out that in Marxist theory the position of labor (or "mode of production") defines the character of any historical era. Thus, slave labor and serf labor characterize the ancient and feudal epochs, respectively. Wage labor, in turn, defines the capitalist era, while true socialist revolution ushers in the era of free labor, where the working class controls the means of production. Instead of free labor, however, these so-called socialist revolutions merely continued the mode of wage labor.

Wage labor reduces the workers to the status of a mere commodity exchanged like any other component in the productive process. Malecki argues that, with some minor exceptions, this description aptly characterizes the position of labor in the so-called socialist countries. In these "socialist" economies, though, a central administrative structure, as opposed to the free market, allocates labor in the productive process. This distinction, however, makes no difference. The workers still lack control of the means of production, still are wage slaves. The label "state capitalism" best describes the relations of production in these countries. In any case, many of the previously "socialist" countries are abandoning the administrative allocation of labor.

Malecki concludes, therefore, that the pseudosocialist revolutions of the twentieth century do not falsify Marxist predictions. Perhaps revolution in advanced capitalist systems is an impossibility, as Huntington argues, but the jury on the issue remains deadlocked. On the other hand, even though empirical ambiguities may not eliminate the Marxist model, they still undermine its credibility as an explanatory theory of revolution.

Adequacy   Structural theories, especially in the Marxist tradition, tend to minimize the significance of individual intention in their explanations of revolutionary transformation. As Theda Skocpol puts it:

> The purposive image is very misleading about both the causes and processes of social revolutions that have actually occurred historically. As for causes, no matter what form social revolutions might conceivably take in the future (say in an industrialized, liberal-democratic nation), the fact is that historically no successful social revolution has ever been "made" by a mass-mobilizing, avowedly revolutionary movement.[84]

Now structuralists do not deny that human beings possess intentions or assign meaning to their actions. Rather, especially in materialist approaches of the Marxist tradition, basic structural realities condition, even determine, forms of individual consciousness. Consequently, our understanding of social outcomes must build on these underlying conditions, not on the second-order states of mind they produce in individuals. Our interest in these mental states concentrates primarily on the "false consciousness" they embody.

The tendency for structural analysis to deny explanatory significance to individual intentionality prompts objections from analysts embracing more interpretive approaches to the study of revolution:

> That revolutions are not made by people with revolutionary intentions does not mean that they are not in the first instance the product of intentional action; that they do not turn out as their participants intended or foresaw does not imply that intentional action has no role in their explanation (the unintended consequences of action are in fact the central preoccupation of rational choice theorists); and that the situations in which the participants in revolutions find themselves are not of their making does not entail that rational action [or, for that matter, "nonrational" intention] had no part in their production.[85]

Indeed, Skocpol's own analysis of the Chinese Revolution demonstrates the difficulty in explaining its outcome without reference to the deliberate actions of the Communist Party leadership and the ideology and organizations they created.[86] The Leninist addition to the Marxist model of a vanguard organization deliberately working to bring about revolutionary transformation provides some account of the possible role of intention in explaining outcome.

A final problem with the adequacy of structural theories concerns their inherent tendency to *reify* their abstractions or categories, that is, to treat them as if they were real. Of course, for a Marxist, categories such as "class" and "state" *are* real. On the other hand, we might regard them simply as ways of conceptualizing complex relations. Perhaps nowhere is the tendency toward reification more obvious than in the treatment of the state as a semiautonomous structure. The "state" strives to maximize its power vis-à-vis other states. The "state" decides this; the "state" competes for that. We might come up with a definition of an economic class independent of the consciousness of its presumed members but rather based solely on their position in the productive process. However, the concept "state" represents complex interactions in which individuals, fulfilling specified roles, deliberately pursue the affairs of state and consciously devise the policies attributed to the "state." The actions of the "state," therefore, clearly represent the conscious intentions of individuals performing roles in the "state." The structural emphasis on reified concepts obscures this reality.

Authenticity   Unlike most other attempts at explanation we reviewed, Marxist theories of revolution explicitly emphasize issues of authenticity in their analysis. The pernicious mystifications of the dominant culture and ideology often mislead the members of the oppressed classes and obscure their true interests and identity. This false consciousness also presumably afflicts bourgeois social scientists who simply help to replicate and reinforce the dominant pattern of productive relations through "theories" that serve as little more than apologias for the status quo.

In the basic Marxist model a true consciousness eventually emerges out of the objective relations of the working class. Moreover, some bourgeois intellectuals—like Marx and Engels—free themselves from delusion through their own efforts.

This latter contention clearly softens the economic determinism characterizing the model. On the other hand, as we noted above, Lenin believed that objective economic conditions would not remove the blinders from the eyes of the proletariat. Rather, the revolutionary vanguard must lead them from false consciousness. In either case authentic social relations would characterize the postrevolutionary era.

As with other theories of false consciousness, we might question the structural standard of critical authenticity itself. When "the masses" fail to hold the values and objectives the revolutionaries deem authentic, it becomes far too easy to dismiss them as deluded. When predicted outcomes do not occur, false consciousness serves as a convenient rationalization. But any theory of false consciousness can lead its adherents to dismiss reality as illusion while mistaking their own illusions for reality. From the perspective of a theory of revolution, critical self-deception leads to mistaken explanation and prediction. From the perspective of revolutionary practice, such delusions lead to disastrous actions on the part of the deluded revolutionaries. More than once in the history of abortive rebellions revolutionaries convinced themselves of the fruitfulness of hostile soil for their radical seeds, only to act in deadly futility.

Generalizability   Structural approaches to revolutionary change, especially those within the Marxist tradition, sometimes aspire for universal applicability to all times and places. Marx himself gives passing attention to a sweeping depiction of historical epochs and their transformation, from the ancient to the contemporary world. On the other hand, he focused his detailed attention on the capitalist system and its presumed contradictions. As we noted above, he also cautioned against applying his analysis in an excessively schematic way (an injunction we have, perhaps, violated).

Some of the best work done within this tradition concentrates on the analysis and comparison of particular historical cases, rather than sweeping generalizations.[87] Skocpol specifically warns against generalizing the arguments she develops to understand and compare the French, Russian, and Chinese revolutions to other contemporary social revolutions (such as those in Mexico, Algeria, and Vietnam), despite superficial similarities.[88] Rather, her structural analysis in its various forms yields some interesting questions that may be relevant to understanding other particular instances of revolution.

While not denying the appeal of such explanatory modesty, it poses its own problems. As Rule points out, it approaches a somewhat circular assertion "that the theory should apply only where the evidence happens to fit."[89] A theory with a limited domain is not inherently flawed, but one that "holds only for certain cases is not very exciting *unless* we can specify in advance what those cases will be. Perhaps what Weber said of the materialist theory of history holds for theories in general: they are not conveyances to be taken and alighted from at will."[90]

♨   ♨   ♨

Structural analysis within the Marxist tradition suffers from some obvious shortcomings: ambiguous and reifying conceptualization, circular argumentation, and empirical failures, as well as a tendency to underestimate the significance of deliberate individual and group action for revolutionary transformation. Nonetheless we should not dismiss structural approaches, for a number of reasons.

First, whatever failures we perceive in postrevolutionary socialist societies, many oppressed people over the past century and around the world have found that this type of analysis makes sense of their situation. We cannot dismiss their response as simply the product of delusion and deception.

Second, structural theories, like other macroapproaches, address directly the problem of the revolutionary transformation of whole societies. Microanalyses of motives and intention cannot easily address such concerns.

Third, though perhaps exaggerating the primacy of material relations, the structural focus on established patterns of socioeconomic interaction which condition, if not determine, people's values, outlook, and political relations adds to our understanding of social processes. The analyses of economic conflict and the role of the state impart important perspectives to the study of radical social change.

Finally, we are not weighing structural analysis against a perfect alternative; all the approaches we have reviewed—micro and macro—suffer from serious limitations.

BRIDGING MICROMOTIVES AND MACROEFFECTS

The opportunity/resource approach focuses explicitly on the Leninist problem of revolutionary organization, drawing upon both micro- and macroanalyses to understand the conditions that favor the emergence and success of a radical social movement.[91] Like rational choice theory, opportunity/resource analysis sees radical social action as rational, but like structural approaches, the interests people pursue are collective rather than individual in nature. These "collective" interests reflect groupings in the social "middle range"; that is, they represent neither simple aggregations of individuals nor whole populations. While they may be class-based, other forms of group identification also exist.

Unlike integration theory, but somewhat similarly to Marxism, the opportunity/resource approach views radical conflict as continuous with other forms of political competition, rather than representing the "breakdown" of a normally peaceful state of affairs. Finally, this approach stresses that contention among groups occurs within the polity as a struggle for power over the whole community. A potentially revolutionary situation arises when two (or more) contenders make mutually exclusive claims to power; that is, each attempts to eliminate the other(s).[92]

Discontent, Opportunity, and Resources in the Emergence of Radical Political Conflict[93]

This approach stresses the importance of opportunity and resources to the emergence of a political movement, radical or otherwise. Consequently it tends to disparage the role of fluctuating discontent in explaining outbreaks of radical politi-

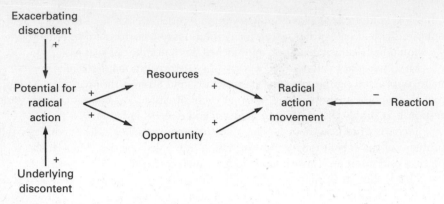

Figure 6.4 Social movement model of revolution.

cal action. For example, Charles Tilly remarks: "Grievances are fundamental to rebellion as oxygen is fundamental to combustion. But just as fluctuations in the oxygen content of the air account for little of the distribution of fire in the workaday world, fluctuations of grievances are not a major cause of the presence or absence of rebellion."[94]

Tilly develops a vivid simile, but his science is somewhat misleading. For most combustion purposes, we can assume that the oxygen level is constant because the fluctuations are insignificant. Significant increases in oxygen content would dramatically affect not only the frequency of fires but also the survival of life on this planet. Beyond being a cautionary lesson on how mistaken metaphors can mislead, this correction implies that fluctuating discontent (which varies more than the level of oxygen in the air) might play a role in a modified mobilization model. Consequently, our social movement model includes discontent, along with opportunity, resources, and reaction (See Figure 6.4).

Discontent   Even assuming that discontent within a particular society is relatively constant over time, we must still account for its origins and level in different societies. Otherwise we would seem to adopt the position that levels of discontent are everywhere the same or that they make no difference in explaining the emergence of radical social movements. Moreover, we should consider the possibility that significant fluctuations occur within the same society over time. Perhaps we can address both of these issues by ascertaining *underlying* and *exacerbating* discontent in a community.

Structural analysis, in particular, focuses on the problem of underlying discontent by identifying forms of exploitation and alienation so deeply embedded in the established order that they provide a constant source of grievance. Marxist depictions of the position of labor in a capitalist system, for example, epitomize this kind of structurally determined discontent.

Even Marxist analysis, however, recognizes that perturbations can affect the levels of grievance felt among oppressed sectors. For example, economic downturns increase the vulnerability and misery of the working classes. The various disequilibrium approaches also recognize and account for some ways in which widely shared feelings of discontent might emerge or increase. Finally, relative deprivation arguments alert us to the possibility that expectations may change, increasing frustration with established patterns of deprivation.

Measuring levels and fluctuations in discontent—whether defined psychologically, culturally, or structurally—is a daunting task and, as we have seen, one that avoids conceptual ambiguity and circularity only with difficulty. Nevertheless, whatever their imperfections, we have reviewed numerous approaches that provide insight into this problem.

Opportunity   Agreeing with structuralists who stress the role of the state in determining the likelihood of revolution, the opportunity/resource model also recognizes that the capacity of the regime to deflect, manipulate, or repress discontent affects the probability of successful mobilization for resistance and transformation. Something must weaken the efficacy of the available instruments of social control to provide the *opportunity* for radical movements to develop.

Many of the events and processes usually cited as disrupting social control include precisely those changes commonly recognized as long- and short-term causes of revolution like industrialization, urbanization, population growth, wars, and international political realignments. More immediate sources of expanded opportunities for resistance arise from divisions within the establishment. The regime itself may be riven by conflict or, as the structural theory of state crisis suggests, deserted by key elements of the dominant sectors of the polity.

Doug McAdam concludes that the expansion of opportunities for resistance resulting from weakening social control has two "facilitative effects." First, these changes "improve the chances for successful social protest by reducing the power discrepancy between insurgent groups and their opponents." Second, the improvement in the relative power position of the radical movement "raises significantly the costs of repressing insurgent action."[95] These two advantages, though, assume that someone possesses the capability to exploit the opportunities created by weakened social control, indicating a third factor contributing to the mobilization of resistance.

Resources   A totally powerless group, if such exists, could not respond to increased opportunities. Those challenging the status quo must already possess some means to seize the opportunities opening up for them. Following McAdam, we note five significant sources of movement strength:[96]

1. *Members*   A movement's resource position will improve if it is able to recruit supporters "by virtue of their involvement in organizations that serve as the associational network out of which [the] new movement emerges," or if it can recruit blocs of members by merging existing groups within the aggrieved community.
2. *Established Solidary Incentives*   Solidary incentives consist of the interpersonal rewards and punishments that hold groups together and thereby help to overcome the free rider problem (see Chapter 5). An

emerging revolutionary movement could draw upon preexisting identifica
tions and enforceable definitions of collective interest.

3. ***Communication Networks***   If the community already possesses established communication networks, then a movement can draw upon these
to facilitate communication of its goals and directives to potential supporters.

4. ***Leaders***   Just as a revolutionary movement could build on the membership of existing organizations, the same organizations may supply recognized leaders who can lend their reputations, skills, and experience to the
emerging movement.

5. ***Cognitive Liberation***   The extent to which a movement can take
advantage of the opportunities available to it partly depends on the "cognitive liberation" of its supporters. This liberation depends on "the subjective meaning [potential members] attach to their situation." Most fundamentally, people must believe that resistance is possible. A virtuous cycle
might arise if the successful organization of revolutionary activities contributes to the cognitive liberation of further potential supporters, leading
to increased support for the movement. Increased support can then translate into more action, and so on. Of course, a defeat could set up a vicious
cycle of defection and further defeat.

In addition to the general idea that resistance is possible, different forms of
resistance place different demands on potential supporters. The attitudes of those
acting on the presumption that the revolution is at hand differ from the beliefs of
those committed to a prolonged struggle. The movement overcomes the free rider
problem more easily in the former than the latter case, at least over the short term.
Of course, if the movement experiences a setback, those committed to immediate
revolutionary gratification will likely defect.

Reaction   Successful mobilization for radical social transformation generates
new challenges. Internally and externally, success may imperil a revolutionary
movement. The creation of formal structures of resistance increases the danger of
oligarchy. Organizational success may generate a leadership faction whose members come to value their own position in the movement more than the realization
of its revolutionary objectives. They may use the institutional power at their disposal to secure their privileges and eliminate challengers. Critics of the Leninist
solution to the rebel's dilemma feared precisely this outcome—the vanguard
transforming itself from leader to dictator.[97]

The co-optation of the oligarchic leadership also threatens the integrity of a
revolutionary movement. "Conserving" reforms may guarantee the leadership's
privileges while compromising the movement's original purpose. The members of
a movement, moreover, may also succumb to the appeal of the modest payoffs of
reform and defect from the revolutionary mission. Oligarchic leadership, moreover, may grow increasingly detached from, and less responsive to, the needs and
feelings of the rank and file, thereby contributing to the erosion of the movement's
base of support.[98]

Apart from these potentially negative organizational dynamics, a revolutionary movement will find that the character of its challenge affects the nature of the repression it faces. A radical attack against the status quo may galvanize even a previously divided regime into more effective repression. Consequently, we might expect that movements advocating more radical transformations and more exclusionist claims to power will have to deflect and defeat more serious repression.[99]

Critique

The social mobilization model draws upon a number of other approaches, both micro and macro, so we need not rehash the conceptual and logical difficulties of these elements. As an empirical theory of revolutionary activity, the mobilization model suggests several propositions:[100]

1. We should expect the participants in radical action to come from sectors of the population defined by preexisting grievances against the status quo.
2. We should expect more radical action to be an outgrowth of less radical action that has been frustrated.
3. We should expect more radical action to be the outgrowth of mutually exclusive claims made by contending sectors.
4. We should expect higher levels of participation from those sectors that already possess some organizational resources.

While each of these claims seems, in principle, falsifiable, developing empirical indicators of relatively ambiguous variables such as preexisting resources or grievances may prove difficult. More serious, perhaps, is the excessively instrumental character of this approach. The theory views radical action as resulting from the rational calculation of collective interests. But just as we cannot explain all individual behavior by the appeal to the rational actor model, we cannot assume collective rationality explains all collective action, assuming actors have overcome the free rider problem in the first place. Considerable amounts of collective violence seem relatively spontaneous in origin, produced by individual and crowd psychology rather than deliberate individual or collective calculation.

Nevertheless, sustained revolutionary activity, as we argued in the previous chapter, must include elements of calculation on the part of both leaders and followers. The social movement model draws upon insights of both micro- and macroapproaches to isolate some key factors influencing the emergence of radical political movements. In addition to providing suggestive links among various approaches, social movement analysis begins to link the concerns of theories of revolution to those of revolutionary theory and practice.

CONCLUSION: EXPLANATION AND UNDERSTANDING

Why do the masses revolt? How are societies transformed? The macrotheories we reviewed offer a number of different answers to these questions (see Table 6.2). Some of these seem to reflect essentially a deterministic bias. Others more read-

Table 6.2   CLASSIFYING EXPLANATIONS OF VIOLENCE AND REVOLUTION (III)
(R=REVOLUTION, PV=POLITICAL VIOLENCE, RCA=RADICAL COLLECTIVE
ACTION)

LEVEL OF ANALYSIS (FOCUS)	DETERMINISTIC	VOLUNTARISTIC
Structure (stable patterns of social arrangement)	• *Demographic/structural disequilibrium* [R][a] • *Structural contradictions* [R] • Regime/dissident balance of power [PV] • Misery thesis [R]	• *Semiautonomous state* [R] • Organization effects [RCA]
Culture (mutually accepted directives)	• *Disequilibrium theories* [R] • Justifications for PV [PV] • Cherry pie thesis, S-R [PV]	• Other-regardingness [RCA] • Cherry pie thesis, S-O-R [PV]
Group (social psychology)	• Insanity thesis, group [PV]	• *Opportunity/resource (vanguard party)* [RCA] • Revolutionary entrepreneurs [RCA] • Conspiracy thesis [R and PV]
Individual (psychology)	• Relative deprivation [PV] • Insanity thesis, individual [PV] • Killer ape thesis [PV]	• The rational revolutionary [RCA]

[a] New material in italics

ily admit the significance of choice, either individual or collective. Both disequilibrium and structural theories, in their basic thrust, tend toward a deterministic understanding of the process of social transformation. A disequilibrium or a structural contradiction develops and intensifies until rectified through social transformation. Individuals seem swept along by cultural or economic forces largely beyond their control and understanding. These broad and impersonal material, social, or cultural forces *make* revolution.

Perhaps no social explanation emphasizing determinism or voluntarism, individual or collective behavior, to the exclusion of the other, ever adequately represents the complexity and ambiguity of social life. As we saw in Chapter 5, more elaborate versions of deprivation and rational choice microtheories enrich their explanatory efforts with additions from macrolevel analysis. Similarly, more complex macroapproaches complement their deterministic tendencies with voluntarist elements like the vanguardist party or the semiautonomous state. Cultural disequilibrium and opportunity/resource approaches, though beginning with a macrolevel approach, emphasizing culture crisis and collective action, respectively, still recognize that ultimately individuals must undertake the radical action.

Given this glut of explanations contradicting, crosscutting, and overlapping one another, each displaying its logical weaknesses, conceptual ambiguities, and empirical shortcomings, we might wish to abandon the search for theories of political violence and revolution. Better, perhaps, to take each case as it comes and build up our understanding, bit by bit, from the facts of the particular situation. We could renounce belief in any social theory to avoid contaminating our understanding of a historical case with preconceived notions of what transpired and why.

Undeniably, advocates of a particular explanatory position sometimes force a recalcitrant reality into their explanatory framework, oblivious to the resulting distortion. We should, perhaps, embrace a kind of "agnosticism" about the value of any particular approach when we confront the intractable diversity of political life. But the notion that we can engage the social world "uncontaminated" by any explanatory orientation is both naive and dangerous. The very determination of what an observed phenomenon "is"—is it violence or not, revolution or not?—reflects some categorical scheme. And explanation begins with categorization. Without some determination of what things "are," we could not even get out of bed in the morning, much less pretend to understand social and political processes.

Efforts to be explicit, systematic, and empirical in developing explanations of social and political life visibly display their shortcomings. The alternative, however, is not pure, unmediated comprehension, but rather a pseudo-understanding hiding the clutter of stereotypes, myths, and prejudices that often pass as unquestioned verities. In the last century the German philosopher G. W. F. Hegel argued that the unexamined prejudices of the common person represent truly abstract thinking, because they are applied without thought or discrimination. The systematic conceptualizations of the philosopher (and, by extension, the social analyst) represent the difficult effort to think more concretely about the world.[101]

Between the hapless ignorance of those who think they directly "know" the world untainted by any conceptual abstractions and the futile certainty of those convinced they possess *the* theory of politics exists an unfortunately wide variety of contending approaches. Taken alone or together, they may not add up to a coherent answer to the puzzles of political violence and revolution, but they at least indicate some important questions to ask. As Rule observes, we know many things about political violence and revolution that are sometimes true, but we don't know when they will hold true.[102] Later, we draw on these theories to help orient us in two case studies of violence and apparent radical transformation (see Part Three).

Revolutionary actors, building on their own understanding of the revolutionary potential in a society, must solve puzzles of leadership, ideology, organization, strategy, and tactics to exploit the opportunities that underlying social forces serve up to them. And, unlike social analysts, they must risk their enterprise and their lives on the validity of their explanatory efforts. These areas of practical concern to the revolutionary actor provide further focus for our efforts to understand the process of radical social transformation in a more concrete manner.

NOTES

1. Michael Thompson, Richard Ellis, and Aaron Wildavsky, *Culture Theory* (Boulder, Colo.: Westview Press, 1990), pp. 207–208.
2. The distinction between social scientific theories of revolution and the revolutionary theory of the participants is that of William H. Friedland, *Revolutionary Theory* (Totowa, N.J.: Allanheld, Osmun, 1982), p. xii.
3. My inventory is a combination and synthesis of those included in Mark N. Hagopian, *The Phenomenon of Revolution* (New York: Dodd, Mead, 1974), pp. 135–150, and Thomas H. Greene, *Comparative Revolutionary Movements: The Search for Theory and Justice,* Third Edition (Englewood Cliffs, N.J.: Prentice Hall, 1990), pp. 152–181. Although I am indebted to these two authors, I take responsibility for any confusion arising from my effort at reorganization, combination, and explication.
4. Richard L. Rubenstein, *The Cunning of History: The Holocaust and the American Future* (New York: Harper Colophon, 1978), pp. 27–28. Rubenstein's argument is heavily influenced by the German sociologist Max Weber. For further citations see Rubenstein's notes.
5. For an intellectual history of this process see Melvin J. Lasky, *Utopia and Revolution* (Chicago: University of Chicago Press, 1976). See also James Billington, *The Fire in the Minds of Men: Origins of the Revolutionary Faith* (New York: Basic Books, 1980).
6. Hagopian, pp. 138–139.
7. See, for example, the argument of Eric R. Wolf, *Peasant Wars of the Twentieth Century* (New York: Harper & Row, 1969).
8. Cf. Norman T. Uphoff and Warren F. Ilchman, "Development in the Perspective of Political Economy," in Norman T. Uphoff and Warren F. Ilchman, eds., *The Political Economy of Development* (Berkeley: University of California Press, 1972), pp. 75–121. Uphoff and Ilchman make an interesting effort to apply the criterion of productivity to noneconomic areas as well.
9. See the discussion of James C. Davies' "J-curve" in the previous chapter's examination of deprivation theory.
10. See, for example, Robert E. Gamer, *The Developing Nations: A Comparative Perspective,* Second Edition (Boston: Allyn and Bacon, 1982).
11. Greene, pp. 154–156.
12. See Jack A. Goldstone, *Revolution and Rebellion in the Early Modern World* (Berkeley: University of California Press, 1991). Goldstone's sophisticated argument concerning the contribution of population growth to disequilibrium is summarized in a later section of this chapter.
13. Hagopian, pp. 143–147.
14. My inventory of accelerators is, again, derived from Greene, pp. 133–151 and Hagopian, pp. 150–166.
15. For a survey of the linkages between war and revolution see Harvey Starr, "The Relationship Between Revolution and War: A Theoretical Overview," presented at the Annual Meeting of the International Studies Association, Vancouver, B.C.,

March 1991. Starr attempts to develop a model that links war and revolution, reminding us not only that war may precipitate revolution, but also the reverse. For example, revolution weakens a country and may well tempt an ambitious and aggressive neighbor to attack (for example, Iraq's aggression against Iran; see Chapter 11). Alternatively, revolutionary fervor may encourage the new regime to try to spread the creed through the gun, whether by subversion or direct aggression.

16. The argument that revolution results when a ruling elite fails to renew itself is commonly associated with the early-twentieth-century sociologist Vilfredo Pareto.

17. The classic study of the importance for a revolution of military defections is Katharine Chorley, *Armies and the Art of Revolution* (Boston: Beacon Press, 1973), originally published in 1943.

18. The crucial significance of the "desertion of the intellectuals" was recognized by both Crane Brinton, *The Anatomy of Revolution* (Englewood Cliffs, N.J.: Prentice-Hall, 1952), and Lyford P. Edwards, *The Natural History of Revolution* (Chicago: University of Chicago Press, 1970).

19. James DeFronzo, *Revolutions and Revolutionary Movements* (Boulder, Colo.: Westview Press, 1991), pp. 19–20.

20. Chalmers Johnson, *Revolutionary Change* (Boston: Little, Brown, 1966), p. 12.

21. Ibid., p. 33.

22. Ibid., pp. 53–54.

23. Ibid., p. 58

24. Ibid., p. 60.

25. Ibid., p. 91.

26. Ibid.

27. Ibid., p. 99.

28. Barbara Salert, *Revolutionaries and Revolutions: Four Theories* (New York: Elsevier, 1976), p. 86.

29. Samuel P. Huntington, *Political Order in Changing Societies* (New Haven, Conn.: Yale University Press, 1968), p. 265.

30. Ibid., p. 266.

31. Ibid., pp. 86–87.

32. Ibid., p. 12.

33. Ibid., pp. 13–24.

34. Ibid., pp. 13–15.

35. Ibid., pp. 266–267.

36. Ibid., pp. 266–274.

37. Ibid., p. 277.

38. Ibid., p. 266.

39. Ibid., p. 265.

40. Thompson, Ellis, and Wildavsky, p. 3.

41. Ibid., p. 5.

42. Ibid., pp. 6–7.

43. Ibid., pp. 26–28.

44. Ibid., pp. 227–231. The authors point out that this reaction happened in response to the excesses of the Cultural Revolution in China, a movement itself inspired by the egalitarian attack on the perceived failure of hierarchy, as well as surviving bourgeois (i.e., individualist) tendencies. A similar reaction may occur in Russia, where individualist reforms seem to produce catastrophe, not the promised prosperity.

45. Ibid., p. 88.

46. See the discussion in Chapter 5.

47. Ibid., pp. 86–93.
48. Ibid., pp. 92–93.
49. Ibid., pp. 265–267.
50. Goldstone cited above, note 12.
51. This summary is based on ibid., pp. 12–17.
52. See especially ibid., pp. 148–149.
53. Ibid., p. 459.
54. Ibid., pp. 141–145.
55. Ibid., pp. 459–460.
56. Ibid., pp. 417–419.
57. Ibid., p. 460.
58. Ibid., pp. 475–476.
59. Ibid., pp. 469–475.
60. See Charles Tilly, "Does Modernization Breed Revolution?" in Jack A. Goldstone, ed., *Revolutions: Theoretical, Comparative, and Historical Studies* (San Diego, Calif.: Harcourt Brace Jovanovich, 1986), pp. 48–51.
61. Salert, p. 86.
62. Thompson, Ellis, and Wildavsky, p. 273.
63. Ibid., pp. 334–346.
64. We might see this more as a difference in emphasis than as a difference in kind. Following Morse Peckham (see Chapter 1), culture could be defined as directions for a performance, social structure as performance according to directions, and directions and performance, of course, take on reality only when embodied in the values and actions of individuals.
65. Karl Marx, "Theses on Feuerbach," in *Karl Marx: Selected Writings*, ed. David McLellan (Oxford: Oxford University Press, 1977), p. 158.
66. Robert C. Tucker, *The Marxian Revolutionary Idea* (New York: W. W. Norton, 1969), p. 3.
67. In addition to Tucker's book, students seeking an overview might consult Robert Freedman, *The Marxist System: Economic, Political, and Social Perspectives* (Chatham, N.J.: Chatham House, 1990), or John McMurtry, *The Structure of Marx's World View* (Princeton, N.J.: Princeton University Press, 1978), for overviews of his basic concepts. Those desiring more of the flesh and blood of the man and his thought should read David McLellan, *Karl Marx: His Life and Thought* (New York: Harper and Row, 1973). A good selection of his writings is Frederic L. Bender, *Karl Marx: The Essential Writings*, Second Edition (Boulder, Colo.: West-view Press, 1986). For a selection of Marxist writings from Marx to Che Guevara and Amilcar Cabral, see David McLellan, ed., *Marxism: Essential Writings* (New York: Oxford University Press, 1988).
68. From the preface to Karl Marx, *A Contribution to the Critique of Political Econo-my*, trans. by N. I. Stone (Chicago: Charles H. Kerr, 1904), pp. 11–13.
69. See, for example, the letter included in Bender, p. 163, where Marx suggests that each historical case or change must be weighed separately: "By studying each of these forms of evolution separately and then comparing them one can easily find the clue to this phenomenon, but one will never arrive there by using as one's mas-ter key a general historico-philosophical theory, the supreme virtue of which con-sists in being super-historical."
70. McMurtry, p. 55.
71. Ibid., p. 73.
72. See especially V. I. Lenin, *What Is to Be Done? Burning Questions of Our Movement*

(New York: International Publishers, 1943), for the fullest development of his argument.

73. Ibid., pp. 54–64.

74. Ibid., p. 76.

75. Ibid., p. 99.

76. See especially Theda Skocpol, *States and Social Revolutions* (New York: Cambridge University Press, 1979). See also most of the essays in Jack A. Goldstone, ed., *Revolutions,* cited above.

77. A widely cited and controversial book that draws this connection is Paul Kennedy, *The Rise and Fall of the Great Powers* (New York: Random House, 1987).

78. For a discussion of this problem see James B. Rule, *Theories of Civil Violence* (Berkeley: University of California Press, 1988), pp. 56–59. Rule focuses, for his purposes, on the relation between class conflict and civil violence, but revolutionary transformation, not violence per se, is the primary focus of Marxist theory.

79. See the discussion of the concept of class in Hagopian, pp. 81–85, and that in Salert, pp. 107–113. For a discussion of how people experience their class see James C. Scott, *Weapons of the Weak: Everyday Forms of Peasant Resistance* (New Haven, Conn.: Yale University Press, 1985), pp. 41–47.

80. Hagopilan, p. 85.

81. Salert, p. 114.

82. V. I. Lenin, *Imperialism: The Highest Stage of Capitalism* (New York: International Publishers, 1939).

83. Edward S. Malecki, "Theories of Revolution and Industrial Societies," *Journal of Politics,* 35 (1973): 948–985.

84. Skocpol, p. 17.

85. Michael Taylor, "Introduction," in Michael Taylor, ed., *Rationality and Revolution* (New York: Cambridge University Press, 1988), p. 1.

86. Skocpol, pp. 252–262.

87. In addition to Skocpol and the book edited by Goldstone noted earlier, see Barrington Moore, Jr., *Social Origins of Dictatorship and Democracy: Lord and Peasant in the Making of the Modern World* (Boston: Beacon Press, 1966). Rule also summarizes some of the numerous empirical studies done within this tradition, pp. 71–76.

88. Skocpol, pp. 287–288.

89. Rule, p. 71.

90. Ibid., p. 89 (emphasis in the original).

91. Cf. Rule, pp. 170–171. See also Charles Tilly, *From Mobilization to Revolution* (Reading, Mass.: Addison-Wesley, 1978), especially Chapter 2.

92. See Tilly, pp. 190–193.

93. This section is based upon Janice Love and Peter C. Sederberg, "Black Education and the Dialectics of Transformation in South Africa, 1982–8," *The Journal of Modern African Studies,* 28 (1990): 305–308.

94. Charles Tilly, "Town and Country in Revolution," in John Wilson Lewis, ed., *Peasant Revolution and Communist Revolution in Asia* (Stanford, Calif.: Stanford University Press, 1974), p. 302.

95. Doug McAdam, *Political Process and the Development of Black Insurgency, 1930–1970* (Chicago: University of Chicago Press, 1982), p. 43.

96. Ibid., pp. 45–48.

97. This position was taken, for example, by the Polish-born German Marxist Rosa Luxemburg. See, for example, the selections "Lenin's Centralism" and "The Russian Revolution" in David McLellan, ed., *Marxism,* pp. 124–133.

98. McAdam, pp. 55–56.

99. Ibid., pp. 56–57.

100. I base these largely, though not entirely, on Rule, pp. 183–191.

101. G. W. F. Hegel, "Who Thinks Abstractly?" in Walter Kaufmann, ed., *Hegel: Text and Commentary* (Garden City, N.Y.: Anchor Books, 1966).

102. Rule, p. 265.

PRACTICE

7

Followers and Leaders in the Revolutionary Process

One way of understanding the practice of revolution is to investigate the dynamics between followers and leaders in a revolutionary movement. First we explore the notion that certain personality types may be disproportionately attracted to revolutionary movements, as well as the idea that the revolutionary leader is also a particular personality type. More concretely, we review the potential contributions of leadership to a revolutionary movement and compare the bases of commitment of followers to leaders. We then speculate on the character of "heroic" leadership and radical transformation. Finally, we identify the negative consequences for a movement dominated by a paramount leader.

LEADERS, FOLLOWERS, AND REVOLUTIONARY TRANSFORMATION

Each revolution has a face. When we think of the Islamic transformation of Iran, the Ayatollah Khomeini glowers at us with deep-set eyes beneath a furrowed brow. The thin, almost ascetic visage of Ho Chi Minh dominates the Vietnamese Revolution. Placid and implacable, the face of Mao Tse-tung rises like a full moon over our image of the Chinese Revolution. Dressed in military fatigues, a bewhiskered Fidel Castro harangues the Cuban masses. And what portrait of the Russian Revolution would be complete without Lenin, goatee pugnaciously thrust forward, spurring the workers and soldiers on in their revolutionary mission? Even where we lack a photographic record, every major revolution still evokes the names of a few personalities without whom, it would seem, the dramatic transformation would not have been possible. Even our own American Revolution has its handful of "founding fathers."

The emphasis on the leader's role in revolution encourages certain kinds of inquiry. Scholars try to solve the puzzle of leadership by identifying the attributes that made leaders great.[1] These attributes include physical characteristics such as height or "hypnotic" eyes, personal qualities like eloquence, and psychological traits like the will to dominate. Such lists of attributes, however, tend to be open-ended. Not all leaders, in any case, possess the attributes, however defined, and not all those who possess the attributes assume positions of leadership. Concentration on personal attributes, finally, tends to drain any *political* significance from the problem of leadership.

Such images of "great men" making revolution, moreover, stand in ironic contrast with most structuralist interpretations of radical transformation. From a structural perspective, the masses, driven by social and economic forces beyond their puny power to control, make history. Leaders are mere epiphenomena. If they appear to be in the forefront of a revolutionary movement, their position merely mimics froth on the leading edge of a massive wave.

Lenin attempted to stake a middle position between the fatalistic proclivities of structural determinism and the more romantic views of revolutionary adventurers. He insisted that revolution could neither be magically induced in an unpropitious social setting nor left to the unguided action of the proletariat. By this argument Lenin defined a semiautonomous role for revolutionary leadership.

We should adopt a kind of "Leninist" position in order to understand the contribution of leadership to the process of revolutionary transformation. Leaders affect outcome; but to understand their impact, we cannot study leaders in isolation. Rather, leaders exist only if they have followers. One promising path of investigation, then, focuses on the character of the relationship between leaders and followers.

The leader/follower relationship raises a number of questions. We might ask whether revolutionary *followers* possess any common attributes that make them susceptible to the appeals of revolutionary leaders. If so, what are these appeals? What contributions, or functions, give leaders a disproportionate impact on the course of events? Given the attributes of the followers and the contributions of leaders, on what bases do followers commit themselves to leaders? Finally, what limits these alternative patterns of commitment?

Leader/follower relationships, however, do not develop in a political vacuum. Aaron Wildavsky argues that particular patterns emerge in the context of alternative regimes.[2] The nature of the regime conditions the type of relations that emerge. We will not find democratic relations in a despotism (or vice versa). A radical change in the nature of leadership can only come with a radical change in regime. Micropolitical leadership helps to explain how leaders induce people to rebel, but only by exploring the macropolitical task of regime transformation can we begin to understand how leadership contributes to revolutionary outcomes.

REVOLUTIONARY FOLLOWERS

A minority commonly makes revolution in the name of the majority. The proportion of the population actively participating is quite small, even where popular support for a rebellion appears widespread. Imagine a series of concentric circles representing the population of a political community. The outermost ring includes the whole population. The next circle within it delineates the population alienated from the established order. The next circle defines the proportion of the alienated who sympathize with the revolutionary movement. Some smaller percentage of these sympathizers act on their beliefs under the right circumstances. Of these potential activists, some will be full-time participants; and of these full-time participants, some will occupy positions of leadership.

The diameters of the circles within the most inclusive one vary with changing circumstances. If no one is alienated, for example, then all the internal circles will collapse into a single point. The various theories reviewed in Part Two suggest alternative explanations for why the internal circles might expand or contract. Deprivation, disequilibrium, and structural theories primarily address the size of the circles of the alienated and the sympathetic. Rational choice and opportunity/resource theories focus more on the relative scale of the activist circles.

All of these theories suggest various hypotheses as to why the percentage of people engaging in revolutionary activity might be quite small, ranging from the limited numbers of alienated to the absence of any incentive or capability of people to act on their alienation. Another approach, however, suggests that certain personality characteristics also affect the level of participation in extreme political activity. Given the same level of alienation and incentives in a particular social setting, some people will more likely engage in radical action than others. They possess, in short, a *revolutionary personality*.

The notion of a revolutionary personality fits into a wider literature on politically relevant personality types, including investigations of the "authoritarian" personality[3] and the "anti-authoritarian" personality.[4] To explore its implications, we first define a hypothetical psychological construct, or "ideal type," of the traits making up the revolutionary personality. Real people more or less closely approximate this psychological construct. Since these traits are not possessed equally by all people, we provide some account of how they might be formed. Finally, we consider the factors determining the distinctiveness, or "abnormality," of the revolutionary participant.

A Revolutionary Personality?

The personality thesis starts from a rather simple premise: People are different. For whatever reasons, whether genetic, social, cultural, or some codetermined mix, people develop different behavioral predispositions, attitudes, and values—the combination of which we label "personality."[5] Given the same structural context, the same level of deprivation, the same presumed set of "rational incentives," people with different personalities respond differently. Some more readily engage in extreme political action than others. This argument suggests that the core activists of a radical movement possess the characteristics of a revolutionary personality.

As an ideal type, revolutionaries combine three substantive and three stylistic traits.[6] *Substantive* traits define the basic content of people's attitudes and values, whereas *stylistic* traits specify the manner in which they hold and express them. Substantively, revolutionary participants possess three basic characteristics regardless of the particulars of their ideology: a polarized worldview, a populist identification, and a positive orientation to power.[7]

1. Polarized Worldview   Revolutionaries polarize the world into good and evil. Whether Marxists, fascists, nationalists, or religious fundamentalists, revolutionaries view their movement as embodying the good, while all those opposed to the movement necessarily incarnate evil. Since adversaries lack any redeeming qualities, compromise with them is quite impossible. After all, any compromise of absolute good necessarily represents a degeneration from the ideal. Moreover, given this polarized worldview, those who fail to conform with revolutionary values must necessarily be evil. No neutral ground exists in this dichotomized community.

The polarized worldview of revolutionaries, according to William Daly, contributes to several other subsidiary tendencies:[8]

1. Revolutionaries tend "to see the cause of all problems, no matter how diverse and logically unrelated, in a single force for evil and to see the solution of all those problems in a single force for good."
2. Revolutionaries tend "to view as moral any behavior that contributes to the victory of the forces of good over the forces of evil and to view as immoral any behavior that delays or endangers that victory."
3. Finally, revolutionaries tend "to insist that all behavior conform strictly and explicitly to the new and highly simplified set of beliefs and values."

2. Populism   Revolutionaries, whatever their ideology, identify with and claim to act in the name of the to-be-emancipated masses, whether class, *Volk*, or community of believers. The glorification of and identification with the masses justify revolutionary activity and provide assurance of ultimate success. Who, after all, can stand against the will of the people? In addition, the belief that one speaks for the people helps to overcome the sense of isolation arising from alienation. Daly argues that revolutionary populism contributes to three related attitudes:[9] First, the emancipated masses become the "key to omnipotence." Mass support guarantees that revolutionaries will ultimately overcome all resistance. Second, mass support serves as "a key to virtue." Those who have such support are authorized to violate the canons of conventional morality. Third, given the practical and moral significance of mass support, revolutionaries attempt to destroy all competitors for the attention and loyalty of the masses.

3. Strong Power Orientation   The combination of a polarized worldview and popular identification with the masses relates to a third substantive trait: a strong, positive orientation to power. With a battle raging between the forces of good and evil and success depending on the unanimous support of the masses, the pursuit of power, the defense of power, and the exercise of power become dominating concerns. Revolutionaries must ruthlessly eliminate both their adversaries in the regime as well as any ideological competitors for mass allegiance.

This strong power orientation, Daly argues, helps to explain two characteristics that appear contrary to the idealism normally associated with revolutionaries—cynicism and elitism.[10] Although revolutionaries act in the name of a set of transcendent principles, whether historical laws or God's word, they seem cynically capable of the utmost brutality in their pursuit of power. After seizing power they seem equally capable of the most sordid acts to maintain their position. Similarly, despite their populism, revolutionaries fear that the masses cannot be trusted to maintain their revolutionary fervor, loyalty, and unity. Consequently they centralize their political organizations, often under the domination of a single leader. Revolutionaries ironically embrace discipline, order, and hierarchy to further the revolution.

Three stylistic tendencies combine with the three substantive traits to complete the psychological typification of the revolutionary personality. Revolutionaries tend to be dogmatic, activist, and destructive in the ways they hold and express their substantive characteristics.

1. Dogmatism   The term *dogmatism* refers essentially to the intolerance of individuals toward views different from their own.[11] Dogmatic people resist changing their beliefs, regardless of the circumstances. Dogmatism usually implies strict adherence to a simplified ideology. Certainly the tendency to polarize the world into good and evil encourages such simplification. Those convinced of the absolute rightness of their worldview are unlikely to tolerate any differences of opinion.

2. Activism   Alienated people (as we noted in Chapter 5) can respond to their alienation in a more or less active fashion. Even extreme alienation need not draw out an active response; rather, the alienated could withdraw from all interaction with the source of their disaffection. Revolutionaries, however, do not shrink from their source of alienation; they confront it. Activist personalities, whether alienated or not, exhibit high energy levels, a belief in their own efficacy, a sense of invulnerability from significant reprisals, high anger levels, and an acceptance of their anger. All these interrelated qualities sustain their commitment to action.[12] Action-oriented people, in comparison with their more passive counterparts, are more willing to take risks.

3. Destructiveness   Action, of course, need not be destructive, but revolutionaries seem ready, even eager, to resort to destructive means to accomplish their ends. While the substantive proclivities of revolutionaries do not automatically generate destructive actions, they certainly seem compatible with them. A polarized worldview, combined with the vigorous pursuit of power, encourages tendencies to destroy competitors both outside and within the movement.

A pure revolutionary personality presumably exhibits all substantive and stylistic traits to a high degree. In contrast, a person could be low on all of these scales, suggesting four basic alienated personality types as illustrated in Figure 7.1.[13] The horizontal axis represents the substantive traits from low to high, and the vertical axis represents the stylistic traits in a similar fashion. We locate the pure authoritarian *revolutionary* type in the upper-right-hand corner.

In the upper-left-hand corner we find those alienated people who share the stylistic but not the substantive traits of the authoritarian revolutionary. This activist *rebel* demonstrates little need to polarize the world, identify with "the people," or to dominate or submit to others. Rebels tend to resist any form of authority. Unlike revolutionaries with their vision of a "brave new world," rebels are less concerned with creating a new order than with bringing down the old. Their anar-

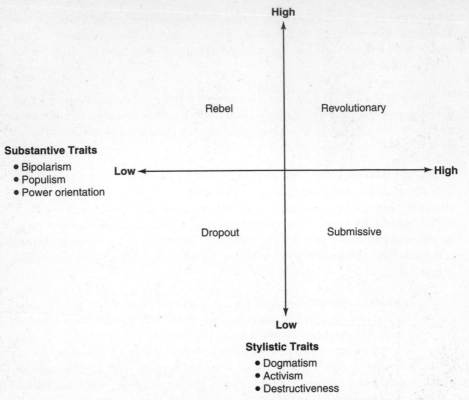

Substantive Traits
- Bipolarism
- Populism
- Power orientation

Stylistic Traits
- Dogmatism
- Activism
- Destructiveness

Figure 7.1 Substance and style in the definition of alienated personality types.

chist tendencies make rebels useful compatriots in the revolutionary struggle for power but definite liabilities in the new revolutionary order.

The lower-left-hand corner of Figure 7.1 defines traits associated with *dropouts*. Unwilling to fight for the new order or live with the old, the dropouts do just that, either individually, by using narcotics or withdrawing into a private world, or collectively, by retreating to a utopian community. Finally, the lower-right-hand corner defines *authoritarian submissives*. These personalities find psychological security in passively submitting to the dominant power, regardless of its character. They support the regime until it fails and then acquiesce in the new revolutionary order. Their bipolar, populist, and power-oriented proclivities, in the absence of activism, culminate in a cult of conformity.

We might consider those exhibiting any of these extreme character types "abnormal" or even pathological. "Normal" alienated people presumably fall within the large center area (see below for a discussion of the two meanings of *normal*) or represent a mix not represented by these four simple types. In disrupted times, however, increased numbers of people might be pushed to extremes of action, withdrawal, or submission (see the discussion of alternative responses to alienation in Chapter 5).

The real mix of personality traits, of course, fails to conform to the neat simplicity of this typology. Revolutionaries, first of all, have no monopoly on either the substantive or the stylistic traits. Vigilante defenders of the establishment may possess both the substance and style of the authoritarian revolutionary, the only difference being that the vigilante identifies with the status quo. Activism characterizes all those significantly involved in political life (or, for that matter, those with a "take charge" attitude in their "private" affairs), whether as establishment participants or revolutionaries. Conservative opponents of radical transformation or even moderate reform often hold their views in a dogmatic fashion. Counterrevolutionaries, as well as the essentially apolitical, can behave destructively. People could exhibit one or two of the substantive or stylistic traits and not the others. Jaundiced political cynics, for example, might view the world in polarized terms but dismiss the "masses as asses" and have no desire for power.

Nevertheless, the characterization of the authoritarian revolutionary personality possesses a certain coherence; that is, the composite makes sense. The traits do not contradict one another, although they are not inevitably combined. Taken together they describe the type of person who could engage in revolutionary activities. Real revolutionaries, of course, need not personify all these traits to the fullest extent; rather, they might approximate this composite to a greater or lesser degree.

The elimination of one or more of the tendencies probably reduces the likelihood that a person would participate in revolutionary activities. On the substantive side, those lacking a polarized worldview or populist tendencies would be less susceptible to the appeals of a revolutionary ideology and more open to compromise. Those who lack a strong power orientation might become romantic revolutionaries, swept up in the glorious cause but unable to compete for power in the New Revolutionary Order. Stylistically, those lacking dogmatism, activism, and at least some capacity for destructiveness could not stomach the sustained egg breaking that necessarily accompanies the making of a revolutionary omelet.

This somewhat unflattering typification, then, depicts the revolutionary as a "perplexing combination of a zealot saint and a power hungry butcher."[14] Revolutionaries appear to be "free-floating" psychotics, present among the alienated in every community, ready to join any extremist movement. Regimes cheerfully promote such an image of the revolutionary, for it excuses them of any blame.

We might reduce the potential conservative bias behind this characterization by considering how personality orientations do not simply reflect inherent dispositions but emerge out of social experience. Revolutionary character traits, moreover, are *stronger or weaker* tendencies that may be *more or less* easily activated. A deteriorating political community may compel political moderates to extremes, prompt relatively passive people to action, and provoke normally peaceful citizens into acts of violent destruction.

The Origins of the Revolutionary Personality

Our exploration of the possible origins of the revolutionary personality draws upon sources ranging from biologically based predispositions to the social construction of the personality. Each perspective provides some insight into the formation of this ideal type, but taken together they fail to yield a unified personality theory. Consequently we must proceed carefully in piecing the puzzle together for we lack all the parts, and those we possess may not make a neat portrait.

Biological Roots of Revolutionary Extremism   Human beings, as we noted in Chapter 1, are biological organisms before they are anything else. We suggested that biological characteristics provide the initial foundation for establishing predictable interaction. We enter a more controversial area when we claim that biology underlies specific personality characteristics. Nevertheless, some aspects of the revolutionary personality appear to have a biological basis, in particular, activism and destructiveness. Moreover, sustained patterns of destructive behavior require sustained levels of activity, even though a person could be active without being destructive or sporadically destructive while otherwise remaining relatively passive.

At the most basic level a strong activist orientation requires some minimum sustained expenditure of energy. We therefore expect some association between certain physiological characteristics or organically based mental states and revolutionary activity.[15] Obviously, severe deprivation and disease enervate the body and inhibit revolutionary activity regardless of the push and pull of other social-psychological factors. Age, too, affects energy levels. The youthfulness of the foot soldiers of war and revolution results not simply from a conspiracy among the old to send the young off to die; rather, the old lack the physical strength and energy required to fight. In addition, various hormones affect both the general energy level and the aggressiveness of animals, including humans. Both heredity and disease influence the level of these chemical energizers.

In addition, research suggests that the primary personality trait of extroversion may be partly determined by heredity.[16] The extroverted person—commonly described as active, assertive, energetic, forceful, and adventuresome—manifests traits associated with a strong activist orientation. In contrast, the introverted person—characterized as quiet, reserved, silent, withdrawn, and retiring—lacks the requisites to go out and rouse the rabble.

Specifically destructive behavior, as opposed to the broader notion of energetic intervention, also has certain biological roots. The capacity for destructive acts seems built into the basic physical structure of the human brain, which shares characteristics with its reptilian and paleomammalian forebears, as well as with the more closely related primates.[17] Capacity alone, of course, does not dictate actual destructive aggression. Human beings, like other animals, are energized for either fight or flight when confronted by a threat.

Other biological elements appear to influence destructive tendencies. Levels of male and female sex hormones, for example, affect the propensity for destructive behavior. Male hormones, especially testosterone, seem particularly associated with destructively aggressive behavior.[18] We must be cautious, however, about overemphasizing male hormonal tendencies, as opposed to culturally determined sex roles, as an explanatory factor. Nonetheless, such biological tendencies may partly explain the disproportionate numbers of males, as well as of the relatively young, among the soldiers of revolution and war. Finally, some forms of psychosis contribute to extremely destructive behavior. Evidence suggests that both schizophrenia and manic-depressive behavior have physiological roots, and people may inherit tendencies toward them.[19]

Erich Fromm argues that the inherited capacity for destructive behavior is primarily defensive in nature, in that threats to vital interests trigger the destructive response. He terms such behavior "benign aggression," because of its purportedly adaptive, life-serving function. This he contrasts with "malignant aggression," which he considers purely destructive and nonadaptive. Malignant destructiveness, because of its maladaptive character, cannot be an inherited personality trait. Therefore, it must be acquired (see below).[20]

Unfortunately, the distinction between benign and malignant destructiveness, though suggestive as an extreme contrast, begins to collapse under close examination. Human learning and technology amplify the range of defensive destructiveness to such an extent that it becomes distinctly maladaptive. In addition, some forms of malignant aggressiveness, like that rooted in psychosis or hormonal imbalance, have a biological basis. Biology, then, takes us only so far in explaining the emergence of the revolutionary personality. We need next to consider how subsequent character formation augments the biological contribution to the revolutionary personality.

Revolutionary Dispositions   The theories of Sigmund Freud stress the importance of basic, even unconscious, drives on personality formation.[21] Freud and his disciples, therefore, accept the argument that biology affects certain behavioral tendencies like aggression. The biological contribution, however, supplies only part of the equation. To complete it we must understand how individuals cope with the conflicts generated by these biological drives. Out of this process certain fundamental personality dispositions presumably emerge. These dispositions shape the subsequent behavior of the individual, including political behavior.

Harold Lasswell, in a classic analysis, represents the emergence of the political personality with the formula $p\}d\}r - P$. Private motives or drives (p) are displaced (d) onto public objects and then rationalized (r) in terms of the public interest, producing political person (P).[22] Lasswell suggests by this formula that political activists work out private needs through their political activity. Presumably if they were able to meet these needs privately, they would not enter the public arena. On the other hand, feelings of inadequacy in the private arena may compel people to seek compensatory political power.

Particular aspects of the revolutionary personality could emerge from this process. Specifically, revolutionaries might experience an exaggerated version of the universal conflict between unacceptable impulses and the social controls on their expression. For Freud such impulses reflected sexual drives and yearnings, most importantly the attraction of the young male to his mother and the consequent rivalry with his father. Desire for the mother combined with resentment of the father leads to the young male's wish to eliminate the father. This desire in turn stimulates both feelings of guilt and fears of reprisal.

This account, of course, describes the classic Oedipal conflict. The young boy represses this conflict throughout the so-called latency period. It reemerges during adolescence, when the passage of puberty again brings sexual urges to the foreground of consciousness. The young adult male, to become personally well adjusted, must come to terms with the conflict with his father, abandon his infantile erotic attachment to his mother, develop normal libidinal ties with another woman, and assume the paternal role himself. Failure to accomplish any or all of this leads to regressive infantile behavior, neurosis, and even psychosis.

The father also represents the child's first experience with authority, so an unresolved Oedipal conflict would seem ripe for displacement into the public arena. Indeed, E. Victor Wolfenstein argues,

> the revolutionist is one who escapes from the burdens of Oedipal guilt and ambivalence by carrying his conflict with authority into the political realm. For this to happen two conditions must exist: the conflict with paternal authority must be alive and unresolvable in the family context as adolescence draws to a close, and there must be a political context in terms of which the conflict can be expressed.[23]

The resolution in the public realm involves dividing political authority into essentially good and evil fathers. The evil father, represented by the existing regime, deserves being the target of previously unacceptable aggressive impulses. On the other hand, the revolutionary movement provides a benign father with whom the revolutionary can identify and to whom he can submit.[24] The revolutionary leader, as opposed to the follower, ultimately assumes a paternal role in the revolutionary movement.[25] The revolutionary leader, then, fully resolves the Oedipal conflict, albeit in a fashion that exacts a toll from the rest of society (see below). Revolutionary followers, from this perspective, remain in a state of arrested development, meliorating their Oedipal conflict by adoption of a bipolar worldview but still unable to grow into fully autonomous adults.

Moving beyond the particular focus on the Oedipal conflict, Erich Fromm speculates that malignant destructiveness originates in the general conflict between impulse and social control. Sadism—"the passion to have absolute and unrestricted control over a living being"—is an extreme response to the experience of repressed impulse.[26]

Anthony Storr suggests several factors that appear associated with development and manifestation of a capacity for sadistic cruelty:[27]

The Absence of Love and Approval Our ability to identify with others and feel what they feel limits our cruelty toward them. Those who have not experienced positive human attachments, especially in childhood, may have an impaired ability to identify with others.

The Need for Obedience Though necessary for social order, obedience to authority also provides an easy excuse for perpetrating cruelty, as the refrain "I was only following orders" makes clear.

Distance from the Victims Those only mildly disposed to cruelty find it easier to carry out their handiwork if they are relatively detached from the target of their attacks. Distance may be physical (studies of B-52 pilots in Vietnam revealed that they experienced significantly less moral conflict and guilt than ground personnel),[28] technological (apparently members of the Nazi *Einsatzgruppen*, who executed their victims face-to-face, suffered more serious psychological reactions than those who operated the gas chambers),[29] or ideological (often the targets of violence are characterized as class enemies, unbelievers, or subhumans unworthy of life).[30]

Victimization as Children   Considerable evidence indicates that childhood victims of cruelty often, though *not* inevitably, develop a capacity for cruelty. Imposition of arbitrary and severe controls on youngsters may contribute to a compensatory desire to exercise such arbitrary power as an adult. Pent-up resentment often vents itself not on the original source of the victimization, like parents or powerful supervisors, but a new victim, perpetuating a cycle of cruelty.

Fear   Sadism certainly feeds on paranoia. Stalin's desire for domination was the other side of his penchant for believing himself surrounded by enemies.

Fromm also identifies a second form of malignant aggressiveness, the necrophilic character. Necrophilia embraces attraction to "all that is dead, decayed, putrid, sickly; it is the passion to transform that which is alive into something unalive; to destroy for the sake of destruction. . . ."[31] A necrophilic lust for destruction, according to Fromm, embodies an even more extreme need to control than sadism.[32] The ultimate way of eliminating the ambiguity and conflicts of living is to destroy life.

Sadistic and necrophilic tendencies, like the Oedipal conflict, may be confined to the private sphere, but Fromm argues that certain political tendencies encourage and even amplify their expression in the public realm. To illustrate his contention, Fromm explores in some depth three of the twentieth century's premier practitioners of malignantly destructive politics: Heinrich Himmler, Adolf Hitler, and Joseph Stalin.

Fromm describes Stalin as a "nonsexual sadist" driven by a fundamental need to demonstrate his absolute dominion over others:

> By his word he could kill them, have them tortured, have them rescued again, have them rewarded; he had the power of God over life and death, the power of nature to make grow and to destroy, to inflict pain and to heal. Life and death depended on his whim.[33]

Himmler's combination of sadism and submissiveness made him, as head of the Nazi SS, the perfect instrument to carry out Hitler's necrophilic projects. Fromm argues that Himmler's essential insecurity contributed both to his subordination to strong "father figures" (especially Hitler) and to a desire to overcome his sense of impotence through the unlimited control over others.[34] Under more benign circumstances, he might have expressed his hostility as an irritating, rule-bound bureaucrat, but unfortunately Hitler's passion for destruction allowed for the full expression of Himmler's (and many others') sadism. Hitler's furious and hateful passion extended not only to the Jews and the Slavs; when faced with defeat he struggled to destroy all of Germany in a final apocalyptic spasm.[35]

Stalin and Hitler may well be the ultimate expression of sadism and necrophilia, respectively, but Fromm suggests that these traits are widely shared, at least to some degree. Many people probably possess some capacity for cruel and destructive behavior. This capacity, though, may exist alongside other qualities of character that appear in direct opposition. Under stress, such as continuous combat, these people might engage in acts of cruelty that they otherwise would not commit. Finally, on a more explicitly Freudian note, fear and resentment of the "paternal" repression of the state may lead some frustrated dissidents to pick up the gun as a "phallic symbol of the ultimate equality."[36]

Malignant aggression, as Fromm describes it, is not a psychological anomaly. Rather, it often addresses, albeit in perverse ways, certain "existential needs" of human beings (see the discussion of these needs in Chapter 1).[37] Those prone to political cruelty, then, may be struggling to overcome their own sense of fear, isolation, and ineffectiveness.

Finally, the revolutionary's dogmatic style may originate in an unresolved identity crisis. Erik Erikson argues that human identity develops through a series of stages, each of which presents a challenge that must be overcome to form an integrated personality.[38] Early stages involve the development of basic trust (or mistrust), autonomy (or shame and doubt), initiative (or guilt), and industry (or inferiority).[39] A pivotal period begins with the onset of puberty, when the youth must establish a stable sense of self at a time of considerable physiological change and psychological stress. Failures in the earlier stages make the resolution of this identity crisis even more difficult. Adolescents, Erikson observes, "are ever ready to install lasting idols and ideals as guardians of a final identity."[40] Again, personal problems may be displaced into the political arena:

> A crisis of identity (when the individual who finds self definition difficult is suffering from ambiguity, fragmentation, and contradiction) makes some adolescents susceptible to "totalism" or to totalistic collective identities that promise certainty. In such collectivities the troubled young find not only an identity but an explanation for their difficulties and a promise for the future.[41]

The content of the dogma appears relatively incidental; rather, the appearance of certainty fulfills a fundamental psychological need.

These psychoanalytic accounts, then, suggest explanations for several traits associated with the revolutionary personality. In somewhat simplistic terms, dogmatic, polarized, destructive revolutionary power seekers emerge from personal failure displaced into the public arena. This depiction still discloses a profoundly conservative bias, especially when combined with the claimed contribution of biology to certain revolutionary traits. Wider social and political relations seem largely absolved of any responsibility for the emergence of revolutionaries. We can reduce this bias, however, through recognition of the social construction of personality.

The Social Construction of the Revolutionary Personality   Even if a revolutionary personality emerges from some private psychological crisis, whether over the repression of impulse or the search for a secure identity, this crisis does not occur in a social vacuum. Distant, punishing paternal relations, for example, may contribute to the emergence of a Oedipal, destructive, and dogma-seeking adolescent. However, shifting the blame from the individual to the father (or mother) hardly removes the conservative bias.

Both Wolfenstein and Fromm recognize the importance of wider political and social relations in the formation of the personality. Wolfenstein notes that the displacement of the Oedipal conflict into the public arena depends on the existence of a political context that supports a polarized conflict with authority (see above). A truly evil regime, for example, facilitates its identification as the "evil father." Similarly, Fromm stresses that the social and political context not only encourages (or suppresses) the expression of destructive tendencies but also makes a profound contribution to their formation. Fromm believes, for example, that modern capitalist society is especially conducive to the development of necrophilic personalities because of its tendency to reduce people to commodities and human relations to questions of technique.[42] Fromm also seems to have in mind some of the particular cultural factors that Gurr considers normative and utilitarian justifications for violence in his model (see Chapter 5).

Such observations suggest that the individual personality develops through interaction within a wider web of social relations. This interactionalist perspective essentially argues that an individual functions as a totality, developing in a continuous and reciprocal engagement with the environment.[43] Social context influences even basic physiological responses. For example, stressful situations induce hormonal excretions that mobilize the body for action (or aggression, broadly defined). "In situations where stress reactions are induced by demand for achievement, males excrete significantly more epinephrine than females, whereas the opposite is the case in situations involving a possible threat to a parent's child."[44] This finding modifies the simple notion that males are biologically inclined to be more aggressive than females to account for the nature of the threat encountered. The interaction between biological disposition and the interpretation of the threat affects the aggressive response (an S-O-R learning model; see Chapter 4).

Widespread social stress, caused by economic depression or rapid social change, makes it more difficult to resolve personal problems in the private sphere. Sociological literature routinely reports on the increase in various social pathologies under such conditions. Rising unemployment brings increased substance abuse, interpersonal violence, crime, and suicide in its wake. To blame such increases in destructive behavior on individual dispositions alone misses the point.

Another common argument suggests that extremist movements most easily mobilize society's dispossessed.[45] Unfortunately for this thesis, most empirical work on civil violence and revolution indicates that participants in extreme political action are not socially isolated. They belong to primary and secondary groups that facilitate their mobilization (see the discussion of the opportunity/resource model in Chapter 6).[46] The completely dispossessed are more likely to sink into fatalistic resignation rather than to rise up in rebellion.

A plausible modification of this thesis focuses on the *security of* social position, not its complete *absence*. Specifically, extremist organizations more easily mobilize those suffering from status insecurity. Secure social status, even on the low end of a social hierarchy, supports the resolution of personal problems in the private sphere. Status insecurity, even for those relatively high in the social hierarchy, increases individual doubt and reinforces personal trauma. Indeed, if processes of social change (outlined in Chapter 6) unsettle whole sectors of society, then these sectors might be mobilized as groups into radical political action.

Insecure sectors of transitional societies include landless peasants, threatened middle classes, nonunionized laborers, and underemployed students and intellectuals. The last group mentioned often serves as the ideological "shock troops" of incipient rebellion.

Radical action, consequently, arises more from the need for secure status than for equal status. The experience of status insecurity, which worsens private psychological tensions, encourages the politization of these supposedly personal problems. Within the radical movement revolutionaries find identity and community absent from their lives in the disrupted wider social order.[47]

Moreover, when the dominant culture fails to prepare people for the world they encounter, they experience a cultural crisis (see the discussion of cultural inadequacy in Chapter 1 and cultural disequilibrium in Chapter 6). Just as status insecurity contributes to social alienation, cultural crisis leads to the experience of a cultural void encouraging the emergence of several revolutionary personality traits. The identification with a dogmatic ideology serves as a substitute for the rejected culture and the moral foundation it once provided. In addition, the glorification of the masses attempts to replace the social support previously provided by sharing beliefs and values with most of the other members of society.[48]

Finally, the decline of established cultural directives and the social organizations that embody them encourages the spread of destructive behavior. Social disruption and cultural decay weaken internalized norms moderating the expression of destructive impulses as well as the effectiveness of the external restraints on destructive behavior. These factors further elicit violent tendencies in members of a revolutionary movement that legitimizes destructive behavior against authorized targets.

Some or all the traits of the revolutionary personality, then, could arise from, or at least be reinforced by, the interaction between individuals and their environment. This possibility suggests that revolutionary "deviance" could become the norm under certain conditions, thereby lessening the conservative bias of the personality approach to revolutionary participation.

"Normal" Deviance? When Society Is Sick

Many of the traits associated with the ideal type of the revolutionary personality represent qualities usually thought of as extreme or deviant. "Normal" people presumably do not embrace dogmatic, polarized views of the world, nor do they engage in destructive behavior. On the other hand, certain revolutionary traits, such as the positive orientation to power and the associated stylistic disposition to high levels of activity, characterize a wide range of people who play major roles in established political organizations.

Further confusion about the "abnormality" of revolutionary personalities arises from the two distinct meanings of the concept of normality.[49] We could define an ideal or optimal political personality and then determine the extent to which any real person deviates from this ideal. If the ideal citizen, for example, is obedient, loyal, kind, peaceful, and tolerant—a real scout—then the revolutionary personality represents a clear abnormality. Alternatively, we might consider normality in simple statistical terms, as a measure of a central tendency. Whether a revolutionary personality represents a significant deviation then depends on the distribution of its distinctive traits in the relevant population.

In simple statistical terms the more widespread revolutionary activity is, the less deviant it becomes. Perhaps the lone assassin or the isolated terrorist cell engages in pathologically deviant behavior. The diagnosis of deviance becomes less plausible, however, as more people embrace the revolutionary worldview, participate in revolutionary organizations, and engage in revolutionary destruction.

Beyond this basic statistical observation, as conditions conducive to development of revolutionary personality traits expand (such as disrupted and unstable social position or the experience of cultural inadequacy), so also will the number of people exhibiting revolutionary characteristics. At some point in this process we must consider whether the established order, rather than the revolutionary participants, represents the real pathology.

Just as people respond differently to the same level of "objective" pain, we might also consider whether people possess different "thresholds" for the manifestation of revolutionary dispositions. As social conditions worsen, as established cultural norms progressively fail to provide adequate guidance, and as the rules and institutions controlling the use of coercion in social relations weaken, more people (and groups) will be attracted by ideologies that promise a secure sense of direction and identity, more people will be driven to action, and more people will be provoked to destructive behavior. In this way the notion of a peculiar revolutionary personality conflates with the microtheories of violence and the macrotheories of revolution discussed in previous chapters.

           🔥   🔥   🔥

Under conditions of severe social and cultural crisis the revolutionary follower begins to look increasingly like the person next door and not some pathological deviant. Nevertheless, from the perspective of an established political order, revolutionary movements still represent politics pushed beyond the limits. Whether these movements emerge, expand, survive, and succeed depends in part on how leaders relate to potential members, address their needs, and mobilize them for effective revolutionary participation.

LEADERS AND FOLLOWERS IN A REVOLUTIONARY MOVEMENT

Leaders or Leadership? Personality or Process?

Revolutionary activists are a relatively distinctive lot who play a "vanguard" (or leadership) role in the wider political community. When we speak of revolutionary *leaders*, then, we single out the vanguard of this vanguard. Oversimplifying further, we commonly focus on a few individuals, or even a single person, who seem to make a particular difference in the movement. Once we are down to a handful of notables, the analysis of personality becomes a powerful temptation. We search for the psychological traits that set revolutionary leaders apart from their followers and the qualities that make them into leaders.[50]

Wolfenstein, as we observed earlier, argues that revolutionaries displace an unresolved Oedipal conflict into the public arena, bifurcating the political world into good and evil realms of authority. The revolutionary leader, as opposed to the follower, must reject subordination. But the inability to follow does not account for the ability to lead. Leaders, in addition, must firmly identify with parental authority.[51] Finally, a paramount leader seeks to eliminate all peers and live in "an emotional world populated only by followers and enemies."[52] These psychological preconditions, of course, represent idealized traits which flesh-and-blood leaders may only approximate. Wolfenstein, for example, argues that Trotsky carried a smaller burden of Oedipal guilt and therefore found it possible to follow Lenin.[53]

Despite such complications these psychological preconditions possess a certain persuasiveness. The so-called antiauthoritarian personality may refuse to follow but also lacks the interest and ability to lead, except perhaps through fluid patterns of influence in essentially egalitarian relationships. Willingness to lead, however, does go far in explaining why some succeed at leadership while others spectacularly fail.

Bruce Mazlish adds some further dimensions to the psychological profile of the revolutionary leader. He argues that prominent revolutionary leaders over the last several hundred years increasingly exhibit the traits of narcissism and asceticism. He terms this personality type "the revolutionary ascetic."[54] Narcissism involves self-love so extreme that other libidinal ties become impossible. Leaders, whether revolutionary or not, who seek public adulation while giving little affection in return reflect narcissistic tendencies. Mazlish, however, takes simple narcissism one step further, suggesting that revolutionary ascetics "displace their self-love onto an abstraction with which they totally identify"—the revolution.[55] The leader appears to act in the name of higher principles while believing *la révolution, c'est moi.*

This abstracted self-love, Mazlish argues, combines with an apparent asceticism—systematic self-denial, dedication to work, and self-sacrifice.[56] The combination makes for potent leadership appeal. The relative absence of normal ties of affection frees the leader from possible distraction and eliminates a source of vulnerability. Moreover, the lack of such ties may make the leader seem "above" the petty interests of ordinary people. The absence of ties of affection also supports the revolutionary leader's rejection of the past.[57] Asceticism justifies the leader's position both in the minds of the followers and in the leader's own mind. The successful imposition of self-discipline and sacrifice gives the leader greater confidence in confronting the external world. Successful self-rule, then, legitimizes the rule of the leader over others.[58]

Narcissism and asceticism take us a bit further in understanding how some important revolutionary leaders earned their position. From Cromwell and Robespierre to Lenin, Mao, Ho, and Khomeini, major historical figures display the tendencies of the revolutionary ascetic. In an analysis of 50 revolutionary leaders of the past 350 years, Mostafa Rejai and Kay Phillips conclude that 27 exhibited evidence of narcissism and 37 traits of asceticism. (They found evidence of an Oedipal conflict in only 6 members of their sample.)[59] Only 20, however, combined both traits of the revolutionary ascetic, suggesting that Mazlish identifies something significant, but not universal, about revolutionary leaders. Indeed, Rejai and Phillips find that 23 members of their study revealed traits of estheticism and romanticism, loved literature and music, and even wrote poetry.[60] These are hardly the inclinations of puritanical asceticism. Half (10) of the revolutionary ascetics show esthetic inclinations as well, suggesting that revolutionary leaders can be more complex and less single-minded than we might think.

Another trait sometimes associated with successful leadership is that of Machiavellianism. Machiavelli, a sixteenth-century Italian political philosopher, advised his prince of the necessity to violate the codes of normal morality when pursuing the interests of the state.[61] The prince, then, must be prepared to lie, to break covenants, to be cruel, even to kill if the political situation demands it. If leaders of established regimes must stifle their moral qualms at times, then the revolutionary leader must be even more capable of transcending conventional morality.[62]

Certainly, any investigation of the major revolutionary leaders of the past century reveals a considerable capacity for ruthlessness shared to some degree by nearly all of them. (Mahatma Gandhi, if a revolutionary, represents one possible exception.) Leaders unable to stomach the evil required in revolutionary conflict are going to be hampered in any power struggle within the movement, as well as in the confrontation with a ruthless regime.

However suggestive we find this summary of the personality characteristics of revolutionary leaders, we might still question whether these traits reveal much about *leadership*. To paraphrase Wildavsky, if we think we can understand the character of leadership by identifying peculiarities of personality rather than the context within which leadership occurs, either the leaders or we are crazy.[63] If, alternatively, we consider leadership as a political process occurring throughout the revolutionary movement, then we need to probe for its essence within the operations of the movement and the challenges it faces. In short, we must scrutinize just what leaders do for the movement. This path of inquiry then leads to the question of why followers commit themselves to leaders and what undermines their commitment.

The Contributions of Leaders to a Revolutionary Movement[64]

Leaders amount to nothing without followers. The crisp directives of the executive depend upon the disciplined response of organizational cadres. The mesmerizing diatribes of the revolutionary agitator become the paranoid rantings of an asylum inmate if they fail to find a receptive audience. Leaders, if leading, must "make things happen that would not otherwise come about."[65] At one level leadership involves an exercise of naked power—leaders induce the followers to do something they otherwise *would* not do. As James MacGregor Burns observes, however, "Even the most fearsome of power devices, such as imprisonment or torture or denial of food and water, may not affect the behavior of a masochist or martyr."[66] Burns adds that good leadership addresses the "wants and needs, the aspirations and expectations—of both leaders and followers."[67] Tyrants, according to Burns, are not leaders, for they direct solely through fear and domination.

Burns' distinction, though morally compelling, cannot be analytically sustained, if we consider leadership simply in terms of outcome within the leader/follower relationship. In any case, even the most fearsome tyrants, like Tchaka, the nineteenth-century Zulu king whose mere gesture meant immediate execution, or Hitler and Stalin, who sent millions to their doom, did not relate to their followers solely on the basis of fear. Moreover, the relation between the most beloved leaders and their followers is unlikely to be free from fear, especially fear of rejection. Mixed motives—love, fear, respect, and simple calculation—probably suffuse all leader/follower relations.

Leadership often consists of something more than the exercise of naked power. In addition to *inducing* people to do what they otherwise *would* not do, leadership also entails *enabling* followers to do what they *could* not otherwise accomplish. Leaders, from this latter perspective, lead because they bring to the relationship something that otherwise would be lacking. One way of understanding the nature of leadership, then, identifies these potential contributions of leaders.[68] James Downton, for example, divides the tasks of rebel leadership into two broad categories. The first concerns the instrumental contributions of leaders:[69]

Goal Setting Leaders define the purposes of collective action. To do so, they may either represent the shared aspirations of potential followers or shape new aspirations.

Communication Leaders tutor their followers, harmonize their often conflicting desires, and relate individual desires to the collective goals. In performing the communication function leaders often serve as "gatekeepers," organizing, interpreting, and validating the information received by the followers. Through the control and interpretation of information, leaders channel the responses of their followers.

Mobilization Once the goals of collective action have been defined and communicated, leaders organize the skills and resources of the followers and energize them to action.

The instrumental tasks of leadership entail overcoming the natural tendency of potential followers to "free ride" (see the discussion of the free rider problem in Chapter 5). Revolutionary entrepreneurs, by defining the value of the collective good of revolution, manipulating selective incentives, and developing organization resources to monitor defections, represent the essence of instrumental leadership.

Leadership often entails something more than pragmatic coordination of common action. Leaders may also provide emotional support and identity to the followers. Downton identifies two major *expressive* functions of leaders:[70]

Ego Support Leaders validate the followers' sense of self-worth. Personal discontent and even self-loathing arise from a number of sources such as perceived discrepancy between performance and aspirations, failure to receive "appropriate" recognition, and the tension arising from the clash between impulse and social norms (between the id and the superego, in Freudian terms). Successful leadership provides avenues for the realization of the followers' aspirations, recognition of their worth, and the rationalization and channeling of their impulses.

Inspiration   Leaders impart meaning to life and purpose to action and sacrifice. All leaders must define or at least support a theodicy, that is, a justification of the "evil" followers inevitably experience in the relationship (see the discussion of explanatory metaphors for revolution in Chapter 4). In addition to these two expressive functions of leadership we might add a third:

Development of a Collective Identity   Leaders make something more of their followers than a simple aggregation of individuals. They contribute to the formation of a sense of collective identity and group solidarity. The creation of a group identity serves to mitigate the free rider problem.

No leader necessarily performs all these tasks equally well. Mark Hagopian, drawing upon the work of Harold Lasswell, Crane Brinton, and others, identifies three basic types of revolutionary leader, depending largely on their contribution to the movement: ideologists, agitators, and administrators.[71]

Ideologists undermine the established regime and articulate a vision of the new order the revolution promises to create. Ideologists define the goals of revolutionary collective action and articulate the basis for revolutionary solidarity.

Agitators communicate the goals of revolutionary action, perhaps translating them into terms the average follower can more easily understand, and mobilize the followers into action. In doing so agitators contribute to the tasks of ego support and inspiration, as well as help generate feelings of solidarity

Finally, *administrators* develop an organization capable of allocating selective incentives and monitoring defections. They also carry out the mundane tasks of coordination, logistics, and communication required for the movement's survival. Whereas ideologists and agitators conceivably perform both instrumental and affective tasks, administrators fulfill essentially instrumental functions.

Hagopian argues that a few revolutionary leaders, like Lenin and Mao, excelled at all three forms of leadership.[72] Trotsky, while an impressive ideologue and agitator, was not as proficient an administrator as Stalin, who in turn lacked the brilliance of Trotsky's revolutionary intellect. Similarly, Chou En-lai in China proved a far more capable administrator than either ideologue or agitator. Fidel Castro and Che Guevara both excelled as agitators, but they were deficient in the other areas of leadership. Che was miserable in a postrevolutionary administrative position in Cuba, and he eventually went off to tilt at other windmills.

If individual leaders possess different talents and make varying contributions to the revolutionary movement, then this conclusion also suggests that all leaders are not equally relevant to every stage of the revolutionary process. Ideologists seem most important during the prerevolutionary era, in identifying and nurturing the conditions contributing to a revolutionary crisis. Agitators come to the foreground once the revolutionary crisis develops and the struggle intensifies. Finally, administrators dominate the task of postrevolutionary power consolidation. These associations do not mean the other tasks can be ignored in any period. Rather, they represent propositions concerning relative emphasis.

The Bases of Follower Commitment

Our discussion of leadership functions indicates what leaders potentially contribute to a movement, but we still must explore why followers commit themselves to particular leaders and what the limits are on their commitment. Essentially, leader/follower relationships take three basic forms: transactional, catalytic/representational, and charismatic (see Table 7.1).[73]

In a *transactional relationship* leaders maintain follower obedience through the manipulation of reasonably concrete rewards and punishments. To establish a transactional relationship, followers must possess an interest in the immediate or short-term gratification of material needs and leaders must have the resources required to fulfill or threaten these needs. Transactional incentives, whether rewards or punishments, must be divisible in nature. Rewards are given *only* to those who follow and punishments inflicted *only* upon those who defect. Transactional followers, therefore, are rational actors, and leaders overcome the potential free rider problem through the manipulation of selective incentives.

The party machines that ruled many American cities in the late nineteenth and early twentieth centuries provide one example of a political movement based primarily on transactional relations. Voters often received immediate payoffs for their electoral support, and leaders would reward activists with patronage positions once the machine successfully controlled city hall. The immediacy of such pure transactions leads Burns to conclude that such relations are usually transitory:

> Their [the leader's and followers'] purposes are related, at least to the extent that the purposes stand within the bargaining process and can be advanced by maintaining that process. But beyond this the relationship does not go. The bargainers have no enduring purpose that holds them together, hence they may go their separate ways. A leadership act took place, but it was not one that binds the leader and the follower in a mutual and continuing pursuit of a higher purpose.[74]

Burns may correctly characterize many transactions as transitory, especially those between relative equals. Nevertheless, he underestimates the significance of the context within which transactions take place. In particular, revolutionaries as rational actors may well share a serious attachment to the ultimate goal of the new revolutionary order (see Chapter 5), but they still become free riders in the absence of selective rewards to offset the selective costs of their participation. Transactions simply become an ongoing requirement to sustain a movement directed at achieving a common goal. The presence of transactional relations, as we noted in Chapter 5, does not necessarily imply the absence of shared values.

Catalytic/representational and charismatic relations resemble each other in several superficial ways.[75] Both relationships often involve expressions of devotion to the leader, who personifies the followers' worldview and gives direction and value to their collective existence. In the *catalytic/representational relationship*, however, the leader inspires such identification by representing (that is, *re-presenting*) the beliefs and aspirations of the followers. The leader articulates the values and attitudes of the followers, giving a voice to the voiceless. In doing so the leader often provides greater definition and order to these values so that they may

Table 7.1 THE CHARACTER OF FOLLOWER COMMITMENT

Forms of relation	Bases of commitment	Crises in relation
Transactional	• Concrete selective incentives (rewards and punishments)	• Resource shortages • Value change among followers
Catalytic/representational	• Followers' beliefs, values, and aspirations	• Incommensurable beliefs and values • Changing beliefs and values
Charismatic	• Personal qualities of leader	• Loss of faith • Loss of leader

223

serve as more effective guides for collective action. Through such articulation and definition the leader catalyzes the followers into coordinated action to accomplish goals they already desire, at least in some inchoate manner.[76]

In a revolutionary movement the explicit articulation of latent but widely shared discontent contributes to the formation of a collective identity among people who previously were unaware of the extent to which they shared interests. In this fashion catalytic/representational relations overcome the free rider problem by "thickening" the incentives to which followers respond. People no longer define their interests in narrow egoistic terms but now rally to a movement that appears to advance their newly recognized collective identity.

This type of leader/follower relationship, however, does not create new values for the followers so much as organize and institutionalize ones they already possess. By doing so a revolutionary movement reorganizes the dominant systems of power and value in a society, exalting the humble and humbling the exalted. The introduction of radically new values, however, seems more the consequence of the charismatic relationship.

Charismatic relationships existed between the founders of the world's great religions—Moses, Christ, Muhammad—and their more avid followers. In these extraordinary cases the disciples believed that their leaders were set apart from ordinary humans by a "gift of grace" implying divinity, or at least privileged access to the Godhead.[77] In more secular charismatic relations followers develop an intense faith in the ability of the leader to identify the correct course of action. The followers believe the leader "to be uniquely capable of cognitively structuring or restructuring the world."[78] Personal qualities of the leader, then, form the basis of follower commitment.

In a pure charismatic relationship the leader endows a system of belief with legitimacy. This contrasts with the catalytic/representational relationship, in which the preexisting values of the followers in effect endow the leader who represents them with legitimacy. Charismatic relations solve the free rider problem by transcending it. While such great faith in the superhuman qualities of the leader might not be, strictly speaking, irrational (perhaps, after all, the leader is God), it certainly differs from conventional rationality whether defined in thin or thick terms. The transcendentally innovative quality of charismatic relations makes them the most potentially revolutionary. For those bound up in a charismatic relationship, the leader can create an entirely new set of values and not merely mobilize a reordering of existing value priorities.

Any particular situation of leader/follower relations may, of course, confound this simple classification. Not only may different followers relate to the same leader on different bases, but even a single follower's commitment may change over time or reflect mixed motives. Indeed, the commitment of the average participant in a revolutionary movement may combine all three forms of attachment.

A more serious conceptual problem complicates this simple framework. Each form of commitment, if considered carefully, seems to slip over into the next category. Indeed, the three types of commitment essentially represent points on a continuum ranging from purely instrumental attachments (transactional) to purely expressive ones (charismatic). For example, concrete incentives might evolve from specific selective incentives ("Ten dollars if you vote for me") to more collective, though no less concrete, goods ("Vote for me and I'll pave your street"). The nature of the relationship evolves further as followers exchange loyalty for increasingly collective and symbolic rewards.

Similarly, a representational form of leadership may more or less literally reflect follower values. In giving voice to the beliefs and aspirations of the followers, a leader also gives them form. If follower values are incoherent to begin with, then the process of representation and articulation grows more creative, and the relationship begins to resemble the charismatic.

Follower commitment weakens in characteristic ways within each relationship. Transactional leader/follower relations depend on the possession of sufficient resources to mobilize support. In pure transactional relations, the leader must command short-term, selective incentives to overcome the tendency to free ride among potential supporters. A revolutionary movement faces a vicious dilemma in the early stages of mobilization. Because of its limited resources, the movement finds it difficult to expand its base of support and thereby increase its resources.

Another crisis looms for a transactional relationship when followers acquire values beyond the desire for immediate individual advantage. As Burns notes (see above), material rewards will not motivate the ascetic, and fearsome threats will fail to persuade a martyr. Apart from these extremes people's values generally shift to more collective and symbolic goods, once their basic material needs are met. They may still respond to selective incentives, if great enough, but they also look for the fulfillment of other, less materialistic values. In short, when people shift to more collective identities and aspirations, they tend to defect from short-term transactional relations.

Catalytic/representational relations, though, face their own peculiar problems. If the followers' commitment depends on the leader's representation and articulation of their values, then this presumes that the values and beliefs of the potential followers possess some minimum compatibility. Incommensurable values and identities may divide the political community. Under such conditions a leader who articulates the values of one faction necessarily alienates its rivals. Intensely alienated people may never coalesce into a unified revolutionary movement, if they are divided by mutual suspicion and hostility.

Changing values also undermine follower commitment in catalytic relations. Leaders may find to their dismay that previously powerful symbols and goals lose their unifying, mobilizing appeal. For example, one strategy to overcome disunity is to organize against a common enemy. The success of this negative strategy, ironically, results in its ultimate failure. The factions within the movement return to their previous discord once they eliminate their common enemy. Alternatively, the potency of collective rewards, like national independence, often diminishes after their initial achievement, as followers turn to more immediate material aspirations. In both instances previously robust catalytic relationships wither the morning after victory.

The charismatic relationship avoids the pitfalls of the other two. The powerful personal appeal of the leader transcends resource limitations and creates unity in a divided community. But the charismatic relationship lasts only so long as the followers believe in the leader's gift of grace. Like the Israelites wandering in the desert, followers may demand repeated demonstrations of the leader's power. And like Moses, the leader may have to produce miracles continually to maintain their faith.

Even if the leader successfully retains the faith of the followers, it only worsens the ultimate charismatic crisis—the loss of the leader. Since the charismatic relation depends on faith in the personal qualities of a particular leader, the loss of that leader essentially destroys the relationship. This contrasts with the other two relations, in which others, at least in principle, could step in and manipulate the incentives or articulate the shared values.

Charismatic relationships usually must be "routinized" to survive the loss of the leader.[79] Routinization demands placing the relationship on some other basis than pure faith. The leader, for example, may endow a set of values with legitimacy, and representation of these values then becomes the new foundation of follower commitment. In a sense, this transforms a religious movement based on faith in the leader into a church based on dogma. Alternatively the successors to a charismatic movement can try to maintain it through the manipulation of more concrete incentives. Of course, successful routinization of a charismatic relationship makes it vulnerable to the other crises (resource shortages or value conflict and change) that it originally transcended.

LEADERSHIP AND REVOLUTIONARY TRANSFORMATION

Leadership, Culture, and Regime

Leadership essentially reflects the cultural context within which it develops.[80] In Chapter 6 we explored four broad cultural types: fatalistic, individualistic, egalitarian, and hierarchical. Wildavsky argues that each of these broad types of culture supports a different political regime and that a particular form of leadership prevails within each regime.[81] Each form of leadership in turn implies a different mix of leader/follower relations. Table 7.2 summarizes these contrasts.

Fatalistic cultures possess slave regimes with despotic leaders. Slaves follow their master largely out of fear, embodying a transactional relationship in which the transactions are mainly, though not entirely, selective punishments. The leader's power is essentially unlimited in scope and continuous in duration.

An individualistic culture, in contrast, entails a pattern of rule that approaches anarchy, in the sense that no leader or law has any ultimate authority over the individual. Anarchy does not mean chaos, for order supposedly emerges out of the free interactions among individuals (for example, the order of the free market). Any leadership that emerges will tend toward the "meteoric." Certain individuals may temporarily direct public affairs to the extent that the others see this management as being to their individual advantage. Followers again establish a trans-

Table 7.2   MODELS OF REGIMES

TRAITS	CULTURE			
	Fatalistic	Individualistic	Egalitarian	Hierarchical
Regime	Slavery	Anarchy	Community	Hierarchy
Leadership	Despotic	Meteoric	Unanimous or charismatic	Bureaucratic
Leader/follower relations	Transactional (punishment more than reward)	Transactional (reward more than punishment)	Catalytic/representational or charismatic	Transactional and/or representational
Scope of power	Unlimited	Limited	Limited or unlimited	Limited
Duration of power	Continuous	Discontinuous	Discontinuous	Continuous

Source: Based on Aaron Wildavsky, *The Nursing Father: Moses as a Political Leader* (Tuscaloosa: University of Alabama Press, 1984), pp. 21–24, and on Michael Thompson, Richard Ellis, and Aaron Wildavsky, *Culture Theory* (Boulder, Colo.: Westview Press, 1990), pp. 5–15. In addition to incorporating other material into this framework, I have taken the liberty of modifying some of Wildavsky's terms to reflect the analysis developed earlier in the chapter.

actional relationship with the leader, but selective rewards will predominate. The power of a meteoric leader is limited in scope and short in duration. The selective advantages produced by a particular leader are usually restricted to a specific task, and followers withdraw their commitment once the leader completes this task.

Egalitarian cultures produce communities founded upon shared values. Given the fundamental equality of the members of the community, Wildavsky argues that only charismatic leadership can develop.[82] Fundamentally equal people follow only the truly blessed: No one else merits the sacrifice of their equality. Other than that, communal action must reflect unanimous consent. This alternative, however, indicates that catalytic/representational leaders might also arise who articulate the universal, uniform values of the community and thereby catalyze unanimous consent. Consequently either catalytic/representational or charismatic relations develop in the egalitarian community. The communal values reflected by the leader limit the scope of the catalytic relationship. The charismatic relationship is, in contrast, potentially unlimited in scope. The duration of each form of leadership, though, remains discontinuous. Neither the catalytic nor the charismatic leader can expect to exercise authority indefinitely.

Finally, hierarchical cultures produce hierarchically structured regimes characterized by bureaucratic leadership. Wildavsky terms the leadership type autocratic, but this seems a misnomer given the limited scope of the leader's authority. Leader/follower relations depend on transactions, but some of these transactions involve collective as well as selective goods, such as the well-being of the hierarchy and the values it embodies. Consequently leaders may represent the values and identities shared by the followers as well as possess knowledge and skill needed to guarantee the smooth operation of the group. The hierarchy in a church provides a good example of such representation and so might the vanguard of a revolutionary movement. The power of the leaders in such a community, though limited in scope, is continuous in duration.

These four cultural types combine in various ways (see Chapter 6), producing greater complexity than this simple classification accommodates. Yet these basic comparisons suggest patterns of internal political coherence that develop within cultural types. Wildavsky observes, "Leaders are shaped by (as they try to shape) particular regimes."[83] Microleadership within a particular culture reflects the dominant patterns of that culture. Perhaps no existing political system embodies a completely unitary culture; nevertheless, we expect to find few egalitarian relations in an essentially despotic regime, or vice versa.

Cultural coherence suggests why so many rebellions fail to change the fundamental patterns of rule characteristic of a political community. Despotism replaces despotism. Dynastic struggles conclude with the institution of a new dynasty, and in bureaucratic revolts the bureaucracy always wins. A true revolution, from this perspective, must transform the nature of the regime.[84] To do this the revolution must radically restructure the dominant culture. Microleadership, trapped within the dominant patterns of political interaction, cannot accomplish this transformation. Revolutionary leadership, however, alters the dominant culture, the nature of the regime, and therefore itself. Revolutionary leaders, indeed, attempt to pull themselves up by their own hair and see the world in new ways.

The great revolutionary leaders who emerge out of this struggle become heroic figures, even when they fail to establish a new regime.

Heroic Leadership and the Challenge of Radical Transformation[85]

Joseph Campbell, in his classic study of heroism, identifies common characteristics of many myths that together form the heroic cycle.[86] Heroes usually emerge in a corrupt or enslaved community. They leave their homeland and wander alone (or with a small band of faithful disciples) in the wilderness, where they face and overcome tests of their courage and wisdom. The struggles of these wanderings purify and transfigure them, and the heroes return home bearing messages of salvation.

Yet the people, and especially the representatives of the established order, do not necessarily embrace them; they are just as likely to crucify them. The heroic message of salvation carries the germ of transformation. Transformation necessarily disrupts the comfortable assumptions and deeply rooted behaviors of the established order. Even when people recognize the need for change, they may resist having the basic rhythms of their lives upset or their cherished beliefs condemned. Heroes stand beyond conventionally defined good and evil, because they develop new standards for judging social relations. The great hero and the great criminal are sometimes indistinguishable—they both violate the standards of the established order.

But heroes differ from simple criminals because of their messages of transformation. The heroic quest involves more than a simple triumph over tribulations and the destruction of a corrupt order. In addition, heroic leaders must institutionalize new values into a new order. The leader as hero, then, creates new values to replace the old ones that failed. The hero as leader establishes these values in a new regime. The successful hero personifies the complete revolutionary.

Of all the leaders of historical record, perhaps Moses is the greatest hero. Exiled from his enslaved people, he returned with a message of freedom and salvation (the Promised Land). Through decades of struggle he proved himself as a revolutionary, as a lawgiver and teacher, as an administrator caring for his people's needs, and ultimately as the founder of a nation.[87]

Many of the "heroes" of contemporary revolutions also approximate this pattern. Early experiences with a corrupt regime kindled the flames of rebellion that sent them into prison or exile. Proving their revolutionary mettle, they honed their message of political salvation. Toppling the old order, they attempted to institute a new, redeemed regime. Lenin, Mao, Ho Chi Minh, Fidel Castro, Vaclav Havel, and Khomeini all recognized the corruption of their homelands; most suffered periods of exile, imprisonment, or both; all developed messages of revolutionary salvation that attracted significant followings; and all were ultimately successful in toppling the older regime.

But did they succeed in instituting a new order? Often the struggle for power compels leaders to embrace methods and organizations that mirror the worst of the old regime. Critics commonly charge Lenin with abandoning the democratic and egalitarian elements of classical Marxism and advancing a new form of despotism—the elite vanguard party—to combat the established despotism of the Czar. Mao lived to see his egalitarian revolutionary ideals steadily eroded by a new version of China's traditional mandarin regime (rule by a hierarchy of intellectuals), a trend he tried to reverse by the Cultural Revolution (c. 1966–1976). Followers as well as leaders backslide into deeply rooted habits after the initial celebration of revolutionary values.

Most revolutions challenge forms of despotism and often represent values of individualism or equality. Yet regimes established on such values seem much more unstable than the other two types, as reflected in the discontinuous patterns of leadership that prevail (see Table 7.2). Usually the new revolutionary order adulterates the purity of these utopian values and embraces some principles of hierarchy.

Even Moses ultimately led the Israelites out of despotism, through periods of anarchy and community, to a new hierarchical order somewhat modified by principles of equality.[88] The promised land still represented a significant change from Egyptian slavery, even though it was not an egalitarian or anarchical utopia. Similarly, when we judge the relative success of contemporary revolutionary heroes, we should not expect too much. Any regime capable of surviving more than a generation probably contains considerable elements of hierarchy. Given the mixed nature of most cultures, a hierarchy could include elements of any of the other three types. The success of revolutionary leadership, then, depends on the extent to which the postrevolutionary regime embodies values and institutions significantly different from its predecessor's. We return to this problem when we assess the outcomes of the revolutions in our two cases (see Chapter 12).

CONCLUSION: THE DANGERS OF A PARAMOUNT LEADER

Leaders, to paraphrase Marx, make the movement, but they do not make it just as they please. Even those who depreciate the role of the hero in history recognize that particular players make key contributions to the movement by articulating goals, communicating programs, mobilizing and coordinating action, and inspiring sacrifice. At the other extreme, even those who argue for the unique quality of charismatic leadership admit that certain conditions favor the emergence of charismatic relations. Charismatic commitments are unlikely to develop among a people comfortable with received values and established social relations.

The debate over the significance of leaders comes down to the issue of substitutability. Those who think history makes leaders believe that given the appropriate conditions someone will arise to fulfill the leadership functions, if not one person, then another. On the other hand, leadership does not seem to be simply a matter of opportunity. Some people may not possess the psychological prerequisites for leadership. Moreover, whatever their willingness to lead, not all people prove equally capable of leadership. Even successful transactional leadership depends on more than the mere possession of the concrete resources required for selective incentives. In addition, people differ with respect to their ability to manipulate available resources and maximize their objectives. Wastrels and fools quickly destroy a political movement dependent on successful transactions. Similarly, not everyone is equally gifted at voicing the aspirations of a united people, much less at developing common ground within a divided community.

The composition and characteristics of the followers certainly affect the emergence and success of leadership, but this admission does not imply that leaders and followers are completely interchangeable. Charismatic relationships, for example, may be impossible to reestablish once a particular leader passes from the scene. Other leaders, too, may be difficult to replace. The unity and success of the movement may depend on the quality of a particular leader or small group of leaders. As leaders grow more difficult to replace, the dangers of paramount leadership increase. In this way current success paves the path to future failure. The problems created by paramount leadership include the following:

1. The Succession Problem   If anyone can fulfill the leadership functions in the revolutionary movement, then no succession problem exists. Alternatively, if the qualities of leadership are unique to a single individual, as they are in a charismatic relationship, then the problem of succession becomes difficult, even impossible, to manage. Between these two extremes the challenge of succession will vary depending on at least two factors. First, regardless of the pool of potential talent the movement must establish clear and accepted means of transmitting authority from one generation of leadership to the next. Second, regardless of the institutionalized path of succession the movement must possess an adequate pool of potential leadership talent.

A hereditary monarchy, for example, may successfully fulfill the first condition, but the talents of the successor are something of a genetic crapshoot. Alternatively, a revolutionary movement may have considerable second-level talent but no clear line of succession. Such seems to have been the case in the Soviet Union. The absence of a clear successor to Lenin resulted in a bitter struggle for power, from which the least desirable successor—Stalin—emerged victorious.

The more important a leader is to the movement, the less likely either condition will be fulfilled. The dominance of the leader discourages the cultivation of successors and at the same time makes it difficult to authorize a process of succession that will hold after the leader's death.

2. Overcentralized Decision Making   The more critical the leader's talents and personal authority are to the movement, the more likely decision making will grow overcentralized. Too much talent and authority at the top often results in too little initiative exercised below. The consequences overburden the leader and discourage the development of leadership skills among promising subordinates. This consequence in turn contributes to the succession problem.

Catalytic and charismatic leader/follower relations raise additional problems. Leaders excessively dependent on either the successful manipulation of inspirational symbols or the exercise of personal gifts often lose touch with the more mundane, instrumental tasks of leadership. Powerful symbols and personal faith may move people to action, but ultimately they cannot feed them.

3. *The Focus of Hope and the Focus of Blame*   Excessive centralization contributes to further risks for a paramount leader. Past success generates expectations for future success. Failure to fulfill these expectations will likely contribute to discontent focused specifically on the leader. The praises of the past become a chorus of condemnation. Leaders who share the credit for success may be better able to evade some of the blame for failure. Those who take all the credit may find they also monopolize the blame. At the extreme, paramount leaders become prime targets for assassination, thereby precipitating the succession crisis.

4. *Sycophancy and the Magnification of Pathology*   Dominant leaders tend to be surrounded by the flatterers and sycophants. Even initially modest and unassuming leaders may find critical opinions drowned out by the din of glorification. Worse, paramount leaders may actually encourage their own cult of personality, grow convinced of their irreplaceability, and become jealous of possible competitors. They then progressively block out information about the failures of their leadership (sycophants only sing of success), ignore the problems of succession and overcentralization, and even eliminate possible successors as potential rivals.

Uncorrected by negative feedback and unconstrained by countervailing institutions, paramount leadership amplifies the personal flaws of the leader. Continuous flattery reinforces character flaws. Once they achieved personal supremacy, for example, Stalin was able to exercise his sadism and Hitler his necrophilia largely unchecked.

         🔥   🔥   🔥

Revolutionary psychology, the functions of leaders, and the bases of follower commitment begin to reveal something of the nature of revolutionary practice. But leaders and followers usually do not relate in some undifferentiated social-psychological synthesis. Rather, the links between followers and leaders are informed by a guiding ideology and structured by a revolutionary organization. Our understanding of the revolutionary practice, then, requires that we next explore these linkages.

NOTES

1. See Aaron Wildavsky, *The Nursing Father: Moses as a Political Leader* (Tuscaloosa: University of Alabama Press, 1984), pp. 183–190, for a critique of alternative approaches to the study of leadership, including that which focuses upon leadership "attributes."
2. Ibid., pp. 190–192.
3. T. W. Adorno et al., *The Authoritarian Personality* (New York: Harper and Brothers, 1950).

4. William P. Kreml, *The Anti-Authoritarian Personality* (London: Pergamon Press, 1977).

5. For a comprehensive review of the recent research on personality in general see Lawrence A. Pervin, ed., *Handbook of Personality: Theory and Research* (New York: The Guilford Press, 1990).

6. The distinction between substantive and stylistic psychological traits parallels that made between construct and stylistic traits in Roger H. Brown, *Social Psychology* (New York: The Free Press, 1965), Chapter 10.

7. This list partly reflects the conclusions of William T. Daly, "The Revolutionary: A Review and Synthesis," *Comparative Politics Series,* Vol. 3, No. 01-025 (Beverly Hills, Calif.: Sage Publications, 1972), pp. 15–17.

8. Ibid., p. 8.

9. Ibid., p. 9.

10. Ibid., pp. 11–12.

11. William P. Kreml, "The Vigilante Personality," in H. Jon Rosenbaum and Peter C. Sederberg, eds., *Vigilante Politics* (Philadelphia: University of Pennsylvania Press, 1976), p. 57.

12. Cf. the discussion in David C. Schwartz, *Political Alienation and Political Behavior* (Chicago: Aldine Publishing Company, 1973), pp. 25–29.

13. This illustration was developed in discussion with William P. Kreml. For his elaboration of some of those ideas see William P. Kreml, *Psychology, Relativism, and Politics* (New York: New York University Press, 1991).

14. Daly, p. 12.

15. See James Chowning Davies, "Biological Perspectives on Human Conflict," in Ted Robert Gurr, ed., *Handbook of Political Conflict: Theory and Research* (New York: The Free Press, 1980), pp. 19–68. See also Albert Somit and Steven A. Peterson, "Biological Correlates of Political Behavior," in Margaret Herman, ed., *Political Psychology: Contemporary Problems and Issues* (San Francisco: Jossey-Bass, 1986), pp. 11–38.

16. Hans J. Eysenck and Michael W. Eysenck, *Personality and Individual Differences: A Natural Science Approach* (New York: Plenum Press, 1985), especially Chapters 1–3. See also Hans J. Eysenck, "Biological Dimensions of Personality," in Pervin, pp. 244–276.

17. Davies, pp. 31–38.

18. Ibid., pp. 40–44.

19. Jon L. Karlson, *Genetics of Human Mentality* (New York: Praeger, 1991), Chapter 6. See also Eysenck and Eysenck.

20. Erich Fromm, *The Anatomy of Human Destructiveness* (New York: Holt, Rinehart and Winston, 1973), pp. 185–188.

21. For a review of contemporary psychoanalytic approaches to personality formation see Drew Westen, "Psychoanalytic Approaches to Personality," in Pervin, ed., pp. 21–65.

22. Harold D. Lasswell, *Psychopathology and Politics* (Chicago: University of Chicago Press, 1930, 1977), pp. 75–76.

23. E. Victor Wolfenstein, *The Revolutionary Personality: Lenin, Trotsky, Gandhi.* (Princeton, N.J.: Princeton University Press, 1971), p. 307.

24. Ibid., pp. 308–309.

25. Ibid., p. 11.

26. Fromm, p. 288.

27. Anthony Storr, "Sadism and Paranoia," in Marius H. Livingston, ed., *International*

Terrorism in the Contemporary World (Westport, Conn.: Greenwood Press, 1978), pp. 232–237. The explanation of his points is mine.

28. Robert Jay Lifton, *The Nazi Doctors: Medical Killing and the Psychology of Genocide* (New York: Basic Books, 1986), pp. 494–495.

29. Ibid., p. 15.

30. Ibid., pp. 434–442.

31. Fromm, p. 332.

32. Ibid., pp. 348–349.

33. Ibid., p. 288.

34. Ibid., pp. 321–322.

35. Ibid., pp. 396–404.

36. Peter Merkl, "Conclusion: Collective Purposes and Individual Motives," in Peter Merkl, ed., *Political Violence and Terror: Motifs and Motivations* (Berkeley: University of California Press, 1986), p. 353.

37. Fromm, pp. 230–242.

38. Erik H. Erikson, *Childhood and Society,* Second Edition (New York: W. W. Norton, 1963).

39. Ibid., pp. 247–261.

40. Ibid., p. 261.

41. Martha Crenshaw, "The Psychology of Political Terrorism," in Herman, ed., pp. 391–392.

42. Fromm, pp. 349–350.

43. David Magnusson, "Personality Development from an Interactional Perspective," in Pervin, ed., p. 196.

44. Ibid., p. 203.

45. William Kornhauser, *The Politics of Mass Society* (Glencoe, Ill.: The Free Press, 1959).

46. For a summary of this evidence see James B. Rule, *Theories of Civil Violence* (Berkeley: University of California Press, 1988), pp. 109–110.

47. Daly, p. 28.

48. Ibid., pp. 21–22.

49. For a more extended discussion of the two meanings see Robert S. Robbins, "Introduction to the Topic of Psychopathology and Political Leadership," in Robert S. Robbins, ed., *Psychopathology and Political Leadership* (New Orleans: Tulane University Press, 1977), pp. 2–3.

50. For a review of the literature on leaders and leadership see Edwin P. Hollander, "Leadership and Power," in Gardner Lindzey and Elliot Aronson, eds., *Handbook of Social Psychology,* Vol. 2: *Special Fields and Applications* (New York: Random House, 1985), pp. 485–538.

51. Wolfenstein, p. 311.

52. Ibid., p. 312.

53. Ibid., p. 311.

54. Bruce Mazlish, *The Revolutionary Ascetic: Evolution of a Political Type* (New York: Basic Books, 1976).

55. Ibid., p. 23.

56. Ibid., pp. 28–34.

57. Ibid., pp. 34–36.

58. Ibid., pp. 38–39.

59. Mostafa Rejai and Kay Phillips, *World Revolutionary Leaders* (New Brunswick, N.J.: Rutgers University Press, 1983), pp. 140–141.

60. Ibid., pp. 140–141, 152–154.
61. See Niccolo Machiavelli, *The Prince,* any edition. For a good critique of Machiavelli see the discussion in Mulford Q. Sibley, *Political Ideas and Ideologies: A History of Political Thought* (New York: Harper & Row, 1970), pp. 294–311. For a review of contemporary research on Machiavellianism as a psychological trait of leaders see Carol Barner-Barry and Robert Rosenwein, *Psychological Perspectives on Politics* (Englewood Cliffs, N.J.: Prentice Hall, 1985), pp. 132–133.
62. For a recent version of the necessity of some degree of immorality in all leadership see F. G. Bailey, *Humbuggery and Manipulation: The Art of Leadership* (Ithaca, N.Y.: Cornell University Press, 1988).
63. Aaron Wildavsky, "A Cultural Theory of Leadership," in Bryan D. Jones, ed., *Leadership and Politics: New Perspectives in Political Science* (Lawrence: University of Kansas Press, 1989), pp. 109–110.
64. This section and the next draw extensively on my argument developed in Peter C. Sederberg, *The Politics of Meaning: Power and Explanation in the Construction of Social Reality* (Tucson: University of Arizona Press, 1984), pp. 164–176.
65. Wildavsky, "A Cultural Theory of Leadership," p. 94.
66. James MacGregor Burns, *Leadership* (New York: Harper & Row, 1978), p. 17.
67. Ibid., p. 19.
68. See, for example, William R. Lassey and Marshal Sashkin, "Dimensions of Leadership," in Lassey and Sashkin, eds., *Leadership and Social Change,* Third Edition (San Diego, Calif.: University Associates, 1983), pp. 11–21.
69. James V. Downton, Jr., *Rebel Leadership: Commitment and Charisma in the Revolutionary Process* (New York: The Free Press, 1973), pp. 26–41.
70. Ibid., pp. 41–52.
71. Mark N. Hagopian, *The Phenomenon of Revolution* (New York: Dodd, Mead, 1974), pp. 329–333.
72. Ibid., pp. 332–333.
73. This categorization is similar to and influenced by that developed by Downton. He distinguishes among three forms of leadership: transactional, inspirational, and charismatic. See especially pp. 74–81.
74. Burns, pp. 19–20.
75. See Downton, pp. 235–237, for another perspective on distinguishing the two.
76. Downton, pp. 77–80.
77. See Max Weber, *Economy and Society,* Vol. 1, Guenther Roth and Claus Wittich, eds. (Berkeley: University of California Press, 1979), pp. 241–245.
78. Ann Ruth Willner, *Charismatic Political Leadership: A Theory* (Princeton, N.J.: Center of International Studies, 1968), p. 7. See also her more recent study *The Spellbinders: Charismatic Political Leadership* (New Haven, Conn.: Yale University Press, 1984).
79. Weber, pp. 246–254. Alternatively, followers could search for a new leader who possesses the qualities of the lost leader. Weber suggests that this is done with the search for a new Dalai Lama, although this ultimately places the relationship on what he terms a traditional basis (what we would consider a form of catalytic/representational relation).
80. Wildavsky, *The Nursing Father,* pp. 19 ff. See also Wildavsky, "A Cultural Theory of Leadership," pp. 100–110.
81. Ibid.
82. Ibid., p. 22.
83. Ibid., p. 19.

84. Ibid., p. 19.
85. This section is based partly upon Sederberg, *The Politics of Meaning*, pp. 162–163.
86. Joseph Campbell, *The Hero with a Thousand Faces*, Second Edition (Princeton, N.J.: Princeton University Press, 1968).
87. See Wildavsky, *The Nursing Father*, pp. 201–203. Muhammad also may be considered a heroic leader. Christ, too, possessed many of the qualities of the heroic revolutionary, but his message was more otherworldly than that of either Moses or Muhammad, who each set up a political order to embody and defend the religious one.
88. Ibid., pp. 24–26.

8

Ideology and Organization: The Links Between Leaders and Followers

The ideology and the organization of the movement link leaders and followers more or less effectively. Often ideology is misleadingly characterized as a narrow, rigid set of false ideas or equated broadly with the content of a political culture. We develop a perspective on ideology that views it more as an action-oriented political philosophy that guides a movement. We review the possible uses and pitfalls of revolutionary ideology for a movement. We then compare the content of a number of revolutionary ideologies. The form and content of an ideology influence the development of revolutionary organizations, the behavioral link between followers and leaders. We identify some of the problems in developing a revolutionary organization and explore the role of organization in moving followers to action.

THE TIES THAT BIND

Revolutionary leaders and followers embrace in an act of political creation. Each engenders the other, and together they spawn the revolutionary movement. The relations between leaders and followers, whether fluid patterns of influence among essential equals or defined patterns of hierarchical subordination, usually involve some kind of exchange. The precise character of the exchange, as we explored in the previous chapter, may be explicit, selective, and concrete or more subtle, collective, and immaterial.

These exchanges, though, do not just happen through some mystical connection, except possibly in the case of the charismatic relation. Moreover, a revolutionary movement faces the challenge of sustaining the patterns of exchange. A spontaneous uprising may shake the foundations of the old order, but a revolution must consolidate power and value in new institutional forms to fulfill its political mission. Moreover, if the *ancien régime* continues to resist, failing to oblige the revolutionaries with its timely collapse, the revolutionary movement must consolidate some power to carry out the revolutionary struggle.

Ideology and organization solidify the links between leaders and followers and sustain the movement in its struggle. The success of revolutionary leaders depends upon, and can be measured by, the appeal of their ideology and the effectiveness of their organization. Clearly, this emphasis on leadership, ideology, and organization runs counter to deterministic theories of revolution. Basic disequilibriums or contradictions produce revolutionary conditions, somewhat independently of the wish or will of either revolutionaries or regime. Nevertheless, specific political actors, the ideas they propagate, and the organizations they generate ultimately shape particular historical outcomes.

Ideological appeal and organizational success, however, do not spring forth in triumph from the head of the revolutionary leader. Rather, leaders forge ideology and organization in the heat of particular historical conditions. The opportunities created by these conditions, the competition from rivals for power in and outside the regime, and the skill and luck of the revolutionaries themselves ultimately determine their success. By exploring the possibilities and pitfalls encountered in developing ideological and organizational ties, we acquire a general orientation to the diversity of historical experience.

IDEOLOGY: DEFINITION AND DEMARCATION

Defining Ideology

Both political analysts and practitioners contend over the ambiguous meaning of ideology.[1] Is ideology truth or falsehood? science or myth? dogmatic or pragmatic? rational or irrational? revolutionary or conservative? Does ideology identify, even create, common interests or do common interests generate a rationalizing ideology? Unfortunately, both political thinkers and actors have used ideology in all of these contradictory senses.[2]

For some, the word *ideology* refers simply to the beliefs, values, and attitudes that shape political activity. They thereby fold the concept into the more inclusive one of "political culture."[3] If everyone holds certain beliefs, values, and attitudes that affect their political activities, then everyone possesses an ideology. "Ideology," here, simply refers to the mental "recipes" or "road maps" that guide our political behavior. These road maps and recipes need not be coherent or consistent; they need not be "true"; they need not even be consciously applied. All politics, from this point of view, becomes ideological politics.

Alternatively, "ideology" often summons up notions of a clearly articulated, but dogmatic and inflexible, creed from which political action is consciously and systematically deduced. Though claiming to embody the truth, an ideology contains oversimplified understandings of the social world, if not outright falsehoods.[4] Ideological politics, from this perspective, contrasts unfavorably with flexible and pragmatic nonideological politics. Pragmatists govern their activities by what seems to work rather than by the dictates of some ideological system.

Neither the broad nor the narrow characterization of ideology serves our purposes. If we equate ideology with political culture, we obscure the role played by systematic doctrine in the formation and activities of a revolutionary movement. Ideologies make up a distinctive part of the broad political culture of a community. Moreover, successful ideologies probably develop specific links with other elements in the culture of which they are a part, lest the people view them as alien imports. Nevertheless, recognizing an ideology's cultural roots differs from equating it with this culture. On the other hand, defining this doctrine from the outset as rigid, unchanging, and wrong-headed simply assumes what we should be investigating. An ideology may be false or misguided, but all ideologies are not equally untrue, except in the trivial sense that no humanly devised system of social explanation captures absolute truth.

The distinctiveness of ideologies arises from four shared characteristics. In contrast with the general notion of political culture, ideologies are *explicit, coherent, value-oriented,* and *action-oriented.*

1. ***Explicit***   An ideology is an explicit statement of beliefs about the world and the values that should guide action in it. People may absorb the biases prevailing in their community but never really examine them nor state any reasons for their preferences and behavior. Ideologies, however, even in their simple, sloganeering form, explicitly articulate the bases for political action.
2. ***Coherent***   These explicit statements present a relatively coherent, consistent, and fairly comprehensive interpretation of the social and political world. We must not mistake relative coherence for perfect consistency. Rather, an ideology appears coherent in comparison with the contradictions contained in the general culture (see Chapter 1, the discussion of cultural incoherence). Now the goal of achieving some degree of internal coherence may contribute to rigidity and dogmatism. Nonetheless, different ideologies exhibit varying degrees of flexibility and openness to revision, even though such flexibility leads to greater risk of inconsistency.
3. ***Value-oriented***   An ideology, as we noted above, is more than a system of beliefs about what the world *is*; it also defines what the world *should be*. An ideology sets forth an explicit system of values, judgments, and goals. This combination of the "is" and the "ought" contributes to the final characteristic of an ideology.
4. ***Action-oriented***   An ideology not only describes and evaluates the world, it also attempts to prescribe and motivate action in it. To paraphrase Karl Marx, science explains the world; normative philosophy evaluates it; but ideology instigates action in it.

Forms of Ideology

Apart from these distinguishing characteristics ideologies take a variety of different forms. For example, an ideology might be *personal* or *collective.* An autonomous individual could formulate a personal guide to political understanding and action, which, though indebted in various ways to elements of the wider culture, is subordinated to none. More typically, though, we think of a political ideology as a system of beliefs and values shared by a group of people.[5]

In addition to being commonly considered a system of shared belief, ideology often implies revolutionary content.[6] This association, though unsurprising, seems too limited. Our definition of ideology applies to any relatively explicit, coherent, value- and action-oriented system of political belief, regardless of whether its mission is to revolutionize, reform, or conserve the established order. Perhaps conservative ideologies lack prominence and frequency because a reasonably well functioning sociopolitical community does not need to create explicit justifications for the status quo. Rather, it can rely on unexamined attitudes of support and deeply ingrained habits of obedience. Those who wish to change this system, whether through reform or revolution, must justify the need for change and the direction it should take. Once they successfully gain power and institutionalize the changes, the ideology that once justified radical transformation converts to a defense of the new status quo.

Ideologies also vary in the degree to which their content is open to revision.[7] Those who view ideology as narrow and inflexible emphasize its nature as predetermined dogma. On the other hand, those who merge the concept of ideology with the broader notion of political culture perhaps incorporate too much flexibility. An intermediate position recognizes that successful ideologies contain *both* predetermined content *and* the capacity for some revision.[8] An ideology must possess some explicit and coherent core of ideas and values. Nevertheless, an effective ideology must be open to revision, especially in its tactical assessments, to serve as an effective guide for action. Some central principles, however, must remain constant to distinguish ideological from purely pragmatic politics.

Finally, a successful ideology includes elements of varying intellectual accessibility.[9] Usually only the intellectual elite of a political movement masters the relatively sophisticated works of ideological analysis that define the core of an ideology. Activists understand the basic principles of the ideological core, as well as recent tactical elaborations. The "revolutionary masses," however, might know little more than the simplistic propaganda of the movement.

The legacy of Karl Marx aptly illustrates these various levels of accessibility. Relatively few intellectuals following in the Marxist ideological tradition fully absorb the imposing scholarship contained in such books as *Capital.* Most Marxist activists, though, probably read *The Communist Manifesto,* and nearly everyone in Marxist movements, even the illiterate, knows the slogan "Workers of the world, unite! You have nothing to lose but your chains!" Books, manifestoes, and slogans represent three levels of increasing ideological accessibility. But even the most accessible level of sloganeering still reflects in some way the principles developed in the more erudite works of ideological analysis.

THE PROMISE AND PROBLEMS OF A REVOLUTIONARY IDEOLOGY

Ideology in Leader/Follower Relationships

Ideology potentially links leaders and followers in a political movement. The development of extensive ideological ties depends on a number of factors. Most fundamentally the potential role of ideology varies according to the basic attributes of the leader/follower relationship. If we view leader/follower relations as ranging along an instrumental/expressive continuum (see Chapter 7), then ideology appears irrelevant at either extreme. In a purely instrumental, transactional relationship, ideas count for little. What matters for the followers are the immediate rewards or punishments manipulated by the leader. At the purely expressive extreme, followers demonstrate a powerful faith in the person of the leader. Again, a systematic interpretation of the social world carries little significance in such a commitment.

The role of ideology grows more significant as we move away from the extremes. A transactional relationship, as we noted in the previous chapter, can evolve from the exchange of purely divisible rewards and punishments to include collective, though still material, incentives (for example, promises to improve public safety or health). The definition of such "public goods" often involves an explicit synthesis of shared beliefs and aspirations, that is, an ideology. At the other extreme a purely charismatic relationship must be "routinized" to survive the inevitable loss of the leader. In one major strategy of routinization the leader attempts to endow a system of beliefs with legitimacy. This charismatically authorized ideology, then, provides a continuing basis for the movement.

Ideology plays a central role in the catalytic/representational relationship. In this relationship the leader represents the aspirations of the followers, giving them shape and voice. A successful representational relation must reconcile differences among the followers and unite them behind a common program. Almost inevitably the product of the leaders' representation of the followers' beliefs will take the form of an ideology. How well this ideology sustains the relationship depends on its performance of certain functions in the movement.

The Uses of Revolutionary Ideology

A revolutionary ideology makes a number of possible contributions to a revolutionary movement. Specifically, ideologies provide a source of explanation, a basis of community, a ground for legitimation, a set of priorities, and a form of inspiration.[10]

As an Explanation of the Political World   Ideologies fill a need to know and understand—an understanding required for effective action. The members of a revolutionary movement need to know the causes of their discontent, the origins of their victimization, and the path of rectification. The revolutionary ideology gives shape to their pain and promises a cure. Potential followers must see the ideology as incorporating salient aspects of their experience. Proposed solutions must also strike followers as relevant and realistic. An ideology, regardless of its internal elegance, that fails to correspond with the experiences of the potential followers will fail to convince them.

In addition, the explanation of exploitation and the recommended course of correction must unite, not divide, the potential revolutionary movement. Usually an isolated sector of society lacks the capability to challenge the regime successfully (see the discussion of the "revolutionary driving force," below). A successful ideology, therefore, must identify unifying interests among apparently disparate groups. In practical terms this means that revolutionary ideologies often stress what they oppose rather than what they support.[11] Common enemies unite people who might otherwise differ on the positive program of social change. In addition, the concentration on the enemy as the embodiment of evil facilitates the polarization necessary for revolutionary transformation.

Critics commonly attack the inadequate explanatory content of revolutionary ideology, especially when communicated to the masses in simplified terms. In particular, revolutionary ideologies polarize the world and eliminate the many nuances and subtleties that supposedly suffuse political relations. Of course, in some sense, *all* social explanations represent simplifications of real-world complexities. A common metaphor for inevitable explanatory shortcomings suggests that a social explanation resembles a map. A map that perfectly represents the detail of the real world would be as large as the area mapped and would hardly serve as a useful guide for action. The real issue revolves around whether any map provides *sufficient* detail for our purposes. A revolutionary "map" may prove sufficient when its explanation captures the essential dynamics of the social system. In short, under conditions of significant social cleavage an ideology that incorporates a polarized worldview may provide a better understanding of essential social realities than supposedly sophisticated social theories.

As a Basis of Community   Revolutionary ideologies explain the social world for their adherents, but intellectual satisfaction alone fails to account for their appeal. Ideology in addition establishes a basis for community and a source of identity. Those susceptible to revolutionary appeals feel alienated from the established order, and an ideology offers a way to overcome the sense of isolation that inevitably accompanies their alienation. Ideology promises a new order that will recognize and value those dispossessed by the old regime. Revolutionary ideology, by dividing the world into friends and enemies, lays down the boundaries of the community of believers and establishes a foundation for solidarity. Once established, a sense of collective solidarity helps to overcome the tendency to free ride on the efforts of others by creating a set of collective incentives counterbalancing the personal costs of participation (see Chapter 5, the discussion of "thickening" rational incentives).

The personal validation and a sense of belonging also help to overcome any explanatory shortcomings encountered by the followers. If an ideology were simply an explanation to be tested against experience, we might expect that explanatory failure (for example, the frequent failures of the predicted revolution to occur or the new revolutionary order to be a paradise) would contribute to wholesale revision or even abandonment of the ideology. Indeed, sustained and repeated failures eventually lead to such outcomes. But where ideological belief reflects emotional attachment as well as intellectual persuasion, then even a series of failures will not necessarily shake the faith of the believers. If an ideology provides a sense of community and identity, then we expect that believers will shift only when they find an alternative source of validation and support.

Leaders, as we noted in Chapter 7, often appeal to followers on emotional, affective grounds as well as pragmatic, instrumental ones. Charismatic relations generate their emotional as well as cognitive appeal from the followers' perceptions of the personal qualities of the leader. The personalistic basis of this emotional attachment constitutes its fatal flaw. An ideology, at least in principle, transcends association with any single leader and provides a more stable foundation for identity and community. To the extent that the members of the movement find meaning and value in an ideology, any leader who represents that ideology can tap into this sense of solidarity.

As Legitimation (and Delegitimation)   In addition to emotional solidarity and explanatory satisfaction, an ideology articulates a reasonably coherent set of values that provides criteria to judge the world. A revolutionary ideology, indeed all ideologies, legitimate a particular social arrangement, and explicitly or implicitly challenge the legitimacy of any other social order. One reason for the strong association between revolutionary politics and ideology is precisely the movement's need to set forth an explicit justification for its attack on the old order. An established regime, as we noted above, relies more extensively on ingrained habits of obedience and the apparent "naturalness" of the existing order. As a political establishment confronts an escalating revolutionary challenge, however, it too feels compelled to develop a more explicit justification for its rule. Indeed, the formulation of conservative ideologies might indicate the seriousness of reformist or revolutionary challenges.

We noted earlier (Chapter 4, explanatory metaphors for revolution) that every stable social order provides some justification for the inevitable experience of evil encountered in our social lives. Insofar as the prevailing "theodicy" successfully legitimates the inequities and suffering associated with the established order, that order will be stable. When people begin to question the reasons given for their suffering, they create an opening for a revolutionary theodicy. This revolutionary theodicy, to succeed, must both challenge the foundation of the establishment theodicy and justify the suffering, sacrifices, and inequities inevitably associated with the revolutionary movement.

Critics sometimes link the legitimating function of ideology to a more self-serving process of rationalization. People naturally tend to view the ideology of their political adversaries as a rationalization of narrow self-interest. From this point of view the preexisting interests of the participants dictate the values contained in their ideology; an ideology simply serves as an after-the-fact justification. While we cannot ignore the capacity of human beings for self-deception, we should avoid completely reducing ideology to a dependent variable. Ideology affects the definition of the interests of its adherents as well as being shaped by these interests.[12]

A successful revolutionary ideology, in particular, usually must create a coalition of common interest and unity among previously divided groups. While such unity cannot be forged in a vacuum—it must build upon existing interests and experiences—it still represents a creative outcome or at least a discovery of a shared fate. The "big ideas" of revolutionary liberation, to appeal to people, must develop out of their "small ideas" involving immediate grievances and aspirations.[13] People will not respond to an ideology remote from their immediate interests. On the other hand, an ideology trapped in the immediacy of particularistic concerns will never succeed in moving the people toward the wider unity and longer-term objectives required for revolutionary transformation. Individual interests and ideology, therefore, interact in complex ways; one does not simply define the content of the other.

As a Set of Priorities for Action   An ideology does not merely explain and evaluate the social world; it aspires to guide action in it. At the very least an ideology establishes certain basic priorities with respect to the investment of the scarce resources. Most importantly, the ideology identifies just who makes up the "revolutionary driving force," that is, the sector or sectors the revolutionaries should attempt to organize (see the discussion of the characteristics of a plausible driving force below).

A systematic and comprehensive revolutionary ideology further defines the basic strategy and tactics of revolutionary transformation. The definition of the driving force reflects the basic ideological explanation of the social world, identifying both the deprived and those responsible for their deprivation. Ideological characterization of the existing social world also helps define the general objectives of the revolutionary movement. Finally, the character of the driving force determines some basic elements of revolutionary strategy (see Chapter 9).

An ideology, however, can go only so far in the definition of tactical options and responses. Tactical success ultimately depends on the ability of leaders to seize the unpredictable opportunities or cope with the unanticipated setbacks that inevitably emerge during the revolutionary struggle. An ideology cannot provide a precise tactical "cookbook" to which the revolutionaries can refer in every situation.

As Inspiration   In addition to explaining, evaluating, and guiding, an ideology also strives to inspire action. The esoteric doctrine that makes up the intellectual core of an ideology may not seem designed to motivate many people. On the other hand, ignorance and incomprehension surely immobilize their victims. People who feel confused and dismayed by the world are unlikely to act in it, whatever their feelings of deprivation. A successful ideology, through explaining their world and guiding action in it, gives people a kind of power over their pain. And action requires power.

Comprehension, though necessary for action, is not sufficient to produce it. In addition, an ideology justifies not only the new revolutionary order but also the sacrifices demanded and the means required to achieve it. Finally, the popular slogans of an ideology attempt to inspire action through simple expressions of power and promise. The slogans of nationalism ("Seek ye first the political kingdom and all else will be given unto ye!"), Communism ("Workers of the world, unite! You have nothing to lose but your chains!"), and participatory democracy ("All power to the people!") succinctly state the primary purposes and understandings of these ideologies in a manner intended to spur action.

The ability to draw upon a persuasive ideology clearly contributes to the successful performance of leadership tasks. Compelling ideologies help leaders define goals, specify means to achieve these goals, and mobilize the necessary energy and resources from their followers. In addition, ideological appeals provide a foundation for an emotionally supportive political community and establish a new sense of identity. Nevertheless, though ideology facilitates the formation of links between followers and leaders in a revolutionary movement, ideological politics also engenders certain potential pitfalls.

The Possible Pitfalls of Ideological Politics

Strains, tensions, and ambiguities commonly accompany ideological politics, especially when the ideology becomes relatively unbending in its interpretation of the world. First, all ideological explanations seek relevance, but their analyses will always be incomplete, misleading, and possibly even false. A flexible ideology will adapt and develop in response to contradictory evidence; more inflexible ideologies tend to substitute ritualistic incantations of received dogma for meaningful analysis.

Some ideologies are so remote from the prevailing social circumstances that any honest consideration would lead to their abandonment. Of course, those who understand the world through an ideology, guide their lives by it, and root their identities in it find it difficult to carry out a detached assessment of the ideology even when confronted with reasonably unambiguous failures of analysis and prediction. Ironically, revolutionary ideologies often claim to uncover the false consciousness induced by the dominant system of values but then seduce their adherents into their own patterns of delusion. In particular, revolutionists sometimes use ideological analysis to exaggerate the revolutionary potential of the masses they claim to represent. Marxist ideologues, for instance, have often exaggerated the revolutionary potential of the working classes in advanced industrial countries.

Psychologically dependent adherents may remain enthralled by an ideology despite explanatory failures, but they will fail to mobilize support from those who find the ideology remote from their immediate experience. Ideological analysis, moreover, need not start off irrelevantly; it may become irrelevant as social circumstances change. Value change, we recall, was one potential weakness in the catalytic/representational leader/follower relationship, in which ideological links assume great importance (see Chapter 7). A nationalist ideology, for example, may provide a convincing source of understanding and affirmation when a liberation movement confronts the imperial oppressor. Once they secure independence, however, people's concerns often turn to more concrete and immediate needs, and they are no longer content to consume only the thin gruel of nationalist symbols.

Revolutionary ideologies often inflate expectations beyond the capacity of the movement to fulfill them. This problem especially arises for a movement unable to produce the promised revolution in the expected time. A revolutionary ideology does not simply engage in a cool assessment of the existing regime; rather, it strives to move the downtrodden to action against it. The desire to inspire action may overwhelm more sober analyses of revolutionary prospects. Promises of immediate success used by revolutionary agitators to motivate potential supporters may discourage long-term commitment. On the other hand, more realistic assessments of the prospects for short-term success may engender feelings of despair and resignation that end up eroding the more plausible long-term prospects.

The problem of inflated expectations does not cease with the seizure of power. Now the revolution must deliver on its promises of postrevolutionary utopia. Many countries of Asia and Africa gained their independence with ideologically inflated expectations of what the achievement of the "political kingdom" would bring, only to encounter intractable problems, divisive conflicts, and inevitable disappointments. Nor do conservative ideologies escape this problem. Though intended to justify the status quo, they often present an idealized version of the existing system. When citizens who have embraced the ideal confront the severely blemished reality, considerable disillusionment results.

Finally, ideological politics generally heightens the scope and intensity of political conflicts. Of course, intensification of conflict is precisely the intent behind a revolutionary ideology, for revolutionary transformation requires as a first step the polarization of the existing community. Nevertheless, this intensification comes with certain costs. Revolutionary ideologies, because of their tendency to interpret the world through a "polarized" lens, politicize many previously private aspects of social life. From a revolutionary perspective everything from parent/child relations and school lessons to the organization of economic production undergoes scrutiny for revolutionary righteousness.

Once the arenas of conflict have multiplied, polarized worldviews endow them with a level of intensity that discourages compromise. Revolutionary ideologues cannot compromise with what they characterize as pure evil, and they end up rejecting half a loaf, preferring none at all. While a rejectionist position may be ideologically exemplary, it often erodes the movement's responsiveness to its followers' needs.

THE CONTENT OF REVOLUTIONARY IDEOLOGY

Most people, at least for the past century, probably identify some form of Marxism as *the* revolutionary ideology. Yet history reminds us of the revolutionary potential in a number of other ideologies. Liberalism not only propelled the American Revolution, but its principles also inspired the recent upheavals in Eastern Europe. The Iranian Revolution shocked the secular West (both Marxist and liberal) through its dramatic demonstration of the potential political power of religious ideals. Anarchism and fascism have also engendered revolutionary turmoil over the past century, the latter ideology inspiring revolutionary change in Italy and Germany between the two world wars. Finally, nationalism, often in combination with another ideology, has energized revolutionary movements around the world in the nineteenth and twentieth centuries.

None of these ideologies, of course, is necessarily revolutionary. At times more moderate versions guide reformist political movements, and once their adherents are entrenched in power, most ideologies become conservative in character. Anarchism, given its opposition to any concentration of political authority, may provide the only exception to these conservative tendencies, but then no anarchist movement has ever controlled a national political community. Although several ideologies might inspire a revolutionary transformation, they conceive both revolutionary context and outcome differently. To illustrate these differences we identify a number of fundamental issues and then compare the six major ideologies on these bases. While this sketch only identifies some essential assumptions of alternative ideologies, we hope thereby to lay a foundation for more detailed analysis in the case studies.

Basic Issues of Ideological Content

Ideologies address common questions, but they arrive at substantially different conclusions. These basic issues not only stimulate ideological analysis, they also engage the attention of social scientists and political philosophers. Scientific analysis alone cannot definitively answer such questions, for they generally transcend the world as it exists and move into the realm of value preferences. Consequently the conclusions drawn by each ideology often reflect both values and purported explanations of the "real" world. The implicit or explicit concerns of any comprehensive revolutionary ideology include the following:[14]

Human Nature   Beliefs about human nature, whether implicit or explicit, condition our attitudes about politics. At one level "human nature" seems susceptible to empirical investigation and scientifically grounded conclusions. Ideologies draw upon science or pseudoscience to defend certain propositions, but ultimately debates revolve around metaphysical, not scientific, issues.

One human nature debate concerns whether humans naturally tend to good or evil (whatever we mean by those terms). Beliefs about inherent human tendencies influence the assessment of the operations of society and government. If human nature inclines people toward "the good," then existing problems result from imperfect, corrupting, and oppressive social and political institutions. Such conclusions support both reformist and revolutionary politics. Alternatively, if humans tend naturally toward evil, then the existing social order restrains the malicious, egotistical tendencies of most people. Such a conclusion generally encourages conservative political attitudes.

Our beliefs about inherent human tendencies affect somewhat how we view the possibility of "redemption." Human beings may be inherently good, but in their prerevolutionary state they are sinful or deluded. All revolutionary ideologies promise some form of human redemption, either individually or within some presumably transcendent collectivity. If the ideology considers human beings individually redeemable, then to some extent the individual stands outside of and is more important than any group. Alternatively, if human beings can be redeemed only through their membership in some group (class, nation, believers, and so forth), then this group subordinates the individual. Not all redemptive belief systems, of course, preach secular redemption. Most religions, for example, confer the blessings of redemption only in some other plane of existence. Revolutionary ideologies, however, promise redemption—the New Revolutionary Order—in this world.

A third human nature problem with profound political implications concerns assumptions about politically relevant inequalities. Again, such assumptions may seem susceptible to scientific investigation, for clearly people are not equally strong, intelligent, or gifted in other ways. But empirically established differences cannot determine what political conclusions we should draw from them. Revolutionary ideologies, indeed all ideologies, define *politically relevant* similarities or differences. Some assume that people possess equal rights and deserve equal treatment regardless of their differences. Others propose that people differ in fundamental ways and that they deserve different treatment, regardless of their other similarities. The former ideologies inspire democratic revolutions against entrenched privilege, whereas the latter emphasize a "leadership principle" justifying the establishment of new structures of political privilege.

The Revolutionary Driving Force[15]   Conclusions about human nature help define the fundamental dispositions of a revolutionary ideology. More pragmatically, a revolutionary ideology specifies the driving force of the revolution—the sector or coalition of sectors capable of propelling the revolutionary process to its conclusion. In this area the explanatory concerns of a revolutionary ideology overlap with theories of revolution developed by social scientists. Both social scientists and social revolutionaries attempt to identify who rebels and why. Scientists want to explain (or understand) and predict; revolutionaries want to organize and inspire. Different ideologies develop different conclusions about the composition of the potential driving force.

Revolutionary ideologies also differ on how they define the character of the revolutionary community. Fundamental assumptions about human nature affect the conception of the community. Revolutionary ideologies, as we noted above, make different assumptions about the primacy of the individual and the existence of politically relevant differences. These assumptions reflect the dispositions of basic cultural types discussed in Chapter 6. A revolutionary ideology may be *individualistic,* rejecting both the primacy of any group identity and the validity of external regulation; *egalitarian,* rejecting external regulation while embracing a strong group identification; or *hierarchic,* embracing both strong group identification and external regulation.[16] No revolutionary ideology, however, reflects either fatalism or autonomy, for the former denies the possibility of secular redemption while the latter rejects social interaction altogether.

Finally, the character of the revolutionary driving force and the community built upon it affects the definition of the revolutionary enemy. Individualistic ideologies reject concentrations of collective power that threaten individual freedom. Egalitarian ideologies reject hierarchies of authority, status, or wealth. Hierarchic ideologies, conversely, denounce the forces sowing discord in the community through destructive egoism or the subversion of rightful authority.

Who Should Rule   Assumptions about human nature, combined with the definition of the composition and character of the driving force, help to determine the basis of legitimacy and illegitimacy in the political community. The problem of who *should* rule entails not only the composition of the rulers but also the source of their right to rule. Different kinds of political community established by various revolutionary ideologies imply different forms of legitimate leadership (see Chapter 7, especially Table 7.2). Individualistic communities, whether revolutionary or not, tend to deny the legitimacy of any continuous pattern of rule. Individual leaders carry out particular tasks necessary to ensure the smooth interactions among rational egoists, but their domain remains severely circumscribed, and they can make no moral claim on other autonomous individuals. Egalitarian communities also reject the imposition of routinized rule, but they may accept those leaders who embody the values and aspirations of the group or personify the group in some charismatic fashion. Finally, legitimate rule in a hierarchic community generally rests on expertise. Those in positions of leadership make some claim to generalized skill and knowledge denied the average member but required for the survival and smooth functioning of the group.

When an ideology defines the basis of legitimacy, by implication it challenges the rightfulness of all other forms of rule. Since revolutionary ideologies polarize the world, illegitimate forms of rule are not simply misguided or inappropriate; rather, they incarnate evil. For extreme individualists no authority structure can make any moral claim on the individual; individualists obey on pragmatic bases alone. An egalitarian community rejects any form of rule that does not embody the defining values of the group. Finally, a hierarchic community condemns rule by those who lack the required wisdom and skills.

The Nature and Role of the State   Revolutions, even those promising to eliminate the centralized state, entail the seizure of state power. Revolutionary ideologies consequently address the nature and role of the state. Ideological assumptions about the essential nature of the state shape revolutionary attitudes toward the state's role and the relation of individuals to it.[17] Organic theories, for example, view the state as a living organism whose existence and needs take priority over the concerns of the individuals who constitute it. The origins of the state seem almost mystical in nature, emerging out of the immemorial traditions of the people and reflecting their collective soul.

Contrary to organicism, instrumentalist theories see individuals as existing prior to the state, which serves as an instrument to meet their needs. An instrumental ideology's disposition toward state power partly depends on whether it adopts an essentially coercion or consensus theory of the state (see Chapter 1, the discussion of different theories of order). According to some instrumentalist theories the state serves the basic needs of all of its members. Other instrumentalist theories see the state as the tool of only one sector of the population. If the state is viewed simply as an instrument of oppression, an ideology might promise to eliminate it after a successful revolution.

Assumptions about the nature of the state entail more than scientific description. They include normative implications about both the proper relation of citizens to the state and the appropriate functions of the state. For example, the requirements of an organic state clearly take precedence over the needs of its members. People's lives have meaning only through their fulfillment of their appropriate functions within the organic order. Before the seizure of power the organic revolutionary movement subsumes its members in a similar fashion.

If, on the other hand, the state is an instrument of its citizens, then the state's meaning and purpose derive from the needs of its members. These citizens possess the right to alter the state to suit their purposes. Instrumentalist ideologies identify whose interests the state serves: a particular sector or class, some majority, or the citizens at large. Similarly, these ideologies define the revolutionary movement as a reflection of a particular sector's interests or that of the whole people.

Finally, assuming that the state exists in the New Revolutionary Order, revolutionary ideologies also describe the appropriate tasks of government. Perhaps the essential issue here concerns the limitations placed on government. Organic ideologies place no theoretical limits on the authority of the government, though certain practical ones may exist. In contrast, some instrumentalist ideologies define inviolable spheres of individual rights. Others, however, do not limit state power, seeing it rather as the instrument of comprehensive social transformation.

The Relation of Truth to Politics   Revolutionary ideologies commonly claim to embody absolute truth, a monopoly position compatible with a polarized worldview. If the ideology splits the world into contending realms of good and evil, then the ideological adversary cannot possess any truth value. Organic ideologies tend toward such absolutism, with political truth assuming an almost mystical nature. Certain instrumentalist ideologies also claim to embody ultimate truths but usually of a more rationalistic, quasi-scientific nature. In either case only a chosen few gain access to these truths.

Other instrumental ideologies avoid claiming a monopoly on truth (though in practice their adherents may act as if they possessed such a monopoly). These limited ideologies consider political insight as incomplete and grant individuals the right to search out and form their own views. Plural value positions can exist within the same community as long as they are tolerant of one another. Modesty about truth content might seem to undermine the revolutionary potential of an ideology, and so it does—in a community where no other sector makes absolutist claims. Somewhat paradoxically the absolutist becomes the polar enemy of an ideology preaching tolerance. A relativist ideology challenges any regime claiming to embody the truth—whether the secular truth of an instrumentalist regime or the transcendent truth of an organic regime.

Revolutionary Ideologies Compared

Revolutionary ideologies include more than a philosophical discourse on these five issues. Such intellectual debates do not, by themselves, constitute a program of action. A revolutionary ideology, in addition, must devote considerable energy to defining appropriate strategy and tactics through which to advance and defend

IDEOLOGY	Human Nature	Revolutionary Driving Force	Who Should Rule	Nature and Role of the State	Relation of Truth to Politics
Liberalism	Basically good, but essentially rational egoists. Unequal in talent but deserving of equal opportunity. Hindered by corrupt institutions.	Potentially, all rational egoists. Revolutionary community basically individualistic. Revolutionary enemy: the absolutist state.	All have right to self-rule. Efficiency requires majority rule or rule by elected "representatives who remain responsible to the people.	Minimal, instrumental state, primarily concerned with facilitating realization of individual goals. Sphere of state activities is limited.	Value relativist. Political truths always partial. Reasonable people can differ. Mandates toleration of different views except, possibly, intolerant, absolutist ideologies.
Anarchism	Basically good, fundamentally moral equals oppressed by illegitimate social and political hierarchies.	All morally autonomous adults. Revolutionary community basically egalitarian. Revolutionary enemy: illegitimate authority structures.	No one has the right to rule over others. Community decisions must "reflect unanimity.	No state. Egalitarian, autonomous communities.	Value relativist among autonomous small communities. Seeks value unanimity within particular community (moral adults can choose to leave). Internally intolerant, externally tolerant.
Marxism-Leninism	Potentially good and collectively rational, but consciousness distorted by dominant ideology and structure. Basically equal, but in need of guidance during the revolutionary struggle.	Members of the oppressed economic class(es) and their allies. Revolutionary community hierarchic in transition, ultimately egalitarian. Revolutionary enemy: capitalist ruling class.	During the transition the revolutionary vanguard rules; when Communism is achieved, transformed into an egalitarian community.	Instrument of class rule. If controlled by revolutionary class, it may be used to aid in transformation. Role unlimited during transition; withers away after achievement of Communism.	Value absolutist. Truth embodied in a doctrine claimed to be rational and scientific, reflecting underlying laws of history. Intolerant of those deemed suffering from false consciousness.
Fascism	Masses basically irrational and unequal; can achieve redemption only through subordination to political movement and its leader.	Members of the Volk (people), usually defined by blood. Revolutionary community hierarchic. Revolutionary enemy: "inferior" races and ideologies that threaten hierarchy (liberalism, Communism).	Masses fit only to follow. Rule by elite and leader who embody the Volk. Leader responsible only to "destiny."	State is the organic emanation of the Volk. No theoretical limits on state's role in coordinating components of the corporate society.	Value absolutist. Truth embodied in the political leader (and movement) that represents the Volk. Intolerant of all others assumed to be inferior.
Nationalism	Members of national community equal to each other, superior to outsiders. Redemption through national autonomy.	Members of the nation, usually defined culturally. Revolutionary community combines hierarchy and equality. Revolutionary enemy: external oppressor ("imperialists").	In principle, people have right to self-rule; in practice the nation's representative-party and leaders rule.	State is the organic manifestation of the nation. Purpose focused on the maximization of national sovereignty, possibly involving a wide role in internal and external relations.	Value absolutist in sphere of national identity, but may make limited claims elsewhere. Possibly tolerant of other nations as long as they don't interfere with sovereignty.
Political religion	Masses basically born evil, but redeemable through community of believers. Usually unequal in community, but equal in God's eyes.	Members of the community of believers. Revolutionary community usually hierarchic. Revolutionary enemy: unbelievers, especially those in power.	Masses fit only to follow. Rule by the religious experts whether priest, prophet, or Imam.	State must be instrument of the religion. Purpose is to maximize realization of religious principles in political life.	Value absolutist. World divided into believers and nonbelievers. No toleration.

its principles as well as to communicating both principles and strategy to the prospective revolutionary community. Yet the answers given to these problems mold the basic shape of the ideology. Subsequent propaganda and practice develop from these principles in the particular context of a revolutionary struggle (see Part Four). A systematic comparison of major revolutionary ideologies, then, provides a basic orientation to contemporary practice. Table 8.1, "Patterns in Revolutionary Principles," illustrates some of the basic contrasts among these ideologies, although this schema abbreviates the complexity of each.[18]

The first four revolutionary ideologies require little further comment, for they represent fairly familiar political doctrines. We need to stress, though, that "anarchism" refers to philosophical anarchism, not the nihilism with which it is sometimes confused. The last two, however, contain certain ambiguities. The basic character of nationalism, for example, depends on the nation represented. Nationalism, moreover, often combines with and energizes other ideologies. Fascism, in particular, incorporates a xenophobic nationalism. Often liberal and even Marxist ideologies also contain nationalist appeals, especially when the revolutionary enemy can also be portrayed as an enemy of the nation. Indeed, we may have difficulty in separating the combined effects.

The doctrine of political religion challenges revolution as a concept of *secular* redemption. The bitter experience with religious wars in the West contributed to a centuries-long struggle to limit the political influence of religious creeds. In the late twentieth century, however, not only Islamic revivalism but also Christianity has challenged the power of secular states in the Middle East, Eastern Europe, and elsewhere. The category of "political religion" recognizes the resurgent political relevance of religious beliefs. Unfortunately, the category lumps together religions and sects within religions, muting the considerable differences among them. Political religions, too, combine with other ideological identities. Christianity combines with elements of Marxism in liberation theology. Polish Catholicism commingles with Polish nationalism. And despite their universalist aspirations Iranian Shi'ites may have to settle for "fundamentalism in one country," just as the Bolsheviks resigned themselves to socialism in one country 70 years ago.

PROBLEMS OF REVOLUTIONARY ORGANIZATION

From Ideology to Organization

Ideas, however captivating and catalyzing, cannot alone link leaders and followers in sustained and effective political action. Prolonged struggle, in particular, demands organization to bind leaders and followers together in the coordinated pursuit of revolutionary objectives. Basil Davidson observes, "The [revolutionary] struggle must be conducted in such a way that the people, increasingly, 'do it themselves.'"[19] We must specify, though, exactly *who* is doing *what* to *whom*.

Three problems make up the challenge of revolutionary organization: Whom to organize? How to organize them? Finally, what to do with the organization?[20]

The first issue concerns the identification of the revolutionary driving force. The second question involves how members of the driving force participate in their revolution. The final question probes into the area of revolutionary strategy and tactics.

The ideological orientation of a particular movement influences how it addresses these challenges. In addition, the social and political context of the struggle affects the practical performance of a revolutionary organization. Ideology clearly guides the identification of the potential revolutionary driving force. To a lesser but important extent, the fundamental form of the revolutionary community affects the structure of revolutionary organization. Ideology also sets forth broad principles of strategic action, but ideological guidance probably exercises less influence on the particular tactical responses to a rapidly changing political environment, even if subsequently rationalized in ideological terms.

Whom to Organize: The Problem of the "Driving Force"[21]

Each revolutionary ideology identifies the political base from which to recruit the revolutionary movement. This base, to fulfill its role as the revolutionary driving force, should possess at least four attributes: discontent, mass, potential coherence, and potential power resources. The plausibility of a significant challenge to the status quo diminishes with the progressive failure to meet any one of these requirements. On the other hand, the mere presence of such attributes does not assure success. The potential driving force must respond to the ideological appeals, and at least a rudimentary structure capable of effective action must exist.

Discontent   The driving force identified by a revolutionary ideology must be disaffected from the established order. Each revolutionary ideology offers an explanation of why its candidate for mobilization *will prove* susceptible to revolutionary appeals. Liberalism and anarchism in their differing ways build upon individual frustration with illegitimate concentrations of political power. For the liberal such concentrations frustrate the rational egoist's opportunities to maximize his or her potential; for the anarchist these concentrations outrage a moral adult's sense of personal autonomy. Marxism offers a theory of collective exploitation that prevents the revolutionary class (or classes) from fulfilling their productive potential. Fascism and nationalism rely on the cumulative resentments of a race or people who cannot control their destiny, and political religions usually presume a growing sense of moral outrage with current corruption.

If the hypothesized discontent has already bubbled into simmering hostility, then the challenge of revolutionary mobilization is reduced. Unfortunately, in the initial stages of revolutionary organization, the targeted driving force often displays few, if any, signs of overt discontent. It may even appear largely supportive of the existing order. At least three factors could account for such support. First, the revolutionary theory could be wrong. Those presumably discontented actually could be authentically contented. Second, free riding might produce acquiescence to the regime. As rational actors they may choose to conform, even though alienated from the regime, because of the selective costs associated with overt rebellion (see the discussion of free riding in Chapter 5). Third, their apparent contentment may be inauthentic, resulting not from some fundamental identity of interests between the presumed revolutionary elements and the status quo but from delusion or false consciousness.

Each of these possible explanations presents a different challenge for the incipient revolutionary organization. In the first instance, authentic contentment, revolutionaries must abandon their dreams of mobilization and wait for underlying social conditions to alter the basic identity of interests between the established regime and the presumed revolutionary sectors. In the second case the revolutionary organization must devise ways of overcoming the free rider problem by, for example, developing selective incentives (positive and negative) or a collective identity to counterbalance rational egoism. In the third case the ideology must somehow "unblind" the potential driving force and lead them to recognize their true interests.

Not surprisingly, few revolutionaries find the option of conceding explanatory failure especially attractive, so they tend to emphasize the other two explanations for nonsupport. In the case of attempting to overcome the free rider problem, nascent revolutionary organizations encounter shortages of the resources needed to offer selective incentives, to supervise activities, and to monitor for defections. Alternatively, the argument that inaction results from delusion of the masses may itself be the product of revolutionary wishful thinking. To paraphrase Hotspur's observation in Shakespeare's *Henry IV,* anyone can call for the people to rise up, but will they rise when they are called?[22]

Critical Mass   Discontented people, of course, exist in every political community. A plausible revolutionary driving force, however, must possess a critical mass sufficient to make a difference. The notion of critical mass obviously begs the question, How much is enough? Most revolutionary ideologies claim that the revolutionary driving force *represents* a majority of the population. The validity of such an assertion not only helps determine the potential power of the movement (see below) but also the revolution's legitimacy. Much smaller numbers, of course, actually participate in the revolution. Similarly, regimes typically claim to rule for all the people, though only a minority actively defends the established order. Generally, minorities claiming to act in the name of majorities engage in both revolutionary action and regime counteraction.

Liberal ideology makes potentially sweeping claims about universal citizenship in the new liberal political order. Anarchism optimistically assumes all people, if liberated from the crippling influence of illegitimate authority, could develop into the autonomous moral adults who constitute its revolutionary base. Marxist economic theory predicts the continuous expansion of the proletariat until it encompasses the vast majority of the population. In the Maoist variant of Marxism the revolutionary movement builds on the numerical mass of the peasant population. Ultimately, Marxism predicts, the proletariat will become the entire human race, ushering in the classless society. Fascism and nationalism, in contrast to the universalist pretensions of the preceding ideologies, distinguish the potential base by race or culture. Religious communities, even ones possessing universal proselytizing aspirations, also possess clearly demarcated boundaries. A credible driving force defined by race, culture, or religion must possess sufficient mass within a particular community; otherwise, at best, it provides only the basis for sectarian, secessionist civil war.

Claims to represent the masses, of course, could be as deluded as the often-wishful thinking about widespread discontent among the potential revolutionary base. The aspirations of liberalism and anarchism may far outstrip the self-consciousness of the average political subject. Indeed, we might cynically conclude that the drastically limited number of morally autonomous adults in the world forecloses any possibility of a successful anarchist revolution. Marxism relies on underlying economic forces to expand its revolutionary base, but often Marxist movements attempt to seize power in countries where the true proletariat, whatever its level of discontent, remains small in number. Mao's Marxist heresy in China made a virtue out of necessity by determining that only the peasants possessed the necessary mass, relegating the urban proletariat to an essentially secondary role.

Perhaps the most serious limitation on potential mass arises from exclusionist definitions of the revolutionary base. An exclusionist ideology both limits the size of the driving force and often generates active opposition from those excluded. Marxist rhetoric emphasizing class conflict makes enemies of those not included in the revolutionary class. Racially or culturally defined political movements have no appeal outside their primordially bound group. Such limitations will not matter if the primordial group constitutes a substantial portion of the community, but if it does not, exclusionist ideologies could consign the movement to a permanent minority status.

Potential Coherence   Mass discontent alone cannot make a revolution. The ability of the revolutionary movement to raise an organized challenge to the state depends in part on the potential coherence of the revolutionary base. Low potential coherence inhibits the organizational efforts of the revolutionary movement, regardless of the discontent among those expected to join. Several factors appear to limit potential coherence: the lack of a common focus for discontent, the presence of conflicts that crosscut the potential revolutionary cleavage, and the relative absence of preexisting social structures and experiences that could facilitate the emergence of revolutionary organization.

The lack of focus is not identical with the absence of latent or overt discontent (see above). Discontent, even if already simmering among the masses, may not support revolutionary mobilization. At the extreme each individual remains trapped in a personal hell of private frustration and resentment with little basis for common identification and cooperation. On the other hand, the experience of deprivation may develop in such a way as to engender a sense of solidarity and common destiny among the suffering. Marx, for example, expected that the shared experience of alienation and exploitation in the workplace would increase the potential for worker solidarity.[23] Similarly, nationalist movements rely on shared resentment against the alien rulers to generate feelings of common interest and destiny. Without some focus for discontent the revolutionary driving force risks degenerating into a battleground of private agendas and personal vendettas. Successful revolutionaries need not be selfless zealots, but they must harness their private motives to some common objective.

Potential coherence, though, depends on more than the existence of a common focus for discontent. Other crosscutting conflicts and identities may undermine the revolutionary cleavage. In particular, such crosscutting identities eroded worker solidarity in Europe. Marx and other socialist revolutionaries correctly recognized that the shared deprivation of the industrial workplace would stimulate the growth of worker organizations. In the last half of the nineteenth century worker solidarity developed largely as predicted: Unions organized in factories then across industries; confederations of industrial unions arose, along with working class–based socialist parties. Ties even developed cross-nationally in the international workers' movement. But when the Great War began in 1914, the workers of the world, for the most part, abandoned proletarian solidarity and went off to fight for their respective nation-states. Economic exploitation and class conflict provided a powerful foundation for organization up to a point, but ultimately other identities and conflicts frustrated international revolutionary coherence. Similarly, racial divisions commonly undercut the unifying potential of economic discontent in the United States. Ironically, once a nationalist movement achieves its goal of independence, class and ideological conflicts as well as other primordial divisions begin to undermine the facade of national solidarity.

Finally, even if the salience of the revolutionary cleavage overwhelms competing conflicts and identities, the potential coherence of the revolutionary driving force depends on preexisting structures and experiences of collective solidarity and action (see the discussion of the opportunity/resource approach in Chapter 6). Marx's skepticism about the revolutionary potential of the peasants as a class arose from the relative absence of this aspect of coherence. He observed, for example, that the French peasants "form a vast mass [living] in similar conditions but without entering into manifold relations with one another. Their mode of production isolates them from one another instead of bringing them into mutual intercourse."[24] For this reason, the peasant mass "is formed by simple addition of homologous magnitudes, much as potatoes in a sack form a sack of potatoes."[25] This, in his mind, contrasted with the experiences of the industrial workers, whose productive relations encouraged not only a *sense* but also the *organization* of class solidarity.

The operations of the revolutionary organization itself may mitigate all these threats to coherence. A revolutionary ideology, in addition to explaining the origins of discontent, thematically unifies apparently disparate deprivations to develop a common focus for frustration. Both the increasing salience of the revolutionary conflict and the ties created by common action erode the potency of crosscutting cleavages. Finally, the organization itself provides the initial experiences of common action among a "homologous" group like the peasants. Nevertheless, low levels of potential coherence in the revolutionary driving force clearly complicate the mission of the movement.

Potential Power Resources   The promise of the revolutionary driving force ultimately depends upon its power. Obviously, the driving force possesses only "potential" power. If it held actual power, there would be little need for a revolution. Alternatively, if the driving force were truly powerless, then revolution would be impossible. Both mass and coherence contribute to the potential power of a driving force, but other power resources also affect the ability of the revolutionary base to challenge the status quo. Marxism, again, aptly illustrates this issue. The proletariat increases in numbers as the capitalist system evolves. The prerevolutionary organizational aptitude and experience of the proletariat also expand, contributing to the growth of class consciousness, a prerequisite for effective revolutionary action. Ultimately, though, the power of the proletariat derives from its position in the productive process. For Marx, labor is the source of all economic value, and when the proletariat effectively wields this power, the capitalist system cannot withstand its force. By effectively withholding its labor, the proletariat brings the economic system to a halt.

In contrast with the hypothesized material power base of organized labor, other revolutionary movements depend on more "idealist" power sources. Liberal revolutions of the late eighteenth, early nineteenth, and late twentieth centuries attracted the support of the intellectual and professional classes, who brought their verbal and organizational expertise to the revolutionary movement. Marxist revolutions, somewhat paradoxically, considering their emphasis on the proletariat, also gained the support of many intellectuals. Fascism, nationalism, and political religions often draw upon preexisting fervor and energies in their targeted revolutionary base.

Strategic position also contributes to the power of a potential revolutionary driving force. What constitutes a strategic position, though, depends on the conception of the revolutionary strategy. In Western-style revolutions (see the discussion in Chapter 6) the uprising starts in the cities and subsequently consolidates power over the countryside. In this process a driving force concentrated in the cities obviously holds a positional advantage over one dispersed throughout the country. In contrast, Eastern-style revolutionary movements gradually mobilize the countryside to surround the old regime in its cities, turning the dispersed peasantry into a strategic resource.

The issue of *potential* power resources again raises the possibility of ideological delusion. No movement could concede the complete powerlessness of the sector in whose name they make revolution. Rather, it must find some redeeming social power—some reason to hope for success. This need for hope encourages, if not outright self-deception, at least the tendency to err on the side of optimism when assessing the respective power positions of the regime and the revolutionary base. In any case neither potential cohesion nor potential power becomes actual until created by the revolutionary organization.

Problems of whom to organize multiply when no single homogeneous candidate for the driving force possesses the mass or power to challenge the regime successfully. The proletariat may lack the numbers. Even if the proletariat possesses the necessary mass, a well-organized and relatively satisfied "labor aristocracy" may have little in common with a nonunionized "lumpenproletariat." The peasantry may be massive in numbers, but even more divided by wealth and status than the urban working classes. The liberal intelligentsia usually lacks the necessary numbers, and other sectors of the population often resent them. In the absence of a homogeneous revolutionary base, the necessary driving force requires a coalition. Workers unite with progressive elements of the bourgeoisie and the peasantry. Landless and small landholding peasants accept alliances with the so-called middle peasantry. Nationalist and religious movements combine different class and status groups united by little more than their common secular or sacred beliefs.

Coalitions, at least in theory, solve problems of mass and power, but they do so at certain obvious costs, especially with respect to coherence. Broadening a revolutionary coalition presumes not only the existence of significant discontent across sectors, but also compatibility among different grievances and interests. Often revolutionary coalitions agree on little more than their enemy, a characteristic particularly evident in nationalist movements. Such "negative" coalitions risk disintegration after the revolution, if not earlier.

Indeed, members of a revolutionary coalition often possess not simply differing, but fundamentally incompatible, interests. Peasants and urban workers, for example, hold opposed economic interests in some critical areas. Specifically, peasants want high prices for agricultural commodities and low prices for industrial goods, and workers desire the reverse. In the so-called Marxist revolutions of the twentieth century, both workers and peasants discovered, to their painful surprise, that the interests of the mobilizing bureaucrats dominating postrevolutionary organizations clashed with their aspirations for the new revolutionary order.

The task of forging a coalition to compensate for the relative weakness of any single sector complicates the formulation of a successful revolutionary ideology and taxes the incipient revolutionary organization. Ideology must now make sense out of multiple grievances and unify diversity in ways that further the possibilities for effective collective action. Organization must somehow mobilize the energies and coordinate the activities of groups that appear to have little in common. Coalitions often compromise both the purity of ideology and the integrity of organization, complicating the second major question of revolutionary mobilization: How to organize?

How to Organize

Three models of revolutionary organization specify the basic options available to an incipient revolutionary movement: elite-vanguard, mass-democratic, and anarchist.[26] Anarchist movements renounce any permanent authority structure and pursue a kind of "antiorganization." Consequently most significant movements of both reform and revolution of the past century resemble one, the other, or some mix of the two other forms. Table 8.2, "Characteristics of Revolutionary Organizations," delineates some essential contrasts among the three options.

Each organizational form reacts against the other two, addressing perceived weakness and potential perversions. Elite-vanguard organizations generally take their inspiration from Leninist revolutionary theory, even when they are not explicitly Marxist in ideology. Mass-democratic organizations, in contrast, commonly trace their roots to the social democratic parties that emerged in Western Europe in the latter part of the nineteenth century and against which Lenin

TABLE 8.2 CHARACTERISTICS OF REVOLUTIONARY ORGANIZATIONS

CHARACTERISTIC	MODEL		
	Elite-Vanguard	Mass-Democratic	Anarchist
Leadership	Professional	Amateur	Transitory
Origin of leaders	Self-appointed or selected by superiors	Elected representatives	Spontaneous emergence
Principles	Ideological purity; exclusive	Broad unifying principles; inclusive	Antiauthority
Membership	"Elite vanguard"	The "masses"	Morally autonomous adults
Origins of members	Selective	Open	Self-selected
Structure	Centralized-clandestine	Decentralized-open	Locally autonomous
Basic dilemma	Organization and ideology dilute appeal	Organization and ideology dilute revolutionary purpose	Organization and ideology dilute sustained activity

directed some of his most vitriolic critiques. Anarchist theory also emerged as a revolutionary force in several countries during this period. Although each form may point to earlier precursors, in some sense they all engaged each other in the same general social milieu.

The elite-vanguard model of organization calls for a "professional" revolutionary leadership. Revolution must be a vocation, not a hobby.[27] Such disciplined professionals emerge from the fires of dedicated revolutionary activity; the fickle fancies of electoral politics could not produce hardened revolutionaries. Only a professional revolutionary elite would hold true to the revolutionary principles, resisting the temptation to slip into reformist compromises with established power. The general members of the revolutionary vanguard must also embody the qualities of dedication and ideological purity. Those who demonstrate dedication to the discipline of the movement constitute the revolutionary vanguard. The movement purges those who weaken, hesitate, or compromise. Finally, a tightly centralized leadership must control the structure of the revolutionary movement to prevent reformist defections. In a hostile political environment the movement's activities turn clandestine and conspiratorial. Unfortunately, in the quest to preserve unity and purity, the vanguard organization often ends up limiting its appeal.

Mass-democratic movements reject the authoritarian implications of vanguardism, fearing that the emphasis on the leadership inevitably contributes to both the alienation of the masses from their own liberation and the emergence of dictatorship.[28] In contrast to elite-vanguard movements, mass-democratic parties rely less on lifelong professionals than on the emergence of talented amateurs. Often followers elect their peers to leadership positions. The underlying principles of this party tend to be broader, more inclusive, and more subject to pragmatic compromises. The party welcomes all who wish to join and support its general principles. Its structure tends to be more decentralized and open to broad participation. The movement eschews conspiracy for the open competition for power. Ironically, pragmatic—even opportunistic—ideology and open organization often combine to dilute revolutionary purpose, just as vanguardists predict.

Anarchist movements condemn the oligarchic tendencies displayed by both the other alternatives.[29] Even mass-democratic parties create permanent, self-perpetuating hierarchies of authority.[30] True anarchists, whether individualist or communitarian in character, reject all such claims of authority. Leaders may arise spontaneously in the movement to address certain problems, but their position of preeminence must be severely constrained and ultimately transitory. Anarchists assert that morally autonomous adults cannot subordinate themselves to any external authority. Clearly, then, the members of an anarchist movement select themselves, and what structures that exist must be small in scale and locally autonomous. The antiauthoritarian organization and ideology of anarchism, despite the potency of its critique of the other organizational modes, dilute its capacity for sustained revolutionary activity. Unfortunately, the creation of structures capable of sustaining revolutionary activity tends to produce precisely the kind of bureaucratic hierarchy anarchism decries.

These three models illustrate the range of organizational options; however, historical cases often combine these types in various ways. The Bolsheviks, for example, approximate the elite-vanguard extreme, but other groups involved in the Russian Revolution were less centralized and dogmatic. Indeed, the soviets (popular councils) formed in Russian cities initially represented relatively spontaneous organs of popular participation—reflecting some democratic and even anarchist impulses—until ultimately captured by the Bolsheviks.[31] On the other hand, conspiratorial vanguardist organizations, to challenge the regime successfully, usually must find a way of broadening their base of support. The Bolsheviks achieved this goal in part by appearing to champion the soviets against the authority of the provisional government after the fall of the Czar.

In many particular revolutionary situations we expect to find these three organizational options tugging at the revolutionary movement. Each addresses weaknesses of the others in various ways. Allowing for mass participation expands the narrow popular base of the vanguard organization. The decentralizing impulses of anarchism reduce the oligarchical tendencies of both vanguard and mass movements. Finally, the elite-vanguard organization combats the loss of revolutionary élan and the limited capacity for sustained revolutionary activity exhibited by the other two approaches. The possibility of such organizational crosscurrents guides our inquiry into the revolutionary cases discussed in Part Four.

CONCLUSION: WHAT TO DO WITH THE ORGANIZATION

The final issue of revolutionary organization concerns the strategy and tactics of revolutionary struggle. Both ideology and organization contribute to the formulation of revolutionary strategy and the choice of particular tactics. Ideology provides an interpretation of the historical situation confronting the revolutionary movement and defines the options available to the movement. As with other explanatory functions, a particular ideology may mislead an incipient revolutionary movement. Traditional Marxist ideology, building on its understanding of the historic role of the proletariat, tends to emphasize the significance of various forms of urban rising as effective revolutionary tactics. The small urban proletariat in China, however, found how vulnerable they were in April 1927, when Nationalist forces launched a general attack on workers' groups and labor unions in Shanghai. Ideology does not necessarily guide strategy in fruitful ways; nonetheless, we must look at the ideological roots of strategies and tactics of revolutionary change.

In addition, patterns of affinity may exist between organizational forms and certain strategies and tactics. Elite-vanguard organizations, because of their conspiratorial and dogmatic character, seem comfortable with certain forms of violence rejected by mass-democratic organizations, such as terrorism and coup d'état. Anarchist movements, however, might engage in decentralized forms of terrorism, but they lack the organizational resources to plot a coup. Anarchist organizations seem most compatible with relatively spontaneous forms of popular uprisings. Alternatively, mass-democratic organizations, to the extent that they manage to retain their revolutionary commitment, would seem attracted to more open forms of struggle such as the general strike. As they compromise their original revolutionary agenda, democratic movements may transfer their political struggle to the arena of parliamentary politics.

Whatever the ideological analysis of political opportunity or the strategic predilections of different organizational formats, the essential strategic problem of revolution remains the same. The next chapter discusses the dimensions of this problem and analyzes the factors affecting the relative success of some major tactics of revolutionary struggle.

NOTES

1. For a careful review of the ambiguities afflicting the concept see John Plamenatz, *Ideology* (New York: Praeger, 1970).
2. For a contemporary review of these various positions see Raymond Boudon, *The Analysis of Ideology*, trans. by Malcolm Slater (Chicago: University of Chicago Press, 1989), especially Chapters 2 and 4.
3. See, for example, William T. Bluhm, *Ideologies and Attitudes: Modern Political Culture* (Englewood Cliffs, N.J.: Prentice Hall, 1974), pp. 3–10.
4. See, for example, Boudon, p. 29.
5. Plamenatz, indeed, makes this sharing a necessary characteristic of an ideology. See Plamenatz, p. 31.
6. Neither Marx nor Karl Mannheim shares this particular bias. Both essentially view ideology as essentially being an apologia for the status quo. Mannheim labels what we term revolutionary ideology as "utopia." See Karl Mannheim, *Ideology and Utopia* (New York: Harcourt, Brace, and World, 1955).
7. This distinction relates somewhat to that between preformed and ad hoc ideologies developed by Hagopian. See Mark N. Hagopian, *The Phenomenon of Revolution* (New York: Dodd, Mead, 1974), pp. 263–269.
8. Hagopian agrees. See ibid., pp. 263–264.
9. Hagopian divides an ideology into three levels: hermetic, esoteric, and exoteric, which represent the range we discuss here. See ibid., pp. 269–271.
10. Other scholars, unsurprisingly, come up with different lists of functions, though the one we discuss overlaps with the basic points of other approaches. See, for example, Thomas H. Greene, *Comparative Revolutionary Movements*, Third Edition (Englewood Cliffs, N.J.: Prentice Hall, 1990), pp. 79–86; Roy C. Macridis, *Contemporary Political Ideologies: Movements and Regimes*, Second Edition. (Boston: Little, Brown, 1983), pp. 9–13; and Mostafa Rejai, *Political Ideologies: A Comparative Approach* (Armonk, N.Y.: M. E. Sharpe, 1991), pp. 17–18.
11. For a discussion of the general function of enemies in ideology see David J. Finlay, Ole R. Holsti, and Richard R. Fagen, *Enemies in Politics* (Chicago: Rand McNally, 1967); see also Murray Edelman, *Constructing the Political Spectacle* (Chicago: University of Chicago Press, 1988), Chapter 4.
12. See Plamenatz, p. 98.
13. Basil Davidson, *The People's Cause: A History of Guerrillas in Africa* (New York: Longman, 1981), pp. 159–160.
14. The fundamental questions of politics, of course, could be framed in a variety of ways. I have chosen the five broad issues here to highlight revolutionary implications. For other related catalogues of basic issues, as well as far more extensive discussions, see Leslie Lipson, *The Great Issues of Politics: An Introduction to Political Science*, Fourth Edition (Englewood Cliffs, N.J.: Prentice Hall, 1970), especially Chapter 1;

and L. T. Sargent, *Contemporary Political Ideologies,* Third Edition (Homewood, Ill.: Dorsey, 1975), Chapter 1.

15. For a discussion of the problem of the "driving force" of a revolution see William H. Friedland, *Revolutionary Theory* (Totowa, N.J.: Allanheld, Osmun, 1982), pp. 1–4. The concept, as Friedland indicates, is fundamentally Marxist in its roots, but it is a relevant concern of any ideology.

16. See the discussion in Michael Thompson, Richard Ellis, and Aaron Wildavsky, *Culture Theory* (Boulder, Colo.: Westview Press, 1990), especially pp. 6–7.

17. The following discussion of organic and instrumental views of the state is indebted to that in T. D. Weldon, *States and Morals: A Study in Political Conflicts* (New York: Whittlesey House, 1947).

18. In addition to the works by Roy Macridis and Lyman Sargent cited earlier (see notes 10, 14), those wishing a more in-depth introduction to each ideology should consult the collection of original writings in Nancy S. Love, ed., *Dogmas and Dreams: Political Ideologies in the Modern World* (Chatham, N.J.: Chatham House, 1991). For an introduction to philosophical anarchism see Robert Paul Wolff, *In Defense of Anarchism* (New York: Harper Torchbooks, 1970). For a still useful comparative discussion of the relation between religion and politics see Donald Eugene Smith, *Religion and Political Development* (Boston: Little, Brown, 1970). For a more recent introduction to Islamic political thought, see Mehran Tamadonfar, *The Islamic Polity and Political Leadership: Fundamentalism, Sectarianism, and Pragmatism* (Boulder, Colo.: Westview Press, 1989).

19. Davidson, p. 161.

20. See Friedland, pp. xi–xii.

21. Friedland provides a review of several candidates for the revolutionary driving force offered by ideologies of essentially Marxist origin. See pp. 1–62.

22. *Glendower:* I can call spirits from the vasty deep. *Hotspur:* Why so can I, or so can any man. But will they come when you do call for them? *Henry IV,* Part I, Act 3, Scene 1, 53–55.

23. For an excellent discussion of this point see Daniel R. Sabia, " Rationality, Collective Action, and Karl Marx," *American Journal of Political Science,* 32 (February 1988): 50–71.

24. Karl Marx, *Eighteenth Brumaire of Louis Bonaparte,* in *Selected Writings,* David McLellan, ed. (New York and Oxford: Oxford University Press, 1977), pp. 317–318.

25. Ibid.

26. For an in-depth discussion of these three forms see Friedland, pp. 63–109.

27. The classic defense of the vanguardist organization is contained in Lenin's monograph *What Is to Be Done?* (New York: International Publishers, 1943).

28. A telling critique of Lenin made by a revolutionary intellectual is probably that of Rosa Luxemburg. See Rosa Luxemburg, *The Russian Revolution, and Leninism or Marxism?* (Ann Arbor: University of Michigan Press, 1961).

29. The anarchist alternative is commonly associated with the thought of Mikhail Bakunin and Pyotr Kropotkin. For selections from these and other anarchist thinkers see Love, pp. 343–411.

30. The classic study of oligarchic tendencies in the late-nineteenth-century German Social Democratic Party is Robert Michels, *Political Parties,* trans. by Eden and Cedar Paul (New York: The Free Press, 1962).

31. Hannah Arendt investigates how Russian Soviets and other manifestations of popular participation and political freedom emerged in various revolutions only to be crushed by authoritarian political elements. See Hannah Arendt, *On Revolution* (New York: Viking Press, 1965), especially pp. 252–285.

9

Strategy and Tactics of Revolutionary Transformation

Revolutionary transformation involves not only the destruction of the old regime, but also the revolutionary reconstruction of the political order. This constructive element in a revolutionary struggle contrasts with the solely destructive goals of conventional war and affects both offensive and defensive strategy and tactics. Once the complex interactions between the constructive and the destructive, the offensive and the defensive, are sorted out, we can evaluate the specific tactics and countertactics of revolutionary struggles. We include in this chapter an assessment of the commonly underrated option of nonviolent coercion.

THE STRATEGY OF REVOLUTIONARY TRANSFORMATION

Radical political ends and coercive political means come together in the strategy of revolutionary transformation. Deliberate strategies of radical change usually involve significant amounts of coercion because the resistance of established interests must be overcome, competitors for power defeated, and the New Revolutionary Order consolidated. Noncoercive accommodation and compromise will not accomplish such tasks, since the consequences of victory and defeat are great. All sides in this high-stakes political struggle, therefore, will likely resort to the "ultimate" power resource of coercion.

Yet the strong probability that coercive tactics dominate strategies of revolutionary transformation does not mean that all revolutionary struggles necessarily follow the same course or involve the same levels of destruction. We have already noted two broad paths to power for a revolutionary movement. In the Western path the old regime collapses and then the revolutionary movement occupies the political center and coercively consolidates its power over the remainder of the country. In contrast, a revolutionary movement following the Eastern path fights its way to power at the center over years of violent struggle from the periphery (see the discussion of Huntington in Chapter 5). Both of these paths to power involve tactics of direct attack.

An often-ignored third path to power and transformation involves tactics of withheld support or noncooperation. Ironically, the Bolsheviks' coup d'état and their subsequent consolidation of power through terror and civil war obscured the role played by tactics of withheld support in Marxist revolutionary theory. In principle the potential resources and strategic position of a growing proletariat should enable it to gain power through such tactics as the general strike. Strikes involve coercion, to be sure, but of a form that differs from that involved in direct attacks like terrorism, insurgency, coup d'état, or conventional civil war.

Whatever the particular tactics of revolutionary struggle, the strategic task confronting the movement (and the opposing regime or establishment) differs substantially from the strategic problem in "normal" international political conflict. These differences in turn affect the selection of any particular tactic or combination of tactics used in a given revolutionary situation. We must therefore first understand the peculiar strategic problem facing revolutionaries before discussing alternative tactics. Once we establish the strategic context, we then assess three major tactical options associated with contemporary revolutionary struggles: terrorism (and counterterrorism), insurgency (and counterinsurgency), and tactics of noncooperation. In conclusion we review some of the factors influencing victory and defeat in a revolutionary struggle.

Michael Mandelbaum observes that any military strategy must address three issues: (1) the political ends sought through coercive means, (2) the specific coercive forces developed and deployed to achieve these ends, and (3) the use of these forces once hostilities break out.[1] The first question links military strategy back into the context of a wider political contest. The third relates general strategy to the particular demands of a dynamic tactical situation.

The coercive strategy of a revolutionary movement pursues two broad political goals, one destructive and one constructive, aiming both to destroy the regime and to create new institutional forms. Without the destructive goal the revolutionary movement will most likely succumb to reformism; without the constructive goal the movement will lapse into nihilism.

In the Western model of revolutionary strategy, destruction of the old largely precedes construction of the new; in the Eastern model, destruction and construction occur simultaneously. The successful construction of new social forms enables the revolutionary movement to mobilize the resources needed to pursue destructive goals, and vice versa. We must be careful, however, not to exaggerate this simple contrast. Even where the old regime collapses, as it did in Russia, the group ultimately filling the power vacuum and eliminating its competitors must initially control relatively significant power resources. Alternatively, a regime confronting an Eastern-style insurgency will probably not fight to its last soldier. It will collapse before any final military defeat, much like the Batista regime in Cuba.

A revolutionary movement faces both defensive and offensive tasks in the development and deployment of its forces. Defensively, the movement must deploy resources to ensure its survival. Offensively, the movement must develop resources to expand its base of support, both quantitatively and qualitatively. Again, we expect to find mutually reinforcing effects. Success at one task contributes to success at the other; failure at one contributes to failure at the other.

The destructive and constructive strategic goals and the defensive and offensive strategic tasks combine to define the context within which particular revolutionary tactics emerge. Table 9.1, "The Strategic Context of Revolutionary Tactics," presents these relationships. The table emphasizes the regime as the opponent of the revolutionary movement, suggesting its primary relevance to the Eastern model of revolution. A revolutionary movement in a Western-style revolution, however, faces similar considerations both before the collapse of the regime and in the subsequent struggle to consolidate power against its competitors.

Destructively, the defensive task of the revolutionary movement involves tactics that erode the regime's ability to attack the movement effectively. Specific examples include political and military actions that diminish the morale of regime forces, attacks designed to tie down the regime forces in static defensive positions, and the creation of disinformation about the position and capabilities of the revolutionary forces. Constructively, defensive tactics must reduce the vulnerability of the movement. Examples include the development of redundant leadership cadres, mobile forces, and intelligence capabilities to warn of regime attacks.

Destructive offensive tactics aim to reduce the regime's control over the population. Revolutionary forces might erode regime control through the specific destruction of the regime's administrative and military forces or through tactics that provoke the regime to respond in ways that further alienate the population. Constructive offensive tactics strive to develop political and military structures that increasingly integrate the population under revolutionary control. These tactics involve actions to engender feelings of revolutionary solidarity, organizations to monitor and punish defections, and structures to mobilize resources and personnel for revolutionary activities.

This table lays out some tactical considerations confronting a revolutionary movement at any stage of its existence. As the movement expands in power, tactical engagements increase in ambition and impact. Any particular tactic, moreover, may fulfill multiple tasks. Thus, tactics that undermine the morale and effectiveness of regime forces also may reduce the regime's control over the population, as well as give increased confidence to the supporters of the revolution.

The strategic goals and tasks of a regime swept up in a revolutionary contest

Table 9.1   THE STRATEGIC CONTEXT OF REVOLUTIONARY TACTICS

TASKS	GOALS	
	Destructive	**Constructive**
Defensive	Erode the regime's ability to attack the movement effectively	Reduce the movement's vulnerability to regime attack
Offensive	Reduce the regime's social control over the population	Create structures that increasingly involve people as participants in revolution

reverse those of the revolutionary movement. Defensively, the regime must reduce the capability of revolutionary forces to attack effectively, while lowering its own vulnerability to attack. Offensively, the regime must eliminate revolutionary control over the population while integrating the population into structures and activities that support the established order. Too often a regime swept up in a revolutionary civil war neglects the constructive goals of counterrevolutionary strategy. This neglect partly explains why the regime finds itself in a revolutionary predicament in the first place.

Virtuous and vicious cycles may develop for both revolutionaries and regime. Destructive success creates opportunities for constructive accomplishments, creating further resources to pursue destructive goals. If the revolutionary movement erodes the regime's ability to undertake effective countermeasures and at the same time reduces the regime's control over the population, then these accomplishments set the stage for further expansion of the movement's constructive capabilities. Alternatively, if the regime successfully attacks the revolutionary movement and reduces its effective sphere of operation, then the regime gains an opportunity to increase its own capabilities and support. Of course, neither side may be able to eliminate its rival or protect itself from attack. Each may retain some minimum level of support needed to sustain its activities, resulting in a prolonged and bloody stalemate.

The understandable attention given to crisis and struggle around the world perhaps leads to an exaggerated sense of the opportunities for revolution. The time is already late when a regime's support crumbles or a revolutionary insurgency roots itself in the countryside. The lowest level of rebellion, after all, is no rebellion at all, a condition of social stability that discourages those isolated elements dreaming about the transformation of the existing order. Under conditions of stability an assessment of the strategic context for revolutionary struggle becomes almost irrelevant.

Terrorism represents the lowest tactical level at which it makes sense to weigh the benefits, risks, and resource requirements of a revolutionary strategy. Rural and sometimes urban insurgency indicate an intensification of the revolutionary struggle and raises a more significant strategic challenge for both revolutionaries and regimes. Full-scale revolutionary civil war embodies the highest level of strategic concern and presumes roughly equivalent forces. Once a struggle reaches this level, the revolutionary movement must have substantially eroded the regime's coercive and institutional resources while significantly enhancing its own.

We should not, however, transform the tactical trinity of terrorism, insurgency, and conventional war into immutable stages of revolutionary conflict. Though terrorism possesses tactical relevance for both Western and Eastern models of revolution, insurgency conforms more with the protracted struggle of the Eastern model. The revolutionary coup probably represents its tactical equivalent in the urban setting of the Western model. Both models culminate in revolutionary civil war; but for the Eastern model civil war represents the final stage of the struggle to seize power at the center, while in the Western model civil war represents the initial stage of power consolidation as the revolutionary regime at the center expands its power over the periphery.

In addition, tactics of noncooperation possess their own levels of intensification, reflecting increasing capabilities of the resistance movement. Just as the lowest level of violent resistance is no violence, the lowest level of noncooperation is obedience. The first acts of actual noncooperation might take the form of covert malingering (thus the old Soviet joke "We pretend to work, and they pretend to pay us"). As resistance escalates, increasing numbers of people may openly demonstrate their withdrawal of consent through demonstrations or other acts of protest. Finally, the general strike, roughly equivalent to full-scale civil war, represents the highest level of withheld obedience.

Such schemes of analysis always simplify the real world. Higher tactical levels do not simply replace lower ones as a "theory" of stages suggests. Rather, as the capability of the revolutionary movement expands, higher level tactics *subsume* the lower. Movements capable of mounting an insurgency, for example, will not automatically forgo terrorist tactics for that reason. Terrorism may retain certain tactical advantages. Moreover, tactical defeats may reverse the progression to a higher level, especially if a movement attempts an escalation prematurely. Finally, though we identified particular patterns of tactical escalation with Western, Eastern, and "third" paths of revolutionary struggle, they may overlap and reinforce one another. The predominantly rural struggles in Cuba and Nicaragua, for example, combined with urban risings and a collapse at the center before the rural insurgency fully achieved the level of a conventional civil war. In addition, strategies of noncooperation figured prominently in both these revolutions.

None of these tactics—terrorism, insurgency, coup d'état, civil war, malingering, demonstrations, and general strikes—possesses any necessary revolutionary content. Any side in a political contest may use these tactics. Tactics gain whatever political character they possess from their ideological and strategic context. Particular tactics take on revolutionary meaning only when used to pursue the destructive and constructive goals of revolution. To illustrate some of these relationships, we investigate the potential roles of terrorism and counterterrorism, insurgency and counterinsurgency, and tactics of noncooperation in a revolutionary struggle.

TERRORISM[2]

Terrorist Tactics: The Problem of Definition

Travelers gunned down as they pass through an international airport. Mutilated bodies of peasants cast into a ditch as a warning to others who contemplate dissent. Such acts do not lend themselves to dispassionate social inquiry. The emotional intensity of terrorist actions reinforces problems of identification. The temptation to take sides is hard to resist, but if we succumb to such a temptation, we may well compromise our understanding. On the other hand, a detached pose suggests an apparent tolerance of heinous behavior. Terrorism, perhaps more than other arenas of human conflict, thrusts us into uncomfortable moral dilemmas.

The interwoven problems of emotion, identification, and moral challenge contribute to the politicization of inquiry. At one level this politicization simply recapitulates the widespread tension in social analysis between the quest for understanding and the desire for policy relevance. When investigating any source of human suffering inquirers often feel challenged to yield "useful" results, that is, results that indicate how to reduce this suffering. In the study of terrorism, though, the pursuit of a political agenda often compromises analysis from the outset. What purports to be an explanation may be little more than political rhetoric intended to advance the purposes of one contender in a political struggle.

All these problems hinder our efforts to understand the potential role of terrorist tactics in revolutionary and counterrevolutionary struggles. At the most basic level some analysts question whether we can even define the category sufficiently to make it a useful tool of analysis. A weary cliché, yet a persistent myth in the study of terrorism, stresses the subjectivity that supposedly afflicts efforts to define the phenomenon. The aphorism "one man's terrorist is another man's freedom fighter" suggests that arbitrary personal or political bias compromises all attempts to formulate the concept. These dubious conceptual foundations then distort all analyses based upon them.

The emotional baggage attendant on the term leads it to be used more for condemnation rather than clarification. The attachment of the label "terrorist" to one's opponent constitutes a moral and political victory.[3] Such victories, though, are purchased at high cost for critical discourse on the problem. Christopher Hitchens argues that the terrorist label "disguises reality and impoverishes language and makes a banality out of the discussion of war and revolution and politics."[4] Little wonder, then, that some conclude that the "very word terror is a hindrance in the investigation of violence."[5]

While the critics of the concept make valuable points, we either need some kind of working definition to delimit the boundaries of terrorist tactics from other forms of coercion, or else we must abandon the term to the mindless pleasures of the polemicists. Unfortunately, the lack of consensus produced by the combination of inherent ambiguity and polemical pressure results in a plethora of definitions. Alex Schmid, in a comprehensive review of the literature in the early 1980s, identifies over a hundred competing definitions. When he published a second edition, the situation had worsened, partly in response to a survey he conducted on definitional issues.[6]

A variety of problems impede our efforts to develop an analytically useful definition of terrorism. First, an understandable but confusing tendency to intermingle explanation, justification, and condemnation mars many definitions. Second, the confusion between the action (terrorism), the actor (the terrorist), and the effect (terror) detracts from our ability to distinguish between terrorism and the larger class of coercive action of which it is a part. In this regard we should focus on the act and recognize that issues of actors and effects constitute areas for inquiry, not definitional attributes. Finally, the option of focusing on particular acts, like hijackings, kidnappings, or bombings, fails to specify exactly what about these particular tactics makes them terrorist.

We must specify those characteristics that distinguish terrorism from other coercive tactics to rescue the concept from both polemicists and those who consider it an empty category. Two traits, each drawing upon the rules of war, appear promising.[7] The most well-established limits on the conduct of warfare involve the targets selected and the means chosen to attack those targets. Specifically, the military contenders should confine their attacks to other combatants, and they should choose discriminating weapons to minimize incidental noncombatant losses.

The principle of noncombatant immunity and the ban on indiscriminate weapons, though related, raise distinct issues. Terrorism consists of those tactics of severe coercion that deliberately violate these two rules of war. Terrorist tactics target noncombatants and attack them with relatively indiscriminate means. These attributes suggest two propositions and two qualifying exceptions:[8]

> *Definition One:* Discriminating acts of coercion aimed at combatants are not terrorist.
>
> *Exception One:* At some point attacks on combatants may become so indiscriminate (for example, counterforce nuclear war) that they become terrorist in effect, if not intent.
>
> *Definition Two:* Undiscriminating and severe coercive attacks deliberately aimed at noncombatants are terrorist.
>
> *Exception Two:* At some point attacks against noncombatants may become so discriminating in choice of target (for example, a tyrant) and means (highly selective assassination), that they can no longer be usefully labeled terrorist.[9]

These propositions both specify the nature of terrorist tactics and identify areas of ambiguity (indiscriminate attacks on presumed combatants or highly discriminating attacks on carefully selected noncombatants). Two key questions remain open: *Who is a noncombatant? And how indiscriminate is too indiscriminate?*

Superficially, the distinction between combatant and noncombatant seems easy to establish. Combatants include the members of the armed forces of either the regime or the revolutionaries. Yet we must be careful not to confuse the role with the person. Prisoners of war or wounded personnel in hospitals, for example, are generally considered noncombatants, regardless of the role they played previously or might play again. If we consider prisoners and wounded noncombatants, then how should we categorize soldiers on "rest and recreation"? Should a bomb planted in a bar frequented mainly by off-duty soldiers be considered a terrorist act?

If military personnel slip into and out of combatant roles, ambiguity increases with respect to the police. Revolutionaries see the police as a coercive organization set up to defend the established order. Consequently the police become combatants in the revolutionary struggle. From the revolutionary perspective, then, a campaign to assassinate police officers is not a terrorist tactic.

Although this logic probably convinces revolutionary partisans, we find it more reasonable to distinguish among the essential tasks performed by particular elements of the police. An unarmed London "bobby" walking his beat seems a relatively remote representative of the armed forces of the regime. On the other hand, branches of police forces of many countries take on paramilitary functions (and armaments) and become direct combatants in the armed struggle between the regime and dissidents. Coercive tactics directed against paramilitary units of the police do not seem terrorist in nature. Similarly, certain irregular forces organized to defend the regime, like the right-wing death squads that have operated throughout Latin America over the past three decades, lose their noncombatant immunity.

The criterion of indiscriminate means presents an even greater ambiguity than noncombatant status, for coercive means clearly entail greater or less discrimination. At what point of indiscriminateness does an act become terrorist? Although bombs exploded in a crowded civilian shopping area or on a civilian airliner typify terrorism, a considerable range lies between such bombings and a single murder by a lone assassin. Although no definitive line can be drawn along this continuum of coercion, we suggest two considerations.

First, relatively indiscriminate coercion directed at combatants generally receives significant, if regrettable, toleration (see Chapter 2, the definition of violence). The terrible weapons of modern conventional warfare, even excluding nuclear weapons, ensure significant noncombatant casualties, especially if they are used in densely populated areas. In contrast to the toleration accorded to relatively indiscriminate combatant coercion, a much more restrictive attitude usually applies to noncombatant targets. Some common forms of terrorism demonstrate significantly more discrimination than the bombings popularly associated with the term. Kidnappings, which received so much attention in the 1980s, generally affect single individuals carefully selected for whom they represent (like Americans or business executives) and for their vulnerability. The victims are usually male (hijackers also often release their female hostages). Despite this degree of selectivity, a significant randomness remains, in that any member of the target group is at risk.

Assassination campaigns pose another interesting problem. The word *assassin* derives from the Arabic, *hashishiyyin*, used to describe an Islamic sect founded toward the end of the eleventh century.[10] This sect dedicated itself to wreaking havoc among the dominant Sunni majority. For nearly two hundred years it waged assassination campaigns against powerful members of the ruling classes. The presence of the Crusaders in the Holy Land meant, inevitably, that some of them too became targets. Many notables apparently paid "protection" money to insure against becoming the next victim. Although they succeeded in terrorizing the ruling elites, the Assassins did not overthrow the dominant order, and they eventually receded into relatively peaceful sectarian communities.

Although their targets were selected from the politico-religious officialdom, their violence cannot be equated with simple tyrannicide. Average subjects might have felt relatively immune, but the breadth of the assassination campaign still appears relatively indiscriminate. We might suggest that the less important the role particular victims play in the maintenance of the ruling structure, the more indiscriminate the coercion directed against them becomes.

The distinctive characteristics of terrorist coercion suggest why it commonly spreads fear greatly disproportionate to the concrete damage done or the probabilities of being a victim. The distinction between combatants and noncombatants provides, perhaps, the last firebreak of a civil order. Once it is breached, no one can feel secure. Terrorism, moreover, often involves innocuous targets such as airplanes, railway depots, and department stores—places people normally consider safe. Terrorist acts not only cause substantive damage, but they also undermine the confidence people have in the familiar. Now people view every place with suspicion, if not alarm.

Varieties of Dissident Terrorism

Terrorist tactics take on revolutionary content only in the context of a political strategy of radical transformation. Dissident groups (or individuals) resorting to terrorism vary according to the comprehensiveness and coherence of their political objectives. While comprehensiveness and coherence represent continuous dimensions, we make several approximate distinctions according to level of political sophistication: psychotic, criminal, nihilist, single-issue, nationalist, and revolutionary (see Figure 9.1). Only the last two levels demonstrate sufficient ideological coherence to be considered part of a revolutionary strategy.

Psychotic Terrorism   Sometimes acts of random, indiscriminate violence result essentially from individual psychosis.[11] In the cases of a lone gunman massacring children in a school yard to satisfy his own inner demons or a demented serial killer, the act contains almost no direct political significance. Psychotic terrorism, though, may possess some indirect political import, if we demonstrate a link between the occurrence of mass murders and a wider culture of violence or systemic deprivation.[12]

Extremist groups that advocate violence against their enemies often attract personalities who find their violent proclivities legitimated.[13] Martin Schechterman suggests three criteria for identifying a terrorist act as irrational: First, the perpetrators fail "to define or stress sought-after political goals in their public rhetoric." Second, the perpetrators "resort to their own defined (self-confirming) code of behavior." Finally, rather than a means to an end, "the act of terrorism is in itself an ultimate satisfaction."[14]

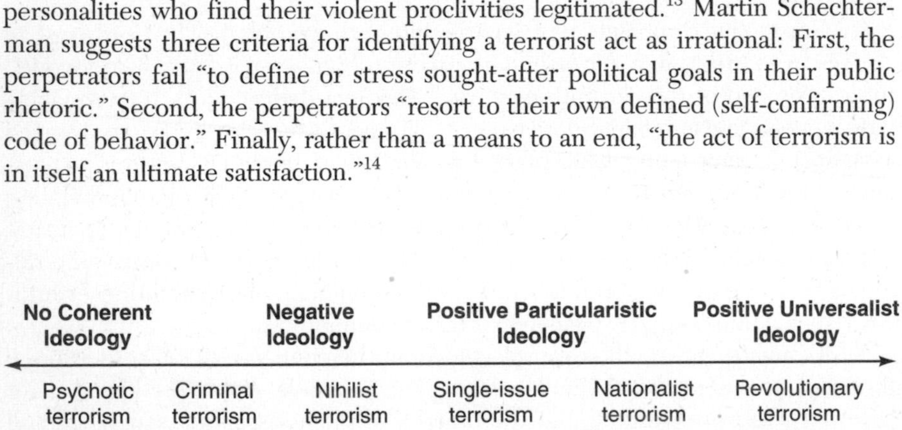

No Coherent Ideology		Negative Ideology	Positive Particularistic Ideology		Positive Universalist Ideology
Psychotic terrorism	Criminal terrorism	Nihilist terrorism	Single-issue terrorism	Nationalist terrorism	Revolutionary terrorism

Figure 9.1 Forms of dissident terrorism.

Criminal Terrorism   Criminal groups generally lack coherent ideological programs and usually simply pursue their own enrichment. Nevertheless, they attend to the operations of the state, especially when it comes to protecting their activities. Such efforts at protection often take the familiar forms of bribery and corruption, but they periodically involve intimidation as well. At some point a program of intimidation can grow so widespread and brutal that it assumes the character of terrorism.

The "narcoterrorism" afflicting the country of Colombia provides an example of criminal terrorism. For years the drug lords of Colombia succeeded in protecting their activities through both the conventional means of corruption and a campaign against those who acted or spoke against them. Gunmen assassinated dozens of judges and journalists. When the government of Colombia finally undertook a tough countercampaign after the 1989 assassination of a leading presidential contender, the terrorist attacks of the drug cartels escalated to include numerous bombings as well as more assassinations.

Those engaged in criminal terrorism do not seek to destroy and then reconstitute the established order. On the contrary, they seem more intent on terrorizing their way into the establishment. This peculiar parasitical relation with the dominant order distinguishes criminal terrorism from other, more ideologically motivated, forms of dissident terrorism.

Nihilist Terrorism   Groups (or individuals) with no systematic political agenda may resort to criminal terrorism. Nihilists, in contrast, possess an agenda, the destruction of the existing order. They devote little, if any, thought to what follows destruction, beyond some vague anticipation that a new and better order will spontaneously arise from the ashes of the old regime. The nineteenth-century Russian anarchist Sergei Nechayev put it clearly. In his *Catechism of the Revolutionist* he declares, "The Organization does not intend to impose on the people any new organization from above. The future organization will without doubt grow out of the popular movement and from life, but this is the task of future generations. Our task is terrible, complete, universal, and merciless destruction."[15]

Contemporary examples of unadulterated nihilism are hard to find. Most of the potential candidates still cling to some shreds of positive ideology, whether these involve vague promises of national liberation or of social transformation. Moreover, attaching the label "nihilist" to "terrorist" often serves no purpose other than to reinforce polemical condemnation. Regimes admitting that a dissident element is in some way "liberationist" or "revolutionary" grant it a degree of authenticity. Consequently most regimes prefer to label dissidents as "criminal" or "nihilist."

Political isolation and the absence of a positive program handicap nihilist groups in their competition with the state. Most people, to paraphrase Nietzsche, prefer any order to no order whatsoever. Unfortunately, the political weakness of the nihilists may make these groups more likely to use highly destructive terrorist tactics. Radicals with more constructive programs and objectives often have too much to lose.

Single-Issue Terrorism   Sometimes extremist political elements organize around a single issue that they attempt to advance through terrorist tactics. In contrast to the nihilists, they possess a positive program, but their narrow cause lacks the comprehensiveness normally associated with the idea of revolution. Of course, a revolutionary movement could incorporate such causes into a more encompassing ideology. For single-issue true believers, however, such incorporation may threaten to dilute their prime value. Alternatively, they may find other aspects of the more inclusive ideology irrelevant or unappealing. Extreme elements of both the right-to-life and environmental movements have engaged in actions (like the bombing of abortion clinics) which appear terrorist in nature.

Nationalist Terrorism   Some dissident appeals more directly challenge the state by outlining an alternative to the existing order. A campaign of violence, including terrorism, may help to solidify support for their alternative. At the risk of some oversimplification, dissidents may be said to develop two basic alternatives, one "particularistic" and the other "universalistic."

In some sense, particularistic ideologies appeal to any solidary group less inclusive than the entire human race. Some ideologies, both secular (Marxism) and sacred (Christianity, Islam), claim to possess universal relevance, whatever the limitations on their appeal in practice. For our purposes, particularistic ideologies consist of those directed at communities other than, and generally less inclusive than, established states. For better or worse the state system remains the dominant political reality of our age. Dissident elements often direct their anger at the state for precisely this reason, but at the same time they wish to establish a claim to their own independent state.[16]

Often groups making particularistic communal appeals include more universalistic elements in their ideologies. Two questions, however, clarify the nature of these "mixed" ideologies. First, without the appeal to communal solidarity, would the other ideological elements alone attract much of a following *within* the community? Second, when combined with the communal appeals, do the other ideological elements attract much of a following *outside* the communal group? If we answer both questions negatively, then we can confidently classify the group as possessing a "particularistic" ideology.

For two centuries ideologies of liberation and self-determination permeated political conflicts in Europe and then spread around the globe. These communal appeals offered compelling rationales for radical action, including terrorism. With the collapse of the Soviet empire, nationalism returned to its area of origin. More than nihilism or, for that matter, the appeals of universal revolution, nationalist ideas and aspirations underlie the extremist politics of our time, whether that of the Basques in Spain, the Palestinians in the Middle East, the Sikhs in India, the Tamils in Sri Lanka, or the Croats and Serbs in the remains of Yugoslavia. If successful in their quest for political autonomy or complete independence, nationalist movements effect a secessionist revolution.

Revolutionary Terrorism   Finally, dissident groups may advocate a program of social transformation that transcends the particularistic concerns of any substate community. They aim not to establish independence from an established state but to seize control of this state and transform it. In some cases the revolutionary vision transcends the boundaries of a single state to encompass a larger, perhaps global, community. The comprehensiveness of revolutionary ideological principles varies, and most contemporary examples of revolutionary dissent fall considerably short of universal appeal. Moreover, sometimes nationalist symbols reinforce apparently universal appeals, as in both the Chinese and Vietnamese revolutions.

Islamic fundamentalism offers a potent contemporary case of mixed appeals, combining a rejection of the corrupting influences of Western culture with the desire to create a just order based on the social principles embodied in the Koranic traditions.[17] Religious principles, to be sure, need not have universal appeal, and indeed, religion has fueled some of the more bitter sectarian conflicts in history. Yet the Islamic revival, and the conflicts it inspires, seems to be more than a simple communal clash like those involving the Basques in Spain, or the Tamils in Sri Lanka, or even that between the PLO and Israel. Islam, despite its divisions, aspires to be a universal religion to which all peoples can convert. The Basques, presumably, do not accept converts.

Secular revolutionary ideals also inspire their proponents to use terrorism as both a tactic of transformation and an instrument of power consolidation (the latter being more an instance of establishment terrorism—see below). Marx, given his emphasis on the basic structural forces underlying successful revolutions, tended to denigrate those who advocated terrorism as a quick and easy way to incite a revolution. Nonetheless, terrorism might intensify class conflict and thereby radicalize the proletariat. Lenin too expressed some skepticism about the efficacy of terrorism, but more on tactical grounds than as a matter of principle.[18]

A simpleminded equation of terrorism with some vaguely conceived radicalism, then, ignores significant differences among the various dissident elements who might resort to terrorist attacks. Such differences prove critical when considering the significance of terrorist tactics in a strategy of revolutionary change. Many acts of dissident terrorism not only fail to achieve revolutionary objectives, they may not have been intended to do so in the first place.

Varieties of Establishment Counterterrorism

Dissidents hold no monopoly on terrorist tactics. Those identifying with the established order may resort to terrorism to defend the status quo. When faced with serious threats to their position, establishment sectors often respond with increasing repression. Establishment terrorism represents an available tactic of repression and involves deliberate and relatively indiscriminate targeting of noncombatants. Since both the regime and private groups identifying with the established order may resort to this tactic, establishment terrorism ranges from completely private acts to totally institutionalized regime policy. Not all the threats that provoke establishment terrorism, however, represent a revolutionary challenge.

Ironically, the full institutionalization of terrorist tactics transforms establishment terrorism from a form of "violence" into "force" (see Chapter 2). When fully integrated into the process of rule, terrorist tactics fall within the dominant definition of "acceptable" coercion. Under its own rules, the regime commits no crime. Less well institutionalized forms of establishment terrorism, however, violate at least formal boundaries regulating the use of coercion and become a kind of establishment violence.

Vigilante Terrorism   Vigilantism consists of establishment violence perpetrated by private citizens, including "off-duty" public officials.[19] Familiar forms of vigilantism commonly involve private citizens stepping in to impose a rough justice when normal law enforcement proves inadequate. Vigilante violence, if effectively targeted on actual criminals (a kind of "combatant"), is not necessarily terroristic.

Sometimes vigilantes target groups who violate no law but simply represent a "deviant" racial, cultural, or political group. Although "crime control" vigilantism may degenerate into indiscriminate attacks on the most unlikely suspects, vigilantism aimed at racial, cultural, or political groups poses a greater likelihood of escalating into vigilante terrorism. Rampages against feared or resented communal groups occur tragically often. Persistent patterns of relatively indiscriminate racial violence in the United States provide a familiar example. Other instances of vigilante terrorism inflicted on deviant groups include Hindu attacks against the Sikhs after the assassination of Indira Gandhi, Malay attacks on the Chinese in Malaysia, the pogrom against suspected Communists in Indonesia in 1965, and mass killing of the Hutus in Burundi in 1972.

Vigilante terrorism, then, includes more than summary justice meted out to a suspicious, but innocent, character; rather, tens of thousands may lose their lives. Moreover, because vigilante mobs appear to defend the established order, law enforcement officials may feel less zealous in controlling their violence. Indeed, sometimes officials covertly participate in vigilante terrorism, in apparent violation of the laws they supposedly uphold.

Covert Official Terrorism   Private and public roles often intersect. When officials use their position to enrich themselves and their friends, we speak of corruption. In a somewhat similar vein, when officials violate the rules governing the use of coercion, we term this official or regime violence. When this violence grows increasingly indiscriminate, it becomes covert official terrorism—covert because the officials recognize that such actions violate formal restrictions on their activities.

Although analytically distinct, vigilante terrorism and covert official terrorism often blend into one another. In Central and Latin America death squads have murdered tens of thousands of people, especially in Brazil, Uruguay, Argentina, El Salvador, and Guatemala. The regimes in these countries sometimes covertly sponsored or organized these death squads, and the campaigns of covert official terrorism in Argentina, Brazil, and Uruguay are well documented.[20] Indiscriminate nonjudicial torture and execution, unfortunately, continue widely throughout the world.[21]

Overt Regime Terrorism   Some brazen regimes openly embrace terrorism as a major enforcement strategy. In vigilante terrorism and even covert campaigns of official terrorism, the regime at least formally recognizes that terrorist tactics violate the laws and norms regulating coercion. Consequently, these types of establishment terrorism represent forms of violence.

By openly embracing terrorism the regime attempts a "magical" transformation, the legalization of establishment terror tactics. The whims of a particular set of rulers, to be sure, cannot automatically redefine the boundaries of acceptable coercion for a community. Long-standing laws and norms also play a considerable part (see Chapter 2). A powerful and determined regime, however, may attempt to expand the definition of "acceptable" coercion. Contemporary history indicates that an official program of coercion indiscriminately aimed at noncombatants sometimes becomes "the law of the land."

Official terrorism of this sort is not the monopoly of the twentieth century. E. V. Walter documents the use of terrorism by the nineteenth-century Zulu ruler Tchaka as a means to break down subregime loyalties and consolidate his personal power.[22] In the twentieth century, however, terrorism as an institutionalized instrument of rule has flourished.[23] The most homicidal examples include the Stalinist purges in the 1930s, Nazi use of terror, and the excesses of the Pol Pot regime in Cambodia between 1976 and 1979.

Genocide   The ultimate expression of establishment terrorism carries the institutionalization of this tactic to an extreme conclusion. Though Tchaka and Stalin used terror to consolidate their power and eliminate any conceivable challenger, their terrorist policy still had some limits. Tchaka was not out to kill all the Zulus, and Stalin did not intend to liquidate the entire structure of the party and government. Genocide transcends such limits. The regime identifies a particular group as undesirable for one reason or another and targets it for complete elimination.

Genocide evokes even more rhetoric and emotion than the concept of terrorism. Irving Louis Horowitz suggests that a structural characterization of genocide should include two points: "First, genocide represents a systematic effort over time to liquidate a national population, usually a minority; second, it functions as a fundamental policy to assure the conformity and participation by the citizenship."[24] Defined in this way, genocide becomes the ultimate form of institutionalized establishment terrorism and represents an intensification of more "routine" forms of official terrorism. The major instance of genocide remains the Nazi holocaust against the Jews of Europe. Some would also include other official pogroms as well, such as that inflicted by the Ottoman Empire on the Armenians during World War I.

Terrorist Tactics and Revolutionary Strategy

Dissident and establishment terrorist tactics serve a variety of possible objectives, not all of which possess any necessary connection to a revolutionary (or counter-revolutionary) strategy. Most of these objectives, moreover, could be pursued by means other than terrorism. Finally, the perpetrators of a particular terrorist event may intend it to serve a number of goals.

Most emotionally, terrorism serves to *express frustration*. Brian Jenkins notes that terrorism is often "born of failure," failure to gain redress of grievances or to protect position and privilege from threat.[25] Terrorist violence, on the part of both dissidents and regimes, can even become an ecstatic end in itself, producing the feeling of transcending normal limits on behavior.[26] And, of course, one act of terrorism often begets a terrorist response in a blood cycle of revenge.

Sometimes the perpetrators give essentially expressive violence a higher rationale of *redemption* (for the dissidents) or *restoration* (for the establishment). Franz Fanon, for example, argues that the psychological cripples of colonization regain their self-respect through acts of violence against their oppressors.[27] In a rough reflection of Fanon's message of redemption, sometimes members of the establishment think that "when law and order are at stake, a society permits its defenders a certain frenzy and ecstasy in protecting the compound of the law."[28]

Terrorist tactics also serve more instrumental objectives. First, terrorism may *publicize* the existence of dissidents with a set of grievances, as well as *demonstrate their capability* for resisting the established order. Similarly, establishment terrorism, when it displays the handiwork of its torturers and death squads, *demonstrates the consequences* of resistance for those tempted to rebel. More extreme campaigns of dissident terrorism may aim at making a *territory ungovernable* or *provoking an ill-conceived campaign of regime repression*. The regime, of course, may respond with an effective, rather than an ill-conceived, campaign of counterterrorism that *makes resistance impossible*.

These rough parallels between the objectives of dissident and establishment terrorism suggest a possible relationship. Three forms of linkage seem plausible: First, dissident and establishment terrorism may stimulate and reinforce each other.[29] Second, dissidents who found terrorism to be a useful tactic of resistance may also use it as an instrument of rule once they gain power. Third, dissident leaders may use forms of establishment terrorism with respect to relations within their own movement.

Having objectives, of course, is not the same as realizing them. Does terrorism work? To paraphrase the old joke: Compared to what? Doing nothing? Peaceful persuasion? Clearly, at some level and related to some objectives, terrorism usually "works." A few bombings may obsess an entire country, as was true in France in the fall of 1986. On the other hand, such provocations may mobilize the enormous power of the state against radical elements, driving their leadership into exile, into jail, or into the grave, as was the fate of the Tupamaro urban guerrillas in Uruguay in the early 1970s. Similarly, establishment terrorism may squeeze potential dissent into sullen acquiescence, as with the Soviet peasants in the 1930s, or it may simply inflame the population further, as happened to some extent in Algeria during the 1950s.

Any assessment of effectiveness, therefore, depends upon an understanding of the special character of each situation; nevertheless, certain general concerns and guidelines provide some orientation to particular instances.

Short- and Long-Term Effects   First, we need to distinguish between short-term and long-term effects. Often short-term success leads to long-term failure. The Tupamaros, noted above, enjoyed some early success against the rather corrupt and ineffective civilian government in Uruguay. They initially cultivated something of a "Robin Hood" image, and their antics in robbing banks and distributing part of the loot or publishing embarrassing government documents amused large segments of the general public. Their increasingly violent challenge, however, provoked a military coup and an effective program of repression (involving establishment terrorism). George Rosie remarks that they "transformed Uruguay from a liberal democracy to a right-wing police state, and their left-wing rhetoric and violence worked the opposite of what they sought to achieve."[30]

On the other hand, short-term failure may contribute to long-term success. Terrorist activities by the Front de Libération Nationale (FLN) in Algiers provoked a brutal and initially successful campaign of counterterror by the French during January–March 1957. The FLN bombing campaign in Algiers ceased, but French brutality "alienated so many Arabs in the process that [the regime's terrorist] 'victory' probably helped to lose the war for France."[31]

These cautionary tales concerning the effects of time on apparent victory or defeat suggest another general consideration. Success in achieving immediate tactical objectives may not contribute to the accomplishment of strategic goals. Tactics and strategy need not bear any necessary relation to one another. Tactics, including terror tactics, can become ends in themselves. The more emotional objectives of terrorist action appear especially susceptible to becoming ends in themselves, displacing any broader, constructive political strategy.

Direct and Indirect Costs   When assessing terrorist (or any other) tactics, we should distinguish between effectiveness (are tactical and/or strategic objectives realized?) and efficiency (are the goals accomplished at minimal cost?). An ineffective tactic, of course, renders the question of efficiency moot. In contrast, excessively costly tactics fail in some sense even if they achieve their objectives.

Often contenders choose terrorist tactics because of their apparently low cost. Despite fears that dissident terrorism might involve weapons of mass destruction, like nuclear bombs, most dissident groups seem content to wreak their havoc with machine guns and car bombs. Though the resources and expertise required for such weapons remain low, they nonetheless can produce dramatic effects. Similarly, some forms of establishment terrorism, especially vigilante and covert regime terrorism, seem economical solutions to the problem of public disorder. Simply killing suspected criminals and other deviants appears more "cost-effective" than going through the trouble and expense of trying and imprisoning them.

Not all forms of terrorism, though, come cheap. Overt regime terrorism often demands an enormous, expensive, and potentially insubordinate enforcement apparatus. The extremely ambitious project of genocide, moreover, requires a major commitment from the regime. The Nazis, for example, diverted resources from the war effort to keep their death camps operating at capacity. Low-level terrorism will also likely fail to achieve ambitious dissident programs, such as revolutionary social transformation. A successful revolutionary strategy usually subordinates terrorist tactics to a far more comprehensive program mobilizing considerable ideological, organizational, and human resources.

Any evaluation of terrorism must also consider the potential indirect costs and consequences. Dissident terrorism, rather than disrupting a regime, may solidify support behind it to deal vigorously with violent dissent. The Red Brigade kidnapping of former Italian premier Aldo Moro in 1978 was tactically brilliant on a number of levels. A well-planned operation, it grabbed global attention. The dumping of Moro's body halfway between the headquarters of the Christian Democratic and Communist parties neatly symbolized the Red Brigade's rejection of establishment politics. Unfortunately for the Red Brigade, the government used the event to galvanize the Italian security forces into a broadly supported and effective counterterrorist campaign.

Establishment terrorism also carries indirect costs. Vigilante violence often contributes to the spread of disorder rather than the restoration of order in a disrupted community. Policies of indiscriminate repression frequently alienate those who might have initially supported regime action against dissent. Widespread regime terror, if it succeeds in atomizing subjects and inculcating fear and suspicion, most likely inhibits cooperation and undermines the regime's own organizational effectiveness. The decimation of the Red Army officer corps in the Stalinist purge, for example, contributed to the initially weak response of the Soviet armies to the Nazi invasion. Terrorism, whether by dissidents or regime, may be a deceptively cheap tactic once the full costs are calculated.

Effectiveness   The fundamental problem in determining the effectiveness of terrorism comes in establishing the precise contribution of particular actions to the achievement of purported goals, whether tactical or strategic. Hannah Arendt argues that "since when we act we never know with any certainty the eventual consequences of what we are doing, violence can remain rational only if it pursues short-term goals."[32] The more precisely defined and immediate the objective, the easier to determine terrorism's contribution.

We can most easily estimate the effectiveness of terrorism at the tactical level, especially where it is used to pursue concrete objectives. Do the terrorists gain publicity? Does the challenge to the state encourage potential supporters? Is the regime provoked into thoughtless repression? Alternatively, are establishment groups able to eliminate opposition figures? Can they crush public dissent? Even "feel good" objectives, such as the venting of frustration or engendering feelings of redemption, constitute immediately realized goals.

The impact of terrorism on the complex and encompassing strategic goals of revolutionary change is more difficult to assess. Nihilist groups who pursue the destruction of the existing order undertake a deceptively simple task. After all, they do not need to trouble themselves with the construction of an alternative social order, nor do they seem to require an extensive organization or direct support of the masses. Isolated nihilists, however, have not succeeded in their destructive aims either in the nineteenth century or in the 1970s. They simply lacked the power to bring down the state, and the absence of popular support meant that the general populace tolerated the use of fairly repressive measures against them. If, however, we wish to contemplate a nightmare scenario, we might consider what such a group could accomplish with weapons of mass destruction—nuclear, biological, or chemical.

If the perpetrators possess more constructive political agendas, terrorism seems most likely to be effective when the following conditions obtain:

1. The theater of action is a society already disrupted by economic crisis or war. 2. The activists are supported by fellow members of some ethnic, religious, or national group. 3. The activists' aims are limited to destabilization of the regime in power or opposition organizations. 4. Their opponents lack the finances, the will, or the political strength to conduct an extended counterterrorism campaign.[33]

These conditions more likely occur in a struggle for national autonomy as opposed to a comprehensive social revolution. In struggles for "self-determination," the dissidents probably will find it easier to develop some ties to the discontented communal group, and they can more easily distinguish the targets of terrorism from their own potential supporters. In contrast, social-revolutionary movements often find that terrorism increases their isolation from presumed supporters. Successful revolutionary movements have used terrorist tactics, but under conditions of strict subordination to a political strategy that places the greatest emphasis on political work and organization among the revolutionary base. As Richard E. Rubenstein observes: "Social revolution is the antithesis of terrorism. It is not small group violence seeking mass support, but mass activism seeking organized defense."[34]

Some specific kinds of terrorism may contribute to destructive strategic goals. Random bombings in urban population centers, for example, raise the defense costs of the regime and tie down large military forces in static defensive positions. Assassination campaigns against civilian administrators may weaken the regime's grip on the population. The elimination of the best representatives of the regime lowers its competence and capability; elimination of the worst, most corrupt officials may encourage popular support for the revolutionaries. The Viet Cong used both types of assassination tactic in the Vietnamese Revolution (see Chapter 10).

The effectiveness of establishment terrorism seems similarly dependent on the degree of social support and the nature of the aims of the perpetrators. Richard Maxwell Brown argues that vigilantism (which is not necessarily terrorist) could be socially constructive if it "dealt directly with a problem of disorder and then disbanded with an increase in the social stability of the locality."[35] Socially destructive vigilantism, in contrast, would generate "such strong local opposition that the result was an anarchic and socially destructive vigilante war."[36] Vigilantism is most likely to be constructive when the vigilantes reflect a community consensus and pursue fairly definite aims. Diffuse aims and community division tend to lead to an escalating cycle of violence, thus defeating the objective of restoring order.

A similar pattern may exist with respect to the effectiveness of both covert and overt regime terror. If a relatively broad consensus supports, or at least tolerates, terrorist actions against a clearly defined and relatively isolated opposition group, a regime may succeed in destroying this opposition without seriously alienating its core supporters. On the other hand, fairly indiscriminate repressive terrorism undertaken by an unpopular regime might well heighten discontent and reinforce its isolation. Many of the citizens of Argentina, for example, appear to have accepted the military intervention in 1976 against the ineffective rule of Isabel Perón as an inevitable response to a deteriorating situation, especially the increasing violence of the radical left. The military's excesses in its "dirty war" against leftists, labor, and liberals, however, progressively alienated the population and contributed to the military regime's eventual downfall.

Finally, and most grimly, we must admit that genocide may be an effective way of eliminating an "undesirable" group. Conditions for "success" include the following: (1) The target group represents a relatively weak minority; (2) the majority population views this group with fear and contempt; and (3) the world community remains relatively indifferent to the victims' fate.[37] In the absence of these conditions, the target group may effectively resist and rebel, the majority population may refuse to cooperate, and outside powers might intervene.

At best, then, it seems that terrorist tactics make marginal contributions to revolutionary strategy. The demonstration of some dissident coercive capability, for example, may weaken a regime's control over the population. If, in response, the regime falls into the trap of ill-considered repression, its legitimacy may decline, further weakening its capacity for social control. Yet terrorism's clandestine nature and its indiscriminate means contribute little to the constructive goals of revolution and run significant risks of alienating potential support. Revolutionary groups limited to terrorist attacks will likely fail to usher in the New Revolutionary Order, though they spread disorder throughout the community. Analogously, counterrevolutionary terror might succeed in expunging resistance, but it probably engenders little positive support for the regime.

INSURGENCY

The Myth of Revolutionary Insurgency—Che Guevara in Bolivia

One hundred years after Marx and Engels asserted that the specter of proletarian revolution haunted Europe, a new phantasm arose to frighten political establishments. In 1949 Communist insurgents triumphed over their numerically and materially superior adversaries in China. This "new" form of revolutionary combat threatened to topple regimes around the world. For the next three decades guerrilla insurgencies spread throughout the Third World, attacking the tottering colonial powers in Vietnam, Indonesia, Malaya, and Portuguese Africa and challenging weak domestic regimes in the Philippines, Cuba, Nicaragua, and elsewhere.

Embattled regimes could not dismiss these revolutionary fighters as mere criminals or simple terrorists. The guerrillas represented a coherent political and ideological challenge, and their intended targets—military units of the regime—

threatened the regime more than isolated terrorist attacks on noncombatants. Revolutionaries, it seemed, had discovered a tactical package that turned their military inferiority into a resource and guaranteed, if not success, the indefinite postponement of defeat. Radical Maoists in China spoke grandly of insurgencies in the "rural" Third World ultimately surrounding the "cities" of the Euro American First World, and American policymakers resolved to demonstrate in Vietnam that they could defeat Communist-led "wars of national liberation."[38]

Guerrilla insurgency, however, is neither new nor inherently revolutionary. It neither guarantees victory nor does it indefinitely postpone defeat. Guerrilla tactics attempt to make a virtue out of the reality of *relative weakness*. For at least 2500 years powerful conventional armies have confronted tenacious adversaries who responded with guerrilla tactics.[39] Guerrilla warfare offers the weaker side a third option to either stand-up, conventional combat leading to probable defeat or outright surrender. The guerrillas—if blessed with sufficient power, skill, and luck—may delay defeat, raise the cost of victory to a discouraging level, or even transform themselves into a more equal adversary to their opponents. They also may lose.

Revolutionary movements usually find themselves to be the militarily weaker side. In a country with limited potential for urban-based revolution, rural insurgency may seem the best tactical option available. Historical experience suggests, however, that guerrilla tactics must be part of a revolutionary strategy, not a substitute for it. Nothing illustrates this better than the bitter and fatal experience of Ernesto "Che" Guevara in Bolivia.

Che was Fidel Castro's compatriot in arms in the Sierra Maestra mountains of Cuba.[40] The victory of Castro's forces over the corrupt Batista regime encouraged Che to draw several conclusions about the promise of revolutionary insurgency:

> Firstly, people's forces can win a war against the army. Secondly, we need not always wait for all the revolutionary conditions to be present; the insurrection itself can create them. Thirdly, in the underdeveloped parts of America the battleground for armed struggle should in the main be the countryside.[41]

Bored and incompetent in his administrative positions in postrevolutionary Cuba, Che undertook to act on his beliefs, first in the Congo (now Zaire) and then in Bolivia. Arriving in Bolivia in November 1966, Che set off with a small force of about 50 to learn the terrain and recruit peasants into the insurgency. Although successfully ambushing a couple of military patrols in March and April of 1967, he and his forces were unable to overcome some essential weaknesses. First, none in the band really knew the country in southeastern Bolivia. Second, the Indian peasants provided infertile ground for the revolutionary message. Already suspicious of outsiders, they were unsympathetic to a foreign-born guerrilla (Che was Argentinean) who did not speak their language and who promised land reform to peasants who already owned their land. Not only did they fail to flock to Che's banner, but by September they were informing on the guerrilla band's movements. Third, Che failed to enlist the support of local leftists like those in the Bolivian Communist Party, who were less than pleased to have their country selected to be the next Vietnam. Little support emerged from the urban intellectuals and workers in the mines. Finally, Fidel Castro, far away in his embattled island, was unable and perhaps unwilling to aid his former comrade.

On the other side, the Bolivian government, though not impressive, possessed a reasonably loyal army assisted by American Special Forces advisers. Bolivia's revolution in the early 1950s had not only distributed land to the Indian peasants but had also raised them out of their second-class, semifeudal status. Che was 15 years too late. Indian informers, coupled with high-tech, infrared surveillance, sharpened military intelligence and led to the destruction of Che's band and his own summary execution in October of 1967, less than a year after his arrival.

Guerrilla insurgency tactics, unconnected with any effective revolutionary strategy and lacking an accurate assessment of revolutionary conditions, neither produced victory nor significantly postponed defeat for Guevara's guerrillas. Such tactics, devoid of strategy or politics, led to destruction. Ironically, advocates of counterinsurgency tactics often commit an error similar to that of Che Guevara. Misunderstanding both the character of a revolutionary strategy and the political context of revolution, advocates of counterinsurgency often search for a tactical formula to assist governments confronted by spreading insurgency. But if an insurgency represents the coercive tactics of an increasingly successful revolutionary strategy, then the embattled regime cannot simply wage counterinsurgency. It must wage counterrevolution.

The Essentials of Guerrilla Tactics

The scale and ambition of guerrilla tactics vary considerably. At the lower end of the scale they emerge out of terrorist attacks on noncombatant targets. At the higher end they approach conventional warfare in terms of the size of the units involved and their willingness to stand and fight to defend territory. A rather broad range of coercive capabilities, organizational resources, and popular support lies between these two extremes. Even at the lower levels of insurgency, though, guerrilla operations demand more of a revolutionary movement than isolated acts of terrorism. An expanding insurgency represents a considerable deterioration in the political and military position of the regime, even though it does not guarantee a revolutionary victory.

Attacks on police stations often provide the first indicator of the move from terrorism to insurgency. Though the regime might claim noncombatant status for the police and condemn such attacks as terrorist, nonetheless the police differ from the normal victims of terrorism. They can shoot back. Later in the struggle, after the revolutionary movement begins to wage pitched conventional battles with the regular armed forces, guerrilla units may continue to harass the regime elsewhere in the country.

The tactical maxims associated with guerrilla warfare essentially codify common sense for the substantially weaker side in a *military* contest. We emphasize "military" because even small-scale hit-and-run guerrilla attacks concentrate on military targets. One theme running through this tactical "cookbook" is the effort of the guerrillas to turn their opponent's strengths against them, a kind of tactical jiujitsu. Commonly identified tactical guidelines include the areas discussed below.[42]

Logistics   Guerrilla insurgents confront a well-equipped foe. In the area of combat technology the regime's forces deploy armor and air power. The guerrillas, in comparison, usually fight only with what they can carry (small arms, machine guns, mortars, and so forth). Foreign supporters of the revolution may contribute supplies (see below), but in a limited and irregular fashion, in contrast with the often continuous and profuse aid received by the regime. Material inferiority leads to several logistical trademarks of guerrilla operations.

1. Self-reliance in Supplies   The inherently undependable nature of resupply of both weapons and nonmilitary necessities encourages self-reliance. This means living off the resources available in the territory of their operations. Food and other supplies may be "taxed" from the peasants or, much better, expropriated from the regime.

2. Use of the Enemy's Supply   Enemy forces provide the best source of supply for the guerrillas. By raiding their adversary's logistical operation for arms and other goods, the guerrillas turn their opponent's material advantage to their own favor. As Mao puts it:

> Our basic directive is to rely on the war industries of the imperialist countries and of our enemy at home. We have a claim on the arsenals of London as well as of Hanyang, and, what is more, it is to be delivered to us by the enemy's own transport corps. This is the sober truth, not a joke![43]

By attempting to combat the dispersed and mobile guerrillas (see below), a regime often disperses its material resources among fortified outposts, local militia, strategic hamlets, and so forth, thereby multiplying the targets for guerrilla resupply.

3. Decentralized Logistics   The nature of guerrilla operations, combined with the necessary self-reliance in supply, contributes to a third logistical principle—decentralized logistics. Guerrillas stockpile supplies, but in relatively small, hidden, and dispersed caches, not large depots like the regime. They also tend to disperse their resupply networks. The so-called Ho Chi Minh Trail in Vietnam, for example, was not a single "trail" but a vast network of pathways dispersed over hundreds of square miles of dense jungle.

4. Efficiency and Austerity   The limited scale and erratic nature of guerrilla logistics impose a powerful need for efficiency and austerity in their operations. Whereas the guerrillas must carefully calculate the costs involved in any operation, the relative wealth of the regime often encourages profligacy.[44] In this way the regime forces waste away their material advantage.

A Vietnam veteran related how a single shot fired at the defensive perimeter of his camp one night brought a flurry of small-arms fire in response. Again a single shot rang out from the jungle, so the Americans called in an armored personnel carrier that rattled away with its heavy machine gun for a few minutes. After a period of silence a third shot struck the American position. This time the guards called in a C-130 armed with Gatling guns to "pacify" the perimeter. After the jungle was mowed down in a storm of lead, silence returned. Later, a dawn patrol found a single guerrilla armed with a World War II bolt-action rifle.[45]

The Application of Force   The numerical and material inferiority of the guerrilla forces also dictates certain tactical choices with respect to the application of force. Again, these tactical maxims attempt to turn guerrilla weakness into strength and the regime's strength into weakness.

1. Nonattachment to Territory   The regime faces the demanding task of defending the entire territory of the state, for it loses credibility even if it cedes control of relatively remote areas to the guerrillas. Population centers and major lines of communication must all be defended. The necessary attachment of the regime to territorial defense fixes a large proportion of its superior forces into positions of static defense. The forces available to seek out the guerrillas may not be numerically superior to those they pursue.

Meanwhile the guerrillas follow the principles of "rove and strike," choosing when and where to fight. Nonattachment to territory generally means that the guerrillas determine the pace and location of military engagements. Even relatively powerful guerrilla forces must resist the temptation to defend territory.[46] A fixed position enables the regime to bring its superior tactical power to bear. As Mao observes, "In guerrilla warfare, we must observe the principle 'To gain territory is no cause for joy, and to lose territory is no cause for sorrow.' To lose territory or cities is of no importance." He goes on to argue that "it is altogether improper to defend cities to the utmost, for this merely leads to sacrificing our own effective strength."[47]

The corollary to nonattachment to territory is to run away when confronted with superior forces. The guerrillas must always be prepared to trade territory for time and survival. As Mao puts it: "'Fight when we can win and run away when we cannot'—this is the popular interpretation of our 'rove and strike' warfare today. No military expert anywhere in the world would approve of only fighting and disapprove of running away, though few people run away as much as we do."[48]

2. Dispersion and Concentration   Mao goes on to say that "all our 'running away' is for the purpose of 'fighting,' and all our strategies and operational directives are formulated on the basis of 'fighting.'"[49] Guerrillas not only "rove"; they also "strike." But they should strike only when they can be assured of an easy victory. Consequently guerrilla insurgents avoid attacking strong positions and they disengage from hard battles. Even a victory in such cases may prove too costly in terms of trained fighters and scarce supplies.[50]

On the other hand, since the regime must disperse its forces to defend territory, opportunites arise for the guerrillas to concentrate locally superior forces on isolated regime outposts or vulnerable supply columns. Samuel Griffith observes, "The enemy's rear is the guerrillas' front; they themselves have no rear."[51] The regime's defensive responsibilities extend its front and therefore its rear. Again, apparent regime strengths create vulnerabilities.

3. Flexibility and Surprise   Nonattachment to territory and the effort to avoid battles with strong forces while engaging isolated detachments place a premium on tactical flexibility and surprise. Mao epitomized the emphasis on flexibility through his three simple maxims of dealing with a superior enemy: "When the enemy advances, we retreat. When the enemy retreats, we pursue. When the enemy halts, we harass him."[52]

Guerrillas attempt to negate the overall superiority of the regime through surprise attacks. Not the pitched battle but the ambush is the hallmark of guerrilla warfare. They must disguise their intentions; as Mao advises, "Cause an uproar in the east, strike in the west."[53] The conventional superiority of the regime forces, ironically, often inhibits their flexibility and capacity to surprise the guerrilla forces. The regime often telegraphs its moves by attempting to mount conventional military sweeps, while the guerrillas enshrine stealth as a cardinal principle of operations.

Intelligence   Both guerrilla logistics and tactics demand secure, accurate intelligence. Usually "military intelligence" refers to information about the enemy's capability and intentions, but in addition intelligence involves several other crucial areas, especially for a guerrilla insurgency.

1. Know Yourself   The principles of guerrilla combat require the insurgents to know themselves, their strengths, and their weaknesses. Failures of self-understanding lead to premature leaps into conventional warfare. Swept away by their success at turning their weaknesses into strengths, guerrillas may undertake a tactical escalation and thereby revert to a position of relative weakness against the regime.

2. Know Your Enemy   Obviously, tactics of dispersal and concentration require precise knowledge of the enemy's location, strength, movements, and intentions. In addition, well-informed insurgents will attempt to ascertain the morale of their opponents and exploit weakness here to their own advantage.

3. Know the Climate and Terrain   Guerrilla combat exploits the opportunities offered by climate and terrain. Guerrilla forces must avoid being caught out in the open, so remote, inaccessible areas favor their operations. In mounting attacks, terrain and weather become important considerations affecting the concentration of locally superior forces. When engaged with the enemy the guerrillas must always secure a line of retreat, given their preference to flee rather than engage in costly fights.

4. Know the People   One of Mao's most famous aphorisms compares the people to the water in which the guerrillas swim like fish. In fact, the guerrillas often resemble the water itself, indistinguishable from the rest of the people in which they circulate. Successful guerrilla insurgencies—ones that stand some chance of not only harassing the regime, but eventually challenging it for power— must gain continuous sustenance from the people in whose name they make revolution. For this reason the most important form of knowledge for the insurgents concerns their revolutionary base. Miscalculation here leads to expressions of popular hostility, isolation from the nurturing "water," and eventual destruction. Mao therefore emphasizes the importance of building a popular base:

> A vital factor in conquering the enemy is the establishment of strong and powerful political work by the army based on a people's war and the solidarity of army and people, the solidarity of commanders and fighters, and the disintegration of the enemy.[54]

In some sense, then, Che Guevara's failure in Bolivia represents a failure of intelligence. He overestimated his own power while underestimating that of his enemies; his knowledge of the terrain and climate was spotty; and ultimately he failed to understand the character of his presumed revolutionary base. From a broader perspective Che failed because of the underdeveloped links between his tactics of guerrilla insurgency and the larger strategic dynamic of revolution.

The Strategic Dynamics of Revolutionary Insurgency

Guerrilla insurgents, if they wish to accomplish something more than simply scurrying around the countryside, must link their tactics to the strategic goals and tasks of revolution. Guerrilla operations need to erode the regime's ability to attack the revolutionary movement, weaken the regime's control over the wider population, and integrate this population into the support structures of the revolution. Several important factors affect the transformation of tactical operations into strategic progress.[55]

Favorable Environment   The insurgents and the regime contend with not only a physical environment but a cultural one as well. The tactical requirements of guerrilla warfare demand familiarity with the environment, but familiarity does not guarantee success. Both the physical and the cultural setting may help or hinder insurgent operations. We must be careful, however, to avoid environmental determinism. Skill and luck can overcome obstacles, and incompetence can waste opportunities.

Inaccessibility, poor communications and transportation systems, and foreign sanctuaries favor guerrilla operations. Alternatively, the more readily the regime can bring its forces to bear, the greater the challenge facing the guerrillas. Accessible terrain and good communications enhance the ability of the government both to counter the mobility of the guerrillas and to maintain regime control over the population. Similarly, the presence of a foreign sanctuary provides the guerrillas an area where they can gain a relative respite from the military pressure of the regime as well as prepare their forces for combat. The existence of such sanctuaries presents the regime with the uncomfortable dilemma of either tolerating guerrilla support bases or risking widening the war.

Ironically, the physical advantages that support the success of guerrilla tactical operations may at some point hinder the extension of tactical success into strategic victory. For example, the very terrain that favors guerrilla operations may limit the ability of the revolutionary organization to expand its control over the population. Often, remote, rugged, and poorly linked locales are also sparsely settled, economically poor, and politically insignificant. Ultimately the revolutionary movement must move from the periphery to the center, both geographically and politically, and this necessarily means that it becomes more accessible to regime countermeasures. Similarly, excessive dependence on foreign sanctuaries may encourage the insurgents to neglect the development of internal support. Without such internal support, the insurgents cannot succeed in their revolutionary mission, but as they attempt to create it, they again become more vulnerable to the regime.

The cultural context of guerrilla operations also affects their chances for success, as Che found in Bolivia. The racial, ethnic, and religious composition of the population offers opportunities for success and risks of failure. Tactical success contributes to the revolutionary mission when such accomplishments solidify the revolutionary base. A divided population provides the opportunity to represent an aggrieved sector but also creates the risk of limiting the movement's appeal. The cultural setting, then, clearly affects a second major factor influencing strategic progress.

Popular Support   Tactical victories by guerrilla bands mean little unless they contribute to the expansion of popular support. Significant guerrilla operations require sources of material and personnel. Often regimes identify insurgents as the tools of some foreign enemy who could not survive without this external support. To the extent that this accusation reflects reality, it represents the relative failure of the insurgents to build an internal foundation for their movement. While external patrons contributed to their victories, the revolutionaries in China, Vietnam, Cuba, and elsewhere could not have presented a revolutionary challenge, much less have succeeded, if they had been simply foreign-supported and controlled puppets.

Successful guerrilla movements build a foundation of support before and during the conduct of their operations. Clearly, leadership and ideology affect their ability to exploit and perhaps reinforce preexisting conflicts and contradictions (see Chapter 8). This generally means developing a relatively inclusive rather than exclusive appeal. Bitterly divided populations, as we noted above, offer dangerous temptations for presumptive revolutionaries, for it is easy to exploit divisions to gain short-term advantage. Usually insurgents with revolutionary aspirations attempt to combine nationalist appeals with the other elements (for example, religious or Marxist-Leninist) making up their ideology. In this way they hope to avoid being limited to a particular minority group. The problem of exclusivity diminishes in significance as the proportion of the total population represented by the revolutionary group increases.

Insurgents identified with a minority element of a divided population, however, limit their revolutionary potential. Around the world—in Sri Lanka, India, Iraq, Turkey, and Sudan—ethnic insurgencies develop strong roots in their particular communal groups, but they usually pose a secessionist rather than revolutionary challenge to the central political authorities. Sometimes these insurgencies, if they represent a cohesive and significant group, succeed in gaining greater autonomy. In Ethiopia in 1991 they actually toppled a discredited central government.

Revolutionaries, as opposed to secessionists, if trapped by such a limited appeal, risk eventual defeat owing to the inherent limits on their base of support. In Malaya during the 1950s, for example, the Communist insurgents were largely composed of ethnic Chinese. The majority Malay population resisted their appeals, even though the insurgents fought against the colonial ruler, Great Britain. The British, successfully playing on the ethnic divisions, isolated and eventually defeated the insurgents.

Successful leadership, especially of a catalytic/representational or charismatic sort, and ideology, particularly an ideology that represents nationalist or other unifying values of the population, generate passive support. Successful guerrilla insurgencies reinforce this support by demonstrating the coercive credibility of the revolutionary movement. But guerrilla operations cannot occur in the first place, nor will the demonstration effect of guerrilla successes translate into an expanded material base, unless passive sympathy can be translated into active engagement. This process depends largely on the quality of the organization behind the insurgents.

Organization   A revolutionary movement cannot achieve its strategic goals unless it overcomes the free rider problem among at least some of its potential supporters. The possible solutions to this problem range from the use of concrete, selective rewards and punishments to the development of feelings of collective solidarity and common destiny among passive supporters (see the discussion of the solutions to the free rider problem in Chapter 5). Almost all the solutions require successful organization.

The ability of an organization to translate passive into active support depends on its scope, complexity, and cohesion.[56] "Scope" refers to the proportion of the population successfully integrated into the organization. "Complexity" identifies the degree of hierarchical and functional specialization in the organization. Finally, "cohesion" reflects the unity and discipline among the members of the organization. Significant guerrilla insurgency requires a degree of organizational scope, complexity, and cohesion far beyond that demanded by most forms of dissident terrorism. The more ambitious and comprehensive the insurgency, the greater will be the demands on the underlying revolutionary organization. To fulfill these demands requires that the movement create structures capable of involving the people in their own liberation. As more people actively support the insurgency, the guerrillas can mount increasingly ambitious operations. Success in these operations contributes in turn to the expansion of support. This virtuous cycle, though, depends on the existence of an organization capable of mounting attacks in the first place and then building on these achievements.

Any assessment of the quality and effectiveness of the organization supporting the guerrillas must contend with two myths. The first myth argues that since only a small proportion of the total population ever engages in direct guerrilla attacks or provides active support for the fighters, guerrilla insurgents must represent only a tiny minority. The small number of people engaging in direct action, however, does not suffice to demonstrate a lack of widespread support. Given the seriousness of the free rider problem in undertaking such deadly activities, a small segment of the population actively engaged in guerrilla resistance may well reflect significant depth and breadth of passive support.

A related myth suggests that the use of coercion to maintain revolutionary discipline also indicates a lack of popular support and legitimacy. "True" revolutionaries supposedly must freely risk their lives for their cause. The nature of the free rider problem suggests, however, that selective coercion may well be necessary to galvanize passive supporters into action. All armies use the threat and practice of severe coercion to maintain discipline among the ranks. The mere presence of internal coercion, even terror, is not sufficient reason to deny the presence of a popular base for the guerrillas. In any case the insurgents' use of coercion in their organization may contrast favorably with the use of coercion by the regime. This raises the final and most important factor in evaluating the strategic context of a guerrilla insurgency.

Relative Regime Effectiveness   Insurgents do not operate in a vacuum. The contribution of guerrilla tactics to the destructive and constructive goals of revolutionary strategy depends in large part on the relative effectiveness of the regime. What Jeffrey Race observes with respect to the National Liberation Front in South Vietnam holds true for any guerrilla insurgency: "To gain victory, the revolutionary movement did not need to be 'good' or 'effective' by any absolute standard; it needed only to be better than the government."[57]

Guerrillas usually suffer in comparison with the regime according to obvious indicators of military and political strength, such as numbers of personnel, material supplies, and territory under nominal control. Yet these indicators may obscure substantial regime weakness in terms of morale, loyalty, organizational effectiveness and efficiency, and depth of support in the general population. On the other hand, no necessary relation exists between the regime's weakness and the insurgents' strength. The general population may view both sides in the political contest with indifference or even hostility.

Nevertheless, the insurgents' exploitation of the geographic and cultural terrain, their ability to attract passive support, and their success in developing organizations capable of translating passive support into action compete with parallel activities of the regime. Though parallel, regime operations generally do not mirror those of the guerrillas. Rather, the regime's predilections, capabilities, and responsibilities shape its actions, which in turn create opportunities for the guerrillas. For example, the conventional military capability and training of the regime's armed forces lead it to favor conventional tactical operations. But, as Race points out, a single guerrilla may control a hamlet except on those brief occasions when government forces engage in a conventional military sweep through the area.[58] If a government exercises power only intermittently, then even geographically central areas may be politically remote from regime control.

Similarly, the regime's commitment to defend established wealth and privilege provides the opportunity for the revolutionary insurgents to offer contingent incentives to maintain active support among the aggrieved population. A "contingent incentive" depends "both on certain kinds of behavior by the target individual and on the continued existence of the sponsoring organization."[59] If the insurgents liberate an area and implement policies (like land reform) that favor previously deprived sectors, the beneficiaries know that their continued enjoyment of these new advantages depends on continued insurgent success. The regime's tendency to reestablish prior privileges if it reasserts its control reinforces popular support for the guerrillas. In this way an effective revolutionary insurgency turns another governmental strength—its base of support—in the guerrillas' favor.

Finally, insurgents can largely negate another source of regime strength—external support—by portraying the government as a tool of foreign powers. Successful revolutionary ideologies, as we observed earlier, often seize the banner of resurgent nationalism from the regime. The regime then faces an uncomfortable dilemma. The more beleaguered it becomes, the more dependent it grows on foreign assistance, but its increased dependency on foreign support validates the insurgents' nationalist appeals.

The Communist victory in China, followed by the French defeat in Indochina and a tenacious, if limited, insurgency in Malaya, sounded an alarm in the United States and elsewhere in the Western alliance. This new form of revolution seemed indisputably potent. A search began for a way to counter this force threatening to swallow up many of the former European colonial possessions and spread revolution throughout the Third World.

The Myth of Counterinsurgency

Faced with revolutionary guerrilla warfare, regimes and their foreign supporters have often responded with various counterinsurgency formulas. In all its variants, counterinsurgency doctrine combines the use of guerrillalike tactics with a political program addressing the roots of the revolutionary appeal.[60] In this way regimes hope to counter the tactical flexibility of the insurgents while redressing the social and political grievances underlying popular discontent. Counterinsurgency tactics supposedly check, even reduce, the guerrillas' coercive capability, while the regime's political program translates this tactical success into an effective counterrevolutionary strategy. A foreign ally often underwrites the counterinsurgency program.

In the abstract, the counterinsurgency formula holds some promise. Since guerrilla tactics attempt to turn regime's conventional military strengths to the guerrillas' advantage, the regime could negate this effort by adopting and adapting the guerrillas' own tactics of mobility, stealth, and surprise. If the revolutionary movement builds its organizational support on the institutional weaknesses of the regime, logic suggests that a counterrevolutionary strategy must correct these same weaknesses. The real world, however, often intrudes between the conception and the implementation of a counterinsurgency strategy.

Perhaps the fundamental limit on counterinsurgency depends on the extent of the guerrilla challenge. Edwin Moise, for example, distinguishes at least four levels of guerrilla operations.[61] The first level involves small, politically isolated bands capable of mounting no more than occasional "pinprick" raids on the regime. Next the guerrilla forces grow strong enough to operate fairly continuously in some areas and develop relations with the local populace. They still lack any permanent political infrastructure. At the third level the insurgents develop a political infrastructure that parallels the regime's in contested territories. Finally, the revolutionary forces develop sufficiently to exclude government forces—both political and military—from a region. In this last stage only a major offensive could displace the guerrilla forces and their political support structure from the area. This final level of insurgency merges into a conventional warfare capability. Of course, an insurgency could be on different levels in separate parts of a country.

Counterinsurgency tactics probably work most effectively at the lower levels of insurgency, before the guerrillas proceed too far in achieving their strategic goals. Once the revolutionary strategic position improves, the regime may lack both the political will and capability to undertake a full-blown counterrevolutionary program.

On the tactical level regime forces, despite continued numerical and material superiority, often lack the capacity to undertake true counterinsurgent operations. A large percentage of the government forces must defend fixed positions, and these defense requirements increase as the insurgents grow in strength. Consequently, as offensive operations demand more resources, the resources available often decline. Second, conventional measures of military superiority indirectly suggest the extent to which the regime's forces are wedded to a conventional military strategy. The established doctrine, armament, and training of the government's army may preclude any effective implementation of counterinsurgency tactics. Finally, a more entrenched insurgency also indicates declining political support for the regime, at least in the areas of guerrilla operations. Reduced morale and discipline among the armed forces may mirror this decline in popular support.

Higher-level insurgency also challenges the regime to reestablish its rule throughout the country. Legitimate, effective regimes do not encounter extensive guerrilla insurgencies. Regimes that do are neither legitimate nor effective. D. Michael Shafer identifies three major components to the political dimension of counterrevolutionary warfare, sometimes termed a battle for the "hearts and minds" of the populace.[62] First, the regime must provide security for the population by reestablishing order and protecting the people from the guerrillas. Second, the regime must provide good government. Administration must expand into areas of relative weakness and eliminate corruption and inefficiency. Finally, the regime must provide for economic progress to address the underlying sources of popular discontent. The regime, moreover, needs to pursue all three objectives simultaneously.

Such a program sounds impressive, but Shafer identifies several problems, particularly where a significant insurgency challenges the regime.[63] First, the policy presumes that the needed administrative and economic reforms serve the immediate interests of the ruling elites. Significant economic reforms obviously threaten elite privileges, and the elite may be unwilling to sacrifice their position. Second, administrative reforms, especially those affecting the military, tread on the powerful interests of sectors upon whom the regime depends for its survival. Moreover, successful administrative reform may simply make the government into a better enforcer of conditions that led to the insurgency in the first place. Third, the policy recommendations ignore the actual relations existing between the government and the general population. If the people identify more with the program of the insurgents than that of the government, then a successful defense of the government's position will not increase the popular sense of security. If the armed forces frequently abuse the people, then enhancing the regime's coercive capability may only increase this abuse. Lastly, the weaker and more corrupt the government, the more it needs reforms but also the less likely it will be able to undertake them.

The regime's foreign patrons, ironically, face similar paradoxes in trying to urge their ally to undertake the political and military program of counterinsurgency.[64] The weaker the regime, the less leverage foreign patrons can exercise over it. Any threat to reduce patron support is ultimately self-defeating, for it only contributes to collapse of the regime. On the other hand, to take over the battle from the regime leads to at least two unhappy consequences. The revolutionaries receive a propaganda boost from the demonstrated foreign domination of the regime. Moreover, while foreign forces may be more effective fighters, they cannot build institutional support for the regime. To the contrary, the more extensive the foreign involvement, the more the regime's political base will atrophy.

The myth of counterinsurgency largely recapitulates the myth of revolutionary insurgency. A few guerrillas running around in the wilderness cannot create revolutionary conditions in an unfavorable environment. Alternatively, if conditions favor guerrilla operations and the expansion of revolutionary activities, the chances for a successful counterinsurgency program decline. Simply put, counterinsurgency succeeds best where it is needed least and succeeds least where it is needed most.

NONCOOPERATION

The Theory and Practice of Noncooperation

An aura of violence surrounds the process of revolutionary transformation. Influenced by both media and myth, popular images of revolution show determined workers defending the barricades, shadowy terrorists inflicting havoc on innocents, or dedicated guerrillas slipping through the jungle. Revolution begets violence and violence propels revolution. Yet both theory and history suggest an alternative path of revolutionary confrontation, one that does not involve tactics of direct attack, such as terrorism, insurgency, conventional warfare, or even relatively spontaneous rioting. Often citizens simply refuse to obey any longer. They do not attack the regime with guns or bombs; rather, they withdraw the support and cooperation upon which the regime depends for its survival.

In a general sense *all* acts of revolutionary resistance demonstrate a spirit of noncooperation. Gene Sharp, the major theorist of the strategy and tactics of withheld support, argues that a widespread refusal to cooperate, apart from any involvement in direct attacks, threatens the survival of a regime. Sharp notes that rulers depend on the general consent of the governed. When the governed withdraw their consent, the consequent loss of authority leads to a disintegration of the regime's power.[65]

> Clearly, every ruler must depend upon the cooperation and assistance of his subjects in operating the economic and administrative system. Every ruler needs the skill, knowledge, advice, labor, and administrative ability of a significant portion of his subjects. The more extensive and detailed the ruler's control is, the more such assistance he will require.[66]

The regime, of course, relies on sanctions, both positive and negative, to ensure obedience. But "the capacity to impose sanctions rests on cooperation. [And] the effectiveness or ineffectiveness of sanctions when available and used also depends on the response of the subjects against whom they are threatened or applied."[67]

Most people usually perform as expected, out of habit, fear of punishment, desire for reward, feelings of moral obligation, or the simple lack of any plausible alternative (see the discussion of order in Chapter 1).[68] Those who wish to transform the status quo must somehow overcome the inertia of a sufficient number of people to mount a plausible challenge. The advocates of violent transformation believe that the refusal to cooperate must be coupled with direct attacks on the regime and its supporters. The theory of noncooperation, in contrast, essentially argues that properly organized and extensive noncooperation, by itself, undermines the regime.

Such a myth of efficacy surrounds violence that most people initially deride the ability of noncooperation to topple a well-armed foe. The refusal to cooperate summons up images of the slaughter of passive lambs. These images compel sympathy, perhaps, but they are unlikely to compel a ruthless and determined regime. Of course, a ruthless and determined regime would also crush any intimation of violent protest, as well. We are so convinced that violence "works," however, that we ignore the numerous cases where it failed to achieve the desired ends. Generally, in any violent confrontation, at least one side loses.

Noncooperation, or withdrawn support, is not a passive but an active assertion of power. Only those with some power can effectively use noncooperation as an instrument to force political change. The power they possess relates to the dependence of the regime on their continued obedience. The noncooperation of marginal groups raises a less threatening challenge than that of sectors more essential to the survival and operations of the regime. However, the desperate violence of marginal groups will also not produce success.

The repression of resistance, moreover, requires the cooperation of the security forces of the regime. If they refuse to cooperate in a program of repression, then the regime crumbles, not as the result of a direct attack, but because its ultimate weapon has withdrawn its support. Those who doubt the potential of noncooperation should recall the dramatic confrontation between the supporters of the Russian government of Boris Yeltsin and the troops mobilized by the coup plotters in August 1991. The people refused to budge, and the troops refused to attack. The coup failed.

In addition to the common confusion between noncooperation and passivity, Sharp identifies a number of other misconceptions.[69] Noncooperation is not simple verbal persuasion but a technique of social power. Such techniques do not assume some absolute moral superiority or that human beings are naturally good. Participants need not be saints, and these tactics can be used to pursue various ends, including selfish ones. Though noncooperation usually takes the form of a protest against a center of power, the tactics by themselves possess no necessary revolutionary thrust. Finally, noncooperation does not presume that the adversary will refrain from physical repression. Just as with tactics of direct attack, proponents of noncooperation must be prepared for vigorous reprisals.

The tactics of noncooperation are many and various. Sharp provides a comprehensive inventory of tactical possibilities ranging from symbolic protests to nonviolent intervention.[70] The more significant include the following:

Persuasion and Protest   These include formal declarations, group representations (deputations, lobbying, picketing); symbolic acts (displays of symbols, prayer, rude gestures); pressure on individual representatives of the regime (tauntings, "hauntings" of officials, and vigils), satirical skits, processions and funerals; protest rallies; and renunciations (like the "silent treatment" or walkouts).

Social Noncooperation   This includes ostracism of offending representatives of the regime or refusal to cooperate with social events and customs.

Economic Noncooperation   This includes a wide variety of economic boycotts (by consumers, producers, middlemen, owners and management, and financial institutions) and strikes (by agricultural or industrial workers and, most potent, the general strike across all forms of economic activity).

Political Noncooperation   This includes the refusal of public support, political boycotts (of elections, government employment, educational institutions, and other government bodies), forms of citizen noncompliance (slow compliance, disguised disobedience, civil disobedience, and so on), and forms of resistance by government personnel (malingering, blocking of communications, general noncooperation, and outright mutiny).

Nonviolent Intervention   This includes fasts, sit-ins, overloading facilities and administrative operations, and ultimately the development of alternative, parallel institutions.

Sharp documents the use of all these techniques as well as many others in historical struggles between various regimes and dissident sectors. None of the tactics guarantees success for the protesters, but then neither terrorism nor guerrilla insurgency inevitably produces the new Jerusalem either.

Noncooperation and the Strategy of Revolutionary Transformation

A strategy of revolutionary transformation involves undertaking defensive and offensive tasks to achieve both destructive and constructive goals (see Table 9.1). Tactics of noncooperation may more effectively realize these goals than alternative means of direct attack.

Defensively, the revolutionary movement must erode the regime's ability to attack the movement while at the same time reducing the movement's own vulnerability to attack. Tactics of noncooperation, since they put the participants at risk without apparently impairing the regime's coercive capacity, might seem especially inadvisable. Effective repression, however, depends on the cooperation of the regime's coercive organizations. Noncooperation may hold greater promise than violent attack for eroding the morale and discipline of the regime's forces. Sharp refers to this potential process as "political jiujitsu." "By combining nonviolent discipline with solidarity and persistence in its struggle, the nonviolent actionists cause the violence of the opponent's repression to be exposed in the worst possible light."[71] In contrast with the tactical jiujitsu of guerrilla insurgency, this political jiujitsu more easily converts tactical success into strategic victory. Political jiujitsu directly influences the support for the dissidents and the regime and not simply immediate advantages or disadvantages on the battlefield.

When faced with a unified protest of people who simply refuse to cooperate, troops may begin to question their orders, defect to the opposition, and even mutiny. Splits may develop in the regime itself over how to handle the refusal of the people to obey. The regime must be careful in its response to noncooperation for fear of alienating its own supporters. Violent attacks on these troops, on the other hand, would seem far more likely to provoke violent retaliation, if only in self-defense. Political neutrals as well as the allies of the regime would more likely see dissident violence as a major threat to order justifying a vigorous response.

Those who refuse to obey the government, of course, cannot depend on the collapse of the regime's repressive forces, either immediately or ever. Noncooperating protestors might appear particularly vulnerable to regime reprisals, since they refuse to meet violence with violence. Again appearances deceive. Though they cannot hide in remote areas like guerrilla insurgents, they can take measures to protect the movement from being destroyed by reprisals.[72] Decentralized, multitiered leadership cadres help ensure that the arrest or destruction of one set of leaders will not decapitate the movement. Tactics of noncooperation require at least as much discipline and an even greater sense of personal responsibility than more violent alternatives. As long as they maintain discipline, movements using noncooperation probably possess greater leadership resources than more authoritarian, clandestine movements. Political jiujitsu again plays a possible role in that the repression of peaceful noncooperation creates new causes for and symbols of resistance.

Offensively, a revolutionary movement tries to reduce the regime's social control over the population while at the same time creating structures that successfully integrate increasing numbers of people in the movement. Sharp argues that noncooperation may more effectively attract the uncommitted and reinforce participation among original sympathizers than would violent tactics.[73] The sight of people suffering for their principles and still refusing to strike back with violence may transform the previously indifferent into at least passive supporters. In addition, the experience of repression may add to grievances and strengthen the resolve of those who suffer it. Again, the political jiujitsu of noncooperation may turn the strength of the regime into a source of weakness, while expanding potential support for the revolutionary movement. Revolutionary violence, in contrast, alienates potential supporters and often leads to acquiescence in vigorous regime countermeasures. Violent attacks, moreover, will likely ignite a blood cycle of retribution and revenge, inhibiting positive institutional support.

The organization of noncooperation, particularly if it involves significant participation, tends to emphasize the search for agreement and relatively open communication, and militates against the emergence of a power elite. Violent tactics, in contrast, encourage centralization and secrecy, qualities that adversely effect the character of any revolutionary order that might emerge. On the other hand, noncooperation demands significant discipline and solidarity and remains susceptible to free riding and defection. Violent organizations, of course, do not escape their own free rider problems. Each depends on effective organization to monitor and prevent defections. Movements implementing noncooperation tactics, though, are less likely to resort to internal violence to maintain discipline. Rather, these movements reduce the free rider problem by relying on process and other-regarding incentives and using the fear of ostracism or shame as sanctions (see the discussion of "thickening" the concept of rationality in Chapter 5).

Successful implementation of a revolutionary strategy of noncooperation depends on a number of factors.[74] First, the *numbers* participating in the strategy affect the ability of the regime to counterattack. Massive participation lowers the vulnerability of any single participant and helps to create a bandwagon effect. Second, the potency of noncooperation depends on the *value* to the regime of the support being withheld. Clearly, the level of participation relates to the question of value, but the strategic position of particular sectors also affects outcome. Particular workers may control more critical sectors of the economy; particular civil servants may hold positions better able to paralyze the administration; particular religious or cultural institutions may possess the ability to withdraw the mantle of legitimacy from the regime. Third, success depends on the *quality* of the organization of noncooperation. The movement must effectively withhold critical support (for example, an effective strike must withdraw the needed labor from the process of production). Moreover, the participants must sustain their noncooperation, even in the face of repression, to give political jiujitsu time to work. Finally, *regime disunity* and the potential for defection among the uncommitted influence the effectiveness of noncooperation. Political jiujitsu works best when the regime loses its nerve and solidarity and the uncommitted detect these weaknesses.

Noncooperation tactics do not guarantee success for revolutionary groups any more than they do for other political actors. Indeed, under conditions of relative stability and social peace, the isolation of groups with revolutionary grievances probably dooms such a path to power . Of course, in these circumstances a fringe group resorting to terrorist or guerrilla violence also faces probable failure. Historically, successful revolutions, in some sense, start with a refusal to obey. This simple refusal to obey, as Sharp amply illustrates, constitutes a power resource in its own right apart from any capacity to carry out direct attacks on the forces of the regime. The effective denial to the regime of expected support and resources ultimately may prove more coercive than a dozen insurgencies. Historical instances of revolutionary upheaval, even though commonly associated with widespread social and political violence, often reveal on closer inspection the important contribution of withdrawn consent and noncooperation.

CONCLUSION: VICTORY AND DEFEAT IN THE REVOLUTIONARY STRUGGLE

Radical political movements constantly fail around the world. Most fundamentally, they fail to get started. If initiated, they fail to expand beyond a narrow ethnic or sectarian base. If they expand beyond this base, they deteriorate into a prolonged and bloody stalemate. If they break this stalemate, they fail to bring about the lofty transformation promised. Despite appalling gaps between rich and poor; despite corrupt, incompetent, and unresponsive regimes; despite the rhetoric of liberation or salvation, most regimes continue indefinitely, often without serious political challenge or with the capability to overcome the challenges encountered.

It anything, the review of the conditions for successful revolution in the preceding chapters overexplained the persistence of failure. We observed that most people, most of the time, prefer stability to uncertainty, a preference that favors *any* established order. Each of the explanations for political violence or radical political transformation sets forth the extreme conditions that underlie such action. Whatever their differences and incompatibilities, both deprivation and rational choice theory outline the significant barriers discouraging risky, radical behavior. Despite their different perspectives the various disequilibrium and structural theories indicate the extremity of the crisis required to produce the context for revolutionary transformation, whether one of collapse at the center or of weakness at the periphery. Finally, the problems of leadership, ideology, organization, strategy, and tactics give some idea of the practical difficulties encountered in constructing a significant alternative to the established order.

In a sense, radical political action, to succeed, must resist succumbing to sequential paths of least resistance. People find it easier to obey and endure than to resist and rebel. If they rebel, they find it easier to destroy than to build. If they build, they find it easier to build on narrow, exclusive identities than on inclusive ones. If they build on inclusive identities, they find it easier to recapitulate old tyrannies and inequities than to fulfill the promise of revolutionary transformation. Often an extreme political movement embarks down the path of resistance only to falter at the next fork in the road.

Despite the odds, some movements travel far down the revolutionary road. Success in achieving the destructive strategic goals depends, first of all, on the weaknesses of the regime. The regime is a "model loser," whether it conveniently collapses at the outset of the struggle because essential political sectors abandon it or a revolutionary civil war progressively erodes its power from the periphery. David Wilkinson aptly characterizes such a regime as a "victim of dynamic decadence and flourishing corruption." The established order lacks "moral unity"; its citizenry is "paralyzed, particularistic, cynical, and desperate," while "greed, localism, factionalism, and class selfishness" afflict the ruling elites. Government institutions "are self-serving, fragmented, bloated, and impotent—too strong for the security of the citizen but too weak for their own." The economy falters under capital flight, decaying production, and falling consumption, while corruption and parasitism flourish. The military, commanded by incompetent and often insubordinate officers, "is too slow, hungry, ignorant, apathetic, and feeble" to prop up the regime or fight effectively.[75]

In contrast, success in achieving the constructive goals of revolutionary transformation depends primarily on the relative strengths of the revolutionary movement in terms of leadership, ideology, and organization. Where the leadership of the regime is corrupt and incompetent, that of the revolution must be seen as dedicated, selfless, and skillful. Where the regime loses its moral position and divides the people, the revolutionary ideology must be seen as providing a new and relatively inclusive basis of solidarity and community. Where the institutions of the regime grow selfish, corrupt, divisive, and ineffective, the revolutionary organizations must demonstrate enthusiasm, effectiveness, discipline, and perhaps even ruthlessness.[76]

In the coming chapters we explore the specific origins of social crisis and the dynamic of weakness and strength in two recent cases of radical political transformation: Iran and Vietnam. Iran appears to approximate the Western path of revolution, though with some telling ideological differences. Vietnam, at least before the massive American intervention, essentially followed the Eastern path. In the final chapter we turn to the issue of outcomes, looking first to the problem of justifying revolutionary ends and extreme, especially violent, means. We then investigate the consequences of apparent revolution in our two cases.

NOTES

1. Michael Mandelbaum, *The Nuclear Question: The United States and Nuclear Weapons, 1946–1976* (New York: Cambridge University Press, 1979), pp. 8–9.
2. Much of this section is based on Peter C. Sederberg, "Terrorism: Contending Themes in Contemporary Research," in Joseph P. Gitler, ed., *Annual Review of Conflict and Conflict Resolution*, Vol. 2 (New York: Garland, 1990), pp. 229–268. More extensive discussion of many of these issues may be found in Peter C. Sederberg, *Terrorist Myths: Illusion, Rhetoric, and Reality* (Englewood Cliffs, N.J.: Prentice Hall, 1989).
3. Brian Jenkins, *International Terrorism: The Other World War* (Santa Monica, Calif.: Rand, November 1985).
4. Christopher Hitchens, "Wanton Acts of Usage," *Harper's,* September 1986, p. 68.
5. J. Bowyer Bell, "Terror: An Overview," in Marius H. Livingston, ed., *International Terrorism in the Contemporary World* (Westport, Conn. and London: Greenwood Press, 1978), p. 39.

6. See Alex P. Schmid, *Political Terrorism: A Research Guide to Concepts, Theories, Data Bases and Literature* (Amsterdam: North-Holland, and New Brunswick, N.J.: Transaction Books, 1983), pp. 119–152. See also Alex P. Schmid and Albert J. Jongman, *Political Terrorism: A New Guide to Actors, Authors, Concepts, Data Bases, Theories and Literature* (Amsterdam: North-Holland, and New Brunswick, N.J.: Transaction Books, 1988), pp. 1–38.

7. See, for example, Michael Walzer, *Just and Unjust Wars*, Second Edition (New York: Basic Books, 1992).

8. Sederberg, *Terrorist Myths*, p. 37.

9. David George, "Distinguishing Classical Tyrannicide from Modern Terrorism," *Review of Politics*, 50 (Summer 1988): 390–419.

10. See Franklin L. Ford, *Political Murder: From Tyrannicide to Terrorism* (Cambridge, Mass.: Harvard University Press, 1985), pp. 100–104.

11. See Ronald M. Holmes and James DeBurger, *Serial Murder* (Beverly Hills, Calif.: Sage Publications, 1988), and Shiva Naipaul, *Journey to Nowhere: A New World Tragedy* (New York: Simon and Schuster, 1980).

12. See, for example, Hugh Davis Graham, "Violence, Social Theory, and the Historians: The Debate over Consensus and Culture in America," in Ted Robert Gurr, ed., *Violence in America*, Vol. 2: *Protest, Rebellion, Reform* (Newbury Park, Calif.: Sage Publications, 1989), pp. 329–351.

13. See Martha Crenshaw, *The Psychology of Terrorism*, Second Edition (San Francisco: Jossey-Bass, 1985).

14. Bernard Schechterman, "Irrational Terrorism," in Martin Slann and Bernard Schechterman, eds., *Multidimensional Terrorism* (Boulder, Colo.: Lynne Rienner, 1987), pp. 20–21.

15. Sergei Nechayev, *The Catechism of the Revolutionist*, reprinted in Phillip B. Springer and Marcello Truzzi, eds., *Revolutionaries on Revolution* (Pacific Palisades, Calif.: Goodyear, 1973), p. 188.

16. Crawford Young, *The Politics of Cultural Pluralism* (Madison: University of Wisconsin Press, 1976), pp. 66–83.

17. David Capitanchik, "Terrorism and Islam," in Noel O'Sullivan, ed., *Terrorism, Ideology and Revolution: The Origins of Modern Political Violence* (Boulder, Colo.: Westview Press, 1986), pp. 115–131.

18. See, for example, the discussion in Peter Calvert, "Terror in the Theory of Revolution," ibid., pp. 27–45. See also Walter Laqueur, *The Age of Terrorism* (Boston and Toronto: Little, Brown, 1987).

19. H. Jon Rosenbaum and Peter C. Sederberg, "Vigilantism: An Analysis of Establishment Violence," *Comparative Politics*, 6 (July 1974): 541–571.

20. For example, see *Nunca Mas: The Report of the Argentine National Commission on the Disappeared* (New York: Farrar, Straus and Giroux, 1986); Jacobo Timmerman, *Prisoner Without a Name, Cell Without a Number,* trans. by Toby Talbot (New York: Alfred A. Knopf, 1981); and Lawrence Weschler, *A Miracle, a Universe: Settling Accounts with Torturers* (New York: Pantheon, 1990).

21. See, for example, *Amnesty International Report, 1991* (New York: Amnesty International USA, 1991).

22. Eugene V. Walter, *Terrorism and Resistance: A Study of Political Violence* (New York: Oxford University Press, 1969).

23. For a survey of the problem see Michael Stohl and George A. Lopez, eds., *The State as Terrorist: The Dynamics of Governmental Violence and Repression* (Westport, Conn.: Greenwood Press, 1984).

24. Irving Louis Horowitz, *Taking Lives: Genocide and State Power,* Third Edition (New Brunswick, N.J.: Transaction Books, 1982), p. 17.
25. Brian Jenkins, *International Terrorism,* pp. 11–12.
26. William F. May, "Terrorism as Strategy and Ecstasy," *Social Research,* 41 (Summer 1974): 277–298.
27. Franz Fanon, *The Wretched of the Earth* (New York: Grove Press, 1978).
28. May, p. 286.
29. For a general exploration of this hypothesis see Ted Robert Gurr, "Persisting Patterns of Repression and Rebellion: Foundations for a General Theory of Political Coercion," in Margaret P. Karns, ed., *Persistent Patterns and Emergent Structures in a Waning Century* (New York: Praeger, 1986).
30. George Rosie, *The Directory of International Terrorism* (New York: Paragon House, 1986), p. 205.
31. Ibid., p. 48.
32. Hannah Arendt, *On Violence* (New York: Harcourt, Brace and World, 1969), p. 79.
33. Richard E. Rubenstein, *Alchemists of Revolution: Terrorism in the Modern World* (New York: Basic Books, 1987), pp. 197–198.
34. Ibid., p. 204.
35. Richard Maxwell Brown, "The History of Violence in America," in Rosenbaum and Sederberg, eds., *Vigilante Politics,* p. 94
36. Ibid., p. 95.
37. Barbara Harf, "Genocide as State Terrorism," in Michael Stohl and George Lopez, eds., *Government Violence and Repression* (Westport, Conn.: Greenwood Press, 1986).
38. For the Chinese position see Lin Piao, *Long Live the Victory of People's War* (Peking: Foreign Languages Press, 1968). For the American appraisal of this purported strategy see Paul Kattenburg, *The Vietnam Trauma in American Foreign Policy, 1945–1975* (New Brunswick, N.J.: Transaction Books, 1980), especially pp. 76–91. American analysis, of course, was strongly influenced by the so-called "domino theory" (see Chapter 4).
39. Perhaps the definitive historical survey of guerrilla war is Robert B. Asprey, *War in the Shadows: The Guerrilla in History,* two volumes (Garden City, N.Y.: Doubleday, 1975).
40. The following account is based on ibid., pp. 970–976.
41. Quoted in ibid., p. 971.
42. The following points represent a distillation and reorganization of points discussed by Nathan Leites and Charles Wolf, Jr., *Rebellion and Authority: An Analytic Essay on Insurgent Conflicts* (Chicago: Markham Publishing Company, 1979), pp. 48–70, and Mao Tse-tung, *Basic Tactics,* trans. by Stuart R. Schram (New York: Frederick A. Praeger, 1966). I also draw on some of the observations and aphorisms collected in William McNaughton, ed. and trans., *Guerrilla War* (Oberlin, Ohio: Crane Press, 1970).
43. Quoted in McNaughton, p. 56.
44. Leites and Wolf, pp. 56–57.
45. Personal communication.
46. Leites and Wolf, pp. 57–60.
47. Mao Tse-tung, pp. 67–68.
48. Quoted in McNaughton, p. 34.
49. Ibid.
50. Mao Tse-tung, pp. 56–57.

51. Samuel B. Griffith, "Introduction," in Mao Tse-tung, *On Guerrilla Warfare*, trans. by Samuel B. Griffith (New York: Frederick A. Praeger, 1961), p. 24.
52. Mao Tse-tung, *Basic Tactics*, pp. 61–65.
53. Ibid., p. 60.
54. Quoted in McNaughton, p 13.
55. This inventory partly reflects that in Bard E. O'Neill, "Insurgency: A Framework for Analysis," in Bard E. O'Neill et al., eds., *Insurgency in the Modern World* (Boulder, Colo.: Westview Press, 1980), pp. 5–26.
56. For a more extensive discussion of these factors see Ted Robert Gurr, *Why Men Rebel* (Princeton, N.J.: Princeton University Press, 1970), Chapter 9, pp. 274–316, especially pp. 283–288.
57. Jeffrey Race, *War Comes to Long An: Revolutionary Conflict in a Vietnamese Province* (Berkeley: University of California Press, 1973), p. xv.
58. Ibid., pp. 144–145.
59. Ibid., p. 174.
60. The best analysis of the origins and weaknesses of counterinsurgency doctrine is D. Michael Shafer, *Deadly Paradigms: The Failure of U.S. Counterinsurgency Policy* (Princeton, N.J.: Princeton University Press, 1988). See also Michael T. Klare and Peter Kornbluh, eds., *Low Intensity Warfare: Counterinsurgency, Proinsurgency, and Antiterrorism in the Eighties* (New York: Pantheon, 1988); for the French doctrine, see Peter Paret, *French Revolutionary Warfare from Indochina to Algeria: The Analysis of a Political and Military Doctrine* (New York: Frederick A. Praeger, 1964).
61. Edwin E. Moise, "Guerrilla Warfare," presented at the Annual Meeting of the Association of Third World Studies, Columbia, S.C., October 12–13, 1990.
62. Shafer, pp. 116–118.
63. Ibid., pp. 118–122.
64. Ibid., pp. 118–120.
65. Gene Sharp, *The Politics of Nonviolent Action* (Boston: Porter Sargent, 1973), p. 13. Sharp labels this withdrawal of support "nonviolent action," but we refer to it as withdrawn support or "noncooperation."
66. Ibid.
67. Ibid., p. 15.
68. Ibid., pp. 19–24.
69. Ibid., pp. 70–71.
70. Ibid., pp. 409–445.
71. Ibid., p. 657.
72. Ibid., pp. 636–640.
73. Ibid., pp. 658–664, 678–690.
74. Cf. ibid., pp. 754–755.
75. David Wilkinson, *Revolutionary Civil War: The Elements of Victory and Defeat* (Palo Alto, Calif: Page-Ficklin Publications, 1975), pp. 118–119.
76. See ibid., pp. 123–126.

PART Four

CASES AND CONCLUSIONS

*I*n the Introduction we previewed two recent cases of revolutionary turmoil—Vietnam and Iran. These two revolutions raise interesting problems of causes and effects, leaders and followers, ideology and organization, and strategy and tactics. The first three parts of the book critically investigated ways of thinking systematically about such issues. We now explore which of these approaches furnish the most appropriate perspective(s) on the two revolutions. Our case studies provide neither definitive history nor theory. Rather, they illustrate some possible ways of understanding revolutionary dynamics in concrete instances.

Our approach to each case approximately parallels the structure of the book. First, we briefly develop the contextual background for each revolution. We then attempt to understand the causes of the revolutionary upheaval. In undertaking this task we draw on several, though not all, of the theoretical perspectives introduced earlier. We analyze the character of leadership, ideology, and organization in the revolutionary process. Finally, we assess the strategy of revolutionary transformation and the character of regime response. Each case study, however, develops somewhat different areas of emphasis and uses different analytical resources. We hope to illustrate in this way alternative paths for organizing inquiry into particular instances of revolution. The analysis of the Vietnamese Revolution, for example, primarily draws upon relative deprivation, cultural disequilibrium, and rational actor approaches. The Iranian case, in contrast, inventories the long-term causes and accelerators of the revolutionary crisis and then draws upon this inventory to develop structural disequilibrium and opportunity/resource interpretations of the crisis and outcome. These brief case studies do not pretend to replace the existing works of historical and political scholarship on the two revolutions. At best, we hope that our analysis provides an initial orientation to complex phenomena. We depend heavily on the work of the true area specialists, and we try to introduce at least some of these resources. Essentially, we strive to stimulate deeper probes into these and other instances of revolution. The cases, then, should serve as the beginning, not the end, of inquiry.

10

Vietnam: The Thirty-Year Revolution*

At first glance Vietnam seems to illustrate the Eastern path of revolutionary struggle. Specifically, a peasant-based revolutionary movement, led by urban intellectuals, takes advantage of regime weakness in the countryside to initiate a rural insurgency. Through many years of bitter, protracted warfare the movement gradually increases its political and military strength until it challenges the regime in conventional combat. A few significant military victories for the revolutionary forces at the point of approximate parity send the regime hurtling down the slippery slope of disintegration and destruction. Though the revolutionary struggle to reach the point of parity is prolonged, the final denouement after parity unfolds rapidly.

Vietnam, however, does not fit neatly into this mold. The Vietnamese Revolution, to be sure, included a prolonged revolutionary insurgency. In fact, it involved at least two distinct insurgencies. Vietnam's revolutionary history, though, is more complex than the straightforward Eastern-style revolutionary model suggests. First, though Viet Minh guerrillas engaged in some armed resistance during World War II, their seizure of Hanoi in August 1945 did not culminate a prolonged struggle. Rather, as the strongest political group in the northern portion of the country, they moved to fill the power vacuum created by the defeat of the French colonial forces by the Japanese in March 1945 and the subsequent Japanese surrender to the Allies in August. The subsequent reimposition of French control forced the Viet Minh out of the cities and into a Maoist-style protracted war.

Second, victory over the French produced only half a country. Initially, Viet Minh supporters in the South hoped for a peaceful reunification of their country. Frustrated in this hope, the revolutionary insurgency began anew in 1959 against the nominally independent, if materially dependent, South Vietnamese government in Saigon. Massive American intervention saved this regime in 1965, just as it teetered on disintegration. This American support kept the Saigon regime in power for another decade. The revolutionary insurgency, then, went through two major phases (1946–1954 and 1959–1965), which provide the focus for our analysis of the revolutionary process in Vietnam.

* With the assistance of Lisa Greene, Yeonsik Jeong, Ewald Leeflang, and Gabriela Tarazona

BACKGROUND[1]

Precolonial History

Contemporary Vietnam, with a population of around 70 million in 1992, curls like an S for over a thousand miles along the eastern edge of the Southeast Asian peninsula. Although the Vietnamese as a people trace their history back over 2000 years, they did not fully occupy the current territory of the country until the end of the eighteenth century. For a thousand years they lived in the northern portion and endured the direct rule of the Chinese. After repeated rebellions the Vietnamese defeated the Chinese in A.D. 939 and gained their independence. Originally centered in the Red River Delta in the northern section of Vietnam (the Tonkin region), the Vietnamese nation began to spread slowly southward down a narrow edge of the peninsula between the mountains and the sea, displacing some indigeneous peoples, until they finally conquered the rich delta farmlands of the Mekong River.

National independence neither ended Chinese influence nor brought much peace to the Vietnamese. Traditional patterns of Vietnamese rule reflected Chinese principles, and Vietnamese rulers continued to pay tribute to China. An emperor ruled through a mandarinate—essentially a hierarchy of officials selected and promoted on the basis of their mastery of Confucian scholarship. Confucian doctrine emphasized order and obedience to rightful authority, particularly to an emperor ruling with the "Mandate of Heaven." Under normal circumstances Confucianism proved profoundly conservative, but if the emperor ever lost the mandate to rule, then Confucianism justified rebellion to restore rightful rule. Indicators of a lost mandate included the absence of social peace, the failure to maintain the irrigation system, or famine and other natural disasters.

Although sometimes unified under a central ruler, Vietnam was often rent by warfare. Constant pressure from China complicated internal dynastic struggles as well as the conflicts engendered by the push south. Territorial expansion led to a series of wars with the Champa kingdom in central Vietnam (the Annam region), culminating with its annexation in the fifteenth century. Subsequently the Vietnamese expanded into the relatively underpopulated Mekong Delta (also called Cochin China), largely at the expense of the Khmer (Cambodian) Empire. By the middle of the eighteenth century, Vietnamese expansion had reached its current southernmost extent at the Gulf of Siam.

One of Vietnam's many dynastic rebellions and civil wars coincided with the culmination of this expansion and conquest. At this time Vietnam was divided, with the North ruled by the Trinh house (or clan) and the South under the domination of the Nguyen house. In 1772 three brothers led a populist rebellion against the Nguyen in the South, and after victory there they marched north and ousted the Trinh. The unified rule established by these three brothers lasted until a survivor of the Nguyen clan, Nguyen Anh, rallied his supporters. After years of struggle he ousted the upstarts and declared himself emperor of a unified Vietnam in 1802. The Nguyen dynasty he founded lasted in some nominal way until 1954. Significantly, a French cleric, Pigneau de Béhaine, and some French volunteers greatly assisted him in his wars.

Despite the vicissitudes of these dynastic struggles the life of the average Vietnamese at the beginning of the nineteenth century centered on the village unit and agricultural activity. In the North, in particular, villages were nearly autonomous units, fulfilling social and political, as well as economic, functions. In areas of more recent expansion the village played a less significant role in the lives of the peasants, but the production of rice remained the primary economic activity. Villagers, like peasants everywhere, largely wished to be left alone, and they resented the imposition of excessive taxes and the depredations of absentee landlords and moneylenders.

Two thousand years of struggle left a complex legacy and a toughened people. Although influenced by Chinese culture and ideas, the Vietnamese tenaciously fought for and later protected their essential autonomy from direct Chinese rule. Though Confucian doctrine mandated obedience to authority, such ideas failed to prevent numerous dynastic civil wars and rebellions. Centuries of conquest and expansion spread the Vietnamese people to their contemporary boundaries. The final phase of conquest and consolidation, though, coincided with growing contacts with European powers, especially the French. The French injected further influences and disruption into the area.

The Impact of French Conquest and Rule

The Nguyen emperors tried to limit the intrusions of the French and the influence of Western ideas, especially Christianity, during the first half of the nineteenth century. Unfortunately, the persecution of Christian missionaries only provided the French with an excuse to intervene repeatedly. In 1859 a Franco-Spanish force conquered Saigon, and the French subsequently expanded their control over the neighboring provinces. A treaty with the emperor Tu Duc in 1862 formally recognized this conquest, giving the French direct sovereignty over the region known as Cochin China. The French then turned their attention to the North, occupying Hanoi first in 1873 and again in 1883. A treaty signed in August of 1883 made the remainder of Vietnam—the regions of Annam and Tonkin—into French protectorates. The emperor survived largely as a figurehead in the central Vietnamese city of Hue. Despite the formal loss of independence, pockets of resistance continued until well into the twentieth century. At the same time that the French consolidated their rule over Vietnam, they also subjugated the remainder of Indochina (Cambodia and Laos).

The imposition of French rule, though nominally indirect in the central and northern regions, profoundly disrupted the economy, culture, and politics of Vietnam. Economically, the French were essentially in the colony *business*. They wanted to make a profit off their colonies, not merely introduce French civilization. To earn these profits the French encouraged the commercialization of agriculture to produce crops for export. They supported the creation of large rubber and rice plantations in the South and imposed taxes to force peasant producers to sell their crops to pay their tax obligations. Wealthy French and Vietnamese landlords bought up the property of peasants who fell into debt, and this consolidation, along with population growth, created a landless rural proletariat to work on the large plantations. The French undermined the economic security of the village as a unit of production and consumption because surpluses were sold for export rather than being retained to cover bad years. Investment in mines and railroads and some industry also helped to create a small working class.

The cultural impact of the French rapidly diminished the significance of the Confucian mandarinate. French education, available to only the fortunate few, replaced Confucian scholarship as the avenue for advancement. In addition to the few French schools, reformed Vietnamese schools provided further, though limited, access to Western education. Those acquiring a Western education grew to resent the lack of high-level opportunities. Ironically, Western education also served to introduce ideas of self-determination, as well as France's own revolutionary tradition. Exposure to the culture of the colonizer, then, reinforced national sentiments and provided a further rationale, if any was needed, for resistance. Economic transformation also produced cultural consequences. The disruption of the traditional peasant economy and the spread of commercial agriculture generated thousands of uprooted people. Some of these turned to opium addiction or to syncretic religious movements, particularly the Cao Dai and the Hoa Hao.

Politically, French rule largely erased whatever legitimacy the Nguyen dynasty previously possessed. Although nominally in charge of political affairs in Annam and Tonkin, in reality the Vietnamese exercised little political authority. The French disrupted traditional patterns of village rule, replacing them with an elected council and executive directly responsible for carrying out colonial policy. In Cochin China, the area directly ruled by the French, they even imposed a French legal code, adjudicated by French judges ignorant of local customs and enforced by French police. Finally, the French organized a native colonial militia to assist them in maintaining their control. This body became the nucleus of the South Vietnamese Army in the 1950s.

Certain Vietnamese benefited from French rule. Some expanded their landholdings in the Mekong Delta region thanks to French hydraulic projects. Those with access to French education enjoyed certain limited opportunities for upward mobility. Even elements of the traditional political elites benefited from collaborating with the French. Importantly, the penetration of French influence was greatest in Cochin China, where they ruled the longest and wrought the greatest economic and social transformation. In sum, French colonialism "introduced economic, political, and social changes which dislocated the traditional mode of life and produced a poorly integrated society in which a small, urban-oriented Westernized elite was largely alienated from the bulk of the village-based population."[2]

The Resurgence of Vietnamese Resistance

Not long after the French quashed the last pockets of resistance they faced new challenges from groups led by partly Westernized intellectuals who invoked nationalist ideals. As in many European colonies around the world, these native elites at first advocated moderate reforms to increase their opportunites within

the existing colonial system. French rejection of these reformist prop
these groups underground and toward more radical action. The major
organization of the 1920s was the Viet Nam Quoc Dan Dang (Vietname
alist Party, or VNQDD). On February 9, 1930, the VNQDD led an ill-fa
ing that the French easily crushed. The subsequent destruction of the VNQDD
organization left the nationalist mantle to be picked up by the Indochinese Communist Party (ICP).

The ICP emerged from the union of three competing Marxist groups in 1930.
Nguyen Ai Quoc (Nguyen the Patriot), the representative of the Communist
International, or Comintern, in Southeast Asia, arranged this union. "Nguyen Ai
Quoc" was the alias adopted by Nguyen Tat Thanh, who later adopted the name
Ho Chi Minh. The ICP instigated peasant demonstrations and worker strikes cul-
minating in peasant revolts in two provinces. Brutal French repression left many
Communists dead and thousands of political prisoners in jail. Though this repres-
sion hurt the ICP, it did not destroy it as earlier measures had the VNQDD.
Although many Communist leaders, including Ho Chi Minh, were forced into
exile in southern China, "the ICP had come to dominate the revolutionary scene
in Vietnam and had laid the foundation for its subsequent claims to historic leadership of the Vietnamese nationalist movement."[3]

The 1040 French defeat in Europe left the colonial authorities in Vietnam to
face the Japanese largely alone. After negotiations, threats, and some fighting, the
French gave in to Japanese demands. In return for complete access to Vietnam's
resources, the Japanese recognized French sovereignty over Indochina and
allowed the colonial administration to continue governing the territory. This
uneasy relationship continued until March 1945, when the Japanese military
seized power throughout Vietnam and prompted the current Nguyen figurehead
emperor, Bao Dai, to declare independence from France. Bao Dai's transformation from French patsy to Japanese patsy impressed few genuine Vietnamese
nationalists. The surrender of Japan a few months later, consequently, created a
vacuum at the center of Vietnamese politics—a vacuum the Communists were
best prepared to fill.

In 1941 the ICP had shifted to a united front strategy aimed at unifying all
progressive elements of Vietnamese society against the colonial regime. In May of
that year they formed the Vietnam Independence League (Viet Nam Doc Lap
Dong Minh Hoi or Viet Minh, for short). They subordinated the Communist
rhetoric of class warfare to the more appealing goal of national independence.
During the war years the Viet Minh focused on expanding their political and military strength in Vietnam. When the Japanese surrendered in August 1945, the
Viet Minh attempted to seize control throughout the country. On August 28 Bao
Dai abdicated in favor of the Viet Minh–led provisional government. Significantly, Viet Minh authority was weakest in the South, though they made up the
strongest element in the Provisional Executive Committee of the South.

Regardless of their compromises and the subsequent reversal of fortune as
the French reasserted their control over the cities, the August Revolution was a
defining moment of the Vietnamese Revolution. John T. McAlister and Paul Mus

argue that the ease with which the Viet Minh came to power demonstrated the passing of "Mandate of Heaven" from the Nguyen dynasty to Ho Chi Minh:

> Let it not be forgotten that from the point of view of the common man in the rice field the abdication of Emperor Bao Dai in 1945 was an important symbolic event. This was especially true because he declared that he wanted to enter the ranks of the newly constituted people as a plain individual. What a mutation for Confucians to reflect upon! How easy for them to imagine that in these events was an expression of the power of the new system, a revolutionary "virtue" supported by a new world in conflict with the old order.[4]

When the French subsequently brought Bao Dai back as "head of state" in 1949, few Vietnamese accepted his attempt to reclaim the mantle of political legitimacy.

The 1954 Geneva agreement ended the first phase of the insurgency with an incomplete revolutionary victory. The temporary division of the country at the seventeenth parallel gave an opportunity for anti-Communist Vietnamese—who, though a minority, still numbered in the hundreds of thousands, especially among Vietnamese Catholics—a chance to regroup. Bao Dai, still the nominal head of state in the southern half of the country, appointed a Vietnamese Catholic, Ngo Dinh Diem, as premier in June 1954.

Diem, though a strong opponent of the Viet Minh, had never collaborated with the French and therefore possessed some credible nationalist credentials. Although initially relatively powerless in the fluid political situation that prevailed in the South, he gradually consolidated his power, gained control over the army and the police, and received the strong backing of the United States. In 1955 he felt sufficiently secure to defy the emperor and hold a plebiscite on the future of the imperial dynasty. Diem won the plebiscite, proclaimed the Republic of Vietnam in October of that year, and became its first president.

After refusing to hold the expected referendum on the future of a united Vietnam, Diem, backed by increasing amounts of assistance from the United States, turned his attention to the destruction of the Viet Minh organization in the South. The Democratic Republic of Vietnam (North Vietnam), for its part, resisted renewing the insurgency in the South. Their own internal policies, including a disastrous land reform program, preoccupied them, and they lacked enthusiasm for a conflict that could well involve the United States. Finally, events in the South forced their hand, and a new revolutionary insurgency began in the South under the aegis of the National Liberation Front (NLF).

Political support for the NLF grew rapidly after 1959, as did their armed forces. The expansion of the NLF challenge between 1960 and 1964 indicates that support for the Diem regime failed to spread into the villages and among the peasants of South Vietnam. Diem and his American advisers labeled the guerrillas as the Viet Cong, or Vietnamese Communists, partly to distinguish the second phase of the revolutionary insurgency from the war against French colonialism. Whatever the value of this label for American consumption, the Vietnamese recognized the continuity between the two insurgencies and Diem's severely compromised credentials as a nationalist. Neil Sheehan reports the questioning of an old peasant by a South Vietnamese Army (ARVN) captain who wanted to know about the guerrillas operating in the area. Both the captain and the peasant repeatedly referred to the guerrillas as "Viet Minh." Sheehan, puzzled, asked a Vietnamese reporter why they both used this name, since he assumed they were pursuing the notorious Viet Cong.

"The Americans and the government people in Saigon call them the Viet Cong," he said, "but out here everyone still calls them the Viet Minh."

"Why?" I asked.

"Because they look like the Viet Minh, they act like the Viet Minh, and that's what these people have always called them," he said.

The ARVN captain knew that the Viet Minh were back; that was why he had been so cautious. Cao [the ARVN division commander] knew that the Viet Minh were back; that was why he was more afraid than he would normally have been. Diem knew the Viet Minh were back; that was another reason he wanted to keep his army intact. Only the Americans knew neither the Vietnamese they were depending on to work their will, nor the Vietnamese enemy they faced.[5]

UNDERSTANDING THE VIETNAMESE REVOLUTION—CAUSES

In one sense the Vietnamese Revolution is easy to explain. Nationalist struggles against colonial rulers erupted throughout the European empires following World War II as oppressed people sought their liberation. The mere desire for national liberation, however, cannot account for the specific dynamics of any particular struggle. Rather, we must explain why people would engage in such extreme and risky political activity rather than remain passive in the face of repression. Moreover, we need to determine why the liberation struggle took the form and course it did. Finally, we need to provide some grasp of the elements that contributed to eventual victory. The preceding background to the revolution in Vietnam identifies some particular puzzles that need attention; it hardly solves them.

More systematic analysis of the revolution in Vietnam involves three interrelated areas of inquiry. First, what factors enabled the Vietnamese revolutionary movement to mobilize the people for revolutionary activities? Second, what role did leadership, ideology, and organization play in this mobilization? Third, what combination of strategy and tactics produced the revolutionary victories?

In attempting an answer to the first puzzle, the factors underlying revolutionary mobilization, we draw upon some of the explanations for revolution and political violence reviewed in Part Two. First, we develop a deprived actor explanation of the forces that made people susceptible to revolutionary appeals. We then contrast two somewhat different interpretations of the revolutionary situation—one based on a type of cultural disequilibrium model and the other emphasizing rational choice—to see how they add to our understanding of the factors contributing to revolutionary mobilization.

Relative Deprivation in the Vietnamese Revolution

Typically, scholars identify a variety of factors contributing to the emergence of the revolutionary crisis in Vietnam. These processes broke down established identities and institutions and made people available for mobilization by a variety of radical movements.[6] Relative deprivation theory provides one means of organizing and understanding these processes. We must, however, be cautious about placing too much faith in this explanation for the Vietnamese Revolution. First, the arguments we make for intensifying feelings of relative deprivation, however plausible, depend on a general assessment of the population's changing economic and social position. They serve as only indirect measures of states of mind. Second, increasing relative deprivation, at best, makes people more susceptible to revolutionary mobilization. By itself, it fails to specify if and when they actually engage in revolutionary activities. Third, even if some people, for whatever reason, cross the threshold from disposition to action, relative deprivation theory cannot explain the comparative success of different appeals. Groups other than the Viet Minh attempted to exploit the social processes that contributed to breakdown and mobilization. Despite these shortcomings relative deprivation theory provides one angle on the origins of the Vietnamese Revolution.

Relative deprivation theory, as we discussed in Chapter 5, incorporates other research questions and levels of analysis. Here we focus on the factors that arguably increased widespread feelings of deprivation just before the attempted establishment of independence in 1945 and the renewal of the insurgency in 1959. Recalling this earlier discussion, we expect relative deprivation to increase as value expectations exceed value capabilities. People possess three types of values, welfare (primarily economic security), power (primarily effective political participation), and interpersonal (primarily a sense of belonging). Felt deprivation increases as people's expectations rise unmatched by a commensurate increase in their capabilities (aspirational deprivation), or as they experience a decline in their capabilities while their expectations remain relatively constant (decremental deprivation). Finally, expectations and capabilities can move in opposite directions simultaneously (progressive deprivation).

The events of the years preceding 1945 provide ample evidence of declining capabilities. Colonialism, by definition, was an exercise in decremental deprivation. A proud and fiercely independent people lost control of their own destiny to an alien conqueror. The loss of independence, moreover, was of relatively recent origin, and the intrusive nature of French rule, penetrating even to the village, constantly reminded the Vietnamese of their subordination.

"High" politics in precolonial Vietnam involved constant rivalries, struggle, dynastic warfare, and external intrusion, especially by the Chinese. In some sense the addition of the French to this equation was not a dramatic change. The villages of Vietnam, however, traditionally enjoyed considerable autonomy from the vicissitudes of imperial politics.[7] The French ended all this. They established accurate population records and therefore tax rolls, and eliminated village self-rule through councils of elders and notables. The peasant villages, then, experienced a double dose of political deprivation, of both national and village independence.

The tax and development policies of the colonial administration contributed to the impoverishment of the mass of the peasants, even though a few large landowners grew rich.[8] Like other colonial powers, the French wished to make Vietnam into a profitable enterprise by stimulating production for export. The French emphasized two crops for export, rice and rubber. Since small peasant proprietors consumed most of what they produced of the former crop, French policy encouraged the development of large estates capable of generating a significant surplus for export. This contrasted dramatically with the traditional policy of Vietnamese emperors to prohibit the export of surpluses, saving them instead for deficit areas or bad years.[9] Rising taxes increased the debt of small landholders, forcing many to sell their land. French hydraulic projects in the South, though they opened new areas for cultivation, benefited primarily large plantations. Landlessness increased, as did the number of peasant proprietors who did not own sufficient land to support their families. By 1940, 500 large landowners controlled 20 percent of the land in Tonkin. In the South the situation was much worse; 2.5 percent of the landholders owned nearly half the land.[10]

The other export crop, rubber, was even more severely concentrated in the hands of a few native landowners and foreign companies.[11] These large plantations required laborers, usually working in wretched conditions for low wages. At one Michelin plantation over 25 percent of the work force died of malnutrition and disease between 1917 and 1944.[12] Given these appalling conditions, owners often used force and deception to recruit the needed workers

Sixty years of French political and economic depredation enriched a few Vietnamese families but left the vast majority much worse off. As if to underline their declining economic capabilities, a bitter famine struck the Vietnamese people in the final year of World War II. Hundreds of thousands of people starved while the French and the Japanese held surplus rice in their granaries. The mass of the population could have had no clearer example of their declining capabilities under the rule of the foreign powers. The Viet Minh in turn could have had no clearer target to raid than these full granaries.

The colonial experience, though, involved more than simply declining capabilities. Many Vietnamese experienced increasing value expectations. French education introduced new ideas and exposed those who benefited from it to Western democratic and revolutionary values. Moreover, as more Vietnamese gained a Western education, their expectations for personal improvement rose only to be dashed by the lack of positions and discriminatory treatment by the French. Many of the leaders of the nationalist groups that began to form in the 1920s came from the disappointed ranks of these intellectuals.[13]

The creation of a mining and industrial sector socialized tens of thousands of Vietnamese workers into the modern workplace, even if under highly exploitative conditions. The growth of the cities, the development of public works, and exposure to the accouterments of French culture all revealed new value opportunities to the Vietnamese. Perhaps the single most important event influencing the expectations of the average Vietnamese was the triumph of the Japanese. Even though the Japanese allowed the French to administer their colony until March 1945, French authority existed only with the sufferance of their erstwhile Asian allies. If any doubt had existed about the ability of an Asian nation to defeat a European power, Japanese actions sweeping away the vestiges of French rule would have ended them.

Finally, the gyrating fortunes of the Viet Minh in 1945–1946 represent a kind of political "J-curve" of deprivation. Recall that James Davies argues that the most volatile prerevolutionary situation arises when a country experiences a sharp reversal after a period of economic advance (see Chapter 5). He predicts that expectations will continue their rise under these conditions even as capabilities plunge, generating intense relative deprivation. Vietnam appears to have experienced a political variation of this phenomenon. The collapse of both French and Japanese power and the abdication of the puppet emperor in favor of Ho Chi Minh and the popular Viet Minh forces ignited the political value expectations of the Vietnamese. The reoccupation of their country first by the British and Chinese and then by the returning French forces constituted a bitter reversal at a time when their political future seemed so bright.

During the three decades of increasing nationalist activity before 1945, the Vietnamese people arguably experienced intensifying and increasingly widespread feelings of relative deprivation of various forms. The mass of the peasants endured decremental economic deprivation as increased landlessness, rising taxes, and the export of rice surpluses eroded their traditional economic status. Local political elites also experienced decremental deprivation with the elimination of traditional village autonomy. New economic groups, like plantation, mine, and factory workers and those fortunate enough to gain some Western education, were exposed to new value opportunities that remained, however, largely beyond their grasp, frustrating their rising expectations. Increasing wealth in the hands of expatriate elites, Chinese merchants, and a small handful of Vietnamese landlords created a growing gap between rich and poor. Finally, the famine of 1945 reinforced feelings of decremental deprivation, while the rise and fall of political opportunity whiplashed the nationalist forces in an experience of progressive deprivation.

The years leading up to the renewal of insurgency in the South also brought repeated blows to the capabilities of the Viet Minh and their sympathizers. Victory on the battlefield failed to produce the expected diplomatic victory at the negotiating table. Forced to accept half a country in 1954, the Viet Minh regime north of the seventeenth parallel nonetheless expected reunification to follow within two years. Diem's successful consolidation of power in South Vietnam frustrated this expectation. More seriously, Diem's attacks on the Viet Minh structure and sympathizers nearly caused the destruction of their apparatus in the South. To make the situation even worse, the United States, a far more powerful adversary than the French, backed Diem in his efforts to consolidate power, abrogate the 1954 Geneva agreement, and eliminate the Viet Minh in the South. North Vietnam had to renew resistance or face the probable destruction of its revolutionary capabilities in the South.

Declining capabilities afflicted more than the revolutionary core in the South. Diem, though initially effective in neutralizing his major competitors for power, followed policies that alienated increasing numbers of people from his regime.[14]

First, Diem's government "grew into a narrow oligarchy composed of his brothers and other relatives."[15] Beyond this immediate circle of nepotism, his regime favored members of the Catholic minority, particularly those Catholics who fled North Vietnam after 1954. Preferential treatment of northern Catholics doubly frustrated the Buddhist majority in the South.

Second, "Diem sought the support of the affluent landowners of the Mekong Delta, whose families were influential in Saigon, and he balked at imposing a rigorous agrarian reform program there that might have won him peasant sympathies."[16] More frustrating than his failure to carry out land reform was Diem's reversal of the land reforms carried out earlier by the Viet Minh. The regime either repossessed land given to the peasants or forced them to pay for it.

Third, his government developed a program of concentrating the peasants in fortified centers, known first as "agrovilles" and later, in their second incarnation, as "strategic hamlets." These programs aimed at isolating the peasants from the influence of Communists. They accomplished the alienation of the peasants by uprooting them from their traditional villages, moving them some distance from their fields, and forcing them to contribute the labor to construct the fortified centers. The idea of isolating the peasants from the Communist revolutionaries in this fashion made sense only if they were distinct from one another. In reality, Liberation Front supporters were largely indistinguishable from the peasant masses, and revolutionary sympathizers in the villages often went right along with their neighbors into the fortified hamlets. Ironically, one of the men in charge of the strategic hamlet program, Colonel Pham Ngoc Thao, was a secret Communist operative "who deliberately propelled the program ahead at breakneck speed in order to estrange South Vietnam's peasants and drive them into the arms of the Vietcong."[17]

Fourth, Diem's authoritarianism increasingly alienated educated sectors of the population. The elections organized by his regime were mere exercises in fraud and coercion and served only to anger those longing for some form of genuine democracy. Calls for reform and greater flexibility went unheard or provoked reprisals against those raising their voices. Security policy meant ensuring the security of Diem's regime against potential competitors in Saigon rather than the effective prosecution of the war against the growing insurgency. Diem's political base, never broad to begin with, progressively narrowed until even his handpicked generals and his American mentors grew sick of him.

This indirect evidence, then, suggests that decremental deprivation spread widely throughout the South Vietnamese population after the partition in 1954. Diem's policies undermined the capabilities of the revolutionary core, Buddhists, peasants, the educated middle class, and growing elements of his own military; and his ineffectual prosecution of the war alienated his American allies. This indirect evidence, however, fails to explain just who became a revolutionary and why, except in the case of those who supported the revolution from the start. Relative deprivation arguments, at best, only suggest that increasing numbers of people became available for mobilization by opposition forces. Not all the opposition to Diem, however, supported the National Liberation Front. Indeed, both the Buddhists who began to demonstrate against the regime in 1963 and the military who ultimately ousted him often professed anti-Communism.

The presence of increasingly intense and widespread feelings of relative deprivation, even if convincingly demonstrated, cannot alone explain revolutionary outbreaks, much less outcomes. Two other approaches might add to our understanding here. First, the evidence of relative deprivation might support an interpretation that Vietnam experienced a severe disequilibrium that only revolutionary reconstruction could correct. Alternatively, we could see conditions in Vietnam as providing the opportunity for political mobilization and explore why the Communists were more successful in exploiting these opportunities than their rivals. The first approach develops a macroperspective on the revolutionary crisis. The second introduces concerns of competitive advantage in the arena of collective action.

Disequilibrium, Culture Crisis, and Revolutionary Reconstruction in Vietnam

Large numbers of alienated, isolated, and angry individuals will not necessarily jell into a revolutionary movement. They could at least as easily slip into apathy and despair. People, moreover, might find other, nonrevolutionary, ways of addressing their discontent. In Vietnam, for example, many discontented people, especially in the South, found some redress for their frustration by joining syncretic movements like the Cao Dai and Hoa Hao. Other, more favored, individuals identified with their colonizers, adopted French culture, and even became French citizens. An account of a revolutionary transformation, then, must explain the comparative advantage enjoyed by the revolutionary alternative over its competitors in mobilizing discontent. Disequilibrium theory offers one possible approach to this puzzle.

The evidence of widespread relative deprivation, especially before the Viet Minh occupation of Hanoi in 1945, attests to the presence of a severely disequilibrated system in Vietnam. In Chalmers Johnson's formulation the introduction of new values and a new division of labor can upset the political and social balances in a system and overwhelm the system's normal mechanisms for adjustment (see Chapter 6). The resulting disequilibrium leads to a deflation of the regime's authority, reinforced by its inability and unwillingness to contemplate conservative reforms. As the crisis worsens, dissident groups offer alternatives to the existing disorder; in short, they promise to reequilibrate the system. Although this description is rather empty in the abstract, the specifics of the prerevolutionary Vietnamese situation provide a more concrete illustration of system disequilibrium.[18]

We have already noted the roots of the traditional Vietnamese state in Confucian political culture.[19] Although authoritarian in character, the centralized state rested relatively lightly on the largely autonomous villages. The primary obligation of the central state was to maintain the ritualistic integrity of the society by keeping the villages from straying from the Confucian model and ideas of virtue. The so-called "small" or "little" tradition of the villages also reflected a strong hierarchical culture, where village elders and dignitaries, ruling through village councils, maintained appropriate balances and limits.

Colonialism severely disrupted the traditional balance between the centralized state and the autonomous villages. The exploitative and incomplete forms of modernization introduced by the French embodied some of the more destructive aspects of Western individualism. Urbanization, the creation of a money-based economy, the spread of usury, the formation of large estates and a landless rural proletariat, and the penetration of central administration into the village all transformed social relations. The peasant became "a taxpayer in the modern sense of the word: one who pays his taxes as an individual rather than as part of a collective anonymity who paid taxes in rice or other products."[20]

In principle an individualistic culture could establish a new social equilibrium, if the emerging individualistic society experiences the benign world it predicts (that is, one where individual effort is rewarded—see Chapter 6) and if individuals have the opportunities to exploit this world. Neither of these conditions, however, prevailed under colonialism. Except for those few who grew wealthy under the new dispensation and the small numbers of Francophile Vietnamese, the colonial system imposed obligations without commensurate opportunities. Moreover, the global depression and World War II demonstrated that the world was not so benign for the colonizers, much less their restive subjects.

On the other hand, colonialism hastened the inevitable engagement with the rest of the world and destroyed the possibility of restoring the traditional political equilibrium. Under these circumstances the normally conservative culture became ripe for more radical alternatives. The ordinary Vietnamese, in circumstances of severe culture crisis, looked for a new cultural equilibrium:

> The moment a "virtue" (in the West one would say a political system) appears to be worn out and another is in view ready to take the place of the old, the previous abuses—which had been put up with until then—are seen in a new light. Then, and only then, they must be remedied with the help of a new principle. Extreme patience is thus replaced by intolerance. First the people tolerate everything. Then they refuse to put up with anything.[21]

In times of crisis, then, this presumably conservative culture could support a revolutionary transformation, but only one that demonstrated its possession of the virtue needed to reequilibrate the system. In this context the events of 1945 that swept away first the French, then the Japanese, and finally the emperor, bringing Ho Chi Minh and his movement to power, signified the authenticity of the Viet Minh alternative.[22] The Mandate of Heaven appeared to descend upon a new dispensation. Of course, this new dispensation's fortunes declined when the Allies facilitated the return of the French. In the renewed contest, however, the Vietnamese people were unlikely to see the mandate restored to the emperor, whom the French again tried to set up as their surrogate. The issue became one of whether the Communists and their allies in the Viet Minh could consolidate their claim to the mantle of legitimacy.

In this struggle for legitimacy the competitor that demonstrates that it completely replaces the discredited order makes the most successful claim. Collaboration with the French or their American successors discredited potential alternatives to the Viet Minh and later the National Liberation Front. A failure to provide a well-defined plan for reestablishing balance in the countryside diminished the position of the sects that also arose in response to the dislocations of colonial modernization. In contrast, because the Communists went "beyond the partial political programs of their competitors and tried determinedly, though not always successfully, to grapple with the symbols and idiom of traditionalist politics, they [had] the most effective revolutionary movement in Viet Nam."[23]

The Communists began to outperform their rivals in the religious movements only after they muted or abandoned the more doctrinaire elements of Marxist class analysis.[24] After 1940 Ho Chi Minh transformed himself from a "cosmopolitan ideologue" into a "backwoods insurrectionist."[25] By forming a nationalist front—the Viet Minh—the Communists recognized the importance of ethnic identity and national liberation. The modified version of socialism put forth by the Viet Minh was consistent with the communalism and hierarchy that characterized Vietnamese culture, even though it changed the specific content of both ownership and rule.[26] The military victories won over the French and later the Saigon government further reinforced their claim as the successor regime.

The deprivation experienced by many sectors of the Vietnamese population, from a disequilibrium perspective, represent more than an aggregation of individual frustration. The deprivations were themselves only symptomatic of the profound disruption wrought by the distorted individualistic and exploitative culture of colonialism. The colonial culture crisis was in some sense irreversible, because restoration of the traditional imperial order was impossible. In this fluid cultural milieu the Communist-led Viet Minh offered the most compelling alternative equilibrium. Their advantage, though, was not absolute, but relative to a weak field of political rivals. Both the French and later the Diem regime demonstrated ample degrees of rigidity, corruption, and incompetence that only worsened their already compromised position.

Disequilibrium, culture crisis, and the revolutionary reconstruction of the social order provide an interesting and largely complementary macroperspective on the deprivation explanation for social upheaval in Vietnam. But this New Revolutionary Order, regardless of how well it resonated with established cultural predilections, represents a public good. Still unanswered is the question of why individual peasants would engage in dangerous collective action in pursuit of even a desirable public good. This question points to a third perspective on the causes of the Vietnamese Revolution.

Reason and Revolution in Vietnam

The general disequilibrium model includes one additional variable contributing to the rise of a revolutionary insurrection—the balance of coercive power between regime and dissidents (see Chapter 6). The relative unity of the contenders reflects their capacity to engage in collective action for a public good, whether revolution or preservation. Recall that a public good generally rewards everyone regardless of their contribution (see Chapter 5). In broad terms both revolution and preservation of the status quo represent public goods. Consequently both the regime and the revolutionaries confront a collective action problem. How can they induce even tacit supporters to make the sacrifices and take the risks of collective action rather than free riding on the efforts of others? The side that most successfully solves the free rider problem possesses a clear competitive advantage over its rivals.

One "solution" to the problem of free riding essentially assumes it away. It posits the existence of a collective identity overriding individual self-interest. Collective identity produces collective action for the public good. Unfortunately, despite myths about the organic unity of the peasant village, most peasants were and are sufficiently self interested to resist making sacrifices for the collective good. Even the Communists recognized that peasants often resisted making individual contributions to the community.[27] As Samuel Popkin observes, "Collective action requires more than consensus or even intensity of need [the bases of the cultural disequilibrium and the relative deprivation explanations]. It requires conditions under which peasants will find it in their individual interests to allocate resources to their common interests and not be free riders."[28] Popkin does not deny that some people contribute out of altruism or solidarity, but he argues that the Viet Minh and their successors in the South, the NLF, also manipulated a range of specific incentives to induce collective action.

The Communists drew upon a variety of selective incentives to mobilize their potential supporters for collective action.[29] Some of the collective projects they undertook, like cooperative planting and harvesting schemes, could restrict their benefits to their participants. Such projects, though, confront another variation of the free rider problem—shirking in a cooperative project. Revolutionary organizations in the villages monitored for defections and shirking. In addition, the revolutionary movement used coercion to punish both supporters of the regime and defectors among their own followers. Again, we must remember that the need for coercion does not, by itself, disprove the existence of general feelings of allegiance. Passive supporters also require prodding, rewards or punishments, to offset their inclination to free ride or shirk.

The Communists also developed selective incentives clearly contingent on the continued success of the overall movement.[30] Policies of land reform, progressive taxation, and other forms of economic redistribution, for example, depended on the survival of revolutionary control in a particular area. Similarly, the new revolutionary system of power and status in the village, involving the expulsion or execution of corrupt officials and moneylenders, presumed the continued exclusion of government forces. Finally, the movement provided protection from the depredations of the government, like conscription or forced labor, in exchange for cooperation with revolutionary projects.

In all these cases the individual beneficiaries linked their personal success with the continued success of the revolutionary movement. As one Vietnamese observed, "If the communists were to go and the government to come back, the peasants would return to their former status as slaves. Consequently they must fight to preserve their interests and their lives, as well as their political power."[31] As Jeffrey Race notes, the most significant aspect about these contingent incentives is that "the contingency itself was lent by the government."[32] By rigidly adhering to its policies of exploitation, the government ensured the loyalty and participation of the beneficiaries of the revolution.

☙   ☙   ☙

The deprivation and disequilibrium approaches help define the context of the revolution in Vietnam, but they cannot adequately account for the motivation of the revolutionary participants. Revolution, especially of the Eastern variety with its prolonged warfare, requires sustained political activity. Neither the anger produced by frustration nor the experience of a disequilibrated social world adequately explains sustained revolutionary activity. Unfortunately, the argument that the manipulation of selective incentives helps to account for such action begs additional questions. Clearly, leadership, organization, and resources help overcome the free rider problem. But why did the movement enjoy a comparative advantage in these areas?

To answer this question, we must further examine the contributions of leaders, ideology, organization, and strategy in the Vietnamese Revolution. We must remember, however, that the revolutionary movement did not have to achieve perfection. It only needed to outperform the government.[33]

UNDERSTANDING THE VIETNAMESE REVOLUTION— LEADERS, IDEOLOGY, AND ORGANIZATION

Leaders and Ideology in the Vietnamese Revolution

Quality leadership can overcome the free rider problem. Leadership quality, though, depends on something more than the concrete resources particular leaders control. Obviously, the availability of selective incentives constitutes an important part of successful leadership, particularly of a transactional sort. Resources alone, however, do not guarantee quality leadership. At the very least, some leaders demonstrate greater skill at maximizing the returns from the concrete selective incentives at their disposal.

Leadership occurs in a cultural context that affects how potential followers assess the credibility of presumptive leaders. Even the most concrete threat or promise involves some judgment of credibility, for the followers must believe that the leaders can and will do what they say. More credible leaders thereby gain an advantage over their less credible rivals, even though the latter may possess more concrete resources.[34] Leaders gain credibility by their ability to relate to the values and aspirations of their potential followers or through their ability to generate follower identification with new values. We labeled the former pattern of leadership catalytic/representational and the latter charismatic (see Chapter 7). In practice the two types of leadership (or leader/follower relationship) merge and mix. Taken together, they reinforce the efficacy of leadership based on selective incentives (transactional).

The relative success of first the Viet Minh and later the National Liberation Front involved more than their ability to manipulate selective incentives. The concrete programs of material improvement and coercive action took on greater efficacy because of the values represented by the revolutionary movement. At the same time, these concrete programs reinforced the ideological position of the movement. Ideology, then, can contribute more than a sense of collective solidarity, transcending the free rider problem by modifying the rational egoist. It also can reinforce the effectiveness of the more concrete solutions to the problem of collective action.

The efficacy of revolutionary leadership, in particular, depends on turning a neat trick. On one hand the followers must see the leader as relevant to their situation, needs, values, and aspirations. On the other, a revolutionary leader must take the existing dispositions of the followers and point them toward a new formulation. If leaders reflect the restricted visions of their followers too closely, they will fail to create something new. If the leaders represent ideas too alien to their potential followers, they will fail to attract much support.

Any revolution in rural Vietnam had to involve the peasants. Initial rebellions against French rule involved rural areas and local elites, but they remained isolated and relatively ineffective and were ultimately crushed. Later, in the 1920s and 1930s, both Marxist and non-Marxist elements organized in the cities and rallied around banners of protest remote from peasant interests. The French successfully repressed these nascent resistance movements as well. As long as the Communists used only a materialist class-based ideology, they failed to make many inroads among the peasants. Once they added cultural themes of ethnic and national identity, they began to provide a more credible vision of the future.[35] Ho Chi Minh demonstrated the genius of his leadership by modifying doctrinaire Communism to form a synthesis of antifeudal principles with a new form of national consciousness.[36]

Ho sought to draw upon the traditional strength and cohesiveness of the peasant village to create a firm foundation for both liberation and revolution.

By using old, persistent concepts, he created the framework for a new spirit of community based on totally new values. His purpose was to link the villagers to a new sense of Viet Nam as a nation by making their traditions relevant to participation in the modern politics of revolution. Instead of the extremely limited participation in politics characteristic of Viet Nam's Confucian kingdoms, Ho wanted mass involvement, and to get it he had to persuade villagers to accept new values by linking them to familiar traditions.[37]

As instructors in this synthesis of the old and the new, the Communist cadres played the role traditionally occupied by the Confucian scholars in the rural areas. They erased the old feudal mandarinate but then filled the social space so created with something functionally familiar. Like the revolutionary scholars of old, the cadres sequestered themselves "in the villages teaching and organizing the peasants over a period of many long years, until the time of land reform and the establishment of agricultural cooperatives. By doing so they raised the peasant struggle to a much higher level, opening it up to entirely new perspectives."[38]

The bearing and behavior of the Communist cadres, up to and including Ho Chi Minh, reinforced the credibility of their synthesized doctrine of liberation and revolution. The relative asceticism and honesty of the cadres reinforced the prestige of the revolutionary leaders. In the simplest terms, honest, self-abnegating leaders more easily convince their followers that contributions will go for the declared purposes. The leaders will not siphon them off for personal enrichment.[39]

Ho probably developed something of a charismatic relation with many of his followers.[40] His cosmopolitan career included travel to America, Europe, and Russia, efforts to place Indochinese independence on the agenda at the Paris Peace Conference in 1919, participation in the founding of the French Communist party, and service in the Comintern (the Communist International) in the 1920s and 1930s. His periods of arrest, exile, wanderings, and return replicate the cycle of a mythic hero (see Chapter 7). On his first return in 1930, he was instrumental in the founding of the Vietnamese Communist party out of several rival Marxist factions. On his second return, in 1941, he brought about the transformation of the Communist Party into the leader of the new nationalist front, the Viet Minh. He demonstrated repeatedly his ability to adapt and recover from setbacks. Many of his immediate subordinates, like General Vo Nguyen Giap, clearly possessed great faith in his leadership. For many ordinary Vietnamese, he embodied national aspirations and possessed extraordinary stature.

The Viet Minh successfully snatched the symbols of national liberation from their potential competitors, and, of course, faced little ideological competition from the French. After the departure of the French the situation grew more complex. Diem, for all his shortcomings, was a genuine nationalist, and South Vietnam was a nominally sovereign state. Ho Chi Minh retained preeminent status as the nationalist leader who brought independence to Vietnam, but the unifying ideological impetus for the renewed struggle in the South differed from that in the original war against the French. The character of the enemy—the French and their puppets—gave clarity to the nationalist goals of the first war. In the second war the national liberation struggle involved a less clear enemy, the nominally independent Saigon regime and the American "neocolonialists," and a less tangible goal, reunification. Although the steady increase in the American presence after 1960 reinforced the nationalist claims of the NLF, the ideological message probably never achieved the clarity of the 1945–1954 period.

The revolutionary movement never monopolized the political field in either period. In quantitative terms their opponents often possessed superior economic and coercive transactional resources. Yet while ideology and deportment enhanced the credibility of the revolutionary leadership, the ideas and actions of their opponents contributed to their own undoing. The creation of a pseudo-independent regime under the discredited emperor, Bao Dai, failed to compensate for the inherently weak value position of the French colonialists. Those Vietnamese who supported the struggle against the Viet Minh because of their Francophile values, Catholic religion, or economic privilege were clearly alienated from the mass of the Vietnamese peasants. The corrupt behavior of many officials of the subsequent Saigon regime, especially when combined with policies favoring the wealthy landholders, contrasted unfavorably with the actions of the revolutionaries.

The official doctrine of the Diem regime—personalism—contributed to the regime's ideological futility. Personalism was an obscure European philosophy originally conceived as an alternative to the materialism of both capitalism and Marxism. Advocated by Ngo Dinh Nhu, the powerful brother of President Diem, the doctrine remained incomprehensible to the Vietnamese peasants and essentially irrelevant to their condition.[41] Although the Diem regime claimed to be nationalist, it remained aloof from the lives of the peasants and often hostile to their interests. The Communists, in contrast, tried with some success to express the abstract ideas of national liberation in the context of particular community interests (for example, land reform and debt forgiveness).

Culture and values, then, play a role in the resolution of the collective action problem. The development of a shared perspective on the world contributes to the formation of collective identity capable of prompting sacrifice for the larger group. The merger of old and new values may galvanize people into new social forms and actions. In addition, the development of shared values and objectives enhances the credibility of the leaders and thereby their ability to manipulate selective incentives for collective action. Alternatively, values and actions that exclude and alienate people undermine the effectiveness of the concrete incentives offered by leaders. In these areas of political competition the edge goes to the Communist revolutionaries and their supporters. The development of their organization and the implementation of their strategy and tactics illustrate how they exploited their advantage.

Organizing the Revolution

In formal terms the revolutionary movement combined elite-vanguard and mass-democratic forms. The Communist Party, in its various incarnations, remained a vanguardist model, emphasizing revolutionary discipline and dedication. On the other hand, the Communists worked through liberation front organizations that strove to involve broad sectors of the population—workers, peasants, students, women, small tradespeople, and so forth—in the liberation struggle. By giving liberation priority over radical reconstruction, the Communists demonstrated their willingness to mute doctrine to achieve their fundamental goals. (When we discuss the consequences of revolution in the final chapter, we will see that after their victories in 1954 and 1975 the Communists tended to revert to more doctrinaire ways.) Moreover, given the necessities of an insurgent struggle, the revolutionary organization of peasant resistance devolved into a movement allowing for considerable local autonomy and initiative and strove to embed itself in the villages.

In 1945 the Viet Minh faced the problem of what to do with the village councils of notables. The French colonial administration, as we noted earlier, essentially destroyed these councils, particularly in Tonkin, by replacing traditional with elected membership. In 1941 Bao Dai restored their former powers to the traditional councils. When the Viet Minh began to organize these villages in the mid-1940s, they had to determine the future of these councils. They decided to eliminate them in favor of new village committees based on a reconstructed system of social status.[42] Landlords and local mandarins lost out in favor of peasants and rural workers. In this way the Communists combined traditional village autonomy with a revolutionized system of values.

Race provides a detailed analysis of how the Communists "outorganized" the government in one province—Long An—between 1959 and 1964. The details of this district organization represent in microcosm the overall success of the revolutionary movement in both stages of the insurgency. Race identifies three critical differences between the revolutionary and the government organizations: different goals, different numerical strength, and different centers of authority.[43]

Race observes that the revolutionaries always judged their organizations on the basis of how each "contributed to the goal of political activity, that is, to the manipulation of contradictions so as to create and support [revolutionary] forces." The government, in contrast, largely focused on administering central policy, most of which, like tax collection, rent enforcement, or conscription, tended to aggravate the peasants' conflict with the government.[44] "Consequently, the more 'effective' local government was—from the viewpoint of the central government, not the local community—the more it aided the party in its goal of altering the balance of forces against the government."[45]

Revolutionary organizations also enjoyed numerical superiority at the village level—"the only level of social significance in rural Vietnam."[46] In one village he studied, for example, Race noted that before the Communists drove them out, a five-member council plus five hamlet chiefs represented the local government. A fifteen-person party branch replaced these. By the time the organization was fully developed, forty more villagers were active in front organizations. In addition the revolutionaries formed a locally based platoon of guerrillas.[47]

Finally, the revolutionaries located authority at the village level to a greater extent than the government. For the government, province and district chiefs were the loci of decision making. In contrast, the village party branch "was the most important echelon and the one at which the initial and usually the binding decisions were made. For example, in such matters as taxation, justice, military recruitment, and land redistribution, a Party village secretary had as much and often far more authority than a government province chief."[48]

The revolutionary movement in Long An, therefore, "structured its forces so that they were inextricably bound into the social fabric of rural communities by ties of family, friendship, and common interest."[49] The survival of these local organizations in turn depended on their continued responsiveness to the community. Otherwise, the villagers could cut off their supplies or betray them to the government. Consequently, the local party branch attempted "to develop bonds of loyalty between individuals and the local community leadership on the basis of the latter's ability to resolve concrete local issues of importance in the peasant's life: land, taxation, protection from impressment into the national army, or a personally satisfying role in the activities of the community."[50] Government organizations, in comparison, generally failed to develop roots in the village and remained dominated by urban interests and personnel.

STRATEGY AND TACTICS IN THE REVOLUTIONARY PROCESS

The comparative advantages enjoyed by the Vietnamese revolutionaries reflected their superior strategic understanding of the problem of revolution. Even though they periodically committed serious tactical blunders, the underlying soundness of their revolutionary strategy allowed for recovery. Their opponents, whether the

French, the Diem regime and its successors, or the Americans, never adjusted their fundamentally flawed strategic assumptions of counterrevolution. The frustrated Americans stalled the revolutionary victory in 1965 by resorting to the massive application of military power, essentially shoving the Saigon regime into the background. The mounting cost in terms of blood, treasure, and political unity at home, however, ultimately forced American withdrawal under the guise of "Vietnamization." Once the war became essentially a Vietnamese affair after 1973, the rootless Saigon regime quickly fell.

The Strategy of Revolutionary Victory

Revolutionaries, particularly those involved in a prolonged struggle, confront a more complex strategic problem than the one faced by the contenders in a conventional war (see Chapter 9). They cannot merely defend; they must replace. They cannot merely destroy; they must build. Only by replacing the organizations of the existing regime can they successfully defend themselves from regime reprisals. Only by building their own base can the revolutionaries acquire the resources to attack and destroy the regime. Offense and defense, destruction and construction interact in complex relations.

The Vietnamese revolutionary struggle continued for decades and went through different adversaries, phases, and problems. By focusing on the period of the second insurgency (1961–1965), we identify some of the characteristic advantages enjoyed by the revolutionary strategy. Race's detailed analysis of Communist success in Long An province during this period provides, perhaps, the best analysis of their revolutionary strategy.

Before the renewed armed struggle in 1959, repressive actions by the Diem regime badly mauled the revolutionary sympathizers and apparatus remaining in Long An. Yet after 1959 the National Liberation Front made rapid progress, until it controlled most of the province by the end of 1964. Government troops, of course, still periodically moved through the rural areas in force, but the guerrillas exercised effective control most of the time.

Race attributes the revolutionaries' success not so much to their military as to their social strategy.[51] Revolutionary military strategy entails the application of force in pursuit of both political and military objectives. The social strategy produces the resources needed to implement the military strategy. Military success, of course, reinforces the social strategy, but only if the social strategy makes sense by itself. Race characterizes the revolutionary social strategy as strongly *preemptive* in character because it pursued "policies to preclude the government from motivating [the] social classes comprising the great majority of the country's population."[52] Revolutionary programs to redistribute wealth, status, and power in the villages and hamlets of Vietnam "ensured that when the conflict crossed into the military phase the majority of the population would choose to fight against the government in defense of its own interests, or at least not choose to fight against the revolution."[53] The social programs and political organization that expanded the political base of the revolutionaries in the rural areas, then, contributed to both defensive and offensive successes.

Defense entails eroding the regime's ability to mount effective attacks while at the same time reducing the vulnerability of the movement to such attacks. The revolutionaries recognized that strategic defense involves more than the concentration of military power to protect an objective. "There is a logical contradiction in 'concentrating one's forces everywhere,' because concentration means centralizing dispersed forces in a limited number of locations."[54] The regime often foundered on this contradiction by attempting to defend extensive lines of communication, urban centers, and territory through purely military means. The forces at the regime's disposal were never sufficient to secure everything militarily.

Strategic security, in contrast, arises from a "sympathetic environment" composed primarily of neutral and supportive people.[55] The blows suffered by the Communist apparatus in the South after the Geneva agreement underlined the significance of strategic security.[56] Initially the North Vietnamese regime expected the elections in the near future and wished to avoid any military provocation that might upset this schedule. Diem, as we noted, consolidated his power in the South, ignored the election requirement, and turned his attention to the remaining Viet Minh apparatus. Most effectively, the government expanded its network of village officials, local administrators, and local police, creating a hostile environment for the quiescent revolutionary forces. In the short term the revolutionary forces suffered serious losses. In the longer term the initial lack of resistance placed the onus of violent repression on the Diem regime. Moreover, the imposition of central control and the reinforcement of the power and position of the landed elites over the villages often served to heighten feelings of resentment among the majority of the peasants.

When the North Vietnamese party leadership finally unfettered the cadres in the South, they knew well whom to strike. The terrorist tactics with which violent resistance began in 1959 were carefully controlled to produce maximum disruption of the government's administrative and political network. Government officials and supporters confronted the choice of either cooperating with the revolutionaries, leaving the hamlets and villages for the more secure towns in the district, or being killed. In this way revolutionaries drove unsympathetic elements from the countryside. In combination with the preemptive social strategy, the initial phase of the armed struggle in the South rooted the insurgency in the rural areas before the movement possessed the tactical capability to challenge the forces of the regime in direct combat. The supportive, or at least neutral, population helped to protect the revolutionary operatives from regime repression while at the same time serving as a source of intelligence on regime activities.

The Strategy of Regime Defeat

The Diem regime during this period did not lack for a strategy. Rather than drifting rudderless, Diem steered directly onto the rocks. He followed a political and social strategy that reinforced the narrow base of his regime and further alienated it from the mass of the rural population. He followed a military strategy intended to secure his regime from factional rivals rather than from the revolutionary threat. American economic and military aid, given with the intention of winning the "hearts and minds" of the people, securing the countryside, and enhancing the effectiveness of the regime, proved unable to reverse Diem's decline.

Diem essentially followed what Race terms a "reinforcement strategy."[57] Michael Shafer, in an analysis of the failures of the Diem regime, also notes that the political and military policies implemented by the regime maintained the status quo where a rather narrow coalition of elites held economic and political power.

> Thus, in Saigon Diem inherited a "national assembly" whose function was not representation, but cooptation of the powerful. Similarly, in the countryside his administrators . . . depended on local elites to maintain order, collect taxes, and supply conscripts. This wedded Diem to the existing local economic and political power structure and tied his interests to those of the village and provincial notables.[58]

By basing his power on the prevailing elite structure, Diem preserved and even enhanced the existing social contradictions in the villages that the revolutionaries then exploited to secure their political base.

To make matters worse, Diem concentrated his attention on protecting his position within the existing power structure rather than developing an effective government.[59] In practice this meant that he appointed relatives to the most sensitive positions and favored Catholics and other refugees from the North throughout the government. Consequently, even southerners hostile to the Communists, like the powerful Buddhist community, began to defect from the regime. He set elements of the bureaucracy off against one another to ensure that they could not conspire against him, a policy that eroded administrative effectiveness. Finally, he tolerated considerable corruption in the hope that no one benefiting from the system would attack it.

Diem most feared a coup d'état. Therefore, his primary military strategy aimed at defeating this threat, even if this hampered the struggle against the rapidly growing challenge from the National Liberation Front. He gave orders to his commanders to avoid engagements where they risked significant casualties. He was convinced, with some reason, that high casualties would weaken the loyalty of the army and encourage conspiracies against him.[60] To further frustrate such conspiracies

> he attacked the chain of command, creating overlapping jurisdictions, multiple channels of communication with the palace, and bypassing the chief of staff altogether. Similarly, he promoted interservice rivalries and civil-military conflicts. Finally, he manipulated the promotion system to weed out charismatic, independent officers and reward Catholics, displaced Northerners, relatives, and loyal incompetents. . . .[61]

These measures helped maintain Diem in power until the end of October 1963. They also eviscerated the effectiveness of the army. Moreover, the military's rapid growth, leading to increased forced conscription and the militarization of rural administration through programs like the strategic hamlets, further reinforced popular hostility. The military increasingly behaved like an army of occupation rather than a defender of the people.[62] Consequently, American policy to strengthen the security of the government of South Vietnam and enhance its military power had an effect opposite to the one intended. Enhancing the security of this onerous status quo undermined the well-being of those to whom the Communists appealed, furthering their social strategy to secure a firm political base of support.

The final irony of this failed strategy emerged when the Americans, tiring of Diem's intransigence and incompetence, sanctioned a coup against him on November 1, 1963. They hoped to replace Diem with an effective military leader, but instead the regime disintegrated. "With the kingpin gone, the palace politics system flew apart, flinging the once carefully counterbalanced factions into violent confrontation. In the melee, there were only losers. What little stability had existed disappeared, and with it the little military, political, and economic capacity the [government] possessed."[63] Seeing an opportunity, the North Vietnamese escalated the conflict, infiltrating some of their own regular troops south. These forces, along with the expanding military capabilities of the NLF, pushed the Saigon regime to the brink. The only choice for the Americans was to walk away or take direct charge of the war. Fatefully for all sides, the Americans took charge.

The Emblems of Strategic Failure: Defeats at Dienbienphu and Ap Bac

Neither the French nor the Saigon regime ever fully understood the nature of the revolutionary challenge they faced nor how their own limitations contributed to revolutionary success. Strategic failure eventually led to tactical defeats. In some sense the real revolutionary victory consisted of the increasing consolidation of political control over the rural population. Nonetheless, we tend to think of wars in terms of battles fought and won, even though in revolutionary war a military victory usually follows a multitude of small political victories. In each of the two insurgencies in Vietnam a battle stands out as emblematic of the regime's strategic political defeat.

The battle of Dienbienphu represents the culmination of the French underestimation of the Viet Minh.[64] They miscalculated Viet Minh intentions, strategy, and capabilities. The French believed that by building a base in a remote highland valley they could penetrate their enemy's rear. They believed that the Viet Minh could not concentrate their forces sufficiently to challenge their paratroops at this base. Most concretely they believed the Viet Minh could not move artillery into the mountains overlooking the French fortifications. They were wrong on all counts.

General Giap, the Viet Minh's military commander, specifically selected Dienbienphu for destruction. Negotiations were beginning with France to end the war, and the Communists wanted a decisive military victory to improve their bargaining position. He deliberately staged diversionary attacks around the country to create the impression of dispersal and to tie down the French forces. Finally, he moved 33 infantry battalions, 6 artillery regiments, and a regiment of engineers to the area around Dienbienphu. His soldiers dragged dozens of cannon up into the mountains overlooking the camp. By the time the battle started in March 1954 the Viet Minh outnumbered the French by more than five to one. Their artillery made the airstrip useless, and overcast weather at this time of year inhibited the effective use of air power.[65] When the French finally surrendered on May 7, they had suffered their most humiliating defeat of the eight-year war.

In the second insurgency a much smaller battle demonstrated the political and military weaknesses of the Saigon regime. For years the South Vietnamese military and their American advisers avowed that if only the stealthy guerrillas would "stand and fight," Saigon's forces would readily win. Whatever the emotional appeal of such a claim, this complaint misses the point. In the early stages of an insurgency guerrillas never stand and fight superior forces, at least if they want to survive. The guerrillas were biding their time, building their forces, and adjusting their tactics to take account of the increased reliance of the South Vietnamese Army on helicopters and armored personnel carriers (APCs). Finally, in January 1963, 350 guerrillas did decide to stand and fight in a rural area known as Ap Bac.[66]

John Paul Vann, the American military adviser working with the local Vietnamese commander, planned the battle to cut off the line of guerrilla retreat, while vastly superior Vietnamese forces engaged in a frontal attack designed to destroy the enemy. The guerrillas, possessing only rifles, light machine guns, and one useless mortar, were outgunned by the South Vietnamese with their helicopters, APCs, and artillery. But the guerrillas stood their ground. They shot down several helicopters and then immobilized the APCs sent to root them out. A Vietnamese captain commanding an APC company hesitated to advance because Diem had recently transferred his company from divisional to central Saigon command as a bit of extra coup insurance. Consequently, the lines of authority for ordering a risky attack were typically murky. Vann, enraged, told the American adviser with the company to "shoot that rotten, cowardly son of a bitch right now and move out."[67] The adviser finally persuaded the Vietnamese to work their way cautiously toward their objective from a different direction. When darkness fell, the guerrillas still held their tree line. Then the local Vietnamese commander essentially allowed them to retreat with their wounded, rather than have his troops fight to contain them in the darkness.

This confrontation epitomized the worsening coercive position of the regime. On one side, the numerically and materially superior Saigon forces fought poorly, despite the urgings of their American advisers. Confused lines of command and responsibility hindered a coordinated attack. Fear of excessive losses limited the willingness to take any risks and encouraged the government troops to allow the guerrillas to slip away. The guerrillas, in contrast, were well led, fought bravely, maintained discipline in the face of frightening odds, maximized the effect of their limited arms, and ultimately inflicted nearly four times the casualties that they absorbed. The defeat demonstrated to Vann that the war was being lost, and that material aid and advice alone would not reverse the decline.

The years immediately following the defeat at Ap Bac brought the Americanization of the Vietnamese revolutionary civil war. The consequences of this Americanization were bitter for all parties. The United States poured tens of billions of dollars, over 55,000 American lives, and a considerable amount of the credibility and integrity of its domestic political institutions into a futile struggle. Unable to invest the resources needed to break a bloody stalemate, the Americans ultimately withdrew and then watched as their proxy regime fell to the North Vietnamese armies.

The North Vietnamese, though they survived, found themselves pounded in a devastating war and won a largely Pyrrhic victory. Perhaps the only thing worse than the costly victory won by the North Vietnamese was the costly defeat suffered by the South Vietnamese regime. And, of course, the Vietnamese peasants, in whose name the revolution and war were fought, gained not the glorious liberation promised on that wonderful day in Hanoi 30 years earlier, but a devastated country, an exhausted authoritarian government, and a future clouded by the continuing enmity of the United States.

NOTES

1. The literature on Vietnam, North and South, is vast. An excellent history of the Vietnamese wars is provided by Stanley Karnow, *Vietnam: A History* (New York: Penguin Books, 1984). A good introduction to the history of the period under consideration is Roy Jumper and Marjorie Weiner Normand, "Vietnam," in George McTurnan Kahin, ed., *Governments and Politics of Southeast Asia,* Second Edition (Ithaca, N.Y.: Cornell University Press, 1964), pp. 373–524. I base this review of history on these two sources as well as James DeFronzo, *Revolutions and Revolutionary Movements* (Boulder, Colo.: Westview Press, 1991), pp. 103–128.
2. Jumper and Normand, p. 383.
3. Ibid., p. 390.
4. John T. McAlister, Jr., and Paul Mus, *The Vietnamese and Their Revolution* (New York: Harper Torchbooks, 1970), p. 68.
5. Neil Sheehan, *A Bright Shining Lie: John Paul Vann and America in Vietnam* (New York: Random House, 1988), pp. 197–198.
6. The classic theoretic statement of this process is in Karl W. Deutsch, "Social Mobilization and Political Development," *American Political Science Review,* 55 (September 1961): 493–514.
7. McAlister and Mus, pp. 55–57.
8. For a description of the consequences of the French economic policies see Eric R. Wolf, *Peasant Wars of the Twentieth Century* (New York: Harper Colophon, 1973), pp. 165–171.
9. Karnow, p. 117.
10. Wolf, p. 166.
11. Ibid., pp. 167–169.
12. Karnow, p. 118.
13. Wolf, pp. 178–179.
14. This summary of Diem's major mistakes is based on Karnow, pp. 230–237.
15. Ibid., p. 230.
16. Ibid., pp. 230–231.
17. Ibid., p. 257.
18. This interpretation of the situation in Vietnam owes something to the "moral economy" approach associated with scholars like Wolf, cited above, and James C. Scott, *The Moral Economy of the Peasant: Rebellion and Subsistence in Southeast Asia* (New Haven, Conn.: Yale University Press, 1976). In this section, though, I am primarily drawing on the book by McAlister and Mus cited earlier.

19. McAlister and Mus, pp. 31–40.
20. Ibid., p. 36.
21. Ibid., p. 61.
22. Ibid., p. 65.
23. Ibid., pp. 114–115.
24. Samuel Popkin, *The Rational Peasant: The Political Economy of Rural Society in Vietnam* (Berkeley: University of California Press, 1979), p. 261.
25. Alexander Woodside, *Community and Revolution in Modern Vietnam* (Boston: Houghton Mifflin, 1976), p. 220.
26. McAlister and Mus, pp. 116–119.
27. Popkin, p. 252.
28. Ibid., p. 253.
29. For a general discussion see ibid., pp. 252–266.
30. Jeffrey Race, *War Comes to Long An: Revolutionary Conflict in a Vietnamese Province* (Berkeley: University of California Press, 1972), pp. 174–176.
31. Quoted in ibid., p. 175.
32. Ibid.
33. Ibid., p. xv.
34. Cf. Popkin, pp. 259–260.
35. Ibid., p. 261.
36. Race, p. 40.
37. McAlister and Mus, p. 24.
38. Nguyen Khac Vien, *Tradition and Revolution in Vietnam* (Washington, D.C.: Indochina Resource Center, 1974), p. 46.
39. Popkin, p. 261.
40. The basic biography of Ho Chi Minh is that of Jean Lacouture, *Ho Chi Minh: A Political Biography* (New York: Random House, 1968).
41. Karnow, p. 265.
42. McAlister and Mus, pp. 58–59.
43. Race, p. 159.
44. Ibid., pp. 159–160.
45. Ibid., p. 160.
46. Ibid., p. 160.
47. Ibid.
48. Ibid., p. 161.
49. Ibid., p. 177.
50. Ibid., p. 179.
51. Ibid., pp. 149–150.
52. Ibid., p. 150.
53. Ibid.
54. Ibid., p. 146.
55. Ibid., pp. 146–147.
56. See ibid., pp. 181–184.
57. Ibid., pp. 155–159.
58. D. Michael Shafer, *Deadly Paradigms: The Failure of U.S. Counter Insurgency Policy* (Princeton, N.J.: Princeton University Press, 1988), p. 255.
59. Ibid., pp. 255–256.
60. Sheehan, pp. 122–125.
61. Shafer, p. 257.
62. Ibid.
63. Ibid., p. 271.

64. Karnow, pp. 189–191.
65. Ibid., pp. 190–198.
66. The account that follows is a brief summary of a detailed analysis in Sheehan, pp. 203–265.
67. Ibid., pp. 233, 236.

11

Iran: The Irony of Revolution[*]

On January 16, 1979, Muhammad Reza Shah fled Iran never to return. His departure marked the end of the Pahlavi dynasty, founded over 50 years earlier by his father. Though serious problems had buffeted the Shah for several years, the apparently rapid demise of his regime caught observers by surprise. Perhaps the most surprised was the Shah himself. As late as June 1978 he had proclaimed, "Nobody can overthrow me. I have the support of 700,000 troops, all of the workers, and most of the people."[1] He left behind a country united in opposition to his continued rule but divided in many other ways. The collapse of the Shah's regime ended the first phase of the Iranian Revolution; the second phase involved the struggle to fill the power vacuum left by his flight.

In many ways the Iranian Revolution follows the Western pattern or model (see Chapter 6).[2] Like the revolutions in France and Russia, the Iranian Revolution overthrew an authoritarian monarch. The old regime collapsed relatively quickly before any clear institutional alternative emerged. The abbreviated struggle to overthrow the regime inflicted far fewer casualties than the bitter losses associated with prolonged Eastern-style revolutionary warfare. Initially, moderate and radical forces contended to fill the power vacuum, but, as often occurs, extremist elements proved to possess the more effective organization and a more ruthless drive for power. The competition to consolidate power in the postrevolutionary era, according to the Western pattern, often leads to an intensified use of terror and sometimes degenerates into a civil war. Iran, though spared a full-scale civil war, experienced a period of severe internal disturbances. A harsh system of revolutionary justice eventually crushed all opposition to the radical regime. Finally, after a period of "rule by the saints," the revolution in Iran seemed to tack off in a more pragmatic, if not truly moderate, direction. Again, such a moderation trend appears consistent with the Western model of revolution.

Although the Iranian Revolution resembles the Western pattern more closely than the Eastern, it includes some important variations. The Shah, though an authoritarian monarch, was no traditionalist. He pursued policies of economic and social modernization that alienated his regime from both the landed elites and traditional religious leaders. These two sectors usually stand as firm pillars

---

[*] With the assistance of Michael J. Edwards, David M. Tefft, and Trey Turner

of support for traditional monarchs. Moreover, some of the forces challenging his rule possessed strong organizations and did not awaken like stunned children to find the political house empty.[3] The Islamic fundamentalists who ultimately prevailed in the post-Pahlavi power struggle possessed a powerful organizational base and a clear idea of the new order they wished to create. Moreover, this power struggle did not simply pit extremists against moderates. Conflict between religious and secular values complicated the division between moderates and extremists. Lastly, though the regime may be less doctrinaire, Muslim clerics still dominate political life. Perceived regime "moderation" arises more from the contrast with previous political attitudes than any resemblance to the expectations of Western secular democracy.

The Western form of the Iranian revolutionary process ironically contrasts with the anti-Western content of the revolutionary outcome. Western revolutions culminate in the triumph of secular rationalists, whether of a liberal or a Marxist sort. The Iranian Revolution, in contrast, brought to power a religiously based regime hostile to both types of Western values. This contrast between form and content suggests at least two puzzles. First, what contributed to the fall of the Shah? Second, what explains the victory of the Islamic fundamentalists? The disequilibrium approach seems pertinent to the first puzzle. The opportunity/resource approach offers a useful way to address both issues. The tactics of confrontation also differed from those of consolidation. Before exploring these problems, however, we first provide some background to the collapse of the Shah's regime.

BACKGROUND TO REVOLUTION[4]

Four factors, combining in volatile ways, provide clues to the underlying causes of the Iranian Revolution: nationalism, Islamic political revival, uneven development, and destabilizing demographic trends. In addition a number of short-term accelerators heightened the crisis of the late 1970s: economic "stagflation," regime ineptitude, elite division and defection, ambiguous support from the Shah's external patron, the United States, and the Shah's own combination of grandiose pretensions and personal weakness.

Long-Term Causes

Nationalism   Iran's strategic position in the Middle East helped make it a center of power and a focus for power struggles for three thousand years. Lying north of the Persian Gulf, bordered by Pakistan and Afghanistan to the east, Azerbaijan, Armenia, and Turkmenistan to the north, and Turkey and Iraq to the west, Iran straddles the land routes between South Asia and the Middle East. The wealth and power generated by this position made Iran through the years both a contender with and a target of powerful neighbors. Sometimes conqueror, as with the ancient Persian and Parthian empires (550 B.C. to 330 B.C. and 247 B.C. to A.D. 224, respectively), and sometimes conquered (by Alexander the Great in 330 B.C. and by the Arabs in the seventh century A.D.), Iran has seldom been ignored.

Although Islamic and Middle Eastern, Iran is not part of the Arab world, and therefore calls for pan-Arab unity have never included Iran. A majority of the population speak Persian, while the Turkish-speaking minority makes up another 25 percent. Other minorities include the Kurds and some Arabs. The historical and cultural pedigree of the Persian people contributes to a distinctiveness that sets them apart from their neighbors.

In the nineteenth century, Iran (called Persia until the twentieth century) became the focus of the "great game" of geopolitics played between Russia and Great Britain. Great Britain, jealous of the security of its imperial "jewel," India, constantly strove to stymie the southward expansion of the Russian Empire. The discovery of significant oil deposits in the twentieth century served to reinforce great power interest in Iran's internal politics. Though never formally incorporated into any European empire, partly because the rivalry between Russia and Britain ensured that neither could directly colonize the territory without risking the strong response of the other, Iranians grew to resent what they saw as the undue influence exercised by these foreign powers.

After the Bolshevik Revolution in 1917, the British became alarmed over the renewed threat to their imperial holdings. Fearing that Communism might spread to Iran and infect India as well, the British supported the overthrow of the incompetent Qajar dynasty by Colonel Reza Khan. In 1926 this foreign-supported upstart crowned himself Shah and proclaimed a new dynasty, the Pahlavi.

Reza's rule for the next 15 years resembled that of Kemal Atatürk, his contemporary in Turkey. Like Atatürk, Reza worked to modernize his country and restrict the influence of religion.[5] He developed a secular code of law, limiting the traditional judicial role of the *ulama* (religious clerics). He set up a system of schools and colleges that broke the religious community's near monopoly on education. He improved roads and built railroads and factories. By renegotiating the British oil concession, he gained somewhat better terms for Iran. He also set the precedent of rewarding family and associates with opportunities to enrich themselves by exploiting these new economic opportunities.

In the 1930s Reza flirted with the new Nazi regime in Germany, inviting hundreds of German advisers to assist in various development projects. This flirtation severely compromised Reza's political position, especially after the Nazi invasion of the Soviet Union in 1941. When the Soviets occupied the northern portion of Iran, he feared not only for his own survival, but for that of his young dynasty as well. In a compromise accepted by the British, still suspicious of the intentions of their new Soviet ally, he abdicated in favor of his ill-prepared son, Muhammad Reza. Consequently, foreign involvement tainted the origins of both Pahlavi monarchs.

When the United States emerged as the paramount power after World War II, it assumed the role previously played by Britain, working to check the expansion of Soviet power into this area. As with its other "imperial" activities around the globe, America's involvement in Iran ensured that it would become the target of enmity as nationalist sentiments intensified. The emergence of the National Front government in a resurgent parliament after World War II eroded the power of the young Shah and challenged the special economic interests of both the British and Americans. Assisted by the CIA, the Shah worked to oust the

National Front government. His initial attempt in August 1953 to dismiss the National Front premier Mohammad Mosaddeq backfired, and the Shah had to flee. Pro-Pahlavi elements in the army, supported by conservative clerics and merchants, rallied to the Shah's banner and eventually defeated those forces supporting the National Front. Upon returning from his brief exile, the Shah, with CIA assistance, set up his secret police (SAVAK), rewarded his friends, and consolidated his power.

Growing American influence and investment over the next two decades reinforced America's position as the primary focus of nationalist resentment. In 1964 the government of Iran issued a Status of Forces law that epitomized for many Iranians the overweening influence enjoyed by America.[6] This agreement effectively extended diplomatic immunity to American military advisers and their staffs and families, exempting them from prosecution under Iranian law.

This law provoked considerable outrage, to which the Ayatollah Khomeini, the subsequent leader of the Islamic Revolution, gave voice. He denounced the agreement as contributing to the "enslavement of Iran" and asserted that if the religious leaders were in charge "it would not be possible for the nation to be at one moment the prisoner of England, at the next, the prisoner of America. . . ."[7] In Khomeini's mind America had emerged as the primary "Satan" bedeviling Iranian internal affairs:

> Are we to be trampled underfoot by the boots of America simply because we are a weak nation and have no dollars? America is worse than the British; the British are worse than the Americans; the Soviet Union is worse than both of them. Each is worse than the other; they are all despicable. But today our business is not with all these forces of evil. It is with America.[8]

His invective prompted the government to send him into exile for the next 14 years.

The surge in oil prices following the Arab-Israeli war of 1973 poured billions of petrodollars into the Shah's coffers. Wisely invested, these resources might have built the legitimacy of the regime on economic performance and compensated for the legitimacy lost through the close association with the United States. Instead, they fueled the Shah's ambition to make Iran into a regional superpower and restore it to the grandeur of the ancient Persian Empire. Age-old symbols of imperial glory, however, proved rather thin gruel for those seething over affronts to Iranian national pride. Indeed, a somewhat more recent source of national identity and cultural guidance—Islam—proved more potent than the Shah's feeble attempts at Persian mythmaking.

Islamic Political Revival   Islam, though one of the world's three great monotheistic religions, conjures up a variety of distorted images in the West, where Christianity predominates. Over a thousand years of political competition and warfare have contributed to and arisen from these distorted images. The Iranian Revolution added to these distortions by highlighting the division within Islam between Sunni and Shi'a. The Sunni branch, commentators have often emphasized, represents the majority of the (presumably moderate) Muslim population worldwide. (A Muslim is any follower of the Islamic faith.) The Western view has tended to transform the Shi'a into a bizarre, deviant, and extremist sect, radically different from "our" Muslims (especially our allies in Egypt and Saudi Arabia).

Such an exaggerated dichotomy, though, underestimates the potential relevance of Shi'a political revival. Though important differences exist between the two branches, we must not overlook their fundamental identity. Most importantly, both are part of the larger Islamic faith. As Asaf Hussain observes, both believe in one supreme divinity (Allah) and accept Muhammad as His primary prophet. (Muslims view Christ and the Jewish prophets as precursors to Muhammad.) Muhammad recited Allah's will, teachings later written down in the Koran, which provides guidance for all aspects of human existence.[9] In addition, the Western tendency to view the Shi'a as fundamentalist and Sunni as moderate obscures the range of belief within Islam as practiced across both branches. Islamic fundamentalists of both conservative and radical persuasions exist among the Sunni. Moderate and reformist elements exist among the Shi'a, even in Iran. The world, as usual, frustrates our simplistic dichotomies. Despite these basic similarities, however, some important differences exist between the two branches.

Hussain characterizes the dispute between the two divisions as political rather than doctrinal.[10] The conflict arose over the rightful heir to Muhammad. After the death of Muhammad in 632, the leaders of the Islamic community selected a successor called a *caliph*. A group of dissenters, though, believed that Ali, a cousin of Muhammad and married to his daughter, Fatima, was the rightful heir. They became known as the Shi'a Ali, the partisans of Ali. The Shi'a believed that only select male descendants of Ali and Fatima could rule as Imams. Ali's selection as the fourth caliph in 656 healed the division for a brief period. After his death, the founder of the Ummayad dynasty usurped the caliphate and again split the Muslim world. The followers of Ali castigated this caliph and his successors as illegitimate hypocrites.

Legitimate or not, the Ummayad caliphs controlled the power of the state. The rivalry reached its almost mythic climax when the caliph Yazid demanded the allegiance of the Imam Husayn, the grandson of the Prophet Muhammad. Husayn refused. He attempted to flee from Mecca to the greater safety of Kufa in Iraq. Yazid's army intercepted his small party at a place in the desert called Karbala. Rather than surrendering, Husayn chose to fight against hopeless odds and was thus martyred. This minor battle assumed major symbolic significance for the Shi'a. "It symbolized a fight between a tyrannous ruler and the liberator, between an Imam and a *munafiqeen* [hypocrite], between a *Tawhidi* leadership (accepting the dominance of God only) and non-*Tawhidi* leaders (accepting human dominance)."[11]

Most of the Imams following Husayn also met violent ends at the hands of the Ummayad caliphs, reinforcing the heritage of persecution and martyrdom. Finally, the twelfth Imam is believed to have entered into *ghaybat* (occultation, a type of transcendent hiding), where he would remain until some later manifestation. Until that time the *ulama*, especially the foremost scholars among them, called the *mujtahids*, would provide leadership. Though not infallible like the Imams, these religious leaders deserved the allegiance of all the faithful.

The Arabs brought Islam to Persia in the seventh century, and it remained a predominantly Sunni country for nearly a thousand years. In the sixteenth century the Safavid dynasty conquered Persia. These new rulers found it convenient to encourage Shi'ism. By making Shi'ism the state religion, the Safavid rulers apparently hoped to boost their own legitimacy while undermining that of their predominantly Sunni rivals in the Ottoman Empire. Shi'ism, though, as subsequent history demonstrated, provides a somewhat unreliable basis for legitimating a monarchy.

The Shi'ite legacy to the revolutionary crisis in Iran consists of a number of factors. First, despite the manipulations of the Safavid monarchs and their successors, Shi'ism challenges all earthly power.[12] Only the Imam can rule legitimately, and since he is absent from the world, all rulers are suspect. Only by demonstrating fealty to Islam and exercising their authority on behalf of the absent Imam can rulers gain some provisional legitimacy. This rejectionist attitude contrasts with the more politically accommodating position of the Sunnis.

A second cultural legacy bequeaths a tradition of martyrdom.[13] Although martyrdom has significance throughout Islam, it holds a position of particular importance for Shi'ism. Husayn's death fighting an illegitimate ruler offers a potent symbol of the sacrifices necessary to resist tyranny, even at overwhelming odds. For a true follower of the Shi'a tradition, every place is a potential "field of struggle where the forces of justice and legitimacy are confronted by the forces of tyranny. Every day of his life is a day of battle in which he should seek either triumph or martyrdom."[14] Hamid Algar remarks that the tendency to reject the legitimacy of de facto rulers when combined with the acceptance of martyrdom in the struggle for justice gave Shi'ism a certain militancy at times in its history.[15]

When the Safavids decided to sanction Shi'ism as the official rite of Islam in Persia, they found few native teachers of the Shi'ite tradition. Consequently they imported Arab scholars from the existing centers of Shi'ite scholarship. These imported scholars provided the origins of the class of *ulama* who began to play an increasingly important role in the history of the country. "Dynasties have come and gone, leaving in many cases little more than a few artifacts behind to account for their existence. But there has been a continuing development of the class of Shi'ia *ulema* [*sic*] in Iran which has been totally without parallel elsewhere in the Islamic world."[16] Though originally imported to serve the geopolitical purposes of the Safavid monarchs, the Shi'ite clergy shortly began to demonstrate their autonomy. At first, they merely reminded the rulers that they held their position in trust as servant of a higher authority; later they began to challenge the ruler's authority directly.[17] In the nineteenth century the *ulama* asserted the position that they were not only the interpreters but also the executors of the Islamic tradition and law.[18]

By the twentieth century the *ulama* had emerged as a political class directly challenging the authority of the monarchs (by this time, the Qajar dynasty). The Constitutional Revolution of 1905–1911 foreshadowed the events of the late 1970s. Middle-class secularists demanded the creation of a parliament and the imposition of constitutional controls on the authority of the Qajar monarch. As a small fringe the secular constitutionalists were vulnerable to repression. Consequently they made an alliance with some of the leading *mujtahids*, who saw an opportunity to safeguard Islam through constitutionalism. This coalition triumphed and imposed constitutional limitations on the monarchy. Though conflict developed between the secular and religious forces, they compromised by guaranteeing in the new constitution that "no laws would be enacted which were repugnant to Islam and that a committee of five mujtahids could consider such laws proposed in the [parliament] and repudiate them wholly or in part."[19] The overthrow of Qajar rule by Reza Khan, however, began to reverse this first effort at constitutionalism.

Uneven Development   Iran's geographic position ensured that cultural as well as military forces would compete for dominance. Islam in general, and the Shi'ite branch specifically, represent externally introduced cultural systems that ultimately secured roots among the Persian people. The competition among the European great powers in the nineteenth century brought new cultural elements into the mix, variously labeled Westernization, modernization, or, most neutrally, development. The discovery of oil reinforced these cultural forces further, because now European companies as well as their governments grew interested in Iran. By the twentieth century Iran was becoming integrated into the world economy, as well as its geopolitical rivalries.

The role of the Pahlavi Shahs in the modernization of their country, the part played by Shi'ite *ulama* and Islamic revivalism in the Iranian Revolution, and the anti-Western rhetoric of the revolutionary participants all appear to support the notion that the revolution represents some kind of atavistic reaction against modernization. What modernization exactly entails, however, remains open to considerable scholarly dispute.[20] Variously identified with industrialization, commercialization of agriculture, the spread of literacy in the general population and technical skills among an intellectual elite, modern bureaucratic organization, secularization, and democratization, this protean cultural force often develops in uneven and disruptive ways. The uneven development of the country, more than modernization as some "essence," contributed to the strains underlying the revolutionary crisis.

Mohsen Milani identifies three ways in which the Pahlavi program of modernization developed unevenly:

First, unable to completely break the back of Iran's traditional society, it created pervasive dualism in the economy, in cultural arenas, and in modes of living and thinking. It increased the power of the modern sector of the economy without destroying the power of the bazaar merchants and shopkeepers, and it somewhat secularized the society but fell short of substantially diminishing the ulema's [sic] power. Second, it led to an uneven development of economic and political systems by modernizing the former without changing the nature of the latter, which remained archaic, traditional, and unyielding to incorporation of various groups into the decision-making process. Third, [it] had a narrow base of support and lacked a solid, supporting ideology. Little was built over the ruins of much that was destroyed, creating in the process, among other things, an ideological vacuum and a sense of confusion and bewilderment for the masses.[21]

The Shah's father initiated the Pahlavi modernization program by bringing new industry to the country, developing a modern educational system, and limiting the influence of the *ulama*. His son, however, reinforced it, particularly after the so-called "White Revolution" of 1963. This program redistributed considerable amounts of land and struck a blow at the landholding classes, traditionally a bulwark of the monarchy. In addition, the Shah's effort to promote new industries and commercial enterprises intruded on the economic interests of another previous supporter, the bazaar merchants. Finally, he poured tremendous amounts of money into industrialization, especially after the increase in oil prices in 1973–1974.

These policies produced significant economic growth and altered the composition of the labor force. The gross domestic product (GDP) increased from an estimated 10.4 billion in 1960 to 51 billion in 1977 (measured in constant 1974 dollars).[22] Agricultural laborers, as a percentage of the total work force, fell from 56.3 to 34 percent between 1956 and 1976, while those involved in manufacturing and industry rose from 33.9 to 53.2 per cent. In 1963 the agricultural sector still accounted for nearly 28 per cent of the GDP. By 1977–1978, this sector had declined to a mere 9.3 percent, while the oil sector had risen from 18.6 to 31.8 percent and industry and mining from 15.8 to 22.5 percent.[23] Superficially, these statistics indicate considerable economic modernization in Iran.

These gross data, however, hide several disjointed developments. First, the industrial sector failed to absorb fully the tremendous flight from the agricultural labor force (which fell in both relative and absolute terms). Rather, changes in the countryside flooded the cities with migrants (see below, "Destabilizing Demographics") who joined the unemployed or underemployed workers in construction, trade, and domestic service.[24] Second, the modernization of the economy rapidly increased the number of highly skilled technical and professional workers. According to one estimate their numbers grew from 628,000 to 1.9 million people (16.5 to 33.2 percent of the work force), again largely concentrated in the urban areas.[25]

Third, the Shah's industrialization program encouraged increased foreign investment in the country and the consequent resentment and fear of foreign domination.[26] Ironically, the Shah's efforts to broaden the base of the Iranian economy only deepened its dependence on foreign capital imports.[27] Fourth, the expansion of economic opportunity unequally benefited the Shah and his cronies. Just as his father had been the country's largest landholder, the Shah, together with his family, became the country's largest industrialist.[28] Finally, the country's economic boom depended on the steady flow of oil revenues. Although given a tremendous boost by the price explosion of 1974, oil prices began to stagnate and then to fall in a few years. The boom became something of a bust, revealing further the economy's continued dependence on outside forces.

The development of modern economic sectors produced a tremendous expansion in overall literacy and in higher education. The literate proportion of the population more than tripled from 1956 to 1977 (14.9 percent to 47.1 percent). Moreover, the literate population disproportionately concentrated in the cities. By 1976 students represented nearly 28 percent of the population over six years of age.[29] In addition, the modernization of the economy increased the number of Iranians traveling abroad (often as students) and spread new communications technologies (radios, tape players, and televisions) widely among the population.[30]

According to a popular Euro-American development myth, economic and social modernization should transform the political system to allow for greater participation. The Shah, however, chose to move in the opposite direction. The increasingly authoritarian character of his regime reinforced the tensions produced by uneven economic and social development. First he tried to weaken the traditionally powerful sectors in Iran. The land reforms of the early 1960s and the effort to develop a modern commercial sector eroded the positions once enjoyed by the large landholders and bazaar merchants, respectively.

In addition, the Shah tried to bring the largely autonomous religious institutions under his control. He reduced the number of religious schools, expanded the state's role in regulating those remaining, and organized a Religious Corps and Religious Propagandists.[31] These two organizations aimed "to spread a conservative, apolitical version of Shi'ism, one that emphasized the compatibility of Shi'ism and monarchical government; to gradually strengthen the intermingling of the institution of Shi'ism with the state bureaucracy; and to demonstrate the commitment of the state to Shi'ism."[32] At the same time that he attempted to reduce the traditional autonomy enjoyed by the clergy, the Shah also glorified the pre-Islamic past (for example, by decreeing a new calendar that began with the rule of the Persian king Cyrus the Great to replace the Islamic calendar) and opened Iran to the proliferation of "decadent" Western culture (movie theaters, bars, and so forth).[33]

Prudence might seem to dictate that the Shah should have expanded his support among the growing modern sectors in Iran as he proceeded to alienate traditional economic and social powers. Instead, he followed policies that, at least in retrospect, seemed designed to alienate these potential supporters as well. We have already noted the compromised character of his nationalist credentials. His economic development program did little to polish this tarnished reputation.

In addition, he reduced meaningful political participation, rather than expanding it.[34] In 1957 he created a two-party system by royal decree. Although both these parties supported him, he grew increasingly intolerant of the intraelite competition they fostered and largely ignored the parties after 1964. Increasingly he ruled by decree, allowing for rubber-stamp approval by the parliament after the fact. In 1975 he abandoned all pretense of two-party democracy and created a one-party system, again by decree. This party, perhaps vaguely influenced by the Leninist model of a vanguard mobilization party, served as little more than a conduit for regime patronage and pressure. Finally, severe political repression maintained this sham of controlled participation. The regime's apparently omnipresent secret police (SAVAK) spread a climate of fear that discouraged dissent, imprisoned many dissenters, and drove others into exile.

Destabilizing Demographics   Population increased significantly between 1959 and 1978. Unfortunately, precise figures, though easy to come by, are difficult to reconcile.[35] UN estimates put the population in 1959 at 19.7 million, growing to 37 million by 1979.[36] Whatever the exact totals, a reasonable consensus exists on several demographic characteristics. First, the Iranian population has grown rapidly over the past several decades, certainly at a rate over 2 percent a year and perhaps 2.5 percent or higher over some periods. Second, this rapid population growth rate means that the majority of the population are under 35 years of age.[37] Third, population growth along with changes in the countryside encouraged significant rural migration to urban areas, producing the lumpenproletariat of first-generation city residents in Tehran and other urban centers. Finally, the rapid expansion of the urban population began to tax the government's ability to provide urban services as well as employment, even with the substantial oil revenues. The provision of housing, sanitation, and power began to fall short of needs in the mid-1970s.[38]

Accelerators of the Revolutionary Crisis

An inventory of the long-term causes of a revolutionary crisis helps to identify the origins of stress in a society. Usually a retrospective analysis of a particular revolution also uncovers factors that accelerated or intensified the experience of stress. While some accelerators recur in a variety of cases, others appear peculiar to a given community. Iran experienced a number of accelerators often found in other revolutionary crises including economic downturn, regime incompetence, and elite division. In addition, the Shah possessed some special weaknesses that contributed to his downfall.

Economic Downturn   Oil fueled the Shah's economic development plans. Revenues from the sale of oil approximated 1 billion dollars in 1968–1969, grew to 5 billion in 1973–1974, and then soared to 20 billion dollars in 1975–1976.[39] The Shah's ambitions expanded along with his revenues. He poured money into grandiose schemes, profligate displays like his lavish celebration of the 2500th anniversary of the Persian Empire, and dreams of military preeminence in the region. All this expenditure, however, fueled inflation, which rose to double-digit levels in the 1970s. In addition, when oil prices began to stagnate after 1976, Iran's revenues began to fall behind planned investments and imports, leading to reductions in public expenditures. The abandonment or postponement of these projects increased unemployment, especially in the construction industry.

At the same time, oil revenues and the development they funded disproportionately benefited the upper classes and some elements of the Westernized professional class.[40] The gap between rich and poor, always wide, grew perceptibly worse during the 1970s. People generally find growing inequality easier to tolerate if their own absolute condition also improves. The faltering of Iran's overheated economy after 1976, however, made these inequities more glaring.

Regime Incompetence   Recently some students of revolution have abandoned the search for general explanations, arguing instead that a combination of bad decisions and worse luck generates a revolutionary crisis.[41] Like forms of more systematic social explanation, the search for illustrations of incompetence usually proceeds after the fact. Not surprisingly, retrospective reflection easily discovers examples of mistaken judgment and outright incompetence. The case of the Shah's fall is no different. Several key errors reinforced the accumulating crisis.

We previously noted the Shah's most fundamental misjudgment—his response to Iran's burgeoning oil wealth.[42] Declining oil prices would have disrupted Iran's economy under any circumstances, but his unwise development plans undoubtedly made the problem much worse. No one compelled him to overheat the economy, create economic bottlenecks, and commit tens of billions of dollars to construction projects dependent on the uninterrupted flow of increasing amounts of petrodollars. Unfortunately, the Shah's dream of transforming Iran into a modern industrial economy in a single generation distorted his development program.

A second error of judgment hastening his downfall ironically involved his efforts at liberalization in 1977.[43] Confident of his power and dismissive of the fragmented opposition, the Shah decided to relax political control. In part, he undertook this liberalization to satisfy Western critics, especially in the American government. Whatever the reason, he lifted restrictions on the opposition and released political prisoners just as economic stagnation intensified. Rather than mollifying the opposition, however, these gestures only made them more dissatisfied with the status quo. The political "space" created allowed both secular and religious dissidents to regroup and reorganize, and paved the way for the protests in the following year.

In a third miscalculation the regime engaged in an unnecessarily provocative attack on the exiled Ayatollah Khomeini in January 1978.[44] An anonymous but regime-sponsored newspaper article questioned Khomeini's moral character and patriotism. The regime clearly underestimated the reaction this scurrilous attack would provoke among the whole religious community. Khomeini's supporters rioted in the religious city of Qom on January 8, 1978, and even moderate clerics rallied to Khomeini's defense. The repression of this riot ignited a year of protests that ultimately drove the Shah from power.

Finally, confronted with rising rebellion, the Shah further inflamed the situation. Basically, he vacillated between conciliation and repression, never able to find an effective strategy for either.[45] The latter angered the growing opposition further, while the former emboldened them to escalate their demands. He gave inconsistent directions to his military concerning the use of force to suppress the essentially nonviolent demonstrators. He searched for some compromise that would preserve his dynasty, if not his personal rule. Even when he fled, he appeared to cling to the hope that he would be able to return, much as he did after his first flight from Tehran in 1953.

Defection of Elites No regime enjoys the fervent support of all the people under its sway. Even bitter opposition, however, need not threaten a ruler who can depend on the continued support of key sectors. In his last years, however, the Shah not only intensified the anger of his old enemies among the clergy and the radical left, he also alienated those who presumably were the natural supporters of his rule.[46] His modernizing reforms after 1963, as we noted earlier, alienated the traditional economic elites in the rural areas and the bazaar. Western-oriented professional elements, even though they dismissed the dogmatism of the religious fundamentalists, defected from the regime because of its growing political authoritarianism. The modern business community smarted under the rather belated stand of the regime against price and tax abuses in the mid-1970s. Middle-level civil servants shared the resentment over the Shah's autocratic rule and grew desperate as the value of their relatively inflexible salaries diminished in the inflation following the oil boom. Even the officer corps and the secret police, the Shah's last bastions of support, began to defect because of their monarch's vacillation in the face of popular opposition and their growing sympathy for these protesters.

Loss of Foreign Support   The international environment can hasten or hinder the development of a revolutionary crisis. In Vietnam massive American intervention temporally snatched victory from the grasp of the revolutionary forces in 1965. Similarly, American covert support proved critical to the Shah's victory over the National Front government in 1953. By 1978, though, American support was wavering.[47] American policy began to shift with the victory of Jimmy Carter in the 1976 presidential election. Carter's emphasis on human rights, though never consistently applied, increased the pressure on the Shah to liberalize his rule. Congressional critics intensified their condemnations of the Shah's abuse of power as well as the carte blanche he received to purchase any arms short of nuclear weapons Factions within Carter's own administration fought over the advisability of Iranian liberalization, sending conflicting messages that reinforced the Shah's own vacillation.

Carter, preoccupied with other foreign policy problems, including arms negotiations with the Soviet Union and Camp David negotiations between Egypt and Israel, paid only limited attention to events in Iran. In the latter part of 1978 William Sullivan, the American ambassador in Tehran, attempted to facilitate a peaceful transition of power from the Shah to the moderate opposition. Consequently, at the same time that social forces of every political coloration buffeted the Shah internally, he found himself bereft of his major foreign supporter.

Idiosyncratic Factors   The Shah's blunders and his bad luck undoubtedly worsened the political crisis he faced in 1978. In addition, commentators identify two other idiosyncratic factors that undermined effective counteraction against the gathering opposition. First, the Shah was apparently a weak and indecisive man. His indecisiveness in the face of a crisis goes back at least to 1952, when demonstrators forced him to reverse his initial decision to dismiss Mosaddeq.[48] Second, by 1978 the Shah knew he was seriously, possibly terminally, ill with cancer. Physical weakness thus reinforced a weak personality. We cannot determine, of course, whether a healthy Shah would have acted differently and more effectively.

        ♨   ♨   ♨

An inventory of long-term causes and short-term accelerators of the revolution in Iran provides a useful background to the crisis. No matter how plausible, though, the inventory remains simply a list. It supplies, however, some of the elements for more systematic examinations of the Iranian Revolution.

UNDERSTANDING THE IRANIAN REVOLUTION

Our inventory of causes and accelerators provides the colors with which to paint a portrait of a disequilibrated social system. Disequilibrium arose from a combination of modernization, demographic pressure, and regime incompetence. State crisis, however, need not culminate in revolution. The opportunity/resource approach helps us identify those sectors most willing and able to seize the opportunities opened by the state crisis and bring about a revolutionary transformation.

Disequilibrium and State Crisis

At first impression, the Iranian Revolution seems to exemplify the pattern whereby the forces of social modernization overwhelm existing political institutions. Recall that Huntington argues that modernization mobilizes new groups into the political arena whose demands for participation exceed the capacity of the existing political institutions to respond (see Chapter 6). In Iran, of course, the Shah's personal contributions to political decay reinforced the strains caused by rapid modernization.

The long-term causes of the revolutionary crisis supply ample evidence of social mobilization. Industrialization, urbanization, education, and modern communication systems created new social groups (professional and technical classes, workers, students, and so forth) and exposed them to potentially destabilizing ideas. At the same time, traditional sectors (religious clerics, the large landowners, and the merchants of the bazaar) found their interests and traditional positions threatened. All sectors placed increasing and sometimes contradictory demands on the regime for greater participation and responsiveness. The moderate modernized elements wished to have greater participation through a Western-style, multiparty parliamentary system with a constitutionally limited (or eliminated) monarch. The traditional economic sectors wished to protect or restore their economic privileges, and the clerical class wanted to subordinate the state to Islamic law.

In the face of these demands for participation the Shah proceeded to *narrow* the institutional base of his regime in the 1960s and first half of the 1970s. Rather than moving toward a meaningful parliamentary system, he ruled increasingly by decree and replaced a token two-party system with a single-party one. Rather than responding to the economic concerns of the traditional economic sectors, he alienated both the traditional and the modern economic bourgeoisie by concentrating wealth in the hands of his family and close cronies and, when economic conditions worsened, imposing restrictions on the operations of the economic sectors outside his family. Rather than ameliorating the grievances of the clergy, he followed policies intended to make religion an instrument of state policy. Admittedly, the Shah could not respond to the contradictory demands of all these sectors, but he increasingly responded to *none* of them. We must, however, avoid concluding that the Iranian Revolution resulted solely from the Shah's idiosyncrasies and mistakes. Rather, his weaknesses worsened a situation made volatile by forces largely beyond his control.

In Huntington's terms, the Pahlavi regime experienced profound political decay after the Shah's return from his brief exile in 1953. This decay accelerated in the 1970s with the economic reversals brought by stagnating oil prices. Specifically, Huntington suggests four broad indicators of the level of institutionalization of a political organization (or state): its adaptability, complexity, autonomy, and coherence (see Chapter 6). The institutionalization of the Pahlavi regime suffered on at least three counts.

The regime failed to adapt to the boom-and-bust cycle of oil prices, a cycle worsened by the regime's unwise development program. Limited external and internal autonomy of the regime further reduced its adaptability. Externally the regime clearly depended excessively on a single export product, oil. In addition, the bloated economic and military ambitions of the Shah created further dependence on external sources of capital and arms. Finally, the Pahlavi dynasty demonstrated a considerable degree of political dependence on external patrons, first Great Britain and the Soviet Union, and later the United States.

Internally, political organizations could not function independently from continual and often counterproductive interference by the Shah. Political parties and the parliament particularly lacked institutional autonomy (most concretely, the ability to set their own agendas). This lack of institutional autonomy contributed to the problem of incoherence. The Shah's tendency to interfere with or to bypass formal institutions led to rapid turnover in top political offices, subversion of parliamentary powers, and inconsistent, vacillating policies.

Huntington's argument that the social mobilization produced by modernization contributes to political decay provides one perspective on the revolutionary crisis in Iran. Political decay, though, still represents a fairly abstract concept. Moreover, not all decay produces a revolutionary crisis. Presumably it must exceed some unspecified (and possibly varying) threshold to bring the state to the point of collapse. We might achieve a greater degree of specificity by turning to measures of political stress developed by Jack Goldstone (see Chapter 6).

Goldstone's study of revolutionary crises in the early modern world convinced him that such traumas develop out of simultaneous disturbances at different levels of society.[49] We have already demonstrated the multifaceted character of the Iranian crisis, including its long-term sources (for example, population growth and uneven development) and short-term accelerators (like regime incompetence and economic downturns). Goldstone, though, proposes a combined index that might represent this complexity in a more systematic fashion. His political stress indicator combines three general variables of state crisis: fiscal distress, intraelite conflict, and mass mobilization potential. The first weakens the state; the second divides normally supportive sectors from the state and each other; and the third supplies the basis to turn an internal elite struggle into a true revolutionary crisis.

Such variables provide little more than a suggestive way of organizing inquiry in the absence of some empirical indicators of each one. Goldstone, however, develops several that seem applicable to the Iranian case. He suggests measuring the level of state fiscal distress on a five-step "desperation" scale.[50] At one end of the scale the state experiences no fiscal problems, whereas at the other the state confronts bankruptcy. In early modern states, fiscal distress often arose because royal revenues depended heavily on relatively inflexible land rents. When inflationary pressures sent expenditures soaring, these inflexible sources of revenue could not keep pace, deficits increased, and the crown would confront the choice of raising new taxes or defaulting. The former alternative risked alienating powerful economic sectors, while the latter demonstrated the regime's incompetence and illegitimacy.

A similar situation occurred in Iran. Instead of inflexible land rents the state increasingly depended on volatile oil prices. During the time of the third Five-Year Development Plan (1963–1967) oil revenues produced 48.1 percent of government income. During the time of the fifth Plan (1973–1977) revenue dependency on oil grew to nearly 78 percent.[51] Increased oil income, as we noted above, prompted a massive increase in government expenditures. According to the International Monetary Fund government expenditures leapt from 504 billion rials in 1973 to 1287 billion rials in 1974, a rise of 155 percent in a single year. Initially revenues more than kept pace; in fact, a small deficit in 1973 turned into a 140-billion-rial surplus. Surpluses soon disappeared. In 1977 expenditures of 2455 billion rials produced a deficit of 355 billion. An expenditure reduction the next year failed to cut this deficit, which increased to 550 billion rials, or 24 percent of expenditures.[52]

The reduction in oil revenues forced the regime to cut back on short-term obligations and to attack elite privileges with new taxation proposals. Tax revenues from salaried groups, for example, more than doubled between 1975 and 1978, despite the economic downturn.[53] These increased taxes, along with other measures to fight inflation, contributed to division between the economic elites and the regime.

Goldstone suggests that university expansion might also indicate a potential increase in intraelite competition.[54] Increased enrollment, though, may be the cause or the effect of heightened elite competition. On one hand, the growing number of those seeking educational credentials may indicate an intensifying struggle for limited elite positions. On the other hand, explosive growth in the number of college graduates may produce increased competition. Iran's student population increased tremendously in the years preceding the revolution. In 1958 only 14.4 thousand students were enrolled in institutions of higher education. By 1977 their numbers had grown over tenfold to 156 thousand.[55] Despite this expansion, competition for the available positions in the colleges and universities remained intense. In 1977, for example, only 60 thousand of the 290 thousand applying for admission were accepted.[56]

While impressive, these statistics provide only indirect measures of elite competition and alienation. Moreover, unlike conditions elsewhere in the Third World, the Iranian economy, at least when expanding, provided sufficient opportunities for the educated and technical population. However, the growth of college- and university-educated people reinforced the size and significance of a sector becoming increasingly disenchanted with the Shah's autocratic rule. In addition, the Shah's capital-intensive development strategy and military ambitions brought many foreign technical personnel into Iran, further fueling the discontent of the educated classes.[57]

Finally, Goldstone suggests that mass mobilization potential may be indicated by the combination of three factors: a decline in real wages, increased urbanization, and an increased proportion of the population under age 35.[58] The logic behind this combination of indicators seems reasonably persuasive, particularly in a Western-style revolution that starts in the cities. A decline in real wages increases frustration, especially after a period of growing prosperity. Urban growth concentrates people geographically and facilitates their mobilization. Finally, younger people generally demonstrate a greater propensity for risky behavior and thus are more easily mobilized to participate in dissident activities. When mobilized in large numbers they affect the calculations of the more timid and contribute to the reduction of the free rider problem (see Chapter 5, the discussion of the bandwagon effect, and below).

The rate of price inflation and the growth in per capita income provide two indirect indicators of movement in real wages. Until the oil boom of the mid-1970s Iran experienced only modest inflation. Between 1963 and 1967 prices rose on the average only 1.5 percent a year. Inflation rose to the still modest rate of 3.7 percent a year in the period 1968–1972. Between 1973 and 1977, however, inflation increased to 15.7 percent a year.[59] Inflation alone, however, does not demonstrate a general decline in real wages, except for those on relatively fixed incomes. But after 1977 the economic expansion stopped. In 1978 the gross domestic product in 1974 prices plunged nearly 17 percent, leading to a 19.2 percent decline in per capita GDP.[60] The period of inflation after 1973 began to erode the real wages of those on relatively fixed incomes (for example, many government employees). The economic downturn that began in 1977 spread this source of grief more widely throughout the society.

We have already noted some of the destabilizing demographic dynamics afflicting Iran. Between 1956 and 1978 population doubled and the urban population tripled. This rapid increase in population changed the age structure as well. By 1976 over 30 percent of Iran's population was between the ages of 15 and 34, the prime age for rebellion.[61] Finally, not only was Iran's population growing younger, but also rural migration to the cities further augmented these destabilizing trends.

Our adaptation of Goldstone's political stress indicator to the Iran case supports the conclusion that the potential for instability increased in the years immediately before the 1979 revolution. The fiscal situation of the state suffered owing to the dependence on oil revenues. Oil dependency also contributed to price inflation and ultimately economic recession. Division among the elites increased, especially between the regime and the established economic elites and intelligentsia. Finally, economic and demographic conditions seemed to favor mass mobilization.

Unfortunately, at least three flaws exist in this portrait of state crisis. First, though economic and social conditions undoubtedly eroded regime stability, especially after 1976, conditions in Iran were not that bad in absolute terms. Fifteen percent inflation looks modest in comparison to many other countries around the world. Indeed, equivalent rates afflicted the United States shortly afterward. (Admittedly, American inflation undermined the Carter administration and contributed to the Reagan "revolution.") Unemployment was low by Third World standards and population growth rates no worse than in other countries without revolutions. Second, some of the worsening economic conditions in the year and a half preceding the fall of the Shah were caused by the revolutionary protests and strikes, not the reverse (see below). Third, most of the economic conditions worsened after the revolution, especially once Iran found itself engaged in a bloody war with Iraq.

This portrayal of revolutionary crisis still lacks something. Goldstone observes, drawing on an earthquake metaphor, that the same stresses affect different state structures differently.[62] Strong states can survive social tremors that topple weak ones. But the after-the-fact conclusion that the Shah's regime was weak, however plausible, is not especially satisfying. The weakness of the state combined with the socioeconomic stresses caused by oil dependency and demographic changes created an opportunity for opposition groups to mobilize. Who mobilized *what* for *which ends*, however, determined the course and outcome of the Iranian Revolution.

Opportunity, Resources, and Revolutionary Mobilization

As economics and demographics weakened the state and placed people in a position of potential opposition, more elements of society began to challenge the authority of the Shah. In the early 1970s a number of relatively small guerrilla groups—some secular Marxist and others with leftist Islamic leanings—began to attack the regime.[63] Though these groups, composed largely of student-age members, failed to mount a serious challenge to the regime, they punctured the aura of regime invulnerability. When the Shah, in response to foreign criticism and confident of his security, relaxed some political controls, relatively moderate middle-class opposition groups began to organize and demand greater liberties. Finally, after the imprudent attack on Khomeini's character in January 1978, new protests, organized by clerics, moved to the forefront of the movement for change. Whereas earlier opposition had primarily been a middle-class affair, the mosque-led protests mobilized the urban masses, particularly the recent migrants to Iran's cities.

Ultimately, opposition to the Shah that began with secular Marxist and modernist Islamic guerrilla groups and then spread to include middle-class demands for reform yielded position to an Islamic revivalist revolutionary movement. This outcome seems best explained by the superior resources of the Islamic fundamentalists.[64] They possessed the members, incentives, organizational networks, and leaders to contend successfully first with the Shah's regime and then with other competitors for power (see the discussion of the opportunity/resource model in Chapter 6).

Members   Successful revolutionary movements generally do not burst forth from an atomized social system. Rather, they usually mobilize people as members of preexisting associations, with social identities. In Iran Islam provided this identity. Contrary to the expectations of some modernization theories, growing urbanization and greater literacy failed to lead to an irreversible secularization of Iranian society. Ironically, they appear to have helped revitalize religious activities. Arjomand notes that Islam has traditionally been connected to urban centers. Mosques and seminaries are located in the cities, and urban migration "has thus been historically associated with increasing religious orthodoxy and a more rigorous adherence to the legalistic and puritanical central tradition of Islam."[65] Recent urban migrants played an important part in the Iranian religious renewal.

Even more ironic, the spread of literacy further increased the vitality of religious activities.[66] Religious tracts and books proved immensely popular in the late 1960s and 1970s. Even modern communications technology, particularly cassette tapes of recorded sermons, played an increasing role in promulgating religious beliefs.[67]

Another indicator of modernization involves the multiplication of secondary voluntary associations. In Iran such groups indeed multiplied, but many were religious associations for laypersons. Often these associations developed among the recent migrants to the cities and among the more modest occupations (such as juice sellers, shoemakers, workers at public baths, and so forth).[68]

Finally, even elements of the educated classes took part in the religious revival. Religious associations formed among professionals and students, especially among the children of the more traditional middle classes. One influential contributor to the growing potency of Islamic identity was the Islamic reformer Ali Shari'ati, who advocated a populist theology based on his radical interpretation of the Koran. His validation of the political relevance of Islam to the contemporary world helped prepare the ground for the clerics who took up the cause of the dispossessed after Shari'ati's death in 1977.[69] This potent combination of the modern symbol of "revolution" with the traditional invocation of "Islam" contributed to the self-deception of the secularized opponents of the Shah. The desire of the new middle classes to eliminate the Shah led them into an allegiance with clerics who would later prove hostile to their interests.[70]

Competitors for the loyalties of the potential opposition movement all suffered from certain limitations. The guerrilla groups—both Marxist and radical Islamic—recruited primarily from the disgruntled intelligentsia. They allied with the clerics in the hope of later seizing control of the revolution, but their lack of a broad social base compromised them in the postrevolutionary struggle for power after 1979. The Shah's policies of divide and rule both alienated the new middle classes, inside government and in the private economy, and impaired their ability to act as a coherent sector in defense of their own interests. Swept up with pride in the resurgence of the Islamic nation, they tended to follow the lead of the clerics rather than compete with them. By the time they realized their mistake, the Islamic revivalists had consolidated their grip on power.[71]

Incentives   People need incentives to participate in revolutionary movements. We earlier explored the different types of solution to the free rider problem (see

Chapter 5). In Iran a number of these combined to help motivate potential revolutionary participants. Some of these, given the conventional characterization of rational actors, further underline the irony of the Iranian Revolution. In any case, successful revolutionary action does not have to meet a standard of perfection; rather, the revolutionaries only have to outperform their rivals. Participation, at least at a low level, ultimately grew widespread. Hundreds of thousands, possibly millions, of people joined in anti-Shah activities of one sort or another.

Initially the leaders of the movement against the Shah, particularly Khomeini and his clerical allies, believed they could make a critical contribution to the transformation of Iran. They believed, in terms of one solution to the free rider problem, that their participation significantly increased the probability of achieving the public good of revolution. Events seem to bear out the rationality of their beliefs.

Leaders, though necessary to success, cannot accomplish a revolution by themselves. They must motivate followers whose individual contribution makes no noticeable difference. Solutions to the free rider problem must add selective incentives to the calculation of such potential followers.

The Shi'ite tradition of suffering and martyrdom offers a peculiar twist on this requirement. In the secular West we often dismiss such motivations as irrational. However, we must temper this conclusion in a culture where many believe that sacrifice of one's life in a holy cause leads to the selective good of personal salvation. We might dismiss belief in salvation as nonrational and immaterial and conclude, therefore, that it cannot serve as a concrete selective incentive. Those who believe in personal salvation cannot, after all, demonstrate the empirical validity of their conviction. On the other hand, many of the things that serve as selective incentives in the materialist societies of the West—for example, money—take on material value only within a system of cultural beliefs. Individual perceptions and beliefs shape the meaning, and consequently the incentive value, of even direct pleasure and pain. Importantly, only the clergy could successfully evoke this tradition of martyrdom.[72] The secular opposition forces possessed no equivalent cultural appeal, while almost no one wished to make personal sacrifices for the Shah.

The Shah's indecisiveness further aided the solution of the free rider problem in that he unwittingly lowered the costs of participation. He never embraced a full-scale program of repression, and casualties consequently were relatively low. Moreover, the rapid expansion of protest across the country and civil disobedience within the government itself made it more difficult to apply a systematic policy of repression.[73] Finally, many workers continued to collect their pay even when on strike. "There were thus substantial rewards and no penalty for going on strike and joining the anti-Shah political festival."[74]

Finally, Khomeini and his clerical followers skillfully blended Islamic faith with nationalist aspirations to create an ideological appeal capable of unifying diverse elements of the opposition.[75] This potent combination swept along more secular elements as they discovered their Iranian roots within Islam. Arjomand argues that the fundamental psychological insecurity of the new middle classes, disoriented by both their increased material wealth and the exposure to Western influences, made them easy prey for Khomeini's new myth of "national communion."[76] With victory in hand, however, those buying into the dream of national regeneration discovered that the clerical ideal of the new Islamic Republic impinged on their interests.

Of course, we cannot dismiss the possibility that many of the participants in the demonstrations and strikes were not acting rationally, at least in the narrow sense. The Shah's regime provoked considerable anger among a wide cross section of the population, and this anger may have propelled some of the protesters regardless of costs and benefits. In any case, once the demonstrations and strikes began they created something of a bandwagon or snowball effect.[77] The rapidly changing calculation of success swept along passive neutrals and even those we might have expected to support the Shah, out of fear of missing the revolutionary train as it roared out of the station. Finally, members of the military, the ultimate pillar of Pahlavi power, began to defect in the face of the Shah's inevitable defeat.[78]

Organization   Those sectors that control preexisting organizational resources more successfully exploit emerging political opportunities. The Islamic Revolution enjoyed widespread support throughout the population, especially among recent urban migrants and the traditional middle classes of the bazaar. The Shah, through his authoritarian political system and the activities of SAVAK, eviscerated many potential opposition organizations, including the National Front. Ironically, however, he largely failed to bring the mosques and seminaries under his control.

In the mid-1970s a vast organizational network lay at the disposal of a politicized clergy. One report estimates that

> in 1975, in Teheran alone, there were 983 mosques, each one administered by a *pish-namaz* (prayer leader), usually appointed by a *marja'-e taqlid* [literally, source of imitation; these were clerical jurists with large followings and ranked high in the Shi'ite hierarchy]. Each pish-namaz had a following of his own, the size of which depended on his popularity and the mosque's location. In Teheran, there were also 164 registered permanent takiyes, each with a considerable membership. Altogether, there were 1,147 mosques and takiyes in Teheran, and 8,439 of them throughout Iran. The data do not include hundreds of Islamic associations and hey'ats (religious associations for debates or reading of the holy Quran, etc.). One source has estimated that in 1974 there were about 12,300 hey'ats in Teheran.[79]

Moreover, the economic and social groups existing in the bazaar generally allied themselves with this impressive religious organizational base.

Despite this latent organizational power the Shi'ite hierarchy was not a monolithic vanguardist movement. Although the Ayatollah Khomeini possessed a long tradition of opposition politics, the clergy included more moderate, even modernist, elements. In another ironic twist the Shah and his secret police left the religious structure largely intact, despite periodic attacks from Khomeini and his allies, because they thought it served as a powerful deterrent against the Communists and other left-wing secular forces.[80]

The ill-conceived diatribe against Khomeini in January 1978 helped drive moderate and more extreme Shi'ite clergy together against the common enemy of Islam—the Shah. Khomeini successfully drew the analogy between the Shah and the archetypal enemy of the Shi'a, the caliph Yazid (see above, the section "Islamic Political Revival").[81] Once established in the minds of the devout—

whether moderates or extremists—this equation denied the possibility of any compromise with the royal hypocrite. Khomeini and his fundamentalist supporters then drew upon their organizational resources to mobilize the masses for political action. The mosques provided a vast network that used contemporary telecommunications and other modern means, such as cassette tape recordings of the Ayatollah's sermons, to communicate Khomeini's interpretations of events and directions for further action.

After the overthrow of the Shah, Khomeini and his supporters moved quickly to consolidate the organizational base of their power. Khomeini's supporters created the Islamic Revolutionary Guard (IRG) to counterbalance the coercive resources possessed by the several guerrilla organizations. In two years the Guard numbered around 200,000 armed supporters. Khomeini formed an Islamic Revolutionary Council (IRC), packed with his supporters, to oversee the activities of the interim government until the inauguration of a true Islamic regime. Finally, his supporters created a new political party, the Islamic Republic Party (IRP), to consolidate clerical influence in the postrevolutionary era.

These political organizations proved more capable than their competitors in the struggle for postrevolutionary power. In effect, Khomeini created a system of dual sovereignty from which he checked, challenged, and ultimately ousted the interim governments that followed the Shah's ouster. Like Lenin in the Russian Revolution Khomeini destroyed the power of the moderate political forces, both secular and religious. In an ironic twist on the Western model of revolution he also outmaneuvered and destroyed the radical secular elements, as well.

Leadership   Clearly, Khomeini played a central role in the mobilization and consolidation of the Islamic Revolution. At first impression it seems remarkable that an aging cleric, long in exile, could be anything more than a figurehead for the revolutionary movement. Khomeini developed a catalytic/representational relationship with his millions of followers. Through long decades as revered cleric and scholar, he rose to the position of Grand Ayatollah, the highest position in the Shi'a hierarchy. The attainment of this rank reflects the extent to which the devout viewed him with respect as a teacher of the Islamic faith. Moreover, over the decades he repeatedly gave voice to the growing resentment with the Shah's authoritarian ways and the anger many Iranians felt about foreign, especially American, influence in their country.

If Khomeini had developed only a representational relationship with those wishing to oust the Shah, he would still have played a significant role. But he reached for something more. Revolution not only destroys; it also must construct a new social order. While moderate secular and religious forces wished to replace the Shah's regime with some form of constitutional parliamentary rule, Khomeini aimed for something different—an Islamic theocracy.

Khomeini encouraged his followers to consider whether he might be the contemporary manifestation of the hidden Imam. Those who believed Khomeini to be the Imam moved from a catalytic/representational to a charismatic relationship. The Imam, in the Shi'ite tradition, infallibly communicates Allah's will and thus possesses a true charismatic "gift of grace" through a direct link to the Godhead. This contrasts with the position of even the most respected cleric, who could do no more than fallibly interpret the word of God. Many of those who refused to grant Khomeini this elevated status nonetheless thought him to be the precursor of the Imam, who would liberate Iran.[82]

In this manner Khomeini closed a sacred circle. Just as the Shah was the contemporary manifestation of the hypocrite Yazid, Khomeini himself was the latest manifestation of the blessed leader of true Islam. Only this time the enemy would flee and ultimately die, while a sacred dispensation would be brought first to the people of Iran and later, presumably, to the entire Islamic world. In Khomeini's vision the upheaval in Iran was far more than a rebellion against a domestic autocrat; it was the first stage of a world-revolutionary transformation.

Khomeini's revolutionary asceticism reinforced his leadership claims in both representational and charismatic relations. His long career seems to follow the type closely.[83] Born in 1902 and orphaned when only a teenager, he spent long years in study. After completing his education he became a young instructor in the religious city of Qom, where he soon gained a reputation as a powerful and magnetic teacher. He gave early vent to his political sentiments in a book published in 1941, in which he called for an increased role for the *ulama* in the state. He did not, however, reject monarchical rule out of hand. He largely shunned political activity for the next two decades, but he continued to expand his influence over hundreds, perhaps thousands, of his former students.

His clashes with the Shah in the early 1960s led to his eventual exile in 1964. In exile he continued to exercise his influence over a network of former students who now were clerics in their own positions of influence. While in exile he published another influential political work far more radical in its implications than his earlier work. In it he condemns the monarchy as alien to Islam and argues for an ideal Islamic state under the leadership of the clerical class. Moreover, he declares that all believers must work for the overthrow of non-Islamic regimes.[84]

Where others both in and outside the clergy contemplated compromises with the Shah's regime, Khomeini remained implacable in his opposition. Where others possessed a variety of underdeveloped ideas of what should replace the old regime, Khomeini possessed a clear vision of the Islamic Republic. The uncompromising nature of his opposition positioned Khomeini, more than any other potential competitor, to seize control of the revolution. He *was* the revolutionary ascetic, whose purity of heart, clarity of purpose, and consistency of opposition had earned him his position of leadership. He then artfully exploited his position to destroy first the Shah and then those forces opposed to his vision of an Islamic Republic.

STRATEGY AND TACTICS OF CHALLENGE AND CONSOLIDATION

The strategic emphasis in a Western-style revolution, as we noted in Chapter 9, differs somewhat from that of an Eastern-style struggle. Initially the rebellious elements in a Western-style revolution concentrate on the destruction of the old order. Only after its collapse do the participants really address the construction of a new regime. In part, the relative ease of the regime's defeat accounts for this difference in emphasis. The stubborn resistance of the regime in the Eastern model ensures a prolonged period of revolutionary warfare. The revolutionary movement can win only if it creates a social and military base from which to wage this conflict. In contrast the rapid demise of the regime in the Western model means that the opposition has little time to develop alternative political institutions. Consequently in the Eastern model dual sovereignty develops during the revolutionary war between the old regime and the revolutionary movement. In the Western model dual sovereignty develops after the fall of the old regime, between the moderate and extremist oppositional elements.

We must nonetheless take care not to exaggerate these differences. The contrast between prolonged resistance and rapid collapse involves judgments of degree, not absolute distinctions in kind. As the old regime offers more resistance, the revolutionaries must undertake a constructive strategy to provide a basis for continued revolutionary action. Moreover, although Western-style revolutions appear to involve relatively spontaneous mass participation in resistance activities, we cannot ignore the organizational foundation of this apparent spontaneity.

In Iran the Ayatollah and his close supporters possessed from the beginning some idea of the character of the regime they wished to construct. During the rapidly escalating confrontation with the Shah's regime in 1978 they muted this vision, choosing rather to focus tactically on the immediate goal of eliminating the Pahlavi dynasty. After the fall of the Shah their constructive goals emerged and became the focus of a further struggle over the direction of the Iranian Revolution.

From the Bottom Up: The Tactics of Massive Opposition

Revolutionary movements, most commentators agree, seldom succeed unless they develop coalitions among a variety of interests and direct them toward a common objective. This seems especially true in Western-style revolutions, where the rapid demise of the regime results from its abandonment by nearly all political sectors. Such a coalition more easily develops around a shared hatred than a shared love. The Shah, as we saw, managed to alienate just about every significant group in Iran. Ultimately the moral decay of his regime was such that even the beneficiaries of his patronage chose to ship first their wealth and then themselves out of the country, rather than fight to preserve the Pahlavis.

Khomeini played on this vast oppositional potential in a variety of ways. First, he kept the villainy of the Shah in the forefront of revolutionary propaganda. We have already noted how the clerical forces skillfully drew upon the Shi'ite tradition of victimization by hypocritical state power by portraying the Shah as the contemporary incarnation of the archdemon Yazid. Arjomand observes that "the vilification of the Shah and his regime were much more important than the glorification of Khomeini. For every one slogan for Khomeini, there were probably more than two against the Shah."[85]

Although hatred of the Shah undoubtedly provided the universal thread weaving the revolutionary coalition together, several more positive elements also drew mass support from diverse elements. The equation of the Shah with Yazid generated a contrasting image of a golden age of just Islamic rule.[86] People did not need to embrace theocracy to yearn for a restoration of a moral political order based on the ultimate supremacy of the word of God. Finally, national resentment over the political and cultural influence of foreigners, especially Americans, provided another widely shared sentiment that unified traditional and modernist elements of the opposition.[87]

The Shah's own indecisiveness made such vilification easier. His gestures of liberalization made his enemies bolder; his gestures of repression made them angrier. He never reformed enough to buy off the moderates and isolate the radicals calling for his removal. He never repressed enough to drive the opposition into sullen retreat. His muddling mainly demoralized his supporters.

Unwillingness to fight *for* the Shah, of course, did not necessarily translate into a willingness to fight *against* him. Although the various guerrilla groups used tactics of direct coercion, particularly in attacks against police stations, massive noncooperation ultimately drove the Shah from Iran. Unlike guerrilla warfare, which asks large sacrifices from small numbers of people, the strategy pursued by the Ayatollah asked small sacrifices from large numbers of people, especially *once the protests began snowballing.* The trick, of course, was to get the ball rolling. The regime, as we noted, helpfully provided a considerable push by the attack on Khomeini's character. This attack unified clerical opposition to the Shah, thereby reducing, if not eliminating, the possibility of some accommodation between more moderate clergy and the regime.

Moreover, when regime forces opened fire on a demonstration of theological students in Qom, January 7, 1978, they produced some Shi'ite martyrs. Khomeini skillfully exploited their deaths to create a cycle of expanding protest.[88] Khomeini used their deaths to call for demonstrations in conjunction with the commemoration of the dead held, in Muslim tradition, 40 days after the initial deaths. Thousands demonstrated in various locations across Iran on February 18. The commemoration in the city of Tabriz turned violent, leading to scores of additional deaths. Again Khomeini called for demonstrations on March 29, 40 days after the Tabriz deaths. This time they spread to 55 cities and towns, and involved tens of thousands of people. Several of these turned violent, providing further martyrs for still more massive demonstrations held 40 days later. These demonstrations against the Shah, organized largely through the networks of mosques and other religious organizations, continued to escalate until at least a half million people protested in Tehran on September 7.

This outpouring of people demanding his death finally convinced the Shah to declare martial law in twelve cities. When thousands began to gather the next day in front of the parliament building, the military brutally dispersed them, killing perhaps hundreds. This repression might have discouraged the opposition had it come earlier and been consistently applied, but the apparently avoidable slaughter horrified the Shah (and much of the world), and he began to vacillate again. He ended censorship and released political prisoners. The now freer press reported the released prisoners' tales of torture at the hands of SAVAK, and resentment escalated.

Mass demonstrations of discontent underscored the regime's loss of legitimacy. Strikes and slowdowns paralyzed both the economy and the government.
Initially the bazaar merchants shut down their shops in solidarity with the martyrs
of resistance. As the demonstrations grew, the strikes spread.

> Group after group agitated in step with the rhythm set by Khomeini and excitedly
> went on strike: bank clerks and journalists in the private sector; power plant engi-
> neers and technicians; Customs officials; and Iran Air, National Iranian Oil Compa-
> ny, and Central Bank employees in the public sector. Late in November, the oil work-
> ers joined the movement, resuming their strike and causing shortages in the towns.
> Strikes and slowdowns also paralyzed many of the government agencies and min-
> istries. Iran plunged into anarchy in the closing months of 1978.[89]

Hundreds of people, of course, died in these protests, but these were a relative handful in comparison to the millions involved in the strikes and protests. The
likelihood of paying the ultimate price for protest was relatively small. Of course,
the army could have exacted a terrible toll had its force been more consistently
applied. However, the Shah's vacillation between liberalization and repression, his
fear that excessive reliance on a strong military response might lead to his ouster
in a coup, his commendable unwillingness to shed enormous quantities of blood,
and his concern for foreign opinion helped to prevent a consistent policy of severe
suppression.

Other factors, however, also contributed to the relative absence of ruthless
repression. The breadth and character of the protests largely prevented successful
repression, whatever the will of the monarch. Military force was largely irrelevant
against a massive campaign of civil disobedience involving nearly every significant
urban sector both inside and outside the government.[90] Moreover, when demonstrations occasionally turned violent, the army was ill trained to control urban
mobs with minimum casualties. Consequently, their actions often made matters
worse.

Finally, the Ayatollah specifically directed the protesters to avoid provoking
the army. Unlike the guerrillas who had little compunction about attacking army
barracks, Khomeini reasoned that direct attacks on soldiers would only increase
their solidarity. In contrast efforts to confront them nonviolently, though it might
lead to some further martyrs, would ultimately undermine the soldiers' loyalty and
discipline. He stated, "We must fight the soldiers from within the soldiers' hearts.
Face the soldier with a flower. Fight through martyrdom because the martyr is the
essence of history. Let the army kill as many as it wants until the soldiers are shak-
en to their hearts by the massacres they have committed. Then the army will collapse, and thus you will have disarmed the army."[91]

In the later stages of the campaign against the regime, the clerical forces
moved beyond undermining the reliability of the conscripts to eroding the loyalty
of the officer corps. They began negotiations with sympathetic officers. Meanwhile loyalist officers found themselves targets of individual boycotts by doctors,
pharmacists, oil workers, and even their neighbors.[92]

The final defeat of military loyalists, though violent, resulted largely from the
divisions planted in the military in the preceding months. The Shah fled, leaving
Iran in the care of the newly appointed prime minister, Shahpur Bakhtiar. The

Shah probably hoped that the military would rally around this caretaker regime and restore him to power. Instead, on Khomeini's triumphant return February 1, 1979, he refused to deal with this royalist rump government. Ominously for the Bakhtiar government, the divided officer corps, especially at the lower ranks, began to declare their loyalty to the Islamic Revolution. When the Shah's remaining military allies in the Imperial Guard attempted to repress a pro-Khomeini rebellion among air force cadets, the airmen, joined by the guerrillas and thousands of civilians, resisted. The guerrillas and armed militants defeated the Imperial Guard units, and the remainder of the officer corps declared their neutrality. Bakhtiar's government fell, and he fled the country. The triumph of the revolution seemed complete. But the question still remained: Whose revolution?

From the Top Down: The Tactics of Power Consolidation[93]

The fall of Bakhtiar marked the end of the first phase of the revolution. Enemies of the revolution still existed in abundance—the ailing Shah, the "satanic" United States, and, after Iraq's invasion of Iran in 1980, the regime of Saddam Hussein. Although these enemies helped maintain some revolutionary unity, they could not resolve the constructive problems of revolutionary consolidation. The members of the revolutionary coalition now competed over the future shape of Iranian society. The coalition began to fracture.

Even before Bakhtiar's departure, Khomeini appointed Mehdi Bazargan provisional prime minister. He served as the nominal leader of a government composed largely of elements of the old National Front and other relatively moderate members of the liberation movement. At the same time, as noted earlier, Khomeini selected a group of loyal clergy and laypersons to form an Islamic Revolutionary Council (IRC) to oversee government policy, and his supporters organized a clerical political party (IRP) and a popular militia (IRG). Bazargan, in short, confronted a situation of dual power similar to that faced by the provisional government in Russia after the February 1917 revolution.

Other divisions complicated the split between relatively secularized moderates aiming to create a Western-style parliamentary democracy and the Islamic revivalists who desired an Islamic Republic. On the left, the Mojahedin and other Islamic leftists favored a radically egalitarian Islamic state, and Marxist Fedayeen and the Tudah (Communist) party hoped that the fall of the Shah would lead to a secular socialist revolution. Even the clergy disputed issues of property rights and the appropriate clerical role in the politics of the new republic. To complicate matters further, various ethnic minorities, especially the Kurds in northwestern Iran, took advantage of the weakness at the center to agitate for greater autonomy.

The struggle over the direction of the revolution lasted four years, but by the end of 1982 Khomeini and his Islamic supporters had succeeded in crushing both the secular and moderate religious opposition. Interestingly, the Ayatollah largely stayed above the immediate fray. He used his role as supreme jurist sometimes to moderate the conflict among the various political factions and sometimes to validate one side or the other. Though not entirely consistent, he usually favored those who pushed for clerical supremacy in the new Islamic Republic.

The struggle over Iran's revolutionary future went through several phases. The first lasted from February to December 1979 and ended with what Arjomand refers to as a clerical coup d'état.[94] Bazargan's moderate government fell in November, and the Islamic Revolutionary Council took over direct control of the state. Immediately thereafter the provisional Assembly of Experts ratified the articles of the new constitution that gave extensive powers to the "jurist" (initially Khomeini) who represents the hidden Imam and to a Council of Guardians of the Constitution to check the religious validity of all government actions.

In part due to the political inexperience of the IRP and the technical disqualification of its candidate, an independent, Abol-Hasan Bani-Sadr, won the office of president in January 1980. The IRP and its allies recovered in time to dominate the election for members of the Majles (parliament) in March. Bani-Sadr, who drew considerable support from the professional middle classes, the old National Front supporters, and the Mojahedin, soon found himself locked in a power struggle with the IRP and its political cohorts. This contest continued until his forced resignation in June 1981.

Bani-Sadr's defeat eliminated the secular nationalist forces from effective contention, but the Islamic Mojahedin subsequently entered into an armed struggle against the fundamentalist clerical coalition. From June through December 1982 the struggle for power in Iran entered its bloodiest stage, with thousands more dying than fell in the struggle against the Shah. By the end of the year the worst of the terror had passed, and most significant opposition to the clerical forces suffered defeat, death, or exile.

A variety of factors contributed to the triumph of the clerical forces. Specifically, the IRP's strength "derived from its domination of the institutions of the state and broadcast media, the collaboration of the revolutionary courts, guards and committees, the network of mosques and clerics at its disposal across the country, a near-monopoly on the instruments of coercion, the prestige gained through close identification with Khomeini and, ultimately, sheer brutality."[95] In addition, the IRP managed to retain its image as the representative of the downtrodden, especially among the urban masses.[96]

The forces opposing the consolidation of clerical power also seemed potentially strong. They included some elements of the bazaar, moderate religious leaders, the surviving elements of the National Front, certain professional groups of the new middle classes, and the Mojahedin and breakaway elements of the Marxist Fedayeen. In addition, Bani-Sadr championed the professional military (against the Revolutionary Guard) and undoubtedly believed that this enhanced his power base.[97] Unfortunately for Bani-Sadr, some weaknesses undermined this potential coalition. First, despite his electoral victory, Bani-Sadr lacked his own political base and organization. Second, the army, decimated by purges and burned by its defeat in February 1979, avoided entering the political fray and remained loyal to the Ayatollah. Third, the alliance with the Mojahedin represented more a marriage of convenience rather than full support and may have cost Bani-Sadr support elsewhere. Finally, Bani-Sadr counted on his previous relationship with Kho-meini to protect him from the full wrath of the clerics. In this he miscalculated. Khomeini's distrust of and contempt for the other elements of

Bani-Sadr's political coalition ultimately overrode whatever personal attachment he might have felt. In the end Khomeini threw his support to the clerics against the more moderate president.

As subsequent events demonstrated, the Ayatollah was correct to suspect the loyalty of the Mojahedin. After Bani-Sadr's defeat they immediately began a bloody campaign of terrorist bombings and assassinations directed at high-level members of the IRP and the government. This campaign represented the initial tactical phase of an urban guerrilla strategy.[98] First, through terrorism, they hoped to destabilize the regime and reveal its vulnerability. Second, they planned to engage in tactics of open confrontation and strikes to mobilize the people. Finally, they hoped to instigate a mass uprising to topple the government, much like the one that brought down the Shah.

The terrorist tactics worked in accomplishing the short-term objectives of destabilization, and they certainly created a climate of fear among top government and party leaders. But terror tactics alone (as we discussed in Chapter 9) make little contribution to the constructive strategic mission of revolution. The government responded with equally ruthless repression. It rallied the Revolutionary Guard to engage in direct counterattacks against the guerrillas and used the revolutionary courts to impose a flurry of executions of regime opponents. When the guerrillas tried to move to the urban equivalent of guerrilla warfare by sending out their partisans to instigate riots and demonstrations, they encountered the full wrath of the Revolutionary Guard and club-wielding *Hezbollahis* (partisans of the Party of God, that is, the IRP). Since the guerrillas possessed no significant organizational base among the urban masses, their sacrifices failed to ignite a mass rising.

The Mojahedin, then, lacked sufficient resources to overcome the free rider problem even though many Iranians were discontented with the declining economic conditions and hostile to clerical authoritarianism. By the end of 1982 regime countermeasures had decimated their ranks, and the Mojahedin ceased to be a significant threat. In December Khomeini felt sufficiently secure to issue a declaration curbing the worst abuses of the regime's program of counterterrorism.[99]

The Islamic regime consolidated its power largely from the top down. Unlike the broad-based uprising that chased the Shah from power, the political support for the Islamic Republic was much narrower. The Ayatollah Khomeini retained considerable legitimacy in the popular mind, but the political forces that cleaved to him succeeded by eliminating other competitors for power. Secular political elements, both moderate and extreme, along with their moderate religious allies, were pushed to the political margins, if not killed outright. A religious hierarchy subordinated political authority and enforced its writ through considerable coercion.

NOTES

1. Fereydoun Hoveyda, *The Fall of the Shah* (New York: Wyndam, 1979), p. 13.
2. See Samuel Huntington, *Political Order in Changing Societies* (New Haven, Conn.: Yale University Press, 1968), pp. 266–274.

3. Huntington quotes Pettee to the effect that the revolutionaries in the Western-style revolution often enter the newly emptied political arena "like fearful children" (ibid., p. 268).

4. The revolution in Iran has spurred a considerable range of scholarship, though not as profuse as the literature on Vietnam. A review of the background to the revolutionary process is provided by Said A. Arjomand, *The Turban and the Crown: The Islamic Revolution in Iran* (New York: Oxford University Press, 1988). A study focusing on the struggle to consolidate power after the fall of the Shah is that of Shaul Bakhash, *The Reign of the Ayatollahs: Iran and the Islamic Revolution,* Revised Edition (New York: Basic Books, 1990). A "revisionist" interpetation is provided by Jahangir Amuzegar, *The Dynamics of the Iranian Revolution: The Pahlavis' Triumph and Tragedy* (Albany: State University of New York Press, 1991).

5. Bakhash, p. 21.

6. Ibid., pp. 33–35.

7. Quoted in ibid., p. 34.

8. Quoted in James A. Bill, *The Eagle and the Lion: The Tragedy of American-Iranian Relations* (New Haven, Conn.: Yale University Press, 1988), p. 160. Bill's book provides a good examination of the misunderstanding that has characterized American policy toward Iran.

9. Asaf Hussain, *Islamic Iran: Revolution and Counter-Revolution* (London: Francis Pinter, 1985), p. 22.

10. This summary is based on ibid., pp. 23–26.

11. Ibid., p. 24.

12. Hamid Algar, "Islam and Shi'ism," in Kalim Siddiqui, ed., *The Islamic Revolution in Iran* (London: The Open Press, 1980), p. 2.

13. Ibid., pp. 2–3.

14. Ibid., p. 3.

15. Ibid.

16. Ibid., p. 4.

17. Ibid., pp. 4–5.

18. Ibid., p. 6.

19. Hussain, pp. 28–29.

20. See, for example, the discussion in Amuzegar, pp. 37–52.

21. Mohsen M. Milani, *The Making of Iran's Islamic Revolution: From Monarchy to Islamic Republic* (Boulder, Colo.: Westview Press, 1988), p. 127.

22. Ibid., p. 107.

23. Ibid., pp. 106–109.

24. Ibid., pp. 111–112.

25. Ibid., p. 113.

26. Ibid., p. 109.

27. Ibid.

28. Ibid., p. 108.

29. Ibid., pp. 120–121.

30. Ibid., pp. 121–122.

31. Ibid., p. 118.

32. Ibid.

33. Ibid.

34. Ibid., pp. 122–127.

35. For example, Milani gives two significantly different figures for the total population in the mid-1970s. In one spot he indicates that the 1976 population was just over 33.7 million; two pages later, a table gives the total population in 1977 as 30.7 million (see

pp. 119, 121). Neither of these figures is easy to reconcile with that of Farrokh Moshiri, who estimates the total population in 1978 at 36.5 million. See Farrokh Moshiri, "Iran: Islamic Revolution Against Westernization," in Jack A. Goldstone, Ted Robert Gurr, and Farrokh Moshiri, eds., *Revolutions of the Late Twentieth Century* (Boulder, Colo.: Westview Press, 1991), p. 122. Moshiri, moreover, indicates that the population was 26 million in 1960 and only 27.15 million in 1970, implying a growth rate of less than 5 percent for the entire decade. His data suggests that the population grew by 6.25 million over the next five years, an increase of over 23 percent in a half decade. Either Iranians were very busy making up for lost time, or these figures are suspect.

36. *Demographic Yearbook,* 1970, 1979 (New York: United Nations, 1971, 1980).

37. In 1976 over 25 million of a total population of 33.7 million (or 75 percent) were estimated to be under age 35. See *Demographic Yearbook,* 1979.

38. Amuzegar, however, correctly points out that the demographic trends and the social conditions to which they contributed—rural migration, underemployment, inflation, strained social services—were less severe in Iran than in many other Third World countries. See pp. 53–65. We must recall, though, that these background causes of social strain cannot by themselves explain why and when a revolution occurs. See Chapter 6.

39. James DeFronzo, *Revolutions and Revolutionary Movements* (Boulder, Colo.: Westview Press, 1991), p. 250.

40. Ibid., pp. 250–251. Again, Amuzegar points out that these effects were not as severe as in many other developing countries, and that the working population was still relatively well-off. See pp. 54–56.

41. See the discussion in Jack A. Goldstone, *Revolution and Rebellion in the Early Modern World* (Berkeley: University of California Press, 1991), pp. 13–15.

42. Milani, pp. 159–174.

43. Amuzegar, pp. 242–245.

44. Ibid., pp. 247–249.

45. Ibid., pp. 249–255.

46. Ibid., pp. 269–288.

47. Milani, pp. 180–184.

48. Arjomand, pp. 118–119.

49. Goldstone, pp. 46–50.

50. Ibid., p. 105. I should note that Goldstone develops all these indicators in a more systematic fashion than I attempt here.

51. M. H. Pesaran, "Economic Development and Revolutionary Upheavals in Iran," in Haleh Afshar, ed., *Iran: A Revolution in Turmoil* (London: The Macmillan Press, 1985), p. 24.

52. These IMF figures are reported in Milani, p. 168.

53. Ibid., p. 167.

54. Goldstone, pp. 123–125.

55. *Statistical Yearbook,* 1960, 1981 (New York: United Nations, 1961, 1982).

56. Arjomand, p. 106.

57. Ibid., p. 108.

58. Goldstone, pp. 134–141.

59. Pesaran, p. 26.

60. Hooshang Amirahmadi, *Revolution and Economic Transition: The Iranian Experience* (Albany: The State University of New York Press, 1990), pp. 134, 195.

61. *Demographic Yearbook,* 1979.

62. Goldstone, pp. 148–149.
63. For an analysis of these various groups and their political leanings see Ervand Abra-
    hamian, *Iran: Between Two Revolutions* (Princeton, N.J.: Princeton University Press,
    1982), pp. 480–495. For a review of the history of the protests see Arjomand, pp.
    91–133, and Milani, pp. 179–235.
64. This analysis is similar to that of both Milani and Moshiri. My interpretations, empha-
    sis, and mistakes are, of course, my own.
65. Arjomand, p. 91.
66. Ibid., pp. 91–92.
67. Ibid., pp. 92–93.
68. Ibid., p. 92.
69. Ibid., pp. 93–94, 98.
70. Ibid., p. 105.
71. Ibid., pp. 106–113.
72. Ibid., p. 99.
73. Ibid., pp. 118–119.
74. Ibid., p. 118.
75. Milani, p. 192.
76. Arjomand, p. 110.
77. See, for example, Timur Kuran, "Sparks and Prairie Fires: A Theory of Unanticipated
    Political Revolution," *Public Choice*, 61 (April 1989): 41–74.
78. See Arjomand, pp. 110–120; also Milani, pp. 218–224.
79. Milani, p. 193.
80. Ibid.
81. Arjomand, pp. 99–100.
82. Ibid., p. 101.
83. For a good summary of his life see Bakhash, pp. 19–51.
84. Ibid., pp. 38–39.
85. Arjomand, p. 103.
86. Ibid.
87. Ibid., p. 105.
88. For a more extended review of these events see ibid., pp. 114–128; see also Milani,
    pp. 190–225.
89. Arjomand, pp. 115–116.
90. Ibid., p. 119.
91. Quoted in Dilip Hiro, *Iran Under the Ayatollahs* (London: Routledge and Kegan
    Paul, 1985), p. 100.
92. Arjomand, p. 122.
93. For a detailed history of the period of power consolidation see Bakhash, especially
    Chapters 3–6 and Chapter 9.
94. Arjomand, pp. 139–141.
95. Bakhash, p. 144.
96. Ibid.
97. Ibid., pp. 141–144.
98. Ibid., p. 219.
99. Ibid., pp. 228–230.

12

Tragic Choices, Tragic Outcomes: Political Violence and Revolutionary Change[*]

The resort to coercive means to achieve our political objectives, whether those of revolutionary transformation or preservation of the status quo, raises difficult ethical issues. While these dilemmas cannot be definitively resolved, we identify some of the particular problems of justifying revolution and explore the impact of extreme coercion on revolutionary ends. We then look at what various theories and explanations for violence and revolution suggest about the corruption of revolutionary ends. Finally, we investigate the degree to which outcomes in Vietnam and Iran illustrate some of the ethical problems of revolutionary action.

JUSTIFYING REVOLUTIONARY VIOLENCE

In a striking scene near the close of Goethe's dramatic poem, the dying Faust hears the sounds of "clattering spades" outside his palace. He mistakenly concludes that workers are laboring on his grandiose plan to drain a marsh and create an earthly paradise. They actually are digging Faust's own grave. Comforted by this delusion, he dies.[1] Jon Gunnemann suggests that revolutionaries often labor under a similar delusion. They mistake the sounds of grave diggers for the construction of their new Jerusalem.[2]

This irony captures the tragedy of many revolutions. Despite declarations of universal rights and aspirations for universal justice, revolutions often fall short of their ideals. All too frequently the road to the New Revolutionary Order lies paved with the victims of "revolutionary justice." Revolutions made in the name of liberty create new tyrannies. Revolutions made in the name of equality institutionalize new inequities. Revolutions made in the name of life spread death. Perhaps the revolution eventually moderates its more extreme impulses and makes pragmatic compromises with a recalcitrant reality, compromises that often bend the revolution to the very forces that previously provoked it.

---

[*]With the assistance of Mark N. Crislip.

Even the best of revolutions seem gravely flawed. Consider, for example, the American Revolution. Bravely justified in the name of human liberty and equality, the new American republic tolerated slavery in its Constitution. This pragmatic compromise between slave and free states festered at the heart of the Constitution's "more perfect union" until finally breaking open in a bloody civil war. Even today America continues to pay the price for this gap between its ideals and the social and political conditions it accepts.[3] Apart from such compromises, skeptics might compare the political history and current conditions in Australia and Canada (two other English settler colonies) with those in the United States and wonder if the Revolution was worth the cost in blood or was even necessary to ensure the liberty of the colonists.

Such retrospective second-guessing, of course, plays into a profoundly conservative agenda and tends to deny the authenticity of any revolutionary grievances. Revolutionaries, we must remember, confront real oppression, not hypothetical disappointments, and they often ignore the "lessons of history" while experiencing more immediate tutoring in tyranny. Michael Walzer precisely defines the ethical conundrum confronting revolutionaries and others who employ extreme means to achieve apparently worthy objectives. He notes that "there are some outcomes that must be avoided at all costs" but "there are some costs that can never rightly be paid."[4] Such choices define the essence of tragedy. To overcome an intolerable status quo, revolutionaries often resort to intolerable means that ultimately subvert the very ends used to justify them.

The overused cliché about the ends justifying the means and its equally simplistic rejection, however, fail to illuminate the real dilemmas facing revolutionaries. The debate of ends and means breaks down into at least four interrelated issues: What ends? What circumstances? What means? And what consequences? Perhaps each of these issues deserves its own essay. Here we only indicate some essential points to consider.

What Ends?

Commonly, we do refer to the goals of our actions to justify the means we choose to pursue them. The pursuit of any goal involves the expenditure of our energies and our resources. All political action entails costs, both direct costs in terms of the time, effort, and resources used and opportunity costs in terms of other desirable alternatives which we must therefore forgo. We justify these costs in terms of the value we attach to the ends we pursue. In pure economic terms such comparison of costs and benefits is straightforward. In political calculations, where the ends sought are often abstract collective goods like national liberation and the costs are difficult to estimate, combine, and compare with these ends, the assessment becomes far more difficult.

Although we refer to our ends in justifying our choice of means, this does not mean that any end, however trivial, justifies any means, however costly. The first challenge in the debate over revolutionary choice, then, involves evaluating the ends pursued. At the extreme some political goals seem so reprehensible that they stand condemned by the world community. For example, the goal of racial or ethnic domination, widely accepted as recently as the nineteenth century, now stands in considerable, though clearly not universal, disrepute.

Most revolutions, however, invoke goals that the world's peoples hold in high regard. Revolutionary movements claim to act in the name of national liberation, individual liberty, social justice, or righteous living. Such ideals seem worthy of considerable sacrifice. But how much sacrifice do they justify? Their nebulous character makes it difficult to determine. We also find it difficult to establish whether revolutionaries hold these goals sincerely. Finally, even if revolutionaries sincerely believe in the formal revolutionary objectives, they generally possess less praiseworthy tacit goals, such as revenge, political ambition, personal enrichment, or even the desire to indulge in repressed impulses. The more these tacit goals displace the formal ones, the more we can speak of the corruption of the revolution.

What Circumstances?

Even those goals we find admirable in the abstract may not deserve endorsement once we specify the concrete circumstances of their pursuit. The nature of revolutionary change reinforces this problem. Change becomes revolutionary in character depending on how radically it alters the status quo. (See the discussion of the definition of revolution in Chapter 2.) The status quo, though, does not float freely above the social world; rather, it lies embedded in the values and lives of human beings. Classical conservatives like Edmund Burke correctly observe that the righteous pursuit of revolutionary reconstruction often blindly destroys values and institutions that have emerged over centuries to define the meaning and significance of people's lives.[5] The very nature of *revolutionary* ends, then, raises the cost of their pursuit, in terms of both social and personal disruption. Critics of the status quo, of course, rightly retort that we cannot simply compare the benefits of the existing order with the costs of disrupting it. Rather, the toll of maintaining the status quo and the benefits of the New Revolutionary Order must also weigh in our deliberations.

Since revolutionary change, however meritorious in the abstract, threatens vested interests in a community, it also provokes vigorous opposition. In the Eastern model of revolution this opposition arises from the old regime. In the Western type the opposition intensifies during the struggle for power after the old regime's collapse. In either case, vigorous opposition provokes vigorous efforts to overcome it. In this way radical goals foster extreme means, again raising the costs of pursuing revolutionary objectives.

The circumstances of revolutionary change, then, contribute to the tragedy of revolutionary action. The more bitterly divided the community, the more likely that the contenders for power will use unacceptable means to prevent what they see as an unacceptable outcome. Not all means, however, are equally unacceptable.

What Means?

The nature of revolutionary goals and the circumstances of the revolutionary struggle propel the contenders toward more extreme means, particularly, though not exclusively, physical coercion. Physical coercion harms the lives or other value possessions of the victims (see Chapter 2). Coercion may involve either tactics of direct attack or withheld support. The former directly destroys the target's value position; the latter indirectly erodes it (see Chapter 9). Revolutionary conflict, of course, may draw on all available power resources, not simply the means of physical coercion. Often we see the recourse to physical coercion as our last or ultimate resort, especially under extreme circumstances.

Unlike other ways of exercising power, the use of coercion seems inherently evil. Whereas other resources could improve the targets' position, *in their own estimation*, coercion only damages it. (Bribes, for example, improve people's material position; invoking status convinces them of the correctness of the recommended course of action, and so on. See the discussion of power resources in Chapter 1.) Consequently we usually defend the use of coercion in tragic terms as the *lesser evil* under the circumstances. The inherent evil of coercive tactics places special conditions on their use by either the regime or the revolutionaries.

1. *The resort to coercion must come only after we have exhausted all other, less destructive, means of achieving our objectives.* This condition presumably places a special burden on those advocating revolutionary change in a relatively responsive political order, democratic or otherwise. If other avenues to gain redress of their grievances exist, then the general ethical prescription to "do no harm" takes on added weight. Analogously, the regime should use coercion only when other means of securing compliance have failed. Of course, a relatively responsive political order helps to ensure that revolutionary grievances remain confined to the fringes of the community and that most of the people, most of the time, obey without the threat of severe punishment hanging over their heads.

2. *The resort to coercion must be effective.* Here the question concerns whether coercion, however severe, can achieve the ends pursued. A myth of efficacy, as we noted in Chapter 9, surrounds the resort to coercion, whether force or violence. We often presume that when all else fails, coercion will succeed. We might better start with the presumption that no situation is so bad that the application of coercive means cannot make it worse. Clearly, if coercion cannot achieve the ends, however attractive, then we cannot use it. Under these circumstances we would inflict the costs of coercion with no compensating benefits. The choice of coercion then becomes the greater, not the lesser, evil.

3. *The resort to coercion must be proportionate.* Assuming that coercion provides an effective response, the evil inevitably inflicted by coercion should not exceed the evil so attacked. In most criminal law, for example, "self-defense" justifies homicide only when the victim truly threatened the perpetrator's life. We cannot justifiably kill another person just because of a gratuitous insult, though unfortunately insults often provoke murder. Under conditions of internal warfare, issues of proportionality arise from the cycle of reprisals that often develop. When the Nazis killed ten civilians for every soldier they lost to resistance fighters, they probably violated, among other things, the principle of proportionality.

4. *The resort to coercion must be efficient.* Even if coercion provides an effective response to repression (or rebellion) and if the coercive tactics chosen are proportionate to the threat, all the associated costs must be identified and minimized. Since coercion always inflicts some harm and is justified only as the lesser evil, care must be taken to inflict the least harm possible in accomplishing the objective. If, for example, the police can physically restrain a suspect, they cannot justifiably beat this person senseless.

5. *The use of coercive tactics must be discriminating.*[6] In conventional war this principle entails noncombatant immunity. The combatants in a military struggle can justifiably target one another, but they cannot attack noncombatants. Beyond this criterion some revolutionaries argue that they can legitimately target particular "noncombatants"—like a tyrant—who share special responsibility for upholding an evil political order. Under this broader principle combatants must still take care to avoid harming those who are not responsible for the tyranny. Finally, since war often traps noncombatants in the field of fire, ethical combatants must take every possible measure to minimize incidental or accidental harm to them. For this reason an attack on a city occupied by enemy military forces raises difficult ethical issues, since extensive "collateral" damage seems unavoidable. Similarly, some argue that weapons of mass destruction (nuclear, chemical, and biological weapons) invariably kill indiscriminately and thus are inherently unethical.

These principles, and perhaps others as well, should govern the use of coercion by all combatants in a political conflict. Should, but often don't. The failure to follow such ethical prescriptions arises from more than human perversity, although revolutionary conflicts, in particular, often call out the worst in human beings. In addition, these principles prove difficult to apply in practice.

Take the first principle, that of exhausting all other means before resorting to coercion. Revolutionaries generally lack a clear menu of alternative means that they can tick off, one by one, as they "exhaust" them. Moreover, if other avenues of redress theoretically exist, they may be neither promising nor timely. Does a remote possibility of gaining some measure of redress some day obligate the disaffected to reject the resort to coercion? Conservatives commonly counsel patience, but how much patience must people possess? The African National Congress, for example, took up the "armed struggle" only after 50 years of working for peaceful change in South Africa. Is 50 years long enough?

According to the second principle we should not resort to coercive tactics if they won't work. This seems straightforward enough. Unfortunately, in addition to the myth of efficacy that surrounds coercion, we seldom know what will or will not work in advance. Clearly futile suicide attacks make up only a small proportion of the coercion used in political conflicts around the world. In most circumstances the combatants might honestly believe that their coercion will work. Moreover, they may *want* to believe in coercion's efficacy simply because they have exhausted all noncoercive means of achieving their ends. Finally, we must remember the tragic dimension of intense political struggles. Sometimes when people confront a totally unacceptable outcome, they will choose to go down fighting, even in a hopeless situation, rather than submit. Who can condemn the Jews of the Warsaw Ghetto who fought the Germans, though they probably killed some soldiers who might otherwise have lived, while not improving their own chances for survival one whit?

The principles of proportionality and efficiency also seem clear in the abstract but prove difficult to apply, particularly in the context of combat. Indeed, these moral prescriptions sometimes seem to conflict with military common sense and with each other. For example, in attempting to achieve a tactical objective, costs may be minimized *for both contenders,* if one side can bring overwhelming power to bear on the other. Proportionate response may simply guarantee a bloody stalemate. Consequently, military leaders, whether of regular or irregular forces, tend to err on the side of excessive force. Too much, from their point of view, is better than too little. In the "fog of war," moreover, the combatants cannot carry out the calculus required by considerations of proportionality and efficiency.

Finally, the principle of discrimination seems especially difficult to follow in the kind of irregular warfare characteristic of revolutionary conflicts. Guerrillas, as we noted in Chapter 9, succeed to the extent that they blend into the native population from whom they draw their support. The line between combatant and noncombatant becomes progressively blurred, and regime soldiers may vent their frustration by striking out at everyone. Moreover, both regime and revolutionaries tend to define their enemies rather broadly, condemning people not normally considered combatants. Such tragic results were all too common in Vietnam, for example. In Iran, on the other hand, the Ayatollah admonished revolutionary crowds *not* to strike back at attacking soldiers, in the hopes of undermining military morale. In this case a broader strategic objective overruled a possibly justifiable response.

Even if the contenders follow all the ethical conditions with which we hedge in the choice of coercion, a problem still remains. What effect does the choice of inherently evil means have on the ends of political action?

What Consequences?

The pursuit of radical ends usually generates stiff opposition. If they lack the power to overcome this resistance through noncoercive means, revolutionaries often turn to more destructive tactics. Regimes, when faced with a destructive radical challenge, commonly resort to increasingly severe coercion as well. The more destructive the tactics used, the more likely such evil means will corrupt the ends, no matter how noble. In some sense the dynamics of corruption could contribute to the violation of the principles of efficiency and proportionality, regardless of the perpetrators' intentions. This corruption arises most commonly with severe tactics of direct attack, as opposed to the indirect coercion of withheld obedience. A number of processes appear to account for the corruption of ends.

1. *Destructive coercion creates destructive personalities.*[7] In order to destroy other human beings it "helps" if either we do not view them as sharing fully in our humanity or, even better, we do not view them at all. Ideologies that portray certain people as subhuman or malevolent facilitate their destruc-

tion. Technologies that provide for remote destruction render the victims nearly invisible. At the same time that we dehumanize others, though, we damage our own humanity. Many psychiatrists view inability to identify with others as a pathological condition.[8] Similarly, technologies that make destruction increasingly remote essentially reduce their operators to mere extensions of the machines of destruction.

2. *Destructive coercion attracts destructive personalities.* The processes of destruction do more than dehumanize both perpetrators and victims. Those organizations using such tactics attract pathological personalities looking for an outlet for their destructive impulses. (See the discussion of malignantly destructive personalities in Chapter 7.) As the role of destructive coercion grows more central to an organization's operations, the more likely it is that such personalities will rise to positions of power.

3. *The expanded use of destructive coercion enhances the power of coercive organizations.* Just as destructive personalities find a home in coercive organizations, the power of coercive organizations increases in both the revolutionary movement and the regime as the role of destructive coercion increases. When the political struggle grows more destructive, the military wings of both contenders tend to usurp ever more power. In the regime representative institutions decay and civil liberties suffer, while the power of the army and the police becomes paramount. In a prolonged coercive struggle, whether with the regime as in Vietnam, or with other revolutionary contenders for power as in Iran, the coercive organizations of the revolutionary movement grow increasingly important. In either case the revolutionaries often sacrifice promises of political liberty and social justice on the altar of military necessity.

4. *The increasing use of destructive coercion also contributes to greater centralization and secrecy in both regime and revolutionary movement.*[9] The systematic application of destructive tactics usually demands strong centralization and places a premium on secrecy. Military organizations generally lack open and democratic processes, emphasizing strict command and unquestioning obedience. Practically speaking, if either regime or revolutionaries planned destructive attacks in the open, their opponents could easily counter them.

5. *Destructive attacks legitimate destructive reprisals.* The use of destructive coercion often sets off a bloody cycle of retribution and revenge that becomes difficult to stop. The original purposes are lost, as each outrage justifies equally outrageous retaliation. René Gerard observes that "(v)engeance professes to be an act of reprisal, and every reprisal calls for another reprisal. . . . Vengeance, then, is an interminable, infinitely repetitive process."[10] At the extreme, such a blood cycle threatens to degenerate into an anarchy destructive of the positive goals of both revolutionaries and regime. In the past 20 years, events in Lebanon, Yugoslavia, and Somalia illustrate the potential extremes of this blood cycle.

6. *Destructive coercion damages, perhaps fundamentally, the social and economic infrastructure of the contenders.* War, whether international or

internal, often leaves both victor and vanquished in far worse condition than they started. Sometimes we cannot even distinguish a victor; rather, the contenders fight to a bloody stalemate. These consequences become bitterly ironic in a revolutionary civil war, because the contenders struggle over the same community and territory. At least with international war each side attacks the resources of an external enemy. In a revolutionary war the contenders destroy the resources, both human and material, of the community they ultimately wish to control.

7. *The contenders in a violent political struggle often follow the perverse logic of sunk costs.* At any point in the struggle, the contenders cannot know future costs, but they possess a keen sense of their past sacrifices. Consequently they continue the struggle so that their prior sacrifices will not have been made in vain. Ironically, the logic of attempting to recover sunk costs may seem more compelling as these costs increase.

Perhaps if Ho Chi Minh had foreseen from the beginning the devastation and death the thirty-year liberation struggle would cost his country, he might have hesitated to declare independence in 1945. Even Khomeini might have paused in his uncompromising destruction of the Shah's regime, if he had possessed foreknowledge of the terrible destruction caused by Iraq's cynical attack on the revolution-weakened Iran.

Revolutionaries, of course, never face choices this clear. Rather, they must choose to continue fighting for uncertain victory or admit that their past sacrifices were merely an exercise in futility. Surrender, moreover, may well include costs in addition to those already endured and the abandonment of the movement's political goals. The victorious side may also inflict terrible reprisals on the vanquished. The logic of sunk costs, then, tends to drive the contenders in both external and internal wars to continue the struggle unless faced with overwhelming evidence of certain defeat. Even then, they might choose self-destruction over surrender.

For all these reasons the resort to increasingly destructive coercion seems especially corrupting of the purposes of the revolutionary movement or, for that matter, of the regime. Of course, we cannot equate all forms of coercion. We have already distinguished between tactics of direct attack and those of withheld obedience. In addition, directly destructive coercion varies in its destructive implications. Limiting and controlling the tactics may limit and control their corrupting impact. Nevertheless, the potential for corruption seems undeniably present, further reinforcing the tragic position of those who engage in intolerable acts to end intolerable conditions.

HOW REVOLUTIONS DIE—THE THEORIES

In Part Two we examined a number of explanations for political violence and revolution. Several of these include, explicitly or implicitly, certain theoretical insights into the corruption of revolutionary ends. Paralleling this earlier discussion, we first examine those approaches focusing on the level of individual behavior and then those emphasizing more broadly construed structures and processes.

Corrupting Influences, Corrupting Decisions

Ted Robert Gurr, in his complex relative deprivation model, argues that the intensity and scope of the justifications for political violence in a particular community partly determine whether increased frustration translates into a disposition to political violence. The model suggests that experience with violence provides the major justifications for the subsequent resort to political violence. For example, major variables include "extrapunitiveness" of individual socialization, historical magnitude of political violence in the community, past frequency of political violence, past success with political violence, perceived success of other groups with political violence, and the "density" of portrayals of violence in the media.[11] Gurr, then, provides a systematic representation of the blood cycle of violence. Not only does personal experience with violence contribute to future violence, but indirectly experienced violence—in history, other groups' actions, or the media—also justifies the resort to violence. Gurr notes that violence "consumes" people, "its victims physically, its practitioners mentally, by habituating them to violence as the means and end of life."[12]

His model also suggests that coercion, as a practical matter, more likely violates limits of effectiveness, efficiency, and relevance as the contenders approach relative parity. Parity maximizes the magnitude of political violence.[13] Neither side can eliminate its opponent nor admit defeat. Consequently each continues the struggle with the weapons at its disposal. Under conditions of parity, therefore, strategies of coercion lose their effectiveness in achieving victory even as they probably prove sufficient to prevent defeat. The ends used to justify the costs of coercion recede further over the horizon while, at the same time, these costs mount ever higher. When effectiveness and efficiency in achieving ultimate objectives become secondary to the struggle for survival, concern for the relevance of coercion's victims also probably declines. Under these circumstances, and "(i)n view of the resources available to modern governments and modern revolutionary movements, total victory is highly likely to be pyrrhic victory."[14]

Gurr's deprivation model suggests how the dynamics of violent political struggle might result in costs exceeding any potential benefit. The rational actor approach offers a different perspective into the corruption of revolutionary ends. The effort of the revolutionary movement to overcome the free rider problem (see Chapter 5) contributes to a variety of potential pathologies. Essentially, the free rider problem encourages both leaders and followers to act strategically rather than sincerely in their interactions. Many of the solutions to the free rider problem encourage self-serving leaders, opportunistic followers, authoritarian organizations, and the compromise of revolutionary objectives.[15]

From the rational actor perspective, leaders participate in revolutionary action largely, though not entirely, because of concrete selective incentives. (The rational belief that their participation increases the probability of achieving victory represents one exception.) When selective incentives motivate participation in collective action, the pursuit of personal profit may displace the collective good. Leaders, then, may compromise the revolution to maximize their personal gain. In addition, leaders possess an incentive to disguise their actual motives, manipulate ideological appeals, and spread disinformation to influence the calculations of their potential followers. Interestingly, this hypocrisy includes both disguising their personal greed behind a facade of self-sacrificing rhetoric and obscuring the true nature of the New Revolutionary Order so as not to alienate potential supporters.

Similar corruption arises among revolutionary followers as well. They too participate essentially because of concrete selective incentives (if we exclude the possibility of "thicker" rational incentives). The desire for these incentives encourages the professionalization of protest. The followers won't follow in the absence of selective rewards. The extreme case of professional followers is, of course, the mercenary army that fights for pay, not patriotism. Like their leaders, revolutionary followers disguise their true motives in order to receive the rewards. The bandwagon effect, indeed, depends on the opportunistic calculations of many neutrals and previous opponents of the revolutionary movement. Even sincere revolutionary leaders, therefore, may discover at the moment of their triumph that they lead a movement of dubious loyalty. For this reason, Marxist revolutionaries fear a military Bonaparte who supports the Revolution to advance his personal ambition.

Revolutionary organization helps mobilize the resources needed to provide selective incentives and monitor for defections. Unfortunately, the strategies of revolutionary mobilization tend to corrupt the organization. We have already noted the incentives for leaders to disguise their true motives. Leaders' hypocrisy encourages secretive organizations that deceive followers as to the true purpose of their activities. Moreover, one major solution to the free rider problem involves raising the cost of defection. This solution, however, increases the role of coercion *within* the organization. As the desire for personal reward corrupts the leaders, they tend to become a self-perpetuating oligarchy. The combination of hypocrisy, secretiveness, increased coercion (both internally and externally directed), and oligarchy implies that the revolutionary movement, whatever its formal ideological pretensions, will grow increasingly authoritarian. The logic of collective action seems to lead revolutions made in the name of liberty and equality in the direction of tyranny and inequality.

Clearly, then, the strategies to overcome the free rider problem tend to corrupt the purity of revolutionary ends. Opportunism and goal displacement among both leaders and followers lead the movement to lose sight of their original objectives. The desire for selective incentives may enable the regime to co-opt the revolutionary movement. (Recall that one major regime strategy of preservation entails buying off the moderately discontented as a way of isolating any remaining radicals. See Chapter 1.) The pursuit of selective incentives, moreover, encourages an unsuccessful revolutionary movement to degenerate into social banditry.

If the movement secures power, then the pursuit of selective incentives leads to further compromises of revolutionary objectives as the new rulers attempt to consolidate their position. In part this arises because the leaders begin to enjoy the privileges of power and forsake their revolutionary roots. In part it results from the necessity to form opportunistic coalitions to gain and maintain power. This latter necessity produces a double irony. At first revolutionary leaders may disguise their true revolutionary goals to secure the loyalty of neutrals. Once in power they may find themselves trapped by their own hypocrisy and forced to abandon their revolutionary beliefs to preserve themselves in power. Sometimes, of course, revolutionaries abandon pretense once in power and attempt to follow their previously hidden agenda. If much of their support, however, followed because of the hypocritical promises of the leaders, these followers will probably feel betrayed and react bitterly. As we will see, both Vietnam and Iran experienced this type of postrevolutionary disillusionment.

Much of the corruption at the individual level of participation and decision occurs regardless of whether or not the revolutionary movement comes to power. The corrupting effects of violence and the strategic manipulation of selective incentives affect victors and vanquished alike. If the revolution achieves nominal success in overthrowing the previous regime, additional problems of process and structure also arise to frustrate the realization of revolutionary ideals.

Process and Structure: Revolution and Reality

In a classic metaphor for the revolutionary process, Crane Brinton compares revolution to a fever that builds to a crescendo of virtue and terror and then subsides as more moderate political elements return to power. (See the discussion of organic metaphors for revolution in Chapter 4.)[16] He suggests that revolution, as a process, cannot sustain a high level of idealism and commitment. Ultimately, political exhaustion compromises the revolutionary vision, as people grow weary of the continuous disruption of their lives. "The outsider in the [revolutionary] crisis period is pushed to the limit of his endurance by interference with some of his most prized and intimate routines; the insider is held to a pitch of spiritual effort and excitement beyond his powers of endurance." Brinton suggests that "human beings can endure for but a limited time the concerted attempt to bring heaven to earth. . . ."[17] In a flurry of metaphors he asserts that the revolutionary tide ebbs, the storm calms, the fever breaks, and society snaps back like a "stretched elastic band."[18] Try as they might, revolutionary saints inevitably find their utopia compromised by "clumsy deals," or worse, swept aside by those promising a return to order and efficiency.

Brinton focused his analysis of the revolutionary process on the "Great Revolutions" in France, Russia, and to a lesser extent the United States. More recently Theodore Hamerow has analyzed the "graying" of twentieth-century Marxist revolutions and provided a more specific depiction of the death of revolutionary ideals.[19] In part, ideological disillusionment and the institutionalization of an authoritarian postrevolutionary regime reflect the failures of Marxist revolutionary theory. (See the discussion in Chapter 6.) Marxist revolutionaries generally expected that their particular upheavals were simply the first shots in a cascade of world revolutionary activity. The Bolsheviks hoped for supporting revolutions in the advanced industrial countries of the West. The Chinese

Communists claimed that their revolution would serve as a model for world revolution of the global countryside (that is, the Third World nations) against its cities (the Western industrial powers of the First World). Cuban revolutionaries thought they had perfected the model of revolution of Latin America.

Unfortunately for the theory, and despite some initially promising signs, all these expectations proved unwarranted, as the forces of world capitalism rallied. Each of these revolutionary regimes was forced to turn inward and accept "socialism in one country." Moreover, surrounded by enemies, both real and imagined, they consolidated power and control. These regimes increasingly worried about their own security. Political suppression, at first directed only against clear-cut enemies, expanded to include previous allies who did not adhere to the party line. Ultimately, coercion took aim at members of doubtful loyalty in the ruling party itself.

Marxist theory also promises that the revolution, by unleashing previously fettered productive forces, will usher in an age of economic prosperity. Although most Marxist revolutions improved the material position of the least advantaged sectors, especially in the areas of health and literacy, economic progress remained slow. Inexperienced and doctrinaire leadership contributed to this slow progress. Revolutionary economic theory mandated economic experiments, like the collectivization of agriculture, that required great coercion to implement and ultimately proved unproductive or even disastrous. Consequently the ideology that promised prosperity and economic justice reinforced trends toward political authoritarianism and at the same time generated an economic crisis that forced a choice between economic decline or compromise of revolutionary ideals.

Hamerow also observes that disappointments of theory led first to disillusionment and then to defections in these revolutions. Ideological fervor necessarily dissipated. Even worse, the second generation of postrevolutionary leadership generally succumbed to the privileges of power, while continuing to pay lip service to revolutionary ideals. New forms of social and political inequality emerged, as party and government bureaucrats garnered access to a material life style far beyond that of the masses. Even worse from the perspective of revolutionary ideals, this "new class" tended to perpetuate itself by passing on its privileges to its children.[20] Disillusion, defection, and corruption spread from the elites to the masses. As promises of liberty, equality, and prosperity faded into some hazy future, average citizens lost their revolutionary fervor and devoted increasing energies simply to the struggle to maintain their lives.

Hamerow concludes that after a generation the New Revolutionary Order begins to show "the same signs of senescence and ossification, formalism and rigidity, that had characterized the *ancien régime* prior to its fall."[21] A widening gap appears between official ideals and reality; new distinctions of wealth and status emerge and are consolidated; political power, at first more fluid, becomes more centralized and exclusive; and finally, the moral basis of the new order calcifies into a new orthodoxy. The final abandonment of Marxist revolutionary theory, of course, came first with the economic reforms and then with the revolutions that swept over most of the Communist world in the past 15 years.

Hamerow's study focuses on the historical experience of twentieth-century

Marxist revolutions. We must be careful, therefore, in extracting general claims about the death of all revolutions from this history. Nevertheless, his analysis indicates problems inherent in any revolutionary theory that achieves its first objective of seizing power. The expectations it necessarily generates, along with its incomplete understanding of the political, social, and economic conditions it confronts, seem likely to lead to similar cycles of failed predictions and authoritarian responses, of inevitable disillusionment and consequent defections, of formal orthodoxy and actual corruption.

Disequilibrium theories indicate some reasons for this cycle of disillusionment. In these various approaches (see Chapter 6), revolutionary crises develop when the existing social and political order proves incapable of managing certain fundamental challenges. The resulting crisis creates an opportunity for new social groupings to seize power. We observed that a successful revolutionary movement does not need to perform perfectly. It only needs to outperform its competitors in the regime and in other opposition groups. But once it seizes the commanding heights of a society, the movement then faces the problems that generated the revolutionary opportunity in the first place. Moreover, particularly in a prolonged "Eastern model" revolutionary war, the movement also confronts the problems created by its struggle.

In Samuel Huntington's view, for example, revolutions reflect extreme crises of modernization. Social change creates new social groups and generates escalating demands for participation.[22] These demands may topple the old regime, but they do not then fade away. Rather, the New Revolutionary Order must somehow structure participation, and, as Huntington observes, it generally does this in an authoritarian manner. In his Western model of revolution the solutions to the participatory problem emerge after the old regime has fallen, during the struggle to consolidate power. In the Eastern model the revolutionary movement must solve the participatory problem to challenge the regime effectively. A prolonged revolutionary civil war practically guarantees a militarized, authoritarian solution.

Similarly, Jack Goldstone observes that revolutionary crises in the early modern world originated from the effects of demographic pressure on inflexible political and social structures (Chapter 6). These pressures shook the old regime to its foundations, but its successor also had to deal with the problems reflected in Goldstone's political stress indicator (*psi*—fiscal crisis, elite competition, and mass mobilization potential). History indicates, in Goldstone's view, that the resolution of these problems generally culminated in "populist, usually military, dictatorships."[23]

> Regardless of the aims or ideology of revolutionaries, the task of rebuilding state authority requires the broad-based mobilization of popular and elite groups to support a new regime, as well as the defeat of internal and often external opponents. The exigencies of this struggle generally lead to terror, disorder, and the growing dominance of military men.[24]

Goldstone concludes that revolution has seldom provided a solution to authoritarianism. Rather, the crises that caused the revolution in the first place generally call forth even more authoritarian responses in the successor regimes.[25]

        🔥   🔥   🔥

The corrupting potential of violent means, combined with the probable historical contingencies that lead to revolutionary crises, suggests rather pessimistic conclusions. The use of political violence to achieve revolutionary transformation is, at best, justifiable as a lesser evil. Revolutions often seem the inevitable outcome of external and internal crises combined with regime incompetence and intransigence. The condition of the people, in whose name the revolution is commonly made, often improves little, if at all, and then only after years of painful reconstruction of the damage inflicted by the revolutionary struggle. The ideologies that promise the New Jerusalem inflate, rather than satisfy, expectations. They offer uncertain guidance in a world that generally resists being remade. In a final irony, often the best that people can hope for is a moderation of revolutionary idealism, generally entailing a restoration of some of the same inequalities that originally propelled revolutionary discontent.

Yet such pessimism does not automatically justify the old order. After all, revolutions come about only because of massive regime failure. The regime begins with most of the advantages. From a psychological perspective people prefer order to disorder. The regime, moreover, initially possesses superior resources required for selective incentives to encourage supportive behavior among an apathetic or even hostile population. A regime faces a serious revolutionary challenge only because it squanders these advantages. The regime, moreover, confronts the same corrupting processes that plague revolutionaries. Extreme coercion to preserve the status quo often damages a community at least as much as the resort to violence to change it. The dynamics of the revolutionary crisis push the regime, as well as the revolutionary movement, in the direction of militarized, authoritarian solutions. We have no reason to assume that a regime victory raises fewer ethical quandaries than a revolutionary victory. With these somewhat gloomy thoughts in mind, we turn to a brief review of the revolutionary outcomes in Vietnam and Iran.

REVOLUTIONARY OUTCOMES IN VIETNAM AND IRAN

Vietnam[26]

The fruits of apparent victory, as we noted in Chapter 10, eluded the Vietnamese at least three times, in 1945, 1954, and 1965. Even in 1975 the triumph of the revolutionary North Vietnamese regime over their competitor in Saigon brought a bitter victory. Thirty years of war had blasted the country. The unified Vietnam proclaimed in July 1976 faced a shattered future. Not only had hundreds of thousands of Vietnamese perished directly or indirectly because of the war, but also tens of thousands of tons of bombs and the widespread use of defoliants had devastated the land and infrastructure. The new government confronted the task of rebuilding the country while at the same time coping with tens of thousands of disabled soldiers and civilians, as well as thousands of orphans. The physical consequences of 30 years of revolutionary warfare, then, were brutally obvious.

The prolonged period of revolutionary warfare also left Vietnam with a highly militarized society. Consequently both the past costs of war and the continuing economic drain of a large military burdened the new government. Any hopes that their revolutionary victory foreshadowed the beginnings of a global, or at least regional, revolutionary period proved futile. Rather than finding itself surrounded by fraternal revolutionary allies, Vietnam soon embroiled itself in hostilities against its erstwhile compatriots in Cambodia and in a bitter border conflict with Communist China. Whatever hopes existed for demobilization after 1975 faded in the light of these continued military conflicts. Promise of foreign economic assistance, especially from the United States, evaporated in response to the invasion of Cambodia and the ongoing dispute over American soldiers missing in action (MIAs). With respect to Vietnam's foreign relations, at least, policy seemed to reflect not an ideology of Marxist internationalism but the more traditional nationalistic interests of the fiercely independent Vietnamese.

Internally the record of the Vietnamese revolutionaries in power conforms with many of the patterns observed in other revolutions. The new regime, though, avoided some of the worst excesses. Given the length and the violence of the struggle, observers (often with political agendas to advance) predicted that a "bloodbath" would follow hard on a Communist victory. The enraged victors presumably would turn on their vanquished foes with a vengeance. However, no bloodbath occurred. The victorious revolutionaries, to be sure, were not communitarian pacifists. They sent tens of thousands of civilians and soldiers associated with the Saigon regime to concentration camps for "political reeducation." Some stayed only for a short while, but thousands of higher-level officials were confined for months, even years. Although such treatment seems harsh, it contrasts favorably with the actual bloodbath inflicted by revolutionaries in Cambodia after they seized power in 1975.

The revolutionary regime also revealed some degree of strategic hypocrisy along with doctrinaire impulses. After gaining power in the North in 1954, the Hanoi government undertook a mismanaged and often brutal program of land reform. Intended to redistribute land seized from large landlords, overzealous and poorly trained cadres turned it into a program of rural terror, denunciation, and death. Thousands of peasants, not merely large landlords, lost their lives. Finally the excesses provoked a rebellion in 1956. The regime recognized the seriousness of its errors, and, although it crushed the rebellion, it also retreated from its land tenure program.

Somewhat similarly, the unified regime after 1976 moved quickly to control the private economy of the South. Unfortunately, the effort to "socialize" the southern economy not only led to greater economic inefficiencies but generated tens of thousands of economic refugees. This river of refugees added their numbers to the flow of political refugees fleeing the Spartan rule of their new masters. Perhaps a million people fled, many in fragile boats, producing the shocking images of the Vietnamese "boat people."

The new regime faced international condemnation for this refugee outflow. This condemnation, combined with the economic inefficiencies of doctrinaire socialism, ultimately induced the regime to relax its economic control and allow for a freer economy. Again, the consequences of doctrinal rigidity, though devastating for both those who fled and those who stayed in Vietnam, fell far short of the catastrophe inflicted on the Cambodian people by the Khmer Rouge as they pursued their peculiar form of primitive Communism. (Perhaps as much as one-eighth of the population of Cambodia perished from disease, deprivation, and execution, as the Communists emptied the cities in pursuit of their vision of rural Communism.)

Confronted with internal economic failure and international hostility from both its former enemy the United States and its former ally China, and bled by a troublesome insurgency against the regime it had installed in Cambodia, Vietnam began to moderate its revolution. The collapse of Communist rule in its major ally, the Soviet Union, accelerated this trend. Domestically the regime relaxed both economic and political controls, especially in the South. Vietnam is attempting to reach out to foreign investors and to restore full relations with the United States. The Vietnamese also participated in lengthy negotiations to end the insurgency in Cambodia and ultimately withdrew their troops from this country. So far, Vietnam seems to be fulfilling its obligations under the United Nations–sponsored peace accord for Cambodia.

Stabilization of Cambodia, combined with the relaxation of tensions with China, may promote a significant reduction in the militarization of Vietnam, releasing resources for economic development. Resolution of the outstanding problems with the United States may further open Vietnam to foreign trade and investment. Already the changing political climate has encouraged thousands of Vietnamese who fled their country to visit their homeland and even explore business opportunities. The continuing replacement of the aging revolutionary leadership may further these trends toward moderation. Ironically, these trends also encourage the reemergence of inequality, corruption, and other forms of personal vice initially condemned by the puritanical revolutionary ideology.[27] In a world where the "socialist bloc" counts for increasingly little, the Vietnamese must accommodate themselves to the dominant world capitalist system if they wish to prosper. For a revolution that was both anticolonialist and anticapitalist, this outcome must be somewhat galling.

Does this mean that the revolution was for nothing? No. Though any hopes of prospering in a fraternal international socialist order quickly evaporated, Vietnam threw off first colonial rule and then a narrow, corrupt, foreign-dominated regime. Indulging in historical "what ifs" represents a form of idle speculation. A few observations, however, are pertinent. First, France granted its other colonies independence only after fighting not one, but two, bitter colonial wars (Vietnam and Algeria). When their hopes were dashed for a "new world order" that would grant colonial peoples their independence, Vietnamese nationalists understandably concluded that they could hope to end the evil of foreign rule and exploitation only through armed struggle. After the Saigon regime failed to hold the expected elections on unification and brutally suppressed the Viet Minh infrastructure in the South, the North Vietnamese regime understandably concluded that it could hope to reunify their country only by renewing the armed struggle.

In 1945 Ho Chi Minh and his compatriots did not face the choice between bowing to colonial rule or accepting 30 years of death and devastation. They chose between servile submission and what they considered justifiable resistance. Not even in their nightmares could they have anticipated the costs of their courage. Nor can those who resisted their drive for independence and unity, for good reasons and bad, escape their share of the blame for the costs of this extended struggle.

More pertinent, perhaps, are the criticisms of the doctrinaire economic policies that caused apparently needless suffering. Here, at least, less ideologically blinkered leadership might have avoided such blunders. After all, the Vietnamese had plenty of historical examples from the Soviet Union and China to demonstrate the costs of rigid and coercive social engineering. In their defense, we should observe that the Vietnamese revolutionary regime did not persevere in such policies as rigidly as was the case in either Stalin's Russia or Mao's China, much less Pol Pot's Cambodia.

In his speech declaring Vietnamese independence on September 2, 1945, Ho invoked the American Declaration of Independence. Now, after 50 years of struggle and disappointment, rigidity and compromise, perhaps the Vietnamese people have begun to glimpse a possibility for "life, liberty, and the pursuit of happiness."

Iran[28]

Superficially, as we noted in Chapter 11, the outcome of Iran's revolution follows the cycle of other Western-style revolutions, particularly that in Russia. After the fall of the old order ideological extremists successfully consolidated their power under the domination of a paramount leader. Internally they imposed a rigid regime that declared the supremacy of Islamic law. Externally they sought to spread their revolution to other Muslim countries and even entertained the notion that their revolution served as a model for the entire Third World. Like the Russian Revolution, the Iranian Revolution provoked suspicion among its neighbors. Moreover, internal weakness tempted one of them—Iraq—to settle old territorial disputes through military invasion.

Under the pressure of war and internal power struggles, the clerical political forces grew steadily more oppressive and militarized. Armed thugs (the *hezbollahis*) increasingly settled the debates between clerical elements and their opponents among the secular and Islamic left. Revolutionary justice took its toll of all those suspected of harboring oppositional leanings. The Revolutionary Guard played a growing role in countering the Iraqi invasion, displacing the regular armed forces. Islamic political faith, as interpreted by the Ayatollah and his disciples, provided the direction for social behavior and public policy.

Eventually the inconclusive war, combined with diplomatic isolation from the secular West, the atheistic Soviet Union, and much of the Arab world, began to force a moderation of Iranian foreign policy. "Clericalism in one country," gradually replaced aspirations to export "universal" Islamic revolution.[29] The regime cautiously pursued relations with parts of the capitalist world to gain the resources and expertise needed for economic development. Internally the deprivations wrought by the war, combined with the inadequacies of Islamic economic doctrine, led to a moderation of economic and social policies. Finally, the death of

Khomeini and the electoral victories of Hashemi Rafsanjani—first his own in the presidential election of July 1989 and later that of his supporters in the parliamentary elections of spring 1992—helped consolidate power in the hands of presumed pragmatists.

The first 13 years of the New Revolutionary Order in Iran, then, somewhat resembles the cycle of Western-type revolutions. First, a strategically manipulated oppositional coalition succeeds in ousting a discredited regime. Then more moderate members of this coalition find that the positive program of their erstwhile allies, muted in the oppositional phase, entails more than they can accept. By this time the extremists successfully dominate the levers of power, crush their former allies, and set up an authoritarian system to impose their ideological vision. Internally, doctrinally defined programs and ideologically pure but technically incompetent personnel lead the country into economic disarray. Externally, extremism and revolutionary adventurism provoke hostility and conflict. The deprivations endured by the people in the new order exceed those that drove them to revolution in the first place. Ultimately internal discontent combined with unrelenting foreign hostility brings more moderate and technically competent people to power. The death of the paramount leader provides the final push for the pragmatic reaction. The revolutionary country, appropriately tamed, overcomes its diplomatic isolation and rejoins the international community. Internal consolidation, along with external accommodation, leads to the obvious question of whether all the upheaval and suffering were worth it to produce this compromised outcome.

In some respects, then, the Iranian Revolution appears to be "graying" in ways similar to those experienced by twentieth-century Marxist revolutions. Nevertheless, critical differences exist, an unsurprising observation perhaps, given the religious basis of the Iranian Revolution. In some respects the regime's revolutionary ideology shares certain traits with fascism, not Communism.[30] Like fascism the Islamic creed opposes liberal democracy for its secularism and foreign nature. It suspects the bourgeoisie because of their cosmopolitan leanings. Again, like fascism it invokes slogans of social justice while condemning Marxist ideas of class conflict and equality. Analogous to fascism's substitution of *Volk* (people) for the Marxist concept of class, Islamic ideology emphasizes the Muslim community of believers over other identities. Finally, the paramount role accorded Khomeini in the Islamic New Revolutionary Order resembles the fascist emphasis on the "leadership principle."

Yet despite these interesting similarities with some traits of both contemporary fascist and Communist revolutions, the postrevolutionary experience in Iran contains significant differences as well. First, although clearly the paramount spiritual and political leader of the revolution, the Ayatollah played more the role of an arbitrator among competing sectors than that of a dictator like Lenin or Hitler. Often he appeared to vacillate between competing factions, as during the struggle between Bani-Sadr and the Islamic Republic Party (IRP; see Chapter 11) and in later debates over the appropriate course of economic policy (see below). Living away from the capital city in the religious center of Qom, he deliberately avoided burdening himself with the mundane problems of daily governance. Sometimes when he made pronouncements, like those in 1988 concerning the powers of the Islamic state, their ambiguities allowed for differing interpretations as to how they affected specific policy.[31] Even when he seemed irrevocably clear, as in his pronouncements concerning the need for Saddam Hussein to fall before peace could be pursued with Iraq, he changed in response to altered circumstances and pressure from others.

Significantly, postrevolutionary Iran was not a single-party totalitarian state. Even after the clerical forces consolidated their triumph over other competitors, factions both inside and outside the IRP continued to debate and maneuver. Far from creating a one-party state, the regime effectively abolished the IRP in 1987. The regime has held semicompetitive elections for both the presidency and for the Majles (parliament). These elections, though clearly not free in the Western sense, seem to resemble a kind of "guided democracy." For example, in the parliamentary elections of 1992 several thousand candidates initially sought to run for several hundred seats. The Guardianship Council, however, screened the Islamic credentials of these hopefuls. This council, dominated by allies of Rafsanjani, declared many of his more prominent rivals, along with many others, ineligible, thereby helping to ensure the election of his supporters. Yet after this screening the voters still had some choice.

Parliamentary debates, moreover, have not simply affirmed dictated policy; rather, they have generally been quite lively. Of course, certain topics were off limits, like direct criticisms of Khomeini or of the war effort. One area of ongoing contention involves the economic and social justice policies of the Islamic Republic.[32] Some favor programs of radical redistribution of wealth. Others take the more traditional position supporting private property and, therefore, the unequal distribution of wealth. They advocate expanding the role of the private sector to revitalize the economy. Khomeini, not untypically, seemed divided on the issue. One scholar of Iranian politics suggests that though Khomeini's heart was with the dispossessed, his head embraced the more traditional socioeconomic inclinations of Islamic social doctrine.[33]

Such divisions resulted in more compromised socioeconomic policies than was the case in the doctrinaire socialist revolutions. The government sector expanded greatly, swelled by the confiscation of the property of the Pahlavis and their allies and the increased government domination of foreign trade. Some redistribution of land occurred with the land reform program of 1986, but it failed to meet the aspirations of the social justice radicals. The merchants of the bazaar continued to play an important economic role, and wealth remained unequally distributed, though perhaps not as badly as under the Shah. Rafsanjani in recent years has undertaken further efforts at economic rationalization.

Similar debates and policy fluctuations occurred in the area of foreign policy.[34] As early as 1984 Iran began to moderate its foreign policy in an effort to end its isolation. The government began to distance itself from various acts of terrorism in the Middle East, cautiously attempted to improve relations with Moscow, and even contacted the great Satan, the United States (contacts that later led to the Iran-Contra scandal). At the same time, more radical elements pulled foreign policy in the opposite direction, particularly through Iranian support of the Shi'ites in Lebanon and cooperation with Libya and Syria. American support of Iraq during the war rejuvenated tensions between the two countries. These tensions peaked after an American missile cruiser shot down an Iranian passenger jet in July 1988. Though Iran acquiesced in the U.S.-led war against Iraq in 1990–1991, relations still remain strained. Ironically, with Iraq's defeat at the hands of the Americans, Iran seems poised to pursue one or both of two foreign policy goals. Iran could attempt to spread the Islamic revolution to the Shi'ites of southern Iraq and elsewhere or try to assume the role as dominant military power in the region. This latter objective, ironically, was the dream of the Shah.

A final postrevolutionary element that belies any consistent trend toward moderation concerns policies governing social behavior. Moderate supporters of the revolution against the Shah certainly did not bargain for the strict imposition of an Islamic code of behavior on sex roles, cultural life, and public activity. Such puritanical controls, however, followed the fall of the Shah, particularly after the triumph of the clerical forces. While some fluctuations have occurred in this area as well, 1992 brought about something of a retrenchment. Especially after their defeat in the parliamentary elections, more culturally fundamentalist elements in the clergy and wider society reinforced their policing of public behavior and cultural affairs.

What, then, has the Islamic revolution wrought?[05] Certainly it caused a major circulation of elites. Execution, purge, imprisonment, and exile eliminated the Pahlavi family and their supporters from positions in the economy, bureaucracy, military, and judiciary. Younger elements of the clergy pushed aside older clerical elites. But a circulation of elites simply replaces one elite structure with another. It need not produce a more egalitarian social order.

The revolution also expanded the role of the government by both transferring wealth and functions to the government and extending the state's interest into more arenas of social behavior. The revolution transformed the constitutional structure of the state, brought a clerical sector to power, and subordinated government functions, at least formally, to the injunctions of Islamic principles. Finally, the Islamic revolution in Iran reinforced the already existing trends in the Middle East toward the revival of religiously inspired political movements.

These changes, however, came accompanied by the costs of the terrible war with Iraq, the authoritarianism of the Islamic Republic, and a level of cultural control that exceeds anything under the Shah. Economically, conditions in Iran have yet to improve to the levels enjoyed in the mid-1970s. Radical dreams of Islamic social justice seem placed on permanent hold. The political process, though not a form of single-party totalitarianism, appears dominated once more by a competition among elite factions, albeit new ones. Again, though, we must avoid judging those who first rebelled against the despised Shah on the basis of such retrospective calculations.

CONCLUSION: THE REVOLUTIONARY TRAGEDY

Revolutionary action encounters a tragic dilemma. The more radically it challenges the existing distribution of power and value both within and outside a particular community, the more conflict it provokes, the more violence ensues, and the more likely the revolutionary victory, if it comes at all, will produce a militarized, authoritarian system. On the other hand, the more the revolution moderates its aims, the more preexisting inequities reassert themselves, perhaps suitably cloaked in a new revolutionary rhetoric. Perhaps the best that emerges from the interplay of these two extremes is an outcome that eliminates the worst aspects of the old order while avoiding the worst excesses of revolutionary reconstruction.

The revolutionary outcomes in Vietnam and Iran have undeniably inflicted some significant costs on their peoples. It may excuse little to observe that these costs have been less than those associated with some other revolutions of the twentieth century, like those in Russia, China, and Cambodia. In addition, we must remember that the revolutionaries alone do not shoulder the blame for running up the costs. Any retrospective reassessment must also note that the United States, and France before her, share the responsibility for escalating unnecessary and ultimately futile wars in Vietnam. Similarly, the revolution may have weakened Iran, but Iraq chose to exploit this weakness through a cynical act of aggression. The suggestion that the revolutionaries should have spared their people by surrendering to such external aggression is politically naive and morally unfair. Finally, revolutionaries challenge a regime in the first place only because of the regime's domination by selfish, corrupt, and incompetent elites. These old elites also carry a burden of responsibility for contributing to the revolutionary crisis.

Perhaps it is always thus: Impelled by intolerable conditions, revolutionaries commit their inexcusable actions.[36]

NOTES

1. Johann Wolfgang von Goethe, *Faust,* Part Two, Act Five, Scene 6.
2. Jon Gunnemann, *The Moral Meaning of Revolution* (New Haven, Conn.: Yale University Press, 1979), pp. 173–175.
3. See Andrew Hacker, *Two Nations: Black and White, Separate, Hostile, Unequal* (New York: Charles Scribner's Sons, 1992).
4. Michael Walzer, *Just and Unjust Wars: A Moral Argument with Historical Illustrations,* Second Edition (New York: Basic Books, 1992), p. 325. This is a paraphrase of an argument made by Thomas Nagel.
5. See Edmund Burke, *Reflections on the Revolution in France,* any edition.
6. Walzer provides an extensive discussion of these issues in Chapters 8 through 13.
7. Viola W. Bernard, Perry Ottenberg, and Fritz Redl, "Dehumanization," in Nevitt Sanford and Craig Comstock, eds., *Sanctions for Evil* (San Francisco: Jossey-Bass, 1971), pp. 102–124.
8. Bernard L. Diamond, "Failures of Identification and Sociopathic Behavior," in Sanford and Comstock, eds., pp. 125–135. See also the discussion in Robert Jay Lifton, *The Nazi Doctors: Medical Killing and the Psychology of Genocide* (New York: Basic Books, 1986).
9. Gene Sharp, *The Politics of Nonviolent Action* (Boston: Porter Sargent, 1973), pp. 800–802.
10. René Gerard, *Violence and the Sacred,* trans. by Patrick Gregory (Baltimore, Md.: Johns Hopkins University Press, 1972), p. 14. Gerard's study is a profound exploration of this problem.

11. Ted Robert Gurr, *Why Men Rebel* (Princeton, N.J.: Princeton University Press, 1971). See the summary of his variables on pp. 363–364.
12. Ibid., p. 358.
13. Ibid., p. 366.
14. Ibid., p. 358.
15. This discussion is indebted to the extensive analysis in Mark Lichbach's forthcoming book, *The Rebel's Dilemma* (Ann Arbor: University of Michigan Press), section 8.4.
16. See Crane Brinton, *Anatomy of Revolution*. This book was originally published in 1938 by Prentice Hall. Subsequent page references are to the Vintage paperback edition.
17. Ibid., p. 213.
18. Ibid., pp. 213–214.
19. Theodore S. Hamerow, *From the Finland Station: The Graying of Revolution in the Twentieth Century* (New York: Basic Books, 1990). The following summary is based primarily on Hamerow's conclusions in Chapter 10, pp. 313–353.
20. The phrase is that of the Yugoslavian Communist "apostate," Milovan Djilas.
21. Hamerow, p. 348.
22. See the argument developed in Samuel P. Huntington, *Political Order in Changing Societies* (New Haven, Conn.: Yale University Press, 1968). See also the discussion of Huntington in Chapter 6.
23. Jack A. Goldstone, *Revolution and Rebellion in the Early Modern World* (Berkeley: University of California Press, 1991), p. 479.
24. Ibid.
25. Ibid., p. 480.
26. For summary analyses of the postrevolutionary situation see James DeFronzo, "Vietnam," in his *Revolutions and Revolutionary Movements* (Boulder, Colo.: Westview Press, 1991), especially pp. 141–149. See also H. John LeVan, "Vietnam: Revolution of Postcolonial Consolidation," in Jack A. Goldstone, Ted Robert Gurr, and Farrokh Moshiri, eds., *Revolutions of the Late Twentieth Century* (Boulder, Colo.: Westview Press, 1991), especially pp. 75–85. For a review of the extent of recent political changes see Douglas Pike, "Change and Continuity in Vietnam," *Current History*, 89 (1990): 117–134.
27. Stanley Karnow reports these trends as already developing after the initial period of relaxation of controls in the early 1980s. See *Vietnam: A History* (New York: Penguin, 1983), pp. 33–34.
28. A good review of the events following the fall of the Shah, covering both the consolidation of power by the clerics and the developments in social and economic policy, is provided by Shaul Bakhash, *The Reign of the Ayatollahs: Iran and the Islamic Revolution*, Revised Edition (New York: Basic Books, 1990). Also of value, though somewhat dated, are the essays in Hooshang Amirahmadi and Manoucher Parvin, eds., *Post-Revolutionary Iran* (Boulder, Colo.: Westview Press, 1988).
29. The phrase is that of Gary Sick, "Iran's Quest for Superpower Status," *Foreign Affairs*, 65 (4): 714.
30. This discussion of the parallels with fascism is based on Said Amir Arjomand, *The Turban and the Crown: The Islamic Revolution in Iran* (New York: Oxford University Press, 1988), pp. 203–206.
31. Bakhash, pp. 250–255.
32. Ibid., pp. 246–250.
33. Shahrough Akhavi, personal conversation.
34. Bakhash, pp. 257–274.

35. Ibid., pp. 289–291.
36. This observation echoes a similar one by Marcel Proust: "It is always thus, impelled by a state of mind which is destined not to last, that we make our irrevocable decisions." See *Within a Budding Grove* in *Remembrance of Things Past,* Volume One, trans. by C. K. Scott Moncrieff and Terence Kilmartin (New York: Random House, 1981), p. 622.

Index